ALONG THESE LINES

THIRD EDITION

ALONG THESE LINES

Writing Paragraphs and Essays

John Sheridan Biays
Broward Community College

Carol Wershoven
Palm Beach Community College

PEARSON

Prentice Hall

UPPER SADDLE RIVER, NEW JERSEY 07458

Library of Congress Cataloging-in-Publication Data

Biays, John Sheridan.
    Along these lines : writing paragraphs and essays / John Sheridan Biays, Carol Wershoven.—3rd ed.
        p.   cm.
    Includes index.
    ISBN   0-13-111219-8
        1. English language—Rhetoric—Problems, exercises, etc.   2. English language—Grammar—Problems, exercises, etc.   3. Report writing—Problems, exercises, etc.   I. Wershoven, Carol.   II. Title.

PE1408   .B4933 2003
808'.042—dc21   2002193061

Editor in Chief: Leah Jewell
Senior Acquisitions Editor: Craig Campanella
Assistant Editor: Karen Schultz
Editorial Assistant: Joan Polk
VP/Director of Production and Manufacturing: Barbara Kittle
Production Editor: Maureen Benicasa
Production Assistant: Marlene Gassler
Copyeditor: Krystyna Budd
Prepress and Manufacturing Assistant Manager: Mary Ann Gloriande
Prepress and Manufacturing Buyer: Brian Mackey
Marketing Director: Beth Mejia
Marketing Manager: Rachel Falk
Marketing Assistant: Adam Laitman
Text Permissions Specialist: Kathleen Karcher
Director, Image Resource Center: Melinda Reo
Manager, Rights and Permissions: Zina Arabia
Interior Image Specialist: Beth Boyd-Brenzel
Image Permissions Coordinator: Nancy Seise
Creative Design Director: Leslie Osher
Art Director: Anne Bonanno Nieglos
Interior and Cover Designer: Carmen DiBartolomeo, C2K, Inc.
Cover Art: Piet Mondrian (1872–1944) Tableau II, 1921–25. Private Collection, Giraudon/Bridgeman Art Library, New York. © Artists Rights Society (ARS) New York.
Development Editor in Chief: Rochelle Diogenes
Development Editor: Elizabeth Morgan

This book was set in 11/13 ITC Bookman by Carlisle Communications, Ltd. and was printed and bound by Courier Companies, Inc. The cover was printed by Phoenix Color Corp.

For permission to use copyrighted material, grateful acknowledgment is made to the copyright holders on page 625, which is considered an extension of this copyright page.

Printed in the United States of America
10 9 8 7 6 5 4 3 2 1

ISBN 0-13-111219-8

Pearson Education LTD., London
Pearson Education Australia PTY, Limited, Sydney
Pearson Education Singapore, Pte. Ltd
Pearson Education North Asia Ltd, Hong Kong
Pearson Education Canada, Ltd., Toronto
Pearson Educación de Mexico, S.A. de C.V.
Pearson Education—Japan, Tokyo
Pearson Education Malaysia, Pte. Ltd
Pearson Education, Upper Saddle River, New Jersey

CONTENTS

Preface   xix

Writing in Stages: The Process Approach   1

Introduction   1

Chapter 1   Writing a Paragraph   3

Beginning the Thought Lines: Gathering Ideas   4
Freewriting, Brainstorming, Keeping a Journal   4
Finding Specific Ideas   5
Selecting One Topic   6
Adding Details to a Specific Topic   9

Focusing the Thought Lines   12
Listing Related Ideas   12
Mapping   13
Forming a Topic Sentence   13
Writing Good Topic Sentences   13

Outlines Devising a Plan for a Paragraph   19
Checking Your Details   19
Adding Details When There Are Not Enough   20
Eliminating Details That Do Not Relate to the Topic Sentence   20
From List to Outline   21

Coherence: Putting Your Details in Proper Order   22

Rough Lines Drafting and Revising a Paragraph   27
Drafting a Paragraph   27
Revising   27

Final Lines Proofreading and Polishing a Paragraph   30
Giving Your Paragraph a Title   30
The Final Version of a Paragraph   30
Reviewing the Writing Process   30

Lines of Detail: A Walk-Through Assignment   32

Writing Your Own Paragraph   34

Peer Review Form for a Paragraph   38
WRITING FROM READING: The Writing Process   39
■ "Sticky Stuff" *by Kendall Hamilton and Tessa Namuth*   39

Chapter 2   Illustration   42

What Is Illustration?   42
Hints for Writing an Illustration Paragraph   42

Writing the Illustration Paragraph in Steps   45
Thought Lines Gathering Ideas: Illustration   45
Adding Details to an Idea   45

Creating a Topic Sentence   46

Outlines **Devising a Plan: Illustration**   50

Rough Lines **Drafting and Revising: Illustration**   53
Transitions 54

Final Lines **Proofreading and Polishing: Illustration**   56

Lines of Detail: A Walk-Through Assignment   **58**

Writing Your Own Illustration Paragraph   **58**

Peer Review Form for an Illustration Paragraph   **61**
WRITING FROM READING: Illustration   **62**
■ *"Spanglish" by Janice Castro, with Dan Cook and Cristina Garcia*   **62**

Chapter 3   ## Description   65

What Is Description?   **65**
Hints for Writing a Descriptive Paragraph   65
Using Sense Words in Your Description   69

Writing the Description Paragraph in Steps   **71**

Thought Lines **Gathering Ideas: Description**   71
The Dominant Impression 72

Outlines **Devising a Plan: Description**   74

Rough Lines **Drafting and Revising: Description**   78
Transitions 80

Final Lines **Proofreading and Polishing: Description**   82

Lines of Detail: A Walk-Through Assignment   **83**

Writing Your Own Descriptive Paragraph   **84**

Peer Review Form for a Descriptive Paragraph   **86**
WRITING FROM READING: Description   **87**
■ *"A Present for Popo" by Elizabeth Wong*   **87**

Chapter 4   ## Narration   90

What Is Narration?   **90**
Give the Narrative a Point   90
Hints for Writing a Narrative Paragraph   94
Using a Speaker's Exact Words in Narrative   95

Writing the Narrative Paragraph in Steps   **96**

Thought Lines **Gathering Ideas: Narration**   96
Freewriting for a Narrative Topic   97
Narrowing and Selecting a Suitable Narrative Topic   98

Outlines **Devising a Plan: Narration**   100

Rough Lines **Drafting and Revising: Narration**   103
Revising for Sharper Details   103
Checking the Topic Sentence   104
Using Transitions Effectively in Narration   106
The Draft   107

Final Lines **Polishing and Proofreading: Narration**   108

Lines of Detail: A Walk-Through Assignment   **109**

Writing Your Own Narrative Paragraph   110
Peer Review Form for a Narrative Paragraph   112
WRITING FROM READING: Narration   113
■ "Rocky Rowf" *by Edna Buchanan*   113

Chapter 5   **Process**   118

What Is Process?   118
A Process Involves Steps in Time Order   118
Hints for Writing a Process Paragraph   119
Writing the Process Paragraph in Steps   121
Thought Lines Gathering Ideas: Process   121
Writing a Topic Sentence for a Process Paragraph   122
Outlines Devising a Plan: Process   123
Rough Lines Drafting and Revising: Process   127
Using the Same Grammatical Person   127
Using Transitions Effectively   128
The Draft   131
Final Lines Proofreading and Polishing: Process   131
Lines of Detail: A Walk-Through Assignment   133
Writing Your Own Process Paragraph   134
Peer Review Form for a Process Paragraph   137
WRITING FROM READING: Process   138
■ "How to Write a Personal Letter" *by Garrison Keillor*   138

Chapter 6   **Comparison and Contrast**   142

What Is Comparison? What Is Contrast?   142
Hints for Writing a Comparison or Contrast Paragraph   142
Organizing Your Comparison or Contrast Paragraph   144
Using Transitions Effectively for Comparison or Contrast   148
Writing the Comparison or Contrast Paragraphs in Steps   150
Thought Lines Gathering Ideas: Comparison or Contrast   150
Getting Points of Comparison or Contrast   151
Adding Details to Your Points   153
Outlines Devising a Plan: Comparison or Contrast   155
Rough Lines Drafting and Revising: Comparison and Contrast   159
Comparison or Contrast   159
The Draft   159
Final Lines Proofreading and Polishing: Comparison or Contrast   162
Contrast Paragraph: Point-by-Point Pattern   162
The Same Contrast Paragraph: Subject by Subject   163
Lines of Detail: A Walk-Through Assignment   166
Writing Your Own Comparison or Contrast Paragraph   167
Peer Review Form for a Comparison or Contrast Paragraph   169
WRITING FROM READING: Comparison or Contrast   170
■ "Against All Odds, I'm Just Fine" *by Brad Wackerlin*   170

Chapter 7 Classification   172

What Is Classification?   172
Hints for Writing a Classification Paragraph   172

Writing the Classification Paragraph in Steps   176
Thought Lines Gathering Ideas: Classification   176
Brainstorming a Basis for Classification   176
Matching the Points Within the Categories   177
Writing a Topic Sentence for a Classification Paragraph   177

Outlines Devising a Plan: Classification   179
Effective Order in Classifying   179

Rough Lines Drafting and Revising: Classification   182
Transitions in Classification   182

Final Lines Proofreading and Polishing: Classification   184

Lines of Detail: A Walk-Through Assignment   186

Writing Your Own Classification Paragraph   187

Peer Review Form for a Classification Paragraph   189
WRITING FROM READING: Classification   190
■ "Three Disciplines for Children" *by John Holt*   190

Chapter 8 Definition   193

What Is Definition?   193
Hints for Writing a Definition Paragraph   193

Writing the Definition Paragraph in Steps   198
Thought Lines Gathering Ideas: Definition   198
Using Questions to Get Details   198
The Topic Sentence   199

Outlines Devising a Plan: Definition   201
Rough Lines Drafting and Revising: Definition   203
Transitions   203
The Draft   203

Final Lines Proofreading and Polishing: Definition   208

Lines of Detail: A Walk-Through Assignment   210

Writing Your Own Definition Paragraph   210

Peer Review Form for a Definition Paragraph   212
WRITING FROM READING: Definition   213
■ "Breaking the Bonds of Hate" *by Virak Khiev*   213

Chapter 9 Cause and Effect   217

What Is Cause and Effect?   217
Hints for Writing a Cause or Effect Paragraph?   217

Writing the Cause or Effect Paragraph in Steps   220
Thought Lines Gathering Ideas: Cause or Effect   220
Freewriting on a Topic   220
Designing a Topic Sentence   222

`Outlines` **Devising a Plan: Cause or Effect**   225
The Order of Causes or Effects   225

`Rough Lines` **Drafting and Revising: Cause or Effect**   229
Linking Ideas in Cause or Effect   229
Making the Links Clear   230
Revising the Draft   230

`Final Lines` **Proofreading and Polishing: Cause or Effect**   234
Lines of Detail: A Walk-Through Assignment   235
Writing Your Own Cause or Effect Paragraph   236

Peer Review Form for a Cause or Effect Paragraph   239
WRITING FROM READING: Cause or Effect   240
■ **"Students in Shock"** *by John Kellmayer*   240

Chapter 10   Argument   244

What Is Argument?   244
Hints for Writing an Argument Paragraph   244
Writing the Argument Paragraph in Steps   248

`Thought Lines` **Gathering Ideas: Argument**   248
Grouping Your Ideas   249

`Outlines` **Devising a Plan: Argument**   251
The Order of Reasons in an Argument   252

`Rough Lines` **Drafting and Revising: Argument**   256
Checking Your Reasons   256
Explaining the Problem or the Issue   256
Transitions That Emphasize   257
A Draft   257

`Final Lines` **Proofreading and Polishing: Argument**   260
Lines of Detail: A Walk-Through Assignment   262

Writing Your Own Argument Paragraph   263

Peer Review Form for an Argument Paragraph   265
WRITING FROM READING: Argument   266
■ **"Athletic Heroes"** *by James Beekman*   266
■ **"Too Tired to Appreciate the Revolution"** *by Jeremy Rifkin*   269

Chapter 11   Writing an Essay   272

What Is an Essay?   272
Comparing the Single Paragraph and the Essay   272
Organizing the Essay   273
Writing the Thesis   274
Hints for Writing a Thesis   274
Writing the Essay in Steps   277

`Thought Lines` **Gathering Ideas: An Essay**   277
Listing Ideas   278
Clustering the Ideas   278

`Outlines` **Devising a Plan: An Essay**   281
Hints for Outlining   282
Revisiting the Thought Lines Stage   283

`Rough Lines` **Drafting and Revising: An Essay**   286

Writing the Introduction   286

Where Does the Thesis Go?   286

Hints for Writing the Introduction   287

Writing the Body of the Essay   289

How Long Are the Body Paragraphs?   290

Developing the Body Paragraphs   290

Writing the Conclusion   291

Revising the Draft   293

Transitions Within Paragraphs   294

Transitions Between Paragraphs   295

A Draft Essay   296

`Final Lines` **Proofreading and Polishing: An Essay**   301

Creating a Title   301

The Final Version of an Essay   301

Lines of Detail: A Walk-Through Assignment   305

Writing Your Own Essay   306

Peer Review Form for an Essay   309

WRITING FROM READING: The Essay   310

■ *"Eleven" by Sandra Cisneros*   310

■ *"Never Give Up" by Althea Gibon*   313

Chapter 12   Different Essay Patterns   318

Illustration   318

Hints for Writing an Illustration Essay   318

Writing the Illustration Essay in Steps   319

`Thought Lines` **Gathering Ideas: Illustration Essay**   319

`Outlines` **Devising a Plan: Illustration Essay**   320

`Rough Lines` **Drafting and Revising: Illustration Essay**   321

`Final Lines` **Polishing and Proofreading: Illustration Essay**   322

Writing Your Own Illustration Essay   323

Description   323

Hints for Writing a Description Essay   323

Writing the Descriptive Essay in Steps   324

`Thought Lines` **Gathering Ideas: Descriptive Essay**   324

`Outlines` **Devising a Plan: Descriptive Essay**   324

`Rough Lines` **Drafting and Revising: Descriptive Essay**   325

`Final Lines` **Polishing and Proofreading: Descriptive Essay**   326

Writing Your Own Illustration Essay   327

Narration   328

Hints for Writing a Narrative Essay   328

Writing the Narrative Essay in Steps   328

`Thought Lines` **Gathering Ideas: Narrative Essay**   328

`Outlines` **Devising a Plan: Narrative Essay**   329

`Rough Lines` **Drafting and Revising: Narrative Essay**   330

Final Lines Polishing and Proofreading: Narrative Essay 330

Writing Your Own Narrative Essay 331

Process 332

Hints for Writing a Process Essay 332

Writing the Process Essay in Steps 333

Thought Lines Gathering Ideas: Process 333

Outlines Devising a Plan: Process Essay 333

Rough Lines Drafting and Revising: Process Essay 334

Final Lines Polishing and Proofreading: Process Essay 335

Writing Your Own Process Essay 337

Comparison and Contrast 337

Hints for Writing a Comparison or Contrast Essay 337

Writing the Comparison or Contrast Essay in Steps 338

Thought Lines Gathering Ideas: Comparison or Contrast Essay 338

Getting Points of Comparison or Contrast 339

Outlines Devising a Plan: Contrast Essay 340

Rough Lines Drafting and Revising: Contrast Essay 341

Final Lines Polishing and Proofreading: Contrast Essay 342

Writing Your Own Comparison or Contrast Essay 343

Classification 344

Hints for Writing a Classification Essay 344

Writing the Classification Essay in Steps 344

Thought Lines Gathering Ideas: Classification Essay 344

Outlines Devising a Plan: Classification Essay 345

Rough Lines Drafting and Revising: Classification Essay 346

Final Lines Polishing and Proofreading: Classification Essay 347

Writing Your Own Classification Essay 348

Definition 349

Hints for Writing a Definition Essay 349

Writing the Definition Essay in Steps 350

Thought Lines Gathering Ideas: Definition Essay 350

Outlines Devising a Plan: Definition Essay 351

Rough Lines Drafting and Revising: Definition Essay 352

Final Lines Polishing and Proofreading: Definition Essay 353

Writing Your Own Definition Essay 354

Cause and Effect 355

Hints for Writing a Cause or Effect Essay 355

Thought Lines Gathering Ideas: Cause or Effect Essay 355

Outlines Devising a Plan: Effects Essay 357

Rough Lines Drafting and Revising: Effects Essay 358

Final Lines Polishing and Proofreading: Effects Essay 358

Writing Your Own Cause or Effect Essay 359

Argument 360

Hints for Writing an Argument Essay 360

Writing the Argument Essay in Steps   361
`Thought Lines` Gathering Ideas: Argument Essay   361
`Outlines` Devising a Plan: Argument Essay   362
`Rough Lines` Drafting and Revising: Argument Essay   363
`Final Lines` Polishing and Proofreading: Argument Essay   364
Writing Your Own Argument Essay   365

`Chapter 13`   **Writing from Reading   367**

What Is Writing from Reading?   367
An Approach to Writing from Reading   367
Attitude   367
Prereading   368
Why Preread?   368
Forming Questions Before You Read   369
An Example of the Prereading Step   369
The Results of Prereading   371
Reading   372
An Example of the Reading Step   372
Rereading with Pen or Pencil   372
An Example of Rereading with Pen or Pencil   373
What the Notes Mean   375
Writing a Summary of a Reading   376
`Thought Lines` Gathering Ideas: Summary   376
Making a List of Ideas   376
Selecting a Main Idea   377
`Outlines` Devising a Plan: Summary   379
`Rough Lines` Drafting and Revising: Summary   379
Attributing Ideas in a Summary   379
`Final Lines` Proofreading and Polishing: Summary   380
Writing a Reaction to a Reading   381
Writing on a Related Idea   381
`Thought Lines` Gathering Ideas: Reaction   381
Freewriting   381
Brainstorming   382
Developing Points of Agreement or Disagreement   382
`Outlines` Devising a Plan: Agree or Disagree   383
`Rough Lines` Drafting and Revising: Agree or Disagree   383
`Final Lines` Polishing and Proofreading: Agree or Disagree   383
Writing for an Essay Test   384
Before the Test: The Steps of Reading   384
During the Test: The Stages of Writing   384
Organize Your Time   385
Lines of Detail: A Walk-Through Assignment   386
Writing Your Own Paragraph on "A Ridiculous Addiction"   386
Peer Review Form for Writing From Reading   388
WRITING FROM READING: 389
■ "My Daughter Smokes" *by Alice Walker*   389
■ "Parental Discussion" *by Dennis Hevesi*   393

Writing in Stages: The Bottom Line: Grammar for Writers   397

Introduction   **397**
Contents   **397**

Chapter 14 **The Simple Sentence   399**

Recognizing a Sentence   399
Recognizing Verbs   399
  More on Verbs   400
Recognizing Subjects   401
  More About Recognizing Subjects and Verbs   402
Prepositions and Prepositional Phrases   402
Word Order   405
  More on Word Order   406
  Word Order in Questions   406
  Words That Cannot Be Verbs   407
  Recognizing Main Verbs   408
  Verb Forms That Cannot Be Main Verbs   408

Chapter 15 **Beyond the Simple Sentence: Coordination   414**

Options for Combining Simple Sentences   414
Option 1: Using a Comma with a Coordinating Conjunction   415
  Where Does the Comma Go?   415
  Placing the Comma by Using Subject-Verb (S-V) Patterns   416
Option 2: Using a Semicolon Between Two Simple Sentences   418
Option 3: Using a Semicolon and a Conjunctive Adverb   419
  Punctuating After a Conjunctive Adverb   420

Chapter 16 **Avoiding Run-On Sentences and Comma Splices   424**

Run-on Sentences   424
Steps for Correcting Run-On Sentences   424
Comma Splices   427
Correcting Comma Splices   427

Chapter 17 **Beyond the Simple Sentence: Subordination   432**

More on Combining Simple Sentences   432
Option 4: Using a Dependent Clause to Begin a Sentence   432
Option 5: Using a Dependent Clause to End a Sentence   432
  Using Subordinating Conjunctions   433
  Punctuating Complex Sentences   434
  Combining Sentences: A Review of Your Options   436

Chapter 18 Avoiding Sentence Fragments   443

Recognizing Fragments: Step 1   443

Recognizing Fragments: Step 2   445

Correcting Fragments   448

Chapter 19 Using Parallelism in Sentences   453

Achieving Parallelism   454

Chapter 20 Using Adjectives and Adverbs   462

What Are Adjectives?   462

Adjectives: Comparative and Superlative Forms   463

What Are Adverbs?   465

Hints About Adjectives and Adverbs   466

Don't Confuse Good and Well, or Bad and Badly   467

Not More + -er, or Most + -est   468

Use Than, not Then, in Comparisons   469

When Do I Need a Comma Between Adjectives?   469

Chapter 21 Correcting Problems with Modifiers   471

Correcting Modifier Problems   472

Correcting Dangling Modifiers   474

Reviewing the Steps and the Solutions   477

Chapter 22 Using Verbs Correctly   480

Using Standard Verb Forms   480

The Present Tense   481

The Past Tense   482

The Four Main Forms of a Verb: Present, Past, Present Participle, and Past Participle   483

Irregular Verbs   484

The Past Tense of be, have, do   486

More Irregular Verb Forms   487

Irregular Verb Forms   488

Chapter 23 More on Verbs: Consistency and Voice   493

Consistent Verb Tenses   493

The Present Perfect Tense   497

The Past Perfect Tense   498

Passive and Active Voice   499

Avoiding Unnecessary Shifts in Voice   501

Small Reminders About Verbs   502

Chapter 24 **Making Subjects and Verbs Agree   506**

Pronouns as Subjects   **507**

Special Problems With Agreement   **508**
Finding the Subject   508
Changed Word Order   511

Compound Subjects   **512**

Indefinite Pronouns   **514**

Collective Nouns   **516**

Making Subjects and Verbs Agree: The Bottom Line   **516**

Chapter 25 **Using Pronouns Correctly: Agreement and Reference   522**

Nouns and Pronouns   **522**

Agreement of a Pronoun and Its Antecedent   **523**

Indefinite Pronouns   **523**
Avoiding Sexism   524

Collective Nouns   **525**

Pronouns and Their Antecedents: Being Clear   **528**

Chapter 26 **Using Pronouns Correctly: Consistency and Case   531**

Choosing the Case of Pronouns   **534**
Problems Choosing Pronoun Case   534

Common Errors With Case of Pronouns   **535**

Chapter 27 **Punctuation: The Period and the Question Mark   539**

The Period   **539**

The Question Mark   **540**

Chapter 28 **Punctuation: The Comma   542**

Use a Comma as a Lister   **542**

Use a Comma as a Linker   **543**

Use a Comma as an Introducer   **544**

Use a Comma as an Inserter   **545**
Other Ways to Use a Comma   547

Chapter 29 **Punctuation: The Semicolon and the Colon   550**

The Semicolon   **550**

The Colon   **551**

Chapter 30 **Punctuation: The Apostrophe   554**

The Apostrophe   554

Chapter 31 **Other Punctuation and Mechanics   560**

The Exclamation Mark   560

The Dash   560

Parentheses   560

The Hyphen   561

Quotation Marks   561

Capital Letters   562

Numbers   565

Abbreviations   565

Chapter 32 **Spelling   570**

Vowels and Consonants   570

Spelling Rule 1: Doubling a Final Consonant   570

Spelling Rule 2: Dropping the Final *e*   571

Spelling Rule 3: Changing the final *y* to *i*   572

Spelling Rule 4: Adding *-s* or *-es*   572

Spelling Rule 5: Using *ie* or *ei*   573

How Do You Spell It? One Word or Two?   575

Words Whose Spelling Depends on Their Meaning   575

Commonly Misspelled Words   577

Chapter 33 **Words That Sound Alike/Look Alike   580**

Words That Sound Alike/Look Alike   580

More Words That Sound Alike/Look Alike   586

Chapter 34 **Word Choice   595**

Precise Language   595

Wordiness   596

Clichés   598

Chapter 35 **Sentence Variety   601**

Balancing Long and Short Sentences   601

Using Different Ways to Begin Sentences   601

Begin With an Adverb   603

Begin With a Prepositional Phrase   604

Using Different Ways to Join Ideas   606

Use an *-ing* Modifier   606

Use an *-ed* Modifier   608

Use an Appositive   610

Use a *Who, Which,* or *That* Clause   611

Appendix ESL   **Grammar for ESL Students   614**

Nouns and Articles   614
   Using Articles With Nouns   615

Nouns or Pronouns Used as Subjects   617

Verbs   618
   Necessary Verbs   618
   -s Endings   618
   -ed Endings   618
   Two-word Verbs   620

Contractions and Verbs   621

Prepositions   622
   Prepositions That Show Time   622
   Prepositions That Show Place   623

Credits   625

Index   626

We have been very encouraged by the positive feedback generated by previous editions of this text, and we trust that the third edition of *Along These Lines: Writing Paragraphs and Essays* will offer instructors and students even more opportunities for stimulating interaction. To enable students to write for a specific audience and make connections between process and product, we have increased the amount of collaborative and independent activities. Today's writing classrooms reflect an ever-widening diversity of teaching strategies, learning styles, and student populations; *Along These Lines* respects and accepts the challenges of this unique tapestry.

THE WRITING CHAPTERS

We have retained what you liked most: the meticulous and intensive coverage of the writing process. This step-by-step coverage continues to trace the stages of writing, from generating ideas, to planning and focusing, to drafting and revising, to the final proofreading. The *lines* of the title refer to these stages, which are called **Thought Lines, Outlines, Rough Lines, and Final Lines,** to serve as convenient prompts for each stage. Every writing chapter covering a rhetorical pattern takes the student through all the stages of writing, in detail.

These chapters remain filled with exercises and activities, both individual and collaborative, because we believe that basic writers are more motivated and learn more easily when they are *actively* involved with individual or collaborative tasks. In keeping with these beliefs and with the emphasis on process, this edition of *Along These Lines* offers instructors more choices than ever.

New Features

In response to the suggestions of our colleagues and reviewers, this edition contains these significant changes and refinements:

- A new chapter, "Writing a Paragraph," for instructors who want to introduce students to a basic paragraph before beginning specific patterns
- A new chapter, "Different Essay Patterns," providing examples of each essay pattern, in each step of composition, from generating ideas to proofreading. This chapter is designed for instructors who want to spend more time familiarizing their students with the essay form.
- Double the number of proofreading exercises in each writing chapter
- New sentence-combining exercises in each writing chapter
- Transition exercises in each writing chapter
- More exercises on writing thesis statements
- More photographs used as writing prompts for visual learners

Additional Features

Along These Lines continues to include these distinctive features:

- A lively, conversational tone, including question-and-answer formats and dialogues
- Not much "talk" about writing; instead, no more than two pages of print are without a chart, a box, a list, an example, or an exercise.
- Small, simple clusters of information surrounded by white space rather than intimidating expanses of small print
- Boxed examples of the outline, draft, and final version of the writing assignment in each chapter
- Exercises throughout each chapter, not merely at the end, so each concept is reinforced as soon as it is introduced
- Exercises that are not merely fill-in-the-blanks, but collaborative ones that have students writing with peers, interviewing classmates, reacting to others' suggestions, and building on others' ideas
- Numerous writing topics and activities in each chapter, providing more flexibility for the instructor
- A Peer Review Form in each chapter so students can benefit from a classmate's reaction to their drafts

THE READING SECTIONS

New Features

We have made these changes and additions to the reading sections:

- New readings on invention, technology, writing a personal letter, and adolescents who smoke
- New topics for writing from reading

Additional Features

Along These Lines continues to offer these features:

- A separate and detailed chapter on "Writing From Reading," explaining and illustrating the steps of prereading, reading, annotating, summarizing, and reacting (in writing) to another's ideas
- Vocabulary definitions for each reading selection
- Grouping of selections by rhetorical pattern
- Readings selected to appeal to working students, returning students, and students who are parents, spouses, and veterans Selections focus on such topics as getting an education, generational divisions and definitions, fitting in, or feeling left out.
- Readings that are accessible and of particular interest to this student audience—many of the selections thus come from popular periodicals
- Topics for writing sparked by the content of the writing, designed to elicit thinking, not rote replication of a model

THE GRAMMAR CHAPTERS

New Features

- A new chapter, "Avoiding Run-On Sentences and Comma Splices"
- New, separate chapters on the comma and the apostrophe
- Paragraph-editing exercises at the end of each grammar chapter to connect the grammar principle to writing assignments

Additional Features

Because reviewers especially praised the focus and the exercises of the grammar chapters, these chapters continue to include these features:

- Emphasis on the most important skills for college readiness
- Grammar concepts taught step-by-step, as in "Two Steps to Check for Fragments"
- Numerous exercises, including practice, editing, and collaborative exercises

Instructors will find *Along These Lines* easy to use for several reasons:

- It has so many exercises, activities, assignments, and readings that teachers can select strategies they prefer and adapt them to the needs of different class sections.
- The tear-out exercises reinforce every instructional concept and eliminate the pressure instructors face in preparing supplemental materials.
- The exercises serve as an instant lesson plan for any class period or as individualized work for students in a writing lab.

Along These Lines will appeal to instructors, but more importantly, it will work for students. The basic premise of this book is that an effective text should respect students' individuality and their innate desire to learn and succeed. We hope it helps your students flourish by providing them with a foundation of respect, encouragement, and ongoing collaboration as they work through the writing process.

ACKNOWLEDGMENTS

Many individuals have helped us refine *Along These Lines*, and we are extremely indebted to reviewers and adopters nationwide who have provided invaluable insight. For their collective wisdom, encouragement, and advice, we wish to thank the following dedicated professionals:

Nancy Alexander	Methodist College
Donald Brotherton	DeVry University–Chicago
Pam Feeney	Kellogg Community College
Ray Foster	Scottsdale Community College
Irene Gilliam	Tallahassee Community College
Barbara Hamilton	Jones County Junior College
Marian Helms	College of Southern Idaho
Joel Henderson	Chattanooga State Technical Community College
Evelyn Kelly	Coastal Carolina Community College
Cari Kenner	Texas State Technical College at Harlingen
Dimitri Keriotis	Modesto Junior College
James Mense	St. Louis Community College Florissant Valley
Julie Nichols	Okaloosa-Walton Community College
Richard Rawnsley	College of the Desert
Athene Sallee	Forsyth Technical Community College
Larry Sexton	Gaston College
Carmen Subryan	Howard University
Jeffrey Torricelli	St. Clair County Community College

Joan Polk, editorial assistant, coordinated the reviews and continues to amaze us with her organizational skills and attention to detail.

Craig Campanella, senior English editor, once again proved to be a master at calming fears and gently reminding us of deadlines for both the student edition and the instructor's edition. He's tactful and energetic enough to be in politics, but we're fortunate that he's still showing authors how to maneuver through the publishing maze.

Additionally, we were blessed to work with Maureen Benicasa, a patient and meticulous production editor who had to oversee numerous manuscript revisions and serve as our liaison to various departments near and far. (Thanks for being so sane and rational, Maureen!) We also are very thankful for the many individuals who helped reshape and redesign our book. Among the talented individuals involved in this "makeover" are Kathleen Karcher, permissions editor; Krystyna Budd, copy editor; Carmen DiBartolomeo, designer; Anne Nieglos, art director; and Dee Josephson, proofreader. Thanks also to Karen Schultz for diligently searching the photo archives for us and saving us many hours of legwork; Julie Nichols for her meticulous review of first proof pages; Jan Williams for producing such a detailed and organized index; and to Rachel Falk, marketing manager, for coordinating promotions and introducing us to fellow writing teachers.

Finally, thanks as always to our colleagues and students at Broward Community College and Palm Beach Community College. Your tolerance, encouragement, friendship, and support are extraordinary along *all* lines.

John Sheridan Biays
Carol Wershoven

The Writing Process in Every Chapter...

K

Known for its dedication to the writing process, **Along These Lines** offers students intensive, thorough, step-by-step direction through the writing process in each chapter:

- *Thought Lines:* generating ideas
- *Outlines:* planning and focusing
- *Rough Lines:* drafting and revising
- *Final Lines:* polishing and proofreading.

Thought Lines **Gathering Ideas: Illustration**

Suppose your instructor asks you to write a paragraph about some aspect of clothes. You can begin by thinking about your subject, to gather ideas and to find a focus for your paragraph.

Looking through entries in your journal might lead you to the following underlined entry.

Journal Entry About Clothes

I went to the mall yesterday to look for some good shoes. What a crowd! Some big sale was going on, and the stores were packed. Everybody was pushing and shoving. I just left. I'll go when it's not so crowded. I hate buying clothes and shoes. Wish I could just wear jeans and tee shirts all the time. But even then, the jeans

Outlines **Devising a Plan: Illustration**

When you plan your outline, keep your topic sentence in mind:

People of various backgrounds and ages wear all kinds of tee shirts.

Notice the key words, which are underlined, and which lead to three key phrases:

people of various backgrounds
people of various ages
all kinds of tee shirts

Can you put the details together so that they connect to one of these key

Rough Lines **Drafting and Revising: Illustration**

Review the outline on tee shirts on page _____. You can create a first draft of this outline in the form of a paragraph. At this point, you can combine some of the short, choppy sentences of the outline, add details, and add transitions to link your ideas. You can revise your draft using the following checklist.

✔ **Checklist**

A Checklist for Revising an Illustration Paragraph

✔ **Should** some of the sentences be combined?

✔ **Do** I need more or better transitions?

✔ **Should** I add more details to support my points?

✔ **Should** some of the details be more specific?

Final Lines **Proofreading and Polishing: Illustration**

As you prepare the final version of your illustration paragraph, make any changes in word choice or transitions that can refine your writing. Following is the final version of the paragraph on tee shirts. As you read it, you will notice a few more changes: some details have been added, some have been made more specific, and a transition has been added. In addiiton, a concluding sentence has been added to unify the paragraph. These changes were made as the final version was prepared. (They are underlined for your reference.)

A Final Version of a Paragraph (Changes from the last draft are underlined.)

People of various backgrounds and ages wear all kinds of tee shirts. Athletes and movie stars are seen in them. Musicians often perform in ragged tees, and

...and now in Full Color!

Writing Your Own Illustration Paragraph

1. Examine the photograph below. After you have looked at it carefully, write a paragraph with this topic sentence:

Most malls have a variety of stores and eating places. The photograph may help you think of examples to support the topic sentence.

Exercise 8

👥 *Collaborate*

Adding Details to an Outline

Below are three partial outlines. Each has a topic sentence and some details. Working with a partner or group, add more details that support the topic sentence.

1. **topic sentence:** People caught in the rain find a number of ways to avoid getting wet.

Answers Will Vary.

Possible answers shown at right.

a. Some cover their heads with newspaper.

b. Some crouch against the wall of a big building.

c. Some take off their shoes and race through the puddles.

d. *Some use their briefcases to cover their heads.*

Name: _____ **Section:** _____

PEER REVIEW FORM FOR AN ILLUSTRATION PARAGRAPH

After you have written a draft for your illustration paragraph, let a writing partner read it. When your partner has completed the form below, discuss the comments. Then repeat the same process for your partner's paragraph.

The examples in this paragraph relate to this topic sentence: _____

The new full color design allows students to readily recognize the pedagogical features so important to their learning.

Along These Lines offers students exercises!

The Third Edition is characterized by its abundance of exercises. New *Connect* exercises direct students to the Internet to look into and research a point.

Collaborative exercises in every chapter have students writing and editing with peers, interviewing classmates, reacting to others' suggestions and building on others' ideas. Working with peers involves each student in completing the task, alleviates the anxiety of working in a vacuum, and promotes critical thinking. *Peer Review Forms* help students organize their thoughts and comments.

Print Components for Students

The New American Webster Handy College Dictionary

Available free to students when packaged with **Along These Lines**, this dictionary has over 1.5 million Signet copies in print and over 115,000 definitions, including current phrases, slang, and scientific terms. It offers more than 1,500 new words, with over 200 not found in any other competing dictionary and features boxed inserts on etymologies and language.

Use this ISBN to order **Along These Lines: Writing Paragraphs and Essays, Third Edition** with FREE Dictionary: (0-13-103922-9)

The Prentice Hall ESL Workbook

Available free to students when packaged with **Along These Lines**, this 138-page workbook is divided into seven major units, providing explanations and exercises in the most challenging grammar topics for non-native speakers. With over 80 exercise sets, this guide provides ample instruction and practice in nouns, articles, verbs, modifiers, pronouns, prepositions, and sentence structure.

Stand-alone ISBN: (0-13-092323-0)

Package ISBN for **Along These Lines: Writing Paragraphs and Essays, Third Edition** with FREE ESL Workbook: (0-13-104294-7)

The Prentice Hall Grammar Workbook

Available free when packaged with **Along These Lines**, this 21-chapter workbook is a comprehensive source of instruction for students who need additional grammar, punctuation, and mechanics instruction. Each chapter provides ample explanation, examples, and exercise sets. The exercises contain enough variety to ensure a student's mastery of each concept.

Stand-alone ISBN: (0-13-042188-X)

Package ISBN for **Along These Lines: Writing Paragraphs and Essays, Third Edition** with FREE Grammar Workbook: (0-13-104293-9)

The Prentice Hall TASP Writing Study Guide

Available free to students when packaged with **Along These Lines**, this guide prepares students for the writing portion of the Texas Academic Skills Program test. In addition, it familiarizes the reader with the elements of the test and provides strategies for success. There are exercises for each part of the exam, and then a full-length practice test with answer key so students can gauge their own progress.

Stand-alone ISBN: (0-13-041585-5)

Package ISBN for **Along These Lines: Writing Paragraphs and Essays, Third Edition** with FREE TASP Writing Study Guide: (0-13-104296-3)

The Prentice Hall Florida Exit Test Study Guide for Writing

Free when packaged with **Along These Lines**, this guide is designed to prepare students for the writing section of the Florida Exit test. It also acquaints readers with the parts of the test and provides strategies for success.

Stand-alone ISBN: (0-13-111652-5)

Package ISBN for **Along These Lines: Writing Paragraphs and Essays, Third Edition** with FREE Florida Exit Test Study Guide for Writing: (0-13-104333-1)

Research Navigator™

Research Navigator™ is the one-stop research solution—complete with extensive help on the research process and three exclusive databases including EBSCO's ContentSelect Academic Journal Database, *The New York Times* Search by Subject Archive, and *Best of the Web* Link Library. Take a tour on the web at *http://www.researchnavigator.com*. Your students get FREE ACCESS to Research Navigator™ when you package **Along These Lines** with our exclusive EVALUATING ONLINE RESOURCES: ENGLISH 2003 guide. Contact your local Prentice Hall sales representative for ordering details.

Print Components for Instructors

Annotated Instructor's Edition

The Annotated Instructor's Edition features the answers to all of the exercises and includes marginal annotations to enhance instruction. Written by John Biays and Carol Wershoven, these annotations are derived from their years of experience teaching developmental writing. (0-13-111622-3)

The annotations include:

- *Teaching Tips* with practical, proven ideas for getting the most out of each class session. They include specific activities to help students master the material.

- *Instructor's Discussion Questions* with ideas on promoting class interaction.

- *Instructor's Notes* providing chapter cross-references and suggestions for helping the class run more smoothly.

- *Answers Will Vary* features that alert instructors to the exercises with a range of responses.

Instructor's Resource Manual

An additional free supplement for instructors, the **Instructor's Resource Manual** provides additional teaching strategies, additional collaborative activities, sample syllabi, chapter summaries, and more. (0-13-111620-7)

The Prentice Hall Writing Skills Test Bank

This printed test bank will include hundreds of additional exercises for instructors to give students. Covering many of the basic skills of writing, **The Prentice Hall Writing Skills Test Bank** can be used with any writing text as a source of extra practice or testing. (0-13-111628-2)

To order any of these supplements, please contact your local Prentice Hall sales representative for hard copies or for the user name and password for **English Instruction Central** at *www.prenhall.com/english.*

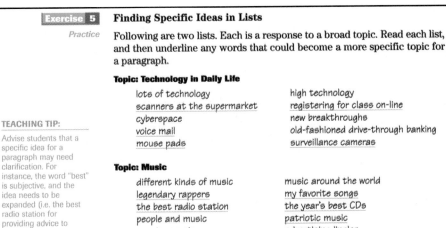

Exercise 5 *Practice*

Finding Specific Ideas in Lists

Following are two lists. Each is a response to a broad topic. Read each list, and then underline any words that could become a more specific topic for a paragraph.

Topic: Technology in Daily Life

lots of technology
scanners at the supermarket
cyberspace
voice mail
mouse pads

high technology
registering for class on-line
new breakthroughs
old-fashioned drive-through banking
surveillance cameras

Topic: Music

different kinds of music
legendary rappers
the best radio station
people and music
country music

music around the world
my favorite songs
the year's best CDs
patriotic music
advertising jingles

TEACHING TIP:

Advise students that a specific idea for a paragraph may need clarification. For instance, the word "best" is subjective, and the idea needs to be expanded (i.e. the best radio station for providing advice to teenagers).

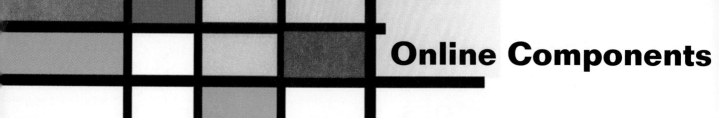

The Companion Website™

www.prenhall.com/biays

With FREE access provided, the **Along These Lines Companion Website™** at *www.prenhall.com/biays* is much more than a resource for study or a launching pad for exploration. Its unique tools and support make it easy for you to integrate our online resources into your course, including:

- **Interactive multiple choice, labeling, and essay exercises** keyed to specific chapters and/or sections of the text allow students the opportunity to take chapter quizzes online with automatic grading.
- **Writing activities** lead developing writers through the steps of the writing process.
- **Relevant and informative weblinks** provide students with additional resources on key concepts presented in the text.
- **A Site Search feature** allows students and instructors to search the Companion Website™ for a particular topic.

The Along These Lines Online Courses

Prentice Hall's online developmental writing course offers you all the advantages of a custom-built program without the hassle of writing it from scratch. Designed specifically for **Along These Lines**, this course supports and augments the text by providing a complete array of writing concepts and exercises at your fingertips—to use just as it is presented or to be customized to your specific course syllabus. Compatible with **BlackBoard™**, **WebCT™**, and **Course Compass™** platforms, this online course includes the following features: chapter introductions, lecture notes, writing workshops, quizzes, essay questions, and course management. Visit *www.prenhall.com/demo* for more information.

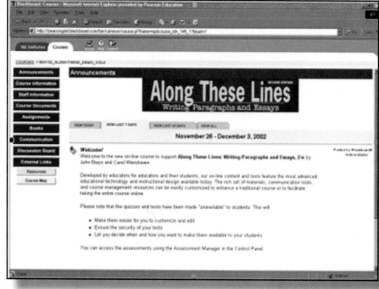

PH WORDS

PH WORDS is an online practice and assessment program covering the entire writing curriculum. Providing instructors the ability to measure and track their students' mastery of all of the elements of writing.

Here's how:

- **ONLINE.** Available 24/7 on the Web.
- **COMPREHENSIVE. PH WORDS** offers over 130 modules covering the entire writing curriculum and 9000+ exercises, including grammar, writing process, patterns of development, and more. Each module has four parts: *Recall, Apply,* and *Write* exercises, which progress from easy to more difficult, and a *Watch Screen*, which offers a one to two minute audio and visual summary of the concept.
- **DIAGNOSTIC. PH WORDS** offers two ways in which students and instructors can assess individual and overall class areas of weakness:
  - Grammar diagnostic tests assess a baseline of knowledge. Once a student takes a diagnostic test, their **PH WORDS** syllabus indicates which grammar concepts they did not master and provides a customized roadmap for improvement.
  - Gradebook Reports—At any point, an instructor can run several reports that will offer a snapshot of where students need the most work. Three basic types are by Skill, by Class, and by Student.

Visit *www.prenhall.com/phwords* and take the **PH WORDS** virtual tour.
To order **Along These Lines: Writing Paragraphs and Essays, Third Edition** with **PH WORDS** for a 50% DISCOUNT, use ISBN: (0-13-103924-5).

Help your students make the grade 24/7 with

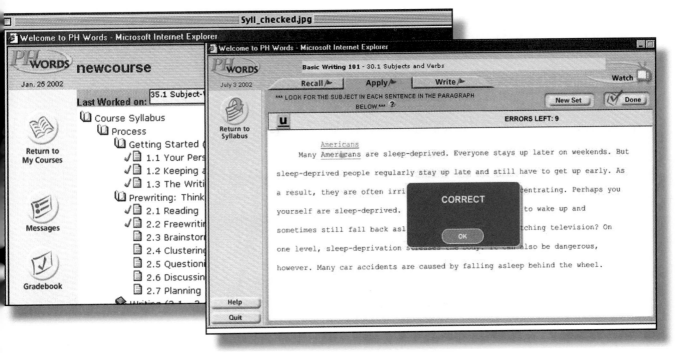

ALONG
THESE
LINES

Writing in Stages

The Process Approach

INTRODUCTION

Learning By Doing

Writing is a skill, and like any skill, writing improves with practice. This book provides you with the practice to improve your writing through several activities. Some activities can be done by yourself, some will ask you to work with a partner or a group, some can be done in the classroom, and some can be done at home. The important point to remember is that *good writing takes practice:* you can learn to write well by writing.

Steps Make Writing Easier

Writing is easier if you *do not try to do too much at once.* Producing a piece of effective writing requires that you think, plan, draft, rethink, focus, revise, edit, and proofread. You can become frustrated if you try to do all these things at the same time.

To make the task of writing easier, *Along These Lines* breaks the process into stages. Throughout this book, the writing process is divided into four major parts:

Thought Lines

In this stage, you *think* about your topic, and you gather ideas. You *react* to your own ideas and add more ideas to your first thoughts. You can also *react* to other people's ideas as a way of generating your own writing material. This is often called *prewriting*.

Outlines

In this stage, you begin to *plan* your writing. You examine your ideas and begin to *focus* them around one main idea. Planning involves combining, dividing, and even eliminating the ideas you started with. It involves more thinking about the point you want to make and the order of details that can best express your point.

Rough Lines

In this stage, the thinking and planning begin to shape themselves into a piece of writing. You complete a *draft* of your work, a rough version of the finished product. And then you think again as you examine the draft and check it. Checking it begins the process of *revision*, "fixing" the draft so that it takes the shape you want and expresses your ideas clearly.

Final Lines

In this stage, the final version of your writing gets one last, careful *review*. When you prepare the final copy of your work, you *proofread* and concentrate on identifying and correcting any mistakes in spelling, mechanics, or punctuation you may have overlooked. This stage is the *final check* of your work to make your writing the best it can be.

These four stages in the writing process—*thought lines, outlines, rough lines, and final lines*—may overlap. You may be changing your plan (the *outlines* stage) even as you work on the *rough lines* of your paper; there is no rule that prevents you from moving back to an earlier stage. Thinking of writing as a series of stages helps you to see the process as a *manageable task*, for it helps you *avoid doing everything at once* and becoming overwhelmed by the challenge.

Throughout the chapters of this text, you will have many opportunities to become familiar with the four stages of effective writing. Working individually and with your classmates, you can become a better writer along <u>all</u> lines.

CHAPTER 1

Writing a Paragraph

Usually, students write because they have a writing assignment requiring them to write on some topic or choice of topics, and the writing is due by a certain day. So assume that you get such an assignment and it calls for one paragraph. You might wonder, "Why a paragraph? Why not something large, like a two- or three-page paper? After all, many classes will ask for papers, not just paragraphs."

For one thing, all essays are a series of paragraphs. If you can write one good paragraph, you can write more than one. The **paragraph** is the basic building block of any essay. It is a group of sentences focusing on *one idea* or one point. Keep this concept in mind: *one idea to a paragraph.* Focusing on one idea or one point gives a paragraph **unity.** If you have a new point, start a new paragraph.

You may ask, "Doesn't this mean a paragraph will be short? How long should a paragraph be, anyway?" To convince a reader of one main point, you need to make it, support it, develop it, explain it, and describe it. There will be shorter and longer paragraphs, but for now, you can assume your paragraph will be somewhere between seven and twelve sentences long.

This chapter will guide you through each stage of the writing process:

- **Thought Lines**—how to generate and develop ideas for your paragraph
- **Outlines**—how to organize your ideas
- **Rough Lines**—how to make and revise rough drafts
- **Final Lines**—how to edit and refine your ideas

We give extra emphasis to the thought lines in this chapter to give you that extra help in getting started that you might need.

BEGINNING THE THOUGHT LINES: GATHERING IDEAS

Suppose your instructor asks you to write a paragraph about your favorite city or town. You already know your **purpose**—to write a paragraph that makes some point about your favorite city or town. You have an **audience** since you are writing this paragraph for your instructor and classmates. Knowing your audience and purpose is important in writing effectively. Often, your purpose is to write a specific kind of paper for a class. But sometimes you may have to write with a different purpose or audience, such as writing instructions for a new employee at your workplace, or a letter of complaint to a manufacturer, or a short biographical essay for a scholarship application.

Freewriting, Brainstorming, Keeping a Journal

Once you have identified your audience and purpose, you can begin by finding some way to *think on paper*. You can use the techniques of freewriting, brainstorming, or keeping a journal to gather ideas.

Freewriting Give yourself fifteen minutes to write whatever comes into your mind on your subject. If your mind is a blank, write, "My mind's a blank. My mind's a blank," over and over until you think of something else. The main goal here is to *write without stopping*. Do not stop to tell yourself, "This is stupid," or "I can't use any of this in a paper." Do not stop to correct your spelling or punctuation. Just write. Let your ideas flow. Write *freely*. Here is an example:

Freewriting About a Favorite City or Town

Favorite city or town. City? I like New York. It's so big and exciting. Haven't been there much, though. Only once. My home town. I like it. It's just another town but comfortable and friendly. Maybe St. Augustine. Lots of fun visits there. Grandparents there. Hard to pick a favorite. Different places are good for different reasons.

Brainstorming **Brainstorming** is like freewriting because you write whatever comes into your head, but it is a little different because you can pause *to ask yourself questions* that will lead to new ideas. When you brainstorm alone, you "interview" yourself about a subject. You can also brainstorm and ask questions within a group. Here's an example:

Brainstorming About a Favorite City or Town

Favorite place.

City or town.

What's the difference between a city and a town?

Doesn't matter. Just pick one. Cities bigger.

How is city life different from town life?

Cities are bigger. More crowded, like Atlanta.

Which do you like better, a city or a town?

Sometimes I like cities.

Why?

There is more to do.

So, what city do you like?

I like New York. St. Augustine.

Is St. Augustine a city?

Yes. A small one.

Do you like towns?

I loved this little town in Mexico.

If you feel as if you are running out of ideas in brainstorming, try to form a question out of what you've just written. *Go where your questions and answers lead you.* For example, if you write, *"There is more to do in cities,"* you could form these questions:

What is there to do? Sports? Entertainment? Outdoor exercise? Meeting people?

You could also make a list of your brainstorming ideas, but remember to *do only one step at a time.*

Keeping a Journal A **journal** is a notebook of your personal writing, a notebook in which you write regularly and often. *It is not a diary, but it is a place to record your experiences, reactions, and observations.* In it, you can write about what you have done, heard, seen, read, or remembered. You can include sayings that you would like to remember, news clippings, snapshots—anything that you would like to recall or consider. A journal provides an enjoyable way to practice your writing, and it is a great source of ideas for writing.

Journal Entry About a Favorite City or Town

I'm not going south to see my grandparents this winter. They're coming here instead of me going to St. Augustine. I'd really like to go there. I like the warm weather. It's better than months of snow, ice, and rain here in Easthampton. I'll miss going there. I've been so many times that it's like a second home. St. Augustine is great around Christmas time.

Finding Specific Ideas

Whether you freewrite, brainstorm, or consult your journal, you end up with something on paper. Follow those first ideas; see where they can take you. You are looking for specific ideas, each of which can focus the general one you started with. At this point, you do not have to decide which specific idea you want to write about. You just want to *narrow your range* of ideas.

You might think, "Why should I narrow my ideas? Won't I have more to say if I keep my topic big?" But remember that a paragraph has one idea; "you want to state it clearly and with convincing details for support." If you try to write one paragraph on the broad topic of city life versus town life, for example, you will probably make so many general statements that you will either say very little or bore your reader with big, sweeping statements. General ideas are big, broad ones. Specific ideas are smaller, narrower. If you scanned the freewriting example on a favorite city or town, you might underline several specific ideas as possible topics:

> Favorite city or town. City? I like <u>New York</u>. It's so big and exciting. Haven't been there much, though. Only once. <u>My home town</u>. I like it. It's just another town but comfortable and friendly. Maybe <u>St. Augustine</u>. Lots of fun visits there. Grandparents there. Hard to pick a favorite. Different places are good for different reasons.

Consider the underlined terms. They are specific places. You could write a paragraph about any one of these places, or you could underline specific places in your brainstorming questions and answers:

> Favorite place.
> City or town.
>
> **What's the difference between a city and a town?**
>
> Doesn't matter. Just pick one. Cities bigger.
>
> **How is city life different from town life?**
>
> Cities are bigger. More crowded, like <u>Atlanta.</u>
>
> **Which do you like better, a city or a town?**
>
> Sometimes I like cities.
>
> **Why?**
>
> There is more to do.
>
> **So, what city do you like?**
>
> I like <u>New York. St. Augustine.</u>
>
> **Is St. Augustine a city?**
>
> Yes. A small one.
>
> **Do you like towns?**
>
> I loved this <u>little town in Mexico.</u>

Each of these specific places could be a topic for your paragraph.

If you reviewed the journal entry on a favorite city or town, you would also be able to underline specific places:

> I'm not going south to see my grandparents this winter. They're coming here instead of me going to <u>St. Augustine</u>. I'd really like to go there. I like the warm weather. It's better than months of snow, ice, and rain here in <u>Easthampton</u>. I'll miss going there. I've been so many times that it's like a second home. St. Augustine is great around Christmas time.

Remember that if you follow the steps, they can lead you to specific ideas.

Selecting One Topic

Once you have a list of specific ideas that can lead you to a specific topic, you can pick one topic. Let's say you decided to work with the list of places you gathered through brainstorming:

> Atlanta
> New York
> St. Augustine
> a little town in Mexico

Looking at this list, you decide you want to write about St. Augustine as your favorite city.

Exercise 1

Practice

Creating Questions for Brainstorming

Following are several topics. For each one, brainstorm by writing at least six questions related to the topic that could lead you to further ideas. The first topic is done for you:

1. topic: dogs

Question 1. Why are dogs such popular pets?

Question 2. What kind of dog is a favorite pet in America?

Question 3. Are dogs hard to train?

Question 4. What dog, in your life, do you remember best?

Question 5. What's the most famous dog on television?

Question 6. Are there dogs as cartoon characters?

2. topic: driving

Question 1. _____

Question 2. _____

Question 3. _____

Question 4. _____

Question 5. _____

Question 6. _____

3. topic: complaining

Question 1. _____

Question 2. _____

Question 3. _____

Question 4. _____

Question 5. _____

Question 6. _____

4. topic: bargains

Question 1. _____

Question 2. _____

Question 3. _____

Question 4. _____

Question 5. _____

Question 6. _____

Exercise 2

Practice

Finding Specific Details in Freewriting

Below are two samples of freewriting. Each is a written response to a different topic. Read each sample, and then underline any words and phrases that could become the focus of a paragraph.

Freewriting Reaction to the Topic of Travel

I like to travel. But I'd rather drive than fly. When I drive, I can decide when to stop and go. When you fly, you can get stuck on the runway for hours and never take off. Then when you're in the air, you can't get out until it's over. Plus, think of airline food. Disgusting soggy sandwiches or tiny bags of pretzels. And there is no leg room. I can drive and find a nice truck stop restaurant.

Freewriting Reaction to the Topic of Pollution

Pollution. Save the planet. Smoke pollutes. Big smokestacks at the edge of the city belch smoke all the time. And even smokers pollute, especially indoors. No-smoking rules are controversial. I used to smoke and never thought about pollution. Noise pollution is a pain, too. People who live next to a highway must hear noise all the time.

Exercise 3

Practice

Finding Specific Details in a List

Below are several lists of words or phrases. In each list, one item is a general term; the others are more specific. Underline the words or phrases that are more specific. The first list is done for you.

1. apple pie
   ice cream
   desserts
   butterscotch pudding
   jello
   chocolate brownies

2. annoying tv jingles
   late-night infomercials
   psychic hotlines
   dogs in commercials
   television commercials

3. stock car racing
   sports
   cheerleaders
   stadium ticket prices
   soccer
   coaches out of control

4. toys
   Barbie dolls
   teddy bears
   action figures
   jump ropes
   miniature trucks

5. auburn
   jet black
   hair color
   platinum blond
   deep brown

6. registration
   financial aid
   student activities fees
   night classes
   placement tests
   required courses

Finding Topics Through Freewriting

The following exercise must be completed with a partner or a group. Below are several topics. Pick one and freewrite on it for ten minutes. Then read your freewriting to your partner or group. Ask your listener(s) to jot down any words or phrases from your writing that could lead to a specific topic for a paragraph.

Your listener(s) should read the jotted-down words or phrases to you. You will be hearing a collection of specific ideas that came from *your* writing. As you listen, underline the words in your freewriting.

Freewriting topics (pick one):

1. a happy occasion

2. a hated chore

3. a special childhood memory

Freewriting on (name of topic chosen): _____

_____

_____

_____

_____

_____

_____

_____

Adding Details to a Specific Topic

You can develop the specific topic you picked in a number of ways:

1. *Check your list* for other ideas that seem to fit with the specific topic you've picked.
2. *Brainstorm*—ask yourself more questions about your topic, and use the answers as detail.
3. *List* any new ideas you have that may be connected to your topic.

One way to add details is to go back and check your brainstorming for other ideas about St. Augustine:

I like St. Augustine.
a small city

Now you can brainstorm some questions that will lead you to more details. The questions do not have to be connected to each other; they are just questions that could lead you to ideas and details:

What's a small city?

It doesn't have skyscrapers or freeways or millions of people.

So, what makes it a city?

Thousands of visitors come there every day.

What's so great about St. Augustine?

You can go to the beach nearby.

Is it a clean, big beach?

Sure. And the water is a clear blue.

What else can you do in St. Augustine?

There's lots of history.

Like what?

A fort. The oldest schoolhouse. Old houses.

Another way to add details is to list any ideas that may be connected to your topic. The list might give you more specific details:

grandparents live there
warm in winter
grandparents feed me
I use their car

If you had tried all three ways of adding detail, you would end up with this list of details connected to the topic of a favorite city or town:

a small city   clear blue water
no freeways   lots of history
no skyscrapers   a fort
not millions of people   oldest schoolhouse
thousands of visitors every day   grandparents live there
can always visit family for free   warm in winter
beach nearby   grandparents feed me
clean, big beach   I use their car

Info BOX

Beginning the Thought Lines: A Summary

The thought lines stage of writing a paragraph enables you to gather ideas. This process begins with several steps:

1. *Think on paper and write down any ideas that you have about a topic.* You can do this by freewriting, by brainstorming, or by keeping a journal.

2. *Scan your writing for specific ideas that have come from your first efforts.* List these specific ideas.

3. *Pick one specific idea.* Then, by reviewing your early writing, by questioning, and by thinking further, you can add details to the one specific idea.

This process may seem long, but once you have worked through it several times, it will become nearly automatic. When you think about ideas before you try to shape them into a paragraph, you are off to a good start. Confidence comes from having something to say, and once you have a specific idea, you will be ready to begin shaping and developing details that support your idea.

Practice

Adding Details to a Topic by Brainstorming

Below are two topics. Each is followed by two or three details. Brainstorm more questions, based on the existing details, that can add more details.

1. topic: advantages of going to college part-time.
    details: saves money
             less stressful

Question 1: <u>How much money can you save?</u>

Question 2: <u>What expenses can you cut?</u>

Question 3: <u>What stresses can be reduced?</u>

Question 4: _____

Question 5: _____

Question 6: _____

2. topic: losing a wallet
    details: frightening experience
             leads to time–consuming chores
             identity is stolen

Question 1: <u>What is frightening about the experience?</u>

Question 2: <u>What are the chores?</u>

Question 3: _____

Question 4: _____

Question 5: _____

Question 6: _____

Adding Details by Listing

Practice

Following are four topics for paragraphs. For each topic, list details that seem to fit the topic.

1. topic: the tastiest fast foods

    details: a. _____   c. _____
                b. _____   d. _____

2. topic: renting videos

    details: a. _____   c. _____
                b. _____   d. _____

3. topic: a good night's sleep

    details: a. _____   c. _____
                b. _____   d. _____

4. topic: good neighbors

details: a. _____ c. _____

b. _____ d. _____

FOCUSING THE THOUGHT LINES

The next step of writing is *to focus your ideas around some point.* Your ideas will begin to take a focus if you reexamine them, looking for *related ideas.* Two techniques that you can use are

- marking a list of related ideas
- mapping related ideas

Listing Related Ideas

To develop a marked list, take another look at the list we developed under the topic of a favorite city or town. The same list is shown below, but you will notice some of the items have been marked with symbols that show related ideas:

N   marks ideas about St. Augustine's **natural** good points

H   marks ideas about St. Augustine's **history**

F   marks ideas about **family** in St. Augustine

Here is the marked list of ideas related to the topic of a favorite city or town:

	a small city	**N**	clear blue water
	no freeways	**H**	lots of history
	no skyscrapers	**H**	a fort
	not millions of people	**H**	oldest schoolhouse
	thousands of visitors every day	**F**	grandparents live there
F	can always visit family for free	**N**	warm in winter
N	beach nearby	**F**	grandparents feed me
N	clean, big beach	**F**	I use their car

You have no doubt noticed that some items are not marked: a small city, no freeways, no skyscrapers, not millions of people, thousands of visitors every day. Perhaps you can come back to them later, or you may decide you do not need them in your paragraph.

To make it easier to see what ideas you have and how they are related, try *grouping related ideas*, giving each list a title, such as the following:

Natural Good Points of St. Augustine

beach nearby   clear blue water
clean, big beach   warm in winter

History in St. Augustine

lots of history   oldest schoolhouse
a fort

Family in St. Augustine

can always visit family for free grandparents live there
grandparents feed me   I use their car

Mapping *(Clustering)*

Another way to focus your ideas is to mark your first list of ideas and then cluster the related ideas into separate lists. You can **map** your ideas like this:

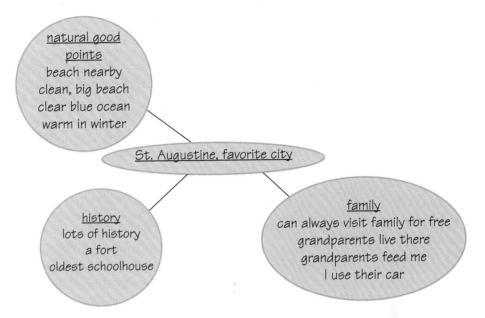

Whatever way you choose to examine and group your detail, you are working toward *a focus*, a *point*. You are asking and beginning to answer the question, "Where do the details lead?" The answer will be the **topic sentence** of your paragraph. It will be the *main idea* of your paragraph.

Forming a Topic Sentence

To form a topic sentence, you can do the following:

1. Review your details and see if you can form some general idea that can summarize the details.
2. Write that general idea as one sentence.

Your sentence that summarizes the details is the **topic sentence.** It makes a general point, and the more specific details you have gathered will support this point.

To form a topic sentence about your favorite city, St. Augustine, follow the steps. First, there are many details about St. Augustine. It is time to ask questions about the details. You could ask yourself, "What kind of details do I have? Can I summarize them?" You might then write the summary as the topic sentence:

> I love St. Augustine because it has sun and sea, history, and family.

Check the sentence against your details. Does it cover your "natural good points" of St. Augustine? Yes. The topic sentence sums them up as *sun and sea*. Does it cover history and family? Yes. The topic sentence says the place has *history and family*.

Writing Good Topic Sentences

Be careful. *Topics are not the same as topic sentences. Topics are the subjects you will write about.* A topic sentence states the *main idea* you have developed on a topic. Consider the differences between the topics and the topic sentences below:

> **topic:** Why courtesy is important
> **topic sentence:** Courtesy takes the conflict out of unpleasant encounters.
> **topic:** Dogs and their owners
> **topic sentence:** Many dog owners begin to look like their pets.

Topic sentences do not announce; they make a point. Look at the sentences below, and notice the differences between the sentences that announce and the topic sentences:

> **announcement:** I will discuss the process of changing a tire.
> **topic sentence:** Changing a tire is easy if you have the right tools and follow a simple process.
> **announcement:** An analysis of why recycling paper is important will be the subject of this paper.
> **topic sentence:** Recycling paper is important because it saves trees, money, and even certain animals.

Topic sentences can be too big to develop in one paragraph. A topic sentence that is *too broad* may take many paragraphs, even pages of writing, to develop. Look at the very broad sentences below, and then notice how they can be narrowed:

> **too broad:** Athletes get paid too much money. (This sentence is too broad because the term "athletes" could mean anything from professional boxers to college football players to neighborhood softball teams; "too much money" could mean any fee that basketball players receive for endorsing products to bonuses that professional football players get if they make the Super Bowl. The sentence could also refer to all athletes in the world at any time in history.)
> **a narrower, better topic sentence:** Last year, several professional baseball players negotiated high but fair salaries.
> **too broad:** I changed a great deal in my last year of high school. (The phrase "changed a great deal" could refer to physical changes, intellectual changes, or emotional changes or to changes in attitude, changes in goals, or just about any other change you can think of.)
> **a narrower, better topic sentence:** In my last year of high school, I overcame my shyness.

Topic sentences can be too small to develop in one paragraph. A topic sentence that is *too narrow* cannot be supported by detail. It may be a fact, which cannot be developed. A topic sentence that is too narrow leaves you with nothing more to say:

> **too narrow:** I hate broccoli.
> **an expanded topic sentence:** I hate broccoli for two reasons.
> **too narrow:** It takes twenty minutes to get out of the airport parking lot.
> **an expanded topic sentence:** Congestion at the airport parking lot is causing problems for travelers.

The thought lines stage begins with free, unstructured thinking and writing. As you work through the thought lines process, your thinking and writing will become more focused.

> ## Info BOX
>
> ### Focusing the Thought Lines: A Summary
>
> The thought lines stage of writing a paragraph enables you to develop an idea into a topic sentence and related details. You can focus your thinking by working in steps:
>
> 1. Mark a list of related details, or try mapping to group your ideas.
>
> 2. Write a topic sentence that summarizes your detail.
>
> 3. Check that your topic sentence is a sentence, not a topic. Make sure that it is not too broad or too narrow, and that it is not an announcement. Check that it makes a point and focuses the details you have developed.

Exercise 7

Practice

Grouping Related Items in Lists of Details

Below are lists of details. In each list, circle the items that seem to fit into one group; then underline the items that seem to belong to a second group. Some items may not belong in either group. The first list is done for you.

1. topic: rainy weekends

no sports activities   cannot jog in neighborhood   *neg. aspects*
picnics cancelled   rains most in autumn
catch up on chores   read a book — *pos. aspects*
not forecast by weathermen   park too wet to visit
go to a mall   watch a movie

2. topic: breakfast

Pepsi and potato chips   juice and toast — *ok*   *Healthy?*
cornflakes and bananas — *ok*   oatmeal — *ok*   *vs. non-*
brunch   large coffee and candy bar — *healthy?*
coffee mugs   granola and fruit — *ok*
tea and a vitamin pill ~   doughnuts and coffee cake

3. topic: falling in love

romantic moments   emotional security   *pro*
shared thoughts   petty arguments   *&*
jealousy   shared dreams   *con*
Valentine's Day   fear of commitment
mutual respect   possessiveness

Exercise 8

Practice

Writing Topic Sentences for Lists of Details

Below are lists of details that have no topic sentence. Write an appropriate topic sentence for each one.

1. topic sentence: _____

People do not have to be in great shape to take walks.
Walking burns calories.
It is good for the heart.
It is good for the bones and muscles.
It doesn't cost anything to walk.
Walking is convenient.

Walking is a convenient, cost-free form of exercise (available to anyone) that burns calories, is good for the heart, & bones & muscles & does not cost...

It requires no exercise equipment or gym membership.
It can be done almost anywhere.

2. topic sentence: _____

_____

Many African-Americans celebrate Juneteenth.
Many Hispanic-Americans celebrate the Three Kings.
The Chinese New Year is a holiday for Chinese-Americans.
Irish-Americans celebrate St. Patrick's Day.
German-Americans enjoy Oktoberfest.
Swedish-Americans celebrate the feast of St. Lucia.

3. topic sentence: _____

_____

Cecilia was the fastest swimmer on the team.
She encouraged all the new team members.
She was a friend to all the old members.
She worked well with the coaches.
She never missed a practice.
She was never late for a meet.
She cheered for all her teammates.

4. topic sentence: _____

_____

Carlos worked twenty hours a week at a service station.
He never missed work.
He took four classes at college.
He was always studying in the student center.
He had two sons, Daniel, 4, and Tyler, 1.
He and his wife Shondra loved their boys.
Carlos was working and studying to make a better life for his family.

Exercise 9

Practice

Turning Topics into Topic Sentences

Below is a list. Some of the items in the list are topic sentences, but some are topics. Put an *X* by the items that are topics. In the lines below the list, rewrite the topics into topic sentences.

1. __X__   Three reasons to learn a second language.

2. _____   Breaking a habit takes will power.

3. __X__   The most rewarding experience of my life.

4. _____   Buying books is a good way to spend your money.

5. __X__   How I learned to cook.

6. _____   My brother discovered his talents on his first job.

7. _____   High school friendships can be lasting ones.

8. _____ Why driving is stressful.

9. _____ I got a B in history because I studied and reviewed.

10. _____ My greatest disappointment was missing my sister's wedding.

Rewrite the topics. Make each one into a topic sentence:

_____

_____

_____

_____

_____

_____

Exercise 10

Practice

Revising Topic Sentences That Are Too Broad

Below is a list of topic sentences. Some of them are too broad to support in one paragraph. Put an *X* by the ones that are too broad. Then, on the lines below the list, rewrite those sentences, focusing on a limited idea, a topic sentence that could be supported in one paragraph.

1. __X__ Working is extremely unpleasant.

2. _____ The most challenging aspect of babysitting was getting the children to go to bed.

3. __X__ Taxes are not fair to many people.

4. _____ Camille's honesty makes her a trustworthy friend.

5. _____ Two speeding tickets set my finances back for months.

6. __X__ Leon believes in the American way of life and wants it for his children.

7. __X__ People should leave their neighbors alone when it comes to little things.

8. _____ Teresa hopes her children will be educated and thoughtful voters.

9. __X__ Violence is ruining America.

10. __X__ My parents fought to keep us out of a gang.

Rewrite the broad sentences. Make each one more limited.

_____

_____

_____

_____

_____

_____

_____

Exercise 11

Practice

Making Announcements into Topic Sentences

Below is a list of sentences. Some are topic sentences. Some are announcements. Put an _X_ by the announcements. Then on the lines below the list, rewrite the announcements, making them into topic sentences.

1. _____ Lying to a spouse is a destructive habit.

2. __X___ The consequences of driving with bald tires will be the subject of this paper.

3. __X___ The need for a new recreation center will be explained.

4. _____ Moving to a new state can be a chance for a fresh start.

5. _____ Ridgefield deserves better cable television service.

6. _____ More benches throughout the city would make it more attractive to pedestrians.

7. __X___ Why clearer road signs are needed in this town is the area to be discussed.

8. __X___ This essay concerns the growing number of bike thefts on campus.

9. _____ A ban on smoking in public parks would protect people who rely on the parks for a natural retreat.

10. __X___ This paper will be about running a marathon.

Rewrite the announcements. Make each one a topic sentence.

_____

_____

_____

_____

_____

_____

Exercise 12

Practice

Revising Topic Sentences That Are Too Narrow

Below is a list of topic sentences. Some of them are topics that are too narrow; they cannot be developed with details. Put an *X* by the ones that are too narrow. Then, on the lines below, rewrite those sentences as broader topic sentences that could be developed in one paragraph.

1. __X__ It snowed when I drove to Denver.

2. _____ On rainy days, I have to pay careful attention to the way I drive.

3. __X__ My apartment is only one room.

4. __X__ Denzel missed the plane because his car broke down on the freeway.

5. _____ Buy-Low is a discount store.

6. _____ Clever use of space made my tiny office look larger.

7. __X__ Nilsa drives a Chevrolet.

8. _____ My old Corolla was a great car for long trips.

9. __X__ Chris takes six vitamins every morning.

10. __X__ Dr. Chan studied at Yale.

Rewrite the narrow sentences. Make each one broader.

_____

_____

_____

_____

_____

_____

Outlines Devising a Plan for a Paragraph

Checking Your Details

Once you have a topic sentence, you can begin working on an **outline** for your paragraph. The outline is a plan that helps you stay focused in your writing. The outline begins to form when you write your topic sentence and write your list of details beneath the topic sentence. You can now look at your list and ask yourself an important question: "Do I have **enough details** to **support** my topic sentence?" Remember, your goal is to write a paragraph of seven to twelve sentences.

Consider this topic sentence and list of details:

> **topic sentence:** People can be very rude when they shop in supermarkets.
>
> **details:** push in line
> express lane
> too many items

Does the list contain enough details for a paragraph of seven to twelve sentences? Probably not.

Adding Details When There Are Not Enough

To add detail, try brainstorming. Ask yourself some questions like these:

> Where else in supermarkets are people rude?
> Are they rude in other lanes besides the express lane?
> Are they rude in the aisles? How?
> Is there crowding anywhere? Where?

By brainstorming, you might come up with this detail:

> **topic sentence:** People can be very rude when they shop in supermarkets.
>
> **details:** push in line
> express lane
> too many items
> hit my cart with theirs in aisles
> block aisles while they decide
> push ahead in deli area
> will not take a number
> argue with cashier over prices
> yell at the bag boy

Keep brainstorming until you feel you have enough details for a seven- to twelve-sentence paragraph. Remember that it is better to have too many details than too few, for you can always delete the extra details later.

If you try brainstorming and still do not have many details, you can refer to your original ideas—your freewriting or journal—for other details.

Eliminating Details That Do Not Relate to the Topic Sentence

Sometimes, what you thought were good details do not relate to the topic sentence because they do not fit or support your point. Eliminate details that do not relate to the topic sentence. For example, the following list contains details that really do not relate to the topic sentence. Those details are crossed out.

> **topic sentence:** Waiters have to be very patient in dealing with their customers.
>
> **details:** customers take a long time ordering
> ~~waiter's salary is low~~
> waiters have to explain specials twice
> customers send orders back
> customers blame waiters for any delays

customers want food instantly
waiters can't react to sarcasm of customers
waiters can't get angry if customer does
~~waiters work long shifts~~
customers change their mind after ordering

From List to Outline

Take another look at the topic sentence and list of details on a favorite city or town:

topic sentence: I love St. Augustine because it has sun, sea, history, and family.

details:

a small city	clear blue water
no freeways	lots of history
no skyscrapers	a fort
not millions of people	oldest schoolhouse
thousands of visitors every day	grandparents live there
can always visit family for free	warm in winter
beach nearby	grandparents feed me
clean, big beach	I use their car

After you scan that list, you are ready to develop the outline of the paragraph.

An outline is a plan for writing, and it can be a type of draft in list form. It sketches what you want to write and the order that you want to present it. *An organized, logical list will make your writing unified since each item on the list will relate to your topic sentence.*

When you plan, keep your topic sentence in mind:

I love St. Augustine because it has <u>sun, sea, history</u>, and <u>family</u>.

Notice the underlined key words, which lead to three key parts of your outline:

sun and sea
history
family

You can put the details on your list together so that they connect to one of these parts:

sun and sea

— beach nearby, clean, big beach, clear blue water, warm in winter

history

— lots of history, a fort, oldest schoolhouse

family

— can always visit family for free, grandparents live there, grandparents feed me, I drive their car

With this kind of grouping, you have a clearer idea of how to organize a paragraph.

Now that you have grouped your ideas with key words and details, you can write an outline.

Info BOX

An Outline for a Paragraph

topic sentence: I love St. Augustine because it has sun, sea, history, and family.

details:

sun and sea
{
It is warm in the winter.
There is a beach nearby.
It is big and clean.
The water is clear blue.

history
{
It has lots of history.
There is a fort.
The oldest schoolhouse is there.

family
{
My grandparents live in St. Augustine.
I stay at their house.
They feed me.
I use their car.

As you can see, the outline combined some of the details from the list. Even with these combinations, the details are very rough in style. As you reread the list of details, you will notice places that need more combination, places where ideas need more explaining, and places that are repetitive. Keep in mind that an outline is merely a very rough organization of your paragraph.

As you work through the steps of designing an outline, you can check for the following:

✓ Checklist

A Checklist for an Outline

✔ **Unity:** Do all the details relate to the topic sentence? If they do, the paragraph will be unified.

✔ **Support:** Do you have enough supporting ideas? Can you add to these ideas with even more specific details?

✔ **Coherence:** Are the details listed in the right order? If the order of points is logical, the paragraph will be coherent.

COHERENCE: PUTTING YOUR DETAILS IN PROPER ORDER

Check the sample outline again, and you will notice that the details are grouped in the same order as the topic sentence: first, details about sun and sea; next, details about history; and then, details about family in St. Augustine. Putting the details in an order that matches the topic sentence is a logical order for this paragraph.

Putting the details in logical order makes the ideas in your paragraph easy to follow. The most logical order for a paragraph depends on the subject of the paragraph. If you are writing about an event, you might use **time order** (such as telling what happened first, second, and so forth); if you are arguing some point, you might use **emphatic order** (such as saving your most convincing idea for last); if you are describing a room, you might use **space order** (such as from left to right or from top to bottom).

The format of the outline helps to organize your ideas. The topic sentence is written above the list of details. This position helps you to remember that the topic sentence is the *main idea*, and the details that support it are written under it. The topic sentence is the most important sentence of the paragraph. You can easily check the items on your list, one by one, against your main idea. You can also develop the *unity* (relevance) and *coherence* (logical order) of your details.

When you actually write a paragraph, the topic sentence does not necessarily have to be the first sentence in the paragraph. Read the paragraphs below, and notice where each topic sentence is placed.

Topic Sentence at the Beginning of the Paragraph

<u>Watching a horror movie on the late show can keep me up all night</u>. The movie itself scares me to death, especially if it involves a creepy character sneaking up on someone in the dark. After the movie, I'm afraid to turn out all the lights and be alone in the dark. Then every little noise seems like the sound of a sinister intruder. Strange shapes seem to appear in the shadows. My closet becomes a place where someone could be hiding. There might even be a creature under the bed! And if I go to sleep, these strange invaders might appear from under the bed or in the closet.

Topic Sentence in the Middle of the Paragraph

The kitchen counters gleamed. In the spice rack, every jar was organized neatly. The sink was polished, and not one spot marred its surface. The stove burners were surrounded by dazzling stainless steel rings. <u>The chef kept an immaculate kitchen.</u> There were no finger marks on the refrigerator door. No sticky spots dirtied the floor. No crumbs hid behind the toaster.

Topic Sentence at the End of the Paragraph

On long summer evenings, we would play softball in the street. Sometimes we'd play until it was so dark we could barely see the ball. Then our mothers would come to the front steps of the row houses and call us in, telling us to stop our play. But we'd pretend we couldn't hear them. If they insisted, we'd beg for a few minutes more, or for just one more game. It was so good to be outdoors with our friends. It was warm, and we knew we had weeks of summer vacation ahead. There was no school in the morning; there would be more games to play. <u>We loved those street games on summer nights.</u>

Info BOX

Since many of your paragraph assignments will require a clear topic sentence, be sure you follow your own instructor's directions about placement of the topic sentence.

Exercise 13

Practice

Adding Details to Support a Topic Sentence

The topic sentences below have some—but not enough—detail. Write sentences to add details to the list below each topic sentence.

1. topic sentence: My habit of being late has hurt me several times.

    a. When I am late for class, I often miss the announcement of a test for the next class meeting.

    b. I was so late that I missed the chance to buy tickets for a sold-out game.

    c. If I'm late, I drive too fast and sometimes get tickets.

    d. _____

    e. _____

    f. _____

    g. _____

2. topic sentence: Raising a baby is expensive.

    a. Babies need medicine.

    b. _____

    c. _____

    d. _____

    e. _____

    f. _____

    g. _____

3. topic sentence: A parent can show his or her love without spending a great deal of money.

    a. Attending a child's school events shows interest.

    b. _____

    c. _____

    d. _____

    e. _____

    f. _____

    g. _____

4. topic sentence: The first day of college can be confusing and tense.

    a. A student may not know how to find the classroom for his or her first class.

    b. The student rushes around, terrified of being late to class.

    c. A new student worries about how hard the classes will be.

    d. _____

    e. _____

    f. _____

    g. _____

Exercise 14

Practice

Eliminating Details That Do Not Fit

Below are topic sentences and lists of supporting details. Cross out the details that do not fit the topic sentence.

1. topic sentence: Computers can limit or harm a small child's growth.
    details: Some children spend too much time indoors on their computers when they could be outdoors.
        They may lose out on the health benefits of exercise.
        They may rely on the computer as a substitute for interacting with real friends.
        In some cases, a child who spends too much time in cyberspace can become very uncomfortable around others.
        As a child, I always had several friends at my house.
        Computers can expose children to questionable pictures or photographs.
        All children should be encouraged to read.

2. topic sentence: Everywhere I look, I see how music influences fashion.
    details: Music celebrities wear a certain style.
        Soon, the style becomes a fad.
        One diva will be famous for her hairstyle.
        Then her fans want their hair styled the same way.
        Another celebrity is photographed in trendy clothing.
        He creates a line of clothing named after him, crossing into the fashion industry.
        Many stars in the music world have to look good.
        If a popular musician wears a certain kind of jewelry, like a necklace or bracelet, many fans want the same jewelry.
        Music is a universal language.

3. topic sentence: People give many reasons for not buckling their safety belts.
    details: Some people say they are in a hurry.
        Others say they are only driving around the block.
        Police officers are very upset when parents do not buckle up their children.

Some people say they have a right not to buckle up if they don't want to.

A few say they don't want to be buckled in if they drive into a lake.

Many say they were about to buckle up, in a minute.

Some just say they forgot.

Air bags are a useful addition to auto safety devices.

Exercise 15

Practice

Coherence: Putting Details in the Right Order

These outlines have details that are in the wrong order. In the space provided, number the sentences in the right order: 1 would be the number for the first sentence, and so on.

1. topic sentence: Our garage sale was a disaster from start to finish.

___7___ By noon, we had nothing left to sell, and people were still coming.

___3___ People began to arrive at 8:30, before we had put out all the merchandise.

___4___ These early arrivals grabbed all the best bargains, even before we had a chance to put on price tags.

___2___ We started setting up at 8:15, thinking we had plenty of time.

___5___ At mid-morning, our yard was full of people, most of them complaining because we had so little left to sell.

___6___ The latest arrivals left, complaining because they had made a trip for nothing.

___1___ We were up at 7:30 A.M., putting Garage Sale signs around the neighborhood.

___8___ We spent the afternoon cleaning up.

___9___ That evening, we swore our next sale would start earlier and include more merchandise.

2. topic sentence: I have a hard time making my own breakfast.

___2___ I know that coffee will help me wake up, so I focus first on making some instant coffee.

___3___ My first challenge is to fill the kettle so I can boil water.

___1___ I arrive in the kitchen barely awake.

___9___ Suddenly, the kettle starts screeching while I try to remove the burnt toast from the toaster.

___4___ I turn on the heat and place the filled kettle on the burner.

___5___ While the water heats up, I decide to have some toast.

___7___ At last, I find some stale bread on the kitchen table.

___6___ But where is the toast? I search the refrigerator and the kitchen counters.

___8___ I pop a slice of the stale bread in the toaster, and I begin to doze off.

3. topic sentence: Losing my car keys was a stressful experience.

_2_ I rushed out the door, grabbing for my car keys on the counter, where I always left them.

_3_ I grabbed some keys, but they were my brother's house keys.

_1_ I was late for work, as usual, so I hurried out of the apartment.

_5_ When I had done a thorough search of the counter, I panicked.

_4_ Trying to be calm, I looked more closely at the counter, searching for my car keys under a pile of mail, behind a stack of magazines, next to the spice rack.

_6_ My next step was a frantic search of my entire apartment and the car.

_7_ Unable to find my keys anywhere, I called my boss to tell him I would be late.

_8_ Then I called a friend, who gave me a ride to work.

Rough Lines Drafting and Revising a Paragraph

Drafting a Paragraph

The outline is a draft in list form. You are now ready to write the list in paragraph form, to "rough out" a draft of your assignment. This stage of writing is the time to draft, revise, edit, and draft again. You may write several drafts in this stage, but don't think of this as an unnecessary chore or a punishment. It is a way of taking the pressure off yourself. By revising in steps, you are reminding yourself that the first try does not have to be perfect.

Review the outline on a favorite city or town on page 22. You can create a first draft of this outline in the form of a paragraph. (Remember that the first line of each paragraph is indented). In the draft of the paragraph below, the first sentence of the paragraph is the topic sentence.

A First Draft of a Paragraph

> I love St. Augustine because it has sun, sea, history, and family. St. Augustine is warm in the winter. There is a beach nearby. It is clean and big. The water is clear blue. St. Augustine has lots of history. There is an old stone fort. The oldest schoolhouse is there. I can always visit my family for free. My grandparents live in St. Augustine. They feed me. I use their car.

Revising

Once you have a first draft, you can begin to think about revising and editing it. **Revising** means rewriting the draft by making changes in the structure, in the order of the sentences, and in the content. **Editing** includes making changes in the choice of words, in the selection of details, in punctuation, and in the pattern and kinds of sentences. It may also include **adding transitions,** which are words, phrases, or sentences that link ideas.

One way to begin revising and editing is to read your work aloud to yourself. Listen to your words, and consider the questions in the following checklist.

> ### ✔️ Checklist
>
> **A Checklist for Revising the Draft of a Paragraph (with key terms)**
> ✔ Am I staying on my point? (unity)
> ✔ Should I take out any ideas that do not relate? (unity)
> ✔ Do I have enough to say about my point? (support)
> ✔ Should I add any details? (support)
> ✔ Should I change the order of my sentences? (coherence)
> ✔ Is my choice of words appropriate? (style)
> ✔ Is my choice of words repetitive? (style)
> ✔ Are my sentences too long? Too short? (style)
> ✔ Should I combine any sentences? (style)
> ✔ Am I running sentences together? (grammar)
> ✔ Am I writing complete sentences? (grammar)
> ✔ Can I link my ideas more smoothly? (transitions)

If you apply the checklist to the first draft of the paragraph on a favorite city or town, you will probably find these rough spots:

- The sentences are very short and choppy.
- Some sentences could be combined.
- Some words are repeated often.
- Some ideas would be more effective if they were supported by more detail.
- The paragraph could use a few transitions.

Consider the following revised draft of the paragraph, and notice the changes, underlined, that have been made in the draft:

A Revised Draft of a Paragraph

topic sentence:	I love St. Augustine, <u>Florida,</u>
detail added	because it has sun, sea, history, and family. <u>St. Augustine is warm in the winter and a big, clean beach with clear blue water is nearby. In addition,</u> St. Augustine has lots of history, including an old stone fort that looks out on the water.</u> It
sentences combined	
transition added	
sentences combined,	
transition added	
details added	<u>also</u> has the oldest schoolhouse <u>in America, a tiny wooden building. Best of all,</u> my
transition added	grandparents live in St. Augustine. They
details added	are <u>my favorite relatives,</u> and <u>they make me feel very welcome. When I am in St. Augustine, I stay with them, enjoy their food, and use their car.</u>
sentences combined	

When you are revising your own paragraph, you can use the checklist to help you. Read the checklist several times; then reread your draft, looking for answers to the questions on the list. If your instructor agrees, you can work with your classmates. You can read your draft to a partner or a group. Your listener(s) can react to your draft by applying the questions on the checklist and by making notes about your draft as you read. When you are finished reading aloud, your partner(s) can discuss the notes about your work.

Practice

Revising a Draft by Combining Sentences

The paragraph below has many short, choppy sentences. The short, choppy sentences are underlined. Wherever you see two or more underlined sentences clustered next to each other, combine the clustered sentences into one clear, smooth sentence. Write your revised version of the paragraph in the spaces above the lines.

Paragraph to Be Revised

My brother is a baseball fanatic. He wakes up in the morning thinking about the game. <u>He reaches for the newspaper. He checks out all the baseball scores.</u> He talks about baseball during breakfast. He can't stop talking and thinking about baseball during work. <u>He talks about his favorite teams during his break. He has baseball conversations during lunch. With customers, he argues about the sport.</u> My brother's clothes reflect his obsession. <u>He has seven baseball caps. There are three baseball jackets in his closet. He owns at least twelve shirts marked with team insignia.</u> For him, it's always baseball season.

 *Collaborate*

Adding Details to a Draft

Complete this exercise with a partner or a group. The paragraph below lacks the kind of details that would make it more interesting. Working with a partner or a group, add the details to the blank spaces provided. When you are finished with the additions, read the revised paragraph to the class.

Paragraph to Be Revised:

Popular movies come in a variety of forms. Some offer exciting action sequences. The action may involve war, in a movie like _____, or a dramatic chase, in films such as _____ and _____. Other popular movies feature tragic love stories. _____ is this kind of film. Every year, one kind of film especially popular with children is the blockbuster cartoon, like _____ or _____. Equally popular are the outrageous comedies that appeal to teens or college students.

Movies such as _____ and _____ are

perfect examples of these comedies. Clearly, there are films to suit all tastes

and ages.

Final Lines   Proofreading and Polishing a Paragraph

The final version of your paragraph is the result of careful thinking, planning, and revising. After as many drafts as it takes, you read to polish and proofread. You can avoid too many last-minute corrections if you check your last draft carefully. Check that draft for the following:

- spelling errors
- punctuation errors
- mechanical errors
- word choice
- a final statement

Take a look at the previous draft of the paragraph on a favorite city or town. Wherever something is crossed out, the draft has been corrected directly above the crossed out material. At the end of the paragraph, you will notice a concluding sentence has been added to unify the paragraph.

Correcting the Last Draft of a Paragraph

               Florida
I love St. Augustine, ~~Fla.,~~ because it has sun, sea, history, and family.
                        winter
St. Augustine is warm in the ~~Winter,~~ and a large, clean beach with clear
blue   *lots*
~~blew~~ water is nearby. In addition, St. Augustine has ~~lot's~~ of history, includ-
                                 has
ing an old stone fort that looks out on the water. It also ~~have~~ the oldest

schoolhouse in America, a tiny wooden building. Best of all, my grandpar-

ents live in St. Augustine. They are my favorite relatives, and they make
      feel
me ~~fell~~ very welcome. When I am in St. Augustine, I stay with them, enjoy
               their
their food, and use ~~there~~ car. St. Augustine has the perfect natural advan-
                         connections
tages, history, and family ~~connection~~ to make it my favorite city.

Giving Your Paragraph a Title

When you prepare the final version of your paragraph, you may be asked to give it a title. The title should be short and should fit the subject of the paragraph. For example, an appropriate title for the paragraph on a favorite city or town could be "My Favorite City" or "The City I Love." Check with your instructor to see if your paragraph needs a title. In this book, the paragraphs do not have titles.

The Final Version of a Paragraph

Following is the final version of the paragraph on a favorite city or town. As you read it, you will notice a few more changes. Even though the paragraph went through several drafts and many revisions, the final copy still reflects some additional polishing: some details have been added, some have been made more specific, and some words have been changed. These changes were made as the final version was prepared. (They are underlined for your reference.)

A Final Version of a Paragraph
(Changes from the previous draft are underlined.)

> I love St. Augustine, Florida, because it has sun, sea, history, and family. St. Augustine is warm in the winter, and a <u>wide</u>, clean beach with clear blue water is <u>ten minutes away</u>. In addition, St. Augustine is <u>filled with</u> history, including an old stone fort that looks out on the water. It also has the oldest schoolhouse in America, a tiny wooden building <u>smaller than a two-car garage</u>. Best of all, my grandparents live in St. Augustine. They are my favorite relatives, and they make me feel very welcome. When I am in St. Augustine, I stay with them, enjoy their <u>delicious Spanish</u> food, and use their car. St. Augustine has the natural advantages, history, and family connections to make it my favorite city.

Reviewing the Writing Process

This chapter has taken you through four important stages in writing. As you become more comfortable with them, you will be able to work through them more quickly. For now, try to remember the four stages.

Info BOX

The Stages of the Writing Process

Thought Lines: gathering and developing ideas, thinking on paper through freewriting, brainstorming, mapping, or keeping a journal.

Outlines: planning the paragraph by combining and dividing details, focusing the details with a topic sentence, listing the supporting details in proper order, and devising an outline.

Rough Lines: writing a rough draft of the paragraph, then revising and editing it several times.

Final Lines: preparing the final version of the paragraph, with one last proofreading check for errors in preparation, punctuation, and mechanics.

Exercise 18

Practice

Proofreading to Prepare the Final Version

Following are two illustration paragraphs with the kind of errors it is easy to overlook when you prepare the final version of an assignment. Correct the errors by writing above the lines. There are eleven errors in the first paragraph and eight errors in the second paragraph.

1. Every time I am on the telephone and I need to write something down, I

am caught in a terible dilemma. First of all, their is never any paper nearby.

Even thou I live in an apartment full of schoolbooks notebooks pads, and typing paper, they're is never any papper near the telephone. I wind up desperately looking for anything I can write on. Sometimes i write on coupons my mother has saved in the kitchen, but coupons are shiny and don't take writing well. If I do manage to find some better paper, I can't find a pen or pencil! Our home is full of pen's and pencil's, but I can never find even a stubbby old pencil or a leaky old ballpoint when I need it. In emergencies, I have taken telephone messages with a crayon and a lipstick.

2. Insufficient parking is a serious prolem for student's at Carlyle College. Very often, students are forced to drive around the filled rows for ten or twenty minutes, looking for a solitary space. if they find one, it is at the end of a long row. And by the time they find it and have walked the long way to there classroom, they are late for class. They run the risk of missing a quiz or being penalize in some other way. For those who cannot find a space, there are even more risky alternatives. Some students parks in a faculty spot or in a fire Lane. These students risk getting a ticket and a fine, but they must weigh this risk against missing class. Carlyle College administrators need to reconize students' parking dilemmas and provide more parking spaces for students who just want to get to class on time.

Lines of Detail: A Walk-Through Assignment

This assignment involves working within a group to write a paragraph.

Step 1: Read the three sentences below. Pick the one sentence you prefer as a possible topic sentence for a paragraph. Fill in the blank for the sentence you chose.

Pick one sentence and fill in the blank:

a. The most frightening movie I've ever seen was

_____ (fill in the title).

b. If money were no problem, the car I'd buy is

_____ (fill in the name of the car).

c. The one food I refuse to eat is

_____ (fill in the name of the food).

Step 2: Join a group composed of other students who picked the same topic sentence you picked. In your class, you'll have "movie" people, "car" people, and "food" people. Brainstorm in a group. Discuss questions that could be used to get ideas for your paragraph.

For the movie topic, sample questions could include "What was the most frightening part of the movie?" or "What kind of movie was it—a ghost story, a horror movie, or another type?" For the car topic, sample questions could include "Have you ever driven this kind of car?" or "Do you know anyone who has one?" For the food topic, sample questions could include "Did you hate this food when you were a child?" or "Where has this food been served to you?"

As you discuss, write the questions, not the answers, below. Keep the questions flowing. Do not stop to say, "That's silly" or "I can't answer that." Try to devise **at least ten questions.**

Ten Brainstorming Questions

1. _____

2. _____

3. _____

4. _____

5. _____

6. _____

7. _____

8. _____

9. _____

10. _____

Step 3: Split up. Alone, begin to think on paper. Answer as many questions as you can, or add more questions and answers, or freewrite.

Step 4: Draft an outline of the paragraph. You will probably have to change the topic sentence to fit the detail you have gathered. For example, your new topic sentence might be something like

_____ was the most frightening movie I have

ever seen; it creates fear by using _____,

_____, and _____.

or

If money were no problem, I would buy a _____ for

its performance, _____ , and _____ .

or

I refuse to eat _____ because _____ .
Remember to look at your details to see where they lead
you. The details will help you to refine your topic
sentence.

Step 5: Prepare the first draft of the paragraph.

Step 6: Read the draft aloud to your writing group, the same people
who met to brainstorm. Ask each member of your group to
make at least one positive comment and one suggestion for
revision.

Step 7: Revise and edit your draft, considering the group's ideas and
your own ideas for improvement.

Step 8: Prepare a final version of the paragraph.

Writing Your Own Paragraph

When you write on any of these topics, follow the four basic stages of the
writing process in preparing your paragraph.

1. Begin this assignment with a partner. The assignment requires an
interview. Your final goal is to write a paragraph that will introduce a class member, your partner, to the rest of the class. In the
final paragraph, you may design your own topic sentence or use
one of the topic sentences below, filling in the blanks with the
material you have discovered:

There are several things you should know about

_____(fill in your partner's name).

or

Three unusual events have happened to

_____ (fill in your partner's name).

Before you write the paragraph, follow these steps:

Step 1: Prepare to interview a classmate. Make a list of six questions
you might want to ask. They can be questions like, "Where
are you from?" or "Have you ever done anything unusual?"
Write *at least six questions* before you start the interview.
List the questions on the following interview form, leaving
room to fill in short answers later.

Interview Form

Question 1: _____

Answer: _____

Question 2: _____

Answer: _____

Question 3: _____

Answer: _____

Question 4: _____

Answer: _____

Question 5: _____

Answer: _____

Question 6: _____

Answer: _____

Additional questions and answers: _____

Step 2: Meet and interview your partner. Ask the questions on your list. Jot down brief answers. Ask *any other questions* you think of as you are talking; write down the answers on the additional lines at the end of the interview form.

Step 3: Change places. Let your partner interview you.

Step 4: Split up. Use the list of questions and answers about your partner as the thought lines part of your assignment. Work on the outline and draft steps.

Step 5: Ask your partner to read the draft version of your paragraph, to write any comments or suggestions for improvement below the paragraph, and to mark any spelling or grammar errors in the paragraph itself.

Step 6: When you have completed a final version of the paragraph, read the paragraph to the class.

2. Below are some topic sentences. Select one and use it to write a paragraph.

Many kinds of people wear _____ for a variety of reasons.

My daily life provides several irritations.

High school students should never forget that _____.

College is a good place to _____ and _____.

3. Write a paragraph on one of the topics below. Create your own topic sentence; explain and support it with specific details.

a favorite activity	a dreaded chore	a sad occasion
a challenging class	a special song	an exciting sport
the best gift	one stress-buster	the best time of day
the ugliest car	a treasured toy	a patriotic moment

4. Examine the two photographs of families above. After you have looked at them carefully, write a paragraph with this topic sentence:

Families can be as varied as their members.

You can write about many kinds of families, not just the kinds shown in the photographs.

5. Examine the photograph of the dog below. After you have looked at it carefully, write a paragraph with this topic sentence:

Some owners treat their pets like people.

The details of the photograph can provide you with some details, but come up with other details on your own.

Name: _____ **Section:** _____

PEER REVIEW FORM FOR A PARAGRAPH

After you have written a draft of your paragraph, let a writing partner read it. When your partner has completed the form below, discuss the comments. Then repeat the same process for your partner's paragraph.

The topic sentence of this paragraph is _____

_____

_____

The detail that I liked best begins with the words _____

_____

The paragraph has _____ (enough, too many, too few)

details to support the topic sentence.

A particularly good part of the paragraph begins with the words _____

_____

I have questions about _____

_____

_____

Other comments on the paragraph: _____

_____

_____

_____

_____

_____

_____

_____

_____

_____

_____

_____

_____

Reviewer's Name: _____

WRITING FROM READING: The Writing Process

Sticky Stuff

Kendall Hamilton and Tessa Namuth

This article is a tribute to three modern products that hold our lives together. One got its start when its creator was walking his dog, another changed its original purpose, and the third was the result of a boring sermon.

Words You May Need to Know (corresponding paragraph number is in parentheses)

bounty (1):   a generous number
ingenious (1):   clever
amalgam (1):   combination
marveled (2):   wondered
burrs (2):   the rough, prickly case around the seeds of certain plants
spawn (2):   produce
dubbed (2):   named
velours (2):   velvet
crochet (2):   small hook
arthritic (2):   people with arthritis, an inflammation of the joints
invective (3):   angry, abusive language
sought (3):   searched
rendered (3):   became
obsolete (3):   out of date, no longer useful

debuted (3):   was introduced
ironically (3):   opposite of what is expected
Great Depression (3):   a period in the United States, beginning in 1929 and continuing through the 1930s, when business, employment, and stock market values were low and poverty was widespread
improvised (4):   created on the spot, without planning
hymnal (4):   a book of hymns, religious songs
colleague (4):   a fellow worker
voila! (4):   French for "there it was!"
ubiquitous (4):   everywhere

1   Never before in the history of humankind has it been so easy to attach one thing to another. Over the past century, inventive minds have brought us a bounty of products designed to keep our daily lives—and who knows, maybe even the universe—together. The paper clip, for instance, is not only an ingenious amalgam of form and function, but it's also a powerful force for order. Below are a few more of the finest products.

2   Anybody who's ever struggled with a stuck zipper or stubborn button owes a debt of gratitude to Georges de Mestral, the Swiss engineer who gave us all an alternative. After a walk in the woods with his dog one day in 1948, de Mestral marveled at the ability of burrs to fastern themselves to his dog's coat and to his own wool clothing. De Mestral shoved a bit of burr under a microscope and saw that its barbed, hooklike seed pods meshed beautifully with the looped fibers in his clothes. Realizing that his discovery could spawn a fastening system to compete with, not replace, the zipper, he devised a way to reproduce the hooks in woven nylon, and dubbed the result Velcro, from the French words *velours* and *crochet*. Today Velcro-brand hook-and-loop fasteners (which is how trademark attorneys insist we refer to the stuff) not only save the arthritic, fumble-fingered or just

plain lazy among us untold aggravation with our clothing, they secure gear—and astronauts—aboard the space shuttle, speed diaper changes, and help turn the machine-gun turrets in the M1A1 tank. Velcro U.S.A., Inc., engineers have even used the product to assemble an automobile. Try doing that with zippers.

3   Some theorize that the world is held together by Scotch tape. If that's not true, it could be: 3M, the company behind the brand, makes enough tape each day to circle the earth almost three times. This was certainly not foreseen by a young 3M engineer named Richard Drew when he invented the tape in 1930. Drew, who'd come up with the first masking tape after overhearing a burst of frustrated invective in an auto-body painting shop, sought to create a product to seal the cellophane that food producers were starting to use to wrap everything from bread to candy. Why not coat strips of cellophane itself with adhesive, Drew wondered, and Scotch tape was born. It was also soon rendered obsolete for its original purpose, as a process to heat-seal cellophane packaging debuted. Ironically, the Great Depression came to the rescue: consumers took to the tape as a dollar-stretcher to keep worn items in service. Ever since, it's just kind of stuck.

4   The Post-it note not only keeps information right where we want it, but it may also be the best thing ever to come out of a dull sermon. Art Fry, a chemical engineer for 3M who was active in his church choir, was suffering through just such a sermon one day back in 1974 when he got to thinking about a problem he'd been having with improvised bookmarks falling out of his hymnal. "I realized what I really needed was a bookmark that would attach and detach lightly, wouldn't fall off and wouldn't hurt the hymnal," recalls Fry, now 66 and retired from 3M. Fry called to mind a weak adhesive developed by his colleague, Spencer Silver. Fry slathered a little of the adhesive on the edge of a piece of paper, and *voila!* He wrote a report about his invention and forwarded it to his boss, also jotting a question on one of his new bookmarks and pressing it down in the middle of one page. His boss scribbled an answer on the note and sent it back to Fry, attached to some other paperwork. Later, over coffee, the two men realized Fry had invented a new communications tool. Today Post-its are ubiquitous—available in eighteen colors, twenty-seven sizes and fifty-six shapes. Some even contain fragrances that smell like pizza, pickles, or chocolate. Soon, perhaps, we'll have our notes and eat them, too.

WRITING FROM READING: "Sticky Stuff"

When you write on any of the following topics, work through the stages of the writing process in preparing your paragraph.

   1. "Sticky Stuff" describes how three products, all used to attach one thing to another," were invented. In a paragraph, write a summary

of the article. Describe the inventor of each product, how he came up with the idea for the product, and how the product was developed and used.

2. Write a paragraph about one item in modern technology you just cannot live without. In your paragraph, explain why this invention is essential in your daily life.

3. "Sticky Stuff" is about three inventions that hold things together. In a paragraph, select one such item (for instance, Scotch tape, duct tape, masking tape, paper clips, or superglue), and describe ways to use it creatively or in an emergency. Use this topic sentence:

    ＿＿＿＿＿＿＿ (name of the item) has several creative and emergency uses.

If your instructor agrees, you might want to brainstorm about one or two items and their uses as a way of getting started.

4. Think of some item that many children take for granted today but that you did not have when you were growing up. (For example, you could write about portable CD players, DVDs, or cable or satellite television.) In a paragraph, describe the item, what it does, and how children take it for granted. Then explain how you amused yourself without this item.

5. Post-it notes are such a small convenience that people may not notice how useful they are. Write a paragraph about one other small convenience (in the office, the car, or the kitchen) that is extremely useful. Explain how it works, and consider how people coped before this item was created.

6. Look around your classroom for five minutes and ask yourself this question: What could be designed better? For instance, how could the desks be improved so that the writing surface is larger? How could the chairs be more comfortable? Are many students loaded with heavy book bags? How could these bags be improved? Are there bulletin boards? Are they effective? Focus on one item in the classroom and write a paragraph about how it could be improved, redesigned, or reinvented.

CHAPTER 2

Illustration

WHAT IS ILLUSTRATION?

Illustration uses specific examples to support a general point. In your writing, you often use illustration since you frequently want to explain a point by a specific example.

Hints for Writing an Illustration Paragraph

Knowing What Is Specific and What Is General A *general* statement is a broad point. The following statements are general:

> Traffic can be bad on Hamilton Boulevard.
> Car insurance costs more today than it did last year.
> It is difficult to meet people at my college.

You can support a general statement with specific examples:

general statement: Traffic can be bad on Hamilton Boulevard.
specific examples: During the morning rush hour, the exit to First Avenue is jammed.
If there is an accident, cars can be backed up for a mile.

general statement: Car insurance costs more today than it did last year.
specific examples: Last year I paid $150 a month; this year I pay $200 a month.
My mother, who has never had a traffic ticket, has seen her insurance premium rise fifty percent.

general statement: It is difficult to meet people at my college.
specific examples: After class, most students rush to their jobs.
There are very few places to sit and talk between classes.

When you write an illustration paragraph, be careful to support a general statement with specific examples, not with more general statements:

not this: general statement: College is harder than I thought it would be.

more general statements: ~~It is tough to be a college student.~~ ~~Studying takes a lot of my time.~~

but this: general statement: College is harder than I thought it would be.

specific examples: I cannot afford to miss any classes. I have to study at least two hours a day.

If you remember to illustrate a broad statement with specific examples, you will have the key to this kind of paragraph.

Exercise 1

Practice

Recognizing Broad Statements

Each list below contains one broad statement and three specific examples. Underline the broad statement.

1. I feel depressed on dark, rainy days.
When it snows, I am filled with excitement and wonder.
Weather has a direct impact on my emotions.
Sun makes me cheerful.

2. My two-year-old son is into everything.
He climbs onto the kitchen table.
I have found him sitting in the laundry basket.
He loves to explore the hall closet.

3. A stranger stopped to help me with my flat tire yesterday.
Random acts of kindness are frequent in our community.
A woman at the market offered to carry an elderly man's groceries to his car.
Somebody knocked on my mother's door to tell her she had left her car lights on.

4. The office printer ran out of ink just before an important deadline.
A sudden power failure caused the loss of an expensive program.
An important backup disk turned out to be blank.
Even computer technology is not always reliable.

5. Many working parents struggle to spend time with their children.
Students do their class work and work full or part-time jobs, too.
Everybody seems to be short of free time these days.
People work overtime because they need the extra money even if they lose their free time.

Exercise 2

Practice

Distinguishing the General Statement From the Specific Example

Each of the following statements is supported by three items of support. Two of these items are specific examples; one is too general to be effective. Underline the one that is too general.

1. **general statement:** Halloween is not just for children anymore.
   support: Costume stores sell or rent costumes to thousands of adults.
   Halloween is a popular adult holiday.
   Many colleges, clubs, and bars have extravagant Halloween parties.

2. **general statement:** A positive attitude is a great asset.
   support: Looking on the bright side is a good thing.
   Smiling can actually improve a person's mood.
   Most people like to be around an optimist, so a positive attitude can lead to more friends.

3. **general statement:** DVDs are becoming increasingly popular.
   support: Video rental stores are giving equal space to DVDs.
   Everybody likes DVDs.
   Many new vans and SUVs are offering DVD players for the road.

4. **general statement:** Music appeals to all ages.
   support: The smallest children love to dance.
   Older people remember the songs they were listening to when they fell in love.
   All generations love some kind of music.

5. **general statement:** Most bookstores sell more than books.
   support: Many sell CDs.
   They sell lots of things.
   Most sell a variety of magazines.

Exercise 3

 *Collaborate*

Adding Specific Examples to a General Statement

With a partner or group, add four specific examples to each general statement below.

1. **general statement:** Some fast foods are full of fat.

   examples: _____

   _____

   _____

   _____

2. **general statement:** Celebrities are used to advertise all kinds of products.

   examples: _____

   _____

   _____

   _____

3. general statement: People who get stopped for speeding have all
kinds of excuses.

examples: _____

_____

_____

_____

4. general statement: Men's haircuts today reflect a wide range of
styles.

examples: _____

_____

_____

_____

WRITING THE ILLUSTRATION PARAGRAPH IN STEPS

Thought Lines ## Gathering Ideas: Illustration

Suppose your instructor asks you to write a paragraph about some aspect
of clothes. You can begin by thinking about your subject to gather ideas
and to find a focus for your paragraph.

Looking through entries in your journal might lead you to the following underlined entry:

Journal Entry About Clothes

I went to the mall yesterday to look for some <u>good shoes</u>. What a crowd! Some big
sale was going on, and the stores were packed. Everybody was pushing and shoving. I just left. I'll go when it's not so crowded. I hate <u>buying clothes and shoes</u>.
Wish I could just wear <u>jeans and tee shirts</u> all the time. But even then, the <u>jeans
have to have the right label</u>, or you're looked down on. There are <u>status labels on
the tee shirts</u>, too. Not to mention <u>expensive athletic shoes</u>.

The underlined terms can lead you to a list:

good shoes   jeans have to have the right label
buying clothes and shoes   status labels on tee shirts
jeans and tee shirts   expensive athletic shoes

Consider the underlined terms. Many of them are specific ideas about
clothes. You could write a paragraph about one item or about several related items on the list.

Adding Details to an Idea

Looking at this list, you might decide you want to write something about
this topic: tee shirts.

To add details, you decide to brainstorm:

Who wears tee shirts?

Athletes, children, teens, movie stars, musicians, parents, old people, restaurant workers.

How much do they cost?

Some are cheap, but some are expensive.

What kinds of tees are there?

Sports tees, concert tees, college names on tees, designer tees, ads on tees.

Why do people wear tees?

They're comfortable and fashionable.

What ads are on tees?

Beer, sporting goods.

What else do you see on tees?

Mickey Mouse, seascapes, political slogans, souvenir pictures or sayings.

You now have this list of ideas connected to the topic of tee shirts:

status labels on tees	concert tees
athletes	college names on tees
children	designer tees
teens	ads on tees
movie stars	comfortable
musicians	fashionable
parents	beer
old people	sporting goods
restaurant workers	Mickey Mouse
cheap	seascapes
expensive	political slogans
sports tees	souvenir pictures or sayings

Creating a Topic Sentence

If you examine this list, looking for *related ideas*, you can create a topic sentence. The ideas on the list include (1) details about the kinds of people who wear tee shirts, (2) details about the cost of tee shirts, and (3) details about what is pictured or written on tee shirts. Not all the details fit into these three categories, but many do.

Grouping the related ideas into the three categories can help you focus your ideas into a topic sentence.

Kinds of People Who Wear Tee Shirts

athletes	movie stars	old people
children	musicians	restaurant workers
teens	parents	

The Cost of Tee Shirts

cheap	some expensive

What Is Pictured or Written on Tee Shirts

ads on tees	beer ads	seascapes
concert tees	sporting goods	political slogans
college names	Mickey Mouse	souvenir pictures or sayings

You can summarize these related ideas in a topic sentence:

People of various backgrounds and ages wear all kinds of tee shirts.

Check the sentence against your detail. Does it cover the people who wear tees? Does it cover what is on the shirts?

Yes. The topic sentence says, "*People of various backgrounds and ages* wear *all kinds* of tee shirts." The topic sentence has given you a focus for your illustration paragraph.

Practice

Finding Specific Ideas in Freewriting

Following are two samples of freewriting. Each is a response to a broad topic. Read each sample, and then underline any words that could become a more specific topic for a paragraph.

Freewriting Reaction to the Topic of Food

What comes to my mind when I think about food? I'm hungry right now. Can I call out for pizza? I get hungry at the strangest times. Late at night. I want ice cream. Chocolate ice cream with chocolate fudge. Or vanilla with pieces of toffee in it. Desserts at 3:00 a.m. I get hungry in class, especially night classes. Food. If the teacher gives us a break in night class, I go to the vending machines. Can you call that food? Emergency food, I guess.

Freewriting Reaction to the Topic of Health

I'm healthy. Health class? I have to take a health class next term. I think it's about nutrition, vitamins, exercise. Health is a hard subject to write about. I just take it for granted that I'll be healthy. I've never really been sick. Just childhood things like chicken pox. One bad case of strep throat. That was awful.

Practice

Finding Specific Ideas in Lists

Following are two lists. Each is a response to a broad topic. Read each list, and then underline any words that could become a more specific topic for a paragraph.

Topic: Technology in Daily Life

lots of technology	high technology
scanners at the supermarket	registering for class on-line
cyberspace	new breakthroughs
voice mail	old-fashioned drive-through banking
mouse pads	surveillance cameras

Topic: Music

different kinds of music	music around the world
legendary rappers	my favorite songs
the best radio station	the year's best CDs
people and music	patriotic music
country music	advertising jingles

Practice

Grouping Related Ideas in Lists of Details

Following are lists of details. In each list, circle the items that seem to fit into one group; then underline the items that seem to fit into a second group. Some items may not fit into either group.

1. topic: losses

lost credit card	lost self-esteem
lost moral standards	lost wallet
lost key chain	lost in the woods
lost in the final inning	lost notebook
lost sense of purpose	lost innocence

2. topic: studying for a test

cramming at 4:00 a.m.	essay test
calmly reviewing the text	notes from class
frantically reading the book	budgeting time to study
trying to memorize it all	getting a good night's sleep
staying up all night	connecting key ideas and terms

3. topic: birthday gifts

a CD by your favorite group	a Lexus SUV
gifts from parents	a romantic gift
airline tickets to Jamaica	new shirts
a special, framed photo	a giant birthday cake
after shave or cologne	a complete entertainment unit

4. topic: traveling to college by bus

can study on the bus	saves gas money
bus can be late	you can be late and miss it
waiting for bus in the rain	walk from bus to school
no parking hassles	variety of bus riders
traffic congestion	bus drivers

Exercise 7   **Writing Topic Sentences for Lists of Details**

Practice

Following are lists of details that have no topic sentences. Write an appropriate topic sentence for each one.

1. topic sentence: _____

_____

The house has a beautiful hardwood floor.
It also has high ceilings.
There is a small but cozy fireplace in the living room.
The entrance hall is spacious.
The kitchen needs a new sink and refrigerator.
There is a leak in the roof over the big bedroom.
Several of the window frames are rotted.
The bathroom tile needs to be replaced.

2. topic sentence: _____

_____

Alicia's boyfriend Keith teases her about her weight.
He is also critical of her intelligence, her personality, and her style.
He even criticizes her friends.
Keith is often late or fails to show up for a date with Alicia.

He gets angry if she questions him about his absence.
He tells her she is too controlling.
He never apologizes for his bad behavior.

3. topic sentence: _____

_____

Alex was once stopped by a police officer.
The officer said Alex had a broken tail light.
He wanted to give Alex a ticket.
Alex started his usual line of jokes and stories.
Soon the officer let Alex off with a warning.
Another time, Alex fell during a soccer game.
He broke a bone in his foot and was rushed to the emergency room.
Instead of complaining about the pain, Alex tried to look on the funny side.
He talked about his "superfoot" and soon had the doctor and nurses laughing.

4. topic sentence: _____

_____

When I took my first airplane trip, a stranger helped me find my connecting flight.
Some good person mailed my wallet (and all its contents) back to me when I lost it.
An elderly customer at the restaurant where I work gave me a ride home when my car wouldn't start.
One day when I was holding my crying baby, a man let me cut ahead in the supermarket line.
The crossing guard on my block always says, "Hi, how are you doing?" when I walk by, even though I don't know him.
A boy in the city went two blocks out of his way to show me the way to the court buildings.

 Choosing the Better Topic Sentence

Practice

Following are lists of detail. Each list has two possible topic sentences. Underline the better topic sentence for each list.

1. possible topic sentences:
a. Americans eat many different foods.
b. Typical American food includes food from many countries.

Mexican food is popular with many ethnic groups.
Many people love tacos and tortillas.
They also crave chili.
Italian food is not just for Italians.
Pizza parlors are everywhere.
Spaghetti is a favorite dish for many.
People of many heritages enjoy Chinese food.
Sweet and sour shrimp and fried rice are available everywhere.
The fortune cookie is as well-known as American apple pie.

2. Possible topic sentences:
   a. In a crisis, it is good to have friends.
   b. A crisis can reveal a person's true friends.

> I had plenty of friends in high school.
> Dave was my basketball buddy; we played every Thursday afternoon.
> Jason and I used to make jokes in our math class.
> I had known Eddie since he had moved into my neighborhood when we were both eight years old.
> Harry and I worked together at the movie theater.
> I ran into Carlos at parties, and we become friends.
> Then I was seriously hurt in a bad car accident.
> Dave came to see me in the hospital, once.
> Jason sent me a funny card.
> Eddie called and said he hadn't had a chance to come to the hospital.
> I never saw Carlos again.
> Only Harry came to see me all through my months of rehabilitation.

3. possible topic sentences:
   a. Big isn't always better.
   b. You never know about life.

> Frank has a huge black dog, a Labrador.
> The dog is very nervous and afraid of loud noises.
> His brother Mike has a little mutt named Sammy.
> Sammy is the fiercest, most protective dog I've ever seen.
> For her birthday, Cherline got an enormous box wrapped in bright blue paper and covered in white ribbons and bows.
> Inside were three new pillows for her bed.
> Her sister Amanda got a small box tied with silk ribbon and decorated with a pink rose.
> In it was a gold-and-diamond bracelet.

`Outlines` Devising a Plan: Illustration

When you plan your outline, keep your topic sentence in mind:

> People of <u>various backgrounds</u> and <u>ages</u> wear <u>all kinds</u> of tee shirts.

Notice the key words, which are underlined, and which lead to three key phrases:

> people of various backgrounds
> people of various ages
> all kinds of tee shirts

Can you put the details together so that they connect to **one** of these key phrases?

people of various backgrounds

— athletes, movie stars, musicians, restaurant workers

people of various ages

  — children, teens, parents, old people

all kinds of tee shirts

  — concert tees, college names on tees, beer ads, sporting goods, Mickey Mouse shirts, surfer tees, souvenir tees, political slogans

With this kind of grouping, you have a clearer idea of how to organize a paragraph.

An Outline for an Illustration Paragraph

topic sentence: People of various backgrounds and ages wear all kinds of tee shirts.

details:	Athletes wear tee shirts.
various	Movie stars are seen in them.
backgrounds	Musicians perform in tee shirts.
	Restaurant workers wear tee shirts.
various	Children and teens wear tee shirts.
ages	Parents and old people wear them.
	There are tee shirts sold at concerts.
	Some shirts have the names of colleges on them.
	Others advertise a brand of beer or sporting goods.
kinds of	Mickey Mouse is a favorite character on them.
tees	Surfers' tee shirts have seascapes on them.
	Some shirts are souvenirs.
	Others have political slogans.

  As you can see, the outline combined some of the details from the list. You can combine other details, avoid repetition, and add more details as you draft your essay.

Exercise 9

 *Collaborate*

Adding Details to an Outline

Below are three partial outlines. Each has a topic sentence and some details. Working with a partner or group, add more details that support the topic sentence.

  1. topic sentence: People caught in the rain find a number of ways to avoid getting wet.

   a. Some cover their heads with newspaper.

   b. Some crouch against the wall of a big building.

   c. Some take off their shoes and race through the puddles.

   d. _____

   e. _____

   f. _____

   g. _____

2. topic sentence: Pets are good for their owners' well-being.

    a. You can get healthy exercise by walking a dog.

    b. Widows and widowers with pets tend to live longer.

    c. A cat who sleeps on your lap makes you feel peaceful.

    d. _____

    e. _____

    f. _____

    g. _____

3. topic sentence: Teenagers are constantly getting the same messages and questions from their parents.

    a. Parents say, "This is my house, and as long as you live in it, you must follow my rules."

    b. They are always asking why teens must sleep so late.

    c. They want to know why their teens have been out so late.

    d. _____

    e. _____

    f. _____

    g. _____

 Exercise 10

Practice

Eliminating Details That Are Repetitive

In the following outlines, some details use different words to repeat an example given earlier in the list. Cross out the repetitive details.

    1. topic sentence: If you have eggs in the refrigerator, you can make a variety of meals.

You can boil the eggs and have egg salad sandwiches.
You can have soft-boiled eggs and toast.
Fried eggs, bacon or sausage, and hash-brown potatoes or grits are a great meal.
Chopped-up hard-boiled eggs and mayonnaise are the filling in egg salad sandwiches.
An omelet with chopped onions, peppers, and tomatoes is a great supper.
Pieces of toast mixed with a soft-boiled egg can be tasty.
Scrambled eggs go with anything: English muffins, ham, waffles, or pancakes.

2. topic sentence: After many mistakes, I've learned to think before I act.

I bought the first car I saw.
It was overpriced and full of hidden mechanical problems.
I chose my college major because everyone else was majoring in business and I was in a hurry to register.
I am not interested in my business courses.
A friend of mine insulted me, and I was so angry that I hit him.
I barely avoided being arrested.
I didn't look around before I got my car.
My mother asked me for a favor, and I blurted out the first excuse I could think of.
I hurt my mother's feelings.
I'm stuck in business classes that bore me.
My temper got me into trouble with a friend and the law.

3. topic sentence: It seems as if everyone I see is carrying some kind of beverage.

Just before their eight A.M. classes, students are swigging diet Pepsi or Mountain Dew.
Later in the day, most students are carrying water or iced tea bottles.
All day, I see people on city streets carrying big, spillproof containers of coffee.
Babies in baby carriages are drinking juice or formula in their baby bottles.
Health nuts are sipping fruit smoothies.
Most people rushing through the city are balancing a giant paper cup of coffee.
A bottle of water or iced tea is essential in most students' backpacks.
Five and six-year-olds stroll while they dribble chocolate milk from the plastic straws in their plastic cups.

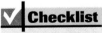 **Drafting and Revising: Illustration**

Review the outline on tee shirts on page 51. You can create a first draft of this outline in the form of a paragraph. At this point, you can combine some of the short, choppy sentences of the outline, add details, and add transitions to link your ideas. You can revise your draft using the following checklist.

✔️ **Checklist**

A Checklist for Revising an Illustration Paragraph

✔ Should some of the sentences be combined?

✔ Do I need more or better transitions?

✔ Should I add more details to support my points?

✔ Should some of the details be more specific?

Transitions

As you revise your illustration paragraph, you may find places where one idea ends and another begins abruptly. This problem occurs when you forget to add **transitions,** which are words, phrases or sentences that connect one idea to another. Using transitions effectively will make your writing clear and smooth. When you write an illustration paragraph, you will need some transitions that link one example to another and other transitions to link one section of your paragraph to another section. Here are some transitions you may want to use in writing an illustration paragraph.

Info BOX

Transitions for an Illustration Paragraph

another example	one instance
a second example	other examples
for example	other kinds
for instance	such as
in addition	the first instance
in the case of	another instance
like	to illustrate
one example	

Look carefully at the following draft of the paragraph on tee shirts, and note how it combines sentences, add details, and uses transitions to transform the outline into a clear and developed paragraph.

A Draft of an Illustration Paragraph

topic sentence	People of various backgrounds and ages wear all kinds of tee shirts. <u>Athletes and movie stars are seen in them.</u> <u>Musicians often per-</u>
sentences combined	
sentences combined	<u>form in them, and restaurant workers some-</u>
details added	<u>times work in tee shirts marked with the</u> <u>name of the restaurant.</u> <u>Children, teens, their</u>
sentences combined	<u>parents, and older people all wear tee shirts</u>.
transition sentence	<u>Almost anything can be printed or pictured</u>
added	<u>on a tee shirt. At concerts, fans can buy tee</u>
details added	<u>shirts stamped with the name of the group</u> <u>on stage.</u> College students can wear the
	name of their college on a shirt. Some shirts
details added	advertise a brand of beer, <u>like Bud</u>, or a
details added	sporting goods company, <u>like Nike</u>. Mickey
	Mouse is a favorite character on tee shirts.
transition added	<u>Other kinds of shirts include shirts with</u>
sentences	<u>seascapes on them, and souvenir shirts, like</u>
combined	<u>the ones that say, "My folks visited Philadel-</u>
details added	<u>phia, and all I got was this lousy tee shirt."</u>
transition	<u>Other shirts</u> have political slogans, <u>like "Save</u>
details added	<u>the Whales."</u>

Exercise 11

Practice

Revising a Draft by Combining Sentences

The paragraph below has many short, choppy sentences, which are underlined. Wherever you see two or more underlined sentences clustered next to each other, combine them into one clear, smooth sentence. Write your revised version of the paragraph in the spaces above the lines.

Mr. Gonzalez, my high school English teacher, had a whole bag of tricks for keeping the class awake and alert. <u>Sometimes a student would fall asleep. The student would be in the back of</u> the classroom. Mr. Gonzalez would stand beside the sleeping student's desk and stare silently. <u>The rest of the class would begin to laugh. The laughing woke up the student.</u> At other times, when Mr. Gonzalez was teaching a grammar lesson, the class would become bored. Mr. Gonzalez would startle everyone by suddenly singing loudly. He was such a terrible singer that we all jumped to attention. Once Mr. Gonzalez really went to extremes. <u>He made the whole class sing. The song was one he had written. It was a song about punctuation.</u> In every class, Mr. Gonzalez's students had to be prepared for surprises.

Exercise 12

Practice

Revising a Draft by Adding Transitions

The paragraph below needs some transitions. Add appropriate transitions (words or phrases) to the blanks.

My girlfriend Elise has some annoying habits. _____ she never lets me finish a sentence. Whenever I start to say something, Elise jumps in with her own idea or with what she thinks I am about to say.

_____, she likes to plan too far ahead. On Monday, she wants to know exactly what we'll be doing on Saturday night. I'm more spontaneous and like to wait until Friday or Saturday to decide. _____, she worries too much. _____, she worries when I am late for school. She also worries when I have a cold. She is afraid it may turn into pneumonia. Elise is clearly a talker, a planner, and a worrier, but these are all minor flaws. She isn't perfect, but she is perfect for me.

Collaborate

Adding Details to a Draft

The paragraph below lacks the kind of details that would make it more interesting. Working with a partner or group, add details to the blank spaces provided. When you are finished, read the revised paragraph to the class.

The cars people drive depend on their age and financial position. The average college student juggling school and a job will likely be driving a

_____ or a _____ . On the other hand, a college-age,

millionaire basketball player can be seen in a _____ . Adults in

their thirties or forties, trying to balance raising their children and earning

enough to pay the bills, will probably be making payments on a

_____ . In contrast, a highly successful mother or father with an

income in the hundreds of thousands will pile the family into a

_____ or a _____ . Retired people living on fixed

incomes often drive _____ while retired rich people might be

behind the wheel of a _____ . Every age has certain cars for its

rich and other ones for its not-so-rich members.

Final Lines Proofreading and Polishing: Illustration

As you prepare the final version of your illustration paragraph, make any changes in word choice or transitions that can refine your writing. Following is the final version of the paragraph on tee shirts. As you read it, you will notice a few more changes: some details have been added, some have been made more specific, and a transition has been added. In addiiton, a concluding sentence has been added to unify the paragraph. These changes were made as the final version was prepared. (They are underlined for your reference.)

A Final Version of a Paragraph (Changes from the last draft are underlined.)

People of various backgrounds and ages wear all kinds of tee shirts. Athletes and movie stars are seen in them. Musicians often perform in <u>ragged tees</u>, and restaurant workers sometimes work in tee shirts marked with the name of the restaurant. Children, teens, their parents, and <u>elderly</u> people all wear tee shirts. Almost anything can be painted or pictured on a tee shirt. At concerts, <u>for example</u>, fans can buy tee shirts stamped with the name of the group on stage. College students can wear the name of their college on a shirt. Some <u>popular</u> shirts advertise a brand of beer, like Bud, or a sporting goods company, like Nike. Mickey Mouse is even a favorite character on tee shirts. Other kinds of tee shirts include <u>surfer</u> shirts with seascapes on them and souvenir shirts, like the <u>surly</u> ones that say, "My folks visited Philadelphia, and all I got was this lousy tee shirt." Other shirts have political slogans, like "Save the Whales." <u>What is written or pictured on tee shirts is as varied as the people who wear them.</u>

Before you prepare the final version of your illustration paragraph, check your latest draft for errors in spelling or punctuation and for any errors made in typing and copying.

Exercise 14

Practice

Proofreading to Prepare the Final Version

Following are two illustration paragraphs with the kind of errors it is easy to overlook when you prepare the final version of an assignment. Correct the errors by writing above the lines. There are eleven errors in the first paragraph and thirteen errors in the second paragraph.

1. The students in this classroom are proof that their are more kinds of pens and pencils then ever. For instance, the blonde girl in the first row is writting with a pen that contains a neon shade of pink ink. The middle-aged man behind her has the stub of an old pencil. He is much more traditonel, but the women behind him has a felt-tipped pen with green ink. Three student's have typical ball-point pens; however, one of those pens is made of thick rubber for an easy grip. Another ball point has a curved shape at the top. The student setting next me has an old-fashioned fountain pen with real, liquid ink. These pens a really in style today and can Be very expensive. This classroom has enough different pens to be a pen store.

2. My family is not like the families I seen on television. For example, television families eat serial for breakfast, or they eat full meals of bacon, eggs, and toast. My brother eats cookies for breakfast, an my Father eats leftovers from last night's dinner. On television, children spill food on the floor, and their mother's smile and clean up the mess with a papper towel. When my brother spills some food on the floor, the dog licks it up before anyone can clean it up. In additon, television familys are always bussy They are always playing sports or cooking or rushing to school or cleaning the bathroom. Noone on television ever sleeps in a old chair in the front of the television or lounges around on the bed. My family is not as active as those energetic parents and children in the screen.

Lines of Detail: A Walk-Through Assignment

Your assignment is to write an illustration paragraph about music.

Step 1: Freewrite or brainstorm on this broad topic for ten minutes.

Step 2: Review your freewriting or brainstorming. Underline any parts that are a specific idea related to the broad topic, music.

Step 3: List all the specific ideas. Choose one as the narrowed topic for your paragraph.

Step 4: Add related ideas to your chosen, narrowed topic. Do this by reviewing your list for related ideas and by brainstorming for more related ideas.

Step 5: List all your related ideas and review their connection to your narrowed topic. Then write a topic sentence for your paragraph.

Step 6: Write a first draft of your paragraph.

Step 7: Revise your first draft. Be sure it has enough details and clear transitions. Combine any choppy sentences.

Step 8: After a final check for any errors in punctuation, spelling, and word choice, prepare the final version of the paragraph.

Writing Your Own Illustration Paragraph

When you write on any of these topics, follow the four basic stages of the writing process in preparing your illustration paragraph.

1. Begin this assignment with a partner or group. Together, write down as many old sayings as you can. (Old sayings include such statements as, "It's not whether you win or lose; it's how you play the game that's important" or "Money can't buy happiness.") If anyone in your group speaks a second language, ask him or her to translate and explain any old sayings from that language.

   Once you have a long list of sayings, split up. Pick one saying; then write a paragraph on that saying. Your paragraph should give several examples that prove the truth of the saying.

2. Below are some topic sentences. Select one and use it to write a paragraph in which you give examples of the topic sentence.

   _____ makes me nervous.

   _____ takes great courage.

   Snow offers many opportunities for outdoor activities.

   A rainy day is a good day to catch up on indoor chores.

   For the worst food in town, go to _____.

3. Select one of the topics listed below. Write a paragraph on some narrowed part of the topic. If you choose the topic of jobs, for example, you might narrow the topic to your experiences working at a supermarket.

jobs	fears	dreams	mistakes
stress	money	television	mysteries
computers	children	celebrities	surprises
fashion	challenges	memories	holidays

4. Examine the photograph below. After you have looked at it carefully, write a paragraph with this topic sentence:

Most malls have a variety of stores and eating places.

The photograph may help you think of examples to support the topic sentence.

5. Examine the photograph below. After you have looked at it carefully, write a paragraph with this topic sentence:

Amusement parks are filled with exciting activities and rides.

The photograph may help you think of examples to support the topic sentence.

Name: _____ Section: _____

PEER REVIEW FORM FOR AN ILLUSTRATION PARAGRAPH

After you have written a draft for your illustration paragraph, let a writing partner read it. When your partner has completed the form below, discuss the comments. Then repeat the same process for your partner's paragraph.

The examples in this paragraph relate to this topic sentence: _____

_____

_____

The paragraph has _____ (enough, too many, too few) details to support the topic sentence.

The most effective example was the one about _____

_____

Three words or phrases of specific detail in the paragraph are

_____

Two transitions (words or phrases) in the paragraph are _____

_____

I have questions about _____

_____

Other comments: _____

_____

_____

_____

_____

_____

_____

_____

_____

_____

_____

_____

_____

_____

Reviewer's Name: _____

WRITING FROM READING: Illustration

Spanglish

Janice Castro, with Dan Cook and Cristina Garcia

The authors of this article discuss the "free-form blend of Spanish and English" that has developed from a mix of cultures. They explain this blend by using many examples.

Words You May Need to Know (Corresponding paragraph numbers are in parenthesis)

bemused (1): confused
Quiero un (1): I want a. . . .
cerveza (1): beer
linguistic currency (2): way of speaking
syntax (3): word order
patter (3): quick talk
Anglo (3): native-born Americans
ir al (4): go to the

counterparts (5): duplicates
phenomena (5): remarkable things
implicit (5): contained
languorous (5): lacking energy
almuerzo (5): lunch
hybrids (6): blends
wielded (9): used
gaffes (9): social mistakes

1   In Manhattan a first-grader greets her visiting grandparents, happily exclaiming, "Come here, *sientate*!" Her bemused grandfather, who does not speak Spanish, nevertheless knows she is asking him to sit down. A Miami personnel officer understands what a job applicant means when he says, "Quiero un part time." Nor do drivers miss a beat reading a billboard alongside a Los Angeles street advertising *CERVEZA—SIX-PACK!*

2   This free-form blend of Spanish and English, known as Spanglish, is common linguistic currency wherever concentrations of Hispanic Americans are found in the U.S. In Los Angeles, where 55% of the city's three million inhabitants speak Spanish, Spanglish is as much a part of daily life as sunglasses. Unlike the broken-English efforts of earlier immigrants from Europe, Asia, and other regions, Spanglish has become a widely accepted conversational mode used casually—even playfully—by Spanish-speaking immigrants and native-born Americans alike.

3   Consisting of one part Hispanicized English, one part Americanized Spanish and more than a little fractured syntax, Spanglish is a bit like a Robin Williams comedy routine: a crackling line of cross-cultural patter straight from the melting pot. Often it enters Anglo homes and families through the children, who pick it up at school or at play with their young Hispanic contemporaries. In other cases, it comes from watching TV; many an Anglo child has learned *uno dos tres* almost as quickly as one two three.

4   Spanglish takes a variety of forms, from the Southern California Anglos who bid farewell with the utterly silly "*hasta la* bye-bye" to the Cuban-American drivers in Miami who *parquean* their *carros* (park their cars). Some Spanglish sentences are mostly Spanish, with a quick detour for an English word or two. A Latino friend may cut short a conversation by glanc-

ing at his watch and excusing himself with the explanation that he must "*ir al* supermarket."

5   Many of the English words transplanted this way are simply handier than their Spanish counterparts. No matter how distasteful the subject, for example, it is still easier to say "income tax" than *impuesto sobre la renta*. At the same time, many Spanish-speaking immigrants have adopted such terms as VCR, microwave and dishwasher for what they view as largely American phenomena. Still other English words convey a cultural context that is not implicit in the Spanish. A friend who invites you to *lonche* most likely has in mind the brisk American custom of "doing lunch" rather than the languorous afternoon break traditionally implied by *almuerzo*.

6   Mainstream Americans exposed to similar hybrids of German, Chinese, or Hindi might be mystified. But even Anglos who speak little or no Spanish are somewhat familiar with Spanglish. Living among them, for one thing, are nineteen million Hispanics. In addition, more American high school and university students sign up for Spanish than for any other foreign language.

7   Only in the past ten years, though, has Spanish begun to turn into a national slang. Its popularity has grown with the explosive increases in U.S. immigration from Latin American countries. English has increasingly collided with Spanish in retail stores, offices and classrooms, in pop music and on street corners. Anglos whose ancestors picked up such Spanish words as *rancho*, *bronco*, *tornado*, and *incommunicado*, for instance, now freely use such Spanish words as *gracias*, *bueno*, *amigo*, and *por favor*.

8   Among Latinos, Spanglish conversations often flow easily from Spanish into several sentences of English and back. Spanglish is a sort of code for Latinos: the speakers know Spanish, but their hybrid language reflects the American culture in which they live. Many lean to shorter, clipped phrases in place of the longer, more graceful expressions their parents used. Says Leonel de la Cuesta, an assistant professor of modern languages at Florida International University in Miami: "In the U.S., time is money, and that is showing up in Spanglish as as economy of language." Conversational examples: *taipiar* (type) and *winshi-wiper* (windshield wiper) replace *escribir a maquina* and *limpiaparabrisas*.

9   Major advertisers, eager to tap the estimated $134 billion in spending power wielded by Spanish-speaking Americans, have ventured into Spanish to promote their products. In some cases, attempts to sprinkle Spanish through commercials have produced embarrassing gaffes. A Braniff Airlines ad that sought to tell Spanish-speaking audiences they could settle back *en* (in) luxuriant *cuero* (leather) seats, for example, inadvertently said they could fly without clothes (*encuero*). A fractured translation of the Miller Lite slogan told readers the beer was "Filling, and less delicious." Similar blunders are often made by Anglos trying to impress Spanish-speaking pals. But if Latinos are amused by mangled Spanish, they also recognize these goofs as a sort of friendly acceptance. As they might put it, *no problema*.

WRITING FROM READING: "Spanglish"

When you write on any of the following topics, work through the stages of the writing process in preparing your illustration paragraph.

1. "Spanglish" gives several reasons for the growth of this blend of languages. In a paragraph, explain how and why Spanglish has become so widespread.

2. Groups often share their own special language. Computer users, for example, use many terms that a non-user would not understand. Police officers, health-care workers, restaurant workers, musicians, and others all use words or terms that are understood only by their group. In a paragraph, write about four key words or phrases used by a specific group. Use a topic sentence like the following:

   There are four key terms in the language of _____ (name the group).

   You can write from your own experience or interview a member of a specific group.

3. In a paragraph, discuss the blending of two languages in your life. You can discuss the language of two cultures or countries (like English and Creole, or English and Portuguese) or of two parts of your life (such as the formal language you use at work and the informal language you use at home). Give several specific examples of each language.

4. In a paragraph, show how two cultures can blend in a person's choice of clothing, music, or family rituals.

5. The authors of "Spanglish" say that "English has increasingly collided with Spanish in retail stores, offices and classrooms, in pop music and on street corners." Working with a partner or group, brainstorm examples to support that statement. For example, ask and answer such questions as "Where and how does Spanish appear in music popular with both Anglos and Hispanics?" and "How is Spanish appearing in offices?"

   When you have at least five examples, work individually on a paragraph that uses the statement as its topic sentence.

6. If English is not your native language, write a paragraph on the problems you have learning English. Give specific examples of each problem.

7. Write a paragraph about the slang you and your friends use. Focus on four key terms.

8. Write a paragraph starting with one of the following topic sentences:

   What we think of as "American" food really includes food from many cultures.

   or

   Americans regularly use words or phrases from other languages. (If you use this topic sentence, avoid using the examples given in "Spanglish.")

CHAPTER **3**

Description

WHAT IS DESCRIPTION?

Description shows a reader what a person, place, thing, or situation is like. When you write description, you try to *show, not tell*, about something. You want to make the reader see that person, place, or situation, and then, perhaps, to make the reader think about or act on what you have shown.

Hints for Writing a Descriptive Paragraph

Using Specific Words and Phrases Your description will help the reader see if it uses specific words and phrases. If a word or phrase is *specific*, it is *exact and precise*. The opposite of specific language is language that is vague, general, or fuzzy. Think of the difference between specific and general in this way:

Imagine that you are browsing through a used car lot. A salesman approaches you.

"Can I help you?" the salesman asks.
"I'm looking for a good, reliable car," you say.
"Well, what kind of car did you have in mind?" asks the salesman.
"Not too old," you say.
"A sports car?" asks the salesman.
"Maybe," you say.

The conversation could go on and on. You are being very general in saying that you want a "good, reliable" car. The salesman is looking for specific details: How old a car do you want? What model of car?

In writing, if you use words like "good" or "nice" or "bad" or "interesting," you will not have a specific description or a very effective piece of writing. Whenever you can, try to use a more precise word instead of a general term. To find a more explicit term, ask yourself such questions as

"What type?" or "How?" The examples below show how a general term can be replaced by a more specific one:

> **general word:** hat (Ask, "What type?")
> **more specific words:** beret, fishing hat, baseball cap

> **general word:** lettuce (Ask, "What type?")
> **more specific words:** iceberg lettuce, Romaine, arugula

> **general word:** ran (Ask, "How?")
> **more specific words:** raced, sprinted, loped

> **general word:** nice (Ask, "How?")
> **more specific words:** friendly, outgoing, courteous

Exercise 1

Practice

Identifying General and Specific Words

Below are lists of words. Put an *X* by the one term in each list that is a more general term than the others. The first one is done for you.

List 1

_____ waiter

__X__ restaurant employee

_____ cook

_____ cashier

_____ dishwasher

List 2

_____ medicine

_____ aspirin

_____ cough syrup

_____ pain lotion

_____ anti-itch creme

List 3

_____ graduate student

_____ eighth-grader

_____ kindergartner

_____ student

_____ freshman

List 4

_____ rose

_____ daisy

_____ carnation

_____ flower

_____ lily

List 5

_____ sneakers

_____ flip-flops

_____ sandals

_____ high heels

_____ shoes

List 6

_____ mathematics

_____ algebra

_____ calculus

_____ geometry

_____ statistics

Exercise 2

Practice

Ranking General and Specific Items

Following are lists of items. In each list, rank the items, from the most general (*1*) to the most specific (*4*).

List 1

_____ story

_____ children's story

_____ fairy tale

_____ *Cinderella*

List 3

_____ college services

_____ academic help

_____ help for students

_____ tutoring

List 2

_____ *Titanic*

_____ movie conflict at sea

_____ lovers fight the sea

_____ exciting movies

List 4

_____ trained dog

_____ dog

_____ dog to help police

_____ drug-sniffing dog

Exercise 3

Collaborate

Interviewing for Specific Answers

To practice being specific, interview a partner. Ask your partner to answer the questions below. Write his or her answers in the spaces provided. When you have finished, change places. In both interviews, your goal is to find specific answers, so you should both be as explicit as you can in your answers.

Interview Questions

1. What is your favorite flavor of ice cream? _____

2. What did you eat and drink for breakfast this morning? _____

_____

3. What is your favorite football team? _____

4. What television personality do you most dislike? _____

_____

5. If you were painting your room, what color would you choose?

_____

6. What fabric do you think is the softest? _____

7. When you think of a fierce dog, what breed comes to mind?

_____

8. When you think of a fast car, what car do you picture?

_____

9. What specific items of clothing are your most comfortable
   clothes? _____

10. What is the hottest city you have visited? _____

_____

4

Practice

Finding Specific Words or Phrases

List four specific words or phrases beneath each general one. You may use brand names where they are appropriate. The first word on List 1 is done for you.

List 1:

general word: blue
specific word or phrase: aquamarine _____

_____

_____

_____

List 2:

general word: said
specific word or phrase: _____

_____

_____

_____

List 3:

general word: toy
specific word or phrase: _____

_____

_____

_____

List 4:

general word: angry
specific word or phrase: _____

_____

_____

_____

List 5:

general word: good-looking
specific word or phrase: _____

_____

_____

_____

 5

Practice

Identifying Sentences That Are Too General

Below are lists of sentences. Put an *X* by one sentence in each group that is general and vague.

1. **a.** _____ Jose is funny.

   b. _____ Jose always has a new joke.

   c. _____ Jose makes faces at me in class.

2. **a.** _____ She criticized anyone who tried to help her at work.

   b. _____ She expected the worst out of her job.

   c. _____ She had a bad attitude.

3. **a.** _____ The car was good-looking.

   b. _____ It had a dazzling silver paint job.

   c. _____ The chrome gleamed in the sun.

4. **a.** _____ Fifteen people were in line at the checkout counter.

   b. _____ Shoppers bumped into each other in the aisles.

   c. _____ The store was crowded.

5. **a.** _____ I want to live life to the fullest.

   b. _____ I want to travel to Africa and study my heritage.

   c. _____ I want to fall in love and raise a family.

Using Sense Words in Your Descriptions

One way to make your description specific and vivid is to *use sense words*. As you plan a description, ask yourself these questions:

What does it **look** like?
What does it **sound** like?
What does it **smell** like?
What does it **taste** like?
What does it **feel** like?

The sense details can make the description vivid. Try to include details about the five senses in your descriptions. Often you can brainstorm sense details more easily if you focus your thinking.

Info BOX

Devising Sense Detail

For the sense of	think about
sight	colors, light and dark, shadows, or brightness
hearing	noise, silence, or the kinds of sounds you hear
smell	fragrance, odors, scents, aromas, or perfume
taste	bitter, sour, sweet, or compare the taste of one thing to another
touch	the feel of things: texture, hardness, softness, roughness, smoothness

Exercise 6

👥 *Collaborate*

Brainstorming Sense Details for a Descriptive Paragraph

With a partner or a group, brainstorm the following ideas for a paragraph. That is, for each topic, list at least six questions and answers that could help you find sense details. Be prepared to read your completed exercise to another group or to the class.

1. topic: The kitchen was the messiest I have ever seen.

Brainstorm questions and answers:

_____

_____

_____

_____

_____

_____

2. topic: The woods at night frightened us.

Brainstorm questions and answers:

_____

_____

_____

_____

_____

_____

3. topic: The fireworks celebration dazzled the children.

Brainstorm questions and answers:

_____

_____

_____

_____

_____

_____

7

Practice

Writing Sense Words

Write sense descriptions for the items below.

1. Write four words or phrases to describe the texture of a cat's fur:

_____

_____

2. Write four words or phrases to describe what a spider looks like:

_____

_____

3. Write four words or phrases to describe the sounds of a traffic jam:

_____

_____

4. Write four words or phrases to describe the taste of chocolate ice cream:

_____

_____

WRITING THE DESCRIPTION PARAGRAPH IN STEPS

Thought Lines ## Gathering Ideas: Description

Writing a description paragraph begins with thinking on paper, looking for specific details and sense descriptions. You can think by brainstorming, freewriting, or writing in a journal. For example, you might decide to write about your brother's bedroom. Brainstorming might lead you to something like the following list of ideas:

Brainstorming a List for a Descriptive Paragraph

- older brother Michael—got a big bedroom
- I shared with my little brother
- stars pasted on the ceiling
- took a long time to fix it up the way he wanted it
- lots of books about science fiction in two bookcases
- movie posters of AI: Artificial Intelligence and The Matrix
- old videos like Raiders of the Lost Ark in bookcases
- his bed had no headboard, made to look like a couch
- Star Trek pillows on the bed

The Dominant Impression

When you think you have enough details, you can begin to think about focusing them. Look over these details and consider where they are taking you. If you were to look at the list above, you might identify ideas that keep appearing in the details:

- stars pasted on the ceiling
- lots of books about science fiction in two bookcases
- movie posters of <u>AI: Artificial Intelligence</u> and <u>The Matrix</u>
- old videos like <u>Raiders of the Lost Ark</u> in bookcases
- <u>Star Trek</u> pillows on the bed

Reading over this list, you realize that all the specific titles of films or television shows are related to fantasy or science fiction. Therefore, one main idea about your brother's bedroom relates to his interest in fantasy or science fiction. This idea is the **dominant impression,** or the main point of the description. It is the topic sentence of the description paragraph. For example, it could be the following:

My brother's bedroom reflected his fascination with fantasy and science fiction.

Once you have a dominant impression, you are ready to add more ideas to explain and support it. You should try to make the added details specific by using sense description where appropriate.

 Exercise 8   **Adding Details to a Dominant Impression**

Practice

Following are sentences that could be used as a dominant impression in a description paragraph. Add more details. Some details to explain and support the dominant impression are already given.

1. dominant impression: The teenager looked like he had dressed in a hurry.

    details: **a.** His shirt was hanging out of his jeans.

            b. The laces of his sneakers were untied.

            c. _____

            d. _____

            e. _____

2. dominant impression: The hallway of the apartment was cluttered.

    details: **a.** A bicycle leaned against one wall.

            b. A skateboard was shoved under the bike.

            c. _____

            d. _____

            e. _____

3. dominant impression: The bakery invited me to come in and buy something.

    details: **a.** The display window was filled with sticky cinnamon rolls.

b. <u>Next to the rolls was a pyramid of dark chocolate brownies.</u>

c. _____

d. _____

e. _____

Creating a Dominant Impression from a List of Details

Following are lists of details. For each list, write one sentence that could be used as the dominant impression created by the details.

1. dominant impression: _____

_____

details: People on beach towels sat elbow to elbow.
A beach volleyball game took up the remaining space.
The lifeguard could barely be seen above the players and sunbathers.
At the water line, parents watched small children build sand castles and wade in the shallow water.
Meanwhile, the deep water was filled with swimmers and people on floats.
CD players and radios blasted above the laughter of children, the shouts of the swimmers, and the victory cries of the volleyball teams.

2. dominant impression: _____

_____

details: The jury returned to their seats, looking down at the floor.
They would not look at the defendant or the lawyers.
No one spoke.
The only sound in the courtroom was the swish of the judge's robes as she returned to her chair.
The defendant turned pale; he clenched his knuckles.
The jury chairperson clenched the verdict in his hand, but his fingers were shaking.
The reporters leaned forward in their seats, waiting for the verdict to be read.

3. dominant impression: _____

_____

details: The leather cover of the album was cracked and dusty.
Inside, the pages of the album nearly crumbled as I turned them carefully.
The photographs that filled the pages had a yellow tint.
The people in the photographs wore clothes in styles I had never seen.
The inscriptions below the photographs were written in a faded black ink.

Outlines **Devising a Plan: Description**

You can use the sentence you created as the dominant impression as the topic sentence of your outline. Beneath the topic sentence, list the details you have collected. Once you have this rough list, check the details, and ask yourself these questions:

> Do all the details relate to the topic sentence?
> Are the details in logical order?

Following are the topic sentence and list of details for the paragraph describing an apartment. The details that are crossed out don't "fit" the topic sentence.

> **topic sentence:** My brother's bedroom reflected his fascination with fantasy and science fiction.

- ~~older brother Michael got a big bedroom~~
- ~~I shared with my little brother~~
- stars pasted on the ceiling
- ~~took a long time to fix it up the way he wanted it~~
- lots of books about science fiction in two bookcases
- movie posters of <u>AI: Artificial Intelligence</u> and <u>The Matrix</u>
- old videos like <u>Raiders of the Lost Ark</u> in bookcases
- ~~his bed had no headboard, made to look like a couch~~
- <u>Star Trek</u> pillows on the bed

Notice what is crossed out. The details about the size of Michael's bedroom, the other brother's bedroom, the time it took Michael to fix up his bedroom, and the bed that looked like a couch do not really have much to do with the topic sentence. The topic sentence is about Michael's fascination with science fiction and fantasy. It is about how his bedroom revealed that fascination.

Remember that as you write and revise, you may decide to eliminate other ideas, to reinsert ideas you once rejected, or even to add new ideas. Changing your mind is a natural part of revising.

Once you have decided upon your best list of details, check their order. Remember that when you write a description, you are trying to make the reader *see*. It will be easier for the reader to imagine what you see if you put your description in a simple, logical order. You might want to put descriptions in order by **time sequence** (first to last), by **spatial position** (top to bottom, or right to left), or by **similar types** (for example, all about the flowers, then all about the trees in a park).

If you are describing a house, for instance, you may want to start with the outside of the house and then describe the inside. You do not want the details to shift back and forth, from outside to inside and back to outside. If you are describing a person, you might want to group all the details about his face before you describe his body. You might describe a meal from first course to dessert.

Look again at the details describing the bedroom. It is logical to use three categories to create a simple order: from the ceiling, to the walls, and to the furniture. Now look at the following outline and notice how this order works.

An Outline for a Descriptive Paragraph

topic sentence: My brother's bedroom reflected his fascination with fantasy and science fiction.

details:		Stars were pasted on the ceiling.
ceiling	{	At night, they glowed in the dark.
		The room appeared to be covered by a starry sky.
walls	{	Movie posters covered the walls.
		There was a poster of Steven Spielberg's film, <u>AI: Artificial Intelligence</u>.
		Another poster, of <u>The Matrix</u>, was framed.
furniture	{	There were lots of books about science fiction in two bookcases.
		I remember <u>Fahrenheit 451</u> and <u>The War of the Worlds</u>.
		Old videos like <u>Raiders of the Lost Ark</u> were also stacked on the bookshelves.
		The bed was piled high with <u>Star Trek</u> pillows.

You probably noticed that the outline has more details than the original list. These details help to make the descriptions more specific. You can add them to the outline and to the drafts of your paragraph.

Once you have a list of details focused on a topic sentence and arranged in some logical order, you can begin writing a draft of your description paragraph.

Exercise 10

Practice

Finding Details That Do Not Relate

Survey the following lists. Each includes a topic sentence and several details. In each list, cross out the details that do not relate to the topic sentence.

1. **topic sentence:** The pond was a tranquil retreat.
   details: Few people knew of this small place.
   It was hidden from the road by a thick wall of trees.
   The road was two bumpy lanes.
   The trees encircled a shady shore of pebbles and greenery.
   Yellow wildflowers bloomed on the edges of the pond.
   The water was lightly ruffled by the breeze.
   I could hear the soft wind in the trees.
   I could hear the buzz of small summer insects.
   I was alone with my own thoughts and dreams.
   Someday I would come back and bring a picnic.

2. **topic sentence:** My Uncle Oscar was a wonderful playmate.
   details: He always had a joke for his nieces and nephews.
   When he ran out of jokes, he had a plan for a new adventure.
   Uncle Oscar died last year.
   Sometimes he would take us exploring in the neighborhood.
   Whenever he came over, he would arrive on time.
   He would push us on the swings for hours.
   He would play video games with us all evening.
   Uncle Oscar was the one who pleaded with our parents to let us stay up longer and play another game.
   He was my mother's brother.

3. topic sentence: Levar was a very spoiled child.

    details: He would interrupt his mother when she was talking to people.

He'd pull at her sleeve or the hem of her dress.

He'd whine, "Mom, Mom, I want to go now" or "Mom, can I have a dollar?"

He had about a hundred toys.

Whenever he broke one, he got a new one right away.

Levar wore designer clothes, even to play in.

Levar had no set bedtime; he was allowed to stay up as long as he wanted.

Levar had a little sister, Denise.

Levar had big black eyes with long, soft lashes.

Exercise 11

Practice

Putting Details in Order

Following are lists that start with a topic sentence. The details under each topic sentence are not in the right order. Put the details in logical order by labelling them, with *1* being the first detail, *2* the second, and so forth.

1. topic sentence: The plane trip went very smoothly. (Arrange the details in time order.)

    details: _____ Our plane departed on time.

_____ We had no turbulent weather in the air.

_____ We arrived at the airport in plenty of time to be assigned good seats.

_____ When we went to claim our luggage, all of it was there.

_____ Our plane arrived on time.

2. topic sentence: The restaurant was dirty and unappealing. (Arrange the details from outside to inside.)

    details: _____ Soot smeared the sign that said, "Burgers and Shakes."

_____ Finger smudges covered the glass front door.

_____ The chrome edges of the counter were caked with food.

_____ As we stood inside the entrance, we smelled the rancid odor of boiling grease.

_____ We approached a counter covered in crumbs.

3. topic sentence: The man showed off his money. (Arrange the details from head to foot.)

    details: _____ His shoes were a glossy, soft leather.

_____ His hair was elaborately styled.

_____ Two diamond earrings shone in his left ear.

_____ His wrist boasted a platinum Rolex.

_____ His shirt was silk.

Exercise 12   **Creating Details Using a Logical Order**

Practice   The following lists include a topic sentence and indicate a required order for the details. Write five sentences of details in the required order.

1. **topic sentence:** The new movie theater will attract customers. (Describe the theater from outside to inside.)

    a. _____

    b. _____

    c. _____

    d. _____

    e. _____

2. **topic sentence:** The day was full of surprises. (Describe the day from beginning to end.)

    a. _____

    b. _____

    c. _____

    d. _____

    e. _____

3. **topic sentence:** The scene after the tornado hit showed people at their best. (First describe what the scene looked like; then describe the people's behavior.)

    a. _____

    b. _____

    c. _____

    d. _____

    e. _____

4. **topic sentence:** The bodyguard was a frightening person. (Describe him from head to foot.)

    a. _____

    b. _____

    c. _____

    d. _____

    e. _____

Rough Lines **Drafting and Revising: Description**

After you have an outline, the next step is creating a first rough draft of the paragraph. At this point, you can begin combining some of the ideas in your outline, making two or more short sentences into one longer one. You can also write your first draft in short sentences and combine the sentences later. Your goal is simply to put your ideas in paragraph form so that you can see how they look and you can check them to see what needs to be improved.

The first draft of a paragraph will not be perfect. If it were perfect, it wouldn't be a first draft. Once you have the first draft, check it, using the following checklist.

✔ Checklist

A Checklist for Revising a Descriptive Paragraph

✔ Are there enough details?

✔ Are the details specific?

✔ Do the details use sense words?

✔ Are the details in order?

✔ Is there a dominant impression?

✔ Do the details connect to the dominant impression?

✔ Have I made my point?

A common problem in writing description is creating a fuzzy, vague description. Take a look at the following fuzzy description:

> The football fans were rowdy and excited. They shouted when their team scored. Some people jumped up. The fans showed their support by cheering and stomping. They were enjoying every minute of the game.

The description could be revised so that it is more specific and vivid:

> The football fans were rowdy and excited. When their team scored, they yelled, "Way to go!" or "Stomp 'em! Crush 'em!" until they were hoarse. Three fans, wearing the team colors of blue and white on their shirts, shorts, and socks, jumped up, spilling their drinks on the teenagers seated below them. During timeouts, the fans chanted rhythmically, and throughout the game they stomped their feet in a steady beat against the wooden bleachers. As people chanted, whooped, and woofed, they turned to grin at each other and thrust their clenched fists into the air.

The vivid description meets the requirements of the checklist. It has sufficient specific details. The details use sense words to describe what the fans looked and sounded like. The details also support a dominant impression of rowdy, excited fans. The vivid, specific details make the point.

Practice

Revising a Paragraph, Finding Irrelevant Sentences

Following are two descriptive paragraphs. In each, there are sentences that are irrelevant, meaning they do not have anything to do with the first sentence, the topic sentence. Cross out the irrelevant sentences in the paragraphs below.

1. Leo looked and sounded like he was trying to control his anger. I know what that's like because I've been furious and had to suppress my feelings. Leo's face was nearly purple with rage, and his eyes were blazing. He spoke very slowly and quietly, but his tone implied that he was holding himself back from an outburst. His jaw was tight, showing his stress. I could hear his shallow breathing as he tried to calm down. Breathing can be the key to changing your frame of mind; it's an important part of meditation.

2. The garage was crammed with junk and dirt. Empty cardboard boxes, collapsing into each other, lined one wall. Other boxes were filled with newspapers and smaller boxes. A workbench against one wall held rusty screwdrivers and an assortment of loose nails and hooks. Above the bench, a pegboard was covered by dangling hammers, clippers, and cords, some of them covered by rags and gardening gloves. My father keeps all his gardening tools in a shed in the yard. A large bag of dog food had spilled its contents across one end of the garage. To avoid this kind of mess, dog food can be stored in large plastic containers. The place was so full of debris that there was hardly room for the one car parked on the oil-stained floor.

Practice

Revising a Paragraph for More Specific Details.

In the following paragraphs, the details that are underlined are not specific. Change the underlined sentences to a more specific description. Write the changes in the lines below each paragraph.

1. My family dressed beautifully for my sister's wedding. My father wore a dark gray suit and a deep red tie. My mother was dressed in an apricot satin dress with matching silk flowers in her hair. My sister and I, the bridesmaids, were in long dresses of pale yellow organdy and wore straw hats with yellow and lavender ribbons. <u>Even my brother looked good.</u>

revisions: _____

_____

2. The classroom was a dreary place. The dull green and gray paint immediately created a sense of an old and faded schoolroom. The blackboards, covered in layers of ancient chalk dust ground into gray patterns by filthy erasers, spoke of neglect and apathy. Even the bulletin boards, which had no tacks, no notices, and no pictures, offered nothing to please the eye. <u>The student desks were awful.</u> The teacher's desk was really a chipped wooden table accompanied by a chipped metal folding chair.

revisions: _____

_____

Transitions

As you revise your description paragraph, you may notice places in the paragraph that seem choppy or abrupt. That is, one sentence may end, and another may start, but the two sentences don't seem to be connected. Reading your paragraph aloud, you may sense that it is not very smooth.

You can make the writing smoother and make the content clearer by using **transitions,** which are words or phrases that link one idea to another idea. They tell the reader what he or she has just read and what is coming next. Here are some transitions you may want to use in writing a description:

Info BOX

Transitions for a Descriptive Paragraph

To show ideas brought together:

and	also	in addition	next

To show a contrast:

although	however	on the contrary	unlike
but	in contrast	on the other hand	yet

To show a similarity:

all	each	like	similarly
both			

To show a time sequence:

after	first	next	then
always	second (etc.)	often	when
before	meanwhile	soon	while

To show a position in space:

above	between	in front of	over
ahead of	beneath	inside	there
alongside	beyond	near	toward
among	by	nearby	under
around	close	next to	up
away	down	on	underneath
below	far	on top of	where
beside	here	outside	

There are many other transitions you can use, depending on what you need to link your ideas. Take a look at a draft of the description pargaraph of a bedroom. Compare it to the outline on pages 74–75. You will notice that more sense details have been added. Transitions have been added, too. Pay particular attention to the transitions in this draft.

A Draft of a Descriptive Paragraph (Transitions are underlined.)

My brother's bedroom reflected his fascination with fantasy and science fiction. Stars were pasted on the ceiling <u>where</u>, at night, they glowed in the dark. <u>Then</u> the room appeared to be covered by a starry sky. Movie posters covered the walls. A poster of Steven Spielberg's film <u>AI: Artificial Intelligence</u> hung <u>next to</u> a poster of <u>The Matrix</u> in a shiny chrome frame. <u>Below</u> the posters, two steel bookcases were full of books about science fiction. I remember <u>Fahrenheit 451</u> and <u>The War of the Worlds</u>. Old videos like <u>Raiders of the Lost Ark</u> were also stacked on the bookshelves. The bed was piled high with <u>Star Trek</u> pillows.

Exercise 15

Practice

Recognizing Transitions.

Underline the transitions in the paragraph below.

Standing at the top of the hill, Nick was surrounded by natural beauty. Beneath him, he could see the valley with the glistening river that wound around the green and white houses. Beyond the houses was the tall steeple of the old church. When Nick raised his glance to the scene closer by, he saw the soft movement of the breeze in the pines surrounding him. Inside the pines he could see glimpses of sun between the tall, dark trees. Nearby, he heard a bird cry. Above him, a flock of sparrows swooped and swirled. Nick felt happy to be alone with so much of nature's greatness.

Exercise 16

Practice

Combining Sentences and Using Transitions

The following description has some choppy sentences that could be combined to create a smoother paragraph. Combine each pair of underlined sentences by revising them in the space above each pair and using appropriate transitions. The first pair is done for you.

The street fair was filled with tempting objects to buy and food to eat. First, there was a booth with bright straw hats. <u>Strollers came by. The vendor popped a hat on each one's head.</u> He told each person the hat looked stunning and tried to make a deal. <u>A stall offering shiny silver bracelets was in the same area. So was a stall selling half-price CDs.</u> Food was a tremendous attraction. <u>Dozens of people crowded around an ice cream truck. A group of people pushed to buy hot pretzels at a pushcart.</u> Food smells filled the air wherever people went. <u>Bakery smells were nearby. So was the odor of pizza.</u> They were irresistible. <u>The spicy aroma of Indian curry came. It was not so close.</u> When people reached the end of the fair, they turned around to walk through it one more time. <u>They had seen, tasted, and bought many things. They wanted to do it all again.</u>

Final Lines **Proofreading and Polishing: Description**

In preparing the final version of a descriptive paragraph, you add the finishing touches to your paragraph, making changes in words, changing or adding transitions, and sharpening details. In the final version of the description paragraph, you will notice these changes:

- The phrase "had lots of books" has been changed to "were crammed with books." (The phrases "lots of" and "a lot" are not specific, and some writers use them repetitively. Try not to use them.)
- "My brother" has been identified by name, Michael.
- A few more sense details have been added.
- Another specific name of a video has been added.
- In the draft paragraph, the ending of the paragraph is a little sudden. The paragraph needs a sentence that pulls all the details together and reminds the reader of the topic sentence. The final version has an added sentence that ties the paragraph together.

A Final Version of a Descriptive Paragraph

(Changes from the draft are underlined.)

My brother <u>Michael's</u> bedroom reflected his fascination with fantasy and science fiction. Stars were pasted on the ceiling where, at night, they glowed in the dark. Then the room appeared to be covered by a starry sky. Movie posters covered the walls. A poster of Stephen Spielberg's <u>AI: Artificial Intelligence</u> hung next to a poster of <u>The Matrix</u> in a shiny chrome frame. Below the posters, two <u>black</u> steel bookcases were crammed with books about science fiction. I remember <u>Fahrenheit 451</u> and <u>The War of the Worlds</u>. Old videos like <u>Raiders of the Lost Ark</u> and <u>Alien</u> were also stacked on the bookshelves. The bed was piled high with <u>huge, soft Star Trek</u> pillows. <u>Anyone entering the room would know at once that Michael liked to escape to fantastic and futuristic places.</u>

Before you prepare the final copy of your own descriptive paragraph, check your last draft for errors in spelling and punctuation, and for any errors made in typing or re-copying.

 Exercise 17 **Proofreading to Prepare the Final Version**

Practice

Following are two descriptive paragraphs with the kinds of errors it is easy to overlook when you write the final version of an assignment. Correct the errors, writing above the lines. There are thirteen errors in the first paragraph and nine errors in the second.

1. I have an old dilapidated sweatshirt that I'll allways cherish for the

memmories it holds. It is a ratty-looking, gray shirt that belongs in the rag pile

but I wore that shirt on many happy occassions. The greasy stain on one sleeve

is a memory of how I got covered in oil when i was working on my first motorcycle The tear at the neck reminds me of a crazy game of football. At the game where I tore the shirt, I also met my current girlfreind. The pale white blotches acrost the front of the shirt are from bleech. But to me they are a memory of the time my girlfriend and I was fooling around at the laundry room and put to much bleach in the washer. Every mark or stain on my shirt has a meaning to me and I'll never through that old shirt away.

2. When I finally got around to cleaning my refrigerator, I was horrified at the items I had been storing. First, I surveyed the boxes and jar's on the door shelves. Among them was a jar of gourmet salsa that some one had given me for Christmas four years ago. I also found a handful of brown rice in a bag and an empty box of vanila puding mix. I did not stop to wonder why I had kep a empty box of pudding mix, or enough brown rice to feed a small mouse. Instead, I moved on to the back of the refrigerator, where I found jars full of a mysterous green and orange fuzz. Behind the jars were shriveled lemons and rock-hard pieces of cheese. Underneath it all was a slice of slimy pizza wrapped in ancient aluminum foil. I had no idea my refrigerator had become such health hazard.

Lines of Detail: A Walk-Through Assignment

Your assignment is to write a paragraph describing a popular place for socializing. Follow these steps:

Step 1: To begin, freewrite about a place where people socialize. For example, you could write about a place where people go to eat, or dance, or swim, or just "hang out."

Step 2: Read your freewriting. Underline all the words, phrases, and sentences of description.

Step 3: List everything you underlined, grouping the ideas in some order. Maybe the details can be listed from inside to outside, or maybe they can be put into categories, like walls, floor, and furniture, or scenery and people.

Step 4: After you've surveyed the list, write a sentence about the dominant impression of the details.

Step 5: Using the dominant impression as your topic sentence, write an outline. Add specific details where you need them. Concentrate on details that appeal to the senses.

Step 6: Write a first draft of your paragraph. Be sure to check the order of your details. Combine short sentences and add transitions.

Step 7: Revise your first draft version, paying particular attention to order, specific details, and transitions.

Step 8: After a final check for punctuation, spelling, and word choice, prepare the final version of the paragraph.

Writing Your Own Descriptive Paragraph

When you write on any of the following topics, work through the stages of the writing process in preparing your descriptive paragraph. Be sure that your paragraph is based on a dominant impression, and put the dominant impression into your topic sentence.

1. Write a paragraph that describes one of the items below:

   a piece of clothing   a hospital waiting room
   a perfect meal   a family member
   a favorite relative   an enemy
   a very young baby   an irritating customer
   what is in your top bureau drawer
   what is in your top kitchen drawer
   the contents of your purse or wallet
   items in the glove compartment of your car
   what you wear on your day off
   your first impression of a school
   a person who was a positive influence in your life

2. Describe a place that creates one of these impressions:

peace	tension	depression
excitement	cheerfulness	hurry
friendliness	danger	safety

3. Describe a person who conveys one of these impressions:

confidence	warmth	pride
hostility	fear	style
shyness	rebellion	intelligence
conformity	strength	beauty

4. Select a photograph of a person or place. You can use a photograph from a magazine or newspaper, or one of your own photographs. Write a paragraph describing that photograph. Attach the photograph to the completed paragraph.

5. Interview a partner so that you and your partner can gather detail, and then write a description paragraph with the title, "My Perfect Room."

   First, prepare a list of at least six questions to ask your partner. Write down the answers your partner gives and use those answers to form more questions. For example, if your partner says her dream room would be a game room, ask her what games she'd like to have in it. If your partner says his perfect room would be a workshop, ask him what kind of workshop.

When you've finished the interview, switch roles. Let your partner interview you. Feel free to add more questions or to follow up on previous ones.

Give your partner his or her interview responses. Take your own responses and use them as the basis for gathering as many details as you can on your perfect room. Finally, build the thought lines part of your paragraph. Then go on to the outline, draft, and final version. Be prepared to read your completed paragraph to your partner.

6. Study the photograph above left. Then write a paragraph that describes and explains the dominant impression of this scene.

7. Look carefully at the face in the photograph above. Write a description that focuses on the aura of the face. Does the face give an impression of wisdom? Pain? Sorrow? Peace? Joy? Strength? You decide, and support your decision by describing the details of the photograph.

Name: _____ Section: _____

PEER REVIEW FORM FOR A DESCRIPTIVE PARAGRAPH

After you've written a draft of your descriptive paragraph, let a writing partner read it. When your partner has completed the form below, discuss the comments. Then repeat the same process for your partner's paragraph.

The dominant impression of the paragraph is this sentence: _____

_____

The details of the description are in a specific order. That order is (for example, top to bottom, time order, etc.) _____

_____

The part of the description I liked best begins with the words _____

_____.

The part that could use more or better details begins with the words _____

_____.

I have questions about _____.

I noticed these transitions: _____

A place where transitions could be added or improved is right before the words _____

_____

Other comments: _____

_____

_____

_____

_____

_____

_____

_____

_____

_____

_____

_____

Reviewer's Name: _____

WRITING FROM READING: Description

A Present for Popo

Elizabeth Wong

The child of Chinese immigrants, Elizabeth Wong was born in Los Angeles, California. She has a master's of fine arts degree and has worked as a writer for newspapers and television. She has also written several plays. In "A Present for Popo," Wong describes a beloved grandmother.

Words You May Need to Know (corresponding paragraphs are in parentheses):

nimbly (1):   quickly, gracefully
vain (2):   proud of one's appearance
co-opted (3):   taken over
niggling (4):   unimportant
dim sum **(6):**   a light meal

terrarium (7):   a small container where plants and small creatures are kept alive under conditions imitating their natural environment

---

1   When my Popo opened a Christmas gift, she would shake it, smell it, listen to it. She would size it up. She would open it nimbly, with all enthusiasm and delight, and even though the mittens were ugly or the blouse too small or the card obviously homemade, she would coo over it as if it were the baby Jesus.

2   Despite that, buying a gift for my grandmother was always problematic. Being in her late 80s, Popo didn't seem to need any more sweaters or handbags. No books certainly, as she only knew six words of English. Cosmetics might be a good idea, for she was just a wee bit vain.

3   But ultimately, nothing worked. "No place to put anything anyway," she used to tell me in Chinese. For in the last few years of her life, Popo had a bed in a room in a house in San Gabriel owned by one of her sons. All her belongings, her money, her very life was now co-opted and controlled by her sons and their wives. Popo's daughters had little power in this matter. This was a traditional Chinese family.

4   For you see, Popo had begun to forget things. Ask her about something that happened 20 years ago, and she could recount the details in the heartbeat of a New York minute. But it was those niggling little everyday matters that became so troubling. She would forget to take her heart medicine. She would forget where she put her handbag. She would forget she talked to you just moments before. She would count the few dollars in her billfold, over and over again. She would ask me for the millionth time, "So when are you going to get married?" For her own good, the family decided she should give up her beloved-one-room Chinatown flat. Popo herself recognized she might be a danger to herself. "I think your grandmother is going crazy," she would say.

5   That little flat was a bothersome place, but Popo loved it. Her window had a view of several import-export shops below, not to mention the grotesque plastic hanging lanterns and that nasty loudspeaker serenading tourists with eighteen hours of top-40 popular hits.

6   My brother Will and I used to stand under her balcony on Mei Ling Way, shouting up, "Grandmother on the Third Floor! Grandmother on the Third Floor!" Simultaneously, the wrinkled faces of a half-dozen grannies would peek cautiously out their windows. Popo would come to the balcony and proudly claim us: "These are my grandchildren coming to take me to *dim sum*." Her neighbors would cluck and sigh, "You have such good grandchildren. Not like mine."

7   In that cramped room of Popo's, I could see past Christmas presents. A full-wall collage of family photos that my mother and I made together and presented one year with lots of fanfare. Popo had attached additional snapshots by way of paper clips and Scotch tape. And there, on the window sill, a little terrarium to which Popo had tied a small red ribbon. "For good luck," as she gleefully pointed out the sprouting buds. "See, it's having babies."

8   Also, there were the utility shelves on the wall, groaning from a wide assortment of junk, stuff and whatnot. Popo was fond of salvaging discarded things. After my brother had installed the shelving, she did a little jig, then took a whisk broom and lightly swept away any naughty spirits that might be lurking on the walls. "Shoo, shoo, shoo, away with you, Mischievous Ones!" That apartment was her independence, and her pioneer spirit was everywhere in it.

9   Popo was my mother's mother, but she was also a second mother to me. Her death was a great blow. The last time I saw her was Christmas, 1990, when she looked hale and hearty. I thought she would live forever. Last October, at ninety-one, she had her final heart attack. The next time I saw her, it was at her funeral.

10   An open casket, and there she was, with a shiny new penny poised between her lips, a silenced warrior woman. Her sons and daughters placed colorful pieces of cloth in her casket. They burned incense and paper money. A small marching band led a New Orleans–like procession through the streets of Chinatown. Popo's picture, larger than life, in a flatbed truck to survey the world of her adopted country.

11   This little 4-foot, 9-inch woman had been the glue of our family. She wasn't perfect, she wasn't always even nice, but she learned from her mistakes, and, ultimately, she forgave herself for being human. It is a lesson of forgiveness that seems to have eluded her own sons and daughters.

12   And now she is gone. And with her—the tenuous, cohesive ties of blood and duty that bound us to family. My mother predicted that once the

distribution of what was left of Popo's estate took place, no further words would be exchanged between Popo's children. She was right.

13   But this year, six of the 27 grandchildren and two of the 18 great-grandchildren came together for a holiday feast of honey-baked ham and mashed potatoes. Not a gigantic family reunion. But I think, for now, it's the one yuletide present my grandmother might have truly enjoyed.

14   Merry Christmas, Popo!

WRITING FROM READING: "A Present for Popo"

When you write on any of the following topics, work through the stages of the writing process in preparing your descriptive paragraph.

1. Elizabeth Wong uses many details about her grandmother's apartment to describe the woman. Write a paragraph in which you use many details about a person's environment (for example, her office, his apartment) to describe that person.

2. Wong's essay includes a description of a funeral in a Chinese-American family. Write a description of some custom or ritual in your family. You could write, for instance, about a wedding, funeral, celebration of a holiday, or religious occasion.

3. "A Present for Popo" is a tribute to a beloved person. Write a description of someone who holds a special place in your life.

4. The grandmother in Wong's essay is an immigrant, a Chinese woman who moved to America. Describe an immigrant that you know. Focus on how the person is a combination of two countries or cultures.

5. Describe an older person you know well. In your description, you can use details of appearance and behavior. Focus on how these details reveal personality.

6. Describe yourself at age ninety. Use your imagination to give details of appearance, behavior, and family relationships.

CHAPTER **4**

Narration

WHAT IS NARRATION?

Narration means telling a story. Everybody tells stories; some people are better storytellers than others. When you write a **narrative** paragraph, you can tell a story about something that happened to you or to someone else, or about something that you saw or read.

A narrative, like a description, relies on specific details, but it is also different from a description because it covers events in a time sequence. While a description can be about a person, a place, or an object, a narrative is always about happenings: events, actions, incidents.

Interesting narratives do more than just tell what happened. They help the reader become involved in the story by providing vivid details. These details come from your memory, your observation, or your reading. Using good details, you don't just tell the story; you *show* it.

Give the Narrative a Point

We all know people who tell long stories that seem to lead nowhere. These people talk on and on; they recite an endless list of activities and soon become boring. Their narratives have no point.

The difficult part of writing a narrative is making sure that it has a point. That point will be included in the topic sentence. The point of a narrative is the meaning of the incident or incidents you are writing about. To get to the point of your narrative, ask yourself questions like these:

What did I learn?
What is the meaning of this story?
What is my attitude toward what happened?
Did it change me?
What emotion did it make me feel?
Was the experience a good example of unfairness, kindness, generosity, or some other quality?

The answers to such questions can lead you to a point. An effective topic sentence for a narrative is

90

not this: I'm going to tell you about the time I flunked my driving test. (This is an announcement; it does not make a point.)

but this: When I failed my driving test, I learned not to be overconfident.

not this: Yesterday my car stalled in rush-hour traffic. (This identifies the incident but does not make a point. It is also too narrow to be a good topic sentence.)

but this: When my car stalled in rush-hour traffic, I was annoyed and embarrassed.

The topic sentence, stating the point of your narrative paragraph, can be placed in the beginning or middle or at the end of the paragraph. You may want to start your story with the point, so that the reader knows exactly where your story is headed, or you may want to conclude your story by leaving the point until last. Sometimes the point can even fit smoothly into the middle of your paragraph.

Consider the narrative paragraphs below. The topic sentences are in various places.

Topic Sentence at the Beginning

<u>When I was five, I learned how serious it is to tell a lie.</u> One afternoon, my seven-year-old friend Tina asked me if I wanted to walk down the block to play ball in an empty lot. When I asked my mother, she said I couldn't go because it was too near dinner time. I don't know why I lied, but when Tina asked me if my mother had said yes, I nodded my head in a lie. I wanted to go play, and I did. Yet as I played in the dusty lot, a dull buzz of guilt or fear distracted me. As soon as I got home, my mother confronted me. She asked me whether I had gone to the sandlot and whether I had lied to Tina about getting permission. This time, I told the truth. Something about my mother's tone of voice made me feel very dirty and ashamed. I had let her down.

Topic Sentence in the Middle

When I was little, I was afraid of diving into water. I thought I would go down and never come back up. Then one day, my father took me to a pool where we swam and fooled around, but he never forced me to try a dive. After about an hour of playing, I walked round and round the edge of the pool, trying to get the courage to dive in. Finally, I did it. <u>When I made that first dive, I felt blissful because I had done something I had been afraid to do</u>. As I came to the surface, I wiped the water from my eyes and looked around. The sun seemed more dazzling, and the water sparkled. Best of all, I saw my father looking at me with a smile. "You did it," he said. "Good for you! I'm proud of you."

Topic Sentence at the End

It seemed that I'd been in love with Reeza for years. Unfortunately, Reeza was always in love with someone else. Finally, she broke up with her boyfriend Nelson. I saw my chance. I asked Reeza out. After dinner, we talked and talked. Reeza told me all about her hopes and dreams. She told me about her family and her job, and I felt very close to her. We talked late into the night. When she left, Reeza kissed me. "Thanks for listening," she said. "You're like a brother to me." <u>Reeza meant to be kind, but she shattered my hopes and dreams.</u>

Exercise   1

Practice

Finding the Topic Sentence in a Narrative Paragraph

Underline the topic sentence in each narrative paragraph below.

Paragraph 1

Last Sunday, my mother insisted that I spend the afternoon with my cousin Lisa, who was visiting from the Dominican Republic. It was the last thing I wanted to do. I barely knew Lisa, and I thought of her as superior and snobbish. The afternoon began with lunch. Lisa, who is very pretty and slim, ordered salad and made me feel fat when I ordered a burger and fries. Throughout the lunch, she said very little, and I felt sure she thought she was too good for the inexpensive restaurant. However, I was wrong. I had to revise my opinion of Lisa when we spent more time together. Just as we were finishing lunch, a rainstorm hit. We were stuck in the restaurant for hours. Over several cups of coffee, Lisa began to open up. I soon realized that she is very shy, and she finally confessed that she felt inferior to me, her American cousin. By the end of the afternoon, we were acting like old friends.

Paragraph 2

I was eager to get a place of my own. I figured that having my own apartment meant I was free at last since there would be no rules, no curfew, no living by someone else's schedule. My first day in the apartment started well. I arranged the furniture, put up all my pictures, and called all my friends. Then I called out for pizza. When it came, I tried to start a conversation with the delivery man, but he was in a hurry. I ate my pizza alone while I watched the late movie. It was too late to call any of my friends, and I definitely wasn't going to call my mother and let her know I wanted some company. In truth, my first day in my apartment showed me the lonely side of living on my own.

Paragraph 3

Yesterday, one person showed me what it means to be a good parent. I was walking in the mall, and just ahead of me a toddler was holding his father's hand and struggling to keep up. Pretty soon, the child got tired and started to cry. Within minutes, his crying had become a full-fledged tantrum. The little boy squatted on the ground, refusing to go any farther, his face purple. Some parents would have shouted at the child, threatened him, or scooped him up and carried him away. This father, however, just sat down on the ground by his son and talked to him, very calmly and quietly. I couldn't hear his words, but I got the feeling he was sympathizing with the tired little boy. Pretty soon, the child's screams became little sniffles, and father and son walked quietly away.

Exercise   2

Practice

Writing the Missing Topic Sentences in Narrative Paragraphs

Following are three paragraphs. If the paragraph already has a topic sentence, write it in the lines provided. If it does not have a topic sentence, create one. (Two of the paragraphs have no topic sentence.)

Paragraph 1

When I got up, I realized I must have turned off my alarm clock and gone back to sleep because I was already an hour behind schedule. I raced into the shower, only to find I had used up the last of the shampoo the day before. I barely had time to make a cup of coffee to take with me in the car. I grabbed the cup of coffee, rushed to the car, and turned the ignition. The car wouldn't start. Two hours later, the emergency service finally came to jump-start the car. I arrived at work three hours late, and the supervisor was not happy with me.

If the paragraph already has a topic sentence, write it here. If it does

not have a topic sentence, create one. _____

_____

_____

Paragraph 2

Since I gave my first speech in my public speaking class, I'm not as shy as I used to be. On the day I was supposed to give my speech, I seriously considered cutting class, taking an F on the speech, or even dropping the course. All I could think of was what could go wrong. I could freeze up and go blank, or I could say something really stupid. In spite of my terror, I managed to walk up to the front of the class. When I started talking, I could hear my voice shaking. I wondered if everyone in the room could see the cold sweat on my forehead. By the middle of the speech, I was concentrating so intensely on *what* to say that I forgot about my nerves. When I finished, I couldn't believe people were clapping! I never believed I could stand up and speak to the entire class. Once I did that, it seemed so easy to talk in a class discussion. Best of all, the idea of making another speech doesn't seem as frightening anymore.

If the paragraph already has a topic sentence, write it here. If it does

not have a topic sentence, create one. _____

_____

_____

Paragraph 3

Last weekend I was driving home alone, at about 10:00 P.M., when a carload of young men pulled up their car beside mine. They began shouting and making strange motions with their hands. At first I ignored them, hoping they'd go away. But then I got scared because they wouldn't pass me. They kept driving right alongside of my car. I rolled up my car windows and locked the doors. I couldn't hear their shouts, but I was still afraid. I was more afraid when I stopped at a red light and they pulled up next to me. Suddenly, one of the men screamed at me, at the top of his lungs, "Hey! You have a broken tail light!"

If the paragraph already has a topic sentence, write it here. if it does

not have a topic sentence, create one. _____

_____

_____

HINTS FOR WRITING A NARRATIVE PARAGRAPH

Everyone tells stories, but some people tell stories better than others. When you write a story, be sure to follow these rules:

- Be clear.
- Be interesting.
- Stay in order.
- Pick a topic that is not too big.

1. Be clear. Put in all the information the reader needs in order to follow your story. Sometimes you need to explain the time or place or the relationships of the people in your story in order to make the story clear. Sometimes you need to explain how much time has elapsed between one action and another. This paragraph is not clear:

> I've never felt so stupid as I did on my first day of work. I was stocking the shelves when Mr. Cimino came up to me and said, "You're doing it wrong." Then he showed me how to do it. An hour later, he told me to call the produce supplier and check on the order for grapefruit. I didn't know how to tell Mr. Cimino that I didn't know what phone to use or how to get an outside line. I also didn't know how to get the phone number of the produce supplier, or what the order for the grapefruit was supposed to be and when it was supposed to arrive. I felt really stupid asking these questions.

What is wrong with the paragraph? It lacks all kinds of information. Who is Mr. Cimino? Is he the boss? Is he a produce supervisior? And, more important, what kind of place is the writer's workplace? The reader knows the place has something to do with food, but is it a supermarket, or a fruit market, or a warehouse?

2. Be interesting. A boring narrative can make the greatest adventure sound dull. Here is a dull narrative:

> I had a wonderful time on prom night. First, we went out to dinner. The meal was excellent. Then we went to the dance and saw all our friends. Everyone was dressed up great. We stayed until late. Then we went out to breakfast. After breakfast we watched the sun come up.

Good specific details are the difference between an interesting story and a dull one.

3. Stay in order. Put the details in a clear order, so that the reader can follow your story. Usually, time order is the order you follow in narration. This narrative has a confusing order:

> My impatience cost me twenty dollars last week. There was a pair of shoes I really wanted. I had wanted them for weeks. When payday came around, I went to the mall and checked the price on the shoes. I had been checking the price for weeks before. The shoes were expensive, but I really wanted them. On payday, my friend, who works at the shoe store, told me the shoes were about to go on sale. But I was impatient. I bought them at full price, and three days later, the shoes were marked down twenty dollars.

There's something wrong with the order of events here. Tell the story in the order it happened: first, I saw the shoes and wanted them; second, the shoes were expensive; third, I checked the price for several weeks; fourth, I got paid; fifth, I checked the price again; sixth, my friend told me the shoes were about to go on sale; seventh, I paid full price right away; eighth, the shoes went on sale. A clear time sequence helps the reader follow your narrative.

4. Pick a topic that is not too big. If you try to write about too many events in a short space, you run the risk of being superficial. You can not describe anything well if you cover too much. This paragraph covers too much:

> Starting my sophomore year at a new high school was a difficult experience. Because my family had just moved to town, I didn't know anybody at school. On the first day of school, I sat by myself at lunch. Finally, two students at another table started a conversation with me. I thought they were just feeling sorry for me. At the end of the first week, it seemed like the whole school was talking about exciting plans for the weekend. I spent Friday and Saturday night at home, doing all kinds of things to keep my mind off my loneliness. On Monday, people casually asked, "Have a good weekend?" I lied and said, "Of course."

This paragraph would be better if it discussed one shorter time period in greater depth and detail. It could cover the first day at school, or the first lunch at school, or the first Saturday night at home alone, when the writer was doing "all kinds of things" to keep from feeling lonely.

Using a Speaker's Exact Words in Narrative

Some of the examples of narrative that you have already seen have included the exact words someone said. You may want to include part of a conversation in your narrative. To do so, you need to know how to punctuate speech.

A person's exact words get quotation marks around them. If you change the words, you do not use quotation marks.

> **exact words:** "You're being silly," he told me.
> **not exact words:** He told me that I was being silly.

> **exact words:** My sister said, "I'd love to go to the party."
> **not exact words:** My sister said she would love to go to the party.

There are a few other points to remember about punctuating a person's exact words. Once you've started quoting a person's exact words, periods and commas generally go inside the quotation marks. Here are two examples:

> Richard said, "Nothing can be done."
> "Be careful," my mother warned us.

When you introduce a person's exact words with phrases like "She said" or "The teacher told us," put a comma before the quotation marks. Here are two examples:

> She said, "You'd better watch out."
> The teacher told us, "This will be a challenging class."

If you are using a person's exact words and have other questions about punctuation, check the information on punctuation in the grammar section of this book.

WRITING THE NARRATIVE PARAGRAPH IN STEPS

Thought Lines **Gathering Ideas: Narration**

Finding something to write about can be the hardest part of writing a narrative paragraph because it is usually difficult to think of anything interesting or significant that you have experienced. By answering the following questions, you can gather topics for your paragraph.

Exercise 3

👥 *Collaborate*

Questionnaire for Gathering Narrative Topics

Answer the questions below as best you can. Then read your answers to a group. The members of the group should then ask you follow-up questions. Write your answers on the lines provided; the answers will add details to your list.

Finally, ask each member of your group to circle one topic or detail on your questionnaire that could be developed into a narrative paragraph. Discuss the suggestions. Repeat this process for each member of the group.

Narrative Questionnaire

1. Did you ever have a close call? When? _____

Write four things you remember about it:

a. _____

b. _____

c. _____

d. _____

Additional details, to be added after working with the group:

_____

_____

2. Have you ever been stuck in traffic? Write four details about what happened before, during, and after:

a. _____

b. _____

c. _____

d. _____

More details, to be added after working with the group:

_____

_____

3. Have you ever had a day when everything went wrong? Write four details about that day:

a. _____

b. _____

c. _____

d. _____

More details, to be added after working with the group:

_____

_____

4. Have you ever applied for a job? Write four details about what happened when you applied for a job:

a. _____

b. _____

c. _____

d. _____

More details, to be added after working with the group:

_____

_____

Freewriting for a Narrative Topic

One good way to discover something to write about is to freewrite. For example, if your instructor asks you to write a narrative paragraph about something that changed you, you might begin by freewriting.

Freewriting for a Narrative Paragraph

Topic: Something That Changed Me

Something that changed me. I don't know. What changed me? Lots of things happened to me, but I can't find one that changed me. Graduating from high school? Everybody will write about that, how boring, and anyway, what was the big deal? I haven't gotten married. No big change there. Divorce. My parents' divorce really changed the whole family. A big shock to me. I couldn't believe it was happening. I was really scared. Who would I live with? They were real calm when they told me. I've never been so scared. I was too young to understand. Kept thinking they'd just get back together. They didn't. Then I got a stepmother. The year of the divorce a hard time for me. Kids suffer in divorce.

Narrowing and Selecting a Suitable Narrative Topic

After you freewrite, you can assess your writing, looking for words, phrases, or sentences that you could expand into a paragraph. The sample writing has several ideas for a narrative:

> high school graduation
> learning about my parents' divorce
> adjusting to a stepmother
> the year of my parents' divorce

Looking for a topic that is not too big, you could use

> high school graduation
> learning about my parents' divorce

Since the freewriting has already called graduation a boring topic, the divorce seems to be a more attractive subject. In the freewriting, you already have some details related to the divorce; add to these details by brainstorming. Follow-up questions and answers might include these:

How old were you when your parents got divorced?

I was seven years old when my mom and dad divorced.

Are you an only child?

My sister was ten.

Where did your parents tell you? Did they both tell you at the same time?

They told us at breakfast, in the kitchen. Both my folks were there. I was eating toast. I remember I couldn't eat it when they both started talking. I remember a piece of toast with one bite out of it.

What reasons did they give?

They said they loved us, but they couldn't get along. They said they would always love us kids.

If you didn't understand, what did you <u>think</u> was happening?

At first I just thought they were having another fight.

Did you cry? Did they cry?

I didn't cry. My sister cried. Then I knew it was serious. I kept thinking I would have to choose which parent to live with. Then I knew I'd really hurt the one I didn't choose. I felt so much guilt about hurting one of them.

What were you thinking?

I felt ripped apart.

Questions can help you form the point of your narrative After brainstorming, you can go back and survey all the details. Do they lead you to a point? Try asking yourself the questions listed earlier in this chapter: What did I learn? What is the meaning of this story? What is my attitude toward what happened? Did it change me? What emotion did it make me feel? Was the experience a good example of something (like unfairness, or kindness, or generosity)?

For the topic of the divorce, the details mention a number of emotions: confusion, pain, shock, disbelief, fear, guilt. The *point* of the paragraph cannot list all these emotions, but it could say

> When my parents announced they were divorcing, I felt confused by all my emotions.

Now that you have a point and several details, you can move on to the outlines stage of writing a narrative paragraph.

Exercise 4

Practice

Distinguishing Good Topic Sentences from Bad Ones in Narration

Below are sentences. Some would make good topic sentences for a narrative paragraph. Others would not; they are too big to develop in a single paragraph, or they are so narrow they can't be developed, or they make no point about an incident or incidents. Put an *X* by the sentences that would not make good topic sentences.

1. _____   I bought a wide-screen television yesterday.

2. _____   I grew up when I was in the Marines.

3. _____   The motorist who stopped to help me on the highway taught me a valuable lesson about trust.

4. _____   My two-year battle for child custody was a nightmare.

5. _____   This is the story of the birth of my son.

6. _____   I saw true compassion when I visited the home for babies with AIDS.

7. _____   Our team's victory over the Rangers demonstrated the power of endurance.

8. _____   I've seen guns ruin the lives of four of my friends in four years.

9. _____   The robbery took place at the deli near my house.

10. _____   I never knew what it was like to be afraid until our house was burglarized.

Exercise 5

Practice

Developing a Topic Sentence From a List of Details

Following are two lists of details. Each has an incomplete topic sentence. Read the details carefully; then complete each topic sentence.

1. topic sentence: When he _____

my brother made me feel _____

details: My brother always borrows my clothes.
Sometimes I wish he wouldn't.
Last week he took my new leather jacket.
I went to my closet, and the jacket wasn't there.
I wanted to wear it that night.
Later, he came home wearing it.
I could have punched him.
He gave it back.
He swore he didn't know it had a big slash in the back.
He acted innocent.
I told him he'd have to pay to fix the jacket.
He still hasn't paid me.

2. topic sentence: A fight at a party showed me _____

_____

details: My friend Tony and I were at a birthday party at his nephew Alex's house.

Everyone was having a good time, eating, drinking, and dancing.

The party became more crowded as cars full of uninvited people showed up.

Four of the strangers pushed their way into the backyard.

One of them came up to Tony and insulted him.

Tony did not react.

Then two of the strangers pushed Tony to the ground.

I grabbed him and pulled him into the house.

Alex went outside to see what was going on.

The next thing I saw was Alex on the ground, being kicked and stomped by a group of men.

The police came, and the strangers ran.

Alex is in the hospital.

I realized that Tony or I could be the one who was hurt.

Outlines **Devising a Plan: Narration**

The topic of how an experience changed you has led you to a point and a list of details. You can now write a rough outline, with the point as the topic sentence. Once you have the rough outline, check it for these qualities:

Relevance: Do all the details connect to the topic sentence?
Order: Are the details in a clear order?
Development: Does the outline need more details? Are the details specific enough?

Your revised outline might look like this:

An Outline for a Narrative Paragraph

topic sentence: When my parents announced that they were divorcing, I felt confused by all my emotions.

details:

background of the narrative
- I was seven when my mom and dad divorced.
- My sister was ten.
- Both my folks were there.
- They told us at breakfast, in the kitchen.
- I was eating toast.
- I remember I couldn't eat anything when they started talking.
- I remember a piece of toast with one bite out of it.

story of the divorce announcement
- My parents were very calm when they told us.
- They said they loved us but couldn't get along.
- They said they would always love us kids.

my reactions at each stage
- It was a big shock to me.
- I couldn't believe it was happening.
- At first I just thought they were having another fight.
- I was too young to understand.
- I didn't cry.
- My sister cried.

$$\left\{\begin{array}{l}\text{Then I knew it was serious.}\\\text{I kept thinking I would have to choose which parent}\\\text{to live with.}\\\text{I knew I'd really hurt the one I didn't choose.}\\\text{I felt so much guilt about hurting one of them.}\\\text{I felt ripped apart.}\end{array}\right.$$

my reactions
(continued)

Once you have a revised outline, you're ready to write a draft of the narrative paragraph.

Exercise 6

Practice

Finding Details That Are Out of Order in a Narrative Outline

The outlines below have details that are out of order. Put the details in correct order by numbering them, using "1" for the detail that should be first, and so on.

1. topic sentence: Getting to see my doctor was a frustrating experience.

details: _____ I arrived early for my 3:00 p.m. appointment.

_____ There were seven people in the waiting room by 3:15 p.m.

_____ I called the doctor's office for an appointment after I had been sick with flu-like symptoms for two days.

_____ The nurse said the soonest I could come in was three days later.

_____ At 3:30 p.m., ten people sat in the waiting room, and no one had yet been called into the doctor's examination rooms.

_____ As I followed the nurse into an examination room, I was relieved that I was getting some attention at last.

_____ "The doctor will be with you shortly," the nurse said as she left me in the examining room.

_____ I waited in the examining room for another thirty minutes.

_____ My name was finally called at 4:30 P.M.

2. topic sentence: Yesterday I saw something that showed me the good side of people.

details: _____ My traffic lane was at a standstill, so I had time to look around.

_____ I was driving down the highway.

_____ As I waited for the traffic to move, I saw a ragged man by the side of the road, holding a sign.

_____ The sign said, "Will Work for Food."

_____ I saw a car pull off the road, right next to the man.

_____ The ragged man shrunk back, as if he were afraid the car would hit him.

_____ The driver motioned to the homeless man through the open window.

_____ The driver of the car rolled down his window on the passenger side.

_____ The homeless man crept over.

_____ The driver handed him a big bag of food from Burger King.

Exercise 7

Practice

Recognizing Irrelevant Details in a Narrative Outline

Below are two outlines. One of them has details that are not relevant to the topic sentence. Cross out the details that do not fit.

1. topic sentence: My father surprised me at my high school graduation.

details: My father has always been a good but somewhat distant father.
He doesn't talk much and is very sparing with his praise.
On the morning of my graduation, he seemed the way he has always been: silent and tough.
His only comment to me was to be sure I didn't forget my cap and gown.
As I walked up to receive my diploma, I spotted him in the crowd; he looked stern and serious.
With my diploma in hand, I made my way back to my seat.
After the ceremony, I looked for my father among the joyful graduates, their families and friends.
I was astonished to see father rushing to greet me.
Tears were streaming down his face as he grabbed my hand.

2. topic sentence: The most embarrassing thing I've ever experienced happened to me in the supermarket checkout line.

details: I always shop with a list of what I need to buy.
The cashier was running the items through the scanner.
Our store uses scanners now instead of cash registers.
When he was finished, he said, "That'll be $23.50."
I reached into my wallet for the money.
All I found was a ten-dollar bill.
I searched frantically through all the folds of my wallet.
There was nothing but the ten-dollar bill.
I was *sure* I had put a twenty in my wallet when I left for the store.
Then I remembered—I had spent the twenty at the gas station.
I whispered to the cashier, "Oops! I didn't bring enough money."
He just looked at me.
The groceries were already bagged.
I had to take them out of the bags and get rid of enough of them to add up to $13.50.
Meanwhile, the people in line behind me wanted to kill me.
At that moment, I wished they had.

Rough Lines **Drafting and Revising: Narration**

After you have a revised outline for your narration paragraph, you can begin working on a rough draft of the paragraph. As you write your first draft, you can combine some of the short sentences of the outline. Once you have a draft, you can check it for places you would like to improve. The list below may help you to check your draft.

> **✔ Checklist**
>
> **A Checklist for Revising the Draft of a Narrative Paragraph**
>
> ✔ Is my narrative vivid?
>
> ✔ Are the details clear and specific?
>
> ✔ Does the topic sentence fit all the details?
>
> ✔ Are the details written in a clear order?
>
> ✔ Do the transitions make the narrative easy to follow?
>
> ✔ Have I made my point?

Revising for Sharper Details

A good idea for a narrative can be made better if you revise for sharper details. In the paragraph below, the underlined words and phrases could be revised to create better details. In the following example, see how the second draft has more vivid details than the first draft.

First Draft: Details Are Dull

A woman at the movies showed me just how rude and selfish people can be. It all started when I was in line with <u>a lot</u> of other people. We had been waiting <u>a long time</u> to buy our tickets. We were outside, and it <u>wasn't pleasant.</u> We were impatient because time was running out and the movie was about to start. Some people were <u>making remarks</u>, and <u>others were pushing</u>. Then <u>a woman cut to</u> the front of the line. The cashier at the ticket window <u>told</u> the woman there was a line and she would have to go to the end of it. The woman <u>said she didn't want to wait because her son didn't want to miss the beginning of the movie.</u>

Second Draft: Better Details

A woman at the movies showed me just how rude and selfish people can be. It all started when I was in line with <u>forty or fifty other people</u>. We had been waiting to buy our tickets for <u>twenty minutes</u>. We were outside, <u>where the temperature was about 90 degrees, and it looked like rain</u>. We were all getting impatient because time was running out and the movie was about to start. <u>I heard two people mutter about how ridiculous the wait was, and someone else kept saying, "Let's go!" The man directly behind me kept pushing me, and each new person at the end of the line pushed the whole line forward, against the</u>

ticket window. Then a woman <u>with a loud voice and a large purse thrust her purse and her body in front of the ticket window.</u> The cashier <u>politely</u> told the woman there was a line and she had to go the end of it. But the woman answered <u>indignantly. "Oh no," she said. "I'm with my son Mickey. And Mickey really wants to see this martial arts movie. And he hates to miss the first part of any movie, so I can't wait. I've got to have those tickets now."</u>

Checking the Topic Sentence

Sometimes you think you have a good idea, a good topic sentence and specific details, but when you write the draft of the paragraph, you realize the topic sentence does not quite fit all the details. When that happens, you can either revise the detail or rewrite the topic sentence.

In the paragraph below, the topic sentence (underlined) does not quite fit all the details, so the topic sentence should be rewritten.

<u>I didn't know what to do when a crime occurred in front of my house.</u> At nine p.m. I was sitting in my living room, watching television, when I heard what sounded like a crash outside. At first I thought it was a garbage can that had fallen over. Then I heard another crash and a shout. I ran to the window, and I looked out into the dark. I couldn't see anything because the street light in front of my house was broken. But I heard at least two voices, and they sounded angry and threatening. I heard another voice, and it sounded like someone moaning. I was afraid. I ran to the telephone. I was going to call 911, but then I froze in fear. What if the police came, and people got arrested? Would the suspects find out I was the one who called the police? Would they come after me? Would I be a witness at a trial? I didn't want to get involved, so I just stood behind the curtain, peeking out and listening. Pretty soon the shouting stopped, but I still heard sounds like hitting. I couldn't stand it any more. I called the police. When they came, they found a young teenager, badly beaten, in the street. They said my call may have saved his life.

The paragraph above has good details, but the story has more of a point than "I didn't know what to do." The person telling the story did, finally, do something. Following is a better topic sentence that covers the whole story.

topic sentence rewritten: I finally found the courage to do the right thing when a crime occurred in front of my house.

Combining Sentences in a Draft of a Narrative

Practice

The following paragraph contains some short, choppy sentences, which are underlined. Wherever you see two or more underlined sentences clustered next to each other, combine them into one clear, smooth sentence. Write your revised version of the paragraph in the spaces above the lines.

Getting lost in the city gave me my first taste of panic. When I was

fourteen, I convinced my mother I was old enough to travel to my aunt's

apartment in the city. <u>My mother gave me clear directions. She wrote the</u>

address on a slip of paper. She also drew a map of the streets I had to cross once I got off the bus. I had been to my aunt's place many times with my family. I was sure I would have no problem. When I got off the bus, I began walking confidently toward my aunt's street. However, after I had walked a few blocks, nothing looked familiar. I convinced myself I had to keep walking until I found a store or restaurant I knew. I walked farther. Everything seemed strange. The streets began to look unfriendly, even dangerous. I felt that people were staring at me. They were staring with hostility. Desperate, I approached a stranger. I asked him for directions. He looked at me for a moment. He laughed. He told me I had gotten off at the wrong bus stop. My aunt's street was fifteen blocks away. I felt relieved. I felt foolish. I felt both emotions about my mistakes and my panic.

Practice

Adding Better Details to a Draft of a Narrative

The following paragraph has some details that could be more vivid. Rewrite the paragraph in the lines below, replacing the underlined details with more vivid words, phrases, or sentences.

Roberto showed he is a great athlete when he lost the wrestling match. The match had been very close, but someone had to lose, and that someone turned out to be Roberto. After the match, the winner, Tom, was getting all the attention. He was acting very full of himself. Roberto was just keeping to himself. Roberto looked hurt. His eyes were sad. Nevertheless, he went to Tom and shook hands. Tom looked mean and didn't say much. Roberto, on the other hand, said the right thing. Then Roberto walked away, his head held high.

Rewrite: _____

_____

_____

_____

_____

_____

_____

_____

Exercise 10

Practice

Writing a Better Topic Sentence for a Narrative

The paragraphs below could use better topic sentences. (In each paragraph, the current topic sentence is underlined.) Read each paragraph carefully, then write a new topic sentence for it, in the lines below.

1. <u>Last week I ran into my old girlfriend.</u> Clarice and I had stopped seeing each other two years earlier. When she left me, I was angry and hurt. I felt I would never find anyone to take her place because we were a perfect match. Then, last Friday, I met her in a coffee shop. While we talked over coffee, I studied her. She was as beautiful and charming as ever. She still had the poise and personality that had attracted me to her in the first place. However, we soon ran out of conversation. She was still living in the neighborhood and was mainly concerned with her social life. I had moved on to college and a demanding job. We had very little in common. Clarice was no longer my perfect mate.

New Topic Sentence: _____

_____

2. <u>I had dinner with my family last week.</u> My two younger brothers, Simon and David, started it by fighting over who was going to sit in the seat next to my father. When we all sat down to eat, my sister provoked my mother by complaining, "Chicken again? All we eat is chicken." Of course, my mother jumped right in and said if my sister wanted to take the responsibility for planning menus and cooking meals, she could go right ahead. Meanwhile, my father was telling David not to kick Simon under the table, and Simon was spitting mashed potatoes at David. I got irritated and said I wished that once, just once, we could eat dinner like a normal family. Then my father and I had an argument about what I meant by a normal family. By that time, Simon had spilled his milk on the floor, and my mother had caught my sister feeding chicken to the dog. We all left the dinner table in a bad mood.

New Topic Sentence: _____

_____

Using Transitions Effectively in Narration

When you tell a story, you have to be sure that your reader can follow you as you move through the steps of your story. One way to make your story easier to follow is to use transitions. Most of the transitions in narration have to do with time. Below is a list of transitions writers often use in writing narration.

Info BOX

Transitions for a Narrative Paragraph

after	before	in the meantime	soon after
again	during	later	still
always	finally	later on	suddenly
at first	first	meanwhile	then
at last	second, (etc.)	next	until
at once	frequently	now	when
at the same time	immediately	soon	while

The Draft

Below is a draft of the paragraph on divorce. As you read it, you will notice that some ideas from the outline on pages 100–101 have been combined, the details have been put in order, and transitions have been added. Exact words of dialogue have been used to add vivid details.

A Draft of a Narrative Paragraph (Transitions are underlined.)

<u>When</u> my parents announced that they were divorcing, I felt confused by all my emotions. <u>At the time</u> of their announcement, I was seven, and my sister was ten. Both my folks were there to tell us. They told us at breakfast, in the kitchen. I was eating toast, but I remember I couldn't eat anything when they started talking. I remember a piece of toast with one bite taken out of it. My parents were very calm when they told us. "We love both you kids very much," my dad said, "but your mother and I aren't getting along." They said they would always love us. The announcement was such a shock to me that I couldn't believe it was happening. <u>At first</u>, I just thought they were having another fight. Because I was too young to understand, I didn't cry. <u>Suddenly</u>, my sister started to cry, <u>and then</u> I knew it was serious. I kept thinking I would have to choose which parent to live with. I knew I'd really hurt the one I didn't choose, <u>so</u> I felt so much guilt about hurting one of them. I felt ripped apart.

 Exercise 11
Practice

Recognizing Transitions in a Narrative Paragraph

Underline the transitions in the following paragraph.

Mrs. Levy's sudden return from vacation sent her sons into a panic. When Mrs Levy called to say she had decided to come home a day early and was on her way home from the airport, Jason and Isaiah were alarmed. They knew they had less than an hour to get the house in order. First, Jason scrambled to collect the empty pizza boxes, Burger King bags, and super-sized drink cups in the living room. Meanwhile, Isaiah rushed from room to room, picking the dirty laundry off the floors and tables and tossing it into the washer. Next, both boys rushed to the kitchen, where Isaiah flung dirty dishes into a sink full of soapy water and Jason swept the cake crumbs, bread crusts, and tortilla chips under the refrigerator. Suddenly, Isaiah remembered he had left his muddy sneakers on the dining room table. He raced to retrieve them before his mother found them drying out on her prized piece of furniture. He was carrying them in one hand at the same time his mother opened the front door.

 Exercise 12
Practice

Adding the Right Transitions to a Narrative Paragraph

In the following paragraph, circle the correct transition in each of the pairs.

I ran into trouble when I was taking my art history test yesterday; later /at once I solved my own problem. I was doing fine after/ at first, completing the matching questions about the painters and their paintings. Then /still I ran into five short-answer questions about the Impressionists, and my mind went blank. I knew I had studied the material, but I couldn't remember a thing. Who or what were the Impressionists? I froze, and the harder I tried to remember, the less confident I felt. I decided to go on to the other questions on the test before /while I lost all my confidence. I took a deep breath and completed the rest of the test, ignoring the five questions about the Impressionists and focusing on what I knew about the remaining questions. Soon after /finally I had done that, I felt much calmer, for I had found the rest of the test fairly easy. I began to feel confident frequently/ again. Before/ Suddenly all that I had studied about the Impressionists came back to me.

Final Lines Polishing and Proofreading: Narration

As you prepare the final version of the narrative paragraph, make any minor changes in word choice or transitions that can refine your writing. Below is the final copy of the narrative paragraph on divorce. Notice these changes in the final version:

- The draft version used both formal and informal words like "folks" and "parents" and "dad" and "father." The final lines uses only "parents" and "father."
- A few details have been added.
- A few details have been changed.
- A transition has been added.

A Final Version of a Narrative Paragraph
(Changes from the draft are underlined).

When my parents announced that they were divorcing, I felt confused by all my emotions. At the time of the announcement, I was seven, and my sister was ten. Both <u>my parents</u> were there to tell us. They told us at breakfast, in the kitchen. I was eating toast, but I remember I couldn't eat anything when they started talking. <u>In fact,</u> I remember <u>staring at</u> a piece of toast with one bite taken out of it. My parents were very calm when they told us. "We both love you very much," my <u>father</u> said. "But your mother and I aren't getting along." They said they would always love us. The announcement was such a shock to me that I couldn't believe it was happening. At first, I just thought they were having another fight. Because I was too young to understand, I didn't cry. Suddenly, my sister started to cry, and then I knew it was serious. I kept thinking I would have to choose which parent to live with. I knew I'd really hurt the one I didn't choose, so I felt <u>terrible</u> guilt about hurting one of them. I felt ripped apart.

Before you prepare the final version of your narrative paragraph, check your latest draft for errors in spelling or punctuation, and for any errors made in typing and re-copying.

Exercise 13 Proofreading to Prepare the Final Version

Practice

Following are two narrative paragraphs with the kind of errors that are easy to overlook when you prepare the final version of an assignment. Correct the errors, writing above the lines. There are eleven errors in the first paragraph and seven in the second.

1. When my girl friend tossed my ring out the window, I knew she was not ready to forgive me one more time. It all started on Saturday, at

MacDonald's when I ran into my girlfriend Lakisha. I could see she was'nt in a good mood. As soon as we sat down, she asked me about Yvonne. A girl I've been seeing behind Lakisha's back. Of course I lied and said that "Yvonne was nothing to me." However, Lakisha said she seen me and Yvonne at the mall the night before, and we looked like we was rommanticly involved. I asked, "How could you tell?" Naturally that was the wrong thing to say since I was admitting Yvonne and I had been together. After I asked that stupid question, Lakisha took my ring off her finger and hurled that ring right threw the window at McDonalds.

2. My son Scott's first day at pre-school was an emotional one for me. i was up early on that day, planning his cloths and worrying about his fears and tears when I dropped him off at his first school. However, when I woke Scott up, I tried to be cheerful. I smiled and acted as if he were about to begin an exciting adventure. "Today is the day you get to make friends and have some fun, I said." Scott didn't seem to unhappy or reluctant as he ate breakfast. He was pleased when I let him wear his faverite baseball cap and shorts. In the car on the way to school, Scott sat quietly, but I could hardly hold back my tears. I was picturing my little boy alone, afraid, crieing in a corner of the classroom. Yet when I handed him over to a friendly teacher, Scott did not protest. He took the teacher's hand and walked, wide-eyed, to a new world.

Lines of Detail: A Walk-Through Assignment

Write a paragraph about an incident in your life that either embarrassed, amused, frightened, saddened, or angered you. In writing the paragraph, follow these steps:

Step 1: Begin by freewriting. Then read your freewriting, looking for both the details and focus of your paragraph.

Step 2: Brainstorm for more details. Then write all the freewriting and brainstorming as a list.

Step 3: Survey your list. Write a topic sentence that makes a point about the details.

Step 4: Write an outline. As you write the outline, check that your details fit the topic sentence and are in clear order. As you revise your outline, add details where they are needed.

Step 5: In the rough lines stage, write and revise a draft of your paragraph. Revise until your details are specific and in a clear order, and your transitions are smooth. Combine any sentences that are short and choppy. Add a speaker's exact words if they will make the details more specific.

Step 6: In preparing the final lines copy, check for punctuation, spelling, and word choice.

Writing Your Own Narrative Paragraph

When you write on any of the following topics, be sure to work through the stages of the writing process in preparing your narrative paragraph.

1. Write about some event you saw that you will never forget. Begin by freewriting. Then read your freewriting, looking for both the details and the focus of your paragraph.

   If your instructor agrees, ask a writing partner or group to (a) listen to you read your freewriting, (b) help you focus it, and (c) help you add details by asking questions.

2. Write a narrative paragraph about how you met your boyfriend or girlfriend or husband or wife. Start by listing as many details as you can, and, if your instructor agrees, ask a writing partner or a group to (a) survey your list of details and (b) ask questions that can lead you to more details.

3. Write about a time when you got what you wanted. Start by listing as many details as you can, and, if your instructor agrees, ask a writing partner or a group to (a) survey your list of details and (b) ask questions that can lead you to more details.

4. Interview an older family member or friend. Ask him or her to tell you an interesting story about his or her past. Ask questions as the person speaks. Take notes. If you have a tape recorder, you can tape the interview, but take notes as well.

   When you've finished the interview, review the information with the person you've interviewed. Ask the person if he or she would like to add anything. If you wish, ask follow-up questions.

   Next, on your own, find a point to the story. Work through the stages of the writing process to turn the interview into a narrative paragraph.

5. Write a narrative paragraph about the couple in the photograph on the next page. Look carefully at their expressions and body language and write about events before, during, and after this scene. You may want to include some dialogue in your paragraph.

6. Write a narrative about the fire in the photograph on the next page. You can include events before, during, and after the dramatic scene in the photograph.

Name: _____   **Section:** _____

PEER REVIEW FORM FOR A NARRATIVE PARAGRAPH

After you have written a draft of your narrative paragraph, let a writing partner read it. When your partner has completed the form below, discuss the responses. Repeat the same process for your partner's paragraph.

I think the topic sentence of this paragraph is _____

_____

_____ . (Write the sentence.)

I think the topic sentence (a) states the point well, (b) could be revised. (Choose one.)

The part of the narrative I liked best begins with the words _____

The part that could use more or better details begins with the words _____

_____

An effective transition was _____

_____ (Write the words of a good transition.)

I have questions about _____

I would like to see something added about _____

I would like to take out the part about _____

I think the narrative is (a) easy to follow, (b) a little confusing (Choose one.)

Other comments: _____

_____

_____

_____

_____

_____

_____

_____

_____

_____

_____

_____

Reviewer's Name: _____

WRITING FROM READING: Narration

Rocky Rowf

Edna Buchanan

Edna Buchanan is famous as a former crime reporter for The Miami Herald *and is the author of non-fiction books and novels about murder and mayhem. In this essay, she writes about a lighter subject: how she met and got to know Rocky Rowf, her dog.*

Words You May Need to Know (corresponding paragraph numbers are in parentheses)

dehydrated (4): lacking water
clambered (7): climbed
nonchalantly (13): coolly, casually
dotes (14): shows great love for
deferential (14): respectful
obsequious (14): slavelike, submissive

abject (14): pitiful
fawning (14): submissive behavior
disdainfully (14): scornfully, arrogantly
pretext (29): excuse
repertoire (34): collection of tricks

1   I was a pushover.

2   I met Rocky on a sizzling Fourth of July weekend. I never intended to take him home with me. He was sprawled under a park bench on South Beach trying to stay cool. I was there to exercise, to bend and stretch in the shade of the sea grape trees, and to look at the blue-green summer sea. Two elderly men, friendly regulars in the park, were sitting on the bench.

3   "Is that your dog?" I asked.

4   They said no. He was so quiet they had barely noticed him. He was panting in the heat, and I grew alarmed as I patted him. His tongue was purple—eggplant purple. I was certain that it meant the animal was dangerously dehydrated. I filled a paper cup several times from a faucet used by bathers to rinse sand off their feet and he drank politely. But his tongue stayed purple.

5   That is its normal color, something I did not learn until later. It may mean he is part chow chow, though he does not look it. He looks like the kind of mutt that everybody has owned at some time in their life: black with buff-colored paws, medium sized, and affable. His ears are floppy, his grin silly. He wore a battered old leather collar with no tag. After he drank, he watched me exercise, then followed as I walked along the seawall. This little romance will end now, I thought, as I returned to my car.

6   When I opened the door, he pushed right past me, scrambling into the front seat. Obviously accustomed to traveling by car, he was determined to have his way. When ordered out, he slunk into the back seat and settled

stubbornly on the floor, on the far side, out of arm's reach. What the heck, I thought, I'll keep him until I find his owner. As we pulled away from the curb, however, I reconsidered: I can't take this dog home. What about all those cats?

7   I stopped at the main lifeguard station, and the dog clambered out after me, trotting right alongside. The guard said he had seen the dog roaming the beach alone for the past three days. He would call Animal Control, he said, and held the dog so I could get away. "Bye, puppy," I said, and headed for the car. My mistake was in looking back. The dog was whimpering and struggling to follow, his eyes fixed on me, pleading.

8   "You sure this isn't your dog?" The lifeguard looked suspicious.

9   I insisted I had never seen that animal before in my life. The lifeguard let go, and the dog bounded to me, wagging his tail.

10   On the way home we stopped at the supermarket for dog food. It was too hot to leave him in the car, so I left him just outside the store and told him to wait. He'll probably be gone, finding a new friend, by the time I get the dog food through the checkout counter, I thought. But as I turned into the next aisle, there he was, trotting past the produce, wriggling with delight when he spotted me. Somebody had opened the door.

11   "Is that your dog?" the store manager wanted to know. I denied it.

12   "Are you sure?" he said, staring pointedly at the dog food and the Milk-Bone box in my cart.

13   He ejected the dog, who was waiting when I came out. I looked around the parking lot vaguely, wondering where I had left my car. He knew. All I had to do was follow as he trotted briskly ahead, found the car, and sat down next to it waiting for me. When we got home, he scampered up the front steps without hesitation and waited as I unlocked the door. It was as though he had lived there all his life. Misty and Flossie were snoozing on the highly polished hardwood floor in the living room when this strange dog walked nonchalantly into their home. Both shot straight up in the air, then fled so fast that for several seconds they ran in place on the slick surface. They skidded into my bedroom and dove out the window. Luckily it was open. The screen landed in the middle of the lawn.

14   After the initial shock, they sized him up at once. He must have lived with other animals, because he dotes on them, especially the smaller ones, and is particularly deferential to cats. He was so obsequious, in fact, rolling on his back in abject surrender whenever they entered the room, that they quickly became disgusted at his fawning. Within two days the cats were stealing his food and stepping disdainfully over him as he napped.

15   For two weeks we walked up and down that stretch of South Beach seawall looking for his owner. Lots of people had seen the friendly dog, but always alone. A middle-aged Puerto Rican busboy with no teeth grinned

and greeted him as Blackie. I thought we had found the owner, but he said he had fed the dog a hamburger and some water at about one o'clock the same morning I found him performing his hungry-and-thirsty act.

16   After two weeks I gave up, took him to the vet [and] got him a license, and he joined the household.

17   He chose his own name. I ran through dozens of appropriate possibilities. None appealed to him. He would not even open his eyes at most. But when I said Rocky, he looked up, wagged his tail, and grinned. So Rocky it is—Rocky Rowf.

18   His past remains a mystery. Housebroken and well-behaved, he did not seem to understand even the most simple commands. Perhaps, I decided, his owner spoke a language other than English. We went to an obedience school, taught by a cop in charge of the Coral Gables police K-9 unit. The only mutt, Rocky was the smartest in the class. However, he did refuse to be a watch-dog. In an attempt to agitate him, they thrust him between a Doberman pin-scher and a German shepherd. The big dogs were ferocious, leaping in frenzies, snarling, and barking. Rocky Rowf sat between them, grinning and drooling. A very laidback dog, he hates trouble, rolling his eyes and whining when the cats quarrel among themselves. If the chips were down and we were attacked by strangers, he would do the sensible thing—run for his life.

19   The day after his first visit to the vet, I got home from the *Herald* after nine o'clock at night. When I opened the back door and called, he did not come bounding in from the yard as usual. I stepped out into the dark and could barely make him out, curled up next to the banana tree. I called to him again and again. He did not move. My heart sank. Frightened, I approached the still form, reached out, and touched the fur ruffled by a summer breeze. It felt cool.

20   He was dead.

21   Poor stray dog, doing fine until I took him home; now he was dead. How did it happen? My mind raced. The vet had said he was in good health thirty-six hours earlier. It had to be poison, or maybe he had been shot. It was too dark to see anything in the yard. I dialed the vet's emergency num-ber. He's dead, I cried accusingly, probably an allergic reaction to the shots you gave him.

22   "What makes you think he's dead?" asked Dr. Hal Nass.

23   "I know a dead dog when I see one!" I screamed.

24   He told me to bring the body to his office. He would get dressed and meet me there; together we would find out what happened.

25   The dog weighed forty-seven pounds. The backyard was dark, and I didn't even own a flashlight. The only neighbor I knew was across the street, in a big house on the bay. When I had moved in months earlier he introduced himself and invited me to call on him if I ever needed help.

26   His wife answered. They had gone to bed early. I said I needed her husband's assistance. I whimpered to him that somebody or something had killed my dog and asked if he had seen any strangers prowling the neighborhood. I told him I had to get the dead dog out of my shadowy and unlit backyard and into my car. Poor Rocky Rowf's last ride would be to the vet for an autopsy.

27   A sympathetic man and a good neighbor, Larry Helfer climbed out of bed, got dressed and brought a flashlight. "I think it was poison," I said, greeting him in tears. "The doctor said he was fine yesterday."

28   I offered him a blanket to wrap the body in. "Where is it?" he said grimly. Out there, I said, pointing. He pushed open the back door, stared into the darkness, then slowly turned and looked at me, his face strange. I stepped past him to look. Sitting at the back door, gazing up at us was Rocky. He was grinning.

29   Never taking his eyes off me, Larry Helfer began to back slowly toward the front door. He obviously believed that, using the pretext of a dead dog, I had lured him out of his bed and across the street, for some unknown purpose.

30   "I could have sworn he was dead. He didn't answer when I called him," I babbled. "He was just lying there."

31   It was his turn to babble. "My, eh, wife, is worried. I better go tell her everything's all right," he said and made a run for it.

32   I caught the vet, just as he was leaving his home. "Never mind," I said.

33   Larry Helfer and his wife avoided me for several years after that. When we did meet by chance, they always asked politely after the health of my dog.

34   Nowadays, I point an index finger at Rocky Rowf and say, "Bang, you're dead!" He falls on the floor, then rolls over on his back. It's one of the best tricks in his repertoire.

35   It wasn't difficult to teach him at all. He already knew how.

WRITING FROM READING: "Rocky Rowf"

When you write on any of the following topics, be sure to work through the stages of the writing process in preparing your narrative paragraph.

1. Write a narrative paragraph about an animal you know that has a distinct personality. To begin, you may want to freewrite about all your memories of this animal.

2. Write a narrative paragraph about how you got a pet. To begin, you may want to list all the steps included in getting your pet.

3. Write the story of an emergency with a pet. If your instructor agrees, you may want to begin by asking a writing partner to interview you, asking questions like these:

> How did you feel during this emergency?
> What was the worst part of the incident?
> Did your feelings change during the emergecny?

Next, you can interview your partner to collect ideas for his or her paragraph.

4. Write the story of how your pet got its name.

5. Write a narrative paragraph that shows that dogs (or cats) are smarter than people.

6. Edna Buchanan writes about a time she helped an animal, a lost dog. Write a narrative paragraph about a time you helped a person who was in trouble.

CHAPTER 5

Process

WHAT IS PROCESS?

A **process** writing explains how to do something or describes how something happens or is done. When you tell the reader how to do something (a **directional process,**) you speak directly to the reader, giving clear, specific instructions about performing some activity. Your purpose is to explain an activity so that a reader can do it. For example, you may have to leave instructions telling a new employee how to close the cash register or use the copy machine.

When you describe how something happens or is done (an **informational process**), your purpose is to explain an activity without telling a reader how to do it. For example, you can explain how a boxer trains for a fight or how the special effects for a movie were created. Instead of speaking directly to the reader, an informational process speaks about "I," "he," "she," "we," or "they" or speaks about a person by name. A directional process uses "you," or, in the way it gives directions, the word "you" is understood.

A Process Involves Steps in Time Order

Whether a process is directional or informational, it describes something that is done in steps, and these steps are in a specific order: a **time order.** The process can involve steps that are followed in minutes, hours, days, weeks, months, or even years. For example, the steps in changing a tire may take minutes, whereas the steps taken to lose ten pounds may take months.

You should keep in mind that a process involves steps that *must follow a certain order*, not just a range of activities that can be placed in any order. This sentence *signals a process:*

Learning to search the Internet is easy if you follow a few simple directions. (Using the Internet involves following steps in order; for example, you cannot search before you turn on the computer.)

This sentence *does not signal a process:*

There are several ways to get a person to like you. (Each way is separate; there is no time sequence here.)

Telling a person, in a conversation, how to do something or how something is done gives you the opportunity to add important points you may have overlooked or to throw in details you may have skipped at first. Your listener can ask questions if he or she does not understand you. Writing a process, however, is more difficult. Your reader is not there to stop you, to ask you to explain further, or to question you. In writing a process, you must be organized and clear.

Hints for Writing a Process Paragraph

1. **In choosing a topic, find an activity you know well.** If you write about something familiar to you, you will have a clearer paragraph.
2. **Choose a topic that includes steps that must be done in a specific time sequence.**

   not this: I find lots of things to do on a rainy day.
   but this: I have a plan for cleaning the garage.

3. **Choose a topic that is fairly small.** A complicated process cannot be covered well in one paragraph. If your topic is too big, the paragraph can become vague, incomplete, or boring.

   too big: There are many stages in the process of a bill before Congress becoming a law.
   smaller and manageable: Willpower and support were the most important elements in my struggle to quit smoking.

4. **Write a topic sentence that makes a point.** Your topic sentence should do more than announce. Like the topic sentence for any paragraph, it should have a point. As you plan the steps of your process and gather details, ask yourself some questions: What point do I want to make about this process? Is the process hard? Is it easy? Does the process require certain tools? Does the process require certain skills, like organization, patience, endurance?

   an announcement: This paragraph is about how to change the oil in your car.
   a topic sentence: You do not have to be a mechanic to change the oil in your car, but you do have to take a few simple precautions.

5. **Include all the steps.** If you are explaining a process, you are writing for someone who does not know the process as well as you do. Keep in mind that what seems clear or simple to you may not be clear or simple to the reader, and be sure to tell what is needed before the process starts. For instance, what ingredients are needed to cook the dish? Or what tools are needed to assemble the toy?
6. **Put the steps in the right order.** Nothing is more irritating to a reader than trying to follow directions that skip back and forth. Careful planning, drafting, and revision can help you get the time sequence right.

7. **Be specific in the details and steps.** To be sure you have sufficient details and clear steps, keep your reader in mind. Put yourself
in the reader's place. Could you follow your own directions or understand your steps?

If you remember that a process explains, you will focus on being
clear. Now that you know the purpose and strategies of writing a
process, you can begin the thought lines stage of writing one.

Exercise 1

Practice

Recognizing Good Topic Sentences for Process Paragraphs

If a sentence is a good topic sentence for a process paragraph, put *OK* on
the line provided. If a sentence has a problem, label that sentence with one
of these letters:

    A This is an **announcement**; it makes no point.

    B This sentence covers a topic that is too **big** for one paragraph.

    S This sentence describes a topic that does *not* require **steps.**

1. _____ I've developed a system for buying groceries that saves me
time and money.

2. _____ How I learned to wash and wax my car is the subject of
this paragraph.

3. _____ There are several reasons for leasing a car.

4. _____ The steps involved in brain surgery are complicated.

5. _____ Beating the traffic on the way to the city means knowing
when and where to detour to the back roads.

6. _____ This paper shows the method of installing a window air
conditioner.

7. _____ Civil rights in America evolved in several stages.

8. _____ There are many things to remember when you enter college.

9. _____ If you learn just a few trade secrets, you can give yourself a
professional manicure at home.

10. _____ Fred learned the right way to apply for a car loan.

Exercise 2

 *Collaborate*

Including Necessary Materials in a Process

Below are three possible topics for a process paragraph. For each topic,
work with a partner or a group and list the items (materials, ingredients,
tools, utensils, supplies) the reader would have to gather before he or she
begins the process. When you've finished the exercise, check your lists with
another group to see if you've missed any items.

    1. topic: making and packing a school lunch for a six-year-old

      needed items: _____

      _____

      _____

2. topic: washing a car

needed items: _____

_____

_____

3. topic: preparing a package for mailing (the package contains a
            breakable item)

needed items: _____

_____

_____

WRITING THE PROCESS PARAGRAPH IN STEPS

Thought Lines   ## Gathering Ideas: Process

The easiest way to start writing a process paragraph is to pick a small topic,
one that you can cover well in one paragraph. Then you can gather ideas by
listing or freewriting or both.

If you decided to write about how to find the right apartment, you
might begin by freewriting.

Then you might check your freewriting, looking for details that have
to do with the process of finding an apartment. You can underline those
details, as in the example that follows.

Freewriting for a Process Paragraph

Topic: Finding the right apartment
You have to <u>look around</u>. <u>Don't pick the first apartment you see</u>. Sean did that,
and he wound up with a dump. <u>Look at a bunch</u>. But <u>not too many</u>, or you'll get
confused. <u>The lease</u>, too. <u>Check it carefully</u>. <u>How much is the security deposit?</u> <u>Do
you want a one bedroom?</u> <u>Friends can help</u> if they know of any nice apartments.
I found my place that way. Maybe somebody you know lives in <u>a good neighbor-
hood</u>. A <u>convenient location can be more expensive</u>. But <u>can save you money on
transportation</u>.

Next, you can put what you've underlined into a list, in correct time
sequence:

before the search

Do you want a one bedroom?
Friends can help
a good neighborhood
convenient location can be more expensive
can save you money on transportation

during the search

look around
Don't pick the first apartment you see.
Look at a bunch.
But not too many

after the search

Check the lease carefully.
How much is the security deposit?

Check the list. Are some details missing? Yes. A reader might ask, "What other ways (besides asking friends) can help you find apartments? What else should you do before you search? When you're looking at apartments, what should you be looking for? What questions should you ask? After the search, how do you decide which apartment is best? And what, besides the security deposit, should you check on the lease?" Answers to questions like these can give you the details needed to write a clear and interesting informational process.

Writing a Topic Sentence for a Process Paragraph

Freewriting and a list can now help you focus your paragraph by identifying the point of your process. You already know what the subject of your paragraph is: finding the right apartment. But what's the point? Is it easy to find the right apartment? Is it difficult? What does it take to find the right apartment?

Maybe a topic sentence could be

Finding the right apartment takes planning and careful investigation.

Once you have a topic sentence, you can think about adding details that explain your topic sentence, and you can begin the outlines stage of writing.

Practice

Finding the Steps of a Process in Freewriting

Read the following freewriting, then reread it, looking for all the words, phrases, or sentences that have to do with steps. Underline all those items. Then once you've underlined the freewriting, put what you've underlined into a list in a correct time sequence.

How I Found a Great Gift for My Father: Freewriting

Birthdays are tough. How do you find the right gift? Especially for a parent. Usually I give my dad a tie or a sweater, something very ordinary which he stashes in the back of his closet. This year he was really surprised when he saw his present draped across the couch. It was a small blanket, called a "throw," with a pattern of footballs and team names. It began when I decided to get my father something he would really use. I started to observe his habits and interests. He gardened; he played cards with some friends. Football was his favorite sport on television. He always fell asleep watching it. He would curl up as if he were cold. Now I had some gift ideas. I went to the stores to see if there were any new gardening gadgets, accessories for card tables, or books on football. Nothing appealed to me. Finally I found the perfect gift. I bought what I knew he would use and like.

Your List of Steps in Time Sequence

_____

_____

_____

_____

_____

_____

Outlines ## Devising a Plan: Process

Using the freewriting and topic sentence on finding the right apartment, you can make an outline. Then you can revise it, checking the topic sentence and the list of details, improving them where you think they can be better. A revised outline of the process of finding an apartment is shown below.

An Outline for a Process Paragraph

topic sentence: Finding the apartment you want takes planning and careful investigation.

details:

before the search
- Decide what you want.
- Ask yourself, "Do I want a one bedroom?" and "What can I afford?"
- A convenient location can be expensive.
- It can also save you money on transportation.
- Friends can help you with names of nice apartments.
- Maybe somebody you know lives in a good neighborhood.
- Check the classified advertisements in the newspapers.
- Look around.

during the search
- Don't pick the first apartment you see.
- Look at several.
- But don't look at too many.
- Check the cleanness, safety, plumbing, and appliances of each one.
- Ask the manager about the laundry room, additional storage, parking facilities, and maintenance policies.

	Compare the two best places you saw.
after the search	Consider the price, location, and condition of the apartments.
	Check the leases carefully.
	Check the amount of the security deposit.
	Check the requirements for first and last month's rent deposits.

The following checklist may help you revise an outline for your own process paragraph.

☑ Checklist

A Checklist for Revising a Process Outline

✔ Is my topic sentence focused on some point about the process?

✔ Does it cover the whole process?

✔ Do I have all the steps?

✔ Are they in the right order?

✔ Have I explained clearly?

✔ Do I need better details?

Practice

Revising the Topic Sentence in a Process Outline

The topic sentence below doesn't cover all the steps of the process. Read the outline details several times; then write a topic sentence that covers all the steps of the process and has a point.

topic sentence: If you want to save money at the supermarket, write a list at home.

details: First, leave a pencil and a piece of paper near your refrigerator.
Each time you use the last of some item, like milk, write that item on the paper.
Before you go to the store, read what's written on the paper and add to the list.
Then rewrite the list, organizing it according to the layout of your store.
Put all the dairy products together on the list, for instance.
Put all the fresh fruits and vegetables together.
At the store, begin with the first items on your list.
Move purposefully through the aisles.
Keep your eyes on your list so you don't see all kinds of goodies you don't need.
Pass by the gourmet items.
Keep going through each aisle, buying only what is on your list.
At the end of the last aisle, check what's in your cart against your list.
Get any item you forgot.

When you stand in the checkout line, avoid looking at the overpriced and tempting snacks that fill the area.

Revised topic sentence: _____

_____

Exercise 5

Practice

Revising the Order of Steps in a Process Outline

The steps in each of these outlines are out of order. Put numbers in the spaces provided, indicating what step should be first, second, etc.

1. topic sentence: The empty lot near our house evolves into a dog park every afternoon.

details: _____ A German shepherd mix is the first arrival.

_____ The shepherd comes with a blonde woman who throws sticks for him.

_____ A teenager with two feisty little terriers releases them to play with the other two dogs.

_____ The terriers' owner throws them a bright green ball.

_____ The shepherd is very excited to see a beagle puppy run into the lot, straining at her leash.

_____ Free of her leash, the beagle begins to dance and leap around the shepherd mix.

_____ Soon all four dogs are racing for the green ball.

_____ After about half an hour, the first exhausted dog, the beagle, is carried home.

_____ The other three continue to play until it begins to get dark.

2. topic sentence: Cody knows exactly how to persuade me to go to the movies.

details: _____ He says, "The paper says there's a new movie opening today. We could go to that."

_____ "It's supposed to be a really good movie," he adds.

_____ Then he says, "If you go to the movies with me, I'll pay."

_____ He starts by looking at the _TV Guide_ and sighing.

_____ "There's nothing on television," he says, so what will we do tonight?"

_____ He looks through the newspaper and asks if I know about any new movies.

_____ I say I don't know about any new movies.

_____ Suddenly, going to the movies seems very attractive to me.

3. topic sentence: Getting my cat to take a pill is a real chore.

     details: _____ I have to hide the pill inside a clump of mashed tuna.

               _____ My cat Princess hates pills.

               _____ She runs when she hears the rattle of the pill container.

               _____ I have to take out one pill, very quietly.

               _____ I coax Princess by allowing her to sniff at the tuna.

               _____ I lure her farther, until I have her out in the open.

               _____ I pop the tuna into her mouth.

               _____ Princess swallows the tuna and the hidden pill.

Exercise 6

Practice

Listing All the Steps in an Outline

Following are three topic sentences for process paragraphs. Write all the steps needed to complete an outline for each sentence. After you've listed all the steps, number them in the correct time order.

1. topic sentence: There are a few simple steps for cleaning your closet.

steps: _____

_____

_____

_____

_____

_____

_____

_____

2. topic sentence: Anyone can make a delicious ice cream sundae.

steps: _____

_____

_____

_____

_____

_____

_____

3. topic sentence: You can devise a plan for getting to work on time.

steps: _____

_____

_____

_____

_____

_____

_____

_____

Rough Lines   **Drafting and Revising: Process**

You can take the outline and write it in paragraph form, and you'll have a first draft of the process paragraph. As you write the first draft, you can combine some of the short sentences from the outline. Then you can review your draft and revise it for organization, details, clarity, grammar, style, and word choice.

Using the Same Grammatical Person

Remember that the _directional_ process speaks directly to the reader, calling him or her "you." Sentences in a directional process use the word "you," or they imply "you."

> **directional:**   _You_ need a good paint brush to get started.
> Begin by making a list. ("You" is implied.)

Remember that the _informational_ process involves somebody doing the process. Sentences in an informational process use words like "I," "we," "he," "she," or "they" or a person's name.

> **informational:**   _Chip_ needed a good paint brush to get started.
> First, _I_ can make a list.

One problem in writing a process is shifting from describing how somebody did something to telling the reader how to do an activity. When that shift happens, the two kinds of processes get mixed. That shift is called a **shift in person.** In grammar, the words "I" and "we" are considered to be in the first person; "you" is the second person; and "he," "she," "it," and "they" are in the third person.

If these words refer to one, they are _singular;_ if they refer to more than one, they are _plural._ The following list may help.

In writing your process paragraph, decide whether your process will be directional or informational, and stay with one kind.

Below are two examples of a shift in person. Look at them carefully and study how the shift is corrected.

shift in person: After *I* preheat the oven to 350 degrees, *I* mix the egg whites and sugar with an electric mixer set at high speed. *Mix* until stiff peaks form. Then *I* put the mixture in small mounds on an ungreased cookie sheet. ("Mix until stiff peaks form" is a shift to the "you" person.)

shift corrected: After *I* preheat the oven to 350 degrees, *I* mix the egg whites and sugar with an electric mixer set at high speed. *I* mix until stiff peaks form. Then *I* put the mixture in small mounds on an ungreased cookie sheet.

shift in person: *A salesperson* has to be very careful when a customer tries on clothes. *The clerk* can't hint that a suit may be a size too small. *You* can insult a customer with a hint like that. (The sentences shifted from "salesperson" and "clerk" to "you.")

shift corrected: *A salesperson* has to be very careful when customers try on clothes. *The clerk* can't hint that a suit may be a size too small. *He or she* can insult a customer with a hint like that.

Using Transitions Effectively

As you revise your draft, you can add transitions. Transitions are particularly important in a process paragraph because you are trying to show the steps in a *specific sequence*, and you are trying to show the *connections* between steps. Good transitions will also keep your paragraph from sounding like a choppy, boring list.

Following is a list of some of the transitions you can use in writing a process paragraph. Be sure that you use transitional words and phrases only when logical to do so, and try not to overuse the same transitions in a paragraph.

Info BOX

Transitions for a Process Paragraph

after	during	last	the second step, etc.
afterward	eventually	later	then
as	finally	meanwhile	to begin
as he/she is	first	next	to start
as soon as	second, etc.	now	until
as you are	first of all	quickly	when
at last	gradually	sometimes	whenever
at the same time	in the beginning	soon	while
before	immediately	suddenly	while I am . . .
begin by	initially	the first step	

When you write a process paragraph, you must pay particular attention to clarity. As you revise, keep thinking about your audience to be sure your steps are easy to follow. The following checklist can help you revise your draft.

**Checklist**

A Checklist for Revising a Process Paragraph

✔ Does the topic sentence cover the whole paragraph?

✔ Does the topic sentence make a point about the process?

✔ Is any important step left out?

✔ Should any step be explained further?

✔ Are the steps in the right order?

✔ Should any sentences be combined?

✔ Have I used the same person throughout the paragraph to describe the paragraph?

✔ Have I used transitions effectively?

Exercise 7

Practice

Correcting Shifts in Person in a Process Paragraph

Following is a paragraph that shifts from being an informational to a directional process in several places. Those places are underlined. Rewrite the underlined parts, directly above the underlining, so that the whole paragraph is an informational process.

Kathleen has an efficient system for paying her bills. As soon as a bill

arrives in the mail, she stacks it in a tray marked "To Pay." Every weekend,

she takes the bills out of the tray and pays them. She could wait and pay

them all at the end of each month, as some people do, but she feels that by

waiting <u>you</u> might miss a bill that is due sooner and have to pay a late penal-
ty. Once she has paid all the bills, she writes "Paid" and the date on her bill
stub. <u>File</u> that customer's stub in a file divided into sections like Electric
Bills, Rent, Telephone Bills, and Car Payments. Once a year, Kathleen surveys that file and discards stubs more than six months old. With her system,
<u>your</u> unpaid bills are all in one place, and <u>you have</u> clear records of paid
bills.

Exercise 8

Practice

Revising Transitions in a Process Paragraph

The transitions in this paragraph could be better. Rewrite the underlined
transitions, directly above each one, so that the transitions are smoother.

In a few simple steps, you can transform scuffed old leather shoes into
shiny new ones. <u>First</u>, you need two soft, clean cloths, a soft brush, and a
container of good, wax-like shoe polish. You want the kind of polish that is
applied with a rag and penetrates the leather, not the kind that is painted on
with a foam tip. <u>Second</u>, spread some newspaper on the table or floor
where you will work. <u>Third</u>, place the shoes on the paper and gently brush
them, removing any dirt or dried-on mud. <u>Fourth</u>, put a little bit of polish on
a clean cloth and apply the polish to a small section of one shoe. Rub the
polish in firmly so that it covers and penetrates small cracks and scuffs in
the leather. Repeat this process until both shoes have been evenly treated
with polish. <u>Fifth</u>, allow the polish to dry for two or three minutes. <u>Sixth</u>,
use a clean cloth to buff and polish the shoes until they glow. <u>Seventh</u>, you
have a shiny pair of shoes with a deep, expensive-looking color.

Exercise 9

Practice

Combining Sentences in a Process Paragraph

The paragraph following has many short, choppy sentences, which are
underlined. Wherever you see two or more underlined sentences clustered
next to each other, combine them into one clear, smooth sentence. Write
your revised version of the paragraph in the spaces above the lines.

The servers at The Barbecue House have a routine that encourages
customers to relax and eat large meals. <u>First, each server greets a table of</u>

patrons. <u>The server hands out menus. He or she takes a drink orders.</u> While the customers wait for their drinks, they have plenty of time to study the extensive menu. <u>In addition, they do not become impatient because they have already seen a server. They know drinks are on the way.</u> As soon as the server returns, he or she recites a list of the day's specials. <u>They always sound delicious. They are always described as juicy, crispy, spicy, or mouth-watering.</u> Later, when the server brings the food, he or she is sure to check that everyone at the table is satisfied, asking, "Is everything all right?" After the table has finished dinner, the server has one more duty. <u>He or she offers three flavors of coffee. He or she describes seven luscious desserts.</u> Few people can resist this smooth and friendly process of offering and serving a meal.

The Draft

Below is a draft of the process paragraph on finding an apartment. This draft has more details than the outline on pages 123–124. Some short sentences have been combined, and transitions have been added.

A Draft of a Process Paragraph

> Finding the apartment you want takes planning and investigation. First of all, you must decide what you want. Ask yourself, "Do I want a one-bedroom apartment?" or "Do I want a studio apartment?" Most important, ask yourself, "What can I afford?" A convenient location can be expensive; on the other hand, that location can save you money in transportation. Before you start looking for a place, do some research. Friends can help you with the names of nice apartments. Be sure to check the classified advertisements in the newspaper. Once you begin your search, don't pick the first place you see. You should look at several places, but looking at too many can make your search confusing. Just be sure to check each apartment's cleanness, safety, plumbing, and appliances. Then ask the manager about the laundry room, additional storage, parking facilities, and maintenance policies. After you've completed your search, compare the two best places you saw. Consider each one's price, location, and condition. Carefully check each lease, studying the amount of the security deposit and deposit for first and last month's rent.

Final Lines **Proofreading and Polishing: Process**

Before you prepare the final copy of your process paragraph, you can check your latest draft for any places in grammar, word choice, and style that need revision.

Following is the final version of the process paragraph on finding the apartment you want. You'll notice that it contains several changes from the previous draft.

- The word "nice" has been changed to "suitable" to make the description more specific.
- The sentence that began "You should look" has been rewritten so that it follows the pattern of the preceding sentences. Three sentences in a row now include the parallel pattern of "Be sure," "don't pick," and "Look at."
- The second use of "be sure" has been changed to "remember" to avoid repetition.
- New details about what to check for in the leases have been added.
- A final sentence that relates to the topic of the paragraph has been added.

A Final Version of a Process Paragraph (Changes from the draft are underlined.)

Finding the apartment you want takes planning and investigation. First of all, you must decide what you want. Ask yourself, "Do I want a one bedroom apartment?" or "Do I want a studio apartment?" Most important, ask yourself, "What can I afford?" A convenient location can be expensive; on the other hand, that location can save you money in transportation. Before you start looking for a place, do some research. Friends can help you with the names of <u>suitable</u> apartments. Be sure to check the classified advertisements in the newspaper. Once you begin your search, don't pick the first place you see. <u>Look at</u> several places, but <u>be aware that</u> looking at too many can make your search confusing. <u>Just remember</u> to check each apartment's cleanness, safety, plumbing, and appliances. Then ask the manager about the laundry room, additional storage, parking facilities, and maintenance policies. After you've completed your search, compare the two best places you saw. Consider each one's price, location, and condition. Carefully check each lease, studying the amount of the security deposit, the deposit for first and last month's rent, <u>and the rules for tenants. When you've completed your comparison, you're ready to choose the apartment you want.</u>

Before you prepare the final copy of your process paragraph, check your latest draft for errors in spelling and punctuation and for any errors made in typing or copying.

Exercise 10

Practice

Proofreading to Prepare the Final Paragraph

Following are two process paragraphs with the kinds of errors that are easy to overlook when you prepare the final version of an assignment. Correct the errors, writing above the lines. There are eight errors in the first paragraph and nine in the second paragraph.

1. I have a foolproof system for making my bed neatly. First, I dump

all the pillow's on the flore. I then pull the bedspread back to the bottom of the bed. Once you've pulled the bedspread back, I can pull back the blanket and the top sheet. Next, i smooth the bottom sheet and pull it tight, tucking the extra material into the corners of the mattress. When the bottom sheet is tucked in tightly, I pull up the top sheet and blanket, smoothing them as I go and making sure they are tucked into the bottom and lower corners of the bed. At the top end of the bed, fold the edge of the top sheet over the blanket, and I smooth the folded sheet and blanket across the bed. Finly, I arrange the bedspread over the bed, making sure the bedspread doesn't drag on one side. In a few move, I have a well-made bed.

2. Pretending to enjoy a dinner you hate can be accomplished if you follow several sneaky steps. First, don't shudder when your father announces he have spent allday making his famous turkey stew. Do not remind him that you have allways despised that recipe. Instead, say something like,"Oh, I remember that stew." It would be a little too phony to say how much you use to love it. When the stew is placed in front of you, begin by moving it around on the plate, meanwhile chewing on a role or salad so that you give the illusion of eating the main coarse. As you pretend to eat, look around you. Is there a hungry dog under the table. Help him out by providing him with a secret meal. If there is no dog, try concealing the stew under some other food on your plate. Put the meat under a potato skin or a lettuce leaf. If you have a paper napkin, consider wrapping it around some stew and concealing the package in your pocket. At the end of the meal, be sure to comment that you're fathers stew is as good as it ever was.

Lines of Detail: A Walk-Through Assignment

Your assignment is to write a paragraph on how to plan a special day. Follow these steps:

Step 1: Focus on one special day. If you want to, you can begin by using your own experience. Ask yourself such questions as these: "Have I ever planned a birthday party? A baby or wedding shower? A surprise party? A picnic? A reunion?

A barbecue? A celebration of a religious holiday?" Have I ever seen anyone else plan such a day? If so, how would you teach a reader about planning for such a day?

Step 2: Once you have picked the day, freewrite. Write anything you can remember about the day and how you or someone else planned it.

Step 3: When you've completed the freewriting, read it. Underline all the detail that refers to steps in planning that event. List the underlined detail, in time order.

Step 4: Add to the list by brainstorming. Ask yourself questions that can lead to more detail. For example, if an item on your list is "Send out invitations early," ask questions like "How early?" and "How do you decide whom to invite?"

Step 5: Survey your expanded list. Then write a topic sentence that makes some point about your planning for this special day. To reach a point, think of more questions like these: "What makes a plan successful?" or "If you are planning for a special day (birthday, barbecue, surprise party, and so forth), what must you remember?"

Step 6: Use the topic sentence to prepare an outline. Be sure that the steps in the outline are in the correct time order.

Step 7: Write a first draft of the paragraph, adding details and combining short sentences.

Step 8: Revise your draft. Be careful to use smooth transitions, and check that you have included all the necessary steps.

Step 9: Prepare and proofread the final version of your paragraph.

Writing Your Own Process Paragraph

When you write on one of these topics, be sure to work through the stages of the writing process in preparing your process paragraph.

1. Write a **directional or informational process** about one of these topics:

packing a suitcase	fixing a clogged drain
preparing for a garage sale	changing the oil in a car
painting a room	washing and waxing a car
taking a test	breaking a specific habit
losing weight	gaining weight
training a roommate	giving a pet a bath
finding the right mate	falling out of love
doing holiday shopping early	getting up in the morning

breaking up with a boyfriend or girlfriend
getting good tips while working as a waiter or waitress
getting ready to go out for a special occasion
sizing up a new acquaintance

2. Write about the wrong way to do something, or the wrong way you (or someone else) did it. You can use any of the topics in the list above, or you can choose your own topic.

3. Imagine that a relative who has never been to your state is coming to visit. This relative will arrive at the nearest airport, rent a car, and drive to your house. Write a paragraph giving your relative clear directions for getting from the airport to your house. Be sure to have an appropriate topic sentence.

4. Interview one of the counselors at your college. Ask the counselor to tell you the steps for applying for financial aid. Take notes or tape the interview, get copies of any forms that are included in the application process, and ask questions about these forms.

    After the interview, write a paragraph explaining the process of applying for financial aid. Your explanation is directed at a high school senior who has never applied for aid.

5. Interview someone whose cooking you admire. Ask that person to tell you the steps involved in making a certain dish. Take notes or tape the interview. After the interview, write a paragraph, *not* a recipe, explaining how to prepare the dish. Your paragraph will explain the process to someone who is a beginner at cooking.

6. Study the photograph below, and notice the connection between the dog and the woman. Then write a process paragraph on how to train a dog to walk on a leash without pulling away.

7. Examine the photograph below, and then write a paragraph on how to exercise effectively to (1) build stamina and endurance or (2) build muscle strength.

Name: _____ Section: _____

PEER REVIEW FORM FOR A PROCESS PARAGRAPH

After you've written a draft of your process paragraph, let a writing partner read it. When your partner has completed the form below, discuss your draft. Repeat the same process for your partner's paragraph.

The steps that are most clearly described are _____

_____

_____

I'd like more explanation about this step: _____

_____

Some details could be added to the part that begins with the words _____

_____

A transition could be added to the part that begins with the words _____

_____

I have questions about _____

_____

The best thing about this paragraph is _____

_____

Other comments _____

_____

_____

_____

_____

_____

_____

_____

_____

_____

Reviewer's Name: _____

WRITING FROM READING: Process

How to Write a Personal Letter

Garrison Keillor

> *Garrison Keillor is best known as host of the radio show,* A Prairie Home Companion, *where his stories of the fictional town of Lake Wobegone and its inhabitants made him famous. He is also a popular writer with a comfortable, friendly style. In this essay, he explains how people, especially shy ones, can write what he calls the "gift" of a personal letter "to be our own sweet selves and express the music of our souls."*

Words You May Need to Know (corresponding paragraph numbers are in parentheses)

trudges (2):   walks with weariness
wahoos (2):   a version of the word "yahoo," meaning a coarse and ignorant person
despite (4):   in spite of
anonymity (4):   being unknown, namelessness
obligatory (5):   required
pulsating (5):   vibrating, quivering
sensate (5):   felt by the senses
sensuous (6):   appealing to the senses

declarative (7):   making a statement
episode (9):   incident, topic
urinary tract (9):   all the organs and ducts involved in the release of urine
indebtedness (9):   owing money or being under some obligation
sibling (9):   brother or sister
relic (10):   an object that has survived over the past 10 years

1   We shy people need to write a letter now and then, or else we'll dry up and blow away. It's true. And I speak as one who loves to reach for the phone, dial the number, and talk. The telephone is to shyness what Hawaii is to February; it's a way out of the woods. *And yet:* a letter is better.

2   Such a sweet gift—a piece of handmade writing, in an envelope that is not a bill, sitting in our friend's path when she trudges home from a long day spent among savages and wahoos, a day our words will help repair. They don't need to be immortal, just sincere. She can read them twice and again tomorrow: "You're someone I care about, Corinne, and think of often, and every time I do, you make me smile."

3   We need to write; otherwise, nobody will know who we are. They will have only a vague impression of us as "A Nice Person" because, frankly, we don't shine at conversation, we lack the confidence to thrust our faces forward and say, "Hi, I'm Heather Hooten; let me tell you about my week." Mostly we say "Uh-huh" and "Oh really." People smile and look over our shoulder, looking for someone else to meet.

4   So a shy person sits down and writes a letter. To be known by another person—to meet and talk freely on the page—to be close despite dis-

tance. To escape from anonymity and be our own sweet selves and express the music of our souls. The same thing that moves a giant rock star to sing his heart out in front of 123,000 people moves us to take ballpoint in hand and write a few lines to our dear Aunt Eleanor. *We want to be known.* We want her to know that we have fallen in love, that we have quit our job, that we're moving to New York, and we want to say a few things that might not get said in casual conversation: "Thank you for what you've meant to me. I am very happy right now."

5   The first step in writing letters is to get over the guilt of *not* writing. You don't "owe" anybody a letter. Letters are a gift. The burning shame you feel when you see unanswered mail makes it harder to pick up a pen and makes for a cheerless letter when you finally do. "I feel bad about not writing, but I've been so busy," etc. Skip this. Few letters are obligatory and they are "Thanks for the wonderful gift" and "I am terribly sorry to hear about George's death" and "Yes, you're welcome to stay with us next month." Write these promptly if you want to keep your friends. Don't worry about other letters, except love letters, of course. When your true love writes, "Dear Light of My Life, Joy of My Heart, O Lovely Pulsating Core of My Sensate Life," some response is called for.

6   Some of the best letters are tossed off in a burst of inspiration, so keep your writing stuff in one place where you can sit down for a few minutes, and – "Dear Roy, I am in the middle of an essay but thought I'd drop you a line. Hi to your sweetie too"–dash off a note to a pal. Envelopes, stamps, address book, everything in a drawer so you can write fast when the pen is hot. A blank white 8" × 11" sheet can look as big as Montana if the pen's not so hot; try a smaller page and write boldly. Get a pen that makes a sensuous line, get a comfortable typewriter, a friendly word processor–whichever feels easy to the hand.

7   Sit for a few minutes with the blank sheet of paper in front of you, and meditate on the person you will write to; let your friend come to mind until you can almost see him or her in the room with you. Remember the last time you saw each other and how your friend looked and what you said and what perhaps was unsaid between you, and when your friend becomes real to you, start to write. Write the salutation, "Dear You," and take a deep breath and plunge in. A simple declarative sentence will do, followed by another and another. Talk about what you're doing and tell it like you were talking to us. Don't think about grammar, don't think about style, don't try to write dramatically; just give us your news. Where did you go, who did you see, what did they say, what do you think?

8   If you don't know where to begin, start with the present: "I'm sitting at the kitchen table on a rainy Saturday morning. Everyone is gone, and the house is quiet." Let your description of the present moment lead to something else; let the letter drift gently along. The toughest letter to crank out is one

that is meant to impress, as we all know from writing job applications; if it's hard work to write a letter to a friend, maybe you're trying too hard to be terrific. A letter is only a report to someone who already likes you for reasons other than your brilliance. Take it easy.

9

Don't worry about form. It's not a term paper. When you come to the end of one episode, just start a new paragraph. You can go from a few lines about the sad state of pro football to the fight with your mother to your cat's urinary tract infection to a few thoughts on personal indebtedness and on to the kitchen sink and what's in it. The more you write, the easier it gets, and when you have a true friend to write to, a *compadre*, a soul sibling, then it's like driving a car; you just press on the gas.

10

Don't tear up the page and start over when you write a bad line; try to write your way out of it. Make mistakes and plunge on. Let the letter cook along and let yourself be bold. Outrage, confusion, love–whatever is in your mind, let it find a way to the page. Writing is a means of discovery, always, and when you come to the end and write "Yours ever" or "hugs and kisses," you'll know something that you didn't when you wrote "Dear Pal."

11

Probably your friend will put your letter away, and it'll be read again a few years from now, and it will improve with age. And forty years from now, your friend's grandkids will dig it out of the attic and read it, a sweet and precious relic that gives them a sudden clear glimpse of you and her and the world we old-timers knew. Your simple lines about where you went, who you saw, what they said, will speak to those children, and they will feel in their hearts the humanity of our times.

12

You can't pick up a phone and call the future and tell them about our times. You have to pick up a piece of paper.

WRITING FROM READING: "How to Write a Personal Letter"

When you write on any of these topics, be sure to work through the stages of the writing process in preparing your process paragraph.

1. While Garrison Keillor does not list the steps to follow in writing a personal letter, he does describe the process in sequence. In a paragraph, give the steps he uses. As you list each step, explain it by giving an example. For your topic sentence, complete this line:

   Writing a personal letter is a good way to _____.

2. A personal letter is written to one special person. Keillor describes it as a gift that says, "You're someone I care about." Write a process paragraph about how to give another kind of special gift to someone special. The gift can be an object or an experience (for example, a visit to a special place or event, a meal, a party).

3. The telephone is a more popular form of personal communication than the letter, but talking on the phone presents certain problems. One of them is the caller who talks on and on when you want to

end the call. Write a paragraph on how to end an endless conversation without being rude or unkind. Be sure that your advice involves steps.

4. Imagine that a close relative has sent your friend a gift that he or she hates. In a paragraph, teach your friend how to write that relative a kind and tactful "thank you" for the awful gift.

5. Garrison Keillor says a letter is a way for shy people to open up. If you consider yourself shy, write a paragraph addressed to more outgoing people, offering them advice on how to converse with a shy person who is reluctant to speak.

6. If you are an outgoing person, think about the process you follow when you meet someone new. You may want to list the steps of this initial conversation, including what you say first, second, and so forth, the kinds of questions you ask and the kind of information you volunteer to keep the conversation going. Then, in a paragraph, explain the steps you follow in your first encounter with a new person.

CHAPTER 6

Comparison and Contrast

WHAT IS COMPARISON? WHAT IS CONTRAST?

To **compare** means to point out *similarities*. To **contrast** means to point out *differences*. **When you compare or contrast, you need to come to some conclusion.** It's not enough to say, "These two things are similar" or "They are different." Your reader will be asking, "So what? What's your point?" You may be showing the differences between two restaurants to explain which is the better buy:

> If you like Mexican food, you can go to either Café Mexicana or Juanita's, but Juanita's has lower prices.

Or you may be explaining the similarities between two family members to explain how people with similar personalities can clash.

> My cousin Bill and my brother Karram are both so stubborn they can't get along.

Hints for Writing a Comparison or Contrast Paragraph

1. Limit your topic. When you write a comparison or contrast paragraph, you might think that the easiest topics to write about are broad ones with many similarities or differences. However, if you make your topic too large, you will not be able to cover it well, and your paragraph will be full of boring statements.

Here are some topics that are too large for a comparison or contrast paragraph: two countries, two periods in history, two kinds of addiction, two wars, two economic or political systems, two presidents.

2. Avoid the obvious topic. Some people think it is easier to write about two items if the similarities or differences between them are obvious, but with an obvious topic, you will have nothing new to say, and you will risk writing a boring paragraph.

Here are some obvious topics: the differences between high school and college, the similarities between *Men in Black* and *Men in Black 2*. If you are drawn to an obvious topic, *try a new angle* on the topic. Write about the unexpected, using the same topic. Write about the similarities between high school and college or about the differences between *Men in Black* and *Men in Black 2*. You may have to do more thinking before you come up with ideas, but your ideas may be more interesting to write about and to read.

3. Make your point in the topic sentence of your comparison or contrast paragraph. Indicate whether the paragraph is about similarities or differences in a topic sentence like this:

Because he is so reliable and loyal, Michael is a much better friend to me than Stefan. (The phrase "much better" indicates differences.)
My two botany teachers share a love of the environment and a passion for protecting it. (The word "share" indicates similarities.)

4. Do not announce in the topic sentence. The sentences below are announcements, not topic sentences:

This paper will explain the similarities between my two botany teachers.
Let me tell you about why Michael is a different kind of friend than Stefan.

5. Make sure your topic sentence has a focus. It should indicate similarities or differences; it should focus on the specific kind of comparison or contrast you will make.

not focused: My old house and my new one are different.
focused: My new home is bigger, brighter, and more comfortable than my old one.

6. In the topic sentence, cover both subjects to be compared or contrasted.

covers only one subject: The beach at Santa Lucia was dirty and crowded.
covers both subjects: The beach at Santa Lucia was dirty and crowded, but the beach at Fisher Bay was clean and private.

Be careful. It is easy to get so carried away by the details of your paragraph that you forget to put both subjects into one sentence.

Practice

Identifying Suitable Topic Sentences for a Comparison or Contrast Paragraph

Following is a list of possible topic sentences for a comparison or contrast paragraph. Some would make good topic sentences. The ones that wouldn't make good topic sentences have one or more of these problems: they are announcements, they don't indicate whether the paragraph will be about similarities or differences, they don't focus on the specific kind of comparison or contrast to be made, they cover subjects that are too big to write about in one paragraph, or they don't cover both subjects.

Mark the problem sentences with an *X*. If a sentence would make a good topic sentence for a comparison or contrast paragraph, mark it *OK*.

1. _____ My sisters, Rebecca and Linda, are very similar.

2. _____ I have two sisters, Rebecca and Linda.

3. _____ My two sisters, Rebecca and Linda, are alike in their athletic ability and outgoing personalities.

4. _____ The United States and Canada are similar in their economic systems, history, and culture.

5. _____ Music World has better bargains and a more helpful staff.

6. _____ This essay will discuss the similarities between my cat and my beagle.

7. _____ Men and women are different in their physical, intellectual, and emotional make-up.

8. _____ On the one hand, there is Montego Bay, Jamaica, and on the other hand, there is Nassau, Bahamas.

9. _____ Mr. Sheridan is a more energetic and enthusiastic teacher than Mr. Smith.

10. _____ My second driving lesson was a big improvement over my first one.

Organizing Your Comparison or Contrast Paragraph

Whether you decide to write about similiarities (to compare) or differences (to contrast), you will have to decide how to organize your paragraph. You can choose between two patterns of organization: subject by subject or point by point.

Subject-by-Subject Organization In the subject-by-subject pattern, you support and explain your topic sentence by first writing all your details on one subject and then writing all your details on the other subject. If you choose a subject-by-subject pattern, be sure to discuss the points for your second subject *in the same order* as you did for the first subject. For example, if your first subject is an amusement park, and you cover (1) the price of admission, (2) the long lines at the rides, and (3) the quality of the rides, when you discuss the second subject, another amusement park, you should write about its prices, lines, and quality of rides *in the same order*.

Look carefully at the outline and comparison paragraph below for a subject-by-subject pattern.

A Comparison Outline: Subject-by-Subject Pattern

topic sentence: Once I realized that my brother and my mother are very much alike in temperament, I realized why they don't get along.

details:

subject 1, James—temper	My brother James is a hot-tempered person. It is easy for him to lose control of his temper.
unkind words	When he does, he often says things he later regrets.
stubbornness	James is also very stubborn. In an argument, he will never admit he is wrong. Once we were arguing about baseball scores.

Even when I showed him the right score, printed in the paper, he wouldn't admit he was wrong. He said the newspaper had made a mistake. James' stubbornness overtakes his common sense.

subject 2,
mother
James has inherited many of his character traits from our mother.

temper
She has a quick temper, and anything can provoke it.

Once, she got angry because she had to wait too long at a traffic light.

unkind words
She also has a tendency to use unkind words when she's mad.

stubbornness
She never backs down from a disagreement or concedes she was wrong.

My mother even quit a job because she refused to admit she'd made a mistake in taking inventory. Her pride can lead her into foolish acts.

After I realized how similar my brother and mother are, I understood how such inflexible people are likely to clash.

A Comparison Paragraph: Subject-by-Subject Pattern

subject 1,
James

Once I realized that my brother and my mother are very much alike in temperament, I realized why they don't get along. My brother James is a hot-tempered person. It is easy for him to lose control of his temper, and when he does, he often

unkind words
stubbornness
says things he regrets. James is also very stubborn. In an argument, he will never admit he is wrong. I remember one time when we were arguing about baseball scores. Even when I showed him the right score, printed in the newspaper, he wouldn't admit he was wrong. James insisted that that the newspaper must have made a mistake in printing the score. As this example shows, sometimes James' stubbornness overtakes James' common sense. It took me a while to realize that my stubborn brother James has inherited many of his

subject 2,
mother—temper
traits from our mother. Like James, she has a quick temper, and almost anything can provoke it. She once got angry because she had to wait too long at a traffic light. She also shares James' habit

unkind words
of saying unkind things when she's angry. And just as James refuses to back down when he's wrong,

stubbornness
my mother will never back down from a disagreement or concede she's wrong. In fact, my mother once quit a job because she refused to admit she'd made a mistake in taking inventory. Her pride is as powerful as James' pride, and it can be just as foolish. After I realized how similar my mother and brother are, I understood how such inflexible people are likely to clash.

Look carefully at the paragraph in the subject-by-subject pattern, and you'll note that it

- begins with a topic sentence about both subjects—James and his mother
- gives all the details about one subject—James
- then gives all the details about the second subject—his mother—in the same order

Point-by-Point Organization In the point-by-point pattern, you support and explain your topic sentence by discussing each point of comparison or contrast, switching back and forth between your subjects. You explain one point for each subject, then explain another point for each subject, and so on.

Look carefully at the outline and the comparison paragraph below for the point-by-point pattern.

A Comparison Outline: Point-by-Point Pattern

topic sentence: Once I realized that my brother and my mother are very much alike in temperament, I realized why they don't get along.

details:

point 1, temper James and mother	My brother James is a hot-tempered person. It is easy for him to lose control of his temper. My mother has a quick temper, and anything can provoke it. Once she got angry because she had to wait too long at a traffic light.
point 2, unkind words James and mother	When my brother gets mad, he often says things he regrets. My mother has a tendency to use unkind words when she's mad.
point 3, stubbornness James and mother	James is very stubborn. In an argument, he will never admit he is wrong. Once we were arguing about baseball scores. Even when I showed him the right score, printed in the paper, he wouldn't admit he was wrong. He said the newspaper had made a mistake. James' stubbornness overtakes his common sense. My mother will never back down from a disagreement or admit she is wrong. She even quit a job because she refused to admit she'd made a mistake in taking inventory. She was foolish in her stubbornness. After I realized how similar my mother and brother are, I understood how such inflexible people are likely to clash.

A Comparison Paragraph: Point-by-Point Pattern

Once I realized that my brother and my mother are very much alike in temperament, I realized why they don't get along. My brother is

point 1
James and mother

point 2
James and mother
point 3
James and mother

a hot-tempered person, and it is easy for him to lose control of his temper. My mother shares James' quick temper, and anything can provoke her anger. Once, she got angry because she had to wait too long at a traffic light. When my brother gets mad, he often says things he regrets. Similarly, my mother is known for the unkind things she's said in anger. James is a very stubborn person. In an argument, he will never admit he's wrong. I can remember one argument we were having over baseball scores. Even when I showed him the right score, printed in the newspaper, he wouldn't admit he had been wrong. He simply insisted the paper had made a mistake. At times like that, James' stubbornness overtakes his common sense. Like her son, my mother will never back down from an argument or admit she was wrong. She even quit a job because she refused to admit she'd made a mistake in taking inventory. In that case, her stubbornness was as foolish as James'. It took me a while to see the similarities between my brother and mother. Yet after I realized how similar these two people are, I understood how two inflexible people are likely to clash.

Look carefully at the paragraph in the point-by-point pattern, and you'll note that it

- begins with a topic sentence about both subjects—James and his mother
- discusses how both James and his mother are alike in these points: their quick tempers, the unkind things they say in a temper, their often foolish stubbornness
- switches back and forth between the two subjects

The subject-by-subject and point-by-point patterns can be used for either a comparison or contrast paragraph. But whatever pattern you choose, remember these hints:

1. Be sure to use the same points to compare or contrast both subjects. If you are contrasting two cars, you can't discuss the price and safety features of one, then the styling and speed of the other. You must discuss the price of both or the safety features, styling, or speed of both.

You don't have to list the points in your topic sentence, but you can include them, like this: "My old Celica turned out to be a cheaper, safer, and faster car than my boyfriend's new Mazda."

2. Be sure to give roughly equal space to both subjects. This rule doesn't mean you must write the same number of words—or even sentences—on both subjects. It does mean you should give fairly equal attention to the details of both subjects.

Since you will be writing about two subjects, this type of paragraph can involve more details than other paragraph formats. Thus, a comparison or contrast paragraph may be longer than twelve sentences.

Using Transitions Effectively for Comparison or Contrast

The transitions you use in a comparison or contrast paragraph, as well as how and when you use them, depend on the answers to two questions:

1. Are you writing a comparison paragraph or a contrast paragraph?

   - When you choose to write a *comparison* paragraph, you use transitional words, phrases, or sentences that point out *similarities*.
   - When you choose to write a *contrast* paragraph, you use transition words, phrases, or sentences that point out *differences*.

2. Are you organizing your paragraph in the point-by-point or subject-by-subject pattern?

   - When you choose to organize your paragraph in the *point-by-point* pattern, you need transitions *within each point and between points*.
   - When you choose to organize in the *subject-by-subject pattern,* you need *most of your transitions* in the *second half* of the paragraph to remind the reader of the points you made in the first half.

Here are some transitions you can use in writing comparison or contrast. There are many others you may think of that will be appropriate for your ideas.

Info BOX

Transitions for a Comparison or Contrast Paragraph

To show similarities:

additionally	both	in the same way	similarly
again	each of	just like	similar to
also	equally	like	too
and	furthermore	likewise	so
as well as	in addition		

To show differences:

although	even though	in spite of	though
but	except	nevertheless	unlike
conversely	however	on the other hand	whereas
different from	in contrast to	otherwise	while
despite	instead of	still	yet

Writing a comparison or contrast paragraph challenges you to make decisions like these: Will I compare or contrast? Will I use a point-by-point or a subject-by-subject pattern? Those decisions will determine what kind of transitions you will use and where you will use them.

Practice

Writing Appropriate Transitions for a Comparison or Contrast Paragraph

Below are pairs of sentences. First, decide whether each pair shows a comparison or contrast. Then combine the two sentences into one, using an appropriate transition (either a word or a phrase). You may have to rewrite parts of the original sentences to create one smooth sentence. The first pair is done for you.

1. Dr. Cheung is a professor of art.
Dr. Mbala is a professor of history.

Combined: Dr. Cheung is a professor of art while Dr. Mbala is a

professor of history.

2. *Dr. Doolittle* featured animals that talked.
In *Babe,* farm animals spoke.

Combined: _____

_____

3. Small children are often afraid to leave their parents.
Teenagers can't wait to get away from their parents.

Combined: _____

_____

4. Phillippe was an intelligent dog who learned all sorts of tricks.
Elvis, our basset hound, refused to do the simplest tricks.

Combined: _____

_____

_____

5. Exercise can help you lower cholesterol levels, fight heart disease, and relieve stress.
A doctor can give you medicine for heart disease, high cholesterol, or stress.

Combined: _____

_____

6. Mrs. Colletti volunteers at the animal shelter.
Mr. Colletti donates his free time to the soup kitchen.

Combined: _____

_____

7. Introduction to Philosophy was a challenging class that developed my skills in reasoning.
College Writing, a tough course, taught me how to think and reason.

Combined: _____

_____

8. Camping out takes work and can be uncomfortable.
Staying in a motel is easy and pleasant.

Combined: _____

_____

9. Staying in a motel costs money.
Camping out takes expensive supplies.

Combined: _____

_____

10. My coworkers at the Sports Store were friendly and supportive.
The people I worked with at Bruno's Subs created a warm and
helpful working environment.

Combined: _____

_____

WRITING THE COMPARISON OR CONTRAST PARAGRAPH IN STEPS

Thought Lines **Gathering Ideas: Comparison or Contrast**

One way to get started on a comparison or contrast paragraph is to list as
many differences or similarities as you can on one topic. Then you can see
whether you have more similarities (comparisons) or differences (contrasts) and decide which approach to use. For example, if you are asked to
compare or contrast two restaurants, you could begin with a list like this:

List for Two Restaurants: Victor's and The Garden

similarities

both offer lunch and dinner

very popular

nearby

differences

Victor's	The Garden
formal dress	informal dress
tablecloths	placemats
food is bland	spicy food
expensive	moderate
statues, fountains, fresh flowers	dark wood, hanging plants

Getting Points of Comparison or Contrast

Whether you compare or contrast, you are looking for points of comparison or contrast, items you can discuss about both subjects. If you surveyed the list on the two restaurants and decided you wanted to contrast the two restaurants, you'd see that you already have these points of contrast:

dress   food
decor   prices

To write your paragraph, start with several points of comparison or contrast. As you work through the stages of writing, you may decide you don't need all the points you've jotted down, but it is better to start with too many points than with too few.

Exercise 3

Collaborate

Developing Points of Comparison or Contrast

Do this exercise with a partner or a group. Below are some topics that could be used for a comparison or contrast paragraph. Underneath each topic, write three points of comparison or contrast. Be ready to share your answers with another group or with the class.

The first topic is done for you.

1. **topic:** Compare or contrast two popular singers (or singing groups).
   Points of comparison or contrast:

   a. the kinds of songs they sing

   b. the kinds of fans they attract

   c. how long they have been popular

2. **topic:** Compare or contrast a movie and its sequel.
   Points of comparison or contrast:

   a. _____

   b. _____

   c. _____

3. **topic:** Compare or contrast two friends.
   Points of comparison or contrast:

   a. _____

   b. _____

   c. _____

4. **topic:** Compare or contrast two college courses.
   Points of comparison or contrast:

   a. _____

   b. _____

   c. _____

5. topic: Compare or contrast two famous athletes.
Points of comparison or contrast:

a. _____

b. _____

c. _____

  Finding Differences in Subjects That Look Similar

Practice

Following are pairs of subjects that seem very similar but that do have differences. List three differences for each pair.

1. Subjects: Burger King and McDonald's

differences: a. _____

b. _____

c. _____

2. subjects: plastic wrap and aluminum foil

differences: a. _____

b. _____

c. _____

3. Subjects: motorcycles and motor scooters

differences: a. _____

b. _____

c. _____

4. Subjects: blankets and quilts

differences: a. _____

b. _____

c. _____

5. Subjects: email and the U.S. Postal Service

differences: a. _____

b. _____

c. _____

Exercise 5 **Finding Similarities in Subjects That Look Different**

Practice

Following are pairs of subjects that are different but have some similarities.
List three similarities for each pair.

1. Subject: attending college part time and attending college full time.

similarities: a. _____

   b. _____

   c. _____

2. Subject: renting a movie and going to a movie

similarities: a. _____

   b. _____

   c. _____

3. Subject: working the night shift and working daytime hours

similarities: a. _____

   b. _____

   c. _____

4. Subject: cats and dogs (as pets)

similarities: a. _____

   b. _____

   c. _____

5. Subject: starting a new business and starting a new relationship

similarities: a. _____

   b. _____

   c. _____

Adding Details to Your Points

Once you have some points, you can begin adding details to them. The details may lead you to more points. If they do not, they will still help you develop the ideas of your paragraph. If you were to write about the differences in restaurants, for example, your new list with added details might look like this:

List for a Contrast of Restaurants

Victor's	The Garden
dress—formal	informal dress
men in jackets, women in dresses	all in jeans
decor—pretty, elegant	place mats, on table is
statues, fountains,	a card listing specials,
fresh flowers on tables,	lots of dark wood, brass,
tablecloths	green hanging plants

food—bland tasting traditional, broiled fish or chicken, traditional steaks, appetizers like shrimp cocktail, onion soup	spicy and adventurous pasta in tomato sauces, garlic in everything, curry, appetizers like tiny tortillas, ribs in honey-mustard sauce
price—expensive everything costs extra, like appetizer, salad	moderate price of dinner includes appetizer and salad

Reading the list about restaurants, you might conclude that some people may prefer The Garden to Victor's. Why? There are several hints in your list. The Garden has cheaper food, better food, and a more casual atmosphere. Now that you have a point, you can put it into a topic sentence. A topic sentence contrasting the restaurants could be

> Some people would rather eat at The Garden than at Victor's because The Garden offers better, cheaper food in a more casual environment.

Once you have a possible topic sentence, you can begin working on the outlines stage of your paragraph.

Writing Topic Sentences for Comparison or Contrast

Practice

Below are lists of details. Some lists are for comparison paragraphs; some are for contrast paragraphs. Read each list carefully; then write a topic sentence for each list.

1. topic sentence: _____

_____

List of Details

frozen yogurt	ice cream
taste—light, milky, a little sour	sweet, heavy, creamy
nutritional value—low fat or fat free, low calorie, a healthy dessert or snack	more fat, higher calories, acceptable as an occasional treat
popularity—younger generation, parents with small children who want a healthy snack, dieters	lovers of gourmet food, people who want to splurge on calories

2. topic sentence: _____

_____

List of Details

frozen yogurt	ice cream
availability—frozen yogurt stores, supermarkets, fast food places, college cafeterias	ice cream stores, supermarkets, college cafeterias, snack bars
ways to buy it—in cones, cups, quarts, pints, in cakes, soft serve	cones, cups, pints, quarts, half gallon, gallon, cakes, a little soft serve

flavors—mostly fruit, some chocolate, some with mixed-in ingredients like Heath bars	chocolate, fruit, mixed-in ingredients like cherries or cookies

3. topic sentence: _____

_____

List of Details

pickup truck	**sport-utility vehicle** (like Bronco, Explorer)
seating—for two room to carry things—large truck bed, can be open space, covered by a canvas cover, or permanently closed	seats four or five large covered space behind seats, but not as big as pickup's space
uses—good for rough terrain, hunting and fishing, hauling and moving, construction work	good for country driving but also for suburban families with space for toys, baby strollers, car seats

4. topic sentence: _____

_____

List of Details

pickup truck	**sport-utility vehicle**
buyers—popular with young people, hunters, farmers	people in their twenties, people who camp or fish
image—a rugged, solid, practical vehicle	tough, rugged, useful
accessories available—CD players, fancy speakers, air conditioning	luxurious interiors, CD players and speakers, air conditioning

Outlines Devising a Plan: Comparison or Contrast

With a topic sentence, you can begin to draft an outline. Before you can write an outline, however, you have to make a decision: what pattern do you want to use in organizing your paragraph? Do you want to use the subject-by-subject or the point-by-point pattern?

The following is an outline of a contrast paragraph in point-by-point form.

An Outline of a Contrast Paragraph: Point-by-Point

topic sentence: Some people would rather eat at The Garden than at Victor's because The Garden offers better, cheaper food in a more casual environment.

details:	Food at Victor's is bland-tasting and traditional. The menu has broiled fish, chicken, traditional steaks. The spices used are mostly parsley and salt. The food is the usual American food, with a little French food on the list. Appetizers are the usual things like shrimp cocktail or onion soup.
point 1: food	Food at The Garden is more spicy and adventurous. There are many pasta dishes in tomato sauce. There is garlic in just about everything. The Garden serves four different curry dishes. It has all kinds of ethnic food. Appetizers include items like tiny tortillas and hot, honey-mustard ribs.
point 2: prices	The prices of the two restaurants differ. Victor's is expensive. Everything you order costs extra. An appetizer and a salad costs extra. Food at The Garden is more moderately priced. The price of a dinner includes an appetizer and a salad.
point 3: environment	Certain diners may feel uncomfortable in Victor's, which has a formal environment. Everyone is dressed up, the men in jackets and ties and the women in dresses. Less formal diners would rather eat in a more casual place. People don't dress up to go to The Garden; they wear jeans.
conclusion	Many people prefer a place where they can relax, with reasonable prices and unusual food, to a place that's a little stuffy, with a traditional and expensive menu.

Once you've drafted an outline, check it. Use the following checklist to help you review and revise your outline.

Checklist

A Checklist for an Outline of a Comparison or Contrast Paragraph

✔ Do I have enough details?

✔ Are all my details relevant?

✔ Have I covered all the points on both sides?

✔ If I'm using a subject-by-subject pattern, have I covered the points in the same order on both sides?

✔ Have I tried to cover too many points?

✔ Have I made my main idea clear?

Using this checklist as your guide, compare the outline with the thought lines list on pages 153–154. You may notice several changes:

- Some details on decor in the list have been omitted because there were too many points.
- A concluding sentence has been added to reinforce the main idea.

Practice

Adding a Point and Details to a Comparison or Contrast Outline

The following outline is too short. Develop it by adding a point of contrast and details to both subjects to develop the contrast.

> **topic sentence:** Carson College is a friendlier place than Wellington College.
>
> **details:** When a person enters Carson College, he or she sees groups of students who seem happy.
> They are sprawled on the steps and on the lawns, looking like they are having a good time.
> They are laughing and talking to each other.
> At Wellington College, everyone seems to be a stranger.
> Students are isolated.
> They lean against the wall or sit alone, reading intently or staring into space.
> The buildings at Carson seem open and inviting.
> There are many large glass windows in each classroom.
> There are wide, large corridors.
> Many signs help newcomers find their way around.
> Wellington College seems closed and forbidding.
> It has dark, windowless classrooms.
> The halls are narrow and dirty.
> There are no signs or directions posted on the buildings.

Add a new point of contrast and details about each college: _____

_____

_____

_____

_____

_____

_____

Practice

Finding Irrelevant Details in a Comparison or Contrast Outline

The following outline contains some irrelevant details. Cross out the details that don't fit.

> **topic sentence:** My daughter's fourth birthday party and my high school graduation ceremony showed that people of all ages celebrate in similar ways.
>
> **details:** Last week, my daughter Nina's friends dressed in their best for her birthday party.
> The girls wore frilly or flowered dresses.
> The boys sported new shirts and clean shoes.
> I always loved to go barefoot when I was a child.
> Years ago, my classmates and I were also elaborately dressed.
> We were self-conscious in our graduation caps and gowns.
> Some of us wore special hoods or colored tassels.

The children at the party were anxious for the fun to get started.

They wanted to play, but their parents had told them to behave.

Some children are too good to be true.

They misbehave at home but are angels in public.

The graduates were eager to get their diplomas.

They fidgeted in their chairs as the guest speaker droned on.

He was the president of a large corporation.

They looked behind them at their families and friends.

But they tried to behave because the Dean of Students had warned them that she would be watching.

When Nina's four-year-old friends heard some music playing, they began to loosen up.

They started to jump around, dance, and giggle.

Soon they were wild with happiness.

When the graduates had all received their diplomas, they let themselves go.

They jumped up, tossed their caps in the air, and hugged each other.

Their parents started taking photographs.

Soon the graduates filled the air with laughter and shouts of victory.

 Exercise 9

Practice

Revising the Order in a Comparison or Contrast Outline

Below is an outline written in the subject-by-subject pattern. Rewrite the part of the outline that is in italics so that the points in the second half follow the order of the first half. You do not have to change any sentences; just rearrange them.

topic sentence: Young people and old people are both victims of society's prejudices.

details: Some people think young people are not capable of mature thinking.

They think the young are on drugs.

They think the young are alcoholics.

The young are considered parasites because they do not earn a great deal of money.

Many young people are in college and not working full time.

Many young people rely on help from their parents.

The young are outcasts because their appearance is different.

The young wear trendy fashions.

They have strange haircuts.

People may think the young are punks.

The way young people look makes other people afraid.

Old people are also judged by their appearance.

They are wrinkled or scarred or frail-looking.

People are afraid of growing old and looking like that.

Therefore they are afraid of the old.

Some people think elderly people are not capable of mature thinking.

They think the old are on too much medication to think straight.

They think the old are senile.

Some people consider the old to be parasites because elderly people do not earn a great deal of money.
Some of the elderly have small pensions.
Some have only Social Security.
The young and the old are often stereotyped.

Rewritten order: _____

_____

_____

_____

_____

_____

_____

_____

_____

_____

_____

_____

DRAFTING AND REVISING

Rough Lines Comparison or Contrast

When you've revised your outline, you can write the first draft of the restaurant paragraph. After making a first draft, you may want to combine more sentences, rearrange your points, fix your topic sentence, or add vivid details. You may also need to add transitions.

The Draft

Here is a draft version of the paragraph on contrasting two restaurants. As you read it, notice the changes from the outline on page: the order of some details in the outline has been changed, sentences have been combined, and transitions have been added.

A Draft of a Contrast Paragraph, Point-By-Point
(Transitions are underlined.)

Some people would rather eat at The Garden than at Victor's because The Garden offers better and cheaper food in a more casual environment. The food at Victor's is bland-tasting and traditional. The menu has broiled fish, chicken, and traditional steaks. The food is the usual American food with a little French food on the list. Appetizers are the usual things like shrimp cocktail and onion soup. The spices used are mainly parsley and salt.

Food at The Garden, <u>however,</u> is more spicy and adventurous. The restaurant has all kinds of ethnic food. There are many pasta dishes with tomato sauce. The menu has five kinds of curry on it. The appetizers include items like tiny tortillas and hot, honey-mustard ribs. <u>And if parsley is the spice of choice at Victor's,</u> garlic is the favorite spice at The Garden. The prices at the restaurants differ, <u>too.</u> Victor's is expensive because everything you order costs extra. An appetizer or a salad costs extra. Food at The Garden, <u>in contrast,</u> is more moderately priced because the price of a dinner includes an appetizer and a salad. <u>Price and menu are important, but the most important difference between the restaurants has to do with environment</u>. Certain diners may feel uncomfortable at Victor's, which has a formal kind of atmosphere. Everyone is dressed up, the men in jackets and ties and the women in dresses. The less formal diners would rather eat in a more casual place like The Garden, where everyone wears jeans. Many people prefer a place where they can relax, with reasonable prices and unusual food, to a place that is a little stuffy, with a traditional and expensive menu.

The checklist below may help you to revise your own draft.

✔️ Checklist

A Checklist for Revising the Draft of a Comparison or Contrast Paragraph

- ✔ Did I include a topic sentence that covers both subjects?
- ✔ Is the paragraph in a clear order?
- ✔ Does it stick to one pattern, either subject by subject or point by point?
- ✔ Are both subjects given roughly the same amount of space?
- ✔ Does all the detail fit?
- ✔ Are the details specific and vivid?
- ✔ Do I need to combine any sentences?
- ✔ Are transitions used effectively?
- ✔ Have I made my point?

Revising the Draft of a Comparison or Contrast Paragraph by Adding Vivid Details

Practice

You can do this exercise alone, with a writing partner or with a group. The following contrast paragraph lacks the vivid details that could make it interesting. Read it; then rewrite the underlined parts in the space above the underlining. Replace the original words with more vivid details.

My new car is giving me the same problems that I had in my old car.

My old car, a Honda Civic, cost at least a hundred dollars a month to keep

on the road. I was constantly paying for some minor but expensive repairs.

One month, the car needed <u>three things</u> repaired. In addition, my Honda

was uncomfortable. The seats were <u>not good</u>, and I always had to sit funny. Another irritation in the Honda was its little quirks. For example, the radio <u>never worked right</u>. I had hoped to put all these problems behind me when I bought my new Nissan Pathfinder, but my hopes were not fulfilled. Just like my old car, my new one costs me <u>a lot </u>to keep on the road. This time the money doesn't go to repairs; it goes to filling the gas tank. I had not realized such a big car would use so much gas. And while the Pathfinder has nice seats, I'm still uncomfortable. I'm not used to sitting so high off the ground. Also, I'm not used to stepping so far down when I get out of the vehicle. Finally, the car shares a radio problem with my old one. The Nissan's radio worked right – for a while. Then someone broke off my antenna, and now the radio doesn't work at all. Thinking of all the similar flaws in my two cars, I have concluded that I must accept them and pray that they will not show up in my next car.

Exercise 11

Practice

Revising a Draft by Combining Sentences

The paragraph below has many short, choppy sentences, which are underlined. Whenever you see two or more underlined sentences clustered next to each other, combine them into one smooth, clear sentence.

My mother and my older sister, Andrea, both treat me like a child. First of all, they both criticize my eating habits. <u>My mother is disturbed when she sees me eating chocolate chip cookies for breakfast. She is upset if I drink Sprite for breakfast. </u>She doesn't believe I am getting the proper nutrition. <u>Andrea eats only health food. She gets concerned about my diet. She is upset when she sees me eating junk food like Whoppers or fried chicken nuggets.</u> My mother and Andrea also monitor my comings and goings. <u>If I am late getting home from work, my mother asks questions. She wants to know if the traffic was bad. She wonders if I had an accident.</u> Similarly, Andrea is always asking why I am leaving late for school or whether I am cutting classes. Worst of all, these two women investigate and evaluate my friends, particularly my girlfriends. My mother will ask, "Whatever happened to that sweet girl you were seeing? I really liked her." My sister is more blunt. She is likely to say, "You'll never find a finer girl than your last girlfriend. You should apologize to her." If she doesn't like a girl I'm seeing, Andrea says, "You can do better than that." Although these comments irritate me, I love my mother and Andrea. <u>I know my mother and sister care about me. I wish they would treat me like an adult.</u>

Final Lines Proofreading and Polishing: Comparison or Contrast

Contrast Paragraph: Point-by-Point Pattern

Following is the final version of the paragraph contrasting restaurants, using a point-by-point pattern. When you read it, you'll notice several changes from the draft on pages 159–160:

- "Usual" or "usually" was used too often, so synonyms were substituted.
- "Onion soup" became "*French* onion soup," to polish the detail.
- "Everything *you* order" was changed to "everything *a person* orders, to avoid sounding as if the reader is ordering food at Victor's.
- "A formal *kind of atmosphere*" became "a formal environment" to eliminate extra words.

A Final Version of a Contrast Paragraph: Point-by-Point
(Changes from the draft are underlined.)

Some people would rather eat at The Garden than at Victor's because The Garden offers better and cheaper food in a more casual environment. The food at Victor's is bland-tasting and traditional. The menu has broiled fish, chicken, and traditional steaks. The food is <u>typical</u> American food with a little French food on the list. Appetizers are <u>standard items</u> like shrimp cocktail and <u>French</u> onion soup. The spices are mostly parsley and salt. Food at The Garden, however, is more spicy and adventurous. The restaurant has all kinds of ethnic food. There are many pasta dishes with tomato sauce. The menu has four kinds of curry on it. The appetizers include items like tiny tortillas and hot, honey-mustard ribs. And if parsley is the spice of choice at Victor's, garlic is the favorite spice at The Garden. The prices at the restaurants differ, too. Victor's is expensive because everything <u>a person</u> orders costs extra. An appetizer or a salad costs extra. Food at The Garden, in contrast, is more moderately priced because the price of a dinner includes an appetizer and a salad. Price and menu are important, but the most important difference between the two restaurants has to do with environment. Certain diners may feel uncomfortable at Victor's, which has a formal <u>environment</u>. Everyone is dressed up, the men in jackets and ties and the women in dresses. Less formal diners would rather eat in a more casual place like The Garden, where everyone wears jeans. Many people prefer a place where they can relax, with reasonable prices and unusual food, to a place that is a little stuffy, with a traditional and expensive menu.

Before you prepare the final copy of your comparison or contrast paragraph, check your latest draft for errors in spelling and punctuation and for any errors made in typing or recopying.

The Same Contrast Paragraph: Subject-by-Subject

To show you what the same paragraph contrasting restaurants would look like in a subject-by-subject pattern, the outline, draft, and final version are shown below.

An Outline: Subject-by-Subject

topic sentence:	Some people would rather eat at The Garden than at Victor's because The Garden offers better, cheaper food in a more casual environment.
details:	Food at Victor's is bland-tasting and traditional. The menu has broiled fish, chicken, and traditional steaks. The spices used are mostly parsley and salt. The food is the usual American food, with a little French food on the list. Appetizers are the usual things like shrimp cocktail and onion soup.
subject 1: **Victor's**	Victor's is expensive. Everything you order costs extra. An appetizer or salad costs extra. Certain diners may feel uncomfortable at Victor's, which has a formal environment. Everyone is dressed up, the men in jackets and ties and the women in dresses.
	Food at The Garden is more spicy and adventurous. There are many pasta dishes in tomato sauce. There is garlic in just about everything. The Garden serves four different curry dishes. It has all kinds of ethnic food. Appetizers include items like tiny tortillas and hot, honey-mustard ribs.
subject 2: **The Garden**	Food at The Garden is moderately priced. The price of a dinner includes an appetizer and a salad. The Garden is casual. People don't dress up to go there; they wear jeans. Many people prefer a place where they can relax, with reasonable prices and unusual food, to a place that's a little stuffy, with a traditional and expensive menu.

A Draft: Subject-by-Subject (Transitions are underlined.)

Some people would rather eat at The Garden than at Victor's because The Garden offers better, cheaper food in a more casual environment. The food at Victor's is bland-tasting and traditional. The menu has broiled fish, chicken, and traditional steaks on it. The food is the usual American food, with a little French food on the list. Appetizers are the usual things like shrimp cocktail and onion soup. At Victor's, the spices are mostly parsley and salt. Eating traditional food at Victor's is expensive, since everything you order costs extra. An appetizer or a salad, for instance, costs extra. Victor's prices make some people nervous, and the restaurant's formal environment makes them uncomfortable. At Victor's, everyone is dressed up, the men in jackets and ties and the women in dresses. <u>The formal atmosphere, the food, and the prices attract some diners, but others would rather go to The Garden for a meal.</u> The food at The Garden is more spicy and adventurous <u>than the offerings at Victor's.</u> The place has all kinds of ethnic food. There are many pasta dishes in tomato sauce, and The Garden serves four different curry dishes. Appetizers include items like tiny tortillas and hot, honey-mustard ribs. <u>If Victor's relies on parsely and salt to flavor its food</u>, The Garden sticks to garlic, which is in just about everything. Prices are lower at The Garden <u>than they are at Victor's</u>. The Garden's meals are more moderately priced because, <u>unlike Victor's</u>, The Garden includes an appetizer and a salad in the price of a dinner. <u>And in contrast to Victor's</u>, The Garden is a casual restaurant. People don't dress up to go to The Garden; everyone wears jeans. Many people prefer a place where they can relax, with unusual food at reasonable prices, to a place that's a little stuffy, with a traditional and expensive menu.

A Final Version: Subject-by-Subject (Changes from the draft are underlined.)

Some people would rather eat at The Garden than at Victor's because The Garden offers better, cheaper food in a more casual environment. The food at Victor's is bland-tasting and traditional. The menu has broiled fish, chicken, and traditional steaks on it. The food is typical American food, with a little French food on the list. Appetizers are the <u>standard</u> things like shrimp cocktail and <u>French</u> onion soup. At Victor's, the spices are mostly parsley and salt. Eating traditional food at Victor's is expensive, since everything <u>a person</u> orders costs extra. An appetizer or a salad, for instance, costs extra. Victor's prices make some people nervous, and the restaurant's formal environment makes them uncomfortable. At Victor's, everyone is dressed up, the men in jackets and ties and the women in dresses. The formal <u>environment</u> and the prices attract some diners, but others would rather go to The Garden for a meal. The food at The Garden is more spicy and adventurous than the offerings at Victor's. The place has all kinds of ethnic food. There are many pasta dishes in tomato sauce, and The Garden serves four different curry dishes. Appetizers include items like tiny tortillas and hot, honey-mustard ribs. If Victor's relies on parsley and salt to flavor its food, The Garden sticks to garlic, which is in just about everything. Prices are lower at The Garden than they are at Victor's. The Garden's meals are moderately priced because, unlike Victor's, The Garden includes an appetizer and a salad in the price of a dinner. And in contrast to Victor's, The Garden is a casual restaurant. People don't dress up to go to The Garden; everyone wears jeans. Many people prefer a place where they can relax, with unusual food at reasonable prices, to a place that's a little stuffy, with a traditional and expensive menu.

Practice

Proofreading to Prepare the Final Version

Following are two comparison or contrast paragraphs with the kinds of errors that are easy to overlook in a final copy of an assignment. Correct the errors, writing your corrections above the lines. There are eleven errors in the first paragraph and nine in the second.

1. My nephew's stuffed dog and my portable CD player meet the same needs in both of us. Brendan, who is four, won't go anywhere without the ragged stufed dog he loves. To him, that dog represents security I have seen him cry so long and so hard that his parents had to turn the car around and drive fifty miles to pick up the dog they forgot. My CD player is my security, and I take it everywere. I even take it to the library when I study; I just plug in the earphones. When Brendan feels tense, he runs to grab his dog. One day Brendans mother was yelling at him, an his face got puckered up and red. Brendan ran out of the room and hid in the corner of the hall-way. He was clutching his dog. While I dont clutch my CD player, I do turn to my mussic to relax whenever I felt anxious. Brendan uses his toy to excape the world. I seen him sit silently for half an hour, holding his dog and starring into space. He is involved in some fantasy with his puppy. Whenever I feel tense, I turn on my music. It soothes me and puts me in a world of my own. I guess adults and children have there own ways of cop-ing with conflict, and they have their own toys, too.

2. The last two Thanksgivings I celebrated were as different as the people who invited me to them. Two years ago, my sister Teresa asked me to come to her house for Thanksgiving dinner. When I arrive, the first think I noticed was an elaborately set table with white linen napkins, china plates, and a centerpiece of fresh flowers and autumn leaves. When we sat down at the table, Teresa set the tone for the formal diner. She made sure that her two sons pulled out chairs for their two great ants, and she slowly passed around the platters of food while her husband carved the turkey. After din-ner, Teresa, who likes to be organized, got everyone to sit queitly in the living room, where we chatted politely about past holidays My sister Camille had a completely diffrent kind of Thanksgiving last year. Camille is a casual person, so I was not surprised to see that when I got to her house, the table was not even sit. Instead, three or four people were coming from the kitchen, loading the table with bowls and platters of food. A pile of plastic utensils and paper plates sat on top of some large paper napkins. In the middle of all this food was a centerpiece of a paper turkey. At dinner time, everyone piled food on a paper plate and sat somewhere in the living room, or den. People kept coming and going, grabbing or offering more food. After dinner, Camille sat back and watched the football game while others played cards or napped. From one holiday to the next, I had witnessed how personalities reveal themselves in family holidays.

Lines of Detail: A Walk-Through Assignment

Write a paragraph that compares or contrasts any experience you've heard about with the same experience as you lived it. For example, you could compare or contrast what you heard about starting college with your actual experience of starting college. You could compare or contrast what you heard about falling in love with your experience of falling in love, or what you heard about playing a sport with your own experience playing that sport. To write your paragraph, follow these steps:

Step 1: Choose the experience you will write about; then list all the similarites and differences between the experience as you heard about it and the experience as you lived it.

Step 2: To decide whether to write a comparison or contrast paragraph, survey your list to see which has more details, the similarities or the differences.

Step 3: Add details to your comparison or contrast list. Survey your list again, and group the details into points of comparison or contrast.

Step 4: Write a topic sentence that includes both subjects, focuses on comparison or contrast, and makes a point.

Step 5: Decide whether your paragraph will be in the subject-by-subject or point-by-point pattern. Write your outline in the pattern you choose.

Step 6: Write a draft of your paragraph. Revise your draft, checking the transitions, the order of the points and the space given to each point for each subject, the relevance and vividness of details. Combine any short, choppy sentences.

Step 7: Before you prepare the final copy of your paragraph, edit for word choice, spelling, punctuation, and transitions.

Writing Your Own Comparison or Contrast Paragraph

When you write on one of these topics, be sure to follow the stages of the writing process in preparing your comparison or contrast paragraph.

1. Contrast what your appearance (or your behavior) makes others think of you and what you are like below the surface of your appearance (or behavior). If your instructor agrees, you can ask a writing partner or group to give you ideas on what your appearance or behavior says about you.

2. Contrast something you did in the past with the way you do the same thing today. For example, you could contrast the two ways (past and present) of studying, shopping, treating your friends, spending your free time, driving a car, or getting along with a parent or child.

3. Compare or contrast any of the following:

two pets	two performers	two movies
two cars	two bosses	two TV shows
two stores	two family members	two jobs
two athletic teams	two birthdays	two classes
two girl/boyfriends	two gifts	two songs

If your instructor agrees, you may want to brainstorm points of comparison or contrast with a writing partner or a group.

4. Imagine that you are a reporter who specializes in helping consumers get the best for their money. Imagine that you are asked to rate two brands of the same supermarket item. Write a paragraph advising your readers which is the better buy. You can rate either two brands of cola, yogurt, potato chips, toothpaste, ice cream, chocolate chip cookies, or paper towels—any item you can get in a supermarket.

Be sure to come up with *enough* points to contrast. You can't, for example, do a well-developed paragraph on just the taste of two cookies. But you can also discuss texture, color, smell, price, fat content, calories, number of chocolate chips, and so on. If your instructor agrees, you may want to brainstorm topics or points of contrast with a group as a way of beginning the writing process. Then work on your own on the outline, draft, and final version.

5. Contrast your taste in music, dress, or ways of spending leisure time, with that of another generation.

6. Interview a person of your age group who comes from a different part of the country. (There may be quite a few people from different parts of the country in your class.) Ask this person about similarities or differences between his or her former home and this part of the country. You could ask about similarities or differences in dress, music, dating, nightlife, ways to spend leisure time, favorite entertainers, or anything else you like.

After the interview, write a paragraph that shows how people of the same age group, but from different parts of the country, either have different tastes in something like music or dress or share the same tastes in that area. Whichever approach you use, be sure to include details you collected in the interview.

7. Examine the photograph of the two buildings. Then write a paragraph contrasting them. You can start by asking such questions as Which is more elegant? Seems less impressive? Is more serene? Is more modern? Use the details of the photograph to support your topic sentence.

8. Look carefully at the photograph of the car. Write a paragraph contrasting the car in the photograph with the car of your dreams.

Name: _____   **Section:** _____

PEER REVIEW FORM FOR A COMPARISON OR CONTRAST PARAGRAPH

After you've written a draft of your paragraph, let a writing partner read it. When your partner has completed the form below, discuss the comments. Then repeat the same process for your partner's paragraph.

I think the topic sentence of this paragraph is _____

_____

_____

The pattern of this paragraph is (a) subject-by-subject, (b) point-by-point. (Choose one.)

The points used to compare or contrast are _____

_____

_____

The part of the paragraph I liked best was about _____

_____

The comparison or contrast is (a) easy to follow, (b) a little confusing. (Choose one.)

I have questions about _____

I would like to see something added about _____

I would like to take out the part about _____

I would like to add or change a transition in front of the words _____

_____

Other comments _____

_____

_____

_____

_____

_____

_____

_____

Reviewer's Name: _____

WRITING FROM READING: Comparison or Contrast

Against All Odds, I'm Just Fine

Brad Wackerlin

When Brad Wackerlin wrote this essay in 1990, he had just graduated from high school. He writes about the differences between society's view of teenagers and the real teens who "do fine" in the real world.

Words You May Need to Know (corresponding paragraph numbers are in parentheses)

baby boomers (1): People born between 1946 and 1964, when the record number of births was called a "baby boom."

generation gap (1): the distance (in attitudes, values, goals, etc.) between two generations

warping (2): twisting out of shape

preconceived (3): formed in advance

---

1   What troubled times the American teenager lives in! Ads for Nike shoes urge us to "Just do it!" while the White House tells us to "Just say no." The baby boomers have watched their babies grow into teens, and history has repeated itself: the punk teens of the '80s have taken the place of the hippie teens of the '60s. Once again, the generation gap has widened, and the adults have finally remembered to remember that teenagers are just no good. They have even coined a name for their persecution of adolescents: "teen-bashing."

2   If what is being printed in the newspapers, viewed on television and repeated by adults is correct, it is against all odds that I am able to write this article. Adults say the average teenager can't write complete sentences and has trouble spelling big words. Their surveys report that I can't find Canada on a map. According to their statistics, my favorite hobbies are sexual intercourse and recreational drug use. It's amazing that I've found time to write this; from what they say, my time is spent committing violent crimes or just hanging out with a gang. In fact, it is even more amazing that I'm here at all, when you consider that the music I listen to is supposedly "warping" my mind and influencing me to commit suicide.

3   Nonetheless, here I am. I write this article to show that a teenager can survive in today's society. Actually, I'm doing quite well. I haven't fathered any children, I'm not addicted to any drugs, I've never worshiped Satan and I don't have a police record. I can even find Canada on a map along with its capital, Ottawa. I guess my family and friends have been supportive of me, for I've never been tempted to become one of those teenage runaways I'm always reading about. Call me a rebel, but I've stayed in school and (can it be true?!) I enjoy it. This month, I graduate from high school and join other graduates as the newest generation of adults. I'm looking forward to four

years of college and becoming a productive member of society. I may not be America's stereotypical teen, but that only proves there is something wrong with our society's preconceived image of today's teenager.

4   My only goal in writing this article is to point out the "bum rap" today's teenager faces. I feel the stereotypical teen is, in fact, a minority. The true majority are the teenagers who, day in and day out, prepare themselves for the future and work at becoming responsible adults. Our time is coming. Soon we will be the adults passing judgment on the teenagers of tomorrow. Hopefully, by then, we will have realized that support and encouragement have a far more positive effect on teenagers than does bashing them.

WRITING FROM READING: "Against All Odds, I'm Just Fine"

When you write on any of the topics below, be sure to work through the stages of the writing process in preparing your comparison or contrast paragraph.

1. Write a paragraph that contrasts society's image of any age group (teens, twenties, thirties, etc.) with the reality. As part of the thought lines stage of writing, interview one or more members of that age group. Before the interview, prepare a list of questions. They can be questions such as these:

   How does television depict your age group?
   What do most people think is wrong with people in your age group?
   Are there stereotypes about how your age group dresses, talks, and so on?

   Prepare at least eight questions before you begin the interview. At the interview, jot down answers, ask follow-up questions, and ask the person(s) being interviewed to review and add to your notes.

2. Contrast your first impression of someone with the way you feel about the person after knowing him or her longer.

3. Show the similarities between teens of today and teens of thirty years ago. If your instructor agrees, brainstorm for similarities with a partner or group.

4. Compare or contrast yourself with the kind of person you think is "typical" of your age group.

CHAPTER 7

Classification

WHAT IS CLASSIFICATION?

When you **classify,** you divide something into different categories, and you do it according to some basis. For example, you may classify the people in your neighborhood into three types: those you know well, those you know slightly, and those you don't know at all. Although you may not be aware of it, you have chosen a basis for this classification. You are classifying the people in your neighborhood according to *how well you know them.*

Hints for Writing a Classification Paragraph

1. Divide your subject into three or more categories or types. If you are thinking about classifying VCRs, for instance, you might think about dividing them into cheap VCRs and expensive VCRs. Your basis for classification would be the price of VCRs. But you would need at least one more type—moderately priced VCRs. Using at least three types helps you to be reasonably complete in your classification.

2. Pick one basis for classification and stick with it. If you are classifying VCRs by price, you cannot divide them into cheap, expensive, and Japanese. Two of the categories relate to price, but "Japanese" does not.

In the following examples, notice how one item does not fit its classification and has been crossed out.

fishermen

fishermen who fish every day
weekend fishermen
~~fishermen who own their own boat~~

(If you are classifying fishermen on the basis of how often they fish, "fishermen who own their own boat" does not fit.)

tests
essay tests
objective tests
~~math tests~~
combination essay and objective tests

(If you are classifying tests on the basis of the type of questions they ask, "math tests" does not fit because it describes the subject being tested.)

3. Be creative in your classification. While it is easy to classify drivers according to their age, your paragraph will be more interesting if you choose another basis for comparison, such as how drivers react to a very slow driver in front of them.

4. Have a reason for your classification. You may be classifying to help a reader understand a topic or to help a reader choose something, or you may be trying to prove a point, to criticize, or to attack.

A classification paragraph must have a unifying reason behind it, and the details for each type should be as descriptive and specific as possible. Determining your audience and deciding why you are classifying can help you stay focused and make your paragraph more interesting.

Exercise 1

Practice

Finding a Basis for Classifying

Write three bases for classifying each of the following topics. The first topic is done for you.

1. **topic to classify:** cats
   You can classify cats on the basis of

   a. Their age _____

   b. Their color _____

   c. How friendly they are _____

2. **topic to classify:** cars
   You can classify cars on the basis of

   a. _____

   b. _____

   c. _____

3. **topic to classify:** action movies
   You can classify action movies on the basis of

   a. _____

   b. _____

   c. _____

4. topic to classify: children
You can classify children on the basis of

a. _____

b. _____

c. _____

Exercise 2

Practice

Identifying What Does Not Fit the Classification

In each list below, one item does not fit because it is not classified on the same basis as the others on the list. First, determine the basis for the classification. Then cross out the one item on each list that does not fit.

1. topic: parties

Basis for classification: _____

list: anniversary parties
birthday parties
small parties
retirement parties

2. topic: hair

basis for classification: _____

list: black
gray
brown
straight

3. topic: jewelry

basis for classification: _____

list: earring
diamond
necklace
bracelet

4. topic: sleepers

basis for classification: _____

list: late sleepers
people who snore
people who toss and turn
people who talk in their sleep

5. topic: police

basis for classification: _____

list: captain
detective
officer of the year
sergeant

Exercise 3

Practice

Finding Categories That Fit One Basis for Classification

In the lines under each topic, write three categories that fit the basis of classification that is given. The first one is done for you.

1. **topic:** cartoons on television
   basis for classification: when they are shown
   categories:

   a. *Saturday morning cartoons*

   b. *weekly cartoon series shown in the evening*

   c. *cartoons that are holiday specials*

2. **topic:** desserts
   basis for classification: how fattening they are
   categories:

   a. _____

   b. _____

   c. _____

3. **topic:** teenagers
   basis for classification: popularity with peers
   categories:

   a. _____

   b. _____

   c. _____

4. **topic:** toys
   basis for classification: price
   categories:

   a. _____

   b. _____

   c. _____

5. **topic:** vacations
   basis for classification: how long they are
   categories:

   a. _____

   b. _____

   c. _____

WRITING THE CLASSIFICATION PARAGRAPH IN STEPS

Gathering Ideas: Classification

First, pick a topic for your classification. The next step is to choose some basis for your classification.

Brainstorming a Basis for Classification

Sometimes the easiest way to choose one basis is to brainstorm about different types related to your topic and to see where your brainstorming leads you. For example, if you were to write a paragraph classifying phone calls, you could begin by listing anything about phone calls that occurs to you:

Phone Calls

sales calls at dinnertime	people who talk too long
short calls	calls I hate getting
calls in middle of night	wrong numbers
long distance calls	waiting for a call

The next step is to survey your list. See where it is leading you. The list on phone calls seems to have a few items about *unpleasant phone calls:*

sales calls at dinner time
wrong numbers
calls in middle of night

Maybe you can label these "Calls I Do Not Want," and that will lead you toward a basis for classification. You might think about calls you *do not* want and calls you *do* want. You think further and realize that you want or do not want certain calls because of their effect on you. You decide to use the effect of the calls on you as the basis for classification. Remember, however, that you need at least three categories. If you stick with this basis for classification, you can come up with three categories:

calls that please me
calls that irritate me
calls that frighten me

By brainstorming, you can then gather details about your three categories:

Added Details for Three Categories

calls that please me

from boyfriend

good friends

catch-up calls—someone I haven't talked to for a while

make me feel close

calls that irritate me

sales calls at dinnertime

wrong numbers

calls that interrupt

invade privacy

calls that frighten me

emergency call in middle of night

"let's break up" call from boyfriend

change my life, indicate some bad change

Matching the Points Within the Categories

As you begin thinking about details for each of your categories, try to write about the same points in each type. For instance, in the list on phone calls, each category includes some details about who made the call:

calls that please me—from good friends, my boyfriend
calls that irritate me—from salespeople, unknown callers
calls that frighten me—from the emergency room, my boyfriend

Each category also includes some details about why you react to them in a specific way:

calls that please me—make me feel close
calls that irritate me—invade privacy
calls that frighten me—indicate some bad change

You achieve unity by covering the same points for each category.

Writing a Topic Sentence for a Classification Paragraph

The topic sentence for a classification paragraph should do two things:

1. It should mention what you are classifying.
2. It should indicate the basis for your classification by stating the basis or listing your categories, or both.

Consider the details on phone calls. To write a topic sentence about the details, you

1. Mention what you are classifying: phone calls,
2. Indicate the basis for classifying by (a) stating the basis (their effect on me) or (b) listing the categories (calls that please me, calls that irritate me, and calls that frighten me). You may also state both the basis and the categories in the topic sentence.

Following these guidelines, you can write a topic sentence like this:

I can classify phone calls according to their effect on me.

or

Phone calls can be grouped into the ones that please me, the ones that irritate me, and the ones that frighten me.

Both of these topic sentences state what you're classifying and give some indication of the basis for the classification. Once you have a topic sentence, you are ready to begin the outlines stage of writing the classification paragraph.

Exercise 4

Collaborate

Creating Questions to Get Details for a Classification Paragraph

Do this exercise with a partner or group. Each list below includes a topic, the basis for classifying that topic, and three categories. For each list, think of three questions that you could ask to get more details about the types. The first list is done for you.

1. **topic:** moviegoers
   basis for classification: what they eat and drink during the movie
   categories: the traditional munchers, the healthy munchers, the really hungry munchers
   questions you can ask:

   a. What does each type eat and drink?

   b. What does each type look like?

   c. Does each group stock up on more supplies during the movie?

2. **topic:** sports fans at a game
   basis for classification: how much they like the sport
   categories: fanatics, ordinary fans, and bored observers
   questions you can ask:

   a. _____

   b. _____

   c. _____

3. **topic:** people at the dentist's office
   basis for classification: how nervous they are
   categories: the mildly anxious, the anxious, and the terrified
   questions you can ask:

   a. _____

   b. _____

   c. _____

4. **topic:** cell phone users
   basis for classification: how often they use the phone
   categories: those who rarely use their cell phones, those who use them moderately, those who use them frequently
   questions you can ask:

   a. _____

   b. _____

   c. _____

5. **topic:** college students
   basis for classification: what they carry in their backpacks
   categories: those who carry the bare essentials, those who carry a few extras, those who carry much more than they need
   questions you can ask:

a. _____

b. _____

c. _____

Exercise 5

Practice

Writing Topic Sentences for a Classification Paragraph

Review the topics, bases for classification, and categories in Exercise 4. Then, using that material, write a good topic sentence for each topic.

Topic Sentences

for topic 1: _____

_____

_____

for topic 2: _____

_____

_____

for topic 3: _____

_____

_____

for topic 4: _____

_____

_____

_____

for topic 5: _____

_____

_____

Outlines **Devising a Plan: Classification**

Effective Order in Classifying

After you have a topic sentence and a list of details, you can create an outline. Think about which category you want to write about first, second, and so on. The order of your categories will depend on what you're writing about. If you're classifying ways to meet people, you can save the best for last. If you're classifying three habits that are bad for your health, you can save the worst one for last.

If you list your categories in the topic sentence, list them in the same order you will use to explain them in the paragraph.

Following is an outline for a paragraph classifying phone calls. The details have been put into categories. The underlined sentences have been added to clearly define each category before the details are given.

An Outline for a Classification Paragraph

topic sentence: Phone calls can be grouped into the ones that please me, the ones that irritate me, and the ones that frighten me.

category 1 details
> There are some calls that please me.
> They make me feel close to someone.
> I like calls from my boyfriend, especially when he calls just to say he is thinking of me.
> I like to hear from good friends.
> I like catch-up calls.
> These are calls from people I haven't talked to in a while.

category 2 details
> There are some calls that irritate me.
> These calls invade my privacy.
> Sales calls always come at dinnertime.
> They offer me newspaper subscriptions or "free" vacations.
> I get at least four wrong number calls each week.
> All these calls irritate me, and I have to interrupt what I'm doing to answer them.

category 3 details
> There are some calls that frighten me.
> They are the calls that tell me about some bad change in my life.
> I once got a call in the middle of the night.
> It was from a hospital emergency room.
> The nurse said my brother had been in an accident.
> I once got a call from a boyfriend.
> He said he wanted to break up.

You can use the following checklist to help you revise your own classification outline.

✔ Checklist

A Checklist for Revising the Classification Outline

✔ Do I have a consistent basis for classifying?

✔ Does my topic sentence mention what I am classifying and indicate the basis for classification?

✔ Do I have enough to say about each category in my classification?

✔ Are the categories presented in the most effective order?

✔ Am I using clear and specific details?

With a revised outline, you can begin writing your draft.

6

Practice

Recognizing the Basis for Classification Within the Topic Sentence

The topic sentences below do not state a basis for classification, but you can recognize the basis nevertheless. After you've read each topic sentence, write the basis for classification on the lines provided. The first one is done for you.

1. topic sentence: Neighbors can be classified into complete strangers, acquaintances, and buddies.

basis for classification: *how well you know them*

2. topic sentence: On any airplane, there are some passengers who bring one small piece of carry-on luggage, others who carry on a couple of large pieces, and some who bring enough carry-on luggage to fill the trunk of a car.

basis for classification: _____

3. topic sentence: At the Thai restaurant, you can order three kinds of hot sauce: hot sauce for beginners, hot sauce for the adventurous, and hot sauce for fire eaters.

basis for classification: _____

4. topic sentence: When it comes to photographs of yourself, there are three types: the ones that make you look good, the ones that make you look fat, and the ones that make you look ridiculous.

basis for classification: _____

5. topic sentence: Internet users can be grouped into those who rely on it for news, those who use it for research, and those who use it for entertainment.

basis for classification: _____

Exercise 7

Practice

Adding Details to a Classification Outline

Do this exercise with a partner or group. In this outline, add details where the blank lines indicate. Match the points covered in the other categories.

topic sentence: My friends can be categorized as best friends, good friends, and casual friends.

details: I know my best friends so well they are like family.
I have two best friends.
We talk about everything, from our problems to our secret ambitions.
I have known my best friends for years.
I can spend time with my best friends any time, good or bad.
I am close to my good friends, but not that close.
I have about six good friends.

I have known all my good friends for at least a year.
I like to be around good friends when I'm in a good mood and want to share it.
Casual friends are people I like but am not close to.
I have about a dozen casual friends.

_____

_____

I like to be around casual friends when I am in a large crowd, so I feel less alone.

Rough Lines Drafting and Revising: Classification

You can transform your outline into a first draft of a paragraph by writing the topic sentence and the details in paragraph form. As you write, you can begin combining some of the short sentences, adding details, and inserting transitions.

Transitions in Classification

Various transitions can be used in a classification paragraph. The transitions you select will depend on what you are classifying and the basis you choose for classifying. For example, if you are classifying roses according to how pretty they are, you can use transitions like "*one lovely kind of rose,*" and "*another, more beautiful kind,*" and "*the most beautiful kind.*" In other classifications, you can use transitions like "the first type," "another type," or "the final type." In revising your classification paragraph, use the transitions that most clearly connect your ideas.

As you write your own paragraph, you may want to refer to a "kind" or a "type." For variety, try other words like "class," "group," "species," "form," or "version" if it is logical to do so.

After you have a draft of your paragraph, you can revise and review it. The checklist below may help you with your revisions.

✔ Checklist

A Checklist for Revising the Draft of a Classification Paragraph

✔ Does my topic sentence state what I am classifying?

✔ Does it indicate the basis of my classification?

✔ Should any of my sentences be combined?

✔ Do my transitions clearly connect my ideas?

✔ Should I add more details to any of the categories?

✔ Are the categories presented in the most effective order?

Below is a draft of the classification paragraph on phone calls with these changes from the outline on page 180:

- An introduction has been added, in front of the topic sentence, to make the paragraph smoother.

- Some sentences have been combined.
- Some details have been added.
- Transitions have been added.
- A final sentence has been added so that the paragraph makes a stronger point.

A Draft of a Classification Paragraph

I get many phone calls, but they fit into three types. Phone calls can be grouped into the ones that please me, the ones that irritate me, and the ones that frighten me. There are some calls that please me because they make me feel close to someone. I like calls from my boyfriend, especially when he calls just to say he is thinking of me. I like to hear from my good friends. I like catch-up calls, the calls from people I haven't talked to in a while that fill me in on what friends have been doing. There are also calls that irritate me because they invade my privacy. Sales calls, offering me newspaper subscriptions and "free" vacations, always come at dinnertime. In addition, I get at least four wrong number calls each week. All these calls irritate me, and I have to interrupt what I'm doing to answer them. The more serious calls are the ones that frighten me. They are the calls that tell me about some bad change in my life. Once, in the middle of the night, a call from a hospital emergency room told me my brother had been in an accident. Another time, a boyfriend called to tell me he wanted to break up. When I get bad news by phone, I realize that the telephone can bring frightening calls as well as friendly or irritating ones.

Exercise 8

Practice

Combining Sentences for a Better Classification Paragraph

The paragraph below has some short sentences that would be more effective if they were combined. Combine each pair of underlined sentences into one sentence. Write the new sentence in the space above the old ones.

In the dog world, there are yipper-yappers, authoritative barkers, and boom-box barkers. <u>Yipper-yappers have a short, high-pitched bark. Their bark sounds like hysterical nagging.</u> Yipping dogs are usually small dogs like miniature poodles or terriers. <u>The fiercely emotional quality of their bark is frightening. I am not too afraid of these dogs.</u> I know they can only get to my ankles if they attack. <u>There is a moderate kind of dog. It is the authoritative barker.</u> This type of dog has a deep bark; it signifies that the dog means business. Boxers, collies, and other medium-size dogs possess this commanding voice. <u>They demand my respect. I am afraid of them. Their low, growling bark and their size make me afraid.</u> The third kind of dog has a

boom-box bark. <u>Its bark is very loud. It can be heard from blocks away.</u>
Dogs that sound like this are usually the enormous ones like Great Danes or
German Shepherds. These dogs strike fear in my heart. They sound intimi-
dating, and they have large bodies and giant teeth. <u>People say you can't</u>
<u>judge a book by its cover. You can tell quite a bit about a dog by its bark.</u>

Exercise 9

Practice

Identifying Transitions in a Classification Paragraph

Underline all the transitions in the paragraph below. The transitions may be
words or groups of words.

　　At the supermarket where I work as a cashier, I classify my customers
according to how they relate to me. First, there are those who are polite and
kind to me. After I say, "Hello, how are you today?" they usually say, "Fine."
Some make a funny comment about the weather or the traffic. This type of
customer often makes pleasant conversation while I ring up the groceries.
Another class of customer doesn't talk at all. As far as this kind is concerned, I do not exist. This kind simply stares right through me or, even
worse, talks on a cell phone as I ring up and bag the groceries. Recently, I
have seen customers glued to their phones throughout their time at the
checkout counter, not even acknowledging me when I announce the total or
hand them their change. The final and most dreaded type of customer is the
angry customer. This kind is angry at me, at the other customers, and possi-
bly at the whole world. Members of this group argue about the price of
every item, complain about how long it takes to ring them up, and criticize
the way I pack their groceries. They always leave shaking their heads in dis-
gust. Dealing with these varieties of customers each day, I am grateful that
most people fit into the first category, the good-natured, pleasant group.

Final Lines

Proofreading and Polishing: Classification

Below is the final version of the classification paragraph on phone calls.
Compare the draft of the paragraph on page 183 to the final version and
you'll notice these changes:

- The first sentence has been rewritten so that it is less choppy, and a word of transition, "My," links the second sentence to the first.
- Some words have been eliminated and sentences rewritten so that they are not too wordy.
- The word choice has been refined: "bad change" has been replaced by "crisis," "someone" has been changed to "a person I care about" to make the detail more precise, and "irritate" has been changed to "annoy" to avoid repetition.

A Final Version of a Classification Paragraph

(Changes from the draft are underlined)

I get many phone calls, but most of them fall into one of three types. My phone calls can be grouped into the ones that please me, the ones that irritate me, and the ones that frighten me. There are some calls I want to receive because they make me feel close to a person I care about. I like calls from my boyfriend, especially when he calls just to say he is thinking of me. I like to hear from my good friends. I like catch-up calls from friends I haven't talked to in a while. There are also calls I don't want because they invade my privacy. Sales calls, offering me newspaper subscriptions and "free" vacations, always come at dinnertime. In addition, I get at least four wrong number calls each week. All these calls annoy me, and I have to interrupt what I'm doing to answer them. The more serious calls are the ones I really don't want to receive. They are the calls that tell me about some crisis in my life. I once got a midnight call from a hospital emergency room, informing me my brother had been in an accident. Another time, a boyfriend called to tell me he wanted to break up. When I get bad news by phone, I realize that the telephone can bring frightening calls as well as friendly or irritating ones.

Before you prepare the final version of your own classification paragraph, check your latest draft for errors in spelling and punctuation, and for any errors made in typing or copying.

Exercise 10

Practice

Proofreading to Prepare the Final Version

Following are two classification paragraphs with the kinds of errors that are easy to overlook when you prepare the final version of an assignment. Correct the errors, writing above the lines. The first paragraph has twelve errors; the second has eleven errors.

1. My experince in school has shown me their are three kinds of pencils, and they are the pencils that work great, the pencils that barely work, and the pencils that dont work at all. The pencil's that work are the ones that are perfectly sharpened to a razor-fine point and have huge, clean erasers at the end. These pencils produce a dark, clear line when I write with them unfortunatly, I never do write with them. Great pencils are the ones I always come accross, all over the house, when i'm looking for something else. The pencils I usually rite with are the damaged pencils. They work, but not well. They need sharpening, or their erasers are worn so far down that using them leaves rips across the page. Sometimes these pencils leave a faded, weak line on the paper. Sometimes the line is so thick it look like a crayon. The third kind of pencil is the worst of all. Pencils in this group just don't work. They have no point. Or if they have a point, it brakes off as soon as I write. They have no eraser. The pencils are so chewed and mutilated they might have been previously owned by woodpeckers. Non-working pencils are the ones I bring to class on test days. I just do'nt seem to have much luck with pencils.

2. I can classify my clothes according to how long I have owned them. My oldest clothes are the most comftable and least presentable ones. I have had them for years. They include soft flannel shirts with worn patches, and baggy shorts with tears at the seams. They are the clothes I wear at home on the weekends. When no one will see me looking so ragged. In public, I wear the clothes I have had for a year or too. My every-day cloths are neat, clean, and without tears or worn spots. They are farely stylish, and I wear them to work and school. My last type of clothes are the new ones. They still have the prices tags on them. They attracted me because they are fashunable and bright. I feel they will make you look good when I wear them for a special occasion. All these kinds of clothes are important to me, for each serves it's purpose.

Lines of Detail: A Walk-Through Assignment

Write a paragraph that classifies bosses on the basis of how they treat their employees. To write the paragraph, follow these steps.

Step 1: List all the details you can remember about bosses you have worked for or known.

Step 2: Survey your list. Then list three categories of bosses, based on how they treat their employees.

Step 3: Now that you have three categories, study your list again, looking for matching points for all three categories. For example, all three categories could be described by this matching point: where the boss works.

Step 4: Write a topic sentence that (a) names what you are classifying and (b) states the basis for classification or names all three categories.

Step 5: Write an outline. Check that your outline defines each category, uses matching points for each category, and puts the categories in an effective order.

Step 6: Write a draft of the classification paragraph. Check the draft, revising it until it has specific details, smooth transitions, and effective word choice.

Step 7: Before you prepare the final copy of your paragraph, check your last draft for any errors in punctuation, spelling, word choice, or mechanics.

Writing Your Own Classification Paragraph

When you write on any of these topics, be sure to work through the stages of the writing process in preparing your classification paragraph.

1. Write a classification paragraph on any of the topics below. If your instructor agrees, brainstorm with a partner or a group to come up with (1) a basis for your classification, (2) categories related to the basis, and (3) points you can make to give details about each of the categories.

horror movies	cars	salespeople
romantic movies	football players	discount stores
children	fans at a concert	soccer players
parents	fans at a sports event	fears
students	neighbors	weddings
teachers	restaurants	insects
drivers	dates	excuses
birthdays	apologies	secrets

2. Adapt one of the topics in question 1 by making your topic smaller. For example, you can classify Chinese restaurants instead of restaurants or classify sports cars instead of cars. Then write a classification paragraph that helps your reader make a choice about your topic.

3. Below are some topics. Each one already has a basis for classification. Write a classification paragraph on one of these choices. If your instructor agrees, work with a partner or group to brainstorm categories, matching points and details for the categories.

Classify

1. Exams on the basis of how difficult they are.
2. Weekends on the basis of how busy they are.
3. Valentines on the basis of how romantic they are.
4. Breakfasts on the basis of how healthy they are.

5. Skin-divers (or some other recreational athletes) on the basis of how experienced they are.
6. Singers on the basis of the kind of audience they appeal to.
7. Parties on the basis of how much fun they are.
8. Television commercials on the basis of what time of day or night they are broadcast.
9. Radio stations on the basis of what kind of music they play.
10. Urban legends on the basis of how illogical they are.

4. Look carefully at the photograph below. Then use its details to write a classification paragraph with this topic sentence:

   College students can be classified according to the way they react to a teacher's lively lecture.

Name: _____   **Section:** _____

PEER REVIEW FORM FOR CLASSIFICATION PARAGRAPH

After you've written a draft of your classification paragraph, let a writing partner read it. When your partner has completed the form below, discuss his or her comments. Then repeat the same process for your partner's paragraph.

This paragraph classifies _____ (Write the topic.)

The basis for classification is according to _____

_____

The matching points are _____

The part that could use more or better details is _____

_____

_____

I have questions about _____

I would like to see something added about _____

_____

I would like to take out the part about _____

_____

The part of this paragraph I like best is _____

_____

Additional comments: _____

_____

_____

_____

_____

_____

_____

_____

_____

_____

_____

_____

Reviewer's Name: _____

WRITING FROM READING: Classification

Three Disciplines for Children

John Holt

John Holt is an educator and activist who believes our system of education needs a major overhaul. In this essay, he classifies the ways children learn from their disciplines, and he warns against overusing one kind of discipline.

Words You May Need to Know (corresponding paragraph numbers are in parentheses)

discipline (1): the training effect of experience

impersonal (1): without personal or human connection

impartial (1): fair

indifferent (1): not biased, not prejudiced

wheedled (1): persuaded by flattery or coaxing

ritual (2): an established procedure, a ceremony

yield (3): give in to, submit

impotent (3): powerless

1   A child, in growing up, may meet and learn from three different kinds of disciplines. The first and most important is what we might call the Discipline of Nature or of Reality. When he is trying to do something real, if he does the wrong thing or doesn't do the right one, he doesn't get the result he wants. If he doesn't pile one block right on top of another, or tries to build on a slanting surface, his tower falls down. If he hits the wrong key, he hears the wrong note. If he doesn't hit the nail squarely on the head, it bends, and he has to pull it out and start with another. If he doesn't measure properly what he is trying to build, it won't open, close, fit, stand up, fly, float, whistle, or do whatever he wants it to do. If he closes his eyes when he swings, he doesn't hit the ball. A child meets this kind of discipline every time he tries to *do* something, which is why it is so important in school to give children more chances to do things, instead of just reading or listening to someone talk (or pretending to). This discipline is a great teacher. The learner never has to wait long for his answer; it usually comes quickly, often instantly. Also it is clear, and very often points toward the needed correction; from what happened he cannot only see what he did was wrong, but also why, and what he needs to do instead. Finally, and most important, the giver of the answer, call it Nature, is impersonal, impartial, and indifferent. She does not give opinions or make judgments; she cannot be wheedled, bullied, or fooled; she does not get angry or disappointed; she does not praise or blame; she does not remember past failures or hold grudges. With her one always gets a fresh start; this time is the one that counts.

2   The next discipline we might call the Discipline of Culture, of Society, of What People Really Do. Man is a social, cultural animal. Children sense around them this culture, this network of agreements, customs, habits, and rules binding the adults together. They want to understand it and be a part of it. They watch very carefully what people around them are doing and want to do the same. They want to do right, unless they become convinced they can't do right. Thus children rarely misbehave seriously in church, but sit as quietly as they can. The example of all those grown-ups is contagious. Some mysterious ritual is going on, and children, who like rituals, want to be part of it. In the same way, the little children that I see at concerts or operas, though they may fidget a little, or perhaps take a nap now and then, rarely make any disturbance. With all those grownups sitting there, neither moving or talking, it is the most natural thing in the world to imitate them. Children who live among adults who are habitually courteous to each other, and to them, will soon learn to be courteous. Children who live surrounded by people who speak a certain way will speak that way, however much we may try to tell them that speaking that way is bad or wrong.

3   The third discipline is the one most people mean when they speak of discipline—the Discipline of Superior Force, of sergeant to private, of "you do what I tell you or I'll make you wish you had." There is bound to be some of this in a child's life. Living as we do surrounded by things that can hurt children, or that children can hurt, we cannot avoid it. We can't afford to let a small child find out from experience the danger of playing in a busy street, or of fooling with the pots on top of a stove, or of eating up the pills in the medicine cabinet. So, along with other precautions, we say to him, "Don't play in the street, or touch things on the stove, or go into the medicine cabinet, or I'll punish you." Between him and the danger too great for him to imagine we put a lesser danger, but one he can imagine and maybe therefore want to avoid. He can have no idea of what it would be like to be hit by a car, but he can imagine being shouted at, or spanked, or sent to his room. He avoids these substitutes for the greater danger until he can understand it and avoid it for its own sake. But we ought to use this discipline only when it is necessary to protect the life, health, safety, or well-being of people or other living creatures, or to prevent destruction of things that people care about. We ought not to assume too long, as we usually do, that a child cannot understand the real nature of the danger from which we want to protect him. The sooner he avoids the danger, not to escape our punishment, but as a matter of good sense, the better. He can learn that faster than we think. In Mexico, for example, where people drive their cars with a good deal of spirit, I saw many children no older than five or four walking unattended on the streets. They understood about cars; they knew what to do. A child whose life is full of the threat and fear of punishment is

locked into babyhood. There is no way for him to grow up, to learn to take responsibility for his life and acts. Most important of all, we should not assume that having to yield to the threat of our superior force is good for the child's character. It is never good for anyone's character. To bow to superior force makes us feel impotent and cowardly for not having had the strength or courage to resist. Worse, it makes us resentful and vengeful. We can hardly wait to make someone pay for our humiliation, yield to us as we were once made to yield. No, if we cannot always avoid using the Discipline of Superior Force, we should at least use it as seldom as we can.

WRITING FROM READING: "Three Disciplines for Children"

When you write on any of the topics below, be sure to work through the stages of the writing process in preparing your classification paragraph.

1. John Holt writes a very clear classification with a clear purpose: he is trying to explain how children should learn. Write a one-paragraph summary of the article. In your summary, include his definitions of all three types of discipline and when they should be used.

2. Holt says that it is very important "in school to give children more chances to do things, instead of just reading or listening to someone talk."

   Write a paragraph classifying your elementary or high school classes according to how much they allowed you to do. Include your opinion of each category in your paragraph.

   If your instructor agrees, begin this assignment with an interview. Ask a writing partner to interview you about your learning experiences as a way of gathering ideas for this topic. Then do the same for your partner. Before any interviewing begins, write at least seven questions to ask your partner.

3. Holt says children want to understand society and to be a part of it. "They watch very carefully what people around them are doing and want to do the same."

   Write a paragraph classifying children according to the behavior they have learned from their parents. If your instructor agrees, freewrite on this topic, and then share your freewriting with a writing partner or group, asking for reactions and further ideas.

4. Instead of classifying disciplines for children, write a paragraph classifying parents according to their attitudes toward their children.

CHAPTER 8

Definition

WHAT IS DEFINITION?

A **definition** paragraph is one that explains *what a term means to you.* You can begin thinking about what a term means by consulting the dictionary, but your paragraph will include much more than a dictionary definition. It will include a personal definition.

You can select several ways to explain the meaning of a term. You can give examples, you can tell a story, or you can contrast your term with another term. If you were writing a definition of perseverance, for example, you could do one or more of the following: you could give examples of people you know who have persevered, you could tell a story about someone who persevered, or you could contrast perseverance with another quality, like impatience. You could also write about times when perseverance is most needed or about the rewards of perseverance.

Hints for Writing a Definition Paragraph

1. Pick a word or phrase that has a personal meaning for you and that allows you room to develop your idea. Remember that you will be writing a full paragraph on this term. Therefore, a term that can be defined quickly, in only one way, is not a good choice. For example, you would not have much to say about terms like "cauliflower" or "dental floss" unless you have strong personal feelings about cauliflower or dental floss. If you didn't have such feelings, your paragraph would be very short.

When you think about a term to define, you might think about some personal quality you admire or dislike. If some quality provokes a strong reaction in you, you will probably have something to write about that term.

2. The topic sentence should have three parts. Include these items:

- the *term* you are defining,
- the broad *class* or *category* into which your term fits,
- the specific *distinguishing characteristics* that make the term different from all the others in the class or category.

Each of the following topic sentences could be a topic sentence for a definition paragraph because it has the three parts.

term   category distinguishing characteristics
Resentment is the *feeling* that life has been *unfair.*

term   category   distinguishing characteristics
A *clock-watcher* is a *worker* who *is just putting in time, not effort.*

3. Select an appropriate class or category when you write your topic sentence.

> **not this:** Resentment is a thing that makes you feel life has been unfair. (Resentment is a feeling or an attitude. Say so.)
>
> **not this:** Resentment is when you feel life has been unfair. ("When" is a word that refers to a time, like noon or 7:00 P.M. Resentment is a feeling, not a time.)
>
> **not this:** Resentment is where a person feels life has been unfair. ("Where" is a word that refers to a place, like a kitchen or a beach. Resentment is not a place; it is a feeling.)
>
> **but this:** Resentment is the feeling that life has been unfair.

4. Express your attitude toward the term you are defining in the "distinguishing characteristics" part of the topic sentence. Make that attitude clear and speciific.

> **not this:** Resentment is the feeling that can be bad for a person. (Many feelings can be bad for a person. Hate, envy, anger, and impatience, for instance, can all be bad. What is special about resentment?)
>
> **not this:** Resentment is an attitude of resenting another person or a circumstance. (Do not define a word with another form of the word.)
>
> **but this:** Resentment is the feeling that life has been unfair.

5. Use specific and concrete examples to explain your definition. *Concrete* terms refer to things you can see, touch, taste, smell, or hear. Using concrete terms and specific examples will make your definition interesting and clear.

You may be asked to define an *abstract* idea like happiness. Even though an abstract idea cannot be seen, touched, tasted, smelled, or heard directly, you can give a personal definition of it by using concrete terms and specific examples:

> **not this:** Happiness takes place when you feel the joy of reaching a special goal. ("Joy" and "special goal" are abstract terms. Avoid defining one abstract term by using other abstract terms.)
>
> **but this:** I felt happiness when I saw my name at the top of the list of athletes picked for the team. Three months of daily, six-hour practices had paid off, and I had achieved more than I had set out to do. (The abstract idea of happiness is linked to a specific, concrete idea of feeling happiness.)

If you remember to show, not tell, your reader what your term means, you'll have a better definition. Be especially careful not to define a term with another form of that term.

Exercise 1

Practice

Recognizing Abstract and Concrete Words

In the list below, put an *A* by the abstract words and a *C* by the concrete words.

1. _____ temptation

2. _____ mansion

3. _____ trust

4. _____ soldier

5. _____ pencil

6. _____ intelligence

7. _____ auditorium

8. _____ sympathy

9. _____ ambition

10. _____ duty

11. _____ fear

12. _____ toddler

13. _____ freedom

14. _____ hurricane

15. _____ ignorance

16. _____ affection

17. _____ remorse

18. _____ newspaper

19. _____ kindness

20. _____ respect

Exercise 2

Practice

Completing a Topic Sentence for a Definition

Following are unfinished topic sentences for definition pargraphs. Finish each sentence so that the sentence expresses a personal definition of the term and has the three requirements for a definition's topic sentence.

1. A pessimist is a person who _____

_____

2. A tailgater is a driver who _____

_____

3. A fixer-upper is a house that _____

_____

4. A best buddy is a friend who _____

_____

5. The life of the party is the guest who _____

_____

6. A two-faced friend is a person who _____

_____

7. A disciplinarian is an authority figure who _____

_____

8. A bargain hunter is a shopper who _____

_____

9. The black sheep in the family is the relative who _____

_____

10. A brat is a child who _____

_____

Exercise 3

Practice

Recognizing Problems in Topic Sentences for Definition Paragraphs

Review the three components that should be included in the topic sentence for a definiiton paragraph. Then read the topic sentences below, put an *X* next to each sentence that has a problem, and underline the part of the sentence that is faulty.

1. _____ Perseverance is the ability to continue in spite of obstacles.

2. _____ Kindness is the quality of being kind to others.

3. _____ Spite is when people feel a mean desire to hurt others.

4. _____ Optimism is the ability to focus on the positive side of every circumstance.

5. _____ Bliss is a feeling of extreme happiness.

6. __ ___ A critical parent is a parent who criticizes his or her children.

7. _____ Insomnia is where a person is unable to sleep.

8. _____ Environmentalism is a movement to preserve the natural world.

9. _____ Consideration is when you are concerned for the impact of your actions on the lives of others.

10. _____ Imagination is the ability to imagine what is possible.

Exercise 4

 *Collaborate*

Writing Examples for Definition Paragraphs

Below are incomplete statements from a definition paragraph. Complete them in the spaces below by writing specific examples. When you have completed the statements, share your work with a group. After each group member has read his or her examples aloud, discuss the examples. Which examples did you like best? Which are the clearest and most specific? Do some examples lead to a different definition of a term than other examples do?

The first part of the exercise has been started for you.

1. I first saw greed in action when _____

_____

_____

_____

_____

Another example of greed was my experience with _____

_____

_____

_____

_____

_____

2. The most hypocritical comment I ever heard was _____

_____

_____

It was hypocritical because _____

_____

_____

A person in the news that I think is hypocritical is _____

_____

because he/she _____

_____

3. The person who represents generosity to me is _____

because this person _____

_____

I was called on to show generosity when _____

_____

_____

4. A situation when a person must be loyal is a _____

_____

_____

I saw loyalty in action when _____

_____

_____

WRITING THE DEFINITION PARAGRAPH IN STEPS

Thought Lines Gathering Ideas: Definition

To pick a topic for your definition paragraph, begin with some personality trait or type of person. For instance, you might define "the insecure person." If you listed your first thoughts, your list might look like this:

the insecure person
someone who is not emotionally secure
wants (needs?) other people to make him or her feel good
no self-respect

Using Questions to Get Details

Often, when you look for ideas to define a term, you get stuck with big, general statements or abstract words, or you simply cannot come up with enough to say. If you are having trouble getting ideas, think of questions about your term. Jot these questions down, without stopping to answer them. One question can lead you to another question. Once you have five or more questions, you can answer them, and the answers will provide details for your definition paragraph.

If you were writing about the insecure person, for example, you could begin with questions like these:

What are insecure people like?
What behavior shows a person is insecure?
How do insecure people dress or talk?
What makes a person insecure?
Why is insecurity a bad trait?
How do insecure people relate to others?
Does insecurity hurt the insecure person? If so, how?
Does the insecure person hurt others? If so, how?

By scanning the questions and answering as many as you can, you can add details to your list. Once you have a longer list, you can review it and begin to group the items on the list. Following is a list of grouped details on the insecure person.

Grouped Details on the Insecure Person

wants (needs?) other people to make him or her feel important

no self-respect

insecure people have to brag about everything

a friend who brags about his car

they tell you the price of everything

they put others down

saying bad things about other people makes insecure people feel better

insecure people can never relax inside

can never enjoy being with other people

other people are always their competitors

must always worry about what others think of them

The Topic Sentence

Grouping the details can help you arrive at several main ideas. Can they be combined and revised to create a topic sentence? Following is a topic sentence on the insecure person that meets the requirements of naming the term, placing it in a category, and distinguishing the term from others in the category:

term   category   distinguishing characteristics

The *insecure person* is a *person* who *needs other people to make him or her feel respected and important.*

Once you have a topic sentence, you can begin working on the outline stage of the paragraph.

Designing Questions to Gather Details

Practice

Following are terms that could be defined in a paragraph. For each term, write five questions that could lead you to details for the definition. The first one has been done for you, as an example.

1. **term:** arrogance

    questions: a. Do I know anyone who displays arrogance?

    b. Is there any celebrity I think is arrogant?

    c. What is an arrogant action?

    d. What kind of remark is an example of arrogance?

    e. Why are people arrogant?

2. **term:** confidence

    questions: a. _____

    b. _____

    c. _____

    d. _____

    e. _____

3. **term:** the rebel

    questions: a. _____

    b. _____

    c. _____

    d. _____

    e. _____

4. **term:** common sense

    questions: a. _____

b. _____

c. _____

d. _____

e. _____

5. term: the risk-taker

questions: a. _____

b. _____

c. _____

d. _____

e. _____

Exercise 6

Practice

Grouping Related Ideas for a Definition Paragraph

Following is a list of ideas for a definition paragraph. Read the list several times; then group all the ideas on the list into one of the three categories below. Put the letter of the category next to each idea.

Categories

 B how ambition can be **bad**
 E an **example** of ambition in action
 P the **positive** qualities of ambition and ambitious people

List

 1. _____ Too much ambition leads to obsession.

 2. _____ Ambitious people have established their goals.

 3. _____ Ambitious people can destroy whatever gets in their way.

 4. _____ I was determined to win a scholarship by scoring high on a national test.

 5. _____ I devised a plan to get my scholarship.

 6. _____ I studied many hours to prepare for the test.

 7. _____ Ambition can motivate people and help them organize their time.

 8. _____ Everyone thought my ambition was unrealistic, but I earned a scholarship.

 9. _____ Achieving an ambition takes discipline.

 10. _____ Ambitious people risk losing their enjoyment of daily life.

OUTLINES:

Devising a Plan: Definition

To make an outline for a definition paragraph, start with the topic sentence and list the grouped details. Often a first outline does not have many examples or concrete, specific details. A good way to be sure you put specific details and concrete examples into your paragraph is to put some shortened version of them into your revised outline. If you compare the following outline to the grouped list of details on page 198, you will see how specific details and concrete examples have been added.

An Outline for a Definition Paragraph

topic sentence: The insecure person is a person who needs other people to make him or her feel respected and important.

details:	Insecure people have to brag about everything.
	An insecure friend may brag about his car.
added detail	Insecure people wear expensive jewelry and tell you what it costs.
added detail	They brag about their expensive clothes.
added detail	They make sure they wear clothes with trendy labels, another kind of bragging.
	Insecure people put others down.
	Saying bad things about others makes insecure people feel better.
added example	When some friends were talking about Susan's great new job, Jill had to make mean remarks about Susan.
	Jill hated having Susan look like a winner.
	Insecure people can never relax inside.
	They can never enjoy being with other people.
	Other people are always their competitors.
added example	Luke can't enjoy any game of basketball unless he is the star.
	Insecure people must always worry about what others think of them.

When you prepare your own definition outline, use the following checklist to help you revise.

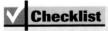

Checklist

A Checklist for Revising a Definition Outline

✔ Does my topic sentence include a category and the characteristics that show how my term is different from others in the category?

✔ Have I defined my term so that it is different from any other term?

✔ Am I being concrete and specific in the details?

✔ Do I have enough examples?

✔ Do my examples relate to the topic sentence?

✔ Are my details in the most effective order?

With a revised outline, you are ready to begin writing a rough draft of your definition paragraph.

 Rewriting a Topic Sentence for a Definition Paragraph

Practice

Below is an outline in which the topic sentence does not make the same point as the rest of the outline. Rewrite the topic sentence so that it relates to the details.

topic sentence: Regret is a feeling of extreme pain.

details: When I was seventeen, I had a chance to go on a major class trip.
The same weekend was my brother's graduation from the police academy.
I chose to go on the class trip.
My brother never said anything, but he was hurt.
To this day, I regret my choice.
I regret many things.
I regret being the class clown instead of earning good grades.
My decision to break up with my girlfriend instead of working things out fills me with regret.
I am sorry I was always too busy to spend time with my grandmother when she asked me to come over.

Rewrite the topic sentence: _____

_____

_____

 Revising an Example to Make It More Concrete and Specific

Practice

The following outline contains one example that is too abstract. In the lines provided, rewrite the example that is too abstract, using more specific, concrete details.

topic sentence: Impulsiveness is the habit of giving in to sudden urges.

details:

example 1   Charlie is an impulsive buyer.
He once walked into a mall just to grab some lunch.
He walked past an electronics store and saw a beautiful new DVD player.
Within minutes, Charlie had bought that DVD player.

example 2   Gary never checks his urge to speak.
Once he was in a tough situation.
He should have kept his mouth shut.
Instead, he said something.
He made the situation worse.

example 3   My Uncle Terrell is the most impulsive person I know.
My uncle was waiting to pick up his cousin at the airport.
Sitting next to him was a beautiful woman.

Without even talking to her, Uncle Terrell decided she
was the one he wanted to marry.
He started a conversation and invited her to dinner.
He proposed a week later.
Last week my uncle Terrell and my aunt celebrated
their twentieth anniversary.

The revised example: _____

_____

_____

_____

_____

Rough Lines   Drafting and Revising: Definition

To write the first draft of your definition paragraph, you can rewrite the outline in paragraph form, combining some of the short sentences and adding
more details. Remember that your purpose in this defintion paragraph is to
explain your personal understanding of a term. Therefore, you want to be
sure that your topic sentence is clear and that your explanation connects
your details to the topic sentence. A careful use of transitions will link your
details to your topic sentence.

Transitions

Since you can define a term in many ways, you can also use many transitions. If you are listing several examples in your paragraph, you can use
transitions like "first," "second," and "finally." If you are contrasting your
term with another, you can use transitions like "on the other hand" or "in
contrast." You may want to alert or remind the reader that you are writing
a definition paragraph by using phrases like "can be defined as," "can be
considered as," "means that," or "implies that."

Because many definitions rely on examples, the transitions below are
ones you may want to use.

Info BOX

Transitions for a Definition Paragraph

a classic case of _____ is _____	in fact	another time
another case	in one case	sometimes
for example	in one	specifically
for instance	one time	

The Draft

Following is a draft of the definition paragraph on the insecure person. When
you read it, you'll notice several changes from the outline on page 201.

- Transitions have been added in several places. Some transitions let
  the reader know an example is coming, some transitions link one

point about the topic to another point, and other transitions connect an example to the topic sentence.

- Examples have been made concrete and specific.
- The word choice has been improved.

A Draft of a Definition Paragraph (Transitions are underlined.)

The insecure person is a person who needs other people to make him or her feel respected and important. The insecure person loves to brag about everything. <u>For instance</u>, a friend may brag about his car. He tells everyone he meets that he drives a Corvette. An insecure person tells you the price of everything. He wears expensive jewelry and tells you what it costs, <u>like</u> the person who always flashes his Rolex watch. <u>Another</u> insecure person will brag about her expensive clothes or make sure she always wears clothes with trendy labels, <u>another kind</u> of bragging. <u>Bragging is not the only way an insecure person tries to look good</u>; he or she may put other people down. Saying bad things about other people can put the insecure person on top. <u>For instance</u>, some friends were recently talking about another friend, Susan, who had just started a great new job Jill had to add some mean remarks about how lucky Susan had been to get the job since Susan really wasn't qualified for it. Jill hated having Susan look like a winner. The insecure person can hurt others <u>but also</u> suffers inside. <u>Such a person</u> can never relax because he or she always sees other people as competitors. <u>An example of this attitude is</u> seen in Luke, a college acquaintance who always plays pickup basketball games. Even though the games are just for fun, Luke doesn't enjoy any game unless he is the star. Luke is a typically insecure person, for he must always worry about what others think of him.

The following checklist may help you to revise the draft of your own definition paragraph.

Checklist

A Checklist for Revising the Draft of a Definition Paragraph

✔ Is my topic sentence clear?

✔ Have I written enough to define my term clearly?

✔ Is my definition interesting?

✔ Could it use another example?

✔ Could it use more details?

✔ Do I need to combine any sentences?

✔ Do I need any words, phrases, or sentences to link the examples or details to the topic sentence?

✔ Do I need any words, phrases, or sentences to reinforce the topic sentence?

Exercise 9

Practice

Adding Examples to a Draft of a Definition Paragraph

Two of the following paragraphs need examples with concrete, specific details to explain their points. Where the lines indicate, write an example with concrete, specific details. Each example should be at least two sentences long. The first paragraph is done for you.

1. Listlessness is the feeling that nothing is worth starting. After a hectic week, I often wake up on Saturday morning feeling listless. I just do not have the energy to do the things I intended to do. I may have planned to wash my car, for example, but I cannot bring myself to get going. I cannot put together the bucket, detergent, brushes, and window cleaner I need to start the process. I tell myself, "Why wash the car? It will probably rain anyway." Another time I feel listless is when I am faced with a big assignment. For instance, I hate to start a term paper because there is so much to do. I have to think of a topic, do research, read, take notes, plan, write, and revise. When I am faced with so many things to do, I don't do anything. I tell myself it is not worth starting because I will probably get a bad grade on the paper anyway. I put off getting started. I let listlessness get the better of me.

2. Complainers are people who must always express their unhappiness with life's imperfections. Complainers can be heard in every crowd. _____

_____

_____

_____ Another

place where complainers are found is in restaurants. _____

_____

_____

_____Complainers

even find fault when they receive a pleasant surprise. _____

_____

_____

_____

_____ It must be

difficult to be a complainer and be forever dissatisfied.

3. "Senioritis" is a disease that afflicts high school students in the last year of high school; its symptoms are restlessness, laziness, and craziness. Students with senioritis have had enough of high school. They are thinking about life after graduation, and so they cannot think about high school any more. Consequently, they are restless in school. _____

_____

_____

_____ Seniors suffering from senioritis just do not want to do any more schoolwork. They are lazy. _____

_____

_____

_____ Senioritis makes people crazy as well as lazy. Senior year is the time when students try all kinds of pranks and stunts. _____

_____

_____

_____ Years after high school, people say, "I can't believe I did such silly things! I must have had senior-itis."

Exercise 10

Practice

Identifying the Words That Need Revision in a Definition Paragraph

The following paragraph has too many vague, abstract words. Underline the words that you think should be replaced with more specific or concrete words or examples.

Self-respect is the ability to acknowledge one's own worth. People who respect themselves know that they are individuals with good and bad things and that they should not be conceited. On the other hand, they should also avoid being overly critical of themselves. Such people respect all parts of themselves. They respect their bodies by living right. They do not abuse their bodies by doing dangerous things. Self-respecting individuals do a lot for their minds, too. They continue to learn by going to school, by observing others at work, by reading, by making new friends, and so forth. In addition, they often nourish their spirit.

Some find meaning in the religion of their childhood; others look for a new faith.

They may experience inner growth by working in other ways. People with self-

respect recognize their physical, intellectual, and spiritual abilities and work to

develop them.

Exercise 11

Practice

Combining Sentences in a Definition Paragraph

The following definition paragraph has some short, choppy sentences that could be combined. These pairs or clusters of sentences are underlined. Combine each pair or cluster into one smooth sentence, and write the new sentence in the lines above the old ones.

A green thumb is a gift for making plants thrive. <u>My father owns a plant</u>

<u>nursery. He has a green thumb.</u> I have seen my father take the most dried-out,

rocky, bare soil and grow amazing flowers in it. <u>Once he received a shipment of</u>

<u>chrysanthemums. The chrysanthemums all looked ragged. They looked spindly.</u>

With loving care, my father nursed those chrysanthemums back to health. His

love for plants is a big part of his gift, but another part of his green thumb is my

father's knowledge of botany. <u>A plant may have a disease. My father knows what</u>

<u>to use to treat the disease.</u> He can identify almost any kind of shrub or tree.

<u>He is constantly reading books. They are books about plants and gardening. He</u>

<u>is constantly reading magazines. They are magazines about gardening and plants.</u>

My father knows and loves the plants he works with, and he brings life to every-

thing he touches with his green thumb.

Exercise 12

Practice

Adding the Right Transitions to a Definition Paragraph

In the following paragraph, circle the correct transition in each of the pairs.

Satisfaction is the sense of having had enough of whatever a person desires.

A boy may feel that he can never have enough vanilla fudge ice cream. He has

never satisfied his desire for this sweet treat. Similarly /In one instance, his

mother may crave just one more pair of shoes for her growing collection. Some

people have small desires while others have large ones. One time/ For example, an athlete who has spent years in training for the Olympics may experience satisfaction only when he or she achieves fame. In fact/ In another case, an ambitious business person may not be satisfied until he or she has twenty million dollars in the bank. Sometimes /Specifically, huge desires can lead to constant disappointment. Another time/ In fact, some people never marry because they are still looking for the perfect mate. They often feel as if life has let them down, but maybe they should have looked for real people and not perfect partners. Other people feel that they have been badly hurt by family members, and they never seem to get over that hurt. No apology can satisfy them, and the family is torn apart. One time Finally, satisfaction is closely connected to what people desire, what is enough to satisfy them, and what compromises they will make.

Final Lines Proofreading and Polishing: Definition

Before you prepare the final version of your definition paragraph, check your latest draft to see if it needs a few changes. You may want to check for good transitions, appropriate word choice, and effective details. If you compare the draft on page 204 to the following final version of the paragraph on the insecure person, you will see a few more revisions:

- The wording has been improved so that it is more precise.
- Transitions have been added to reinforce the topic sentence.
- The word "you" has been taken out so that the paragraph is consistent in person.

A Final Version of a Definition Paragraph (Changes from the draft are underlined.)

The insecure person is a person who needs other people to make him or her feel respected and important. <u>To get respect</u>, the insecure person loves to brag about everything. For instance, a friend may brag about his car. He tells everyone he meets that he drives a Corvette. An insecure person tells <u>people</u> the price of everything. He wears expensive jewelry and tells <u>people</u> what it costs, like the man who always flashes his Rolex watch. Another insecure person will brag about her expensive clothes or make sure she wears clothes with trendy labels, another kind of bragging. Bragging isn't the only way an insecure person tries to look good; he or she may also <u>criticize</u> other people. <u>Criticizing</u> others can put the insecure person on top. For instance, some friends were recently talking about another friend, Susan, who had just started a great new job. Jill had to add some mean remarks about how lucky Susan had been to get the job since Susan really wasn't qualified for it. Jill couldn't stand to have Susan look like a winner. The insecure person <u>like Jill</u> can hurt others but also suffers inside. Such a person can never relax because he or she always sees other people as competitors. An example of this attitude can be seen in Luke, a college acquaintance who always plays pickup basketball games. Even though the games are just for fun, Luke doesn't enjoy any game unless he is the star. Luke is a typically insecure person, for he must always worry about what others think of him.

As you prepare the final version of your definition paragraph, check your latest draft for any errors in spelling and any errors made in typing or copying.

Correcting Errors in the Final Version of a Definition Paragraph

Below are two definition paragraphs with the kinds of errors that are easy to overlook in a final version. Correct the errors by writing above the lines. There are thirteen errors in the first paragraph and nine in the second paragraph.

1. Nerve is a talent for pushing forward when most people would stay back. We've all exclamed "That really takes nerve!" when somebody has cut us off on the road or cut ahead of us in line. Nervey people has an ability to do what most people wouldn't think of doing they can be selfish, rude, or inconsiderate right in front of their victim's. For example, a nervy person can walk right by an older lady and takes the last seat on the buss A nervy person can reach right out and grab the last sale-priced sweater in the store, right out of another custumers hands. nervy people seem to be blind to the rights of others. And why shouldn't they be? After all, the only person they think about is the one they see in the mirror every morning.

2. Thoughtfulness is the ability to consider others' needs and personalities. Thoughtful people really listen to and observe others. They, notice more and remember more then less perceptive people. For example, thoughtful freinds do not forget birthdays, and they give specially selected, personnel gifts. Thoughtful people are tuned in to others' problem, too, and allways have an appropriate response. A thoughtful friend takes a coworker out to lunch when the coworker loses his job. A thoughtful mother make's her son's favorite dessert after his Little League team loses. Thoughtfulness shows up at times of joy too. Thoughtful people offer to babysit so parents can celebrate an anniversary. They bring the camera to a surprise party and send copies of the pictures to everyone. Everyone love the insight and generosity of a person gifted with thoughtfulness.

Lines of Detail: A Walk-Through Assignment

Write a paragraph that gives a personal definition of a secure person. To write the paragraph, follow these steps:

Step 1: List all your ideas about a secure person.

Step 2: Write at least five questions that can add details about a secure person. Answer the questions as a way of adding details to your list.

Step 3: Group your details; then survey your groups.

Step 4: Write a topic sentence that includes the term you are defining, puts the term into a category, and distinguishes the term from others in the category.

Step 5: Write an outline. Begin by writing the topic sentence and the groups of details. Then add more details and specific examples.

Step 6: Write a draft of your paragraph. To revise, check that you have enough examples, that your examples fit your definition, and that the examples are in an effective order. Combine any choppy sentences, and add transitions.

Step 7: Before you prepare the final version of your definition paragraph, check the punctuation, word choice, transitions, and grammar of your latest draft.

Writing Your Own Definition Paragraph

When you write on any of these topics, be sure to work through the stages of the writing process in preparing your definition paragraph.

1. Define an abstract term using concrete, specific details. Choose from the following list. You can begin by looking up the term in a dictionary, to be sure you understand the dictionary meaning. Then write a personal definition.

   You can begin by freewriting. If your instructor agrees, you can read your freewriting to a group for reactions and suggestions. If you prefer, you can begin by brainstorming a list of questions to help you define the term. Again, if your instructor agrees, you can work with a group to develop brainstorming questions. Here is the list of abstract terms:

loyalty	generosity	fun
charm	style	patience
boredom	charisma	persistence
rudeness	consideration	determination
ambition	selfishness	jealousy
suspicion	fear	loneliness
failure	shame	irritation
anger	self-deception	self-discipline
initiative	bliss	prejudice

2. Write a definition of a type of person. Develop your personal definition with specific, concrete details. You can choose one of the following types or choose your own type.

Freewriting on the topic is one way to begin. If your instructor agrees, you can read your freewriting to a group for reactions and suggestions. You can also begin by brainstorming a list of questions to help you define your term. If your instructor agrees, you can work with a group to develop brainstorming questions. Here is the list of types of people:

the procrastinator	the bully	the daredevil
the braggart	the bodybuilder	the jock
the chocaholic	the neatness fanatic	the apologizer
the organizer	the fitness fanatic	the joker
the inventor	the manipulator	the dreamer
the worrywart	the whiner	the buddy
the workaholic	the old reliable friend	the fan
the compulsive liar	the Mr./Ms. Fixit	the achiever

3. Think of one word that best defines you. In a paragraph, define that word, using yourself as a source of examples and details. To begin, you may want to freewrite about several words that define you; then you can select the most appropriate one.

4. Study the photograph below. Then write a paragraph that defines the emotion you see in the picture. Be sure to pick a word to identify the emotion first.

Name: _____ Section: _____

PEER REVIEW FORM FOR A DEFINITION PARAGRAPH

After you've written a draft of your definition paragraph, let a writing partner read it. When your partner has completed the form below, discuss the comments. Then repeat the same process for your partner's paragraph.

In the topic sentence, the term being defined is placed in this category or class: _____

_____

In the topic sentence, the characteristic(s) that make(s) the term different from others in its class or category is/are _____

_____

_____

The most enjoyable or interesting part of this definition starts with the words _____

_____

The part that could use a clear example or more details starts with the words _____

_____

I have questions about _____

_____

I would like to take out the part about _____

_____

_____

_____

Other comments: _____

_____

_____

_____

_____

_____

_____

_____

Reviewer's Name _____

WRITING FROM READING: Definition

Breaking the Bonds of Hate

Virak Khiev

Khiev, who immigrated to America at age ten, wrote this essay when he was a nineteen-year-old senior at the Blake School in Minneapolis, Minnesota. As you read his essay, you will notice how he defines the American Dream and two kinds of war.

Words You May Need to Know (corresponding paragraph numbers are in parentheses)

carrion (4): dead flesh
stereotype (5): an established image of someone or something, believed in by many people
unscrupulous (5): without a conscience
mentality (6): attitude, way of thinking

adversaries (7): enemies
immortalized (9): given the ability to live forever.
"the melting pot" (10): an image of America in which all the races and ethnic groups blend in harmony
mind-set (10): attitude

---

1 Ever since I can remember, I wanted the ideal life: a big house, lots of money, cars. I wanted to find the perfect happiness that so many people have longed for. I wanted more than life in the jungle of Cambodia. America was the place, the land of tall skyscrapers, televisions, cars, and airplanes.

2 In the jungles of Cambodia I lived in a refugee camp. We didn't have good sanitation or modern conveniences. For example, there were no inside bathrooms—only ones made from palm-tree leaves, surrounded by millions of flies. When walking down the street, I could smell the aroma of the outhouse; in the afternoon, the five- and six-year-olds played with the dirt in front of it. It was the only thing they had to play with, and the "fragrance" never seemed to bother them. And it never bothered me. Because I smelled it every day, I was used to it.

3 The only thing that bothered me was the war. I have spent half of my life in war. The killing is still implanted in my mind. I hate Cambodia. When I came to America nine years ago at the age of ten, I thought I was being born into a new life. No more being hungry, no more fighting, no more killing. I thought I had escaped the war.

4 In America, there are more kinds of material things than Cambodians could ever want. And here we don't have to live in the jungle like monkeys, we don't have to hide from mortar bombing and we don't have to smell the rotten human carrion. But for the immigrant, America presents a different type of jungle, a different type of war and a smell as bad as the waste of Cambodia.

5   Most Americans believe the stereotype that immigrants work hard, get a good education and have a very good life. Maybe it used to be like that, but not anymore. You have to be deceptive and unscrupulous in order to make it. If you are not, then you will end up like most immigrants I've known: living in the ghetto in a cockroach-infested house, working on the assembly line or in the chicken factory to support your family, getting up at three o'clock in the morning to take the bus to work and not getting home until 5:00 p.m.

6   If you're a kid my age, you drop out of school to work because your parents don't have enough money to buy you clothes for school. You may end up selling drugs because you want cars, money, and parties, as all teenagers do. You have to depend on your peers for emotional support because your parents are too busy working in the factory trying to make money to pay the bills. You don't get along with your parents because they have a different mentality: you are an American, and they are Cambodian. You hate them because they are never there for you, so you join a gang as I did.

7   You spend your time drinking, doing drugs and fighting. You beat up people for pleasure. You don't care about anything except your drugs, your beers and your revenge against adversaries. You shoot at people because they've insulted your pride. You shoot at the police because they are always bothering you. They shoot back, and then you're dead like my best friend Sinerth.

8   Sinerth robbed a gas station. He was shot in the head by the police. I'd known him since the sixth grade from my first school in Minneapolis. I can still remember his voice calling me from California. "Virak, come down here, man," he said. "We need you. There are lots of pretty girls down here." I promised him that I would be there to see him. The following year he was dead. I felt sorry for him. But as I thought it over, maybe it is better for him to be dead than to continue with the cycle of violence, to live with hate. I thought, "It is better to die than live like an angry young fool, thinking that everybody is out to get you."

9   When I was like Sinerth, I didn't care about dying. I thought that I was on top of the world, being immortalized by drugs. I could see that my future would be spent working on the assembly line like most of my friends, spending all my paycheck on the weekend and being broke again on Monday morning. I hated going to school because I couldn't see a way to get out of the endless cycle. My philosophy was "Live hard and die young."

10   I hated America because, to me, it was not the place of opportunities or the land of "the melting pot," as I had been told. All I had seen were broken beer bottles on the street and homeless people and drunks using the sky as their roof. I couldn't walk down the street without someone yelling out, "You gook" from his car. Once again I was caught in the web of hatred. I'd become a mad dog with the mind-set of the past: "When trapped in the

corner, just bite." The war mentality of Cambodia came back: get what you can and leave. I thought I came to America to escape war, poverty, fighting, to escape the violence, but I wasn't escaping; I was being introduced to a newer version of war—the war of hatred.

11   I was lucky. In Minneapolis, I dropped out of school in the ninth grade to join a gang. Then I moved to Louisiana, where I continued my life of "immortality" as a member of another gang. It came to an abrupt halt when I crashed a car. I wasn't badly injured, but I was underage, and the fine took all my money. I called a good friend of the Cambodian community in Minneapolis for advice (she'd tried to help me earlier). I didn't know where to go or whom to turn to. I saw friends landing in jail, and I didn't want that. She promised to help me get back in school. And she did.

12   Since then I've been given a lot of encouragement and caring by American friends and teachers who've helped me turn my life around. They opened my eyes to a kind of education that frees us all from ignorance and slavery. I could have failed so many times except for those people who believed in me and gave me another chance. Individuals who were willing to help me have taught me that I can help myself. I'm now a twelfth grader and have been at my school for three years; I plan to attend college in the fall. I am struggling to believe I can reach the other side of the mountain.

WRITING FROM READING: "Breaking the Bonds of Hate"

When you write on any of these topics, be sure to work through the stages of the writing process in preparing your paragraph.

1. In a paragraph, trace the turning points in Virak Khiev's life. Consider all the changes in his life and whether they made his life better or worse.

2. Khiev defines "the bonds of hate," a hate that kept him from achieving a good life. He says that he was a prisoner of his hatred for the country that denied him what he hoped for and of his hatred for his parents. He hated the endless cycle of poverty and struggle he found in the ghetto.
    Write your own paragraph defining the bonds of hate. That is, write a personal definition of the kind of hatred that can keep a person in chains.

3. By explaining what a gang does and why he joined one, Khiev defines the term "gang." Write your own definition of a gang.

4. Write a paragraph that gives your personal definition of the American Dream. Use examples from your life or the lives of people you know.

5. Khiev says that "for the immigrant, America presents a different type of jungle, a different type of war, and a smell as bad as the waste of Cambodia."

Write a paragraph defining "the immigrant's experience of America." Define the term using the experiences of one or more immigrants as examples. Your definition does not have to be similar to Khiev's. If you are an immigrant to America, you can use your own experiences as examples. If you are not an immigrant, interview one or more immigrants, taking notes and/or taping the interviews to gather details. Your classmates or teachers may include people to interview. Before you interview, have at least six questions to ask.

6. Khiev defines the luck in his life as the help of other people, particularly one woman who was a friend to the Cambodian community. In a paragraph, define the luck in your life.

CHAPTER 9

Cause and Effect

WHAT IS CAUSE AND EFFECT?

Almost every day, you consider the causes or effects of events so that you can make choices and take action. In writing a paragraph, when you explain the **reasons** for something, you are writing about **causes.** When you write about the **results** of something, you are writing about **effects.** Often in writing, you consider both the causes and effects of a decision, an event, a change in your life, or change in society, but in this chapter, you will be asked to *concentrate on either causes (reasons) or effects (results).*

Hints for Writing a Cause or Effect Paragraph

1. Pick a topic you can handle in one paragraph. A topic you can handle in one paragraph is one that (a) is not too big and (b) doesn't require research.

Some topics are so large that you probably can't cover them in one paragraph. Topics that are too big include ones like

Why People Get Angry
Effects of Unemployment on My Family

Other topics require you to research the facts and to include the opinions of experts. They would be good topics for a research paper, but not for a one-paragraph assignment. Topics that require research include ones like

The Causes of Divorce
The Effects of Television Viewing on Children

When you write a cause or effect topic, choose a topic you can write about by using what you already know. That is, make your topic smaller and more personal. Topics that use what you already know are ones like the following:

Why Children Love Video Games
The Causes of My Divorce

What Enlistment in the Navy Did for My Brother
How Alcoholics Anonymous Changed My Life

2. Try to have at least three causes or effects in your paragraph. Be sure you consider immediate and remote causes or immediate and remote effects. Think about your topic and gather as many causes or effects as you can *before* you start drafting your paragraph.

An event usually has more than one cause. Think beyond the obvious, the **immediate cause,** to more **remote causes.** For example, the immediate cause of your car accident might be the other driver who hit the rear end of your car. But more remote causes might include the weather conditions or the condition of the road.

Situations can have more than one result, too. If you take Algebra I for the second time and you pass the course with a C, an **immediate result** is that you fulfill the requirements for graduation. But there may be other, **more remote results.** Your success in Algebra I may help to change your attitude toward mathematics courses, or may build your confidence in your ability to handle college work, or may lead you to sign up for another course taught by the same teacher.

3. Make your causes and effects clear and specific. If you are writing about why short haircuts are popular, don't write, "Short haircuts are popular because everybody is getting one" or "Short haircuts are popular because they are a trend." If you write either of those statements, you have really said, "Short haircuts are popular because they are popular."

Think further. Have any celebrities been seen with this haircut? Write the names of actors, athletes, or musicians who have the haircut, or find out the name of the movie and the actor who started the trend. By giving specific details that explain, illustrate, or describe a cause or effect, you help the reader understand your point.

4. Write a topic sentence that indicates whether your paragraph is about causes or effects. You should not announce, but you can *indicate:*

> **not this:** The effects of my winning the scholarship are going to be discussed. (an announcement)
> **but this:** Winning the scholarship changed my plans for college. (indicates effects will be discussed)

You can *list* a short version of all your causes or effects in your topic sentence, like this:

> The high price of concert tickets has enriched a few performers and promoters, excluded many fans, and threatened the future of live entertainment.

You can just *hint* at your points by summarizing them, like this:

> The high price of concert tickets has brought riches to a few but hurt many others.

Or you can use words that *signal* causes or effects.

> **words that signal causes:** reasons, why, because, motives, intentions
> **words that signal effects:** results, impact, consequences, changed, threatened, improved

Exercise 1

Practice

Selecting a Suitable Topic for a Cause or Effect Paragraph

Below is a list of topics. Some are suitable for a cause or effect paragraph. Some are too large to handle in one paragraph, some would require research, and some are both too large and would require research. Put an *X* next to any topic that is not suitable.

1. _____ Why Dinosaurs Appeal to My Child

2. _____ Effects of Smoking Cigarettes

3. _____ Reasons I Attend College Part-Time

4. _____ The Impact of Technology on Education

5. _____ The Causes of Drug Abuse

6. _____ The Effects of AIDS on Our Society

7. _____ How Magic Johnson Changed My Perceptions of AIDS

8. _____ Why Marriages Fail

9. _____ The Causes of Anorexia

10. _____ The Impact of Violent Movies on Children

Exercise 2

Practice

Recognizing Cause and Effect in Topic Sentences

In the list below, if the topic sentence is for a cause paragraph, put a C next to it. If the sentence is for an effect paragraph, put an E next to it.

1. —— Adopting a stray dog had startling consequences for my family.

2. —— I decided to get a tattoo out of a desire to look different, to do something exciting, and to shock my parents.

3. —— Jack has several motives for proposing marriage.

4. —— Until I actually owned one, I never knew how a computer could change a person's work habits.

5. —— The television's remote control device has created conflicts in my marriage.

6. —— Children enjoy horror movies because the movies allow them to deal with their fears in a nonthreatening way.

7. —— Fast food restaurants are popular because they are cheap, they are convenient, and they are familiar.

8. —— The birth of my little sister had an unexpected impact on my family life.

9. _____ I am beginning to understand why my mother was a strict disciplinarian.

10. _____ Animal rights protesters have changed the fashion industry.

WRITING THE CAUSE OR EFFECT PARAGRAPH IN STEPS

Thought Lines Gathering Ideas: Cause or Effect

Once you've picked a topic, the next—and very important—step is getting ideas. Because this paragraph will contain only causes *or* effects and details about them, you must be sure you have enough causes or effects to write a developed paragraph.

Freewriting on a Topic

One way to get ideas is to freewrite on your topic. Since causes and effects are so clearly connected, you can begin by freewriting about both and then choose one—causes or effects—later.

If you were thinking about writing a cause or effect paragraph on owning a car, you could begin by freewriting something like this:

Freewriting on Owning a Car

A car of my own. Why? I needed it. Couldn't get a part time job without one. Because I couldn't get to work. Needed it to get to school. Of course I could have taken the bus to school. But I didn't want to. Feel like a grown-up when you have a car of your own. Freedom to come and go. I was the last of my friends to have a car. Couldn't wait. An old Camaro. But I fixed it up nicely. Costs a lot to maintain. Car payments, car loan. Car insurance.

Now you can review the freewriting and make separate lists of causes and effects you wrote down:

causes (reasons)
needed to get a part time job
needed to get to school
my friends had cars

effects (results)
feel like a grown-up
freedom to come and go
costs a lot to maintain
car payments
car loan
car insurance

Because you have more details on the effects of owning a car, you decide to write an effects paragraph.

Your list of effects can be used several ways. You can add to it if you think of ideas as you are reviewing your list. You can begin to group ideas in your list and then add to it. Following is a grouping of the list of effects. Grouping helps you see how many effects and details you have.

effects of getting my own car

effect 1:	I had to pay for the car and related expenses.
details:	costs a lot to maintain
	car payments
	car loan
	car insurance

effect 2:	I had the freedom to come and go.
details:	none

effect 3:	I felt like a grown-up.
details:	none

Will these effects work in a paragraph? One way to decide is to try to add details to the ones that have no details. Ask questions to get those details.

effect 2:   I had the freedom to come and go.

What do you mean?

Well, I didn't have to beg my father for his truck any more. I didn't have to get rides from friends. I could go to the city when I wanted. I could ride around just for fun.

effect 3: I felt like a grown up.

What do you mean, "like a grown up"?

Adults can go where they want, when they want. They drive themselves.

If you look carefully at the answers to the questions above, you'll find that the two effects are really *the same*. By adding details to both effects, you'll find that both are saying that owning a car gives you the adult freedom to come and go.

So the list needs another effect of owning a car. What else happened? How else did things change when you got your car? You might answer:

I worried about someone hitting my car.
I worried about bad drivers.
I wanted to avoid the scratches you get in parking lots.

With answers like these, your third effect could be

I became a more careful driver.

Now that you have three effects and some details, you can rewrite your list. You can add details as you rewrite.

List of Effects of Getting My Own Car

effect 1:	I had to pay for the car and related expenses.
details:	costs a lot to maintain
	car payments
	car loans
	car insurance
effect 2:	I had the adult freedom to come and go.
details:	didn't have to beg my father for his truck
	didn't have to get rides from friends

effect 3:   could go to the city when I wanted
could ride around for fun

effect 3:   I became a more careful driver.

details: worried about someone hitting the car
worried about bad drivers
wanted to avoid the scratches cars get in parking lots

Designing a Topic Sentence

With at least three effects and some details for each effect, you can create a topic sentence. The topic sentence for this paragraph should indicate that the subject is the *effects* of getting a car. You can summarize all three effects in your topic sentence, or you can just hint at them. A possible topic sentence for the paragraph can be

> Owning my own car cost me money, gave me freedom, and made me more careful about how I drive.

or

> Once I got a car of my own, I realized the good and bad sides of ownership.

With a topic sentence and a fairly extensive list of details, you are ready to begin the outlines step in preparing your paragraph.

Exercise 3

Collaborate

Designing Questions for a Cause or Effect Paragraph

Below are four topics for cause or effect paragraphs. For each topic below, write five questions that could lead you to ideas on the topic. (The first one is completed for you.) After you've written five questions for each topic, give your list to a member of your writing group. Ask him or her to add one question to each topic and then to pass the exercise on to the next member of the group. Repeat the process so that each group member adds to the lists of all the other members.

Later, if your instructor agrees, you can answer the questions (and add more questions and answers) as a way to begin writing a cause or effect paragraph.

1. **topic:** the effects of email on the workplace
   questions that can lead to ideas and details:

   a. Does everyone know how to use email?

   b. What is email used for at work?

   c. Does email save money at work?

   d. Do some workers misuse email?

   e. Can a boss spy on employees through their email?

   additional questions: With email, can some people work at home?

   Will offices be eliminated because of email?

   Does email save paper?

2. **topic:** why college students work part or full time
   questions that can lead to ideas and details:

   a. _____

   b. _____

   c. _____

   d. _____

   e. _____

   additional questions: _____

   _____

   _____

3. **topic:** the effects of road rage on drivers
   questions that can lead to ideas and detail:

   a. _____

   b. _____

   c. _____

   d. _____

   e. _____

   additional questions: _____

   _____

   _____

4. **topic:** why Americans are eating more meals away from home
   questions that could lead to ideas and detail:

   a. _____

   b. _____

   c. _____

   d. _____

   e. _____

   additional questions: _____

   _____

   _____

Creating Causes or Effects for Topic Sentences

For each of the following topic sentences, create three causes or effects, depending on what the topic sentence requires. The first one is completed for you.

1. **topic sentence:** Working out at the gym has both improved and complicated my life.

   a. I am in better physical shape than I have been in years.

   b. The physical exercise also gives me a mental boost.

   c. I now have to find time to fit my workouts into my busy schedule.

2. **topic sentence:** Small children may fear the dark for a number of reasons.

   a. _____

   _____

   b. _____

   _____

   c. _____

   _____

3. **topic sentence:** There are several reasons why some students are afraid to speak in class.

   a. _____

   _____

   b. _____

   _____

   c. _____

   _____

4. **topic sentence:** Credit cards can have negative effects on those who use them.

   a. _____

   _____

   b. _____

   _____

   c. _____

5. topic sentence: Taking too many college courses at one time can have serious consequences.

a. _____

_____

b. _____

_____

c. _____

_____

Outlines   **Devising a Plan: Cause or Effect**

With a topic sentence and a list of causes (or effects) and details, you can draft an outline of your paragraph. Once you have a rough outline, you can work on revising it. You may want to add to it, to take out certain ideas, to rewrite the topic sentence, or to change the order of the ideas. The following checklist may help you to revise your outline.

✔ Checklist

A Checklist for Revising the Outline of a Cause or Effect Paragraph

✔ Does my topic sentence make my point?

✔ Does it indicate whether my paragraph is about causes or effects?

✔ Does the topic sentence fit the rest of the outline?

✔ Have I included enough causes or effects to make my point?

✔ Have I included enough details?

✔ Should I eliminate any ideas?

✔ Is the order of my causes or effects clear and logical?

The Order of Causes or Effects

Looking at a draft outline can help you decide on the best order for your reasons or results. There is no single rule for organizing reasons or results. Instead, you should think about the ideas you are presenting and decide on the most logical and effective order.

For example, if you are writing about some immediate and some long-range effects, you might want to discuss the effects in a **time order.** You might begin with the immediate effect, then discuss what happens later, and end with what happens last of all. If you are discussing three or four effects that are not in any particular time order, you might save the most important effect for last, for an **emphatic order.** If one cause leads to another, then use the **logical order** of discussing the causes.

Compare the following outline on owning a car to the list of effects on pages 221–222. Notice that in the outline, the carefree side of owning a car comes first, and the cares of owning a car, the expense and the worry, come later. The topic sentence follows the same order.

An Outline for an Effects Paragraph

revised topic sentence: Owning my own car gave me freedom, cost me money, and made me careful about how I drive.

effect 1	I had the adult freedom to come and go.
details	I didn't have to beg my father for his truck. I didn't have to get rides from my friends. I could go to the city when I wanted. I could ride around for fun.
effect 2	I had to pay for the car and related expenses.
details	A car costs a lot to maintain. I had car payments. I had a car loan to pay. I had car insurance.
effect 3	I became a more careful driver.
details	I worried about someone hitting the car. I worried about bad drivers. I wanted to avoid the scratches cars can get in a parking lot.

Once you have a revised outline of your cause or effect paragraph, you are ready to begin writing your draft.

Exercise 5

Practice

Writing Topic Sentences for Cause or Effect Outlines

There are two outlines below. They have no topic sentences. Read the outlines carefully several times. Then write a topic sentence for each.

1. topic sentence: _____

_____

_____

details: When I don't get enough sleep, I get irritable.
Little things, like my friend's wise remarks, make me angry.
At work, I am not as patient as I usually am when a customer complains.
Lack of sleep also slows me down.
When I'm tired, I can't think as fast.
For instance, it takes me ten minutes to find a number in the phone book when I can usually find one in a minute.
When I'm tired, I am slower in restocking the shelves at the store where I work.
Worst of all, I make more mistakes when I'm tired.
Last Monday, I was so tired I locked myself out of my car.
Also, a sleepless night can cause me to ring up a sale the wrong way.
Then I have to spend hours trying to fix my mistake before my boss catches it.

2. topic sentence: _____

_____

_____

> **details:** Denise wasn't really interested in what I like to do.
> She hated sports.
> She always complained when we went to football games together.
> Denise was not much fun to be with.
> Whenever we were together, we wound up fighting over some trivial thing.
> For example, we once spent a whole evening fighting about what movie we should see.
> My main reason for breaking up was Denise's lack of trust in me.
> Denise couldn't believe I cared about her unless I showed her, every minute.
> She made me call her at least three times a day.
> She needed to know where I was at all times.
> She was jealous of the time I spent away from her.

Exercise 6

Practice

Revising the Order of Causes or Effects

Below are topic sentences and lists of causes or effects. Reorder each list according the directions given at the end of the list. Put a 1 by the item that would come first, a 2 by the next one, and so forth.

1. topic sentence: My brother went on a diet for several reasons.

_____ He couldn't exercise for as long as he was used to.

_____ His clothes were too tight.

_____ A doctor told him his weight was raising his cholesterol to a dangerous level.

Use this order: From least important to most important.

2. topic sentence: Cell phones have had a serious impact on driving.

_____ Some areas are banning the use of cell phones by drivers.

_____ Many accidents involved distracted drivers talking on their cell phones.

_____ People began to use cell phones while they drove because the phones were so convenient.

Use this order: Time order.

3. topic sentence: Losing my job had negative and positive effects on me.

_____ I was in a state of shock, since I had no idea I'd be laid off.

_____ I eventually realized the job had been a dead-end job and I could do better.

_____ I went from shock to a feeling of failure.

Use this order: The order indicated by the topic sentence, from bad to good.

Exercise 7   **Developing an Outline**

Practice

The outlines below need one more cause or effect and details for that cause or effect. Fill in the missing parts.

1. topic sentence: A promotion at work can be both rewarding and frightening.

effect 1:   Moving up is a sign that others respect a person's work.
details   My father was thrilled to be promoted to assistant manager.
His boss had told him the promotion was a reward for good work.
It also signaled his boss's faith in him.

effect 2:   In addition, a promotion is a chance to use more of
details   one's talents and skills.
I was delighted to move up in the shipping company I worked for.
I knew I would no longer be locked into the same dull, daily routine.
Instead, I could make some of my own decisions.

effect 3: _____

_____

details (at least two sentences) _____

_____

_____

_____

_____

2. topic sentence: People give many reasons for running red lights.

cause 1:   Some claim it was safe to do so.
details   They say they were all alone on a deserted road.
They say there was no traffic coming or going.
Therefore, they say, they didn't need to stop.

cause 2:   Many drivers swear they didn't see the light.
details   Some swear they were distracted by their children misbehaving in the car.
Others blame the dog; they say it jumped on them.
A few say they were changing the station on the radio and didn't look up in time.

cause 3: _____

_____

details (at least three sentences): _____

_____

_____

_____

_____

Rough Lines **Drafting and Revising: Cause or Effect**

Once you have an outline in good order, with a sufficient number of causes or effects and a fair amount of detail, you can write a first draft of the paragraph. When the first draft is complete, you can read and reread it, deciding how you'd like to improve it. The checklist below may help you revise.

✔ Checklist

A Checklist for Revising the Draft of a Cause or Effect Paragraph

✔ Does my topic sentence indicate cause or effect?

✔ Does it fit the rest of the paragraph?

✔ Do I have enough causes or effects to make my point?

✔ Do I have enough details for each cause or effect?

✔ Are my causes or effects explained clearly?

✔ Is there a clear connection between my ideas?

✔ Have I shown the links between my ideas?

✔ Do I need to combine sentences?

✔ Do I need an opening or closing sentence?

Linking Ideas in Cause or Effect

When you write about how one event or situation causes another or about how one result leads to another, you have to be very clear in showing the connections between events, situations, or effects.

One way to be clear is to rely on transitions. Some transitions are particularly helpful in writing cause and effect paragraphs.

Info BOX

Transitions for a Cause or Effect Paragraph

For cause paragraphs:

because	for	for this reason	since
due to			

For effect paragraphs:

as a result	hence	then	thus
consequently	in consequence	therefore	so

Making the Links Clear

Using the right transition is not always enough to make your point. Sometimes you have to write the missing link in your line of thinking so that the reader can understand your point. To write the missing link means writing phrases, clauses, or sentences that help the reader follow your point.

> **Not this:** Many mothers are working outside the home. Consequently, microwave ovens are popular.
>
> **But this:** Many mothers are working outside the home and have less time to cook. Consequently, microwave ovens, which can cook food in minutes, are popular.

The hard part of making clear links between ideas is that you have to put yourself in your reader's place. Remember that your reader cannot read your mind, only your paper. Connections between ideas may be very clear in your mind, but you must spell them out on paper.

Revising the Draft

Below is a draft of the paragraph on owning a car. When you read it, you'll notice many changes from the outlines stage on page 226:

- The details on "car payments" and "a car loan" said the same thing, so the repetition has been cut.
- Some details about the costs of maintaining a car and about parking have been added.
- The order of the details about the costs of a car has been changed. Now, paying for a car comes first, and maintaining it comes after.
- Sentences have been combined.
- Transitions have been added.

A Draft of an Effects Paragraph (Transitions are underlined.)

> Owning my own car gave me freedom, cost me money, and made me more careful about how I drive. <u>First of all</u>, my car gave me the adult freedom to come and go. I didn't have to beg my father for his truck or get rides from my friends any more. I could go to the city or even ride around for fun when I wanted. <u>On the negative side,</u> I had to pay for the car and related expenses. I had to pay for the car loan. I also paid for car insurance. <u>A car costs a lot to maintain, too.</u> I paid for oil changes, tune ups, tires, belts, and filters. <u>With so much of my money put into my car,</u> I became a more careful driver. I worried about someone hitting the car and watched out for bad drivers. <u>In addition,</u> I wanted to avoid the scratches a car can get in a parking lot, so I always parked far away from other cars.

Making the Connections Clear

Practice

Following are ideas that are connected, but the connection is not clearly explained. Rewrite each pair of ideas, making the connection clear.

> **1.** I never wrote a research paper in high school. Therefore, I did poorly in U.S. history in college.

Rewritten: _____

_____

_____

_____

(**Hint:** Did your U.S. history class require a research paper? Did you know how to write one?)

2. Young teens see actors and actresses smoking cigarettes in popular movies. The actors and actresses seem sophisticated and confident, so the young teens begin smoking.

Rewritten: _____

_____

_____

_____

(**Hint:** Do the young teens want to look sophisticated and confident?)

3. I drank three cups of coffee last night. Consequently, I couldn't sleep.

Rewritten: _____

_____

_____

_____

(**Hint:** Do you usually or rarely drink coffee at night? What substance in the coffee kept you awake?)

4. Pine Tree College was nearer home than Lake College. As a result, I went to Pine Tree College.

Rewritten: _____

_____

_____

(**Hint:** Did you want to go to a college close to home? Did you want to save money by attending college and living at home? Did you want a shorter trip to school?)

5. Some people believe the government interferes in the private life of the individual. Thus these people refuse to follow a seat belt law.

Rewritten: _____

_____

_____

_____

_____

_____

_____

(**Hint:** Do these people think a seat belt law is an interference in their private life?)

Practice

Revising a Paragraph by Adding Details

Each of the paragraphs below is missing details. Add details, at least two sentences, to each paragraph.

1. Becoming a parent has made me a happier, more cautious, and more ambitious person. I had never believed the friends who told me that parenthood would change my life, but they were right. First of all, parenthood has brought the joy of watching my child grow and change every day. I am constantly amazed when I realize that I am a part of this little person. My happiness is mixed with caution because I am protective of my child. I now listen to the weather report every day because I don't want my child to catch cold in the snow or sniffle in the rain. I scan every room in my apartment to clear it of the stray pencil or china coffee mug that my baby might pick up. Being a parent has made me more careful than I have ever been, and also more ambitious. _____

_____

_____

_____

Now that I have a child, I feel that I have been reborn as a more fulfilled, careful, and motivated person.

2. The school board had good reasons for closing Franklin High School. First, the school was extremely overcrowded. Franklin High was designed to hold 2,000 students; last year, it held 4,500. Expanding it to accommodate a population that continues to grow would be more expensive than building a new school. The school was not only too small; it was also in the wrong place. When it opened thirty-five years ago, Franklin High was surrounded by neighborhoods with families, but shortly after, the neighborhood changed. Today the school is surrounded by empty lots and decaying warehouses. Franklin has not kept up with the changing times in another respect. It lacks the modern technology a good school needs.

_____

_____

Although it is always difficult to see a high school close, Franklin High is too crowded, poorly located, and outdated to save.

 Exercise 10   **Revising a Draft by Combining Sentences.**

Practice   Combine the underlined sentences in the following paragraph. Write your combinations in the space above the original sentences.

There are powerful reasons why automobile manufacturers sell their products in television commercials featuring dogs. One reason is that dogs immediately create good feeling. <u>The dogs used are funny-looking. Some are cute. Some are beautiful.</u> Almost everyone likes dogs, so seeing a dog, viewers begin to feel good while they also see the car carrying the dog. The good feeling is transferred. The dogs in the cars are also associated with good times. Sometimes a dog is with children. <u>The children and dog are on their way to a picnic. Maybe they are going to a beach. Or they may be on their way to a Little League game.</u> At other times the dog is in the front seat with a pretty girl, and loud music plays as the two cruise down the road. Soon the dogs and cars in these commercials are linked to fun. In addition, the dogs represent the freedom of riding in a car. They always look happy riding in the automobiles. <u>Many of them are seen with their heads leaning out the car window. Their ears are flapping in the breeze.</u> The dogs seem to be grinning with the pleasure of a carefree ride. In these commercials, the happy dogs represent the good times and free moments we can all experience in a new car.

Final Lines **Proofreading and Polishing: Cause or Effect**

Following is the final version of the paragraph on owning a car. When you contrast the final version with the draft on page 230, you'll notice several changes:

- An introductory sentence has been added.
- Some sentences have been combined.
- Transitions have been revised.
- Some words have been changed so that the language is more precise.

Changes in style, word choice, sentence variety, and transitions can all be made before you decide on the final version of your paragraph. You may also want to add an opening or closing sentence to your paragraph.

A Final Version of an Effects Paragraph (Changes from the draft are underlined.)

> When I bought my first car, I wasn't prepared for all the changes it made in my life. Owning my own car gave me freedom, cost me money, and made me careful about how I drive. First of all, my car gave me the adult freedom to come and go. I didn't have to beg my father for his truck or get rides from my friends any more. I could go to the city or even ride around for fun when I wanted. On the negative side, I had to pay for the car and related expenses. I had to pay for both the car loan and car insurance. A car costs money to maintain, too. I paid for oil changes, tune ups, tires, belts, and filters. With so much of my money put into my car, I became a more careful driver. I worried about someone hitting the car and watched out for bad drivers. To avoid dangers in the parking lot as well as on the road, I always parked my car far away from other cars, keeping my car safe from scratches.

Before you prepare the final copy of your paragraph, check your latest draft for errors in spelling and punctuation and for any errors made in typing or copying.

Practice

Correcting a Final Copy of a Cause or Effect Paragraph

Following are one cause paragraph and one effects paragraph with the kinds of errors that are easy to overlook when you prepare the final version of an assignment. Correct the errors, writing above the lines. There are nine errors in the first (cause) paragraph and eleven errors in the second (effects) paragraph.

1. I signed up for an Introduction to Computers class this semster

so that I could get some useful skills. One reason I took the Course is

that, I want to be able to use my son's computer. He is ten years old and

knows all about e-mail and the Internet, but I don't know anything. At thirty,

I should be able to keep up with my son. I also want to know some thing my

son doesn't know, and that is how to do word processing. Now that I am in college, I have many written assinments that would be much easier if I knew word processing. A basic knowledge of computers would also be a important asset in my future. Right now I am in a low-paying job, but I think I get a better job if I had some computer skills. I know that banks, stores, schools, buisnesses, and hospitals all want to hire people who know how to use technolgy. I believe learning computer skills would help me at home, at school, and at work.

2. A major traffic jam can have a number of affects. Of coarse, the tie-up directly affects those caught in it and the drivers forced to find alternite routes. These people experience frustration and even rage as they realize they will be late for work, school, or other responsibility. When they finally excape the traffic snarl they take their nasty moods with them. They should consider themselves lucky to get out with no damage but lost time. Others has more to complain about. They get caught in the overheating cars or minor accidents that occur when traffic cannot move. these poor drivers have to deal with tow trucks, repair services, and even insurance agents. While most people think of a traffic jam's effect on drivers, not many think of it's effect on law enforcement. The local police or highway patrol must not only find the cause of the gridlock but deal with impatient drivers. While some search for the source of the traffic snarl. Other officers direct the masses of cars to merge or take a detour. A traffic jam calls for patience in every direction.

Lines of Detail: A Walk-Through Assignment

Write a paragraph on this topic: "Why Americans Are Eating More Meals Away from Home". To write your paragraph, follow these steps:

Step 1: Go back to Exercise 3, Topic 4, on page 223. It is the same topic as this assignment. If you have already done that exercise, you have 5 or more questions that can lead you to ideas and details. If you haven't done the exercise, do topic 4 now.

Step 2: Use the answers to your questions to prepare a list of ideas and details. Put the items on your list into groups of reasons and related details. Add to the groups until you have at least three reasons (and related details) why Americans are eating more meals away from home.

Step 3: Write a topic sentence that fits your reasons.

Step 4: Write an outline. Check that your outline has sufficient details and that you have put the reasons in the best order.

Step 5: Write a rough draft of your paragraph. Revise it until you have enough specific details to explain each reason, and make sure the links between your ideas are smooth and clear. Check whether any sentences should be combined and whether your paragraph could use an opening sentence or a concluding one.

Step 6: Before you prepare the final copy of your paragraph, check your latest draft for word choice, punctuation, transitions, and spelling.

Writing Your Own Cause or Effect Paragraph

When you write on any of the following topics, be sure to work through the stages of the writing process in preparing your cause or effect paragraph.

1. Write a cause paragraph on one of the following topics. You create the topic by filling in the blanks.

   Why I Chose _____

   Why I Stopped _____

   Why I Enjoy _____

   Why I Started _____

   Why I Hate _____

   Why I Bought _____

   Why I Decided _____

2. Write a one-paragraph letter of complaint to the manufacturers of a product you bought or the company that owns a hotel, restaurant, airlines, or some other service you used. In your letter, write at least three reasons why you (1) want your money refunded or (2) want the product replaced. Be clear and specific about your reasons. Be sure your letter has a topic sentence.

   If your instructor agrees, read a draft of your letter to a writing partner, and ask your partner to pretend to be the manufacturer or the head of the company. Ask your partner to point out where your ideas are not clear or convincing and where you make your point effectively.

3. Think of a current fad or trend. The fad can be a popular style of clothing, a kind of movie, a kind of music, a sport, a pastime, a gadget, an invention, an appliance, and so on.

Write a paragraph on the causes of this fad or trend or the effects of it.

If your instructor agrees, begin by brainstorming with a group. Create a list of three or four fads or trends. Then create a list of questions to ask (and answer) about each fad or trend. If you are going to write about causes, for example, you might ask questions like these:

What changes in society have encouraged this trend?
Have changes in the economy helped to make it popular?
Does it appeal to a specific age group? Why?
Does it meet any hidden emotional needs? For instance, is it a
    way to gain status or to feel safe or powerful?

If you are going to write about effects, you might ask questions like these:

Will this trend last?
Has it affected competitors?
Is it spreading?
Is the fad changing business, education, or the family?
Has it improved daily life?

4. If you have ever had one of the following experiences, write a paragraph about its effects on you.

moving to a new place	losing a friend
losing a job	starting a job
being a victim of a crime	breaking a bad habit
winning a contest	entering a relationship
undergoing surgery	ending a relationship

5. After looking at the photograph below, write a paragraph on why soccer is or is not popular in a particular country.

6. After looking at the photograph below, write a paragraph on the positive effects of the very young and the old creating a bond.

Name: _____   **Section:** _____

PEER REVIEW FORM FOR A CAUSE OR EFFECT PARAGRAPH

After you've written a draft of your cause or effect paragraph, let a writing partner read it. When your partner has completed the form below, discuss the comments. Then repeat the same process for your partner's paragraph.

This is a cause paragraph/an effect paragraph. (Circle one.)

In this paragraph, the causes or effects are _____

_____

_____

_____

(Briefly list all of them.)

The topic sentence uses these words to indicate cause or effect:_____

_____

_____(Write the exact words.)

The cause or effect that is most clearly explained is _____

_____

I would like to see more details added to _____

_____

I have questions about _____

I would like to take out the part about _____

Other comments: _____

_____

_____

_____

_____

_____

_____

_____

_____

Reviewer's Name: _____

WRITING FROM READING: Cause or Effect

Students in Shock

John Kellmayer

In this 1989 essay, John Kellmayer, an educator, explores the reasons why college students are stressed beyond their limits. He also discusses how colleges are reacting to student problems.

Words You May Need to Know (corresponding paragraph numbers are in parentheses)

warrant (6):   demand, call for, require

magnitude (9):   great importance

biofeedback (10):   A method of monitoring one's blood pressure, heart rate, and so on, as a way of monitoring and controlling stress

1   If you feel overwhelmed by your college experiences, you are not alone—many of today's college students are suffering from a form of shock. Going to college has always had its ups and downs, but today the "downs" of the college experience are more numerous and difficult, a fact that the schools are responding to with increased support services.

2   Lisa is a good example of a student in shock. She is an attractive, intelligent twenty-year-old college junior at a state university. Having been a straight-A student in high school and a member of the basketball and softball teams there, she remembers her high school days with fondness. Lisa was popular then and had a steady boyfriend for the last two years of school.

3   Now, only three years later, Lisa is miserable. She has changed her major four times already and is forced to hold down two part-time jobs in order to pay her tuition. She suffers from sleeping and eating disorders and believes she has no close friends. Sometimes she bursts out crying for no apparent reason. On more than one occasion, she has considered taking her own life.

4   Dan, too, suffers from student shock. He is nineteen and a freshman at a local community college. He began college as an accounting major but hated that field. So he switched to computer programming because he heard the job prospects were excellent in that area. Unfortunately, he discovered that he had little aptitude for programming and changed majors again, this time to psychology. He likes psychology but has heard horror stories about the difficulty of finding a job in that field without a graduate degree. Now he's considering switching majors again. To help pay for school, Dan works nights and weekends as a sales clerk at K-Mart. He doesn't get along with his boss, but since he needs the money, Dan feels he has no choice except to stay on the job. A few months ago, his girlfriend of a year and a half broke up with him.

5   Not surprisingly, Dan has started to suffer from depression and migraine headaches. He believes that in spite of all his hard work, he just isn't getting anywhere. He can't remember ever being this unhappy. A few times he considered talking to somebody in the college psychological counseling center. He rejected that idea, though, because he doesn't want people to think there's something wrong with him.

6   What is happening to Lisa and Dan happens to millions of college students each year. As a result, one-quarter of the student population at any time will suffer from symptoms of depression. Of that group, almost half will experience depression intense enough to warrant professional help. At schools across the country, psychological counselors are booked up months in advance. Stress-related problems such as anxiety, migraine headaches, insomnia, anorexia, and bulimia are epidemic on college campuses. Suicide rates and self-inflicted injuries among college students are higher now than at any other time in history. The suicide rate among college youth is fifty percent higher than among non-students of the same age. It is estimated that each year more than five hundred college students take their own lives. College health officials believe that these reported problems represent only the tip of the iceberg. They fear that most students, like Lisa and Dan, suffer in silence.

7   There are three reasons today's college students are suffering more than in earlier generations. First is a weakening family support structure. The transition from high school to college has always been difficult, but in the past there was more family support to help get through it. Today, with divorce rates at a historical high and many parents experiencing their own psychological difficulties, the traditional family is not always available for guidance and support. And when students who do not find stability at home are bombarded with numerous new and stressful experiences, the results can be devastating.

8   Another problem college students face is financial pressure. In the last decade tuition costs have skyrocketed—up about sixty-six percent at public college and ninety percent at private schools. And at the same time that tuition costs have been rising dramatically, there has been a cutback in federal aid to students. College loans are now much harder to obtain and are available only at near-market interest rates. Consequently, most college students must work at least part-time. And for some students, the pressure to do well in school while holding down a job is too much to handle.

9   A final cause of student shock is the large selection of majors available. Because of the magnitude and difficulty of choosing a major, college can prove a time of great indecision. Many students switch majors, some a number of times. As a result, it is becoming commonplace to take five or six years to get a degree. It can be depressing to students not only to have taken courses that don't count towards a degree but also to be faced with

the added tuition costs. In some cases these costs become so high that they force students to drop out of college.

10   While there is no magic cure-all for student shock, colleges have begun to recognize the problem and are trying in a number of ways to help students cope with the pressures they face. First of all, many colleges are upgrading their psychological counseling centers to handle the greater demand for services. Additional staff is being hired, and experts are doing research to learn more about the psychological problems of college students. Some schools even advertise these services in student newspapers and on campus radio stations. Also, third- and fourth-year students are being trained as peer counselors. These peer counselors may be able to act as a first line of defense in the battle for students' well-being by spotting and helping to solve problems before they become too big for students to handle. In addition, stress-management workshops have become common on college campuses. At these workshops, instructors teach students various techniques for dealing with stress, including biofeedback, meditation, and exercise.

11   Finally, many schools are improving their vocational counseling services. By giving students more relevant information about possible majors and career choices, colleges can lessen the anxiety and indecision often associated with choosing a major.

12   If you ever feel that you're "in shock," remember that your experience is not unique. Try to put things in perspective. Certainly, the end of a romance or failing an exam is not an event to look forward to. But realize that rejection and failure happen to everyone sooner or later. And don't be reluctant to talk to somebody about your problems. The useful services available on campus won't help you if you don't take advantage of them.

WRITING FROM READING: "Students in Shock"

When you write on any of the topics below, be sure to work through the stages of the writing process in preparing your cause or effects paragraph.

1. Write a one-paragraph summary of "Students in Shock." Include the three significant reasons college students are in distress, and discuss how colleges are reacting to student stress. Remember to use logical and effective transitions throughout your summary.

2. Write a paragraph about the main causes of stress in your life. To begin, list everything that caused you stress in the past twenty-four hours. Do not think about whether the cause was minor or major; just list all the causes you can remember. If you felt stress waiting for a traffic light to change, for example, write it down.

   When you have completed your list, read it to a writing partner or group. Ask your listener(s) to help you identify three or more causes of stress in your life. Then work alone to prepare your paragraph.

3. Write a paragraph on the positive effects of your attending college. Be sure you have at least three effects.

4. Write a paragraph on the negative effects of your attending college. Be sure you have at least three effects.

5. Write a letter to your college instructors. Your letter will be a paragraph giving at least three reasons why students seem tired in class.

6. Stress has different effects on different people. Freewrite about the effects of college stress on you and people you know. Use your freewriting to plan and write a paragraph on the effects of college stress. Use you and your friends' experiences as examples of the different effects of college stress.

CHAPTER 10

Argument

WHAT IS ARGUMENT?

A written **argument** is an attempt to *persuade* a reader to think or act in a certain way. When you write an argument paragraph, your goal is to get people to see your point so that they are persuaded to accept it and perhaps to act on it.

In an argument paragraph, you take a stand. Then you support your stand with reasons. In addition, you give details for each reason. Your goal is to persuade your reader by making a point that has convincing reasons and detail.

Hints for Writing an Argument Paragraph

1. Pick a topic you can handle. Your topic should be small enough to be covered in one paragraph. For instance, you can't argue effectively for world peace in just one paragraph.

2. Pick a topic you can handle based on your own experience and observation. Topics like legalizing drugs, gun control, capital punishment, or air pollution require research into facts, figures, and expert opinions to make a complete argument. They are topics you can write about convincingly in a longer research paper, but for a one-paragraph argument, pick a topic based on what you've experienced yourself:

not this topic: Organized Crime
but this topic: Starting a Crime Watch Program in My Neighborhood

3. Do two things in your topic sentence: name the subject of your argument, and take a stand. The following topic sentences do both:

subject   takes a stand
The college cafeteria should serve more healthy snacks.

subject   takes a stand
High school athletes who fail a course should not be allowed to play on a school team.

You should take a stand, but *don't* announce it:

> **not this:** This paragraph will explain why Springfield needs a teen center.
>
> **but this:** Springfield should open a teen center. (This is a topic sentence with a subject and a stand.)

4. Consider your audience. Think about why these people should support your points. How will they be likely to object? How will you get around these objections? For instance, you might want to argue to the residents of your community that the intersection of Hawthorne Road and Sheridan Street needs a traffic light. Would anyone object?

At first, you might think, "No. Why would anyone object? The intersection is dangerous. There's too much traffic there. People risk major accidents getting across the intersection." But if you think further about your audience, which is the people in your community, you might identify these objections: Some town residents may not want to pay for a traffic signal. Some drivers may not want to spend extra time waiting for a light to change.

There are several ways to handle objections:

> You can *refute* an objection. To refute it means to prove it isn't valid; it isn't true. For instance, if someone says that a light wouldn't do any good, you might say that a new light has already worked in a nearby neighborhood.
>
> Sometimes it's best to admit the other side has a point. You have to *concede* that point. For instance, traffic lights do cost money. And waiting for a light to change does take time.
>
> Sometimes you can *turn an objection into an advantage*. When you acknowledge the objection and yet use it to make your own point, you show that you've considered both sides of the argument. For instance, you might say that the price of a traffic signal at the intersection is well worth it because that light will buy safety for all the drivers who try to cross Hawthorne Road and Sheridan Street. Or you might say that waiting a few moments for the light to change is better than waiting many minutes for an opening in the heavy traffic of the intersection.

5. Be specific, clear, and logical in your reasons. As always, think before you write. Think about your point and your audience. Try to come up with at least three reasons for your position.

Be careful that your reasons do not overlap. For instance, you might write the following:

topic sentence:	College students should get discounts on movie tickets.
audience:	Owners of movie theaters.
reasons:	1. Many college students can't afford current ticket prices.
	2. The cost of tickets is high for most students.
	3. More people in the theater means more popcorn and candy sold at the concession stand.

But reasons 1 and 2 overlap; they are really part of the same reason.

Be careful not to argue in a circle. For instance, if you say, "One reason for having an afterschool program at Riverside Elementary School is that we need one there," you've just said, "We need an afterschool program because we need an afterschool program."

Finally, be specific in stating your reasons:

not this: One reason to start a bus service to and from the college is to help people.

but this: A bus service to and from the college would encourage students to leave their cars at home and use travel time to study.

Exercise 1
Practice

Recognizing Good Topic Sentences in an Argument Paragraph

Some of the topic sentences below are appropriate for an argument paragraph. Some are for topics that are too large for one paragraph, and some are for topics that would require research. Some are announcements. Some do not take a stand. Put *OK* next to the sentences that would work well in an argument paragraph.

1. _____ People should try to cure their own addictions.

2. _____ The empty lot by the post office is a serious problem.

3. _____ We must stop offshore oil drilling in American waters.

4. _____ Bicycle safety should be taught at Deerfield Elementary School.

5. _____ We need stricter penalties for criminals.

6. _____ Something must be done about aggressive drivers.

7. _____ The City Parks and Recreation Department should put more picnic tables at Veterans' Park.

8. _____ College students deserve more financial aid.

9. _____ Crescent College needs a larger financial aid staff.

10. _____ The reasons to ban skateboarding at Miller Mall will be the subject of this essay.

Exercise 2
Collaborate

Recognizing and Handling Objections

Below are the topic sentences of arguments. Working with a group, list two possible objections to each argument that might come from the specific audience identified. Then think of ways to handle each objection, either by refuting it, conceding it, or trying to turn it to your advantage. On the lines provided, write the actual sentence(s) you would use in a paragraph.

1. **topic sentence:** The college library, which is currently open until 10:00 P.M., should be open until midnight every night.
   audience: The deans, vice president and president of the college.
   possible objections from this audience:

   a. _____

   b. _____

answering objections:

a. _____

_____

b. _____

_____

2. **topic sentence:** The local mall [you pick a specific mall] needs more security officers to patrol inside and outside the mall.
   audience: the owners of the mall
   possible objections from this audience:

   a. _____

   b. _____

   answering objections:

   a. _____

   _____

   b. _____

   _____

3. **topic sentence:** Atlantic Township should ban parking at the beach parking lot after midnight.
   audience: teen residents of Atlantic Township
   possible objections from this audience:

   a. _____

   b. _____

   answering objections:

   a. _____

   _____

   b. _____

   _____

4. **topic sentence:** Dogs in Riverdell must be on a leash in all public parks.
   audience: Dog owners in Riverdell
   possible objections from this audience:

   a. _____

   b. _____

answering objections:

a. _____

_____

b. _____

_____

5. topic sentence: Clearbrook patients who wait more than an
hour for their scheduled doctor's appointment should not have
to pay for the appointment unless the doctor was dealing with
an emergency.
audience: The doctors of Clearbrook
possible objections from this audience:

a. _____

b. _____

answering objections:

a. _____

_____

b. _____

_____

WRITING THE ARGUMENT PARAGRAPH IN STEPS

Thought Lines   Gathering Ideas: Argument

Imagine that your instructor has given you this assignment:

> Write a one-paragraph letter to the editor of your local newspaper.
> Argue for something in your town that needs to be changed.

One way to begin is to brainstorm for some specific thing that you can
write about:

Is there a part of town that needs to be cleaned up?
Should something be changed at a school?
What do I notice on my way to work or school that needs improvement?
What could be improved in my neighborhood?

By answering these questions, you may come up with one topic, and then
you can list ideas on it:

topic

Cleaning Up Roberts Park

ideas

dirty and overgrown
benches are all cracked and broken
full of trash
could be fixed up
people work nearby
they would use it

You can consider your audience and possible objections:

audience

local people of all ages who read the local paper

possible objections from this audience

would cost money
more important things to spend money on

answering objections

Money would be well spent to beautify the downtown.
City children could play there in the fresh air and in nature; workers could eat lunch there.

Grouping Your Ideas

Once you have a list, you can start grouping the ideas on your list. Some of the objections you wrote down may actually lead you to reasons that support your argument. That is, by answering objections, you may come up with reasons that support your point. Following is a list with a point to argue, three supporting reasons, and some details about cleaning up Roberts Park.

A List for an Argument Paragraph

point:	We should fix up Roberts Park.
reason	Improving the park would make the downtown area more attractive to shoppers.
details	Shoppers could stroll in the park or rest from their shopping. Friends could meet in the park for a day of shopping and lunch.
reason	City children could play in the park.
details	They could get fresh air. They could play in a natural setting.
reason	Workers could get lunch outdoors.
details	Several office complexes are nearby. Workers would take a break outdoors.

With three reasons and some detail for each, you can draft a topic sentence. Remember that your topic sentence for an argument should (1) name your subject and (2) take a stand. Below is a topic sentence about Roberts Park that does both.

subject   **takes a stand**

Roberts Park should be cleaned up and improved.

With a topic sentence, you are ready to move on to the outlines stage of preparing an argument paragraph.

Practice

Distinguishing Between Reasons and Details

Each list below has three reasons and details for each reason. Write *reason 1*, *reason 2*, or *reason 3* next to the reasons on each list. Then write *detail for 1*, *detail for 2*, or *detail for 3* by the items that give detail about each reason. There may be more than one sentence of details connected to one reason.

1. **topic sentence:** The city needs to pick up garbage at my apartment complex three times a week, not twice.

   _____ Garbage spills out past the dumpster.

   _____ People throw their garbage on top of already loaded dumpsters; the bags fall and split open.

   _____ Uncovered garbage that piles up is a health hazard.

   _____ Too much garbage accumulates when the schedule allows for only two pickups.

   _____ Flies buzz over the garbage, a sign of dangerous contamination that can spread.

   _____ The roaches from the garbage area spread into the apartments, carrying disease.

   _____ Trash piles make people lose pride in their neighborhood.

   _____ Apartment residents are starting to litter the parking lot because they've lost respect for their homes.

   _____ One long-time resident is thinking of moving to a better neighborhood.

2. **topic sentence:** Children under ten years of age should not be permitted in the Mountain Mall unless they are accompanied by an adult.

   _____ It is not safe for children to be alone in the mall.

   _____ Unsupervised children cause trouble for mall merchants.

   _____ Children left alone in the mall are not always happy with their freedom.

   _____ I've seen one nine-year-old boy roam the mall for hours, looking forlorn.

   _____ Sometimes pairs of sad young girls wait by the food court for an hour until Mom, who is late, remembers to pick them up.

   _____ Once I saw two seven-year-old boys walk back and forth in front of my store for half an hour with nothing to do.

_____ Children have been kidnapped in malls.

_____ If a child gets sick at the mall, will he or she know what to do?

_____ Bored children run through stores, chasing each other.

_____ I saw one child shoplifting.

Exercise 4

Practice

Finding Reasons to Support an Argument

Give three reasons that support each point. In each case, the readers of your local newspaper will be the audience for an argument paragraph.

1. point: Local elections should create an option for voting online.

    reasons: a. _____

                    b. _____

                    c. _____

2. point: Our state must ban the sale of all fireworks.

    reasons: a. _____

                    b. _____

                    c. _____

3. point: Parenting should be a required course for all high school students.

    reasons: a. _____

                    b. _____

                    c. _____

4. point: Public education should start with preschool, at age three.

    reasons: a. _____

                    b. _____

                    c. _____

Outlines **Devising a Plan: Argument**

With a topic sentence and a list of reasons and detail, you can draft an outline. Then you can review it, making whatever changes you think it needs. The checklist following may help you to review and revise your outline.

> ✓ **Checklist**
>
> **A Checklist for Revising an Argument Outline**
>
> ✔ Does my topic sentence make my point? Does it state a subject and take a stand?
>
> ✔ Have I considered the objections to my argument so that I am arguing intelligently?
>
> ✔ Do I have all the reasons I need to make my point?
>
> ✔ Do any reasons overlap?
>
> ✔ Are my reasons specific?
>
> ✔ Do I have enough details for each reason?
>
> ✔ Are my reasons in the best order?

The Order of Reasons in an Argument

When you are giving several reasons, it is a good idea to keep the most convincing or most important reason for last. Saving the best for last is called using **emphatic order.** For example, you might have these three reasons to tear down an abandoned building in your neighborhood: (1) The building is ugly. (2) Drug dealers are using the building. (3) The building is infested with rats. The most important reason, the drug dealing, should be used last for an emphatic order.

Following is an outline on improving Roberts Park. When you look at the outline, you'll notice several changes from the list on page 249:

- Since the safety of children at play is important, it is put as the last detail.
- Some details have been added.
- A sentence has been added to the end of the outline. It explains why improving the park is a good idea even to people who will never use the park themselves. It is a way of answering these people's objections.

An Outline for an Argument Paragraph

topic sentence: Roberts Park should be cleaned up and improved.

reason	Improving the park would make the downtown area more attractive to shoppers.
details	Shoppers could stroll through the park or rest there after shopping. Friends could meet at the park for a day of shopping and lunch.
reason	Workers from nearby offices and stores could eat lunch outdoors.
details	Several office complexes are nearby. An hour outdoors is a pleasant break from work.
reason	City children could play there.

details	They would get fresh air.
	They would play on grass, not on asphalt.
	They would not have to play near traffic.
final idea	An attractive park improves the city, and all residents benefit when the community is beautified.

Exercise 5

Practice

Working with the Order of Reasons in an Argument Outline

Below are topic sentences and lists of reasons. For each list, put an X by the reason that is the most significant, the reason you would save for last in an argument paragraph.

1. topic sentence: Crandall Airport must provide better lighting at its long-term parking lot.

reason 1: _____ Car break-ins would be less likely in a well-lighted parking lot.

reason 2: _____ Bright lights would protect people from physical assault.

reason 3: _____ Better lights would make it easier for people to find their cars.

2. topic sentence: Our town's library needs a collection of DVDs that can be checked out.

reason 1: _____ More young people would use the library if it had DVDs.

reason 2: _____ DVDs are very popular.

reason 3: _____ DVDs include specially edited versions of block-buster movies, with interviews and background, for film study.

3. topic sentence: Parents should not let their children play in the sun for hours.

reason 1: _____ Too much sun in childhood can lead to skin cancer later in life.

reason 2: _____ Too much sun, even in childhood, can cause premature wrinkling in adults.

reason 3: _____ The sun can cause headaches and irritability in all age groups.

4. topic sentence: Seven-year-olds should be given a small allowance to spend as they wish.

reason 1: _____ Seven-year-olds see other children their age with spending money.

reason 2: _____ Children need to learn to handle money responsibly.

reason 3: _____ Learning about making change is good practice in math skills.

Exercise 6

Practice

Recognizing Reasons That Overlap

Below are topic sentences and lists of reasons. In each list, two reasons overlap. Put an X by the two reasons that overlap.

1. topic sentence: Dollar Days Discount Store needs more sales and service staff.

a. _____ A lack of cashiers leads to long lines at the few checkout counters.

b. _____ Customers with questions can rarely find a salesperson to direct them to the correct part of the store.

c. _____ Many of the items in the store are not marked with a price.

d. _____ Customers wait in endless lines to pay for their purchases.

2. topic sentence: The college cafeteria should lower its prices.

a. _____ Prices are too high for most students.

b. _____ Lower prices would actually mean a profit for the cafeteria because more students would use the cafeteria.

c. _____ Many students cannot afford to eat in the cafeteria.

d. _____ The cafeteria has to compete with nearby, cheaper restaurants.

3. topic sentence: Our college needs a larger, lighted sign at the entrance.

a. _____ Some residents of our town have never heard of our college, so a large sign would be good publicity.

b. _____ Visitors to the college have a hard time finding it.

c. _____ Students who are preoccupied sometimes drive right past the entrance to their college at night.

d. _____ A better sign would make people more aware of the college.

Exercise 7

Practice

Identifying a Reason That Is Not Specific

For each of the following lists, put an X by the reason that is not specific.

1. topic sentence: The senior class should hold a senior citizens' day to bring elderly people to school for a day of fun and entertainment.

a. _____ Teenagers would enjoy talking to older people, especially since many teens do not have much contact with their own grandparents.

b. _____ Planning a day's entertainment would teach teens how to organize a major event.

    c. _____ The older people would benefit from the day.

    d. _____ Each generation would learn not to stereotype the other.

2. topic sentence: American college students should learn a foreign language.

    a. _____ Countries that compete with us economically, like Japan or Germany, have a competitve edge because their children routinely learn English.

    b. _____ It is often easier for a person to get a good job if he or she speaks two languages.

    c. _____ Learning a new language broadens a person's horizons.

    d. _____ Most Americans, at home or at work, have to interact with immigrants or visitors who do not speak English.

3. topic sentence: Woodhaven needs a daycare center that is open twenty-four hours a day.

    a. _____ Many parents work the night shift, but daycare centers do not take them into account.

    b. _____ Small children need a place to stay.

    c. _____ Other parents have nighttime emergencies and have nowhere to leave their children.

    d. _____ A round-the-clock daycare center might reduce the number of children left home alone at night.

Exercise 8

Practice

Adding Details to an Outline

Following is part of an outline. It includes a topic sentence and three reasons. Add at least two sentences of details to each reason. Your details may be examples or description.

topic sentence: The staff at Bargain Supermarket should enforce the "Nine Items or Less" rule at the express checkout lane.

    reason: Customers who follow the rule must suffer because of people who don't obey the rule.

    details: _____

    _____

    details: _____

    _____

    reason: Not enforcing the rule can create unpleasant confrontations among customers.

    details: _____

    details: _____

    _____

reason: If it fails to enforce the rule, Bargain Supermarket may lose customers.

details: _____

_____

details: _____

_____

Rough Lines Drafting and Revising: Argument

Once you are satisfied with your outline, you can write the first draft of your paragraph. When you have completed it, you can begin revising the draft so that your argument is as clear, smooth, and convincing as it can be. The checklist below may help you with your revisions.

✔ Checklist

A Checklist for Revising the Draft of an Argument Paragraph

✔ Do any of my sentences need combining?

✔ Have I left out a serious or obvious reason?

✔ Should I change the order of my reasons?

✔ Do I have enough details?

✔ Are my details specific?

✔ Do I need to explain the problem or issue I am writing about?

✔ Do I need to link my ideas more clearly?

✔ Do I need a final sentence to stress my point?

Checking Your Reasons

Be sure that your argument has covered all the serious or obvious reasons. Sometimes writers get so caught up in drafting their ideas they forget to mention something very basic to the argument. For instance, if you were arguing for a leash law for your community, you might state that dogs who run free can hurt people and damage property. But don't forget to mention another serious reason to keep dogs on leashes: Dogs who are not restrained can get hurt or killed by cars.

One way to see if you have left out a serious or obvious reason is to ask a friend or classmate to read your draft and to react to your argument. Another technique is to put your draft aside for an hour or two and then read it as if you were a reader, not the writer.

Explaining the Problem or the Issue

Sometimes your argument discusses a problem so obvious to your audience that you do not need to explain it. On the other hand, sometimes you need to explain a problem or issue so that your audience can understand your point. If you tell readers of your local paper about teenage vandalism at Central High School, you probably need to explain what kind of vandalism has occurred and how often. Sometimes it is smart to convince readers of the seriousness of a situation by explaining it a little so that they will be more interested in your argument.

Transitions That Emphasize

In writing an argument paragraph, you can use different transitions, depending on how you present your point. But no matter how you present your reasons, you will probably want to *emphasize* one of them. Below are some transitions that can be used for emphasis.

Info BOX

Transitions to Use for Emphasis

above all	finally	most important	most significant
especially	mainly	most of all	primarily

For example, by saying, "*Most important*, broken windows at Central High School are a safety problem," you put the emphasis for your audience on this one idea.

A Draft

Following is a draft of the argument paragraph on Roberts Park. When you read it, you'll notice these changes from the outline on pages 252–253:

- A description of the problem has been added.
- Details have been added.
- Short sentences have been combined.
- Transitions, including two sentences of transition, have been added. "Most important" and "best of all"—transitions that show emphasis—have been included.

A Draft of an Argument Paragraph (Transitions are underlined.)

Roberts Park was once a pretty little park, but today it is overgrown with weeds, cluttered with trash and rusty benches. Roberts Park should be cleaned up and improved. Improving the park would make the downtown area more attractive to shoppers. Shoppers could stroll through a renovated park or rest there after shopping. Friends could <u>also</u> meet there for a day of shopping and lunch. <u>Shoppers are not the only ones who could enjoy the park.</u> Workers from nearby offices and stores could eat lunch outdoors. Several office complexes are near the park, and workers from these offices could bring their lunch to work and eat outside in good weather. I think many people would agree that an hour spent outdoors is a pleasant break from work. <u>Most important</u>, city children could play in an improved Roberts Park. They would get fresh air while they played on grass, not asphalt. <u>Best of all</u>, they would not have to play near traffic. <u>Children, shoppers, and workers would benefit from a clean-up of Roberts Park, but so would others</u>. An attractive park improves the city, and all residents benefit when a community is beautified.

| Exercise 9 | **Adding an Explanation of the Problem to an Argument Paragraph** |

Practice

This paragraph could use an explanation of the problem before the thesis. Write a short explanation of the problem in the lines provided.

_____

_____

_____

_____

  Directional and exit signs on Lake Highway must be designed with larger lettering. Larger lettering would help a significant number of our residents. Lake Valley has many older residents whose vision is not perfect. Signs in large letters would make driving easier for those who are currently straining to see the right exit, only to find it as they pass it. Another group that would appreciate bigger lettering is the visitors to the area. Many of them are struggling to find their way to a motel, restaurant, or store they've never seen, and they are not sure where to turn. Better signs would reduce their confusion and make their visit more pleasant. Most of all, larger lettering would result in safer driving. If signs were larger, drivers would see them sooner. Thus they could change lanes sooner and more safely as they merged into the correct lane or got to an exit ramp. Many of the accidents caused by drivers suddenly switching lanes would be avoided. Better signs would then lead to safer, smoother driving.

| Exercise 10 | **Recognizing Transitions in an Argument Paragraph** |

Practice

Underline all the transitions—words, phrases, or sentences—in the paragraph below. Put a double line under any transitions that emphasize.

  At the start of each workday, millions head to their jobs with good intentions. However, many start the day already tired and stressed and therefore unable to make their best efforts. They are living proof that workers in America need four weeks' annual paid vacation. Employees need more time off because they are facing more stress in the workplace. Many are working longer hours; some hold a second job to supplement their income. Bosses demand more productivity and new skills. Employees face further stress at home, too. When both parents work outside the home, they strain to find time for their children and their household duties. When one parent works, the family may face economic hardship due to the loss of income of the stay-at-home parent. Single parents struggle to cope alone. Those without partners or children may seem lucky, but they, too, fight to pay the bills and find time for a personal life. More vacation time would destress these workers, but most of all, it would also benefit employers. Exhausted, burnt-out workers cannot give their best when they are struggling just to get through the day. On the other hand, people who have sufficient time to rest return to work with renewed energy. Thus everybody—employees and employers—profits from more vacation for workers.

Revising a Draft by Combining Sentences

Practice

In the following paragraph, combine each cluster of underlined sentences into one clear, smooth sentence. Write your combinations in the space above the original sentences.

My dog loves to ride in the car. He sticks his head out the window. He feels the breeze ruffle his fur. Unfortunately, he can't travel much because our town has no beach, green fields, or public park that allows dogs. Sandy Heights needs a dog park. A dog park would give dogs a place to run freely. Hundreds of residents in this town have dogs. These dogs can walk only on a leash. They can walk only on narrow sidewalks. They need a place in the open. A dog park would give dogs freedom as well as a place to socialize. Most dogs love to meet other dogs. They love to sniff other dogs. They love to run with other dogs. They love to play with other dogs. A dog park is their idea of heaven. Dogs parks are good not just for dogs and dog lovers. Dog parks can also improve the quality of life for people who don't own dogs. No one wants to hear a neighbor's dog bark all day. No one likes a neighbor's dog digging holes in other people's backyards. Such behavior is often the last resort of dogs that are bored or lack exercise. In contrast, dogs that get to visit dog parks are happy, and so are their owners and neighbors.

Adding a Final Sentence to an Argument Paragraph

Practice

The paragraph below can use a final sentence to sum up the reasons or to reinforce the topic sentence. Add that final sentence.

I am twenty years old, and I live with my parents while I work and attend college. Living at home, I am comfortable and save money, but I am in constant conflict with my parents. Parents of grown children who live at home should remember that these children are adults. Attempting to monitor grown children as if they were still in middle school does not work. My parents continually ask me, "Where are you going? When will you be back?" They want to know when I plan to study or how I am spending my money. The more questions they fire at me, the less I tell them. Questioning doesn't achieve its goal, and trying to control an adult child doesn't work, either. I have heard the warning, "You are still living under our roof, and as long as you do, you must follow our rules." This is a logical point, but most of the time, I am *not* under their roof. I am at my job, at school, or with friends, so my folks must learn to trust me not control me. The most significant reason why parents should respect their children's adult status is that respect leads to cooperation. I am always happy when my parents praise one of my decisions—a decision made without their nagging. When they don't push me, I am more likely to make choices they would approve of.

_____

_____

_____

_____

Final Lines Proofreading and Polishing: Argument

Following is the final version of the argument paragraph on Roberts Park. When you read it, you'll notice several changes from the draft on page 257:

- Some words have been changed to improve the details.
- The first sentence has been changed so that it is more descriptive and uses a parallel pattern for emphasis.

A Final Version of an Argument Paragraph
(Changes from the draft are underlined.)

> Roberts Park was once a pretty little park, but today it is overgrown with weeds, <u>littered with trash, and cluttered with rusty benches.</u> Roberts Park should be cleaned up and improved. Improving the park would make the downtown area more attractive to shoppers. Shoppers could stroll through a <u>restored</u> park or rest there after shopping. Friends could also meet at the park for a day of shopping and lunch. Shoppers are not the only ones who could enjoy the park. Workers from nearby offices and stores could eat lunch outdoors. Several office complexes are near the park, and workers from these offices could bring <u>a bag</u> lunch to work and eat outside in good weather. I think many people would agree that an hour spent outdoors is a pleasant break from work. Most important, city children could play in an improved Roberts Park. They would get fresh air while they played on grass, not asphalt. Best of all, they would not have to play near traffic. Children, shoppers, and workers would benefit from a clean-up of Roberts Park, but so would others. An attractive park improves the city, and all residents benefit when a community is beautified.

Before you prepare the final copy of your argument paragraph, check your latest draft for errors in spelling and punctuation, and for any errors made in typing or copying.

Exercise 13

Practice

Proofreading to Prepare the Final Version

Following are two paragraphs with the kinds of errors that are easy to overlook when you prepare the final version of an assignment. Correct the errors, writing above the lines. There are twelve errors in the first paragraph and eleven in the second paragraph.

1. Our college should put a pencil sharpener in every classroom. First of all putting a sharpener in each class would help many students. Most student take notes and tests in pencil. Often, a pencil point breaks or gets worn down while a student is writing. A pencil sharpener in the room takes care of the problem. Second, a pencil sharpner would eliminate distractions in class. For instance, I was in my math class yesterday when my pencil point broke. I dind't have another pencil, and there was no sharpener in the room. I had to interrupt the lesson to ask to borow a pencil. last of all, a pencil sharpner in each room would solve the problem of wandering students. At least once a day, a student comes into one of my classes, politely asking, "Does this room have a pencil sharpener? Its embarrassing to have to do this. And its worse to wander desperately threw the halls, trying to find one of the few rooms with a sharpener. Pencil sharpeners wouldn't cost the college much, but they would certainly make a diference.

2. My local Cable Television Service, Friendly Cable Company, needs to live up to the terms of its contract with subscribers. For one thing, Friendly Cable Company promises fast service, but their response is slow. When I call the company I have to go through an entire menu of sales offers, before I get to press number five for cable service. Than I am placed on hold for as long as twenty minutes. When I finally reach a service representative, I am given a service appointment that is three days later. Friendly Cable isn't very fast, and it isn't too friendly, either. Once I asked to speak to the Manager. The representative said I couldn't speak to the manager, but I could leave my number, and the manager would get back to me. The manager never call me. Most important, the Friendly Cable Company contract provides cable television in return for money. The contract says that if I

don't pay my cable bill, I don't get to watch cable television. I always pay

my bill, but I do'nt always get functioning cable television. Twice in this

month alone, my cable has been out. I think Friendly Cable owes me some

money for the times when I didn't get my money's worth. I like watching

cable television, but I wish my cable service did it's job.

Lines of Detail: A Walk-Through Assignment

Write a one-paragraph letter to the editor of your local newspaper. Argue for some change you want for your community. You could argue for a traffic light, turn signal, or stop sign at a specific intersection. Or you could argue for bike paths in certain places, a recycling program, more bus service, or for any other specific change you feel is needed. To write your paragraph, follow these steps:

Step 1: Begin by listing all the reasons and details you can about your topic. Survey your lists and consider any possible objections. Answer the objections as well as you can, and see if the objections can lead you to more reasons.

Step 2: Group your reasons, listing the details that fit under each reason. Add details where they are needed and check to see if any reasons overlap.

Step 3: Survey the reasons and details and draft a topic sentence. Be sure that your topic sentence states the subject and takes a stand.

Step 4: Write an outline. Then revise it, checking that you have enough reasons to make your point. Also check that your reasons are specific and in an effective order. Be sure that you have sufficient details for each reason. Check that your outline includes answers to any significant objections.

Step 5: Write a draft of your argument. Revise the draft until it includes any necessary explanations of the problem being argued, all serious or obvious reasons, and sufficient specific details. Also check that the most important reason is stated last. Add all the transitions that are needed to link your reasons and details.

Step 6: Before you prepare the final copy of your paragraph, decide whether you need a final sentence to stress your point and whether your transitions are smooth and logical. Refine your word choice. Then check for errors in spelling, punctuation, and grammar.

Writing Your Own Argument Paragraph

When you write on any of the topics below, be sure to work through the stages of the writing process in preparing your argument paragraph.

1. Write a paragraph for readers of your local newspaper, arguing for one of the following:
   a. a ban on all advertising of alcohol
   b. mandatory jail terms for those convicted of drunk driving
   c. a ban on smoking in all enclosed public places, including restaurants and bars
   d. a tax on all dog or cat owners who do not have their animals neutered, to be used to support animal shelters

2. In a paragraph, argue one of the following topics to the audience specified. If your instructor agrees, brainstorm your topic with a group before you start writing. Ask the group to "play audience," reacting to your reasons, raising objections, and asking questions.

   topic a: Early morning classes should be abolished at your college.
   audience: the dean of academic affairs

   topic b: Attendance in college classes should be optional.
   audience: the instructors at your college

   topic c: College students should get discounts at movie theaters.
   audience: the owner of your local movie theater

   topic d: Your college should provide a daycare facility for students with children.
   audience: the president of your college

   topic e: Businesses should hire more student interns.
   audience: The president of a company (name it) you'd like to work for

   topic f: You deserve a raise.
   audience: your boss

3. Write a paragraph for or against any of the following topics. Your audience for the argument is your classmates and your instructor.

   For or Against
   a. seat belt laws
   b. hidden cameras to catch drivers who run red lights
   c. dress codes in high school
   d. uniforms in elementary schools
   e. mandatory student activities fees for commuter students at colleges and universities
   f. a law requiring a month waiting period between buying a marriage license and getting married
   g. a higher tax on cigarettes to be used to pay the health costs of smokers with smoking-related illnesses

4. Study the photograph below. Then argue for some way to solve this congestion. You may want to argue for widening the road, better public transportation, carpooling, staggered work hours, or another solution.

5. Study the photograph below. Pretend this alley is near your home, and argue for a way to keep it clean.

Name: _____   **Section:** _____

PEER REVIEW FORM FOR AN ARGUMENT PARAGRAPH

After you've written a draft of your argument paragraph, let a writing partner read it. When your partner has completed the form below, discuss the comments. Then repeat the same process for your partner's paragraph.

The topic sentence has this subject: _____

It takes this stand: _____

The most convincing part of the paragraph started with the words _____

and ended with the words _____.

After reading this paragraph, I can think of an objection to this argument. The objection is _____

_____

The paragraph has/has not handled this objection. (Choose one.)

The part of the argument with the best details is the part about_____

_____

The part that could use more or better details is the part about _____

_____

The order of the reasons (a) is effective or (b) could be better. (Choose one.)

I have questions about _____

Other comments: _____

_____

_____

_____

_____

_____

_____

_____

_____

_____

_____

_____

Reviewer's Name: _____

WRITING FROM READING: Argument

Athletic Heroes

James Beekman

James Beekman was a junior in high school when he wrote this essay. It was one of thirty-three selected from more than 12,000 entries in a Newsweek *magazine contest. In his essay, Beekman argues that we overemphasize sports at all levels and should return to the idea of playing sports for fun, not for money and winning.*

Words You May Need to Know (corresponding paragraph numbers are in parentheses)

accolades (4):   awards, honors
generate (6):   create

salary caps (7):   upper limit of a
salary range

1   Almost every child grows up with a professional athlete as his or her hero. Why do some kids choose a hero they don't even know? Maybe it's because society dictates what is popular. I think that sports in general receive too much recognition, not only nationally, but locally, and this preoccupation with athletics distracts society from other equally important activities.

2   This trend toward sports starts when children are very young. At an early age, every child usually picks a sport he or she likes and at which he or she can excel. It is only natural, then, that the child will choose a professional athlete in that sport as a hero. There is nothing wrong with this except that some children, and even their parents, become too interested in that sport and less focused on school. An example of this is the large number of children who play on traveling soccer, hockey, and baseball teams. They spend hours on the road away from home and families. Sports are exciting and can be great for building talent, but I think sports should be reserved for recreation and should not be a substitute for education.

3   Sports receive too much recognition in high school. I am a junior in high school. I have participated in sports all my life. My involvement in sports began when I was three years old and took swimming lessons. Then I moved on to soccer when I was four and to baseball when I was six. I even played basketball in elementary school. I continued to play soccer, baseball, and basketball through the eighth grade and managed to run track a couple of years as well. I have great memories of how much fun these sports were, but I also remember that the coaches' focus on winning became more pronounced the older I became. I thought sports were intended to be fun, but now I question this. I noticed a drastic change in attitude about sports when I entered high school. It seems that the coaches of high school sports make sports more than just an extracurricular activity.

4   Sports seem to receive more attention than other activities in high school. One of these activities is the debate team. I am not part of this team, but I know the members work very hard and practice as many hours as any of the athletes. An activity in which I am involved is the high school show choir. We practice after school from six to fifteen hours a week, and then travel out of town for competitions on weekends. The show choir has consistently won top awards and championships and even has a better record than most of the high school sports teams. And yet who receives all the accolades? One has only to turn to the second section of the *Courier,* our local newspaper, to answer this question. The high school athletes are given front-page coverage. Both the football and the basketball teams had school pep rallies before their big games. There was even a special rally for the boys' soccer team when it went to the state tournament. There have never been any special rallies given for the show choir and its sixty members, yet they have repeatedly won contests.

5   The most important thing that is being denied in the overemphasis on high school sports is academic achievement. Many students who excel academically receive far less attention than the stars of the athletic teams. The goal of schools should be to educate the students and not to sensationalize sports. Colleges award many sports scholarships as well as scholarships for academic achievements, and supposedly their main purpose is education. It is possible that some students who do not excel academically but who are eager to learn might be denied an opportunity to attend college, while a star athlete who is not motivated academically might be given a full scholarship.

6   On the professional level, money and winning seem to be the most important goal. Whatever happened to the old idea of playing a sport for fun? Professional athletes seem to be motivated by making the most money for the least amount of work. Most sports last only one season of a few months. The rest of the year the athletes are free to travel and make television commercials and public appearances. Many of these athletes also endorse products to generate additional income. In general, most professional athletes today in basketball, football, baseball, and hockey make more than a million dollars per year. Deion Sanders just signed a $35 million contract with the Dallas Cowboys. In baseball, Ken Griffey, Jr. just signed a multiyear contract with the Seattle Mariners for which he will receive more than $7 million a year. These are the most highly paid players in their sport, but other team members are not far behind. Professional golfer Greg Norman made about $1.6 million in tournament wins last year but raked in an estimated $40 million from his endorsements.

7   Not only do these sports heroes make enormous sums of money, but they also seem to want even more. Last year the major-league baseball teams went on strike for more money before the World Series was even

played. The National Hockey League went on strike over salary caps. Hard-working Americans don't make nearly as much as the professional athletes and receive no attention at all.

8   Sports should be for recreation and fun. More recently, sports figures have become more focused on securing large salaries and less focused on entertainment. Almost every child has a star athlete as his or her hero. Maybe if children were better informed about these heroes, they would look elsewhere for a hero. And who would that hero be? Just maybe that hero could be someone as extraordinary as their parents.

WRITING FROM READING: "Athletic Heroes"

When you write on any of the following topics, work through the stages of the writing process in preparing your argument paragraph.

1. Beekman says, "The most important thing that is being denied in the overemphasis on high school sports is academic achievement." Write a paragraph in which you (1) argue for more emphasis on academic achievement in high school or (2) argue that the emphasis on high school sports is healthy for all high school students.

2. Write a paragraph arguing one of the following:

   _____ (name a professional athlete) is too highly paid.

   _____ (name a professional athlete) deserves his/her pay.

   Coaches in children's sports place too much emphasis on winning.

   Sports receive more attention than any other activity in high school and this situation is unfair/fair.

3. In some high schools, successful athletes may be part of an exclusive group. Write a paragraph arguing that this focus on winning athletes can make other students feel inferior and rejected.

4. Write a paragraph arguing that children should have, instead of sports heroes, other heroes. Be specific in naming who the "other heroes" may be.

5. Write a paragraph arguing that playing a sport for fun is worthwhile, no matter how good an athlete one is.

Too Tired to Appreciate the Revolution?

Jeremy Rifkin

Jeremy Rifkin, author of The Age of Access *and president of the Foundation for Economic Trends, questions whether our "24/7" lifestyle may be costing us too much of our humanity. He argues that while we are "beginning to organize life at the speed of light," we feel as if we are constantly running out of time.*

Words You May Need to Know (corresponding paragraph numbers are in parentheses)

cyberspace (1): electronic communications

loom (1): come into view in a threatening way

compressing (2): forcing into less space

accelerating (2): increasing the speed

processing (2): performing operations on

techno gurus (2): recognized leaders in technology

nanosecond (2): one billionth of a second

enslaving (2): making into slaves

embedded (5): firmly enclosed

interdependent (5): relying on one another

temporal (5): lasting only for a time

Descartes (5): René Descartes, a French philosopher and mathematician of the seventeenth century

dictum (5): a statement made with authority

telltale (6): revealing

angst (6): a feeling of anxiety often mixed with depression

attributable (6): connected to, caused by

information overload (6): being weighed down with too much knowledge, too many facts, and too much data

burnout (6): physical or emotional exhaustion

adverse (6): harmful

diminished (6): decreased

attention deficit hyperactivity disorder (7): a condition characterized by overactivity and a short attention span

neural (7): connected to the nerves or nervous system

condition (7): accustom

social conservatives (8): people who believe in traditional values

civility (8): courteous behavior

defer (8): to submit to the opinion or wishes of someone else, out of respect

reflect (8): to form carefully considered thoughts

lexicon (8): vocabulary

hair-trigger (8): responding to the slightest stimulation or provocation

1 The whole world is rushing to join the Information Age revolution. Everyone wants to be connected. Indeed, the only debate today is how to ensure that everyone has access to the world of cyberspace. But an equally important issue is beginning to loom: Is too much access as big a problem as too little? Is it possible that we are speeding up human activity at such a rate that we risk doing grave harm to ourselves and to society?

2 Recently, scientists showed that they can alter the speed of light, either by stopping it for an instant or by boosting it along. These experiments are

opening the door to new technologies that could vastly speed up both computing and communications in the coming century. We are, in other words, beginning to organize life at the speed of light—compressing time, accelerating activity and processing greater stores of information. The techno gurus promised us that instant access would lighten our loads and give us back more time. Is it possible, instead, that the nanosecond culture is enslaving us in a web of ever-accelerating connections from which there seems to be no easy escape?

3   A new term—24/7—has entered our vocabulary. Around-the-clock activity, twenty-four hours a day, seven days a week. Our always-operating fax machines, e mail, voice mail, PCs, Palm Pilots and cellular phones; our twenty-four-hour trading markets, ATMs, online banking services and e-commerce; our television sets that are always left on; our open-all-night restaurants and drug stores that we can go to any time we want—all of this hollers for our attention. Yet because these devices and services only increase the diversity, pace and flow of commercial and social activity, we feel as if we have less time available to us than any other humans in history.

4   For example, online messaging is a great convenience. However, now we find ourselves spending much of our day frantically responding to each other's e-mail. The cell phone is a great time-saver. However, now we can be reached by anyone at any time. I've heard businessmen answer work-related phone calls while sitting on the toilet seat in the men's room. Does anyone doubt that time is fast becoming the most scarce resource?

5   Today, we find ourselves firmly embedded in a far more complex, interdependent temporal world made up of ever-changing webs of human relationships and activity, a world in which every available minute becomes an opportunity to make another connection. Descartes' dictum, "I think, therefore I am," has been replaced by a new dictum, "I am connected, therefore I exist."

6   The telltale signs of our new time angst are everywhere. Stress-related illness is rising dramatically, much of it attributable, say the experts, to information overload and burnout. In the United States, forty-three percent of all adults suffer adverse health effects because of stress, and job stress is estimated to cost industry billions annually in absenteeism, diminished productivity, employee turnover, and medical costs. Around-the-clock activity has led to a serious decline in the number of hours devoted to sleep. In 1910, the average adult was sleeping nine to ten hours a night. Now the average adult in a highly industrial country gets less than seven. That's hundreds more waking hours a year. But we are still biologically designed to go to sleep after sunset and awake at sunrise. Massive sleep deprivation, brought on by the frantic new pace of living, is increasingly being linked to serious illnesses including diabetes, cancer, strokes, and depression.

7   Nowhere is the "speed of light" society having a greater impact than with the dot-com generation. Millions of kids, especially boys, are being diagnosed

with attention deficit hyperactivity disorder in the United States. Is it any wonder? If a child grows up in an environment surrounded by the fast pace of television, video games, computers, and constant media stimulation, chances are that his neural development will condition him to a short attention span.

8   Social conservatives talk about the decline in civility, blaming it on the loss of a moral compass and of religious values. Has anyone asked whether the hyper-speed culture is making all of us less patient and less willing to listen and defer, consider and reflect? "Road rage," "desk rage," and "air rage" have become part of the popular lexicon as more and more people act out their stress with violent outbursts. In a click-click culture, everyone is poised toward a hair-trigger response. Maybe we need to ask what kind of "connections" really count and what types of "access" really matter. If this new technology revolution is only about speed and hyper-efficiency, then we lose something even more precious than time—our sense of what it means to be a caring human being.

WRITING FROM READING: "Too Tired to Appreciate the Revolution?"

When you write on any of these topics, work through the stages of the writing process in preparing your paragraph.

1. In a paragraph, explain what Jeremy Rifkin means when he says that our "24/7," instant-access lifestyle has its harmful effects. Refer to some of his examples in your explanation.

2. Respond to Rifkin's criticism of the new world of instant access and easy communication. Write a paragraph about the benefits of two or three of the technological advances (for instance, instant messaging, cell phones, e-commerce) he questions.

3. Rifkin talks about the rise in stress-related illness and burnout today. In a paragraph, propose one way to relieve this stress and reduce the incidence of burnout.

4. Write a paragraph that argues for one of the following:
   a. less technology (computers, video games, television, DVD players) in homes with children under twelve years of age
   b. a shorter work week
   c. more telecommuting (that is, performing job activities at home)
   d. four weeks' annual vacation for workers (instead of the traditional two weeks)
   e. one day per week without computers or cell phones
   f. a required class in stress management for all high school students

5. Rifkin cites statistics about the increasing number of people who suffer from sleep deprivation. Many people say they just do not have time to get more sleep. In a paragraph, propose cutting back on one activity so that people could get more sleep. You could argue for reducing time spent answering email, surfing the Internet, watching television, and so forth. Be sure to explain the benefits of spending less time on this activity as part of your argument.

CHAPTER **11**

Writing an Essay

WHAT IS AN ESSAY?

You write an essay when you have more to say than can be covered in one paragraph. An **essay** can consist of one paragraph, but in this book, we take it to mean a writing of more than one paragraph. An essay has a main point, called a *thesis*, supported by subpoints. The subpoints are the *topic sentences*. Each paragraph in the *body*, or main part, of the essay has a topic sentence. In fact, each paragraph in the body of the essay is like the paragraphs you've already written because each one makes a point and then supports it.

COMPARING THE SINGLE PARAGRAPH AND THE ESSAY

Read the paragraph and the essay that follow, both about Bob, the writer's brother. You will notice many similarities.

A Single Paragraph

I think I'm lucky to have a brother who is two years older than I am. For one thing, my brother Bob fought all the typical child-parent battles, and I was the real winner. Bob was the one who made my parents understand that seventeen-year-olds shouldn't have an 11:00 P.M. curfew on weekends. He fought for his rights. By the time I turned seventeen, my parents had accepted the later curfew, and I didn't have to fight for it. Bob also paved the way for me at school. He was such a great athlete that I benefited from his reputation. When I tried out for the basketball team, I had an advantage before I hit the court. I was Bob Cruz's younger brother, so the coach thought I had to be pretty good. At home and at school, my big brother was a big help to me.

An Essay

Some people complain about being the youngest child or the middle child in the family. These people believe older children get all the attention and grab all the power. I'm the younger brother in my family, and I disagree with the complainers. I think I'm lucky to have a brother who is two years older than I am.

For one thing, my brother Bob fought all the typical child-parent battles, and I was the real winner. Bob was the one who made my parents understand that seventeen-year-olds shouldn't have an 11:00 P.M. curfew on weekends. He fought for his rights, and the fighting wasn't easy. I remember months of arguments between Bob and my parents as Bob tried to explain that not all teens on the street at 11:30 are punks or criminals. Bob was the one who suffered from being grounded or who lost the use of my father's car. By the time I turned seventeen, my parents had accepted the later curfew, and I didn't have to fight for it.

Bob also paved the way for me at school. Because he was so popular with the other students and the teachers, he created a positive image of what the boys in our family were like. When I started school, I walked into a place where people were ready to like me, just as they liked Bob. I remember the first day of class, when the teachers read the new class rolls. When they got to my name, they asked, "Are you Bob Cruz's brother?" When I said yes, they smiled. Bob's success opened doors for me in school sports, too. He was such a great athlete that I benefited from his reputation. When I tried out for the basketball team, I had an advantage before I hit the court. I was Bob Cruz's younger brother, so the coach thought I had to be pretty good.

I had many battles to fight as I grew up. Like all children, I had to struggle to gain independence and respect. In my struggles at home and at school, my big brother was a big help to me.

If you read the two selections carefully, you noticed that they make the same main point, and they support that point with two subpoints.

> **main point:** I think I am lucky to have a brother who is two years older than I am.

> **subpoints:** 1. My brother Bob fought all the typical child-parent battles, and I was the real winner.
> 2. Bob also paved the way at school.

You noticed that the essay is longer because it has more details and examples to support the points.

ORGANIZING AN ESSAY

When you write an essay of more than one paragraph, the **thesis** is the focus of your entire essay; it is the major point of your essay. The other important points that relate to the thesis are in topic sentences.

> **Thesis:** Working as a salesperson has changed my character.
> **Topic sentence:** I have had to learn patience.
> **Topic sentence:** I have developed the ability to listen.
> **Topic sentence:** I have become more tactful.

Notice that the thesis expresses a bigger idea than the topic sentences below it, and it is supported by the topic sentences. The essay has an introduction, a body, and a conclusion.

1. **Introduction:** The first paragraph is usually the introduction. The thesis goes here.

2. **Body:** This central part of the essay is the part where you support your main point (the thesis). Each paragraph in the body of the essay has its own topic sentence.

3. **Conclusion:** Usually one paragraph long, the conclusion reminds the reader of the thesis.

WRITING THE THESIS

There are several characteristics of a thesis:

1. It is expressed in a sentence. A thesis is *not* the same as the topic of the essay or the title of the essay

    topic: quitting smoking
    title: Why I Quit Smoking
    thesis: I quit smoking because I was concerned for my health, and I wanted to prove to myself that I could break the habit.

2. A thesis *does not announce*; it makes a point about the subject.

    announcement: This essay will explain the reasons why young adults should watch what they eat.
    thesis: Young adults should watch what they eat so they can live healthy lives today and prevent future health problems.

3. A thesis *is not too broad*. Some ideas are just too big to cover well in an essay. A thesis that tries to cover too much can lead to a superficial or boring essay.

    too broad: People all over the world should work on solving their interpersonal communications problems.
    acceptable thesis: As a Southerner, I had a hard time understanding that some New Yorkers think slow speech is ignorant speech.

4. A thesis *is not too narrow*. Sometimes, writers start with a thesis that looks good because it seems specific and precise. Later, when they try to support such a thesis, they can't find anything to say.

    too narrow: My sister pays forty dollars a week for a special formula for her baby.
    acceptable thesis: My sister had no idea what it would cost to care for a baby.

Hints for Writing a Thesis

1. You can **mention the specific subpoints** of your essay in your thesis. For example, your thesis might be

I hated *Hannibal* because the film was ultraviolent and it glorified criminals.

With this thesis, you have indicated the two subpoints of your essay: *Hannibal* was ultraviolent; *Hannibal* glorified criminals.

2. You can **make a point** without listing your subpoints in your thesis. For example, you can write a thesis like this:

I hated *Hannibal* because of the way it turned the unspeakable into entertainment.

With this thesis, you can still use the subpoints stating that the movie was ultraviolent and glorified criminals. You just don't have to mention all your subpoints in the thesis. Be sure to check with your instructor about the type of thesis you should devise.

Exercise 1

Practice

Recognizing Good Thesis Sentences

Following is a list of thesis statements. Some are acceptable, but others are too broad or too narrow. Some are announcements; others are topics, not sentences. Put a *G* next to the good thesis sentences.

1. _____ How students can make the most of their financial aid will be discussed in this essay.

2. _____ My sister won a golf scholarship to a private college.

3. _____ Technology is a necessity in today's fast-paced society.

4. _____ Why mosquitoes are a serious health threat in our community.

5. _____ Drug abuse is an international crisis.

6. _____ College essay assignments are easier to prepare because of computers.

7. _____ The government should stop making pennies, since they have outlived their usefulness.

8. _____ St. Augustine, Florida, is the oldest city in the United States.

9. _____ The advantages of speaking two languages.

10. _____ Learning to play a musical instrument can bring a person much pleasure.

Exercise 2

Practice

Selecting a Good Thesis Sentence

In each pair of thesis statements below, put a *G* next to the good topic sentence.

1. a. _____ Road rage incidents and people under stress.

   b. _____ People under stress are more likely to be involved in incidents of road rage.

2. a. _____ Drinking bottled water is a popular but expensive habit.

   b. _____ Pollution of the oceans, rivers, and lakes of the world is threatening to change life as we know it.

3. a. _____ The challenges of being a foreign student will be discussed in this essay.

   b. _____ Foreign students face academic, social, and financial challenges.

4. a. _____ The Need for a Better Highway System in Leesboro

b. _____ Leesboro needs to expand and restructure its highway system.

5. a. _____ I failed my third sociology test last Friday.

b. _____ Sociology has too many strange terms, boring statistics, and complicated studies for me to remember.

6. a. _____ The old house needs basic repairs in several areas.

b. _____ Where the old house needs basic repair work is the subject of this paper.

7. a. _____ The differences between a foster child and an adopted child in the state legal system.

b. _____ In the state legal system, there are three significant differences between a foster child and an adopted child.

8. a. _____ A homemade pie looks, tastes, and smells better than a store-bought pie.

b. _____ Why Homemade Pies are Better Than Store-Bought Ones

9. a. _____ Gold jewelry and its quality

b. _____ There are three signs that a piece of jewelry is real gold.

10. a. _____ Child abuse is a problem in families of every social class.

b. _____ The local child abuse hotline is helping to save lives.

Exercise 3

Practice

Writing a Thesis That Relates to the Subpoints

Following are lists of subpoints that could be discussed in an essay. Write a thesis for each list. Remember that there are two ways to write a thesis: you can write a thesis that includes the specific subpoints, or you can write one that makes a point without listing the subpoints. As an example, the first one is done for you, using both kinds of topic sentences.

1. one kind of thesis: _If you want a pet, a cat is easier to care for than a dog._

another kind of thesis: _Cats make better pets than dogs because cats don't need to be walked, don't mind being alone, and don't make any noise._

subpoints: **a.** Cats don't have to be walked and exercised, like dogs do.

> **b.** Cats are independent and don't mind being home alone, but a dog gets lonely.
>
> **c.** Cats are quieter than dogs.

2. thesis: _____
_____

subpoints: **a.** Neighbors will often collect your mail when you're out of town.

b. In an emergency, neighbors can lend you the tools you need.

3. thesis: _____
_____

subpoints: **a.** Neighbors will often collect your mail when you're out of town.

b. In an emergency, neighbors can lend you the tools you need.

c. Neighbors can be nosy and critical.

d. Neighbors can invade your living space.

4. thesis: _____
_____

subpoints: **a.** Employers look for workers who are prepared to work hard.

b. Employers will hire people with the right training.

c. Employers want workers who have a positive attitude towards the job.

5. thesis: _____
_____

subpoints: **a.** The local television news gives me the weather forecast.

b. It tells me about crimes in my neighborhood.

c. It informs me of major car accidents.

WRITING THE ESSAY IN STEPS

In an essay, you follow the same steps you learned in writing a paragraph—thought lines, outlines, rough drafts, and final version—but you adapt them to the longer essay form.

Thought Lines   Gathering Ideas: An Essay

Often you begin by _narrowing a topic_. Your instructor may give you a large topic so that you can find something smaller, within the broad one, that you would like to write about.

Some students think that because they have several paragraphs to write, they should pick a big topic, one that will give them enough to say.

But big topics can lead to boring, superficial, general essays. A smaller topic can challenge you to find the specific, concrete examples and details that make an essay effective.

If your instructor asked you to write about college, for instance, you might *freewrite* some ideas as you narrow the topic:

Narrowing the Topic of College

what college means to me—too big, and it could be boring
college vs. high school—everyone might choose this topic
college students—too big
college students who have jobs—better!
problems of working and going to college—OK!

In your freewriting, you can consider your purpose—to write an essay about some aspect of college—and audience—your instructor and classmates. Your narrowed topic will appeal to this audience because many students hold jobs and because instructors are familiar with the problems of working students.

Listing Ideas

Once you have a narrow topic, you can use whatever process works for you. You can brainstorm by writing a series of questions and answers about your topic, you can freewrite on the topic, you can list ideas on the topic, or you can combine any of these processes.

Following is a sample listing of ideas on the topic of the problems of working and going to college.

problems of working and going to college

early classes	weekends only time to study
too tired to pay attention	no social life
tried to study at work	apartment a mess
got caught	missed work for makeup test
got reprimanded	get behind in school
slept in class	need salary for tuition
constantly racing around	rude to customers
no sleep	girlfriend ready to kill me
little time to do homework	

Clustering the Ideas

By clustering related items on the list, you'll find it easier to see the connections between ideas. The following items have been clustered (grouped), and they have been listed under a subtitle.

Problems of Working and Going to College: Ideas in Clusters

problems at school	problems at work
early classes	tried to study at work
too tired to pay attention	got caught
slept in class	got reprimanded
little time to do homework	missed work for makeup test
get behind in school	rude to customers

problems outside of work and school

weekends only time to study

no social life

apartment a mess

girlfriend ready to kill me

When you surveyed the clusters, you probably noticed that some of the ideas from the original list were left out. These ideas, on racing around, not getting enough sleep, and needing tuition money, could fit into more than one place and might not fit anywhere. You might come back to them later.

When you name each cluster by giving it a subtitle, you move toward a focus for each body paragraph of your essay. And by beginning to focus the body paragraphs, you start thinking about the main point, the thesis of the essay. Concentrating on the thesis and on focused paragraphs helps you to *unify* your essay.

Reread the clustered ideas. When you do so, you'll notice that each cluster is about problems at a different place. You can incorporate that concept into a thesis with a sentence like this:

Students who work while they attend college face problems at school, at work, and at home.

Once you have a thesis and a list of details, you can begin working on the outlines part of your essay.

Exercise 4

Collaborate

Narrowing Topics

Working with a partner or a group, narrow these topics so that the new topics are related, but smaller and are suitable for short essays that are between four and six paragraphs long. The first topic is narrowed for you.

1. topic: summer vacation
   smaller, related topics:

   a. *a car trip with children*

   b. *finding the cheapest flight to Mexico*

   c. *my vacation job*

2. topic: driving
   smaller, related topics:

   a. _____

   b. _____

   c. _____

3. topic: sports
   smaller, related topics:

   a. _____

   b. _____

   c. _____

4. topic: nature
smaller, related topics:

a. _____

b. _____

c. _____

5. topic: money
smaller, related topics:

a. _____

b. _____

c. _____

Exercise 5

Practice

Clustering Related Ideas

Below are two topics, each with a list of ideas. Mark all the related items on the list with the same number (*1*, *2*, or *3*). Some items might not get any number. When you've finished marking the list, write a title for each number that explains the cluster of ideas.

1. topic: giving a speech

_____ audience may be large

_____ begin by thinking of a good topic

_____ right before you speak, take a deep breath

_____ make eye contact with your audience as you speak

_____ make a list of what you want to say

_____ organize your list onto note cards

_____ relax as you get up to speak

_____ speak slowly

_____ as you wait to speak, remember all speakers are nervous

_____ stand confidently

The ideas marked *1* can be titled _____

The ideas marked *2* can be titled _____

The ideas marked *3* can be titled _____

2. topic: why a new job is stressful

_____ boss may be bad tempered

_____ you may feel all your coworkers are watching you

_____ you don't know anyone who works there

_____ you think you can't learn the new routines

_____ a different computer program is challenging

_____ the rules may be strictly enforced by the boss

_____ the salary may be low

_____ you may think all the coworkers are gossiping about you

_____ you may be afraid you won't get the work done quickly enough

_____ the boss may have strong dislikes

The items marked *1* can be titled _____

The items marked *2* can be titled _____

The items marked *3* can be titled _____

Outlines   Devising a Plan: An Essay

In the next stage of writing your essay, draft an outline. Use the thesis to focus your ideas. There are many kinds of outlines, but all are used to help a writer organize ideas. When you use a **formal outline,** you show the difference between a main idea and its supporting detail by *indenting* the supporting detail. In a formal outline, Roman numerals (I, II, III, and so on) and capital letters are used. Each Roman numeral represents a paragraph, and the letters beneath the numeral represent supporting details.

The Structure of a Formal Outline

first paragraph	I. Thesis
second paragraph	II. Topic sentence
details	A.
	B.
	C.
	D.
	E.
third paragraph	III. Topic sentence
details	A.
	B.
	C.
	D.
	E.
fourth paragraph	IV. Topic sentence
details	A.
	B.
	C.
	D.
	E.
fifth paragraph	V. Conclusion

Hints for Outlining

Developing a good, clear outline now can save you hours of confused, disorganized writing later. The extra time you spend to make sure your outline has sufficient details and that *each paragraph stays on one point* will pay off in the long run.

1. Check the topic sentences. Keep in mind that each topic sentence in each body paragraph should support the thesis sentence. If a topic sentence is not carefully connected to the thesis, the structure of the essay will be confusing. Here are a thesis and a list of topic sentences; the topic sentence that does not fit is crossed out:

thesis:	I. A home-cooked dinner can be a rewarding experience for the cook and the guests.
topic sentences:	II. Preparing a meal is a satisfying activity.
	III. It is a pleasure for the cook to see guests enjoy the meal.
	IV. ~~Many recipes are handed down through generations.~~
	V. Dinner guests are flattered that someone cooked for them.
conclusion:	VI. Dining at home is a treat for everyone at the table or in the kitchen.

Since the thesis of this outline is about the pleasure of dining at home, for the cook and the guests, topic sentence IV doesn't fit: it isn't about the joy of cooking *or* of being a dinner guest. It takes the essay off track. A careful check of the links between the thesis and the topic sentences will help keep your essay focused.

2. Include enough details. Some writers believe that they don't need many details in the outline. They feel they can fill in the details later, when they actually write the essay. Even though some writers do manage to add details later, others who are in a hurry or who run out of ideas run into problems. For example, imagine that a writer has included very few details in an outline, like this outline for a paragraph:

II. A burglary makes the victim feel unsafe.
    A. The person has lost property.
    B. The person's home territory has been invaded.

The paragraph created from that outline might be too short and lack specific details, like this:

    A burglary makes the victim feel unsafe. First of all, the victim has lost property. Second, a person's home territory has been invaded.

If you have difficulty thinking of ideas when you write, try to tackle the problem in the outline. The more details you put into your outline, the more detailed and effective your draft essay will be. For example, suppose the same outline on the burglary topic had more details, like this:

II. A burglary makes the victim feel unsafe.
    A. The person has lost property.
    B. The property could be worth hundreds of dollars.

more details about burglary	C. The victim can lose a television or camera or VCR. D. The burglars may take cash. E. Worse, items with personal value, like family jewelry or heirlooms, can be stolen.
more details about safety concerns	F. Even worse, a person's territory has been invaded. G. People who thought they were safe know they are not safe. H. The fear is that the invasion can happen again.

You will probably agree that the paragraph will be more detailed, too.

3. Stay on one point. It is a good idea to check the outline of each body paragraph to see if each paragraph stays on one point. Compare each topic sentence, which is at the top of the list for the paragraph, against the detail indented under it. Staying on one point gives each paragraph unity.

Below is the outline for a body paragraph that has problems staying on one point. See if you can spot the problem areas.

III. Sonya is a generous person.
    A. I remember how freely she gave her time when our club had a car wash.
    B. She is always willing to share her lecture notes with me.
    C. Sonya gives ten percent of her salary to her church.
    D. She is a member of Big Sisters and spends every Saturday with a disadvantaged child.
    E. She can read people's minds when they are in trouble.
    F. She knows what they are feeling.

The topic sentence of the paragraph is about generosity. But sentences E and F talk about Sonya's insight, not her generosity.

When you have a problem staying on one point, you can solve the problem in two ways:

1. Eliminate details that do not fit your main point.
2. Change the topic sentence to cover all the ideas in the paragraph.

For example, you could cut out sentences E and F about Sonya's insight, getting rid of the details that do not fit. As an alternative, you could change the topic sentence in the paragraph so that it relates to all the ideas in the paragraph. A better topic sentence is "Sonya is a generous and insightful person."

Revisiting the Thought Lines Stage

Writing an outline can help you identify undeveloped places in your plan, places where your paragraphs will need more details. You can devise these details in two ways:

1. Go back to the writing you did in the thought lines stage. Check whether items on a list or ideas from freewriting can lead you to more details for your outline.
2. Brainstorm for more details by using a question-and-answer approach. For example, if the outline includes "My apartment is a mess," you might ask, "Why? How messy?" Or if the outline includes "I have no social life," you might ask, "What do you mean? No friends? No activities? Or what about school organizations?"

The time you spend writing and revising your outline will make it easier for you to write an essay that is well developed, unified, and coherently structured. The checklist below may help you to revise.

> ☑|**Checklist**
>
> **A Checklist for Revising the Outline of an Essay**
>
> ✔ **Unity:** Do the thesis and topic sentences all lead to the same point? Does each paragraph make one, and only one, point? Do the details in each paragraph support the topic sentence? Does the conclusion unify the essay?
>
> ✔ **Support:** Do the body paragraphs have enough supporting details?
>
> ✔ **Coherence:** Are the paragraphs in the most effective order? Are the details in each paragraph arranged in the most effective order?

A sentence outline on the problems of working and going to college follows. It includes the thesis in the first paragraph. The topic sentences have been created from the titles of the ideas clustered earlier. The details have been drawn from ideas in the clusters and from further brainstorming. The conclusion has just one sentence that unifies the essay.

An Outline for an Essay

paragraph 1	I. Thesis: Students who work while going to college face problems at school, at work, and at home.
paragraph 2 topic sentence details	II. Trying to juggle job and school responsibilities creates problems at school. A. Early classes are difficult. B. I am too tired to pay attention. C. Once I slept in class. D. I have little time to do homework. E. I get behind in school assignments.
paragraph 3 topic sentence details	II. Work can suffer when workers attend college. A. I tried to study at work. B. I got caught by my boss. C. I was reprimanded. D. Sometimes I come to work very tired. E. When I don't have enough sleep, I can be rude to customers. F. Rudeness gets me in trouble. G. Another time, I had to cut work to take a make-up test.
paragraph 4 topic sentence details	IV. Working students suffer outside of classes and the workplace. A. I work nights during the week. B. The weekends are the only time I can study. C. My apartment is a mess since I have no time to clean it. D. Worse, my girlfriend is ready to kill me because I have no social life.

E. We never even go to the movies anymore.

F. When she comes over, I am busy studying.

V. I have learned that working students have to be very organized to cope with their responsibilities at college, work, and home.

Exercise 6

Practice

Completing an Outline for an Essay

Following is part of an outline that has a thesis and topic sentences, but no details. Add the details and write in complete sentences. Write one sentence for each capital letter. Be sure that the details are connected to the topic sentence.

 I. Thesis: Video cameras have several beneficial uses in American society.

 II. Americans use their video cameras to record memorable family events.

A. _____

B. _____

C. _____

D. _____

E. _____

 III. Video cameras are being used to prevent or detect crimes.

A. _____

B. _____

C. _____

D. _____

E. _____

 IV. Video cameras have given ordinary people an entry into many television programs.

A. _____

B. _____

C. _____

D. _____

E. _____

 V. The video camera has changed the way Americans celebrate family rituals, has contributed to the prevention and detection of crime, and has made ordinary people into television directors, reporters, and performers.

Focusing an Outline for an Essay

Practice

The outline below has a thesis and details, but it has no topic sentences for the body paragraphs. Write the topic sentences.

> I. Thesis: After my last meal at Don's Diner, I swore I'd never eat there again.
>
> II. _____
>
> _____
>
>   A. My friend and I were kept waiting for a table for half an hour.
>   B. During that time, several tables were empty, but no one bothered to clear the dirty dishes.
>   C. We just stood in the entrance, waiting.
>   D. Then, when we were seated, the waitress was surly.
>   E. It took fifteen minutes to get a menu.
>   F. The plates of food were slammed down on the table.
>   G. The orders were mixed up.
>
> III. _____
>
> _____
>
>   A. The hamburger was full of gristle.
>   B. The French fries were as hard as cardboard.
>   C. Our iced tea was instant.
>   D. The iced tea powder was floating on top of the glass.
>   E. The lettuce had brown edges.
>   F. Ketchup was caked all over the outside of the ketchup bottle.
>
> IV. I never want to repeat the experience I had at Don's Diner.

Rough Lines   Drafting and Revising: An Essay

When you are satisfied with your outline, you can begin drafting and revising the essay. Start by writing a first draft of the essay, which includes these parts: introduction, body paragraphs, and conclusion.

WRITING THE INTRODUCTION

Where Does the Thesis Go?

The thesis should appear in the introduction of the essay, in the first paragraph. But most of the time it should not be the first sentence. In front of the thesis, write three or more sentences of introduction. Generally, the thesis is the *last sentence* in the introductory paragraph.

Why put the thesis at the end of the first paragraph? First of all, writing several sentences in front of your main idea gives you a chance to lead into it, gradually and smoothly. This will help you build interest and gain the reader's attention. Also, by placing the thesis after a few sentences of introduction, you will not startle the reader with your main point.

Finally, if your thesis is at the end of the introduction, it states the main point of the essay just before that point is supported in the body paragraphs. Putting the thesis at the end of the introduction is like putting an arrow pointing to the supporting ideas in the essay.

Hints for Writing the Introduction

There are a number of ways to write an introduction.

1. You can begin with some general statements that gradually lead to your thesis:

general statements	Students face all kinds of problems when they start college. Some students struggle with a lack of basic math skills; others have never learned to write a term paper. Students who were stars in high school have to cope with being just another social security number at a large institution. Students with small children have to find a way to be good parents and good students, too. Although all these problems are common, I found
thesis at end	an even more typical conflict. <u>My biggest problem in college was learning to organize my time.</u>

2. You can begin with a quotation that smoothly leads to your thesis. The quotation can be from someone famous, or it can be an old saying. It can be something your mother always told you, or it can be a slogan from an advertisement or the words of a song.

quotation	Everybody has heard the old saying, "Time flies," but I never really thought about that statement until I started college. I expected college to challenge me with demanding course work. I expected it to excite me with the range of people I would meet. I even thought it might amuse me with the fun and intrigue of dating and romance. But I never expected college to exhaust me. I was
thesis at end	surprised to discover that <u>my biggest problem in college was learning to organize my time.</u>

Note: You can add transition words or phrases to your thesis, as in the example above.

3. You can tell a story as a way of leading into your thesis. You can open with the story of something that happened to you or to someone you know, a story you read about or heard on the news.

story	My friend Phyllis is two years older than I am, so she started college before I did. When Phyllis came home from college for the Thanksgiving weekend, I called her with plans for fun, but Phyllis told me she planned to spend most of the weekend sleeping. I didn't understand her when she told me she was worn out. When I started college myself, I understood her perfectly. Phyllis was a victim of that old college ailment:

	not knowing how to handle time. I developed the same disease. <u>My biggest problem in college was learning to organize my time.</u>
thesis at end	

4. You can explain why this topic is worth writing about. Explaining could mean giving some background on the topic, or it could mean discussing why the topic is an important one.

	I do not remember a word of what was said during my freshman orientation, and I wish I did. I am sure somebody somewhere warned me about the problems I would face in college. I am sure somebody talked about getting organized. Unfortunately, I didn't listen, and I had to learn the hard way. I hope other students will listen and learn and be spared my
explain	
thesis at end	hard lesson and my big problem. <u>My biggest problem in college was learning to organize my time.</u>

5. You can use one or more questions to lead into your thesis. You can open with a question or questions that will be answered by your thesis. Or you can open with a question or questions that catch the reader's attention and move toward your thesis.

	Have you ever stayed up all night to study for an exam, then fallen asleep at dawn and slept right through the time of the exam? If you have, then you were probably the same kind of college student I was. I was the student who always ran into class three minutes late, the one who begged for an extension on the term paper, the one who pleaded with the teacher to postpone the test. I just could not get things done on schedule. <u>My</u>
question thesis at end	
thesis at end	<u>biggest problem in college was learning to organize my time.</u>

6. You can open with a contradiction of your main point as a way of attracting the reader's interest and leading to your thesis. You can begin with an idea that is the opposite of what you will say in your thesis. The opposition of your opening and your thesis creates interest.

	People who knew me in my freshman year probably felt really sorry for me. They saw a girl with dark circles under her bloodshot eyes, a girl who was always racing from one place to another. Those people probably thought I was exhausted from overwork. But they were wrong. My problem in college was definitely not too much work; it
contradiction	
thesis at end	was the way I handled my work. <u>My biggest problem in college was learning to organize my time.</u>

Exercise 8

Practice

Writing an Introduction

Following are five thesis sentences. Pick one. Then write an introductory paragraph on the lines provided. Your last sentence should be the thesis sentence. If your instructor agrees, read your introduction to others in the class who wrote an introduction to the same thesis, or read your introduction to the entire class.

Thesis sentences

1. Young girls are becoming dangerously preoccupied with their weight.
2. Three kinds of music appeal to my friends.
3. A pet can brighten a person's life.
4. One family member has been my greatest role model.
5. People should be more careful in protecting their homes from thieves.

(Write an introduction) _____

_____

_____

_____

_____

_____

_____

WRITING THE BODY OF THE ESSAY

In the body of the essay, the paragraphs *explain, support, and develop your thesis*. In this part of the essay, each paragraph has its own topic sentence. The topic sentence in each paragraph does two things:

1. It focuses the sentences in the paragraph.
2. It makes a point connected to the thesis.

The thesis and the topic sentences are ideas that need to be supported by details, explanations, and examples. You can visualize the connections among the parts of an essay like this:

Introduction with Thesis

Body
- Topic Sentence
- Details
- Topic Sentence
- Details
- Topic Sentence
- Details

Conclusion

When you write topic sentences, you can help to organize your essay by referring to the checklist below.

 **Checklist**

A Checklist for the Topic Sentences of an Essay

✔ Does the topic sentence give the point of the paragraph?

✔ Does the topic sentence connect to the thesis of the essay?

How Long Are the Body Paragraphs?

Remember that the body paragraphs of an essay are the place where you explain and develop your thesis. Those paragraphs should be long enough to explain your points, not just list them. To do this well, try to make your body paragraphs *at least seven sentences long.* As you develop your writing skills, you may find that you can support your ideas in fewer than seven sentences.

Developing the Body Paragraphs

You can write well-developed body paragraphs by following the same steps you used in writing single paragraphs for the earlier assignments in this course. By working through the stages of gathering ideas, outlining, drafting, revising, editing, and proofreading, you can create clear, effective paragraphs.

To focus and develop the body paragraphs, as you revise, ask the questions in the following checklist.

 **Checklist**

A Checklist for Developing Body Paragraphs for an Essay

✔ Does the topic sentence cover everything in the paragraph?

✔ Do I have enough details to explain the topic sentence?

✔ Do all the details in the paragraph support, develop, or illustrate the topic sentence?

 Exercise 9

Practice

Creating Topic Sentences

Following are thesis sentences. For each thesis, write topic sentences (as many as indicated by the numbered blanks). The first one is done for you.

1. thesis: Cats make good pets.

topic sentence 1: <u>Cats are independent and don't mind being home alone.</u>

topic sentence 2: <u>Cats are easy to litter-train.</u>

topic sentence 3: <u>Cats are fun to play with.</u>

2. thesis: Mr. Thompson is willing to help his students both inside the classroom and during his office hours.

topic sentence 1: _____

_____

topic sentence 2: _____

_____

3. thesis: It is easy to recognize the student who is in college to have a good time.

topic sentence 1: _____

_____

topic sentence 2: _____

_____

topic sentence 3: _____

_____

4. thesis: The ideal roommate has several characteristics.

topic sentence 1: _____

_____

topic sentence 2: _____

_____

topic sentence 3: _____

_____

5. thesis: Moving to a new town has its good and bad points.

topic sentence 1. _____

_____

topic sentence 2. _____

_____

topic sentence 3. _____

_____

topic sentence 4. _____

_____

WRITING THE CONCLUSION

The last paragraph in the essay is the **conclusion.** It does not have to be as long as a body paragraph, but it should be long enough to tie the essay together and remind the reader of the thesis. You can use any of these strategies in writing the conclusion:

1. You can restate the thesis, in new words. Go back to the first paragraph of your essay and reread it. For example, this could be the first paragraph of an essay:

introduction	Even when I was a child, I did not like being told what to do. I wanted to be my own boss. When I grew up, I figured that the best way to be my own boss was to own my own business. I thought that being in charge would be easy. I now know how difficult being an independent busi-
thesis at end	nessperson can be. <u>Independent business own-</u> <u>ers have to be smart, highly motivated, and</u> <u>hard-working.</u>

The thesis, underlined above, is the sentence that you can restate in your conclusion. Your task is to *keep the point but put it in different words.* Then work that restatement into a short paragraph, like this:

restating the thesis	People who own their own business have to be harder on themselves than any employer would ever be. Their success is <u>their</u> own responsibility; they cannot blame company policy or rules because they set the policy and make the rules. <u>If</u> <u>the business is to succeed, their intelligence,</u> <u>drive, and effort are essential.</u>

2. You can make a judgment, valuation, or recommendation. Instead of simply restating your point, you can end by making some comment on the issue you've described or the problem you've illustrated. If you were looking for another way to end the essay on owning one's own business, for example, you could end with a recommendation:

ending with a recommendation	People often dream of owning their own business. Dreaming is easy, but the reality is tough. <u>Those who want to succeed in their own</u> <u>venture should find a role model.</u> Studying a role model would teach them know-how, ambition, and constant effort lead to success.

3. You can conclude by framing your essay. You can tie your essay together neatly by *using something from your introduction* as a way of concluding. When you take an example, or a question, or even a quotation from your first paragraph and refer to it in your last paragraph, you are "framing" the essay. Take another look at the introduction to the essay on owning your own business. The writer talks about not liking to be told what to do, being one's own boss, and believing that being in charge would be easy. The writer also mentions the need to be smart, highly motivated, and hard-working. Now consider how the ideas of the introduction are used in this conclusion:

frame	Children <u>who do not like to take directions</u>
frame	may think that <u>being their own boss will be easy.</u>
frame	Adults who try to start a business soon discover that they must be totally self-directed; that is, they
frame	must be strong enough to <u>keep learning</u>, to <u>keep</u>
frame	<u>pushing forward</u>, and to <u>keep working.</u>

Exercise 10

Practice

Choosing a Better Way to Restate the Thesis

Following are five clusters. Each cluster consists of a thesis sentence and two sentences that try to restate the thesis. Each restated sentence could be used as part of the conclusion to an essay. Put a *B* next to the sentence in each pair that is a better restatement. Remember that the better choice repeats the same idea as the thesis but does not rely on too many of the same words.

1. thesis: Students choosing a college major should consider their abilities, their interests, and their financial goals.

restatement 1: _____ Before they choose a major, students should think about what they do well, what they like to do, and what they want to earn.

restatement 2: _____ Abilities, interests, and financial goals are things students choosing a major should consider.

2. thesis: One of the best ways to meet people is to take a college class.

restatement 1: _____ Taking a class in college is one of the best ways to meet people.

restatement 2: _____ College classes can make strangers into friends.

3. thesis: The three household chores I hate the most are cleaning closets, dusting, and folding laundry.

restatement 1: _____ Taking care of cluttered closets, dusty furniture, and wrinkled laundry makes me crazy.

restatement 2: _____ Cleaning the closets, dusting, and folding the laundry are the three household chores I hate the most.

4. thesis: My first job taught me the importance of being on time.

restatement 1: _____ On my first job, I learned how important it is to be on time.

restatement 2: _____ Punctuality was the key lesson of my first job.

5. thesis: Saving even a small amount of money each month is better than not saving at all.

restatement 1: _____ Saving a little money every month can be better than not saving at all.

restatement 2: _____ No matter how small it is, a monthly deposit in a bank account is better than living from paycheck to paycheck.

Revising the Draft

Once you have a rough draft of your essay, you can begin revising it. The following checklist may help you to make the necessary changes in your draft.

✔️ Checklist

Checklist for Revising the Draft of an Essay

✔ Does the essay have a clear, unifying thesis?

✔ Does the thesis make a point?

✔ Does each body paragraph have a topic sentence?

✔ Is each body paragraph focused on its topic sentence?

✔ Are the body paragraphs roughly the same size?

✔ Do any of the sentences need combining?

✔ Do any of the words need to be changed?

✔ Do the ideas seem to be smoothly linked?

✔ Does the introduction catch the reader's interest?

✔ Is there a definite conclusion?

✔ Does the conclusion remind the reader of the thesis?

Transitions Within Paragraphs

In an essay, you can use two kinds of transitions: those within a paragraph and those between paragraphs.

Transitions that link ideas *within a paragraph* are the same kinds you've used earlier. Your choice of words, phrases, or even sentences depends on the kind of connection you want to make. Here is a list of some common transitions and the kind of connection they express:

Info BOX

Common Transitions Within a Paragraph

To join two ideas:

again	another	in addition	moreover
also	besides	likewise	similarly
and	furthermore		

To show a contrast or a different opinion:

but	instead	on the other hand	still
however	nevertheless	or	yet
in contrast	on the contrary	otherwise	

To show a cause-and-effect connection:

accordingly	because	for	therefore
as a result	consequently	so	thus

To give an example:

for example	in the case of	such as	to illustrate
for instance	like		

To show time:			
after	first	recently	subsequently
at the same time	meanwhile	shortly	then
before	next	soon	until
finally			

Transitions Between Paragraphs

When you write something that is more than one paragraph long, you need transitions that link each paragraph to the others. There are several effective ways to link paragraphs and remind the reader of your main idea and of how the smaller points connect to it. Restatement and repetition are two ways.

1. Restate an idea from the preceding paragraph at the start of a new paragraph. Look closely at the two paragraphs below and notice how the second paragraph repeats an idea from the first paragraph and provides a link.

> If people were more patient, driving would be less of an ordeal. If, for instance, the driver behind me didn't honk his horn as soon as the traffic light turned green, both he and I would probably have lower blood pressure. He wouldn't be irritating himself by pushing so hard. And I wouldn't be reacting by slowing down, trying to irritate him even more, and getting angry at him. When I get impatient in heavy traffic, I just make a bad situation worse. My hurry doesn't get me to my destination any faster; it just stresses me out.

transition
restating an idea

> <u>The impatient driver doesn't get anywhere; neither does the</u> impatient customer at a restaurant. Impatience at restaurants doesn't pay. I work as a hostess at a restaurant, and I know that the customer who moans and complains about waiting for a table won't get one any faster than the person who makes the best of the wait. In fact, if a customer is too aggressive or obnoxious, the restaurant staff may actually slow down the process of getting that customer a table.

2. Use synonyms and repetition as a way of reminding the reader of an important point. For example, in the next two paragraphs, notice how certain repeated words, phrases, and synonyms all remind the reader of a point about facing fear. The repeated words and synonyms are underlined.

> Some people just <u>avoid</u> whatever they <u>fear.</u> I have an uncle who is <u>afraid</u> to fly. Whenever he has to go on a trip, he does anything he can to <u>avoid</u> getting on an airplane. He will drive for days, travel by train, take a bus trip. Because he is so <u>terrified</u> of flying, he lives with <u>constant anxiety</u> that some day he may have to fly. He is always thinking of the one emergency that could force him to <u>confront what he most dreads.</u> Instead of <u>dealing directly with his fear,</u> he lets it <u>haunt</u> him.

Other people are even worse than my uncle. He won't <u>attack his fear</u> of something external. But there are people who won't <u>deal with their fear</u> of themselves. My friend Sam is a good example of this kind of person. Sam has a serious drinking problem. All Sam's friends know he is an alcoholic. But Sam <u>will not admit</u> his addiction. I think he is <u>afraid to face</u> that part of himself. So he <u>denies</u> his problem, saying he can stop drinking any time he wants to. Of course, until Sam has the courage to <u>admit what he is most afraid of</u>, his alcoholism, he won't be able to change.

A Draft Essay

Below is a draft of the essay on working and going to college. As you read it, you'll notice many changes from the outline on page 284–285:

- An introduction has been added, phrased in the first person, "I," to unify the essay.
- Transitions have been added within and between paragraphs.
- General statements have been replaced by more specific ones.
- Word choice has been improved.
- A conclusion has been added. Some of the ideas added to the conclusion came from the original list of ideas about the topic of work and school. They are ideas that do not fit in the body paragraphs but are useful in the conclusion.

A Draft of an Essay (Thesis and topic sentences are underlined.)

I work thirty hours a week at the front desk of a motel in Riverside. When I first signed up for college classes, I figured college would be fairly easy to fit into my schedule. After all, college students are not in class all day, as high school students are. So I thought the twelve hours a week I'd spend in class wouldn't be too much of a load. But I was in for a big surprise. <u>My first semester at college showed me that students who work while going to school face problems at school, at work, and at home.</u>

<u>First of all, trying to juggle job and school responsibilities creates problems at school.</u> Early morning classes, for example, are particularly difficult for me. Because I work every weeknight from six to midnight, I don't get home until 1 A.M., and I can't fall asleep until 2 A.M. or later. I am too tired to pay attention in my 8 A.M. class. Once, I even fell asleep in that class. My work hours create other conflicts. They cut into my study time, so I have little time to do all the assigned reading and papers. I get behind in these assignments, and I never seem to have enough time to catch up. Consequently, my grades are not as good as they could be.

Because I both work and go to school, I have problems doing well at school. But <u>work can also suffer when workers attend college.</u> Students can bring school into the workplace. One night I tried to study at work, but my boss caught me reading my biology textbook at the front desk. I was reprimanded, and now my boss doesn't trust me. Sometimes I come to work very tired. When I don't get enough sleep, I can be rude to hotel guests who give me a hard time. Then the rudeness can get me into trouble. I remember one particular guest who reported me because I was sarcastic to her. She had spent a half hour complaining about her bill, and I had been too tired to be patient. Once again, my boss reprimanded me. Another time, school interfered with my job when I had to cut work to take a makeup test at school. I know my boss was unhappy with me then, too.

As a working student, I run into trouble on the job and at college. <u>Working students also suffer outside of college and the workplace.</u> Since I work nights during the week, the weekends are the only time I can study. Because I have to use my weekends to do schoolwork, I can't do other things. My apartment is a mess since I have no time to clean it. Worse, my girlfriend is ready to kill me because I have no social life. We never even go to the movies anymore. When she comes over, I am busy studying.

With responsibilities at home, work, and college, I face a cycle of stress. I am constantly racing around, and I can't break the cycle. I want a college education, and I must have a job to pay my tuition. The only way I can manage is to learn to manage my time. <u>I have learned that working students have to be very organized to cope with their responsibilities at college, work, and home.</u>

Exercise 11

Practice

Identifying the Main Points in the Draft of an Essay

Below is the draft of a four-paragraph essay. Read it, then reread it and underline the thesis and the topic sentences in each body paragraph and in the conclusion.

Until this year, I had never considered spending my free time helping others in my community. Volunteer work, I thought, was something retired folks and rich people did to fill their days. Just by chance, I became a volunteer for the public library's Classic Connection, a group that arranges read-a-thons and special programs for elementary school children. Although I don't receive a salary, working with some perceptive and entertaining third graders has been very rewarding in other ways.

Currently, I meet with my small group of four girls and three boys each Saturday morning from ten to eleven o'clock, and they have actually taught me more than I ever thought possible. I usually assign the children various passages in an illustrated children's classic like *The Little Prince*, and I help them with the difficult words as they read aloud. When I occasionally read to them, they follow right along, but when it's their turn, they happily go off track. I've learned that each child has a mind of his or her own, and I now have much more respect for day care workers and elementary school teachers who must teach, entertain, and discipline thirty rowdy children all day long. I'm tired after one hour with just seven children.

I have also learned the value of careful planning. I arrive at each session with a tape recorder and have them record a sound effect related to the story we'll be reading. At certain points during the session, we stop to hear the sound effects. They love to hear themselves and seem more focused on reading when I use this method. I feel more relaxed when I am well prepared and the sessions go smoothly.

I have enjoyed making several new friends and contacts through the Classic Connection. I've become friendly with the parents of the kids in my reading group, and one of the fathers has offered me a good-paying job at his printing business. He even mentioned he could be flexible about my schedule. I asked him if he could help me put a collection together of the group's most outrageous original stories, and he said he'd be glad to do it in *his* free time. I've thus learned that the spirit of volunteerism is indeed contagious.

I plan to keep volunteering for the Classic Connection's programs and look forward to a new group that should be starting soon. I don't know if I'm ready to graduate to an older group. After all, third graders still have much to teach me.

 Exercise 12

Practice

Adding Transitions to an Essay

The following essay needs transitions. Insert the transitions where indicated. Be sure to add the kind of transition—word, phrase, or sentence—indicated.

When I finished high school, I was determined to go to college. What I hadn't decided was *where* I would go to college. Most of my friends were planning to go away from home to attend college. They wanted to be responsible for themselves and to be free of their parents' supervision. Like my friends, I thought of going away to college. But I finally decided to go to a college near my home. I chose a college near home for several reasons.

_____ (add a phrase), I can save money by attending a community college near home. _____ (add a word) I am still living at home, I do not have to pay for room and board at a college dorm or to pay rent at an apartment off campus. I do not have to pay for the transportation costs of visits home. My friends who are away at school tell me about all the money they are spending on the things I get at home for free. These friends are paying for things like doing their laundry or hooking up their cable television. _____ (add a phrase) my college expenses are basically just tuition, fees, and books. I think I have a better deal than my friends who went away to college.

_____

_____

_____ (add a sentence). By attending college near home, I have kept a secure home base. I think it would be very hard for me to handle a new school, a new town, a new set of classmates, and a new place to live all at the same time. I have narrowed my challenges to a new school and new classmates. _____ (add a word) I come home after a stressful day at college, I still have Mom's home cooking and Dad's sympathy to console me. I still sleep in my own comfortable—and comforting—room. Students who go away to school may have more free-dom, _____ (add a word) I have more security.

_____

_____

_____ (add a sentence). My decision to stay home for college gave me a secure job base as well. For the past year, I've had a job I like very much. My boss is very fair, and she has come to value my work enough to let me set my own work schedule. _____ (add a word or phrase), she lets me plan my work schedule around my class schedule. If I had moved away to attend college, I would have had to find a new job. _____

_____ (add a word or phrase) I would have had a hard time find-

ing a boss as understanding as the one I have now.

There are many good reasons to go to a college away from home.

_____ (add a word or phrase) there are probably as

many good reasons to go to one near home. I know that I'm happy with my

decision. It has paid off financially and helped me maintain a secure place

to live and to work.

Exercise 13

Practice

Recognizing Synonyms and Repetition Used to Link Ideas in an Essay

In the following essay, underline all the synonyms and repetition (of words
or phrases) that help remind the reader of the thesis sentence. (To help you,
the thesis is underlined.)

Last summer, my mother planned a new kind of vacation for us. She,

my sister, and I were all going to visit relatives in the Dominican Republic.

These relatives lived in the country. They had no computer, no cable televi-

sion, and only one old truck for six family members. I dreaded this trip. <u>Yet

my time in the country exposed me to a happy and satisfying lifestyle.</u>

In this rural lifestyle, I saw a whole new kind of family interaction.

Mealtimes showed this relationship at its best. There were no fast food

places nearby, and each meal was prepared from scratch. My aunts and

great aunts cooked, my uncles barbecued, and my cousins sat around the

table and the yard, laughing and gossiping. As we ate, we shared stories and

jokes. Teens didn't separate from adults; all ages mingled. We were all

content to be together, enjoying this traditional way of life.

Being with my extended family was pleasant; so was being in the beau-

tiful countryside. The air was different from the city pollution I was used to.

In the city, I walked my dog on a leash and kept my cat indoors. Here my rel-

atives had three dogs who cheerfully explored the village and greeted the

neighbors' dogs like old friends. The cats came and went as they pleased.

There were also pigs and cows and chickens, and the mix created a noisy but joyful atmosphere. At night, when everything was quiet, I sat outside with my cousins, enjoying the stars and the fulfillment of a day in the country.

Before my trip to the Dominican Republic, I would never have believed that I could find happiness without my email, my cell phone, and my hectic social life with my friends. However, I now know that there is another way of life, simpler and slower, that appeals to me. It offers the satisfaction that comes from being close to family and to nature.

Final Lines Proofreading and Polishing: An Essay

When you are satisfied with the final version of your essay, you can begin preparing a good copy. Your essay will need a title. Try to think of a short title that is connected to your thesis. Since the title is the reader's first contact with your essay, an imaginative title can create a good first impression. If you can't think of anything clever, try using a key phrase from your essay.

The title is placed at the top of your essay, about an inch above the first paragraph. Always capitalize the first word of the title and all other words *except* "the," "an," "a," or prepositions (like "of," "in," "with") that are under five letters. Do not underline or put quotation marks around your title.

The Final Version of an Essay

Following is the final version of the essay on working and going to college. When you compare it to the draft on pages 296–297, you will notice some changes:

- In the first paragraph, the words "I thought" have been added to make it clear that the statement is the writer's opinion.
- One topic sentence, in paragraph two, has been revised so that it includes the word "students" and the meaning is more precise.
- Words have been changed to sharpen the meaning.
- Transitions have been added.
- A title has been added.

A Final Version of an Essay (Changes from the draft are underlined.)

Problems of the Working College Student

I work thirty hours a week at the front desk of a motel in Riverside. When I first registered for college classes, I figured college would be fairly easy to fit into my schedule. After all, I thought, college students are not in class all day, like high school students are. So I <u>assumed</u> the twelve hours a week I'd spend in class wouldn't be too much of a load. But I was in for a big surprise. My first semester at college showed me that students who work while going to college face problems at school, at work, and at home.

First of all, <u>students who try</u> to juggle job and school responsibilities <u>find trouble</u> at school. Early morning classes, for example, are particularly difficult for me. Because I work every week night from six to midnight, I don't get home until 1 A.M., and I can't fall asleep until 2 A.M. or later. <u>Consequently,</u> I am too tired to pay attention in my eight o'clock class. Once, I even fell asleep in that class. My work hours create other conflicts. They cut into my study time, so I have little time to do all the assigned reading and papers. I get behind in the assignments, and I never seem to have enough time to catch up. <u>As a result,</u> my grades are not as good as they could be.

Because I both work and go to school, I have problems doing well at school. But work can also suffer when workers attend college. Students can bring school into the workplace. <u>I've been guilty of this practice and have paid the price.</u> One night I tried to study at work, but my boss caught me reading my biology textbook at the front desk. I was reprimanded, and now my boss doesn't trust me. Sometimes I come to work very tired, <u>another problem.</u> When I don't get enough sleep, I can be rude to <u>motel</u> guests who give me a hard time. Then the rudeness can get me into trouble. I remember one particular guest who reported me because I was sarcastic to her. She had spent a half hour complaining about her bill, and I had been too tired to be patient. Once again, my boss reprimanded me. Another time, school interfered with my job when I had to cut work to take a makeup test at school. I know my boss was unhappy with me then, too.

As a working student, I run into trouble on the job and at college. Working students also suffer outside of classes and the workplace. <u>My schedule illustrates the conflicts of trying to juggle too many duties.</u> Since I work nights during the week, the weekends are the only time I can study. Because I have to use my weekends to do schoolwork, I can't do other things. My apartment is a mess since I have no time to clean it. Worse, my girlfriend is ready to kill me because I have no social life. We never even go to the movies anymore. When she comes over, I am busy studying.

With responsibilities at home, work, and college, I face a cycle of stress. I am constantly racing around, and I can't break the cycle. I want a college education, and I must have a job to pay my tuition. The only way I can manage is to learn to manage my time. <u>In my first semester at college, I've realized</u> that working students have to be very organized to cope with the responsibilities of college, work, and home.

Before you prepare the final copy of your essay, check your latest draft for errors in spelling and punctuation and for any errors made in typing or copying.

Practice

Proofreading to Prepare the Final Version

Following are two essays with the kinds of errors that are easy to overlook when you prepare the final version of an assignment. Correct the errors, writing above the lines. There are nineteen errors in the first essay and seventeen in the second.

"Three Myths About Young People"

Today, when a person says the word "teenager" or refers to "college kids," that person may be speaking with a little sneer. Young people have acquired a bad reputation. Some of the repution may be deserved, but some of it may not be. Young people are often judged according to myths, beliefs that are not true. Older people should not believe in three common myth's about the young.

We are always hearing that young people are irresponsable, but their are many teens and people in their early twenties who disprove this statement. In every town, there are young people who hold full-time jobs and support a family. There are even more young people who work and go to school. All of my friends have been working since their sophmore year of High School. The fact that not one of them has ever been fired from a job implies they must be pretty good workers. Furthermore, young people today are almost forced to be responsible they must learn to work and pay for their clothes and college tuition.

Another foolish belief is that all young people take drugs. Hollywood movies encourage this myth by including a drug-crazed teenager in almost every movie. Whenever television broadcasts a public service advertisement about drugs, the drug user shown is a young person. In reality, many young people have chosen not to take drugs. For every teen with a problem of abuse, there is probally another teen who has never taken drugs or who has conquered a drug problem. In my high scool, an anonymous student poll showed that more than half of the students had never experimented with drugs.

Some older adults label young people irresponsible and addicted. Even more people are likely to say that the young are apathetic, but such critics are wrong. The young are criticized for not carring about political or social issues, and for being unconscience of the problems we all face. yet high school and college students are the ones who are out there, cleaning up the litter on the highways or beaches, whenever there is a local clean-up campaign. During the holidays, every school and college collects food, clothing, and toys for the needy students organize these drives, and students distributes these items. On many weekends, young people are out on the highways, collecting for charities.

Granted, there are apathetic, addicted, and irresponsible young people. But a whole group should not be judged by the actions of a few. Each young person deserve to be treated as an individual, not as an example of a myth.

Everyday Pleasures

As I hurry through each day, I focus on the demands and difficulties that face me. I thinks about driving in rush hour, or studying for a quizz. I rarely stop to consider the many moments of enjoyment that fill each day. These simple pleasures compensate for all life's stressful moments.

Even as I get ready for the day ahead, I enjoy the sootheing comfort of a hot shower. The stream of hot waters soothes my aching muscles. I adjust the shower head so that warm needles of water masage my back. The rising steam surrounds me. I fill my body restoring itself and I never want to leave. Yet when I face the cold air outside the shower, drying off with the soft bath towels leaves me feeling clean and new

When I return home, my dogs greeting allways makes me smile. I hear him bark as I turn the key in the lock. Then he sees me and wriggles his entire body with joy. I feel a wet nose against my hand and look into two, deep brown eyes. He seems to be smiling at me. To my dog, my return means a long walk, some fun with a ball, and a good dinner. My dog's happiness makes me happy.

The evening has its own enjoyments. My couch is deep and wide with many pillows, perfect for laying in front of the television. I stretch out and turn on a movie, my dog at my feet. The movie is silly, but it does'nt matter. I burrow into the pillows. Soon my dog and me are both asleep on the couch.

As I face the irritations of my day, I forget the moments of pleasure, comfort, and happiness that I expereince. Because they are routine and ordinary, they are easy to forget. However stopping to remember these times makes me appreciate the good I have in my life.

Lines of Detail: A Walk-Through Assignment

Choose two radio stations popular with people your age. They can be two stations that broadcast music or two stations that broadcast talk shows. Write a four-paragraph essay describing who listens to each station. To write the essay, follow these steps:

Step 1: Begin with some investigation. Listen to two stations, either talk or music, popular with your age group. Before you listen, prepare a list of at least six questions. The questions will help you gather details for your essay. For any radio station, you can ask:

What kinds of products, restaurants or services are advertised?

Does the station offer any contests?

Does the station sponsor any events?

For two music stations, your questions might include these:

What groups or individuals does the station play?

What kind of music does it play?

For two talk-radio stations, your questions might include these:

What are the talk-show hosts like? Are they funny or insulting or serious?

What topics are discussed?

What kinds of people call in?

Listen to the stations you chose, and as you listen, take notes. Answer your own questions, and write down anything about each station that catches your interest or that seems relevant.

Step 2: Survey your notes. Mark the related ideas with the same number. Then cluster the information you have gathered, and give each cluster a title.

Step 3: Focus all your clusters around one point. To find a focus, ask yourself whether the listeners of the two stations are people of the same social class, with the same interests, the same educational background, the same ethnic or racial background.

Try to focus your information with a thesis like one of these:

_____ (station name) and _____

(station name) appeal to the same audience.

_____ (station name) and _____

(station name) appeal to different audiences.

_____ (station name) and _____

(station name) use different strategies to appeal to the

same kind of listeners.

_____ (station name) appeals to young people

who _____, but _____ (station name)

appeals to young people who _____.

While _____ (station name) is popular with

middle-aged listeners interested in _____,

_____ (station name) appeals to middle-aged

listeners who like _____.

Step 4: Once you have a thesis and clustered details, draft an outline. Revise your draft outline until it is unified, expresses the ideas in a clear order, and has enough supporting details.

Step 5: Write a draft of your essay. Revise the draft, checking it for balanced paragraphs, relevant and specific details, a strong conclusion, and smooth transitions.

Step 6: Before you prepare the final lines version of your essay, check for spelling, word choice, punctuation, and mechanical errors. Also, give your essay a title.

Writing Your Own Essay

When you write on any of these topics, be sure to work through the stages of the writing process in preparing your essay.

1. Take any paragraph you wrote for this class and develop it into an essay of four or five paragraphs. If your instructor agrees, read the paragraph to a partner or group, and ask your listener(s) to suggest points inside the paragraph that could be developed into paragraphs of their own.

2. Write an essay using one of the following thesis statements:

   If I won a million dollars, I know what I would do with it.
   Most families waste our natural resources every day simply by going through their daily routines.
   Television's coverage of football [or basketball, tennis, or any other sport you choose] could be improved by a few changes.

   The one place I'll never visit again is _____ because

   _____.

   All bad romances share certain characteristics.

   If I could be someone else, I'd like to be _____ for several reasons.

3. Write an essay on earliest childhood memories. Interview three classmates to gather details and to focus your essay. Ask each one to tell you about the earliest memory he or she has of childhood. Before you begin interviewing, make a list of questions like these: What is your earliest memory? How old were you at the time of that recollection? What were you doing? Do you remember other people or events in that scene? If so, what were the others doing? Were you indoors? Outdoors? Is this a pleasant memory? Why do you think this memory has stayed with you? Use the details collected at the interviews to write a five-paragraph essay with a thesis sentence like one of the following:

Childhood memories vary a great deal from person to person.

The childhood memories of different people are surprisingly similar.

Although some people's first memories are painful, others remember a happy time.

Some people claim to remember events from their infancy, but others can't remember anything before their third or fourth, fifth, etc. birthday.

4. Freewrite for ten minutes on the two best days of your life. After you've completed the freewriting, review it. Do the two days have much in common? Or were they very different? Write a four-paragraph essay based on their similarities or differences, with a thesis like one of these:

The two best days of my life were both _____. (Focus on

similarities.)

While one of the best days of my life was _____, the

other great day was _____. (Fill in with differences.)

5. Write an essay on one of the following topics:

Three Careers for Me	The Three Worst Jobs
Three Workplace Hazards	Three Workplace Friends
Three Lucky People	Three Wishes
Three Family Traditions	Three Decisions for Me

6. Look closely at the top photograph on page 308. Write a five-paragraph essay in which you describe a situation that the picture may represent. In one body paragraph, you can write about how these two people met and decided to head for New York; in another paragraph, about what they are hoping for as they stand together hitchhiking; and in another paragraph, about what may happen to them next.

7. Look closely at the bottom photograph on page 308. Write a four-paragraph essay in which you describe the relationship between the people in the photograph. You can use your imagination, but try to base your imaginings on the facial expressions and body language of the people.

8. Narrow one of the following topics and then write an essay on it.

nature	dreams	crime	music	celebrities
fears	family	lies	health	romance
habits	books	money	animals	travel
students	teachers	games	secrets	fashion

Name: _____ Section: _____

PEER REVIEW FORM FOR AN ESSAY

After you've written a draft of your essay, let a writing partner read it. When your partner has completed the form below, discuss the comments. Then repeat the same process for your partner's paragraph.

The thesis of this essay is _____

_____

The topic sentences for the body paragraphs are _____

_____

_____

_____

_____

The topic sentence in the conclusion is _____

_____

The best part of the essay is the _____ (first, second, third, etc.) paragraph.

I would like to see details added to the part about _____.

_____.

I would take out the part about _____.

The introduction is (a) good or (b) could be better. (Choose one.)

The conclusion is (a) good or (b) could be better. (Choose one.)

I have questions about _____

Additional comments: _____

_____

_____

_____

_____

_____

_____

_____

Reviewer's Name: _____

WRITING FROM READING: The Essay

Eleven

Sandra Cisneros

Sandra Cisneros, the child of a Mexican father and a Mexican-American mother, grew up in Chicago. She has worked as a teacher to high school dropouts and in other areas of education and the arts. A poet and writer of short stories, Cisneros incorporates her ethnic background into her writing. Her story "Eleven" is about a birthday gone wrong.

1   What they don't understand about birthdays and what they never tell you is that when you're eleven, you're also ten, and nine, and eight, and seven, and six, and five, and four, and three, and two, and one. And when you wake up on your eleventh birthday you expect to feel eleven, but you don't. You open your eyes and everything's just like yesterday, only it's today. And you don't feel eleven at all. You feel like you're still ten. And you are—underneath the year that makes you eleven.

2   Like some days you might say something stupid, and that's the part of you that's still ten. Or maybe some days you might need to sit on your mama's lap because you're scared, and that's the part of you that's five. And maybe one day when you're all grown up maybe you will need to cry like if you're three, and that's okay. That's what I tell Mama when she's sad and needs to cry. Maybe she's feeling three.

3   Because the way you grow old is kind of like an onion or like the rings inside a tree trunk or like my little wooden dolls that fit one inside the other, each year inside the next one. That's how being eleven years old is.

4   You don't feel eleven. Not right away. It takes a few days, weeks even, sometimes even months before you say Eleven when they ask you. And you don't feel smart eleven, not until you're almost twelve. That's the way it is.

5   Only today I wish I didn't have only eleven years rattling inside me like pennies in a tin Band-Aid box. Today I wish I was one hundred and two instead of eleven because if I was one hundred and two I'd have known what to say when Mrs. Price put the red sweater on my desk. I would've known how to tell her it wasn't mine instead of just sitting there with that look on my face and nothing coming out of my mouth.

6   "Whose is this?" Mrs. Price says, and she holds the red sweater up in the air for all the class to see. "Whose? It's been sitting in the coatroom for a month."

7   "Not mine," says everybody. "Not me."

8   "It has to belong to somebody," Mrs. Price keeps saying, but nobody can remember. It's an ugly sweater with red plastic buttons and a collar and sleeves all stretched out like you could use it for a jump rope. It's maybe a thousand years old and even if it belonged to me I wouldn't say so.

9   Maybe because I'm skinny, maybe because she doesn't like me, that stupid Sylvia Saldívar says, "I think it belongs to Rachel." An ugly sweater like that, all raggedy and old, but Mrs. Price believes her. Mrs. Price takes the sweater and puts it right on my desk, but when I open my mouth nothing comes out.

10   "That's not. I don't, you're not. . . . Not mine," I finally say in a little voice that was maybe me when I was four.

11   "Of course it's yours," Mrs. Price says. "I remember you wearing it once." Because she's older and the teacher, she's right and I'm not.

12   Not mine, not mine, not mine, but Mrs. Price is already turning to page thirty-two, and math problem number four. I don't know why but all of a sudden I'm feeling sick inside, like the part of me that's three wants to come out of my eyes, only I squeeze them shut tight and bite down on my teeth real hard and try to remember today I am eleven, eleven. Mama is making a cake for me tonight, and when Papa comes home everybody will sing Happy birthday, happy birthday to you.

13   But when the sick feeling goes away and I open my eyes, the red sweater's still sitting there like a big red mountain. I move the red sweater to the corner of my desk with my ruler. I move my pencil and books and eraser as far from it as possible. I even move my chair a little to the right. Not mine, not mine, not mine.

14   In my head I'm thinking how long till lunchtime, how long till I can take the red sweater and throw it over the schoolyard fence, or leave it hanging on a parking meter, or bunch it up into a little ball and toss it in the alley. Except when math period ends Mrs. Price says loud and in front of everybody, "Now, Rachel, that's enough," because she sees I've shoved the red sweater to the tippy-tip corner of my desk and it's hanging all over the edge like a waterfall, but I don't care.

15   "Rachel," Mrs. Price says. She says it like she's getting mad. "You put that sweater on right now and no more nonsense."

16   "But it's not—"

17   "Now!" Mrs. Price says.

18   This is when I wish I wasn't eleven, because all the years inside me—ten, nine, eight, seven, six, five, four, three, two, and one—are pushing at the back of my eyes when I put one arm through one sleeve of the sweater that smells like cottage cheese, and then the other arm through the other and stand there with my arms apart like if the sweater hurts me and it does, all itchy and full of germs that aren't even mine.

19   That's when everything I've been holding in since this morning, since when Mrs. Price put the sweater on my desk, finally lets go, and all of a sudden I'm crying in front of everybody. I wish I was invisible but I'm not. I'm eleven and it's my birthday today and I'm crying like I'm three in front of

everybody. I put my head down on the desk and bury my face in my stupid clown-sweater arms. My face all hot and spit coming out of my mouth because I can't stop the little animal noises from coming out of me, until there aren't any more tears left in my eyes, and it's just my body shaking like when you have the hiccups, and my whole head hurts like when you drink milk too fast.

20   But the worst part is right before the bell rings for lunch. That stupid Phyllis Lopez, who is even dumber than Sylvia Saldívar, says she remembers the red sweater is hers! I take it off right away and give it to her, only Mrs. Price pretends like everything's okay.

21   Today I'm eleven. There's a cake Mama's making for tonight, and when Papa comes home from work we'll eat it. There'll be candles and presents and everybody will sing Happy birthday, happy birthday to you, Rachel, only it's too late.

22   I'm eleven today. I'm eleven, ten, nine, eight, seven, six, five, four, three, two, and one, but I wish I was one hundred and two. I wish I was anything but eleven, because I want today to be far away already, far away like a runaway balloon, like a tiny *o* in the sky, so tiny-tiny you have to close your eyes to see it.

WRITING FROM READING: "Eleven"

When you write on any of these topics, work through the stages of the writing process in preparing your essay.

1. Write about a time when you didn't feel your age. You can call the essay "Seventeen" or "Eleven," or whatever your chronological age was, but write about why you felt you were a different age.

2. Write about a time, or several times, when an older person was wrong and you were right.

3. Write about a teacher you will always remember.

4. Write an essay on three things that children (or teens) fear.

5. You may have heard the saying "You're only as old as you feel." Interview three people. Ask them their age; ask them how old they feel and why. Use the information you gather to write an essay about people and age.

6. Cisneros writes that "the way you grow old is kind of like an onion or like the rings inside a tree trunk." Write an essay about three memorable "rings," three experiences, when you grew in some significant way.

7. Write an essay about two emotions that Rachel, the girl in "Eleven," feels. Use details from "Eleven" to describe and explain these emotions.

Althea Gibson: Never Give Up

Varla Ventura

Ventura writes about one of the heroes of the sports world, Althea Gibson. Gibson, Ventura writes, changed from "'bad girl' to tennis sensation" and later became a mentor and coach to a generation of African-American women tennis players.

Words You May Need to Know (corresponding paragraph numbers in parentheses.)

sharecropper (2): a farmer who rents land and pays the rent with a share of the crop

truant officers (2): officers who check on a child's regular attendance at school

dire (3): terrible, dreadful

naysayers (3): those with negative comments

patrons (3): people who support another with money or efforts

chafed (4): became irritated and annoyed by

heinous (4): wicked

decrying (4): speaking with disapproval of

Babe Zaharias (5): a famous all-around sportswoman who decided to become a professional golfer in order to make a living

LPGA (5): Ladies' Professional Golf Association

---

1   From the ghetto to the tennis court, Althea Gibson's story is pure heroism. At a time when tennis was dominated not by whites but by upperclass whites at that, she managed to serve and volley her way to the top.

2   Born in 1927 to a Southern sharecropper family, Althea struggled as a girl with a restless energy that took years for her to channel into positive accomplishments. The family's move to Harlem didn't help. She was bored by school and skipped a lot; teachers and truant officers predicted the worst for Althea, believing that she was a walking attitude problem whose future lay as far as the nearest reform school.

3   Although things looked dire for Althea, she had a thing or two to show the naysayers. Like many heroes, Althea had to bottom out before she could get to the top. She dropped out of school and drifted from job to job until, at a mere fourteen, she found herself a ward of New York City's Welfare Department. This turned out to be the best thing that could have happened to Althea—a wise welfare worker not only helped her find steady work, but also enrolled her into New York's police sports program. Althea fell in love with paddle ball and, upon graduating to real tennis, amazed everyone with her natural ability. The New York Cosmopolitan Club, an interracial sports and social organization, sponsored the teen and arranged for her to have a tennis coach, Fred Johnson. Althea's transformation from "bad girl" to tennis sensation was immediate; she won the New York State Open Championship one year later. She captured the attention of two wealthy patrons who agreed to sponsor her if she finished high school. She did in 1949—and went on to accept a tennis scholarship to Florida Agricultural and Mechanical University.

4   Althea's battles weren't over yet, though. She aced nine straight Negro national championships and chafed at the exclusion from tournaments closed to non-white players. Fighting hard to compete with white players, Althea handled herself well, despite being exposed to racism at its most heinous. Her dignified struggle to overcome segregation in tennis won her many supporters of all colors. Finally, one of her biggest fans and admirers, the editor of *American Lawn Tennis* magazine, wrote an article decrying the "color barrier" in tennis. The walls came down. By 1958, Althea Gibson won the singles and doubles at Wimbledon and twice took the U.S. national championships at the U.S. Open as well.

5   Then, citing money woes, she retired; she just couldn't make a living at women's tennis. Like Babe Zaharias, she took up golf, becoming the first black woman to qualify for the LPGA. But she never excelled in golf as she had in tennis, and in the seventies and eighties she returned to the game she truly loved, serving as a mentor and coach to an up-and-coming generation of African American women tennis players.

6   Through sheer excellence and a willingness to work on behalf of her race, Althea Gibson made a huge difference in the sports world for which we are all indebted.

WRITING FROM READING "Althea Gibson: Never Give Up"

When you write on any of these topics, work through the stages of the writing process in preparing your essay.

1. Write an essay about several obstacles Gibson overcame in her lifetime.

2. As a child and teenager, Gibson did not appear to be headed for success. Write an essay about another person who did not appear to be headed in the right direction but who turned his or her life around. The person does not have to be a celebrity or someone involved in sports.

3. Throughout her struggles and victories, Gibson showed certain strong personal qualities that enabled her to survive and thrive. Write an essay about these qualities; in your details, show how each quality turned up at crucial times in her life. (A personal quality is a trait such as dignity or confidence.)

4. Write about a time when you or someone you knew refused to give up.

5. Althea Gibson is credited with helping to break the "color barrier" in tennis. Write an essay about someone who helped to break a barrier. To begin, you can work with a group to brainstorm about barriers. Consider color, gender, or ethnic barriers and think about people who have helped to break down a barrier. Breaking a barrier does not have to involve a confrontation; it can also mean succeeding at a profession usually closed to certain people or living a life that breaks a stereotype.

Send Your Children to the Libraries

Arthur Ashe

Arthur Ashe was the first African-American Davis Cup participant and the first black male to win the U.S. Open and Wimbledon. Besides being a champion tennis player, he was a graduate of the University of California, Los Angeles, a writer, and a political activist. "Send Your Children to the Libraries," written in 1977, is addressed to African-American parents, but its message can be applied to all parents and children today who dream only of a career in sports.

Words You May Need to Know

pretentious (1): showy
dubious (1): doubtful, uncertain
emulate (2): imitate

viable (4): practical, realistic
benchwarmer (7): an athlete who does not get much playing time

1   Since my sophomore year at University of California, Los Angeles, I have become convinced that we blacks spend too much time on the playing fields and too little time in the libraries. Please don't think of this attitude as being pretentious just because I am a black, single professional athlete. I don't have children, but I can make observations. I strongly believe the black culture expends too much time, energy, and effort raising, praising, and teasing our black children as to the dubious glories of professional sport.

2   All children need models to emulate—parents, relatives, or friends. But when the child starts school, the influence of the parent is shared by teachers and classmates, by the lure of books, movies, ministers, and newspapers, but most of all by television. Which televised events have the greatest number of viewers? Sports—the Olympics, Super Bowl, Masters, World Series, pro basketball playoffs, Forest Hills. ABC-TV even has sports on Monday night prime time from April to December. So your child gets a massive dose of O. J. Simpson, Kareem Abdul-Jabbar, Muhammad Ali, Reggie Jackson, Dr. J. and Lee Elder and other pro athletes. And it is only natural that your child will dream of being a pro athlete himself.

3   But consider these facts: For the major professional sports of hockey, football, basketball, golf, tennis, and boxing, there are roughly only 3,170 major league positions available (attributing 200 positions to golf, 200 to tennis, and 100 to boxing). And the annual turnover is small. We blacks are a subculture of about 28 million. Of the 13 1/2 million men, 5 to 6 million are under 20 years of age, so your son has less than one chance in 1,000 of becoming a pro. Less than one in a thousand. Would you bet your son's future on something with odds of 999 to 1 against you? I wouldn't.

4   Unless a child is exceptionally gifted, you should know by the time he enters high school whether he has a future as an athlete. But what is more

important is what happens if he doesn't graduate or doesn't land a college scholarship and doesn't have a viable alternative job career. Our high school dropout rate is several times the national average, which contributes to our unemployment rate of roughly twice the national average.

5   And how do you fight the figures in the newspapers every day? Ali has earned more than $30 million boxing, O. J. just signed for 2 1/2 million, Dr. J. for almost $3 million, Reggie Jackson for $2.8 million, Nate Archibald for $400,000 a year. All that money, recognition, attention, free cars, girls, jobs in the off season—no wonder there is Pop Warner football, Little League baseball, National Junior Tennis League tennis, hockey practice at 5:00 A.M., and pickup basketball games in any center city at any hour.

6   There must be some way to assure that the 999 who try but don't make it to pro sports don't wind up on the street corners or in the unemployment lines. Unfortunately, our most widely recognized role models are athletes and entertainers—"runnin'" and "jumpin'" and "singin'" and "dancin.'" While we are 60 percent of the National Basketball Association, we are less than 4 percent of the doctors and lawyers. While we are about 35 percent of major league baseball, we are less than 2 percent of the engineers. While we are about 40 percent of the National Football League, we are less than 11 percent of construction workers such as carpenters and bricklayers. Our greatest heroes of the century have been athletes—Jack Johnson, Joe Louis, and Mohammed Ali. Racial and economic discrimination forced us to channel our energies into athletics and entertainment. These were the two ways out of the ghetto, the ways to get that Cadillac, those alligator shoes, that cashmere sport coat.

7   Somehow, parents must instill a desire for learning alongside the desire to be Walt Frazier. Why not start by sending black professional athletes into high schools to explain the facts of life? I have often addressed high school audiences, and my message is always the same. For every hour you spend on the athletic field, spend two in the library. Even if you make it as a pro athlete, your career will be over by the time you are 35. So you will need that diploma. Have these pro athletes explain what happens if you break a leg, get a sore arm, have one bad year or don't make the cut for five or six tournaments. Explain to them the star system, wherein for every O. J. earning millions there are six or seven others making $15,000 or $20,000 or $30,000 a year. But don't just have Walt Frazier or O. J. or Abdul-Jabbar address your class. Invite a benchwarmer or a guy who didn't make it. Ask him if he sleeps every night. Ask him whether he was graduated. Ask him what he would do if he became disabled tomorrow. Ask him where his old high school athletic buddies are.

8   We have been on the same roads—sports and entertainment—too long. We need to pull over, fill up at the library and speed away to Congress and the Supreme Court, the unions and the business world. Don't worry:

we will still be able to sing and dance and run and jump better than any-body else.

9   I'll never forget how proud my grandmother was when I graduated from U.C.L.A. in 1966. Never mind the Davis Cup in 1968, 1969, and 1970. Never mind the Wimbledon title, Forest Hills, etc. To this day, she still doesn't know what those names mean. What mattered to her was that of her more than thirty children and grandchildren, I was the first to be grad-uated from college, and a famous college at that. Somehow, that made up for all those floors she scrubbed all those years.

WRITING FROM READING: "Send Your Children to the Libraries"

When you write on any of the following topics, be sure to work through the stages of the writing process.

1. Write an essay explaining Ashe's reasons for emphasizing aca-demics over sports.

2. Ashe was a role model in sports and is also remembered as a writer and a crusader for equality. Write an essay about another role model who is admirable in more than one area.

3. Ashe asks his readers to consider the realities of a career in pro-fessional sports. Write an essay about another career that many people dream of, and explain the difficulties of this career. You can write about the fantasy side of this career, the difficulties of entering this career, and the realities of working in this career.

4. Write a reply to Ashe's essay. In your reply, explain why, in spite of the odds, young people of all races dream of a career in profes-sional athletics.

5. Write an essay about three people who are not athletes but who should be role models for young people.

CHAPTER 12

Different Essay Patterns

You can write essays in a number of patterns, but any pattern will develop more successfully if you follow the writing steps in preparing your essay. The following examples take you through the steps of preparing an essay in each pattern. Each essay expands on its related paragraph pattern in an earlier chapter of this book.

ILLUSTRATION

Hints for Writing an Illustration Essay

1. Use specific examples to support a general point. Remember that a *general* statement is a broad point, and a *specific* example is narrow.

> **general statement:** The weather was terrible yesterday.
> **specific example:** It rained for six hours.

> **general statement:** I am having trouble in my math class.
> **specific example:** I can't understand the problems in Chapter 12.

2. Be sure that you support a general statement by using specific examples instead of merely writing another general statement.

> **not this: general statement:** The weather was terrible yesterday.
> **more general statements:** ~~It was awful outside. Yesterday brought nasty weather.~~
> **But this: general statement:** The weather was terrible yesterday.
> **specific examples:**　　It rained for six hours.
> 　　　　　　　　　　Several highways were flooded.

3. Be sure that you have sufficient examples and that you develop them well. If you use one or two examples and do not development them effectively, you will have a skimpy paragraph. You can use fewer examples and develop each one, or you can use more examples and develop them less extensively.

not this: a skimpy paragraph:

The weather was terrible yesterday. It rained for six hours. Several highways were flooded.

but this: a paragraph with few examples, each one well developed:

The weather was terrible yesterday. It rained for six hours. The rain was heavy and harsh, accompanied by high winds that lashed the trees and signs on stores and restaurants. The downpour was so heavy that several highways were flooded. Drivers who usually take the Collins Road Expressway were diverted to a narrow city street and crawled home at 30 m.p.h. Additionally, traffic on the interstate highway was at a standstill because drivers slowed to gawk at the numerous accidents caused by the lack of visibility and water-slicked roads.

or this: a paragraph developed with more examples:

The weather was terrible yesterday. It rained for six hours, and several highways were flooded. Cedar Forest Elementary School closed early because of a leak in the auditorium's roof. The standing water also collected in low-lying residential areas where some children put on their swimsuits and splashed in four to six inches of water. Their parents, meanwhile, were trying to sweep the water out of porches and patios and praying that more rain would not seep into their houses. The high winds that accompanied the rain snapped tree branches and littered the area with debris. Two small "For Sale" signs were blown into the drive-through window at Burger King.

WRITING THE ILLUSTRATION ESSAY IN STEPS

Thought Lines Gathering Ideas: Illustration Essay

If you were asked to write an illustration essay about some aspect of clothes, you might first freewrite to narrow the topic and then decide to write about *tee shirts*. Brainstorming and listing your ideas about tee shirts might lead you to group your ideas into three categories:

Listing and Grouping Ideas for an Illustration Paragraph

Topic: Tee Shirts

Kinds of People Who Wear Tee Shirts

athletes	movie stars	old people
children	musicians	restaurant workers
teens	parents	

The Cost of Tee Shirts

cheap	some expensive

What Is Pictured or Written on Tee Shirts

ads on tees	beer ads	seascapes
concert tees	sporting goods	political slogans
college names	Mickey Mouse	souvenir pictures or sayings

You can summarize these ideas in a thesis sentence:

People of various backgrounds and ages wear all kinds of tee shirts.

This thesis sentence contains three parts: (1) people of various backgrounds, (2) people of all ages, and (3) all kinds of tee shirts. The part about the cost of tee shirts has been left out of the thesis. As you work toward a thesis, you can decide what to include and what to leave out. The three parts of the thesis may lead you to topic sentences for your outline.

With thesis sentence and a list of ideas, you are now ready to write an outline for your essay.

Outlines Devising a Plan: Illustration Essay

Following is an outline for an illustration essay on tee shirts.

An Outline for an Illustration Essay

paragraph 1	I. Thesis: People of various backgrounds and ages wear all kinds of tee shirts.

paragraph 2
topic sentence
and details
people of
various
backgrounds
	II. The rich and poor, famous and unknown, all wear tee shirts.
	  A. Famous athletes can be seen in tee shirts, signing autographs after a game.
	  B. Members of the local Little League team wear tees.
	  C. Movie stars are seen in them.
	  D. Musicians perform in tee shirts.
	  E. Restaurant workers wear tee shirts.
	  F. Famous political leaders work out in tee shirts.

paragraph 3
topic sentence
and details
people of all ages
	III. Every age group feels comfortable in tee shirts.
	  A. Mothers dress their babies in soft, washable little tees.
	  B. Older children wear a favorite tee shirt until it falls apart.
	  C. A teen wardrobe would not be complete without the latest style in tee shirts.
	  D. Parents wear them to clean and do chores.
	  E. Old people can be seen jogging or gardening in tees.

paragraph 4
topic sentence
and details
all kinds of
tee shirts
	IV. Almost anything can be printed or pictured on a tee shirt.
	  A. There are tees sold at concerts.
	  B. Some shirts have the names of colleges on them.
	  C. Others advertise a brand of beer or sporting goods.
	  D. Mickey Mouse is a favorite character on them.
	  E. Surfers' tee shirts have seascapes on them.
	  F. Some shirts are souvenirs.
	  G. Others have political slogans.

paragraph 5 conclusion	V. Anyone can find a tee shirt suited to his or her age and lifestyle, and that shirt can carry almost any message.

The outline combined some of the details from the list with new details gathered during the outlining process. As you write and revise your draft, you can continue to add details. You can also combine sentences, add transitions, and work on word choice.

Rough Lines Drafting and Revising: Illustration Essay

Following is a revised draft of the essay on tee shirts. As you read it, you'll notice many changes from the outline on page 320:

- An introduction has been added.
- Transitions have been added within and between paragraphs.
- Details have been added.
- Sentences have been combined.
- A concluding paragraph has been added.

A Draft of an Illustration Essay (Thesis and topic sentences are underlined.)

Fashion fads come and go. One year, everyone wears ripped jeans, and another year, striped soccer shirts are in. Whatever is most popular this year will most likely be out of style by next year. However, there is one piece of clothing that never goes out of style: the tee shirt. <u>People of various backgrounds and ages wear all kinds of tee shirts.</u>

<u>The rich and poor, famous and unknown all wear tee shirts.</u> While famous athletes dressed in tees sign autographs after a big game, children of the local Little League proudly sport their team shirts. Movie stars wear tees to their movie premieres. Musicians, both famous and struggling, perform in tee shirts. Meanwhile, many restaurant workers wear the restaurant's name or logo on their uniform tee. Even famous politicians have been photographed jogging or working out in tee shirts.

Tees appeal to all classes, and they also appeal to all generations. <u>Every age group feels comfortable in tee shirts.</u> Mothers dress their babies in soft little tee shirts. Older children often become so attached to a favorite tee that they wear it until it falls apart. In addition, a teen wardrobe would not be complete without the latest style in tee shirts. Parents wear them to clean the house, do the shopping, and wash the car. Older people in tees can be seen jogging through the neighborhood or gardening in their front yard.

All kinds of people wear tees, just as the shirts themselves come in all varieties. <u>Almost anything can be pictured or printed on a tee shirt.</u> At concerts, tee shirts with the performer's name on them cost a lot of money. Another popular kind of tee carries the name of a college. Other tees advertise a brand of beer, like Bud, or a sporting goods company, like Nike. Mickey Mouse is a favorite character on tee shirts, and not just on children's tees. Still other kinds of shirts include surfer tee shirts with seascapes on them, and souvenir tees, like the ones that say, "My folks visited Philadelphia, and all I got was this lousy tee shirt." Some shirts have political slogans, like "Save the Whales."

Fads can fade, but the tee shirt is everywhere. It has become so popular that it is almost a uniform. Its popularity is connected to its variety. <u>Anyone can find a tee shirt suited to his or her age and lifestyle, and that shirt can carry almost any message.</u>

`Final Lines` **Polishing and Proofreading: Illustration Essay**

Following is the final version of the essay on tee shirts. When you compare it to the draft on page 321, you will notice some changes:

- Some of the word choice has been polished to make a description more precise or to eliminate an awkward phrase.
- One phrase, "cost a lot of money," was changed to "can be expensive" to eliminate the use of "a lot," a phrase that some writers rely on too heavily.
- A transition was added to the conclusion.
- The conclusion includes a new, final sentence to stress the link between tee shirts' popularity and their variety.
- A title has been added.

A Final Version of an Illustration Essay (Changes from the draft are underlined.)

Tee Shirts Galore

Fashion fads come and go. One year, everyone wears ripped jeans, and another year, striped soccer shirts are in. Whatever is most popular this year will most likely be out of style by next year. However, there is one piece of clothing that never goes out of style: the tee shirt. People of various backgrounds and ages wear all kinds of tee shirts.

The rich and poor, famous and unknown all wear tee shirts. While famous athletes dressed in tees sign autographs after a big game, children of the local Little League proudly sport their team shirts. Movie stars wear tees to their <u>glamorous</u> movie premieres. Musicians, both famous and struggling, perform in tee shirts. Meanwhile, many restaurant workers wear the restaurant's name or logo on their uniform tee. Even famous politicians have been photographed jogging or working out in tee shirts.

Tees appeal to all classes, and they also appeal to all generations. Every age group feels comfortable in tee shirts. Mothers dress their babies in soft little tee shirts. Older children often become so attached to a favorite tee that they wear it until it falls apart. In addition, a teen wardrobe would not be complete without the latest style in tee shirts. Parents wear them to clean the house, do the shopping, and wash the car. Older people in tees can be seen jogging through the neighborhood or gardening in their front yard.

All kinds of people wear tees, just as the shirts themselves come in all varieties. Almost anything can be pictured or printed on a tee shirt. At concerts, tee shirts with the performer's name on them <u>can be expensive</u>. Another popular kind of tee carries the name of a college. Other tees advertise a brand of beer, like Bud, or a sporting goods company, like Nike. Mickey Mouse is a favorite character on tee shirts <u>for all ages</u>. Still other kinds of shirts include surfer tee shirts with seascapes on them, and souvenir tees, like the ones that say, "My folks visited Philadelphia, and all I got was this lousy tee shirt." Some shirt have political slogans, like "Save the Whales."

Fads can fade, but the tee shirt is everywhere. It has become so popular that it is <u>like a uniform</u>. <u>Yet</u> its <u>universal appeal</u> is connected to its variety. Anyone can find a tee shirt suited to his or her age and lifestyle, and that shirt can carry almost any message. <u>Therefore, each tee shirt is a uniform that reflects the person who wears it.</u>

WRITING AN ILLUSTRATION ESSAY

When you write on any of these topics, work through the stages of the writing process in preparing your essay.

1. Complete one of the following statements and use it as the thesis for an illustration essay.

Finding a job can be _____.

People in love often _____.

Students under pressure sometimes _____.

A sense of humor can _____.

Fitting in is _____.

In a crisis, there are always people who _____.

2. Choose one of the following topics. Narrow it to a more specific topic and then write a thesis statement about it. Use that thesis to write an illustration essay.

families	loneliness	nature
weddings	babies	adolescents
young adults	laws	crime
change	technology	health

3. To begin this assignment, work with two or three classmates. Brainstorm as many typical, general statements as you can. You are looking for the kinds of generalizations we have all heard or even said. For example, "Your college years are the best years of your life" or "Old people are the worst drivers on the road." List as many as you can. Then split up. Pick one of the general statements and write a thesis that challenges the truth of the statement. For example, your thesis could be "The college years are not the best of a person's life" or "Old people are not always bad drivers." Use the thesis for an illustration essay.

4. To begin this assignment, look around your classroom. Now, write a general statement about some aspect of the classroom: the furniture, the colors used to decorate, the condition of the room, what the students carry to class, the students' footwear, facial expressions, hair styles, and so forth. Write a five-paragraph essay using that general statement as your thesis and supporting it with specific examples from your observation.

DESCRIPTION

Hints for Writing a Description Essay

1. Use many specific details. Because an essay is usually longer than one paragraph, you will need to develop an essay with more details. To ensure that your details create an effective description, make them specific.

2. Decide on a clear order. Without a clear order, a descriptive essay will become a jumble of details spread over several paragraphs. Decide on a clear order (from inside to outside, from top to bottom, and so forth) and stick to it. Each body paragraph can focus on one part of that order.

WRITING THE DESCRIPTIVE ESSAY IN STEPS

Thought Lines Gathering Ideas: Descriptive Essay

If you were going to write an essay describing your brother's bedroom, you might first brainstorm a list

Brainstorming a List for a Descriptive Essay

Topic: My Brother's Bedroom

- older brother Michael—got a big bedroom
- I shared with my little brother
- stars pasted on the ceiling
- took a long time to fix it up the way he wanted it
- lots of books about science fiction in two bookcases
- movie posters of <u>AI: Artificial Intelligence</u> and <u>The Matrix</u>
- old videos like <u>Raiders of the Lost Ark</u> in bookcases
- his bed had no headboard, made to look like a couch
- <u>Star Trek</u> pillows on the bed

After surveying the list, you want to think about what point it makes. The main point of the list is the *dominant impression.* For this list, the dominant impression could be this sentence:

My brother's bedroom reflected his fascination with fantasy and science fiction.

This sentence could be the thesis sentence of the descriptive essay.

Outlines Devising a Plan: Descriptive Essay

Following is an outline for a descriptive essay on a brother's bedroom.

An Outline for a Descriptive Essay

paragraph 1

I. Thesis: My brother's bedroom reflected his fascination with fantasy and science fiction.

paragraph 2

topic sentence

and details

the ceiling

II. The ceiling created a fantasy.
A. Stars were pasted on the ceiling.
B. In the daylight, they were nearly invisible.
C. At night, they glowed in the dark.
D. The room appeared to be covered by a starry sky.
E. On many nights, my brother and I would lie on the floor.
F. We would pretend his room was a spaceship and the stars were the planets.

paragraph 3

topic sentence

and details

the walls

III. The walls were the most obvious sign of my brother's interests.
A. They were covered in movie posters from fantasy or science fiction films.
B. There was a poster of Steven Spielberg's film <u>AI: Artificial Intelligence</u>.
C. My brother had seen the movie five times.

D. At a garage sale, he had found an old poster of <u>ET</u>.

E. It was also on the wall.

F. Another poster, of <u>The Matrix</u>, was framed.

G. The walls made me feel as if I were in the lobby of a movie theater.

paragraph 4

topic sentence

and details

the furniture

IV. The furniture was ordinary, but it had some fantastic touches.

A. There were two battered old bookcases ready for the junk pile.

B. They were full of books about science fiction.

C. I remember <u>Fahrenheit 451</u> and <u>The War of the Worlds</u>.

D. Old videos like <u>Raiders of the Lost Ark</u> were also stacked on the bookshelves.

E. My brother had the same standard single bed that I had.

F. His was piled high with <u>Star Trek</u> pillows.

paragraph 5

conclusion

V. My brother created his own fantastic world in his room.

The outline combined some of the details from the list with new details gathered during the outlining process. As you write and revise your draft, you can continue to add details. You can also combine sentences, add transitions, and work on word choice.

Rough Lines **Drafting and Revising: Descriptive Essay**

Following is a revised draft of the essay on a brother's bedroom. As you read it, you'll notice many changes from the outline on pages 324–325:

- An introduction has been added.
- Transitions have been added within and between paragraphs.
- Details have been added.
- Sentences have been combined.
- A concluding paragraph has been written.

A Draft of a Descriptive Essay (Thesis and topic sentences are underlined.)

Whenever my older brother and I would watch television, we would fight over what to watch. I always wanted to watch wrestling, but my brother was bigger than I was, so we ended up watching <u>Deep Space Nine</u> or <u>Alien 2</u>. He would watch even the oldest reruns of <u>The Twilight Zone</u> because he loved the strange, the unreal, and the scientific. Even <u>my brother's bedroom reflected his fascination with fantasy and science fiction.</u>

<u>The ceiling of his room created a fantasy.</u> Stars were pasted on the ceiling. In the daylight, they were nearly invisible. In the night, they glowed in the dark so that the room appeared to be covered by a starry sky. On many nights, my brother and I would lie on the floor. We would pretend his room was a spaceship and the stars were the planets.

Although the ceiling gave a hint of my brother's dreams, and that hint was visible at night, there was another hint. <u>The walls were the most visible</u>

sign of my brother's interests. They were covered in movie posters from fantasy or science fiction films. There was a poster of Steven Spielberg's film <u>AI: Artificial Intelligence.</u> My brother had seen the movie five times, and the poster hung over his bed. At a garage sale, he found an old poster of <u>ET</u>. It and the <u>AI</u> poster hung over his bed. Another poster, of <u>The Matrix</u>, was framed and covered the opposite wall. The posters made me feel as if I were in the lobby of a movie theater.

Unlike the wall decorations, <u>the furniture was ordinary, but my brother had given it some fantastic touches.</u> He had two battered old bookcases ready for the junk pile. They were like any other boy's furniture except that they were full of books about science fiction. I particularly remember <u>Fahrenheit 451</u> and <u>The War of the Worlds</u>. Old videos like <u>Raiders of the Lost Ark</u> were also stacked on the bookshelves. And even though my brother had the same standard single bed that I had, his was different. It was piled high with <u>Star Trek</u> pillows.

Any boy's room reveals his interests. However, few boys are as determined as my brother was in transforming his room into something else. <u>My brother created his own fantastic world in his room.</u>

Final Lines   Polishing and Proofreading: Descriptive Essay

Following is a final version of the essay on a brother's bedroom. When you compare it to the draft on pages 325–326, you will notice some changes:

- The introduction used the word "even" twice, an awkward repetition. A change in word choice and a new transition to the thesis statement eliminated the repetition.
- A final sentence was added to the second paragraph. The paragraph needed a few more details, and the new sentence helped to reinforce the thesis, too.
- A change in word choice in the third paragraph eliminates the repetition of "visible."
- The third paragraph also repeated the detail that the <u>AI</u> poster hung over the bed. The repetition was cut.
- New details were added to the third paragraph.
- A sentence of specific details was added to the conclusion; so were other details.
- A title has been added.

A Final Version of a Descriptive Essay (Changes from the draft are underlined.)

My Brother's Heavenly Bedroom

Whenever my older brother and I would watch television, we would fight over what to watch. I always wanted to watch wrestling, but my brother was bigger than I was, so we ended up watching <u>Deep Space Nine</u> or <u>Alien 2</u>. He would watch the oldest reruns of <u>The Twilight Zone</u> because he loved the strange, the unreal, and the scientific. <u>This love was so strong that</u> even my brother's bedroom reflected his fascination with fantasy and science fiction.

The ceiling of his room created a fantasy. Stars were pasted on the ceiling. In the daylight, they were nearly invisible. In the night, they glowed in the dark so that the room appeared to be covered by a starry sky. On many nights, my brother and I would lie on the floor. We would pretend his room was a spaceship and the stars were the planets. <u>At these moments, I became a partner in his imaginary world.</u>

Although the ceiling gave a hint of my brother's dreams, and that hint was <u>apparent</u> at night, there was another, <u>stronger</u> hint. The walls were the most visible sign of my brother's interests. They were covered in movie posters from fantasy or science fiction films. There was a poster of Steven Spielberg's film <u>AI: Artificial Intelligence</u>. My brother had seen the movie five times. At a garage sale, he found an old, ragged poster of <u>ET</u>. <u>He cut the poster's ragged edges and covered it in plastic.</u> It and the <u>AI</u> poster hung over his bed. Another poster, <u>a dark vision</u> of <u>The Matrix</u>, was framed and covered the opposite wall. The posters made me feel as if I were in the lobby of a movie theater.

Unlike the wall decorations, the furniture was ordinary, but my brother had given it some fantastic touches. He had two battered old bookcases ready for the junk pile. They were like any other boy's furniture except that they were full of books about science fiction. I particularly remember <u>Fahrenheit 451</u> and <u>The War of the Worlds</u>. Old videos like <u>Raiders of the Lost Ark</u> were also stacked on the bookshelves. And even though my brother had the same standard single bed that I had, his was different. It was piled high with <u>Star Trek</u> pillows.

Any boy's room reveals his interests. <u>There may be a basketball, some video games, and a poster or two</u>. However, few boys are as determined as my brother was in transforming his room into <u>his private space</u>. My brother created his own fantastic world in his room.

WRITING A DESCRIPTIVE ESSAY

When you write on any of these topics, work through the stages of the writing process in preparing your essay.

1. Begin this essay with a partner. Describe your ideal man or woman to your partner. Ask your partner to (1) jot down the details of your description and (2) help you come up with specific details by asking you follow-up questions each time you run out of ideas. Work together for at least ten minutes. Then change roles. Let your partner describe his or her ideal man or woman to you and take notes for your partner. Then split up and use the details you collected to write an essay.

2. Describe a place you would never want to return to. Be sure to use specific details that explain why this place is terrible, unpleasant, or unattractive.

3. If you were allowed to take only three items (furniture, pictures, photographs, jewelry, and so forth) from your home, what would these things be? Write an essay describing them and their importance to you.

4. Describe one of the following:

a place that you loved when you were a child
a room that makes you feel comfortable
a place you go to when you feel stressed
a favorite pet
your workplace
your favorite place outdoors
the place you go to study

5. Describe someone you know well and who has two sides to him or her. These sides may be the private and the public sides, the happy and sad sides, the calm and angry sides, and so forth. Give specific details for both sides of this person.

6. We all associate certain people with certain rooms. For instance, you may associate your mother with her kitchen or her home office, or your brother with the garage, where he works on his car. You may picture your father in the den, where he likes to relax. Choose a person you know well, and then decide which room you associate with this person. Then write an essay showing how the details of that room relate to the person's personality, interests, and goals.

NARRATION

Hints for Writing a Narrative Essay

1. Give the essay a point and stick to it. A narrative essay tells a story. A story without a point becomes a list of moments that lead nowhere. Once you have your point, check that your use of details does not lead you away from the point.

2. Divide your narrative into clear stages. In an essay, you divide your narrative into several paragraphs. Check that each body paragraph has a clear focus (in the topic sentence) and that you have a clear reason for your division. You may decide to divide your body paragraphs into (a) before, during, and after or (b) the first part of the story, the middle part, the ending.

WRITING THE NARRATIVE ESSAY IN STEPS

Thought Lines Gathering Ideas: Narrative Essay

If you were asked to write a narrative essay about something that changed you, you might begin by freewriting.

Freewriting for a Narrative Essay

Topic: Something That Changed Me

Something that changed me. I don't know. What changed me? Lots of things happened to me, but I can't find one that changed me. Graduating from high school? Everybody will write about that, how boring, and anyway, what was the big deal? I haven't gotten married. No big change there. Divorce. My parents' divorce really changed the whole family. A big shock to me. I couldn't believe it was happening. I was really scared. Who would I live with? They were real calm when they told me. I've never been so scared. I was too young to understand. Kept thinking they'd just get back together. They didn't. Then I got a stepmother. The year of the divorce a hard time for me. Kids suffer in divorce.

Reviewing your freewriting, you decide to write on the topic of your parents' divorce. Once you have this topic, you begin to brainstorm about your topic, asking yourself questions that can lead to further details about the divorce.

With more details, you can decide that your essay will focus on the announcement of your parents' divorce and the emotions you felt. You devise the following topic sentence:

When my parents announced that they were divorcing, I felt confused by all my emotions.

Outlines **Devising a Plan: Narrative Essay**

Following is an outline for a narrative essay on an announcement of divorce. As you read it, note how it divides the announcement into three parts: (1) the background of the announcement, (2) the story of the divorce announcement, and (3) the emotions connected to the announcement.

An Outline for a Narrative Essay

paragraph 1

I. Thesis: When my parents announced that they were divorcing, I felt confused by all my emotions.

paragraph 2
topic sentence
and details
background of
the announcement

II. I will never forget how one ordinary day suddenly became a terrible one.
   A. I was seven when my mom and dad divorced.
   B. My sister was ten.
   C. Both of my parents were there.
   D. They told us at breakfast, in the kitchen.
   E. I was eating toast.
   F. I remember I couldn't eat anything after they started talking.
   G. I remember a piece of toast with one bite out of it.

paragraph 3
topic sentence
and details
story of the
announcement

III. When my parents first spoke, I was in shock.
   A. They were very calm when they told us.
   B. They said they loved us, but they couldn't get along.
   C. They said they would always love us kids.
   D. It was an unreal moment to me.
   E. I couldn't believe it was happening.
   F. At first I just thought they were having another fight.
   G. I was too young to understand.
   H. I didn't cry.

paragraph 4
topic sentence
and details
my emotions

IV. When the reality hit me, my emotions overwhelmed me.
   A. My sister cried.
   B. Then I knew it was serious.
   C. I kept thinking I would have to choose which parent to live with.
   D. I knew I would really hurt the one I didn't choose.
   E. I loved them both.
   F. I felt so much guilt about leaving one of them.
   G. I also needed both of them.
   H. I felt ripped apart.

paragraph 5
conclusion

V. When my parents' marriage fell apart, so did I.

The outline combined some of the details from the freewriting with other details gathered through brainstorming and during the outlining process. As you write and revise your draft, you can continue to add details. You can also combine sentences, add transitions, and work on word choice.

Rough Lines Drafting and Revising: Narrative Essay

Following is a revised draft of the essay on an announcement of divorce. As you read it, you'll notice many changes from the outline on page 329:

- An introduction has been added.
- Transitions within the paragraphs have been added.
- Details have been added.
- Some dialogue has been added.
- A concluding paragraph has been added.

A Draft of a Narrative Essay (Thesis and topic sentences are underlined.)

Divorce can be really hard on children. <u>When my parents announced that they were divorcing, I felt confused by all my emotions.</u>

<u>I will never forget how one ordinary day suddenly became a terrible one</u>. I was seven, and my sister was ten on that day. Both of my parents told us at breakfast, in the kitchen. I clearly remember that I was eating toast, but once they started talking, I couldn't eat anything. I can still recall holding a piece of toast with one bite out of it. I stared at the toast stupidly as I listened to what they had to say.

<u>When my parents first spoke, I was in shock</u>. They were very calm when they told us. "We love both of you very much," my dad said, "but your mother and I aren't getting along." "But we will always love you," my mother added. The announcement was such an unreal moment that I couldn't believe it was happening. My parents used to fight a lot, so at first I just thought they were having another fight. I was too young to understand. In fact, I didn't even cry.

<u>When the reality hit me, my emotions overwhelmed me</u>. My sister began to cry, and I suddenly knew it was serious. I kept thinking I would have to choose which parent to live with, and I knew I would really hurt the one I didn't choose. I loved them both. I was filled with guilt about hurting one. I also needed both parents so much that I dreaded separating from one of them. I believed that the one I didn't choose would hate me. I felt ripped apart.

<u>In one morning, my world changed</u>. One minute, I was an ordinary seven-year-old having breakfast with his family. The next, I was experiencing powerful emotions no child should feel. When my parents' marriage fell apart, so did I.

Final Lines Polishing and Proofreading: Narrative Essay

Following is the final version of the essay on an announcement of divorce. When you compare it to the draft above, you will notice some changes:

- The introduction has been developed and improved.
- More specific details have been added.
- The word "dad" has been replaced with "father," so that the language is more formal.

- The phrase "a lot" was changed to "often," since "a lot" is an overused phrase.
- The word "fight" was replaced by "argument" so that "fight does not appear twice in one sentence.
- The first word in paragraph 4 has been changed from "When" to "Then" so that the openings of paragraphs 3 and 4 are not repetitive.
- The word "it" in paragraph 4 has been replaced by "the situation" so that the sentence is clearer.
- To improve the style in paragraph 4, some sentences have been combined.
- A title has been added.

A Final Version of a Narrative Essay (Changes from the draft are underlined.)

An Emotional Morning

No childhood is perfect, and part of growing up is facing disappointment, change, and loss. However, there is one loss that can be overwhelming. Divorce can be really hard on children. When my parents announced that they were divorcing, I felt confused by all my emotions.

I will never forget how one ordinary day suddenly became a terrible one. I was seven, and my sister was ten on that day. Both of my parents told us at breakfast, in the kitchen. I clearly remember that I was eating toast, but once they started talking, I couldn't eat anything. I can still recall holding a piece of whole wheat toast with one bite out of it. I stared at the toast stupidly as I listened to what they had to say.

When my parents first spoke, I was in shock. They were very calm when they told us. "We love both of you very much," my father said, "but your mother and I aren't getting along." "But we will always love you," my mother added. The announcement was such an unreal moment that I couldn't believe it was happening. My parents used to fight often, so at first I just thought they were having another argument. I was too young to understand. In fact, I didn't even cry.

Then the reality hit me, and my emotions overwhelmed me. My sister began to cry, and I suddenly knew the situation was serious. I kept thinking I would have to choose which parent to live with, and I knew I would really hurt the one I didn't choose. Because I loved them both, I was filled with guilt about hurting one. I also needed both parents so much that I dreaded separating from one of them. I believed that the one I didn't choose would hate me. I felt ripped apart.

In one morning, my world changed. One minute, I was an ordinary seven-year-old having breakfast with his family. The next, I was experiencing powerful emotions no child should feel. When my parents' marriage fell apart, so did I.

A NARRATIVE ESSAY

When you write on any of these topics, work through the stages of the writing process in preparing your essay.

1. This assignment begins with an interview. Ask one (or both) of your parents to tell you about the day you were born. Be prepared to ask questions. (For example, were you expected that day, or did you surprise your family? Was there a rush to the hospital?) Get as many details as you can. Then write a narrative essay about that day.

2. Write about a time you learned an important lesson. Use the events of that time to explain how you learned the lesson.

3. Write the story of an argument (one you were involved in or one you observed) and its consequences.

4. Write about a crime you witnessed or were a victim of. Be sure to include details about what happened after the crime was committed.

5. Write about an incident in your life that seemed to be fate (that is, meant to happen).

6. Write the story of an accident. The accident can be one you were involved in or one you observed. It can be any kind of accident: a car accident, a sports injury, and so forth.

7. Write on any of the following topics:

your first day at work	your first day at school
the best day of your life	the worst day of your life
the day you witnessed a victory	a day you made a friend
a day you lost a friend	a day with a pleasant surprise

PROCESS

Hints for Writing a Process Essay

1. Remember that there are two kinds of process essays: a **directional** process essay tells the reader how to do something; an **informational** process essay explains an activity without telling the reader how to do it. Whether you write a directional process essay or an informational process essay, be sure to make a point. That point is expressed in your thesis.

When you write a process essay, it is easy to confuse a topic with a thesis:

topic: How to change the oil in your car.
thesis: You don't have to be an expert to learn how to change the oil in your car.

topic: How gardeners squirrel-proof their backyards.
thesis: Gardeners have to think like squirrels to keep the critters away from plants and trees.

2. Find some logical way to divide the steps into paragraphs. If you have seven steps, you probably don't want to put each one into a separate paragraph, especially if they are short steps. You would run the risk of having a list instead of a well-developed essay. To avoid writing a list, try to cluster your steps according to some logical division.

For instance, if you are writing about how to prepare for a successful party, you could divide your steps into groups like (1) what to do a week before the party, (2) what to do the day before the party, and (3) what to do the day of the party. Or if you are writing about how to make a carrot cake, you could divide the steps into (1) assembling the ingredients, (2) making the cake, and (3) baking and frosting the cake.

3. Develop your paragraphs by explaining each step thoroughly and by using details. If you are explaining how to make a cake, you can't simply tell the reader to mix the combined ingredients well. You need to explain how long to mix and whether to mix with a fork, spoon, spatula, or electric mixer. Fortunately, an essay gives you the time and space to be clear. You will be clear if you put yourself in the reader's place and anticipate his or her questions.

WRITING THE PROCESS ESSAY IN STEPS

Thought Lines Gathering Ideas: Process

If you were writing a process essay about finding an apartment, you might first freewrite your ideas on the topic. Brainstorming and listing your ideas might lead you to group your ideas into three categories organized in time order:

Listing and Grouping Ideas for a Process Essay

Topic: Finding an Apartment

before the search
Do you want a one bedroom?
Friends can help
a good neighborhood
a convenient location can be more expensive
Can save you money on transportation

during the search
look around
Don't pick the first apartment you see.
Look at a bunch.
But not too many

after the search
Check the lease carefully.
How much is the security deposit?

After some more thinking, you could summarize these ideas in a thesis:

> Finding the apartment you want takes planning and careful investigation.

With a thesis sentence and some ideas clustered in categories, you can write an outline for your essay.

Outlines Devising a Plan: Process Essay

Following is an outline for a process essay on finding an apartment.

An Outline for a Process Essay

paragraph 1   I Thesis: Finding the apartment you want takes
planning and careful investigation.

paragraph 2 topic sentence and details before the search	II. You can save yourself stress by doing some preliminary work. A. Decide what you want. B. Ask yourself, "Do I want a one bedroom?" and "What can I afford?" C. Weigh the pros and cons of your wishes. D. A convenient location can be expensive. E. It can also save you money on transportation. F. Friends can help you with the names of nice apartments. G. Maybe somebody you know lives in a good neighborhood. H. Check the classified advertisements in the newspapers.
paragraph 3 topic sentence and details during the search	III. On your search, be patient, look carefully, and ask questions. A. Look around. B. Don't pick the first apartment you see. C. Look at several. D. But don't look at too many. E. Check the cleanness, safety, plumbing, and appliances of each one. F. Ask the manager about the laundry room, additional storage, parking facilities, and maintenance policies.
paragraph 4 topic sentence and details after the search	IV. When you've seen enough apartments, take time to examine your options. A. Compare the two best places you saw. B. Consider the price, locations, and condition of the apartments. C. Check the leases carefully. D. Are pets allowed? E. Are there rules about getting roommates? F. Check the amount of the security deposit. G. Check the requirements for the first and last month's rent deposit.
paragraph 5 conclusion	V. With the right strategies and a thorough search, you can get the apartment that suits you.

The outline used each cluster of steps as one body paragraph. A topic sentence for each body paragraph made some point about that group of steps. It also added many new details gathered during the outline process. As you write and revise your draft, you can continue to add details. You can also combine sentences, add transitions, and work on word choice.

Rough Lines   **Drafting and Revising: Process Essay**

Following is a revised draft of the essay on finding an apartment. As you read it, you'll notice many changes from the outline above:

- An introduction has been added.
- Transitions have been added within and between paragraphs.
- Details have been added.

- Sentences have been combined.
- A concluding paragraph has been added.

A Draft of a Process Essay (Thesis and topic sentences are underlined.)

Some people drive around a neighborhood until they see an apartment complex with a "Vacancy" sign. They talk to the building manager, visit the apartment, and sign a lease. Soon they are residents of their new apartment, and often they are unhappy with their home. These people went about their search the wrong way. <u>They did not realize that finding a suitable apartment takes planning and careful investigation.</u>

<u>You can save yourself stress by doing some preliminary work.</u> First of all, decide what you want. Ask yourself, "Do I want a one-bedroom apartment?" and "What can I afford?" Weigh the pros and cons of your wishes. You may want a convenient location, but that can be expensive. On the other hand, that location can save you money on transportation. When you've decided what you want, rely on friends to help you with your search. They can help you with the names of nice apartments. Maybe somebody you know lives in a good neighborhood and can help you find an apartment. In addition, check the classified advertisements in the newspapers. They are full of possibilities.

<u>In your search, be patient, look carefully, and ask questions.</u> It's important to look around and not to pick the first apartment you see. Look at several so that you can get a sense of your options. However, don't look at so many apartments that they all become a blur in your memory. As you visit each apartment, check its cleanness, safety, plumbing, and appliances. You don't want an apartment that opens onto a bad area or one with a leaky refrigerator. Be sure to ask the apartment manager whether there are a laundry room, storage area, and sufficient assigned parking and guest parking. Check to see if a maintenance person lives on the premises.

<u>When you've seen enough apartments, take the time to examine your options.</u> First, compare the two best places you saw. Now that you have narrowed your search, consider the price, location, and condition of each apartment. Check the leases carefully. If you have or are thinking of getting a pet, check to see if pets are allowed. Check the rules about roommates, too. Next, check to see how much money you will have to put up initially. Does the lease specify the amount of the security deposit? Does it require a payment of first and last month's rent? The answers to these questions can help you reach a decision.

Once you have followed the steps of the process, you are ready to make your choice. While these steps take more time than simply picking the first place you see on the street, they are worth it. <u>With the right strategies and a thorough search, you can get the apartment that suits your needs.</u> All that remains is to settle into your new home.

Final Lines **Polishing and Proofreading: Process Essay**

Following is the final version of the essay on finding an apartment. When you compare it to the draft above, you will notice some changes:

- A transition has been added to the beginning of paragraph 2 so that there is a smoother movement from the thesis at the end of paragraph 1 and the topic sentence of paragraph 2.

- The words "nice," "good," and "bad" have been changed to more specific ones.
- More details have been added to the end of paragraph 3.
- A title has been added.

A Final Version of a Process Essay (Changes from the draft are underlined.)

How to Find a Suitable Apartment

Some people drive around a neighborhood until they see an apartment complex with a "Vacancy" sign. They talk to the building manager, visit the apartment, and sign a lease. Soon they are residents of their new apartment, and often they are unhappy with their home. These people went about their search the wrong way. They did not realize that finding a suitable apartment takes planning and careful investigation.

<u>When it comes to choosing an apartment</u>, you can save yourself stress by doing some preliminary work. First of all, decide what you want. Ask yourself, "Do I want a one-bedroom apartment?" and "What can I afford?" Weigh the pros and cons of your wishes. You may want a convenient location, but that can be expensive. On the other hand, that location can save you money on transportation. When you've decided what you want, rely on friends to help you with your search. They can help you with the names of <u>suitable</u> apartments. Maybe somebody you know lives in an <u>attractive</u> neighborhood and can help you find an apartment. In addition, check the classified advertisements in the newspapers. They are full of possibilities.

In your search, be patient, look carefully, and ask questions. It's important to look around and not to pick the first apartment you see. Look at several so that you can get a sense of your options. However, don't look at so many apartments that they all become a blur in your memory. As you visit each apartment, check its cleanness, safety, plumbing, and appliances. You don't want an apartment that opens onto a <u>dark and deserted</u> area or one with a leaky refrigerator. Be sure to ask the apartment manager whether there are a laundry room, storage area, and sufficient assigned parking and guest parking. Also check whether a maintenance person lives on the premises <u>or if a rental agency handles emergencies and repairs</u>.

When you've seen enough apartments, take the time to examine your options. First, compare the two best places you saw. Now that you have narrowed your search, consider the price, location, and condition of each apartment. Check the leases carefully. If you have or are thinking of getting a pet, check to see if pets are allowed. Check the rules about roommates, too. Next, check to see how much money you will have to put up initially. Does the lease specify the amount of the security deposit? Does it require a payment of first and last month's rent? The answers to these questions can help you reach a decision.

Once you have followed the steps of the process, you are ready to make your choice. While these steps take more time than simply picking the first place you see on the street, they are worth it. With the right strategies and a thorough search, you can get the apartment that suits your needs. All that remains is to settle into your new home.

WRITING A PROCESS ESSAY

When you write on any of these topics, work through the stages of the writing process in preparing your essay.

1. Write a directional or informational process essay about one of these topics:

trying out for a team	childproofing a room
finding the best airfare	painting a room
setting up a new computer	teaching someone to drive
finding a roommate	applying for a loan
selling a car	proposing marriage
getting a good night's sleep	cutting and styling hair
giving yourself a manicure	learning to ski
learning to surf	learning to skateboard
learning to dance	overcoming shyness
installing a car's sound system	writing a thank-you note
having a pleasant first date	registering for class

2. You may work through some process at work. For example, you may have to open or close a store, clean a piece of machinery, fill out a report, use a specific computer program, or follow a process in making telemarketing calls. You may have to maintain the appearance of a work area, like aisles in a supermarket, or follow a procedure in dealing with complaints. If you follow a process at work, write an essay that teaches the process to a new employee.

3. Think of a time when you had to make an important decision. Write an essay about how you reached that decision. You can write about the circumstances that led to your having to make a choice and about the steps you took to come to a decision. That is, what did you consider first? Did you weigh the good and bad points of your options? What was your first choice? Did you stick with that decision or change your mind? Trace the steps of your thought process.

4. Is there someone you know who has an irritating habit or is hard to live with? For instance, you may be living with someone who leaves the kitchen a mess or working with someone who always loses items (staplers, pens) and borrows yours. Write an essay in which you teach this person the steps to breaking the bad habit or changing the annoying behavior.

COMPARISON AND CONTRAST

Hints for Writing a Comparison or Contrast Essay

1. Use the thesis of your comparison or contrast essay to make a statement. Your essay must do more than explain the similarities or differences of two people, places, or things. It must make some statement about the two. For instance, if you are writing about the differences between your first and second semester of college, your thesis may be that a person can change radically in a short time.

2. Use your points of comparison or contrast as a way to organize your body paragraphs. A comparison or contrast essay needs points;

each point focuses on a specific similarity or difference. For example, you might use three points to compare two dogs: their appearance, their temperament, and their abilities. You can write one body paragraph on each of these points of comparison.

3. Use a point-by-point pattern. That is, each body paragraph can explain one point of comparison or contrast. The topic sentence can summarize the point, and the details about the two subjects (people, places, or things you are comparing) can support the topic sentence. These details can be grouped so that you first discuss one subject and then the other. You might, for example, compare the appearance of two dogs. An outline for one body paragraph might look like the following:

topic sentence
point: appearance
subject 1:
my German shepherd

subject 2:
my border collie

II. My German shepherd and my border collie are similar in appearance.
   A. Max, my shepherd, has long, shiny black and brown hair.
   B. His ears stand up as if he is always alert.
   C. His eyes are dark and intelligent.
   D. Sheba, my collie, has glossy black and white hair.
   E. Her pointed ears make it seem as if she is always listening to something.
   F. Her black eyes are knowing and wise.

WRITING THE COMPARISON OR CONTRAST ESSAY IN STEPS

Thought Lines **Gathering Ideas: Comparison or Contrast Essay**

One way to get started on a comparison or contrast essay is to list as many differences or similarities as you can on one topic. Then you can see whether you have more similarities (comparisons) or differences (contrasts) and decide which approach to use. For example, if you decide to compare or contrast two restaurants, you could begin with a list like this:

Listing Ideas for a Comparison or Contrast Essay

Topic: Two restaurants: Victor's and The Garden

Similarities

both offer lunch and dinner

very popular

nearby

Differences

Victor's	The Garden
formal dress	informal dress
tablecloths	place mats
food is bland	spicy food
expensive	moderate
statues, fountains, fresh flowers	dark wood, hanging plants

Getting Points of Comparison or Contrast

Whether you compare or contrast, you are looking for points of comparison or contrast, items you can discuss about both subjects.

If you surveyed the list on the two restaurants and decided you wanted to contrast the two restaurants, you'd see that you already have these points of contrast:

dress   food
decor   prices

To write your essay, start with several points of comparison or contrast. As you work through the stages of writing, you may decide you don't need all the points you've jotted down, but it is better to start with too many points than with too few.

Once you have some points, you can begin adding details to them. The details may lead you to more points. If they do not, they will still help you develop the ideas of your paragraph. If you were to write about the differences in restaurants, for example, your new list with added details might look like this:

Listing Ideas for a Contrast Essay

Topic: Two Restaurants

Victor's	The Garden
dress—formal	informal dress
men in jackets, women in dresses	all in jeans
decor—pretty, elegant	place mats, on table is a card
statues, fountains	listing specials, lots of
fresh flowers on tables	dark wood, brass, green
tablecloths	hanging plants
food—bland tasting	spicy and adventurous
traditional, broiled fish or	pasta in tomato sauces, garlic
chicken, traditional steaks,	in everything, curry,
appetizers like shrimp cocktail,	appetizers like tiny
onion soup	tortillas, ribs in honey-mustard sauce
price—expensive	moderate
everything costs extra,	price of dinner includes
like appetizer, salad	appetizer and salad

Reading the list about restaurants, you might conclude that some people may prefer The Garden to Victor's. Why? There are several hints in your list. The Garden has cheaper food, better food, and a more casual atmosphere. Now that you have a point, you can put it into a topic sentence. A topic sentence contrasting the restaurants could be

> Some people would rather eat at The Garden than at Victor's because The Garden offers better, cheaper food in a more casual environment.

Once you have a possible topic sentence, you can begin working on the outlines stage of your essay.

Outlines Devising a Plan: Contrast Essay

Following is an outline for a contrast essay on two restaurants.

An Outline for a Contrast Essay

paragraph 1	I. Thesis: Some people would rather eat at The Garden than at Victor's because The Garden offers better, cheaper food in a more casual environment.
paragraph 2 topic sentence and details food Victor's	II. The menus at the two restaurants reveal significant differences. A. Food at Victor's is bland-tasting and traditional. B. The menu has broiled fish, chicken, and traditional steaks. C. The spices used are mostly parsley and salt. D. The food is the usual American food, with a little French food on the list.
The Garden	E. Food at The Garden is more spicy and adventurous. G. There are many pasta dishes in tomato sauce. H. There is garlic in just about everything. I. The Garden serves five different curry dishes. J. It has all kinds of ethnic food. K. Appetizers include items like tiny tortillas and hot honey-mustard ribs.
paragraph 3 topic sentence and details price Victor's	III. There is a contrast in prices at the two restaurants. A. Victor's is expensive. B. Everything you order costs extra. C. An appetizer or a salad costs extra. D. Even a potato costs extra.
The Garden	E. Food at The Garden is more moderately priced. G. The price of a dinner includes an appetizer and a salad. H. All meals come with a potato, pasta, or rice.
paragraph 4 topic sentence and details environment Victor's	IV At Victor's and The Garden, meals are served in opposing environments. A. Certain diners may feel uncomfortable in Victor's, which has a formal atmosphere. B. Everyone is dressed up, the men in jackets and ties and the women in dresses. C. Even the children in the restaurant are in their best clothes and sit up straight. D. Less formal diners would rather eat in a more casual place.
The Garden	E. People don't dress up to go The Garden; they wear jeans. F. Some come in shorts and sandals. G. The children often wear sneakers and caps. H. They wriggle in their seats and even crawl under the table.
paragraph 5 conclusion	V. Many people prefer a place where they can relax, with reasonable prices and unusual food, to a place that's a little stuffy, with a traditional and expensive menu.

The outline added some new details gathered during the outlining process. The topic sentences of the body paragraphs are based on the points of contrast on the earlier list. One point of contrast, the decor of the restaurants, has been omitted. The details about decor may be useful in the introduction or conclusion of the essay.

As you write and revise your draft, you can continue to add details. You can also combine sentences, add transitions, and work on word choice.

Rough Lines Drafting and Revising: Contrast Essay

Following is a revised draft of the essay on two restaurants. As you read it, you'll notice many changes from the outline on page 341:

- An introduction has been added, and it contains some of the details on decor gathered earlier.
- Transitions have been added within and between paragraphs.
- Details have been added.
- Sentences have been combined.
- The word choice has been improved.
- A concluding paragraph has been added.

A Draft of a Contrast Essay (Thesis and topic sentences are underlined.)

There are two well-known restaurants in town. One, Victor's, is an elegant place with white linen tablecloths and fresh flowers on each table. The other, The Garden, has paper place mats on the tables. The only other item on the tables is a small card listing the day's specials. While it might seem that Victor's is a more attractive setting for a meal, The Garden has its advantages. Some people would rather eat at The Garden than at Victor's because The Garden offers better, cheaper food in a more casual environment.

The menus at the two restaurants reveal significant differences. Food at Victor's is bland-tasting and traditional. The menu offers broiled fish, baked chicken, and typical steaks like T-bone and sirloin. The spices used are mostly parsley and salt. Victor's cooks standard American food with a little French food on the list; for example, the appetizers include an American favorite, shrimp cocktail, and a French onion soup. While food at Victor's relies on old, safe choices, food at The Garden is more spicy and adventurous. There are many pasta dishes in tomato sauce. Garlic appears in just about everything from mashed potatoes to pork roasts. The Garden serves five different curry dishes. In fact, it has all kinds of ethnic food; tiny tortillas and ribs dipped in honey and hot Chinese mustard are the most popular appetizers.

Food choices are not the only difference at Victor's and The Garden; there is also a contrast in prices at the two restaurants. Victor's is expensive. Everything you order, such as an appetizer or a salad, costs extra. Even a baked potato costs extra. An entree like a steak, for example, comes on a platter with a sprig of parsley. If you want a potato or a vegetable, you have to pay extra for it. Food at The Garden is more moderately priced. The price of a dinner includes an appetizer and a salad; in addition, all meals come with a potato, pasta, or rice, so there are few pricey extras.

The cost of a meal at Victor's is different from one at The Garden, and the atmosphere in which the meal is enjoyed is different, too. At the two places, meals are served in opposing settings. Certain diners may feel uncomfortable in Victor's, which has a formal atmosphere. Everyone is dressed up, the men in jackets and ties, and the women in dresses. Even the children at Victor's are dressed in their best and sit straight up in their chairs. Less formal diners would rather eat in a more casual place, like The Garden. People don't dress up to go to The Garden; they wear jeans or shorts and sandals. The children often wear sneakers and baseball caps. They wriggle in their seats and even explore under the table.

Sometimes adults want to let go, just as children do. They want to sit back, not up, stretch their legs in casual clothes, not jackets and ties or dresses, and explore new food choices, not the same old standards. The Garden appeals to that childlike need for physical comfort and adventurous dining, at a moderate cost. <u>People</u> choose it over Victor's because they <u>prefer a place where they can relax, with reasonable prices and unusual food, to a place that's a little stuffy, with a traditional and expensive menu.</u>

Final Lines Polishing and Proofreading: Contrast Essay

Following is a final version of the essay on two restaurants. When you compare it to the draft on pages 341–342, you will notice some changes:

- More specific details have been added.
- Two sentences in paragraph 3 have been revised so that the shift to "you" is eliminated.
- The phrase "explore under the table" in paragraph 4 has been changed to "explore the spaces under the table" for clarity.
- One sentence in the conclusion has been revised so that it has a stronger parallel structure.
- A title has been added.

A Final Version of a Contrast Essay (Changes from the draft are underlined.)

Victor's and The Garden: Two Contrasting Restaurants

There are two well-known restaurants in town. One, Victor's, is an elegant place with white linen tablecloths and fresh flowers on each table. The other, The Garden, has paper place mats on the tables. The only other item on the tables is a small card listing the day's specials. While it might seem that Victor's is a more attractive setting for a meal, The Garden has its advantages. Some people would rather eat at The Garden than at Victor's because The Garden offers better, cheaper food in a more casual environment.

The menus at the two restaurants reveal significant differences. Food at Victor's is bland-tasting and traditional. The menu offers broiled fish, baked chicken, and typical steaks like T-bone and sirloin. The spices used are mostly parsley and salt; <u>pepper, garlic, and curry are nowhere to be found.</u> Victor's cooks standard American food with a little French food on the list; for example, the appetizers include an American favorite, shrimp cocktail, and a French onion soup. While food at Victor's relies on old, safe choices, food at The Garden is more spicy and adventurous. There are many pasta dishes, <u>from linguini to lasagna,</u> in <u>a rich</u> tomato sauce. Garlic appears in just about everything from mashed potatoes to pork roasts. The Garden serves five different curry dishes. In fact, it has all kinds of ethnic food; tiny tortillas and ribs dipped in honey and hot Chinese mustard are the most popular appetizers.

Food choices are not the only difference at Victor's and The Garden; there is also a contrast in prices at the two restaurants. Victor's is expensive. Everything <u>a person orders</u>, such as an appetizer or a salad, costs extra. Even a baked potato costs extra. An entree like a steak, for example, comes on a platter with a sprig of parsley. <u>Anyone who wants</u> a potato or a vegetable has to pay extra for it. Food at The Garden is more moderately priced. The price of a dinner includes an appetizer and a salad; in addition, all meals come with a potato, pasta, or rice, so there are few pricey extras.

The cost of a meal at Victor's is different from one at The Garden, and the atmosphere in which the meal is enjoyed is different, too. At the two places, meals are served in opposing settings. Certain diners may feel uncomfortable in Victor's, which has a formal atmosphere. Everyone is dressed up, the men in jackets and ties, and the women in <u>fancy</u> dresses. Even the children at Victor's are dressed in their best and sit straight up in their chairs. Less formal diners would rather eat in a more casual place, like The Garden. People don't dress up to go to The Garden; they wear jeans or shorts and sandals. The children often wear sneakers and baseball caps. They wriggle in their seats and even explore <u>the spaces</u> under the table.

Sometimes adults want to let go, just as children do. They want to sit back, not up, stretch their legs in casual clothes, <u>not hold their breath in tight ties or fancy dresses</u>, and explore new food choices, not <u>settle for</u> the same old standards. The Garden appeals to that childlike need for physical comfort and adventurous dining, at a moderate cost. <u>People</u> choose it over Victor's because they <u>prefer a place where they can relax, with reasonable prices and unusual food, to a place that's a little stuffy, with a traditional and expensive menu.</u>

Writing a Comparison or Contrast Essay

When you write on any of these topics, work through the stages of the writing process in preparing your essay.

1. Compare or contrast any of the following:

two holidays	satellite and cable television
two video games	two Internet providers
two personal goals	two clothing styles
two weddings	two surprises
two movie theaters	two role models
two expensive purchases	two houses you've lived in
two coworkers	two assignments

2. Find a baby picture of yourself. Study it carefully; then write an essay about the similarities between the baby you were and the adult you are today. You can use physical similarities or similarities in personality or attitude as expressed in the photo. If your instructor agrees, you can ask a classmate to help you find physical resemblances between you as you are today and the baby in the picture.

3. Compare or contrast the person you were two years ago to the person you are today. You might consider such points of comparison as your worries, fears, hopes, goals, or relationships.

4. Begin this assignment by working with a partner or group. Brainstorm to make a list of four or five top performers (singers, actors, or comedians) popular with one age group (young teens, high school students, college students, people in their twenties or thirties, and so forth—your group can decide on the age group). Once you have the list, write individual essays comparing or contrasting two of the people on the list.

5. Compare or contrast the way you spend a weekday with the way you spend a day off. You can consider what you do in the morning, after-noon, and evening as points of comparison or contrast.

CLASSIFICATION

Hints for Writing a Classification Essay

1. Be sure to have a point in your classification. Remember that you need to do more than divide something into three or more types, according to some basis, and explain and describe these types. You must have a reason for your classification. For example, if you write about three types of digital cameras, you may be writing to evaluate them, and your point may state which type is the best buy. If you are classifying weight-loss programs, you may be studying each type so that you can prove that two types are dangerous.

2. A simple way to structure your classification essay is to explain each type in a separate body paragraph. Then use the same kind of details to describe each type. For instance, if you describe the medical principles, food restrictions, and results of one type of weight-loss pro-gram, describe the medical principles, food restrictions, and results of the other types of weight-loss programs.

WRITING THE CLASSIFICATION ESSAY IN STEPS

Thought Lines **Gathering Ideas: Classification Essay**

First, pick a topic for your classification. The next step is to choose some basis for your classification. For example, if you were to write a paragraph classifying phone calls, you could write about phone calls on the basis of their effect on you. With this basis for classification, you can come up with three categories:

> calls that please me
> calls that irritate me
> calls that frighten me

By brainstorming, you can then gather details about your three categories:

Added Details for Three Categories of a Classification Essay

Topic: Phone Calls

calls that please me
from boyfriend
good friends
catch-up calls—someone I haven't talked to for a while
make me feel close

calls that irritate me
sales calls at dinnertime
wrong numbers
calls that interrupt
invade privacy

calls that frighten me
emergency call in middle of night
"let's break up" call from boyfriend
change my life, indicate some bad change

With these categories and details, you can write a thesis that (1)mentions what you are classifying and (2)indicates the basis for your classifying by listing all three categories or by stating the basis, or both. Here is a thesis that follows the guidelines:

Phone calls can be grouped into the ones that please me, the ones that irritate me, and the ones that frighten me.

This thesis mentions what you are classifying, *phone calls*. It indicates the basis for classification, the effect of the phone calls, by listing the types: *the ones that please me, the ones that irritate me, and the ones that frighten me.* Here is another thesis that follows the guidelines:

I can classify phone calls according to their effect on me.

This thesis also mentions what you are classifying, *phone calls*, but it mentions the basis for classification, *their effect on me*, instead of listing the types.

Once you have a thesis sentence and a list of ideas, you are ready to begin the outlines stage of writing the classification essay.

Outlines **Devising a Plan: Classification Essay**

Following is an outline for a classification essay on phone calls.

Info BOX

An Outline for a Classification Essay

paragraph 1	I. Thesis: Phone calls can be grouped into the ones that please me, the ones that irritate me, and the ones that frighten me.
paragraph 2 topic sentence and details pleasing calls	II. Calls that please me make me feel close to someone. A. I like calls from my boyfriend, especially when he calls to say he is thinking of me. B. I like to hear from good friends. C. My two best friends call me at least twice a day. D. I like catch-up calls. E. These are calls from people I haven't talked to in a while. F. A friend I hadn't seen in a year called me from Ecuador to say "Happy Birthday." G. We talked for a long time.
paragraph 3 topic sentence	III. Some calls irritate me because they invade my privacy.

---

and details

irritating calls

A. Sales calls always come at dinnertime.

B. They offer me newspaper subscriptions or "free" vacations.

C. The calls start with a friendly voice, talking fast.

D. By the time I find out what the caller is selling, my dinner is cold.

E. I get at least four wrong number calls each week.

F. Some of the callers don't even apologize.

G. These calls annoy me because I have to interrupt what I'm doing to answer them.

paragraph 4

topic sentence

and details

frightening calls

IV. The calls that tell me about some bad change in my life frighten me.

A. I once got a call in the middle of the night.

B. It was from a hospital emergency room.

C. The nurse said my brother had been in an accident.

D. That was the most terrifying call of my life.

E. I once got a call from a boyfriend.

F. He said he wanted to break up.

G. His words hurt me.

paragraph 5

V. A phone is just an instrument; its effect on the person who receives a call makes it a good or bad instrument.

The outline combined some of the details from the list with new details gathered during the writing process. It used the three categories as the basis for the topic sentences for the body paragraph. These topic sentences have two parts: (1) the name of the category, like pleasing calls, and (2) the effect of calls in this category. For example, here is one topic sentence:

(1) the category   (2) the effect of calls in this category
Calls that please me make me feel close to someone.

Since the point of the essay is to show the effect of different kinds of calls, this topic sentence is effective.

As you write and revise your draft, you can continue to add details. You can also combine sentences, add transitions, and work on word choice.

Rough Lines   **Drafting and Revising: Classification Essay**

Following is a revised draft of the essay on phone calls. As you read it, you'll notice many changes from the outline on pages 345–346.

- An introduction has been added.
- Transitions have been added within and between paragraphs.
- Details have been added.
- Sentences have been combined.
- A concluding paragraph has been added.

A Draft of a Classification Essay (Thesis and topic sentences are underlined.)

I am lost without a phone. My friends swear that I must have been born holding a tiny phone to my ear. Although I am constantly talking on the phone, I am not always enjoying the process. Not all my phone calls are enjoyable. In fact, <u>the calls can be grouped into the ones that please me, the ones that irritate me, and the ones that frighten me.</u>

<u>Calls that please me make me feel close to someone.</u> For example, I like calls from my boyfriend, especially when he calls to say that he is thinking of me. I also like to hear from good friends. My two best friends call me at least twice a day, and it is amazing that we can always find something to talk about. Catch-up calls, calls from people I haven't seen in a while, are another kind of call I enjoy. Recently, a friend I hadn't seen in a year called me from Ecuador to say "Happy Birthday." It was so good to hear from her that we talked for a long time.

The ring of a phone can bring me warm feelings, but it can sometimes bring irritation. <u>Calls that irritate me invade my privacy.</u> Sales calls, for instance, always come at dinnertime. They offer me newspaper subscriptions or "free" vacations that always have a hidden cost. This kind of call always starts with a friendly voice, talking fast. By the time I figure out what the caller is selling, my dinner is cold. Also in this category are wrong number calls. I get at least four of these a week, and some of the callers don't even apologize for bothering me. These calls annoy me because I have to interrupt what I'm doing to answer them.

Finally, there are the worst calls of all. <u>The calls that frighten me tell me about some bad change in my life.</u> I once got a call in the middle of the night. It was from a hospital emergency room; the nurse told me my brother had been in an accident. That was the most terrifying call of my life. Another time, a boyfriend called to say he wanted to break up. His cold words surprised and hurt me.

I rely on the telephone, but it is not always good to me. Ever since I received the call about my brother's accident, I tremble when the phone rings late at night. However, I have come to realize that <u>a phone is just an instrument; its effect on the person who receives a call makes it a good or bad instrument.</u>

Final Lines Polishing and Proofreading: Classification Essay

Following is the final version of the essay on phone calls. When you compare it to the draft above, you will notice some changes:

- Some of the word choice has been polished to make a detail more specific, to eliminate repetition, or to eliminate an awkward phrase.
- A final sentence has been added to paragraph 4 to reinforce the point that both examples in the paragraph are about a life-changing phone call.
- The last sentence in the concluding paragraph has been revised to make a more precise statement about the basis for the classification: the effect of each type of phone call.
- A title has been added.

A Final Version of a Classification Essay (Changes from the draft are underlined.)

Phone Calls: The Good, The Bad, and the Ugly

I am lost without a phone. My friends swear that I must have been born holding a tiny phone to my ear. Although I am constantly talking on the phone, I am not always enjoying the process. Not all <u>the conversations</u> are <u>pleasant.</u> In fact, the calls can be grouped into the ones that please me, the ones that irritate me, and the ones that frighten me.

Calls that please me make me feel close to someone. For example, I like calls from my boyfriend, especially when he calls to say that he is thinking of me. I also like to hear from good friends. My two best friends call me at least twice a day, and it is amazing that we can always find something to talk about. Catch-up calls, calls from people I haven't seen in a while, are another kind of call I enjoy. Recently, a friend I hadn't seen in a year called me from Ecuador to say "Happy Birthday." It was so good to hear from her that we talked for <u>an hour.</u>

The ring of a phone can bring me warm feelings, but it can sometimes bring irritation. Calls that irritate me invade my privacy. Sales calls, for instance, always come at dinnertime. They offer me newspaper subscriptions or "free" vacations that always have a hidden cost. This kind of call always starts with a friendly voice talking fast. By the time I figure out what the caller is selling, my dinner is cold. Also in this category are wrong number calls. I get at least four of these a week, and some of the callers don't even apologize for bothering me. These calls annoy me because I have to interrupt what I'm doing to answer them.

Finally, there are the worst calls of all. The calls that frighten me tell me about some <u>crisis</u> in my life. I once got a call in the middle of the night. It was from a hospital emergency room; the nurse told me my brother had been in an accident. That was the most terrifying call of my life. Another time, a boyfriend called to say he wanted to break up. His cold words surprised and hurt me. <u>Both of these calls brought me news that changed my life, and the news was totally unexpected.</u>

I rely on the telephone, but it is not always good to me. Ever since I received the call about my brother's accident, I tremble when the phone rings late at night. However, I have come to realize that a phone is just an instrument; <u>it conveys a message.</u> Its effect on the person who <u>receives that message</u> makes it a <u>welcome, annoying, or dreaded</u> instrument.

WRITING A CLASSIFICATION ESSAY

When you write on any of these topics, work through the stages of the writing process in preparing your essay.

1. Write a classification essay on any of the topics below. If your instructor agrees, brainstorm with a partner or group to come up with a basis for your classification and categories related to the basis.

your clothes	your dreams	your mistakes
your relatives	your coworkers	your travels
photographs	discount stores	snacks
cartoon heroes	websites	workouts
ghost stories	bargains	gossip
recipes	talk shows	music videos
visits to the dentist	war movies	teen idols

2. You may not know it, but you are probably an expert on something. For example, you may work in a jewelry store and know all about diamonds. You may be a paramedic and know about medical emergencies. If you are a veterinarian's assistant, you know about cats and dogs. If you collect Barbie dolls, you are an expert on these toys. Consider what you know best through your work, hobbies, education, or leisure activities, and write a classification essay about a subject in that area. If you know about diamonds, you can classify engagement rings. If you work at a veterinarian's office, you can classify pet owners or poodles.

3. Below are some topics. Each one already has a basis for classification. Write a classification essay on one of the choices.

Classify
a. baby-sitters on the basis of how competent they are
b. small children on the basis of their behavior in a restaurant
c. teenage boys on the basis of their favorite sport
d. government offices (like the driver's license office, courthouse) on the basis of how efficient they are
e. roads on the basis of how safe they are
f. fads on the basis of how long they last
g. auto repair shops on the basis of their reliability
h. classrooms on the basis of how comfortable they are
i. uniforms on the basis of how attractive they are
j. uniforms on the basis of how comfortable they are

4. This assignment requires a little research. Write an essay that classifies some product according to price. That is, you can classify home computers (or hair dryers, bookbags, hiking boots, motorcycles, and so forth) according to their cost. Pretend that you are writing to advise readers who may want to buy this product and want the best deal for their money. Research the details of this product in different price ranges; for example, explain what the most expensive computer includes and how useful these features are, and then explain what mid-priced and low-priced computers offer for their price. Use your essay to recommend the best deal for the money.

DEFINITION

Hints for Writing a Definition Essay

1. Write a personal definition, not a dictionary definition. To develop a definition essay, you need to define a term that can be explained by more than the words in the dictionary. You can develop your essay with concrete terms and specific examples that help define the term.

terms that won't work in a personal definition:
photosynthesis, DNA, the Colt revolver, the Renaissance

terms that will work in a personal definition:
self-pity, patience, the team player, the pessimist

2. Include in your thesis (1) the term you are defining, (2) the broad class or category into which your term fits, and (3) the specific distinguishing characteristics that make the term different from all others in the class or category. Each of the following sentences could be the thesis for a definition essay.

term   category   distinguishing characteristics

Envy is the desire for what others have.

term   category   *distinguishing characteristics*

A nit-picker is a person who worries excessively about minor details.

3. Form your body paragraphs from different aspects of your term; for example, if you defined patience, you might write one paragraph on the times when patience is necessary and another paragraph on the times when people need to stop being patient and take action. If you write about temptation, you might write one paragraph on how to resist temptation and another paragraph on when to give in to temptation.

WRITING THE DEFINITION ESSAY IN STEPS

Thought Lines Gathering Ideas: Definition Essay

To pick a topic for your definition essay, you can begin with some personality trait or type of person. For instance, you might define "the insecure person." If you listed your first thoughts, your list might look like this:

the insecure person
someone who is not emotionally secure
wants (needs?) other people to make him or her feel good
no self-respect

Often, when you look for ideas to define a term, you get stuck with big, general statements or abstract words, or you simply cannot come up with enough to say. If you are having trouble getting ideas, think of questions about your term. Jot these questions down without stopping to answer them. One question can lead you to another question. Once you have five or more questions, you can answer them, and the answers will provide details for your definition paragraph.

If you were writing about the insecure person, for example, you could begin with questions like these:

What are insecure people like?
What behavior shows a person is insecure?
How do insecure people dress or talk?
What makes a person insecure?
Why is insecurity a bad trait?
How do insecure people relate to others?
Does insecurity hurt the insecure person? If so, how?
Does the insecure person hurt others? If so, how?

By scanning the questions and answering as many as you can, you can add details to your list. Once you have a longer list, you can review it and begin to group the items on the list. Following is a list of grouped details on the insecure person.

Grouped Details for a Definition Essay

Topic: The Insecure Person

wants (needs?) other people to make him or her feel important
no self-respect

insecure people have to brag about everything
a friend who brags about his car
they tell you the price of everything

they put others down
  saying bad things about other people makes insecure people feel better

insecure people can never relax inside
  can never enjoy being with other people
  other people are always their competitors
  must always worry about what others think of them

Grouping the details can help you arrive at several main ideas. Can they be combined and revised to create a topic sentence? Following is a thesis on the insecure person that meets the requirements of naming the term, placing it in a category, and distinguishing the term from others in the category:

term   category   distinguishing characteristics

The insecure person is a person who needs other people to make him or her feel respected and important.

Once you have a thesis sentence, you can begin working on the outlines stage of the paragraph.

Outlines **Devising a Plan: Definition Essay**

Following is an outline for a definition essay on the insecure person.

Info BOX

An Outline for a Definition Essay

paragraph 1

I. Thesis: The insecure person is a person who needs other people to make him or her feel respected and important.

paragraph 2
topic sentence
and details

II. Insecure people have to brag about everything.
  A. An insecure friend may have to brag about his car.
  B. He is sure to tell you how fast it can go.

bragging

  C. Insecure people wear expensive jewelry and tell you what it cost.
  D. A man will tell you what his ring cost; a woman will tell you what her boyfriend paid for her ring.
  E. They make sure they wear clothes with trendy labels.
  F. They have to have shirts with the designer's logo on the pocket and jackets with the designer's name spread across the front.
  G. This is another kind of bragging.

paragraph 3
topic sentence
and details
putting others
down

III. Insecure people put others down.
  A. They make mean remarks about other people's looks, clothes, or style.
  B. Saying bad things about others makes insecure people feel better.

C. When some friends were talking about Susan's great new job, Jill had to make mean remarks about Susan.

D. Jill hated having Susan look like a winner.

E. Jill wanted all the attention and admiration for herself.

F. I work with a man who is always spreading cruel gossip.

G. His attacks on others are a cowardly way of making himself look good.

paragraph 4
topic sentence
and details
never relaxing

IV. Insecure people can never relax inside.

A. They can never enjoy being with other people.

B. Other people are always their competition.

C. Luke plays pickup basketball games.

D. He can't enjoy any game of basketball unless he is the star.

E. When someone on his team scores, he is not pleased.

F. Instead, he becomes aggressive and selfish.

G. Another person I know is always loud and crude at parties.

H. He is so desperate to be liked that he turns himself into an obnoxious character that he thinks is the life of the party.

paragraph 5

V. Insecure people must always worry about what others think about them.

The outline combined some of the details from the list with new details and examples gathered during the outlining process. As you write and revise your draft, you can continue to add details. You can also combine sentences, add transitions, and work on word choice.

Rough Lines   Drafting and Revising: Definition Essay

Following is a revised draft on the essay on the insecure person. As you read it, you'll notice many changes from the outline above.

- An introduction has been added.
- Transitions have been added within and between paragraphs.
- Details have been added.
- Sentences have been combined.
- A concluding paragraph has been added.

A Draft of a Definition Essay (Thesis and topic sentences are underlined.)

Everybody knows at least one person who seems to feel so superior that no one could ever reach his or her status. Sometimes this person annoys others; at other times, this person hurts them. While it seems to be pride that motivates this person to irritate and belittle others, it is really insecurity disguised as ego. <u>The insecure person is a person who needs other people to make him or her feel respected and important.</u>

One sign of the insecure person is bragging. <u>Insecure people have to brag about everything.</u> An insecure friend may have to brag about his car and will be sure to tell everyone how fast it can go. Some insecure people wear expensive jewelry and brag about what it cost. A man may boast about what his ring cost; a woman will mention what her boyfriend paid for her ring. Others filled with insecurity brag about their expensive clothes. They make sure they wear clothes with trendy labels. They have to have shirts with the designer's logo on the pocket or jackets with the designer's name spread across the front. This is another kind of bragging.

<u>Insecure people</u> not only like to build themselves up, but they also <u>have to put others down.</u> They make mean remarks about other people's looks, clothes, and style. Saying bad things about others makes insecure people feel better. Recently, some friends were talking about our classmate Susan's great new job. While most of us were happy for Susan, Jill had to add some comments about how lucky Susan had been to get the job since Susan was not qualified for it. Because she wants all the attention and admiration for herself, Jill hated having Susan looking like a winner. Another insecure person is a man I work with who is always spreading cruel gossip. His attacks on others are his cowardly way of making himself look good.

The constant need to shine in other people's opinion means that <u>insecure people can never relax inside.</u> Other people are always their competition for attention or approval. One such person is Luke, a college acquaintance who always plays on our pickup basketball games. Even though the games are just for fun, Luke can't enjoy any game of basketball unless he is the star. When someone on his team scores, he isn't pleased. Instead, he becomes aggressive and selfish. He wants to win every game singlehanded. Another person who is eager to shine is always loud and crude at parties. He is so desperate to be liked that he turns himself into an obnoxious character that he thinks is the life of the party.

Insecure people can be mean and obnoxious, but they are mainly sad. <u>Insecure people must always worry about what others think of them.</u> Because they care so much about others' opinions, they cannot be spontaneous or open. They must get very tired of hiding their fears behind their bragging and criticizing. They must also be very lonely.

Final Lines **Polishing and Proofreading: Definition Essay**

Following is the final version of the essay on the insecure person. When you compare it to the draft above, you will notice some changes:

- Sentences in paragraph 2 have been combined for a smoother style.
- The word "this" in the last sentence of paragraph 2 has been replaced with a more specific phrase: "This obsession with designer clothes."
- Some of the word choice has been polished to avoid repetition or to be precise.

A Final Version of a Definition Essay (Changes from the draft are underlined.)

The Insecure Person

Everybody knows at least one person who seems to feel so superior that no one could ever reach his or her status. Sometimes this person annoys others; at other times, this person hurts them. While it seems to be pride that motivates this person to irritate and belittle others, it is really insecurity disguised as ego. The insecure person is a person who needs other people to make him or her feel respected and important.

<u>One sign of the insecure person is bragging, for insecure people have to brag about everything.</u> An insecure friend may have to brag about his car and will be sure to tell everyone about <u>its powerful engine.</u> Some insecure people wear expensive jewelry and brag about what it cost. A man may boast about what his ring cost; a woman will tell mention what her boyfriend paid for her ring. Others filled with insecurity <u>show off</u> their expensive clothes. They make sure they wear clothes with trendy labels. They have to have shirts with the designer's logo on the pocket or jackets with the designer's name spread across the front. This <u>obsession with designer clothes</u> is another kind of bragging.

Insecure people not only like to build themselves up, but they also have to put others down. They make mean remarks about other people's looks, clothes, and style. <u>Making nasty comments</u> about others makes insecure people feel better. Recently, some friends were talking about our classmate Susan's great new job. While most of us were happy for Susan, Jill had to add some comments about how lucky Susan had been to get the job since Susan was not qualified for it. Because she wants all the attention and admiration for herself, Jill hated having Susan looking like a winner. Another insecure person is a man I work with who is always spreading cruel gossip. His attacks on others are his cowardly way of making himself look good.

The constant need to shine in other people's opinion means that insecure people can never relax inside. Other people are always their competition for attention or approval. One such person is Luke, a college acquaintance who always plays on our pickup basketball games. Even though the games are just for fun, Luke can't enjoy any game of basketball unless he is the star. When someone on his team scores, he isn't pleased. Instead, he becomes aggressive and selfish. He wants to win every game singlehanded. Another person who is eager to shine is <u>my cousin Jamie, a generally good-natured person who</u> is always loud and crude at parties. He is so desperate to be liked that he turns himself into an obnoxious character that he thinks is the life of the party.

Insecure people can be mean and obnoxious, but they are mainly sad. Insecure people must always worry about what others think of them. Because they care so much about others' opinions, they cannot be spontaneous or open. They must get very tired of hiding their fears behind their bragging and criticizing. They must also be very lonely.

WRITING YOUR DEFINITION ESSAY

When you write on any of these topics, work through the stages of the writing process in preparing your essay.

1. What is the one quality you most admire in other people? Is it courage, kindness, drive, or another character trait? Decide on that quality and write an essay defining it.

2. Define any of the terms listed below, using specific details and examples. You can begin by looking up the term in a dictionary to be sure you understand the dictionary meaning. Then write a personal definition.

guilt	satisfaction	longing
worry	stress	contentment

paranoia	trust	shyness
boldness	confidence	will power
sympathy	brotherhood	compassion
nerve	perseverance	generosity

3. Write a definition of a specific type of person. Develop your definition by using specific details and examples. Following is the list of types.

the tattletale	the guardian angel	the loner
the natural athlete	the ideal mate	the planner
the big brother or sister	the computer geek	the nagger
the control freak	the hypochondriac	the sneak
the good sport	the lost soul	the patriot
the rebel	the tightwad	the critic

4. We often use terms that we understand and that we assume everyone knows, but that may not have a clear definition. Write your definition of such a term. Examples of these terms are listed below, but you can also choose you own terms. Here are some sample terms:

street smarts	a people person	fashion sense
people skills	negative vibes	personal issues

CAUSE AND EFFECT

Hints for Writing a Cause or Effect Essay

1. **Choose either causes or effects.** If you try to do both in a short essay, you will make your task more difficult. In addition, you need a longer and more complex essay to cover both causes and effects adequately.

2. **Use each cause or effect as the focus of one body paragraph.** You can develop the paragraph by explaining and describing that cause or effect.

Writing the Cause or Effect Essay in Steps

Thought Lines **Gathering Ideas: Cause or Effect Essay**

If you were thinking about writing a cause or effect paragraph on owning a car, you could begin by freewriting something like this:

Freewriting for a Cause or Effect Essay

Topic: Owning a Car
A car of my own. Why? I needed it. Couldn't get a part time job without one. Because I couldn't get to work. Needed it to get to school. Of course I could have taken the bus to school. But I didn't want to. Feel like a grown-up when you have a car of your own. Freedom to come and go. I was the last of my friends to have a car. Couldn't wait. An old Camaro. But I fixed it up nicely. Costs a lot to maintain. Car payments, car loan. Car insurance.

Now you can review the freewriting and make separate lists of causes and effects you wrote down:

causes (reasons)

needed to get a part time job
needed to get to school
my friends had cars

effects (results)

feel like a grown-up
freedom to come and go
costs a lot to maintain
car payments
car loan
car insurance

Because you have more details on the effects of owning a car, you decide to write an effects paragraph.

After brainstorming questions to help you gather more effects and details, you are ready to write another list:

List of Effects for an Effects Essay

Topic: Owning a Car

effect 1: I had to pay for the car and related expenses.
details: costs a lot to maintain
     car payments
     car loan
     car insurance

effect 2: I had the adult freedom to come and go.
details: didn't have to beg my father for his truck
     didn't have to get rides from friends
     could go to the city when I wanted
     could ride around for fun

effect 3:   I became a more careful driver.
details: worried about someone hitting the car
     worried about bad drivers
     wanted to avoid the scratches cars get in parking lots

With at least three effects and some details for each effect, you can create a thesis. The thesis for this paragraph should indicate that the subject is the *effects* of getting a car. You can summarize all three effects in your thesis, or you can just hint at them. A possible thesis sentence for the paragraph can be

Owning my own car cost me money, gave me freedom, and made me more careful about how I drive.

The thesis summarizes all three effects. Another possible thesis hints at the effects:

Once I got a car, I realized the good and bad sides of ownership.

With a thesis sentence, three effects, and a list of details, you are ready to write an outline for your essay.

`Outlines` Devising a Plan: Effects Essay

Following is an outline for an effects essay on owning a car.

An Outline for an Effects Essay

paragraph 1	I. Thesis: Owning my own car gave me freedom, cost me money, and made me a more careful driver.
paragraph 2 topic sentence and details effect 1: freedom	II. The wonderful part of owning a car was the adult freedom it gave me. A. I didn't have to beg my father for his truck. B. Every time I asked him, he seemed reluctant to lend it to me. C. He was always worried that I would get the interior dirty. D. I didn't have to get rides from my friends. E. I was really tired of begging rides from my buddies, and I am sure they were sick of driving me around. F. I could go to the city whenever I wanted. G. I could even ride around for fun.
paragraph 3 topic sentence and details effect 2: costs	III. I had to pay for the car and related expenses. A. A car costs a lot to maintain. B. There are oil changes and tune-ups. C. My car needed new tires. D. I had car payments. E. I had a car loan to pay. F. I had car insurance. G. I took a second job. H. I had to work overtime to pay the insurance bills.
paragraph 4 topic sentence effect 3: cautiousness	IV. I became a more careful driver. A. I worried about someone hitting the car. B. I could see my beautiful car dented and dinged. C. I began to worry about bad drivers. D. I became more nervous on the road. E. I worried about parking lots. F. I wanted to avoid the scratches cars can get in parking lots. G. I parked at the end of the row, away from other cars.
paragraph 5 conclusion	V. Owning a car gave me adult freedom, but it gave me adult responsibilities and worries, too.

The outline put each effect into a separate body paragraph. It combined some of the details from the list with details gathered during the outlining process. As you write and revise your draft, you can continue to add details. You can also combine sentences, add transitions, and work on word choice.

Rough Lines   **Drafting and Revising: Effects Essay**

Following is a revised draft of the essay on owning a car. As you read it, you'll notice many changes from the outline on page 357:

- An introduction has been added.
- Transitions have been added within and between paragraphs.
- Details have been added.
- Sentences have been combined.
- A concluding paragraph has been added.

A Draft of an Effects Essay (Thesis and topic sentences are underlined.)

Ever since I was six years old, I have dreamed of owning my own car. The day I got my driver's license was one of the happiest days of my life. All that was left, I thought, was having a car of my own. That day came, too, and it changed my life. <u>Owning my own car gave me freedom, cost me money, and made me a more careful driver.</u>

<u>The wonderful part of owning a car was the adult freedom it gave me.</u> First of all, I didn't have to beg my father for his truck any more. Every time I asked him, he seemed reluctant to lend it to me. He was always worried that I would get the interior dirty. Second, I no longer had to get rides from my friends whenever I wanted to go somewhere. I was really tired of begging rides from my buddies, and I am sure they were sick of driving me around. With my own car, I could go to the city whenever I wanted. I could even ride around for fun.

On the more serious side, <u>I had to pay for the car and related expenses.</u> A car costs a lot to maintain. There are oil changes and tune-ups to keep the car in good running condition. Two months after I got my car, I had to buy four new and very expensive tires. Of course, I had monthly payments on my car loan. I also had to pay for car insurance which, because of my young age, was unbelievably expensive. My insurance cost so much that I had to work overtime to pay it.

Now that I was paying for the car I drove, <u>I became a more careful driver.</u> I became worried about someone hitting the car; I could imagine my beautiful car dented and dinged. These thoughts made me worry about bad drivers and become more nervous on the road. Parking lots made me nervous, too. To avoid the scratches cars can get in parking lots, I parked at the end of the row, away from other cars.

Owning a car gave me adult freedom, but it gave me adult responsibilities and worries, too. Even with the stress of car payments, insurance payments, and car maintenance, I would never give up my car. My fear of dents and scratches can't keep me from the joy of driving whenever and wherever I want. I'm happy to accept the responsibilities that come with being on the road in my own car.

Final Lines   **Polishing and Proofreading: Effects Essay**

Following is the final version of the essay on owning a car. When you compare it to the draft above, you will notice some changes:

- Some of the word choice has been polished to replace a vague term like "costs a lot" with the more specific "costs hundreds of dollars" or to avoid repetition of words like "worry" and "expensive."

- Details have been added; for instance, in paragraph 2, there are new details about what makes a car dirty and about how friends feel ("acting like a taxi service") when they are constantly asked for rides.
- A sentence has been added to paragraph 4 to support the topic sentence. The focus of the paragraph is on careful driving, and the body of the paragraph gives many examples of the fears of a new-car owner, but it needed one more detail to show the change in the owner's driving.
- A title has been added.

A Final Version of an Effects Essay (Changes from the draft are underlined.)

Owning a Car: My New Lease on Life

Ever since I was six years old, I have dreamed of owning my own car. The day I got my driver's license was one of the happiest days of my life. All that was left, I thought, was having a car of my own. That day came, too, and it changed my life. Owning my own car gave me freedom, cost me money, and made me a more careful driver.

The wonderful part of owning a car was the adult freedom it gave me. First of all, I didn't have to beg my father for his truck any more. Every time I asked him, he seemed reluctant to lend it to me. He was always worried that I would dirty the interior with food wrappers and empty soda cans. Second, I no longer had to get rides from my friends whenever I wanted to go somewhere. I was really tired of begging rides from my buddies, and I am sure they were sick of acting like a taxi service. With my own car, I could go to the city whenever I wanted. I could even ride around for fun.

On the more serious side, I had to pay for the car and related expenses. A car costs hundreds of dollars to maintain. There are oil changes and tune-ups to keep the car in good running condition. Two months after I got my car, I had to buy four new and very expensive tires. Of course, I had monthly payments on my car loan. I also had to pay for car insurance which, because of my young age, was unbelievably high. My insurance cost so much that I had to work overtime to pay the bill.

Now that I was paying for the car I drove, I became a more careful driver. I became worried about someone hitting the car; I could imagine my beautiful car dented and dinged. These thoughts made me fear bad drivers and become more nervous on the road. I began to drive more defensively, and instead of challenging aggressive drivers, I began to avoid them. Parking lots made me nervous, too. To avoid the scratches cars can get in parking lots, I parked at the end of the row, away from other cars.

Owning a car gave me adult freedom, but it gave me adult responsibilities and worries, too. Yet even with the stress of car payments, insurance payments, and car maintenance, I would never give up my car. My fear of dents and scratches can't keep me from the joy of driving whenever and wherever I want. I'm happy to accept the responsibilities that come with being on the road in my own car.

WRITING A CAUSE OR EFFECT ESSAY

When you write on any of these topics, work through the stages of the writing process in preparing your essay.

1. Think of a time when you had to make an important choice. Then write an essay explaining the reasons for your choice. Your essay can include an explanation of your options as well as the reasons for your choice.

2. Write an essay about the effects on you (or someone you know well) of one of the following:

learning to swim	learning to read
learning a new language	learning to use a computer
learning to dance	learning to sing
learning to play a new sport	learning to meditate
learning to play a musical instrument	

3. Write an essay on one of the following topics:

why Some Students Are Nervous About Speaking in Class
why Most Children No Longer Walk or Ride Bicycles to School
why Many High School Students Have Part-Time Jobs
why Many _____ (Teens, Young People, Families, Older People, Hispanics—you name the group) Like to Watch _____ (you name the television show).
why College Students May Feel Lonely

4. Think of a singer, rapper, singing group, or musician that is popular with people of your age and background. Write an essay explaining that person or group's popularity.

5. Explain why a certain sport (you choose the sport) is no longer as popular as it used to be.

ARGUMENT

Hints for Writing an Argument Essay

1. **Pick a topic based on your own experience and observation.** Although you may not realize it, you have a wide range of experience because you play many roles: consumer, student, parent, child, husband or wife, parent, worker, driver, pet owner, athlete. These and many other roles may fit you. In each of your roles, you may have noticed or experienced something that can lead to a topic.

2. **Be sure to take a stand in your thesis.**   That is, don't merely state a problem, but make a point about how to solve or eliminate it:

   not this: The potholes on Johnson Road are terrible.
   but this: The Department of Public Works must fix the potholes on Johnson Road immediately.

   not this: Skateboarders have nowhere to go in Mason Heights.
   but this: Mason Heights needs a skateboard park.

3. **Use the reasons in your argument to focus your body paragraphs.**   If you have three reasons, for instance, you can write three body paragraphs.

4. **Consider your audience's objections.**   Always ask yourself who the audience is for your argument. If you are arguing that your office needs a new copier, you will probably be writing to your supervisor. If you are arguing for an after-school program at your child's elemen-

tary school, you will probably be writing to the school board. Think about why your audience should support your points as well as how your audience might object.

There are several ways to handle objections. If you can *refute* an objection, that is, prove that it isn't valid, you have removed a major obstacle. Sometimes you might have to admit the other side has a valid objection by *conceding* it. Even by conceding, however, you win confidence by showing that you know both sides of the argument and are open-minded enough to consider another point of view.

Another way to handle an objection is to *turn an objection into an advantage*. That is, you can admit the objection is valid but use it to reinforce your own point. If you are arguing for a new copier and your supervisor says it is too expensive, you can agree that it is expensive but that the office is losing time and money constantly repairing the old copier. Turning an obstacle into an advantage shows that you are informed, open-minded, and quick-thinking.

Even if you do not openly refer to objections in your argument essay, being aware of possible objections helps you to frame your points effectively by keeping your audience in mind.

WRITING THE ARGUMENT ESSAY IN STEPS

Thought Lines Gathering Ideas: Argument Essay

Imagine that your instructor has given you this assignment:

Write a one-paragraph letter to the editor of your local newspaper. Argue for something in your town that needs to be changed.

One way to begin is to brainstorm for some specific thing that you can write about. You can ask questions such as these: Is there a part of town that needs to be cleaned up? Should something be changed at a school? What do I notice on my way to work or school that needs improvement? What could be improved in my neighborhood?

By answering these questions, you may come up with one topic, and then you can list ideas on it.

topic

Cleaning Up Roberts Park

ideas

dirty and overgrown
benches are all cracked and broken
full of trash
could be fixed up
people work nearby
they would use it

You can consider your audience and possible objections:

audience

local people of all ages who read the local paper.

possible objections from this audience

would cost money
more important things to spend money on

answering objections

Money would be well spent to beautify the downtown. City children could play there in the fresh air and in nature; workers could eat lunch there.

Once you have a list, you can start grouping the ideas on your list. Some of the objections you wrote down may actually lead you to reasons that support your argument. That is, by answering objections, you may come up with reasons that support your point. Following is a list with a point to argue, three supporting reasons, and some details about cleaning up Roberts Park.

A List for an Argument Essay

Topic: Cleaning Up a Park

point:	We should fix up Roberts Park.
reason:	Improving the park would make the downtown area more attractive to shoppers.
details:	Shoppers could stroll in the park or rest from their shopping. Friends could meet in the park for a day of shopping and lunch.
reason:	City children could play in the park.
details:	They could get fresh air. They could play in a natural setting.
reason:	Workers could get lunch outdoors.
details:	Several office complexes are nearby. Workers would take a break outdoors.

With your reasons and details, you can draft a thesis sentence:

Roberts Park should be cleaned up and improved.

With a thesis sentence, three reasons, and details, you are ready to move on to the outlines stage of preparing an argument essay.

Outlines Devising a Plan: Argument Essay

Following is an outline for an argument essay on cleaning up a park.

An Outline for an Argument Essay

paragraph 1 I. Thesis: Roberts Park should be cleaned up and improved.

paragraph 2 II. Improving the park would make the downtown area more attractive to shoppers.
topic sentence
and details A. If the city could clean, landscape, and refurnish the park, it would be a natural refuge for shoppers.

reason 1 B. It is located in the middle of the shopping district.
a place for C. Those who already shop in the city could stroll through the park or rest there after shopping.
shoppers D. Soon, shoppers would tell their friends about the attractive, new-looking park.

E. Eventually, friends could agree to meet at the park for a day of shopping and lunch.

F. City shops and department stores would see business improve.

G. Business would be good for restaurants, too.

paragraph 3

topic sentence

and details

III. Workers from nearby offices and stores could eat lunch outdoors.

A. Several office buildings are nearby.

reason 2

a place for

works

B. During the lunch break, many people, even those who bring their lunch, want to get out of the office or store.

C. Everyone wants to get up and forget the job for a little while.

D. Some want fresh air.

E. Others want to read a book or magazine while they eat.

F. Others want to get some exercise by walking a little.

G. Others just want to observe nature and people.

H. An improved park could meet all these needs.

paragraph 4

topic sentence

and details

IV. City children could play there.

A. City children live in apartments.

B. They don't have backyards to enjoy.

C. They are reduced to playing in dangerous streets or on narrow sidewalks.

reason 3

a place for

children

D. Many aren't allowed outside at all.

E. They go from sitting all day at school to sitting at home.

F. In the park, children could interact rather than sit alone inside watching television and playing video games.

G. They could play on grass, not asphalt.

H. They would not have to play near traffic.

Paragraph 5

conclusion

V. Roberts Park used to be the city's landmark, and it could be, once again.

The outline combined some of the details from the list with new details gathered during the outlining process. It focused each body paragraph on one reason to clean up the park. As you write and revise your draft, you can continue to add details to each reason. You can also combine sentences, add transitions, and work on word choice.

Rough Lines Drafting and Revising: Argument Essay

Following is a revised draft of the essay on cleaning up a park. As you read it, you'll notice many changes from the outline on pages 262–263.

- An introduction has been added.
- Transitions have been added within and between paragraphs.
- Details have been added.
- A concluding paragraph has been added.

A Draft of an Argument Essay (Thesis and topic sentences are underlined.)

Roberts Park was once a pretty little park, with a fountain, dark wood benches, carefully landscaped paths, and lush trees and flowers. Today, however, the fountain is cracked and dry, the benches are faded and splintered, and the paths are overgrown. Trash fills the flowerbeds. <u>Roberts Park should be cleaned up and improved.</u>

There are several reasons why a better park would make a better city. <u>First, improving the park would make the downtown area more attractive to shoppers.</u> If the city could clean, landscape, and refurnish the park, it would be a natural refuge for shoppers. It is right in the middle of the shopping district, making it convenient for those who already shop in the city to stroll through the park or rest there. Soon, shoppers might tell their friends about the attractive, new-looking park. Eventually, friends could agree to meet at the park for a day of shopping and lunch. City shops and department stores would see an increase in business, and restaurants would benefit, too.

Those who do business in the city would appreciate a renovated park as well. <u>Workers from nearby offices and stores could eat lunch outdoors.</u> Several high-rise office buildings are nearby, full of office workers. During their lunch break, many people, even those who bring their lunch, want to get out of the office or store. Everyone wants to get up and forget the job for a little while. Some want fresh air while others want to read a book or magazine while they eat. The more ambitious want to get some exercise by walking a little; however, many people just want to observe nature and people. An improved park could meet all these needs.

The most important reason to clean up the park is to help children. <u>City children could play in Roberts Park.</u> City children, who live in apartments, don't have backyards to enjoy. If they go outside, they are reduced to playing in dangerous streets or on narrow sidewalks. Many aren't allowed outside at all. They go from sitting all day at school to sitting at home. In a restored park, children could interact rather than sit alone at home, watching television and playing video games. They could play on grass, not asphalt. Best of all, they would not have to play near traffic.

Today, the words "Roberts Park" describe a run-down, ragged plot of broken benches, weeds, and trash. But the place could be a haven for children, shoppers, and workers. Once the park was green, the fountain shimmered, and the benches shone. <u>Roberts Park used to be the city's landmark, and it could be, once again.</u>

Final Lines Polishing and Proofreading: Argument Essay

Following is the final version of the essay on cleaning up a park. When you compare it to the draft above, you will notice some changes:

- The introduction needed a transition from the description of the park to the thesis. A transition sentence has been added.
- One sentence in paragraph 2 has been revised to eliminate extra words.
- Also in paragraph 2, the words "shop," "shoppers," and "shopping" became repetitive, so one phrase, "these people," replaced one use of "shoppers."
- Some details have been added and word choice improved.
- A new sentence of details has been added to paragraph 4.
- A transition has been added to paragraph 4.
- A title has been added.

A Final Version of an Argument Essay (Changes from the draft are underlined.)

The Case for Renovating Roberts Park

Roberts Park was once a pretty little park, with a <u>bubbling</u> fountain, dark wood benches, carefully landscaped paths, and lush trees and flowers. Today, however, the fountain is cracked and dry, the benches are faded and splintered, and the paths are overgrown. Trash fills the flowerbeds. <u>It is time to make this place park-like again.</u> Roberts Park should be cleaned up and improved.

There are several reasons why a better park would make a better city. First, improving the park would make the downtown area more attractive to shoppers. If the city could clean, landscape, and refurnish the park, it would be a natural refuge for shoppers. <u>Because it is right in the middle of the shopping district, those who already shop in the city would be likely to stroll through the park or rest there.</u> Soon, <u>these people</u> might tell their friends about the attractive, new-looking park. Eventually, friends could agree to meet at the park for a day of shopping and lunch. City shops and department stores would see an increase in business, and restaurants would benefit, too.

Those who do business in the city would appreciate a renovated park as well. Workers from nearby offices and stores could eat lunch outdoors. Several high-rise office buildings are nearby, full of office workers. During their lunch break, many people, even those who bring their lunch, want to get out of the office or store. Everyone wants to get up and forget the job for a little while. Some want fresh air while others want to read a book or magazine while they eat. The more ambitious want to get some exercise by walking a little; however, many people just want to observe nature and people. An improved park could meet all these needs.

The most important reason to clean up the park is to help children. City children could play in Roberts Park. City children, who live in apartments, don't have backyards to enjoy. If they go outside, they are reduced to playing in dangerous streets or on narrow sidewalks. Many aren't allowed outside at all. They go from sitting all day at school to sitting at home. In a restored park, children could interact rather than sit alone at home, watching television and playing video games. <u>They would get some much-needed exercise.</u> <u>In addition,</u> they could play on grass, not asphalt. Best of all, they would not have to play near traffic.

Today, the words "Roberts Park" describe a run-down, ragged <u>site full of</u> broken benches, weeds, and trash. But the place could be a haven for children, shoppers, and workers. Once the park was green, the fountain shimmered, and the benches shone. Roberts Park used to be the city's landmark, and it could be, once again.

WRITING AN ARGUMENT ESSAY

When you write on any of these topics, work through the stages of the writing process in preparing your essay.

1. Write an essay for readers of your local newspaper, arguing for or against one of the following:

    a. a citywide curfew for every person under eighteen
    b. cameras that photograph the license plates of drivers who run red lights
    c. a ban on using a cell phone while driving
    d. an online traffic school

2. As a consumer, you purchase a number of products and services. Think of one product (like toothpaste, a calculator, a table) or a service (like a flight on a plane, a car repair, or a meal in a restaurant) that you feel needs improvement. Write an essay in the form of a letter to the president of the company that produces the product or offers the service. Argue for the improvement you want. Be specific. For example, if you are dissatisfied with a brand of cereal, you might want less deceptive packaging, a lower price, or less sugar in the cereal.

3. Write to the president of a company whose advertising offends you. The advertising can be television or print advertising. In an essay in the form of a letter, argue for removing that advertising.

4. Argue for one of the following college issues. Your audience will be the president, vice presidents, and deans at your college. Topics to argue:

open parking (with the exception of handicapped spaces) at your college
a laptop (at a minimal rental fee and with a security deposit) for each
  registered student
a twenty-four-hour study area with computers available
security escorts for all evening students who ask for them to get to
  their cars

5. If you are a parent, a husband or wife, a partner, an employee, an employer, a student, a pet lover, a driver, or a traveler, you have most likely noticed something in one of your roles that has irritated or upset you. Write an argument essay about how to change that place, rule, policy, procedure, situation, and so forth, that has irritated or upset you.

Writing from Reading

WHAT IS WRITING FROM READING?

One way to find topics for writing is to draw on your ideas, memories, and observations. Another way is to write from reading you have done. You can *react* to it; you can *agree or disagree* with something you have read. In fact, many college assignments or tests ask you to write about an assigned reading: an essay, a chapter in a textbook, an article in a journal. This kind of writing requires an active, involved attitude toward your reading. Such reading is done in steps:

1. Preread.
2. Read.
3. Reread with a pen or pencil.

After you have completed these three steps, you can write from your reading. You can write about what you have read, or you can react to what you have read.

AN APPROACH TO WRITING FROM READING

Attitude

Before you begin the first step of this reading process, you have to have a certain **attitude.** That attitude involves thinking of what you read as half of a conversation. The writer has opinions and ideas; he or she makes points, just like you do when you write or speak. The writer supports his or her points with specific details. If the writer were speaking to you in a conversation you would respond to his or her opinions or ideas. You would agree, disagree, or question. You would jump into the conversation, linking or contrasting your ideas with those of the other speaker.

The right attitude toward reading demands that you read the way you'd converse: *you become involved.* In doing this, you "talk back" as you read, and later you react in your own writing. Reacting as you read will keep you focused on what you are reading. If you are focused, you will remember more of what you read. With an active, involved attitude, you can begin the step of prereading.

Prereading

Before you actually read an assigned essay, a chapter in a textbook, or an article in a journal, magazine, or newspaper, take a few minutes to look it over, and be ready to answer the questions in the prereading checklist.

✔ Checklist

A Prereading Checklist

✔ How long is this reading?

✔ Will I be able to read it in one sitting, or will I have to schedule several time periods to finish it?

✔ Are there any subheadings in the reading? Do they give any hints about the reading?

✔ Are there any charts? Graphs? Boxed information?

✔ Are there any photographs or illustrations with captions? Do the photos or captions give me any hints about the reading?

✔ Is there any introductory material about the reading or its author? Does the introductory material give me any hints about the reading?

✔ What is the title of the reading? Does the title hint at the point of the reading?

✔ Are any parts of the reading underlined, italicized, or emphasized in some other way? Do the emphasized parts hint at the point of the reading?

Why Preread?

Prereading takes very little time, but it helps you immensely. Some students believe it is a waste of time to scan an assignment; they think they should jump right in and get the reading over with. However, spending just a few minutes on preliminaries can save hours later. Most important, prereading helps you to become a *focused reader.*

If you scan the length of an assignment, you can pace yourself. And if you know how long a reading is, you can alert yourself to its plan. A short reading, for example, has to come to its point fairly soon. A longer essay may take more time to develop its point and may use more details and examples.

Subheadings, charts, graphs, illustrations, and boxed or other highlighted material are important enough that the author wants to emphasize them. Looking over that material *before* you read gives you an overview of the important points the reading will contain.

Introductory material or introductory questions will also help you know what to look for as you read. Background on the author or on the subject may hint at ideas that will come up in the reading. Sometimes even the title of the reading will give you the main idea.

You should preread so that you can start reading the entire assignment with as much knowledge about the writer and the subject as you can get.

When you then read the entire assignment, you will be reading *actively*, for more knowledge.

Forming Questions Before You Read

If you want to read with a focus, it helps to ask questions before you read. Form questions by using the information you gained from prereading.

Start by noting the title and turning it into a question. If the title of your assigned reading is "Reasons for the Alien and Sedition Acts," you can turn that title into a question: "What were the reasons for the Alien and Sedition Acts?"

You can turn subheadings into questions. If you are reading an article on beach erosion, and one subheading is "Artificial Reefs," you can ask, "How are artificial reefs connected to beach erosion?"

You can form questions from graphs and illustrations. If a chapter in your history book includes a photograph of a Gothic cathedral, you can ask, "How are Gothic cathedrals connected to this period in history?" or "Why are Gothic cathedrals important?" or "What is Gothic architecture?"

You can write down these questions, but it's not necessary. Just forming questions and keeping them in the back of your mind helps you read actively and stay focused.

An Example of the Prereading Step

Take a look at the article below. Don't read it; *preread* it.

A Ridiculous Addiction

by Gwinn Owens

Gwinn Owens, a retired editor and columnist for The Baltimore Evening Sun, *writes this essay about his experiences in parking lots, noting that the American search for a good parking space "transcends logic and common sense."*

Words You May Need to Know (corresponding paragraph numbers are in parenthesis)

preening (2): primping, making oneself appear elegant
perusing (2): reading
stymied (3): hindered, blocked, defeated
addiction (5): a compulsive habit
coveted (6): desired, eagerly wished for
transcends (6): rises above, goes beyond the limits of
atavistically (7): primitively

acrimonious (8): bitter, harsh
holy grail (8): a sacred object that the Knights of the Round Table devoted years to finding
antithesis (9): opposite
ensconced (10): securely sheltered
idiocy (11): foolish behavior
contempt (13): scorn, lack of respect
emporium (14): store

1   Let us follow my friend Frank Bogley as, on the way home from work, he swings into the shopping mall to pick up a liter of Johnny Walker, on sale at the Bottle and Cork. In the vast, herringboned parking area

there are, literally, hundreds of empty spaces, but some are perhaps as much as a forty-second walk from the door of the liquor store. So Bogley, a typical American motorist, feels compelled to park as close as possible.

2   He eases down between the rows of parked cars until he notices a blue-haired matron getting into her Mercedes. This is a prime location, not more than twenty-five steps from the Bottle and Cork. Bogley stops to await her departure so as to slip quickly into the vacated slot. She shuts the door of her car as Bogley's engine surges nervously. But she does not move. She is, in fact, preening her hair and perusing a magazine she just bought.

3   The stymied Bogley is now tying up traffic in that lane. Two more cars with impatient drivers assemble behind him. One driver hits his horn lightly, then angrily. Bogley opens his window and gives him the finger, but reluctantly realizes that the Mercedes isn't about to leave. His arteries harden a little more as, exasperated, he gives up and starts circling the lot in search of another space, passing scores of empty ones which he deems too far from his destination. Predictably, he slips into the space for the handicapped. "Just for a moment," he says to his conscience.

4   The elapsed time of Bogley's search for a convenient parking space is seven minutes. Had he chosen one of the abundant spaces only a few steps farther away, he could have accomplished his mission in less than two minutes, without frazzled nerves or skyrocketing blood pressure—his as well as those who were backed up behind him. He could have enjoyed a little healthful walking to reduce the paunch that is gestating in his middle.

5   Frank Bogley suffers an acute case of parking addiction, which afflicts more Americans than the common cold. We are obsessed with the idea that it is our constitutional right not to have to park more than ten steps from our destination.

6   Like all addictions, this quest for the coveted spot transcends logic and common sense. Motorists will pursue it without concern over the time it takes, as if a close-in parking space were its own sweet fulfillment. They will park in the fire lane, in the handicapped space or leave the car at the curb, where space is reserved for loading.

7   The quest atavistically transcends politeness and civility. My local paper recently carried a story about two motorists who, seeing a third car about to exit a spot, both lusted for the vacancy. As soon as the departing vehicle was gone, one of the standbys was a little faster and grabbed the coveted prize. The defeated motorist leaped from his car, threw open his rival's door and punched him in the snoot. He was charged with assault. Hell hath no fury like a motorist who loses the battle for a close-in parking space.

8   The daily obsession to possess the coveted slot probably shortens the life of most Americans by at least 4.2 years. This acrimonious jockeying, waiting, backing, maneuvering for the holy grail of nearness jangles the nerves, constricts the arteries and turns puppylike personalities into snarling mad dogs.

9   I know a few Americans who have actually kicked the habit, and they are extraordinarily happy people. I am one, and I owe my cure to my friend Lou, who is the antithesis of Frank Bogley. One day I recognized Lou's red Escort in the wallflower space of the parking lot of our local supermarket. There was not another vehicle within 80 feet.

10   In the store I asked him why he had ensconced his car in lonely splendor. His answer made perfect sense: "I pull in and out quickly, nobody else's doors scratch my paint and I get a short walk, which I need." Lou, I might point out, is in his 60s and is built like twenty-five—lean and fit.

11   These days, I do as Lou does, and a great weight has been lifted. Free of the hassle, I am suddenly aware of the collective idiocy of the parking obsession—angry people battling for what is utterly without value. I acquire what does have value: saving of time, fresh air, peace of mind, healthful exercise.

12   The only time I feel the stress now is when I am a passenger with a driver who has not yet taken the cure. On one recent occasion I accepted a ride with my friend Andy to a large banquet at which I was a head-table guest. The banquet hall had its own commodious parking lot, but Andy is another Frank Bogley.

13   He insisted on trying to park near the door "because it is late." He was right; it *was* late, and there being no slots near the door, he then proceeded to thread his way through the labyrinth of the close-in lot, as I pleaded that I didn't mind walking from out where there was plenty of space. He finally used five minutes jockeying his big Lincoln into a Honda-size niche. Thanks to Andy's addiction, I walked late into the banquet hall and stumbled into my conspicuous seat in the midst of the solemn convocation. My attitude toward him was a mixture of pity and contempt, like a recovering alcoholic must feel toward an incipient drunk.

14   These silly parking duels, fought over the right not to walk more than fifteen steps, can be found almost anywhere in the fifty states. They reach their ultimate absurdity, however, at my local racquet and fitness club. The battle to park close to the door of the athletic emporium is fought as aggressively as at the shopping mall. Everyone who parks there is intending to engage in tennis, squash, aerobic dancing, muscle building or some other kind of athletic constitutional. But to have to exercise ahead of time by walking from the lot to the door is clearly regarded by most Americans as unconstitutional.

The Results of Prereading By prereading the article, you might notice the following:

> The title is "A Ridiculous Addiction."
> The author was a newspaper writer from Baltimore.
> There are many vocabulary words you may need to know.
> The essay is about parking lots.
> The introductory material says Americans' search for a desirable
>   parking space goes beyond the limits of common sense.

You might begin reading the article with these questions in mind:

> What is the addiction?
> How can an addiction be ridiculous? An addiction is usually considered something very serious, like an addiction to drugs.
> What do parking spaces have to do with addiction?
> What is so illogical about looking for a good parking space?

Reading

The first time you read, try to get a sense of the whole piece you are reading. Reading with questions in mind can help you do this. If you find that you are confused by a certain part of the reading selection, go back and reread that part. If you do not know the meaning of a word, check the vocabulary list to see if the word is defined for you. If it is not defined, try to figure out the meaning from the way the word is used in the sentence.

If you find that you have to read more slowly than the way that you usually do, don't worry. People vary their reading speed according to what they read and why they are reading it. If you are reading for entertainment, for example, you can read quickly; if you are reading a chapter in a textbook, you must read more slowly. The more complicated the reading selection, the more slowly you will read it.

An Example of the Reading Step

Now read "A Ridiculous Addiction." When you've completed your first reading, you will probably have some answers to the prereading questions you formed, like those below:

Answers to Prereading Questions

> The author says that the ridiculous addiction is the need to find the best parking space.
> He means it's ridiculous because it makes parking a serious issue and because people do silly things to get good parking spots.
> People are illogical in getting parking because they'll even be late for an event in order to get a good space. Or they get upset.

Rereading with Pen or Pencil

The second reading is the crucial one. At this point, you begin to *think on paper* as you read. In this step, you make notes or write about what you read. Some students are reluctant to do this, for they are not sure *what* to note or write. Think of making these notes as a way of learning, thinking, reviewing, and reacting. Reading with a pen or pencil in your hand keeps you alert. With that pen or pencil, you can do the following:

> Mark the main point of the reading.
> Mark other points.
> Define words you don't know.
> Question parts of the reading you're not sure of.
> Evaluate the writer's ideas.
> React to the writer's opinions or examples.
> Add ideas, opinions, or examples of your own.

There is no single system for marking or writing as you read. Some readers like to underline the main idea with two lines and to underline other important ideas with one line. Some students like to put an asterisk (a star) next to important ideas while others like to circle key words.

Some people use the margins to write comments like "I agree!" or "Not true!" or "That's happened to me." Sometimes readers put questions in the margin; sometimes they summarize a point in the margin next to its location in the essay. Some people make notes in the white space above the reading and list important points, and others use the space at the end of the reading. Every reader who writes while he or she reads has a personal system; what these systems share is an attitude. *If you write as you read, you concentrate on the reading selection, get to know the writer's ideas, and develop ideas of your own.*

As you reread and write notes, don't worry too much about noticing the "right" ideas. Think of rereading as the time to jump into a conversation with the writer.

An Example of Rereading with Pen or Pencil

For "A Ridiculous Addiction," your marked article might look like the following:

A Ridiculous Addiction

Gwinn Owens

Let us follow my friend Frank Bogley as, on the way home from work, he swings into the shopping mall to pick up a liter of Johnny Walker, on sale at the Bottle and Cork. In the vast, herringboned parking area there are, literally, hundreds of empty spaces, but some are perhaps as much as a 40-second walk from the door of the liquor store. So Bogley, <u>a typical American motorist, feels compelled to park as close as possible.</u>

the bad habit

He eases down between the rows of parked cars until he notices a blue-haired matron getting into her Mercedes. This is a prime location, not more than 25 steps from the Bottle and Cork. Bogley stops to await her departure so as to slip quickly into the vacated slot. She shuts the door of her car as Bogley's engine surges nervously. But she does not move. She is, in fact, preening her hair and perusing a magazine she just bought.

The stymied Bogley is now tying up traffic in that lane. Two more cars with impatient drivers assemble behind him. One driver hits his horn lightly, then angrily. Bogley opens his window and gives him the finger, but reluctantly realizes that the Mercedes isn't about to leave. His arteries harden a little more as, exasperated, he gives up and starts circling the lot in search of another space, passing scores of empty ones which he deems too far from his destination. <u>Predictably, he slips into the space for the handicapped.</u> "Just for a moment," he says to his conscience.

I hate this!

<u>The elapsed time of Bogley's search for a convenient parking space is seven minutes.</u> Had he chosen one of the abundant spaces only a few steps

*wasted
time
irritation*

farther away, <u>he could have accomplished his mission in less than two min-utes, without frazzled nerves or skyrocketing blood pressure—his as well as those who were backed up behind him.</u> He could have enjoyed a little healthful walking to reduce the paunch that is gestating in his middle.

Frank Bogley suffers an acute case of parking addiction, which afflicts more Americans than the common cold. <u>We are obsessed with the idea that it is our constitutional right not to have to park more than 10 steps from our destination.</u>

<u>Like all addictions, this quest for the coveted spot transcends logic and common sense.</u> Motorists will pursue it without concern over the time it takes, as if a close-in parking space were its own sweet fulfillment. <u>They will park in the fire lane or in the handicapped space or leave the car at the curb, where space is reserved for loading.</u>

example

The quest atavistically <u>transcends politeness and civility.</u> My local paper recently carried a story about two motorists who, seeing a third car about to exit a spot, both lusted for the vacancy. As soon as the departing vehicle was gone, one of the standbys was a little faster and grabbed the coveted prize. The defeated motorist leaped from his car, threw open his rival's door, and punched him in the snoot. He was charged with <u>assault.</u> Hell hath no fury like a motorist who loses the battle for a close-in parking space.

The daily obsession to possess the coveted slot probably shortens the life of most Americans by at least 4.2 years. This acrimonious jockeying, waiting, backing, maneuvering for the holy grail of nearness <u>jangles the nerves, con-stricts the arteries and turns puppylike personalities into snarling mad dogs.</u>

opposite

I know a few Americans who have actually kicked the habit, and they are extraordinarily happy people. I am one, and I owe my cure to my friend Lou, who is the (antithesis) of Frank Bogley. One day I recognized Lou's red Escort in the wallflower space of the parking lot of our local supermarket. There was not another vehicle within 80 feet.

*breaking
the habit:
advan-
tages*

In the store I asked him why he had ensconced his car in lonely splen-dor. His answer made perfect sense: "<u>I pull in and out quickly, nobody else's doors scratch my paint and I get a short walk, which I need.</u>" Lou, I might point out, is in his 60s and is built like 25—lean and fit.

*more
advantages*

These days, I do as Lou does, and a great weight has been lifted. Free of the hassle, I am suddenly aware of the collective idiocy of the parking obsession—angry people battling for what is utterly without value. I acquire what does have value: <u>saving of time, fresh air, peace of mind, healthful exercise.</u>

*back to
bad habit*

The only time I feel the stress now is when I am a passenger with a dri-ver who has not yet taken the cure. On one recent occasion I accepted a ride with my friend Andy to a large banquet at which I was a head-table guest. The banquet hall had its own commodious parking lot, but Andy is another Frank Bogley.

He insisted on trying to park near the door "because it is late." He was right; it *was* late, and there being no slots near the door, he then proceeded to thread his way through the labyrinth of the close-in lot, as I pleaded that I didn't mind walking from out where there was plenty of space. He finally used five minutes jockeying his big Lincoln into a Honda-size niche. Thanks to Andy's addiction, I walked late into the banquet hall and stumbled into my conspicuous seat in the midst of the solemn convocation. My attitude toward him was a mixture of pity and contempt, like a recovering alcoholic must feel toward an incipient drunk.

How true!

These silly parking duels, fought over the right not to walk more than 15 steps, can be found almost anywhere in the 50 states. They reach their ultimate absurdity, however, at my local racquet and fitness club. The battle to park close to the door of the athletic emporium is fought as aggressively as at the shopping mall. Everyone who parks there is intending to engage in tennis, squash, aerobic dancing, muscle building or some other kind of athletic constitutional. But to have to exercise ahead of time by walking from the lot to the door is clearly regarded by most Americans as unconstitutional.

more on bad habit

What the Notes Mean

In the sample above, the underlining indicates sentences or phrases that seem important. The words in the margin are often summaries of what is underlined. The words "wasted time," "irritation," and "effects," for instance, are like subtitles or labels in the margin.

Some words in the margin are reactions. When Owens describes a man who parked illegally in a handicapped spot, the reader notes, "I hate this!" When the writer talks about a Lincoln trying to fit into a Honda-sized spot, the reader writes, "How true!" One word in the margin is a definition. The word "antithesis" in the selection is defined as "opposite" in the margin.

The marked-up article is a flexible tool. You can go back and mark it further. You may change your mind about your notes and comments and find other, better or more important points in the article.

You write as you read to involve yourself in the reading process. Marking what you read can help you in other ways, too. If you are to be tested on the reading selection or asked to discuss it, you can scan your markings and notations at a later time for a quick review.

Exercise 1 *Practice*

Reading and Making Notes

Following is the last paragraph of "A Ridiculous Addiction." First, read it. Then reread it and make notes on the following:

1. Underline the sentence that begins the long example in the paragraph.
2. Circle a word you don't know and define it in the margin.
3. In the margin, add your own example of a place where people fight for parking spaces.
4. At the end of the paragraph, summarize the point of the paragraph.

Paragraph from "A Ridiculous Addiction"

These silly parking duels, fought over the right not to walk more than 15 steps, can be found almost anywhere in the 50 states. They reach their ultimate absurdity, however, at my local racquet and fitness club. The battle to park close to the door of the athletic emporium is fought as aggressively as at the shopping mall. Everyone who parks there is intending to engage in tennis, squash, aerobic dancing, muscle building, or some other kind of athletic constitutional. But to have to exercise ahead of time by walking from the lot to the door is clearly regarded by most Americans as unconstitutional.

Main point of the paragraph: _____

_____

WRITING A SUMMARY OF A READING

There are a number of ways you can write about what you've read. You may be asked for a summary of an article or chapter, or for a reaction to it, or to write about it on an essay test. For each of these, this chapter will give you guidelines so that you can follow the stages of the writing process.

A **summary** of a reading tells the important ideas in brief form. It includes (1) the writer's main idea, (2) the ideas used to explain the main idea, and (3) some examples used to support the ideas.

When you preread, read, and make notes on the reading selection, you have already begun the thought lines stage for a summary. You can think further, on paper, by listing the points (words, phrases, sentences) you've already marked on the reading selection.

Thought Lines **Gathering Ideas: Summary**

Marking a List of Ideas

To find the main idea for your summary and the ideas and examples connected to the main idea, you can mark related items on your list. For example, the expanded list below was made from "A Ridiculous Addiction." Four symbols are used:

K marks the **kinds** of close spots people will take.

X marks all **examples** of what can happen when people want a good spot.

– marks the **negative** effects of the close-parking habit.

+ marks the **advantages** of breaking the habit.

A List of Ideas for a Summary of "A Ridiculous Addiction"

K no close spots, takes handicapped

X seven minutes looking for close spot

– wasted time, could have found
  another in two minutes

X got mad

X an assault over a spot

– jangles nerves, constricts
  arteries, and makes people mad
  dogs kicking the habit

+ get in and out fast

X made others wait	+ no scratched car doors
X they got angry	+ good exercise
Americans obsessed with right	+ saving time
to good spot	+ fresh air
transcends logic	+ peace of mind
no common sense	+ healthful exercise
K park in fire lane	X late for big dinner
K leave car at curb	X fitness clubs the
K loading zone	silliest—won't wait
− impolite	

The marked list could be reorganized, like this:

kinds of close spots people will take

handicapped
fire lane
curb
loading zone

examples of what can happen when people want a good spot

seven minutes of wasted time
others, waiting behind, get mad
an assault over a spot
late for a big dinner
members of the fitness club won't walk

negative effects of the close-parking habit

wasted time
impolite
jangles nerves, constricts arteries
makes people mad dogs

advantages of breaking the habit

get in and out fast
no scratched car doors
good exercise
saving time
fresh air
peace of mind
healthful exercise

Selecting a Main Idea

The next step in the process is to select the idea you think is the writer's main point. If you look again at the list of ideas, you'll note a cluster of ideas that are unmarked:

1. Americans obsessed with the right to a good spot
2. transcends logic
3. no common sense

You might guess that they are unmarked because they are more general than the other ideas. In fact, these ideas are connected to the title of the essay: "A Ridiculous Addiction," and they are connected to some of the questions in the prereading step of reading: "What's the addiction?" and "How can an addiction be ridiculous?"

Linking the ideas may lead you to a main idea for the summary of the reading selection:

Americans' obsession with finding a good parking spot makes no sense.

Once you have a main idea, check that main idea to see if it fits with the other ideas in your organized list. *Do the ideas in the list connect to the main idea?* Yes. "Kinds of close spots people take" explains how silly it is to break the law. "Examples of what can happen" and "negative effects" show why the habit makes no sense, and "advantages of breaking the habit" shows the reasons to conquer the addiction.

Once you have a main point that fits an organized list, you can move to the outlines stage of a summary.

Practice

Marking a List of Ideas and Finding the Main Idea for a Summary

Below is a list of ideas from an article called "How to Land the Job You Want." Read the list, and then mark the items on the list with one of these symbols:

X   examples of people looking for or getting jobs
S   steps in getting a job
A   advice from employers

After you've marked all the ideas, survey them, and think of a main idea. Try to focus on an idea that connects to the title, "How to Land the Job You Want."

List of Ideas

_____ Laid-off engineer used his personality to get a sales job.

_____ Insurance company manager says applicants can walk in without appointment.

_____ Find the hidden job market.

_____ Unemployed teacher found a job through his insurance agent.

_____ Bank worker got a job through his club.

_____ Prepare specifically for each interview.

_____ Locate hidden openings.

_____ Company director says a good letter of application is crucial.

_____ Make résumé strong and polished.

_____ Put yourself in employer's place in writing a résumé.

_____ Cabinetmaker checked phone books of nine cities for companies in his field.

_____ Use the library to research job opportunities.

Main idea: _____

Outlines Devising a Plan: Summary

Below is a sample of the kind of outline you could do for a summary of "A Ridiculous Addiction." As you read it, you'll notice that the main idea of the thought lines stage has become the topic sentence of the outline, and the other ideas have become the details.

Outline for a Summary of "A Ridiculous Addiction"

topic sentence: Americans' obsession with finding a good parking spot makes no sense.

details:

examples
- Many bad or silly things can happen when people try for a good spot.
- One person wasted seven minutes.
- He made other drivers angry.
- Someone else got involved in an assault.
- Someone else was late for a big dinner.
- Silly people, on their way to a fitness club, will avoid the walk in the fitness club parking lot.

negative effects
- Looking for a close spot can make people impolite or turn them into mad dogs.
- It can jangle drivers' nerves or constrict arteries.
- Some people will even break the law and take handicapped spots or park in a fire lane or loading zone.

advantages of kicking the habit
- If people can give up the habit, they can gain advantages.
- A faraway spot is not popular, so they can get in and out of it fast.
- Their cars won't be scratched.
- They get exercise and fresh air by walking.

In the preceding outline, some ideas from the original list have been left out (they were repetitive) and the order of some points has been rearranged. That kind of selecting and rearranging is what you do in the outlines stage of writing a summary.

Rough Lines Drafting and Revising: Summary

Attributing Ideas in a Summary

The draft of your summary paragraph is the place where you combine all the material into one paragraph. This draft is much like the draft of any other paragraph, with one exception: When you summarize another person's ideas, be sure to say whose ideas you are writing. That is, *attribute the ideas to the writer.* Let the reader of your paragraph know

1. the author of the selection you are summarizing, and
2. the title of the selection you are summarizing.

You may wish to do this by giving your summary paragraph a title like this:

A Summary of "A Ridiculous Addiction," by Gwinn Owens

(Note that you put the title of Owens' essay in quotation marks.)

Or you may want to put the title and author into the paragraph itself. Following is a draft of a summary of "A Ridiculous Addiction" with the title and author incorporated into the paragraph.

A Draft of a Summary of "A Ridiculous Addiction"

"A Ridiculous Addiction" by Gwinn Owens says that Americans' obsession with finding a good parking spot makes no sense. Many bad or silly things can happen when people try for a good spot. One person wasted seven minutes. He made other drivers angry. Someone else got involved in an assault. Someone else was late for a big dinner. Silly people, on their way to a fitness club, will avoid the walk in the club parking lot. Looking for a close spot can make people impolite or turn them into mad dogs. It can be stressful. Some people even break the law and take handicapped spots or park in a fire lane or loading zone. If people can give up the habit, they can gain advantages. A faraway spot is not popular, so they can get in and out of it fast. Their cars won't be scratched. They get exercise and fresh air by walking.

When you look this draft over and read it aloud, you may notice a few problems:

1. It is wordy.
2. In some places, the word choice could be better.
3. Some of the sentences are choppy.
4. It might be a good idea to mention that the examples in the summary were given by Gwinn Owens.

Revising the draft means rewriting it to eliminate some of the wordiness, to combine sentences or smooth out ideas, and to insert the point that the author, Gwinn Owens, gave the examples used in the summary. When you state that Owens created the examples, you are being clear in giving the author credit for his ideas. Giving credit is a way of attributing ideas to the author.

Note: When you refer to an author in something that you write, use the author's first and last name the first time you make a reference. For example, you write "Gwinn Owens" the first time you refer to this author. Later in the paragraph, if you want to refer to the same author, use only his or her last name. Thus, a second reference would be to "Owens."

Final Lines   **Proofreading and Polishing: Summary**

Look carefully at the final version of the summary. Notice how the sentences have been changed and words added or taken out. "Owens" is used to show that the examples given came from the essay.

A Final Version of a Summary of "A Ridiculous Addiction"

"A Ridiculous Addiction" by Gwinn Owens says that Americans' obsession with finding a good parking spot makes no sense. Owens gives many examples of the unpleasant or silly things that can happen when people try for a good spot. One person wasted seven minutes and made the other drivers angry. Someone else got involved in an assault; another person was late for an important dinner. At fitness club parking lots, people coming for exercise are missing out on the exercise of walking through the parking lot. Looking for a good spot can turn polite people into impolite ones or even into mad dogs. The search is not only stressful; it can also lead people to break the law by taking handicapped, fire lane, or loading zone spots. If people broke the habit and took spots farther away from buildings, they would have several advantages. No one wants the faraway spots, so drivers can get in and out fast, without any scratches on their cars. In addition, people who break the habit get exercise and fresh air.

Writing summaries is good writing practice, and it also helps you develop your reading skills. Even if your instructor does not require you to turn in a polished summary of an assigned reading, you may find it helpful to summarize what you have read. In many classes, midterms or other exams cover many assigned readings. If you make short summaries of each reading as it is assigned, you will have a helpful collection of focused, organized material to review.

WRITING A REACTION TO A READING

A summary is one kind of writing you can do after reading, but there are other kinds. You can react to a reading by writing on a topic related to the reading or by agreeing or disagreeing with some idea within the reading.

Writing on a Related Idea

Your instructor might ask you to react by writing about some idea connected to your reading. If you read "A Ridiculous Addiction," for example, your instructor might have asked you to react to it by writing about some practice or habit that irritates you. You can begin to gather ideas by freewriting.

Thought Lines   Gathering Ideas: Reaction

Freewriting

You can freewrite in a reading journal, if you wish. To freewrite, you can

- Write key points made by the author.
- Write about whatever you remember from the reading selection.
- Write down any of the author's ideas that you think you might want to write about someday.
- List questions raised by what you have read.
- Connect the reading selection to other things you have read or heard or experienced.
- Write any of the author's exact words that you might like to remember, putting them in quotation marks.

A freewriting that reacts to "A Ridiculous Addiction" might look like this:

Freewriting for a Reaction to a Reading

"A Ridiculous Addiction"—Gwinn Owens

People are silly in fighting for parking spaces. Owens says these are "silly parking duels." They get mean. Take handicapped spots. Angry. They fight over spots. Get angry when people sit in their cars and don't pull out of a spot. They jam big cars in small spaces, cars get damaged. They're "angry people battling for what is utterly without value." Why? To make a quick getaway?

Freewriting helps you review what you've read, and it can give you topics for a paragraph that is different from a summary.

Brainstorming

After you freewrite, you can brainstorm. You can ask yourself questions to lead you toward a topic for your own paragraph. For instance, brainstorming on the idea "angry people battling for what is utterly without value" could look like this:

Brainstorming After Freewriting

Owens says people fighting for spaces are "battling for what is utterly without value." So why do they do it? Is there any other time drivers battle for what has no value?
Sure. On the highway. All the time.

How?
They weave in and out. They cut me off. They tailgate. They speed.

What are they fighting for?
They want to gain a few minutes. They want to get ahead. Driving is some kind of contest to them.

Then don't they get some kind of satisfaction in the battle?
Not really. I often see them at the same red light I've stopped at. And their driving is very stressful for them. It raises their blood pressure, and it makes them angry and unhappy. They can't really win.

Could you write a paragraph on drivers who think of driving as a contest? If so, your brainstorming, based on your reading and freewriting, has led you to a topic.

Developing Points of Agreement or Disagreement

Another way to use a reading selection to lead you to a topic is to review the selection and jot down any statements that provoke a strong reaction in you. You are looking for sentences with which you can agree or disagree. If you already marked "A Ridiculous Addiction" as you read, you might list these statements as points of agreement or disagreement:

Points of Agreement or Disagreement

"Hell hath no fury like a motorist who loses the battle for a close-in parking space."—agree
"This quest for the coveted spot transcends logic and common sense."—disagree

Then you might pick one of the statements and agree or disagree with it in writing. If you disagreed with the second statement, "This quest for the coveted spot transcends logic and common sense," you might develop the thought lines part of writing by listing your own ideas. You might focus on why a close parking space is important to you. With a focus and a list of reasons, you could move to the outlines part of writing from reading.

Outlines **Devising a Plan: Agree or Disagree**

An outline might look like the one below. As you read it, notice that the topic sentence and ideas are your opinion, not the ideas of the author of "A Ridiculous Addiction." You used his ideas to come up with your own thoughts.

An Outline for an Agree or Disagree Paragraph

Topic sentence: Sometimes a close parking spot is important.

details:

convenience	{ I may have heavy bags to carry from the store.
car safety	{ Cars can be vandalized. Vandalism and burglary are more likely if the car is parked at a distance.
personal safety	{ I can be attacked in a parking lot. Attacks are more likely at night. Muggings are more likely if I am parked far away.

Rough Lines **Drafting and Revising: Agree or Disagree**

If your outline gives you enough good points to develop, you are on your way to a paragraph. If you began with the ideas above, for example, you could develop them into a paragraph like this:

A Draft for an Agree or Disagree Paragraph

Sometimes a close parking spot is important. The short distance to a store can make a difference if I have heavy bags or boxes to carry from the store to my car. Convenience is one reason for parking close. A more important reason is safety. In my neighborhood, cars are often vandalized. Sometimes, cars get broken into. Cars are more likely to get vandalized or burglarized if they are parked far from stores. Most of all, I am afraid to park far from stores or restaurants because I am afraid of being attacked in a parking lot, especially at night. If I am far away from buildings and other people, I am more likely to be mugged.

Final Lines **Polishing and Proofreading: Agree or Disagree**

When you read the paragraph above, you probably noticed some places where it could be revised:

- It could use more specific details.
- It should attribute the original idea about parking to Gwinn Owens, probably in the beginning.
- Some sentences could be combined.

Following is the final version of the same paragraph. As you read it, notice how a new beginning, added details, and combined sentences make it a smoother, clearer, and more developed paragraph.

Final Version for an Agree or Disagree Paragraph

Gwinn Owens says that people who look for close parking spaces are foolish, but I think that sometimes a close parking spot is important. The short distance to a store can make a difference if I have heavy bags or boxes to carry from the store to my car. Convenience is one reason for parking close, but the more important reason is safety. In my neighborhood, cars are often vandalized. Antennas get broken off; the paint jobs get deliberately scratched. Sometimes, cars get broken into. Radios and CD players are stolen. Cars are more likely to get vandalized or burglarized if they are parked far from stores. Most of all, I am afraid to park far from stores or restaurants because I am afraid of being attacked in a parking lot, especially at night. If I am far away from buildings or other people, I am more likely to be mugged.

Reading can give you many ideas for your own writing. Developing those ideas into a polished paragraph requires the same writing process as any good writing, a process that takes you through the stages of thinking, planning, drafting, revising, editing, and proofreading.

WRITING FOR AN ESSAY TEST

Most essay questions require a form of writing from reading. That is, your instructor asks you to write about an assigned reading. Usually, an essay test requires you to write from memory, not from an open book or notes. Such writing can be stressful, but breaking the task into steps can eliminate much of the stress.

Before the Test: The Steps of Reading

If you work through the steps of reading days before the test, you are halfway to your goal. Prereading helps to keep you focused, and your first reading will give you a sense of the whole selection. The third step, rereading with a pen or pencil, can be particularly helpful when you are preparing for a test. Most essay questions will ask you to summarize a reading selection or to react to it. In either case, you must be familiar with the reading's main idea, supporting ideas, examples, and details. If you note these by marking the selection, you are teaching yourself about the main point, supporting ideas, and structure of the reading selection.

Shortly before the test, review the marked reading assignment. Your notes will help you to focus on the main point and the supporting ideas.

During the Test: The Stages of Writing

Answering an essay question for a test may seem very different from writing at home. After all, on a test, you must rely on your memory and write within a time limit, and these restrictions can make you feel anxious. However, by following the stages of the writing process, you can meet that challenge calmly and confidently.

Thought Lines Before you begin to write, think about the question: Is the instructor asking for a summary of a reading selection? Or is he or she asking you to react to a specific idea in the reading by describing or developing that idea with examples or by agreeing or disagreeing? For example, in an essay question about "A Ridiculous Addiction," you might be asked (1) to explain what Gwinn Owens thinks are the advantages and disadvantages of seeking a close parking space (a summary), (2) to explain what he means when he says that fighting for parking turns drivers into mad dogs (a reaction, where you develop and explain one part of the reading), or (3) to agree or disagree that close spaces are utterly without value (a reaction, so you have to be aware of what Owens said on this point).

Once you've thought about the question, list or freewrite your first ideas about the question. At this time, don't worry about how "right" or "wrong" your writing is; just write your first thoughts.

Outlines Your writing will be clear if you follow a plan. Remember that your audience for this writing is your instructor and that he or she will be evaluating how well you stick to the subject, make a point, and support it. Your plan for making a point about the subject and supporting that point can be written in a brief outline.

First, reread the question. Next, survey your list of freewriting. Does it contain a main point that answers the question? Does it contain supporting ideas and details?

Next, write a main point and then list supporting ideas and details under the main point. Your main point will be the topic sentence of your answer. If you need more support, try brainstorming.

Rough Lines Write your point and supporting ideas in paragraph form. Remember to use effective transitions and to combine short sentences.

Final Lines You will probably not have time to copy your answer, but you can review it, proofread it, and correct any errors in spelling, punctuation, and word choice. This final check can produce a more polished answer.

Organize Your Time

Some students skip steps: they immediately begin writing their answer to an essay question, without thinking or planning. Sometimes they find themselves stuck in the middle of a paragraph, panicked because they have no more ideas. At other times, they find themselves writing in a circle, repeating the same point over and over. Occasionally, they even forget to include a main idea.

You can avoid these hazards by spending time on each of the stages. Planning is as important as writing. For example, if you have half an hour to write an essay, you can divide your time like this:

   5 minutes: thinking, freewriting, listing
   10 minutes: planning, outlining
   10 minutes: drafting
   5 minutes: reviewing and proofreading

Focusing on one stage at a time can make you more confident and your task more manageable.

Lines of Detail: A Walk-Through Assignment

Here are two ideas from "A Ridiculous Addiction":

1. The typical American has a compulsion about finding a convenient parking space.
2. People who search for good parking spots become mean and nasty.

Pick one of the ideas, with which you agree or disagree. Write a paragraph explaining why you agree or disagree. To write your paragraph, follow these steps:

Step 1: Begin by listing at least two reasons why you agree or disagree. Use your own experience with parking lots to come up with your reasons. For example, for statement 1, you could ask yourself these questions: Are all Americans concerned with parking spaces? How do you know? Is it a compulsion or just practical behavior? For statement 2, you might ask questions like these: Have you ever seen nastiness in parking lots? Have you ever experienced it? What actions were mean? Answering such questions can help you come up with your reasons for agreement or disagreement.

Step 2: Read your list to a partner or group. With the help of your listener(s), you can add reasons or details to explain the reasons.

Step 3: Once you have enough ideas, transform the statement you agree or disagree with into a topic sentence.

Step 4: Write an outline by listing your reasons and details below the topic sentence. Check that your list is in a clear and logical order.

Step 5: Write a draft of your paragraph. Check that you have attributed Gwinn Owens' statement, that you have enough details, and that you have combined any choppy sentences. Revise your draft until the paragraph is smooth and clear.

Step 6: Before you prepare the final copy, check your last draft for errors in spelling, punctuation, and word choice.

Writing Your Own Paragraph on "A Ridiculous Addiction"

When you write on one of these topics, be sure to work through the stages of the writing process in preparing your paragraph.

1. Gwinn Owens writes about Americans' addiction to the close-in parking space. Write about another addiction that Americans have. Instead of writing about a topic like drug or alcohol addiction, follow Owens' example and write about a social habit that is hard to break. You might, for instance, write about these habits:

driving while talking on a phone	tailgating
weaving in and out of traffic	speeding
driving too slowly	pushing in line
running yellow traffic lights	littering
talking during a movie	arriving late

Once you've chosen a habit, brainstorm, alone or with a partner, for details. Think about details that could fit these categories:

why the habit is foolish	where and when people act this way
why the habit is dangerous	advantages of breaking the habit

Ask yourself questions, answer them, and let the answers lead to more questions. Once you've collected some good details, work through the stages of writing a paragraph.

2. Gwinn Owens writes about a great invention, the car, and about the parking problems caused by cars. Below are several other recent inventions that can cause problems. Your goal is to write a paragraph about *the problems one of these inventions can cause.*

   To start, pick two of the inventions below. Alone, or with a partner or group, brainstorm both topics: ask questions, answer them, and add details so that each topic can lead you to enough ideas for a paragraph.

   After you've brainstormed, pick the topic you like better and work through the stages of preparing a paragraph.

   Topics to brainstorm: problems that could be caused by voice mail, car alarms, automatic teller machines, cell phones, pagers, or email.

PEER REVIEW FORM FOR WRITING FROM READING

After you've written a draft version of your paragraph, let a writing partner read it. When your partner has completed the form below, discuss the comments. Repeat the same process for your partner's paragraph.

This paragraph (pick one) (1) summarizes, (2) agrees or disagrees, or (3) writes about an idea connected to a reading selection.

I think this paragraph needs/does not need to include the title and author of the reading selection.

The topic sentence of this paragraph is _____

_____

_____

The best part of this paragraph started with the words _____

_____

One suggestion to improve this paragraph is _____

_____

Other comments: _____

_____

_____

_____

_____

_____

_____

_____

_____

_____

_____

_____

_____

Reviewer's Name: _____

WRITING FROM READING

To practice the skills you've learned in this chapter, follow the steps of pre-reading, reading, and rereading with a pen or pencil as you read the following selections.

My Daughter Smokes

Alice Walker

Alice Walker, the award-winning writer of fiction and nonfiction, is best known for her novel The Color Purple. *In this essay, she describes a family habit that has passed through the generations. She also connects that habit to poverty and oppression through the years.*

Words You May Need to Know (corresponding paragraph numbers are in parentheses)

Queen Victoria (2): queen of England from 1837 to 1901

consort (2): the husband or wife of a royal person; Prince Albert was Queen Victoria's husband

pungent (2): sharp smelling or tasting

coupled with (3): joined with

dapper (3): neat and trim

perennially (5): continually

toxic (11): poisoned or poisonous

chronic (11): constant

bronchitis (12): an inflammation of the membrane lining of the air passages beyond the windpipe that lead to the lungs

emphysema (12): a defect in the lung system

emaciated (12): thin and wasted away

eradicating (13): destroying, exterminating

futility (14): uselessness

empathy (15): identification with and understanding of another's situation

venerated (15): treated with reverence

denatured (15): deprived of its natural character or traits

mono-cropping (15): growing a single crop on a farm or in a region

kin (16): relatives, things of a similar kind

cajole (18): to persuade by flattery or promise, to coax

literally (18): actually, truly

1   My daughter smokes. While she is doing her homework, her feet on the bench in front of her and her calculator clicking out answers to her algebra problems, I am looking at the half-empty package of Camels tossed carelessly close at hand. Camels. I pick them up, take them into the kitchen, where the light is better, and study them—they're filtered, for which I am grateful. My heart feels terrible. I want to weep. In fact, I do weep a little, standing there by the stove holding one of the instruments, so white, so precisely rolled, that could cause my daughter's death. When she smoked Marlboros and Players, I hardened myself against feeling so bad; nobody I knew ever smoked these brands.

2   She doesn't know this, but it was Camels that my father, her grandfather, smoked. But before he smoked "ready-mades"—when he was very young and very poor, with eyes like lanterns—he smoked Prince Albert

tobacco in cigarettes he rolled himself. I remember the bright-red tobacco tin, with a picture of Queen Victoria's consort, Prince Albert, dressed in a black frock coat and carrying a cane. The tobacco was dark brown, pungent, slightly bitter. I tasted it more than once as a child, and the discarded tins could be used for a number of things: to keep buttons and shoelaces in, to store seeds, and best of all, to hold worms for the rare times my father took us fishing.

3   By the late forties and fifties, no one rolled his own any more (and few women smoked) in my hometown, Eatontown, Georgia. The tobacco industry, coupled with Hollywood movies in which both hero and heroine smoked like chimneys, won over completely people like my father, who were hopelessly addicted to cigarettes. He never looked as dapper as Prince Albert, though; he continued to look like a poor, overweight, overworked colored man with too large a family; black, with a very white cigarette stuck in his mouth.

4   I do not remember when he started to cough. Perhaps it was unnoticeable at first. A little hacking in the morning as he lit his first cigarette upon getting out of bed. By the time I was my daughter's age, his breath was a wheeze, embarrassing to hear; he could not climb stairs without resting every third or fourth step. It was not unusual for him to cough for an hour.

5   It is hard to believe there was a time when people did not understand that cigarette smoking is an addiction. I wondered aloud once to my sister—who is perennially trying to quit—whether our father realized this. I wondered how she, a smoker since high school, viewed her own habit.

6   It was our father who gave her her first cigarette, one day when she had taken water to him in the fields.

7   "I always wondered why he did that," she said, puzzled, and with some bitterness.

8   "What did he say?" I asked.

9   "That he didn't want me to go to anyone else for them," she said, "which never really crossed my mind."

10   So he was aware it was addictive, I thought, though as annoyed as she that he assumed she would be interested.

11   I began smoking in eleventh grade, also the year I drank numerous bottles of terrible sweet, very cheap wine. My friends and I, all boys for this venture, bought our supplies from a man who ran a segregated bar and liquor store on the outskirts of town. Over the entrance there was a large sign that said COLORED. We were not permitted to drink there, only to buy. I smoked Kools because my sister did. By then I thought her toxic darkened lips and gums glamorous. However, my body simply would not tolerate smoke. After six months, I had a chronic sore throat. I gave up smoking, gladly. Because it was a ritual with my buddies—Murl, Leon, and "Dog" Farley—I continued to drink wine.

12   My father died from "the poor man's friend," pneumonia, one hard winter when his bronchitis and emphysema had left him low. I doubt he had much lung left at all, after coughing for so many years. He had so little breath that, during his last years, he was always leaning on something. I remember once, at a family reunion, when my daughter was two, that my father picked her up for a minute—long enough for me to photograph them—but the effort was obvious. Near the very end of his life, and largely because he had no more lungs, he quit smoking. He gained a couple of pounds, but by then he was so emaciated no one noticed.

13   When I travel to Third World countries, I see many people like my father and daughter. There are large billboards directed at them both: the tough, "take-charge," or dapper older man, the glamorous, "worldly" young woman, both puffing away. In these poor countries, as in American ghettos and on reservations, money that should be spent for food goes instead to the tobacco companies; over time, people starve themselves of both food and air, effectively weakening and addicting their children, eventually eradicating themselves. I read in the newspaper and in my gardening magazine that cigarette butts are so toxic that if a baby swallows one, it is likely to die, and that the boiled water from a bunch of them makes an effective insecticide.

14   My daughter would like to quit, she says. We both know the statistics are against her; most people who try to quit smoking do not succeed. There is a deep hurt that I feel as a mother. Some days it is a feeling of futility. I remember how carefully I ate when I was pregnant, how patiently I taught my daughter how to cross a street safely. For what, I sometimes wonder; so that she can wheeze through most of her life feeling half her strength, and then die of self-poisoning, as her grandfather did?

15   But, finally, one must feel empathy for the tobacco plant itself. For thousands of years, it has been venerated by Native Americans as a sacred medicine. They have used it extensively—its juice, its leaves, its roots, its (holy) smoke—to heal wounds and cure diseases, and in ceremonies of prayer and peace. And though the plant as most of us know it has been poisoned by chemicals and denatured by intensive mono-cropping and is therefore hardly the plant it was, still, to some modern Indians it remains a plant of positive power. I learned this when my Native American friends, Bill Wahpepah and his family, visited with me for a few days and the first thing he did was sow a few tobacco seeds in my garden.

16   Perhaps we can liberate tobacco from those who have captured and abused it, enslaving the plant on large plantations, keeping it from freedom and its kin, and forcing it to enslave the world. Its true nature suppressed, no wonder it has become deadly. Maybe by sowing a few seeds of tobacco in our gardens and treating the plant with the reverence it deserves, we can redeem tobacco's soul and self-respect.

17   Besides, how grim, if one is a smoker, to realize one is smoking a slave.

18   There is a slogan from a battered women's shelter that I especially like: "Peace on earth begins at home." I believe everything does. I think of a slogan for people trying to stop smoking: "Every home a smoke-free zone." Smoking is a form of self-battering that also batters those who must sit by, occasionally cajole or complain, and helplessly watch. I realize now that as a child I sat by, through the years, and literally watched my father kill himself; surely one such victory in my family, for the rich white men who own the tobacco companies, is enough.

Note: Three months after reading this essay, Alice Walker's daughter stopped smoking.

WRITING FROM READING: "My Daughter Smokes"

When you write on any of the topics below, be sure to work through the stages of the writing process in preparing your paragraph.

1. Write a summary of Alice Walker's essay. Be sure to include (a) her description of her daughter's habit (b) the story of her father's decline, and (c) her point about the misuse of the tobacco plant.

2. Walker writes of addicted smokers as people who end up "eradicating themselves" by spending the money that should go for food on tobacco. Write about another way that people end up destroying themselves; that is, describe people who, in some way, deprive themselves of what they need. You might want to consider another serious addiction or such conditions as anorexia, bulimia, obsession with fitness, etc.

3. Working with a partner or a group, brainstorm a list of behaviors that people your age might laugh about or justify with a joke but which are dangerous. Then write individual paragraphs on one of those behaviors and how and why its risks are often ignored.

4. Imagine that your father is Alice Walker's father. Write him a letter about his smoking. Include all the feelings about his smoking that you never expressed when he was alive.

5. Pick one of the statements below (both are from "My Daughter Smokes") and use it to write an agree or disagree paragraph.

    "Smoking is a form of self-battering that also batters those who must sit by, occasionally cajole and complain, and helplessly watch."

    "Peace on earth begins at home."

6. If you have a habit that you (or others) feel you should break, write about that habit. You can consider why you don't want to or can't break it, its dangers, and its satisfactions.

Parental Discretion

Dennis Hevesi

Dennis Hevesi is a writer for The New York Times. *In this essay, he writes about how the family structure changes when a parent goes back to school.*

Words You May Need To Know (corresponding paragraph numbers are in parentheses)

discretion (title): the right to make one's own decision

wrought (4): inflicted

havoc (4): disorder, confusion

diehard (4): stubbornly committed, dedicated

feminists (4): people who fight for women's rights

genes (8): a unit in the body that controls the development of hereditary traits

maternal (14): motherly

anthropology (15): a study of the origins and physical and cultural development of humankind

Renaissance (17): a period of European history, roughly from the late 1300s to 1600

1   When the letter came saying that Pamela Stafford, after all her part-time study at night, had been accepted at the age of 34 as a full-time student by the University of California at Berkeley, her two teen-age sons leaped into the air, slapped palms in a high-five and shouted: "We did it! We did it!"

2   "I'm not sure they included me," she said.

3   Several months ago, when Gary Hatfield, also 34, and a sophomore at the Ohio State University, in Columbus, was telling his son, Seth, 11, why he was spending so much time studying, "He patted me on the shoulder and said: 'Dad, I understand. You want to finish school,'" Mr. Hatfield recalled, adding, "Blessed is the child's forgiving nature."

4   In hundreds of homes throughout the nation, as the rolls of those signing up for continuing education courses grow, getting mom or pop off to school has often wrought a kind of joyous havoc on family life and forced the sort of realignment of expectations that would warm the hearts of diehard feminists.

5   Dads or children are doing the shopping, the cooking, the cleaning, the laundry. Teen-agers have become the family chauffeur, or at least make sure the car is available when a parent has to get to class. Schedules have been turned on end. Children have even adopted parental roles—nagging when homework hasn't been done.

6   Mr. Hatfield, an English major, wants to teach high school or college English. "I'll sometimes get jabbed if I make a spelling or grammatical mistake," he said. "Seth will say, 'Hey, English teacher . . .'"

7   What can come through the difficulties and the role reversals is a shared commitment, a strengthened bond and a deepened appreciation for education. "When I went back to school, my older son went from being a C and D student to making honor roll," said Ms. Stafford, who is divorced and lives in Albany, near the university. "The younger guy, well, not as much improvement. But he did develop a more serious attitude toward school. Now, it's sort of a given that what you really do in life is finish school first."

8   And when the boys—Joseph, 18, and Christopher, 14—run into what Ms. Stafford called "the geek mentality" of friends who think doing well in school is totally lame, they are equipped to respond. "Joseph once told his friend," Ms. Stafford said, " 'Hey, my mom is smart. It's in the genes. I can't help being smart.' "

9   Mom is indeed smart. Out of a possible 4.0, Ms. Stafford is maintaining a 3.9 grade-point average as an English major at Berkeley, where she is also on staff as an administrative assistant.

10   "I felt really guilty about taking night courses," she said. "Then, at the end of that first semester, I got an A in ancient Mediterranean literature, and my sons developed an investment in my education. They sort of fired me as a mother and recreated me as a student."

11   Joseph, now a freshman at St. Mary's College in nearby Moraga, said: "I had to cook, wash dishes, pretty much take care of myself and my brother, too. There were times when I wished she was around, when things would happen that I couldn't handle."

12   Joseph said Christopher "was always a hyper kid. So I just had to be real patient. I talked to him about girls, about drugs. He doesn't do the silly stuff he used to do to get attention, like kitchen gymnastics—you know, dancing and flipping around the house like an idiot. Sometimes we fought. But he and I loved each other enough to punch each other and then hug."

13   During midterms and finals, Ms. Stafford said, the boys "would mysteriously disappear" so that she could study. "I like to deejay," Joseph said, "you know, sound-mixing in my room. I had to do this with the headphones the entire time. There could be no noise."

14   Between classes, Ms. Stafford would call home "and try to at least bring a maternal presence into the conversation: 'Have you done your homework? Have you done your chores?' But they would say, 'Hey, we don't need you. Goodness, the things we go through putting a parent through school.' "

15   Sometimes it seemed that Seth Hatfield wasn't so much putting his father through school as accompanying him. "Last quarter, I was taking an anthropology course," Mr. Hatfield said, "and one of the evenings I would take Seth to that class. He would sit and do his homework at the table with me. And the teacher was so nearsighted that she would walk by and give him handouts, just like one of the students."

16   Mr. Hatfield, who is divorced and lives in Columbus, has worked as a landscaper, a salesman, a counselor to juvenile delinquents, and a social worker at a home for the mentally retarded. With a part-time job, a little money in the bank and a grant from Ohio State, he returned to college in 1987 and is maintaining a grade-point average of 3.2.

17   "I get hit with anxiety attacks," he said, "because here I am plowing through Renaissance literature and wishing I was sitting with my son playing a game."

18   But Seth doesn't complain, and his exposure to college has had benefits. "I found out from his teachers that he speaks proudly of going to Ohio State with his dad," Mr. Hatfield said. "Just walking across campus, with him wearing his Ohio State sweatshirt, gives me the opportunity to familiarize him with what the place really is. We go plunder through the library. He knows the computer catalogue search system can lead him to information on Superman."

19   "I might go there when I grow up," Seth said. "When my dad gets his education, if he becomes a teacher, he'll have a larger income, and I might even have him as a teacher. Maybe I'll borrow money from him for lunch."

20   Mr. Hatfield realizes that Seth, who lives with his mother about a mile away, is his first priority. "I will cut class to go to his band concert," he said. "Those things are too precious. I can take an incomplete in a course and make it up. I can't take an incomplete as a parent and ever make that up."

WRITING FROM READING: "Parental Discretion"

When you write on any of the following topics, be sure to work through the stages of the writing process in preparing your paragraph.

1. Write a summary paragraph of Hevesi's article. Be sure to include Hevesi's points about the good and bad effects of parents' returning to college.

2. No matter how old you are, attending college presents certain challenges. If you are the "traditional" college age of eighteen or nineteen, you may face the challenge of adjusting to a place that is not like high school. If you are in your twenties, you may be facing other challenges: earning money for college, living at home and going to college, balancing the demands of a family, work, and school. Students in their thirties, forties, fifties, sixties, and seventies all have different problems when they go to college. Write a paragraph about the problems one age group faces in attending college. You may use a topic sentence like this one:

   It's not easy being eighteen (or twenty-five, or thirty, or sixty— you fill in the age) and going to college.

   If your instructor agrees, you might interview a writing partner about the difficulties his or her age group faces in going to college. Then your partner can interview you. By interviewing, each of you can help the other gather details.

3. As an alternative to topic 2, choose a topic sentence that is closer to your experience, like one of these:

It's not easy working full time and going to college.
It's not easy being in a wheelchair and going to college.
It's not easy being a single parent and going to college.

4. Begin this assignment by working with a group. Plan a paragraph with this topic sentence:

Today, the term "college student" can include many kinds of people.

In your group, have each member support the topic sentence by talking about himself or herself. You might mention age, reason for going to college, ethnic background, college major, hobbies, special talents, family background, and so on. As each member describes himself or herself, write down the details. Ask follow-up questions and write down the answers. After you have gathered enough specific examples, write your paragraph.

The Bottom Line

Grammar for Writers

Introduction

Overview

In this section, you'll be working with "The Bottom Line," the basics of grammar that you need to be a clear writer. If you are willing to memorize certain rules and work through the activities here, you will be able to apply grammatical rules automatically as you write.

Using "The Bottom Line"

Since this portion of the textbook is divided into self-contained segments, it does not have to be read in sequence. Your instructor may suggest you review specific rules and examples, or you may be assigned various segments as either a class or a group assignment. Various approaches are possible, and thus you can regard this section as a user-friendly grammar handbook for quick reference. Mastering the practical parts of grammar will improve your writing; you will feel more sure of yourself because you will know the bottom line.

CONTENTS

Chapter 14 The Simple Sentence   399

Chapter 15 Beyond the Simple Sentence: Coordination   414

Chapter 16 Avoiding Run-On Sentences and Comma Splices   424

Chapter 17 Beyond the Simple Sentence: Subordination   432

Chapter 18 Avoiding Sentence Fragments   443

Chapter 19 Using Parallelism in Sentences   453

Chapter 20 Using Adjectives and Adverbs   462

Chapter 21 Correcting Problems with Modifiers   471

Chapter 22 Using Verbs Correctly   480

Chapter 23 More on Verbs: Consistency and Voice   493

Chapter 24 Making Subjects and Verbs Agree   506

Chapter 25 Using Pronouns Correctly: Agreement and Reference   522

Chapter 26 Using Pronouns Correctly: Consistency and Case   531

Chapter 27 **Punctuation: The Period and the Question Mark** 539

Chapter 28 **Punctuation: The Comma** 542

Chapter 29 **Punctuation: The Semicolon and the Colon** 550

Chapter 30 **Punctuation: The Apostrophe** 554

Chapter 31 **Other Punctuation and Mechanics** 560

Chapter 32 **Spelling** 570

Chapter 33 **Words That Sound Alike/ Look Alike** 580

Chapter 34 **Word Choice** 595

Chapter 35 **Sentence Variety** 601

APPENDIX **Grammar for ESL Students** 614

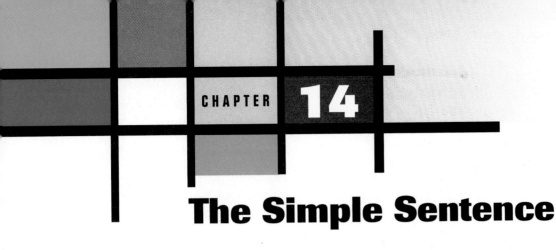

CHAPTER 14

The Simple Sentence

Identifying the crucial parts of a sentence is the first step in many writing decisions: how to punctuate, how to avoid sentence fragments, how to be sure that subjects and verbs "agree" (match). To move forward to these decisions requires a few steps back—to basics.

RECOGNIZING A SENTENCE

Let's start with a few basic definitions. A basic unit of language is a **word.**

> **examples:** *car, dog, sun*

A group of related words can be a **phrase.**

> **examples:** *shiny new car; snarling, angry dog; in the bright sun*

When the group of words contains a subject and a verb, it is called a **clause.** When the word group has a subject and a verb and makes sense by itself, it is called a **sentence** or an independent clause. When the word group has a subject and a verb but does not make sense by itself, it is called a dependent clause.

If you want to check to see whether you have written a sentence and not just a group of related words, you first have to check for a subject and a verb. It is often easier to locate the verbs first.

RECOGNIZING VERBS

Verbs are words that express some kind of action or being. Verbs about the five senses—sight, touch, smell, taste, sound—are part of the group called **being verbs.** Look at some examples of verbs as they work in sentences:

action verbs:
We *walk* to the store every day.
The children *ran* to the playground.

being verbs:

My mother *is* a good cook.
The family *seems* unhappy.
The soup *smells* delicious.

Exercise 1

Practice

Recognizing Verbs

Underline the verbs in each of the following sentences.

1. A van <u>pulled</u> into traffic.
2. Most of the time, she <u>swims</u> in the pool.
3. He <u>looks</u> upset about the accident.
4. Your brother Freddie <u>was</u> the fastest runner in town.
5. Noise <u>fills</u> the streets on holidays.
6. The cinnamon rolls <u>smell</u> wonderful.
7. Some workers <u>love</u> the night shift.
8. Teens <u>are</u> frequent moviegoers in the summer.
9. This plate <u>feels</u> greasy.
10. College students <u>handle</u> responsibilities at school and at home.

More on Verbs

The verb in a sentence can be more than one word. First of all, there can be **helping verbs** in front of the main verb, the action or being verb. Here is a list of some frequently used helping verbs: *is, am, are, was, were, do, must, might, have, has, shall, will, can, could, may, should, would.*

I *was watching* the Super Bowl. (The helping verb is *was.*)
You *should have called* me. (The helping verbs are *should* and *have.*)
The president *can select* his assistants. (The helping verb is *can.*)
Leroy *will graduate* in May. (The helping verb is *will.*)

Helping verbs can make the verb in a sentence more than one word long. But there can also be more than one main verb:

Andrew *planned* and *practiced* his speech.
I *stumbled* over the rug, *grabbed* a chair, and *fell* on my face.

Exercise 2

 *Collaborate*

Writing Sentences with Helping Verbs

Complete this exercise with a partner or a group. First, ask one person to add at least one helping verb to the verb given. Then work together to write two sentences using the main verb and the helping verb(s). Appoint a spokesperson for your group to read all your sentences to the class. Notice how many combinations of main verb and helping verb you hear.

The first one is done for you.

1. verb: called

verb with helping verb(s): <u>has called</u>

sentence 1: <u>Sam has called me twice this week.</u>

sentence 2: <u>She has called him a hero.</u>

2. verb: thinking

verb with helping verb(s): _____

sentence 1: _____

sentence 2: _____

3. verb: complete

verb with helping verb(s): _____

sentence 1: _____

sentence 2: _____

4. verb: experienced

verb with helping verb(s): _____

sentence 1: _____

sentence 2: _____

5. verb: taken

verb with helping verb(s): _____

sentence 1: _____

sentence 2: _____

RECOGNIZING SUBJECTS

After you can recognize verbs, it is easy to find the subjects of sentences because subjects and verbs are linked. If the verb is an action verb, for example, the subject will be the word or words that answer the question "Who or what is doing that action?"

The truck stalled on the highway.

Step 1: Identify the verb: *stalled*
Step 2: Ask, "Who or what stalled?"
Step 3: The answer is the subject: The *truck* stalled on the highway. The *truck* is the subject.

If your verb expresses being, the same steps apply to finding the subject.

Spike was my best friend.

Step 1: Identify the verb: *was*
Step 2: Ask, "Who or what was my best friend?"
Step 3: The answer is the subject: *Spike* was my best friend. *Spike* is the subject.

Just as there can be more than one word to make up a verb, there can be more than one subject.

examples: *David* and *Leslie* planned the surprise party.
My *father* and *I* worked in the yard yesterday.

Exercise 3
Practice

Recognizing the Subjects in Sentences

Underline the subjects in the following sentences.

1. Andrea could have written a better report.

2. They will return the videos in the morning.

3. Without warning, a man blocked the path.

4. In some ways, children are wiser than their parents.

5. Tension can affect the body and mind.

6. Pharmacies keep a record of their sales.

7. Apologizing can often repair a damaged friendship.

8. After the accident, grief and guilt haunted the driver.

9. Something is causing the problem with the television.

10. Nobody knows the real story of the escape.

More About Recognizing Subjects and Verbs

When you look for the subject of a sentence, look for the core word or words; don't include descriptive words around the subject. The idea is to look for the subject, not for the words that describe it.

> The dark blue *dress* looked lovely on Anita.
> Dirty *streets* and grimy *houses* destroy a neighborhood.

The subjects are the core words *dress*, *streets*, and *houses*, not the descriptive words *dark blue, dirty,* and *grimy.*

PREPOSITIONS AND PREPOSITIONAL PHRASES

Prepositions are usually small words that often signal a kind of position or possession, as shown in the following list:

Info **BOX**					
Some Common Prepositions					
about	before	beyond	inside	on	under
above	below	during	into	onto	up
across	behind	except	like	over	upon
after	beneath	for	near	through	with
among	beside	from	of	to	within
around	between	in	off	toward	without
at					

A prepositional phrase is made up of a preposition and its object. Here are some prepositional phrases. In each one, the first word is the preposition; the other words are the object of the preposition.

Prepositional Phrases

about the movie	of mice and men
around the corner	off the record
between two lanes	on the mark
during recess	up the wall
near my house	with my sister and brother

There is an old memory trick to help you remember prepositions. Think of a chair. Now, think of a series of words you can put *in front of* the chair:

around the chair	*with* the chair
behind the chair	*to* the chair
between the chairs	*near* the chair
by the chair	*under* the chair
of the chair	*on* the chair
off the chair	*from* the chair

Those words are prepositions.

You need to know about prepositions because they can help you identify the subject of a sentence. There is an important grammar rule about prepositions:

> **Nothing in a prepositional phrase can ever be the subject of the sentence.**

Prepositional phrases describe people, places, or things. They may describe the subject of a sentence, but they *never include* the subject. Whenever you are looking for the subject of a sentence, begin by putting parentheses around all the prepositional phrases.

> The restaurant (around the corner) makes the best fried chicken (in town.)

The prepositional phrases are in parentheses. Since *nothing* in them can be the subject, once you have eliminated the prepositional phrases, you can follow the steps to find the subject of the sentence:

> What is the verb? *makes*
> Who or what makes the best fried chicken? The *restaurant*. *Restaurant* is the subject of the sentence.

By marking off the prepositional phrases, you are left with the *core* of the sentence. There is less to look at.

> (Behind the park), a *carousel* (with gilded horses) delighted children (from all the neighborhoods).
> subject: *carousel*

> The *dog* (with the ugliest face) was the winner (of the contest).
> subject: *dog*

Exercise 4 · Recognizing Prepositional Phrases, Subjects, and Verbs

Practice

Put parentheses around all the prepositional phrases in the following sentences. Then underline the subject and verb and put an *S* above each subject and a *V* above each verb.

1. The dog in the back seat of the car has a red bandana around his neck.

2. None of the people in the store asked for any items from the back room.

3. Two of the clowns in the circus jumped into a crazy car.

4. During the movie, someone rolled a plastic cup from the back of the theater to the front row.

5. The mystery beneath the crime was solved by a detective with experience in identity theft.

6. Craig gave the money to the clerk and put the sandwich on a tray.

7. The last passengers rushed through the airport toward the departure gate.

8. The people in the apartment above mine shouted at each other every night.

9. On weekends, I often visit my girlfriend at her home near Chattanooga.

10. The partnership between Marlon and Ronnie covered all their plans except the financial arrangement.

Exercise 5
Collaborate

Writing Sentences with Prepositional Phrases

Complete this exercise with a partner. First, add one prepositional phrase to the core sentence. Then, ask your partner to add a second prepositional phrase to the same sentence. For the next sentence, let your partner add the first phrase, and you add the second. Keep reversing the process throughout the exercise. When you have completed the exercise, be ready to read the sentences with two prepositional phrases to the class. The first one has been done for you as an example.

1. core sentence: Rain fell.

Add one prepositional phrase: Rain fell on the mountains.

Add another prepositional phrase: From a dark sky, rain fell on the mountains.

2. core sentence: The door was locked.

Add one prepositional phrase: _____

Add another prepositional phrase: _____

_____

3. core sentence: The ship sank.

Add one prepositional phrase: _____

Add another prepositional phrase: _____

_____

4. core sentence: Students are concerned.

Add one prepositional phrase: _____

_____

Add another prepositional phrase: _____

_____

5. core sentence: The spy gave me an envelope.

Add one prepositional phrase:_____

_____

Add another prepositional phrase: _____

_____

WORD ORDER

When we speak, we often use a very simple word order: first, the subject; then, the verb. For example, someone would say, "I am going to the store." *I* is the subject that begins the sentence; *am going* is the verb that comes after the subject.

But not all sentences are in such a simple word order. Prepositional phrases, for example, can change the word order.

sentence: Among the contestants was an older man.

Step 1: Mark off the prepositional phrase(s) with parentheses: (Among the contestants) was an older man. Remember that nothing in a prepositional phrase can be the subject of a sentence.

Step 2: Find the verb: *was*

Step 3: Who or what was? An older *man* was. The subject of the sentence is *man*.

After you change the word order of this sentence, you can see the subject (S) and verb (V) more easily.

                S   **V**
An older *man was* among the contestants.

 Exercise 6
Practice

Finding Prepositional Phrases, Subjects, and Verbs in Complicated Word Order

Put parentheses around the prepositional phrases in the following sentences. Then underline the subjects and verbs and put an *S* above each subject and a *V* above each verb.

1. Down the road from the college is a health food store.

2. Behind the bedroom is a small patio.

3. Inside the cabinet are canned soups and boxes of crackers.

4. Near the back of the garden is a small flowering tree with tiny pink blossoms on its top branches.

5. Above the hills shone a round yellow moon with a halo of mist around it.

6. From the back of the classroom came the sound of whispering.

7. Between the pages of the book was a pressed red rose.

8. In Norman's top drawer is a photograph of his ex-girlfriend.

9. Among my grandmother's letters was a an old birthday card from me.

10. With the heavy rain came street flooding.

More on Word Order _w/ There/ Here_

The expected word order of subject first, then verb changes when a sentence starts with *There is/are, There was/were, Here is/are, Here was/were.* In such cases, look for the subject after the verb:

> V · S · S
> There *are* a *bakery* and a *pharmacy* down the street.

> V · S
> Here *is* the *man* with the answers.

If it helps you to understand this pattern, change the word order:

> S · S · V
> A *bakery* and a *pharmacy are* there, down the street.

> S · V
> The *man* with the answers *is* here.

There/ Here will never be the subject

You should also note that even if the subject comes after the verb, the verb has to "match" the subject. For instance, if the subject refers to more than one thing, the verb must also refer to more than one thing.

> There *are* a *bakery* and a *pharmacy* down the road. (Two things, a bakery and a pharmacy, *are* down the road.)

Word Order in Questions

Questions may have a different word order. The main verb and the helping verb may not be next to each other.

> **question:** Do you like pizza?
> **subject:** *you*
> **verbs:** *do, like*

If it helps you to understand this concept, think of answering the question. If someone accused you of not liking pizza, you might say, "I *do like* it." You would use two words as verbs.

question: Will he think about it?
subject: *he*
verbs: *will, think*

question: Is Maria telling the truth?
subject: *Maria*
verbs: *is, telling*

Practice

Recognizing Subjects and Verbs in Complicated Word Order: A Comprehensive Exercise

Underline the subjects and verbs and put an *S* above the subjects and *V* above the verbs.

1. Behind the fancy menu and the high prices was a restaurant with bad food.

2. Has Jimmy met the newest member of the team?

3. Near the bottom of the box was a jar of pennies.

4. Around the back of house there were a porch and a garden shed.

5. Inside her heart was a longing for understanding.

6. Here are the checks for the rent and phone bill.

7. From three states came eager reporters with their cameras.

8. There were many questions about the disappearance of the man.

9. Is there something on your mind?

Words That Cannot Be Verbs

Sometimes there are words that look like verbs in a sentence, but they are not verbs. Such words include adverbs (words like *always, often, nearly, rarely, never, ever*), which are placed close to the verb but are not verbs. Another word that is placed between a helping verb and a main verb is *not*. *Not* is not a verb.

When you are looking for verbs in a sentence, be careful to eliminate words like *often* and *not*.

He will not listen to me. (The verbs are *will listen.*)
Althea can always find a bargain. (The verbs are *can find.*)

Be careful with contractions:

They *have*n't *raced* in years. (The verbs are *have raced. Not* is not a part of the verb, even in contractions.)

Don't you *come* from Arizona? (The verbs are *do come.*)
Won't he ever *learn*? (The verbs are *will learn. Won't* is a contraction for *will not.*)

Recognizing Main Verbs

If you are checking to see if a word is a main verb, try the *pronoun test.* Combine your word with this simple list of pronouns: *I, you, he, she, it, we, they.* A main verb is a word such as *drive* or *noticed* that can be combined with the words on this list. Now try the pronoun test.

> For the word *drive:* I drive, you drive, he drives, she drives, it drives, we drive, they drive
> For the word *noticed:* I noticed, you noticed, he noticed, she noticed, it noticed, we noticed, they noticed

But words like *never* cannot be used, alone, with the pronouns:

> ~~I never, you never, he never, she never, it never, we never, they never~~
> (Never did what?)

Never is not a verb. *Not* is not a verb either, as the pronoun test indicates:

> ~~I not, you not, he not, she not, it not, we not, you not, they not~~
> (These combinations do not make sense because *not* is not a verb.)

Verb Forms That Cannot Be Main Verbs

There are forms of verbs that cannot be main verbs by themselves, either. **An -*ing* verb, by itself, cannot be the main verb,** as the pronoun test shows:

> For the word *voting:* ~~I voting, you voting, he voting, she voting, we voting, they voting~~

If you see an -*ing* verb by itself, correct the sentence by adding a helping verb:

> Scott ~~riding~~ his motorcycle. (*Riding,* by itself, cannot be a main verb.)
> **correction:** Scott *was riding* his motorcycle.

Another verb form, called an infinitive, also cannot be a main verb. An **infinitive** is the form of the verb that has *to* placed in front of it.

> **Info BOX**
>
> **Some Common Infinitives**
>
> | | | |
> |---|---|---|
> | to care | to vote | to repeat |
> | to feel | to play | to stumble |
> | to need | to reject | to view |

Try the pronoun test, and you'll see that infinitives cannot be main verbs:

> For the infinitive *to vote:* ~~I to vote, you to vote, he to vote, she to vote, we to vote, they to vote~~

So if you see an infinitive being used as a verb, correct the sentence by adding a main verb.

> We ~~to vote~~ in the election tomorrow. (There is no verb, just an infinitive.)
> **correction:** We *are going* to vote in the election tomorrow. (Now there is a verb.)

The infinitives and the -ing verbs do not work as main verbs. You must put a verb with them to make a correct sentence.

Exercise 8

Practice

Correcting Problems with *-ing* or Infinitive Verb Forms

Most—but not all—of the sentences below are faulty; an *-ing* verb or an infinitive may be taking the place of a main verb. Rewrite the sentences with errors.

1. Someone from the club to announce the meeting dates for next semester.

   rewritten: _____

   _____

2. Lisa and Mauricio leaving the movie at the most exciting part.

   rewritten: _____

   _____

3. For two hours, I have been thinking about an old friend from high school.

   rewritten: _____

   _____

4. Some of the people on our street want to call the police about the noisy family at the end of the block.

   rewritten: _____

   _____

5. On good days, the injured football player to walk without a cane.

   rewritten: _____

   _____

   _____

6. After a short press conference, the star of the movie rushing into the theater with tears in her eyes.

rewritten: _____

_____

7. One of the wealthiest people in the community to donate a million dollars to the hospital for a children's cancer center.

rewritten: _____

_____

8. Without a word of explanation, the owner closing the popular restaurant.

rewritten: _____

_____

9. One of these days, Connie is going to install the new speakers in her car.

rewritten: _____

_____

10. On top of the high bookcase, my gray kitten smiling down at me with an expression of triumph.

rewritten: _____

_____

Exercise 9

Practice

Finding Subjects and Verbs: A Comprehensive Exercise

Underline the subjects and verbs in these sentences and put an *S* above each subject and a *V* above each verb.

1. Have they ever seen a house with a tile roof?

2. After the holidays, they're taking a trip to Cozumel.

3. Behind all Joe's excuses is a fear of flying.

4. The detective wants to interview all the witnesses.

5. Won't you stay for a few more minutes?

6. Senator Kolsky has often spoken about children's safety.

7. The dean will never change the policy on parking tickets.

8. There are two answers to that question.

9. Farah could have been shopping for a computer last night.

10. There were a pizza, a microwave dinner, and a bag of vegetables in the freezer.

11. Tanya answered the door and greeted her nephews with hugs.

12. Beneath the grit and grime was a beautiful hardwood floor.

13. In the bright sun, the house and garden seemed fresh and inviting.

14. Shy people can often become the most interesting friends.

15. My son has never liked mustard on hotdogs.

16. You have rarely spoken with so much confidence.

17. Without his credit card, Bill can't pay for the gas.

18. Here was the man with the extra set of car keys.

19. In the early morning, my father brewed the coffee, toasted the bread, and set the table for breakfast.

20. In the first place, you should never have listened to him.

Exercise 10

Create Your Own Text

Complete this activity with two partners. Below is a list of rules you've just studied. Each member of the group should write one example of each rule. When your group has completed three examples for each rule, trade your completed exercise with the members of another group and check their examples while they check yours. The first rule has been done for you, as a sample.

Rule 1: The verb in a sentence can express some kind of action.

examples:

a. _Janelle drives to work every day._

b. _Last week my cat killed a mouse in the basement._

c. _My little sister dyed her hair with Kool-Aid._

Rule 2: The verb in a sentence can express some state of being or one of the five senses.

examples:

a. _____

b. _____

c. _____

Rule 3: The verb in a sentence can consist of more than one word.

examples:

a. _____

b. _____

c. _____

Rule 4: There can be more than one subject of a sentence.

examples:

a. _____

b. _____

c. _____

Rule 5: If you take out the prepositional phrases, it is easier to identify the subject of a sentence, since nothing in a prepositional phrase can be the subject of a sentence.

examples: (Write sentences with at least one prepositional phrase
and put parentheses around the prepositional phrases.)

a. _____

b. _____

c. _____

Rule 6: Not all sentences have the simple word order of subject first,
then verb.

examples: (Give examples of more complicated word order.)

a. _____

b. _____

c. _____

Rule 7: Words like *not, never, often, always,* and *ever* are not verbs.

examples: (Write sentences using those words, but underline the correct verb).

a. _____

b. _____

c. _____

Rule 8: An -*ing* verb form by itself or an infinitive (*to* preceding the verb) cannot be a main verb.

examples: (Write sentences with -*ing* verb forms or infinitives, but underline the main verb.)

a. _____

b. _____

c. _____

Exercise 11   **Recognizing Subjects and Verbs in a Paragraph**

Connect   Underline the subjects and verbs in this paragraph and put an *S* above each subject and a *V* above each verb.

Writing with a felt-tipped pen can be hazardous to a person's skin and possessions. Many people use felt-tipped pens for their smooth, gliding stroke. However, there are some drawbacks to these pens. The ink in them is liquid and powerful. It has been known to smear on the writer's fingers or wrists and leave a bright slash of color. A careless writer may also leave an ink smear across a page. The pens have a tendency to leak. Leaving an uncapped pen on the page of an open book can leave an ink blob on the paper. The uncapped pen can leak onto a shirt or slacks and destroy the clothes in a minute. Felt-tipped pens are easy to use. On the other hand, isn't a pencil safer?

CHAPTER 15

Beyond the Simple Sentence: Coordination

A group of words containing a subject and verb is called a **clause.** When that group makes sense by itself, it is called a sentence or an independent clause.

The kind of sentence that has one independent clause is called a **simple sentence.** If you rely too heavily on a sentence pattern of simple sentences, you risk writing paragraphs like this:

> I am a college student. I am also a salesperson in a mall. I am always busy. School is time-consuming. Studying is time-consuming. Working makes me tired. Balancing these activities is hard. I work too many hours. Work is important. It pays for school.

Here is a better version:

> I am a college student and a salesperson at a mall, so I am always busy. School and study are time-consuming, and working makes me tired. Balancing these activities is hard. I work too many hours, but that work is important. It pays for school.

OPTIONS FOR COMBINING SIMPLE SENTENCES

Good writing involves sentence variety; it means mixing a simple sentence with a more complicated one, a short sentence with a long one. Sentence variety is easier to achieve if you can combine related, short sentences into one.

Some students avoid such combining because they are not sure how to do it. They do not know how to punctuate the new combinations. It is true that punctuation involves memorizing a few rules, but once you know them, you will be able to use them automatically and write with more confidence. Here are three options for combining simple sentences and the punctuation rules to follow in each case.

OPTION 1: USING A COMMA WITH A COORDINATING CONJUNCTION

memorize

You can combine two simple sentences with a comma and a coordinating conjunction. The coordinating conjunctions are *and, but, or, nor, for, yet,* and *so.*

To coordinate means to join equals. When you join two simple sentences with a comma and a coordinating conjunction (*CC*), each half of the combination remains an independent clause, with its own subject (S) and verb (V).

Here are two simple sentences:

    S   V   S   V
He cooked the dinner. *She washed* the dishes.

Here are the two simple sentences combined with a comma and with the word *and*, a coordinating conjunction (CC):

    S   V   CC S   V
He cooked the dinner, *and she washed* the dishes.

The combined sentences keep the form they had as separate sentences; that is, they are still both independent clauses, with a subject and verb and with the ability to stand alone.

The word that joins them is the **coordinating conjunction.** Remember it is used to join *equals*. Look at some more examples. These examples use a variety of coordinating conjunctions to join two simple sentences:

sentences combined with *but:*

  S   V   , CC S V
I rushed to the bank, *but I was* too late.

sentences combined with *or:*

  S   V   , CC S   V
She can write a letter to Jim, *or she can call* him.

sentences combined with *nor:*

  S   V   , CC V S V
I didn't like the book, *nor did I like* the movie made from the book. (Notice what happens to the word order when you use nor.)

sentences combined with *for:*

   S   V   , CC S V
Sam worried about the job interview, *for he saw* many qualified applicants in the waiting room.

sentences combined with *yet:*

   S   V   , CC S   V
Leo tried to please his sister, *yet she* never *seemed* appreciative of his efforts.

sentences combined with *so:*

  S V   , CC S V
I was the first in line for the concert tickets, *so I got* the best seats in the stadium.

Where Does the Comma Go?

Notice that the comma comes *before* the coordinating conjunction (*and, but, or, nor, for, yet, so*). It comes before the new idea, the second independent clause. It goes where the first independent clause ends. Try this punctuation check. After you've placed the comma, look at the combined sentences. For example:

> She joined the army, and she traveled overseas.

Then split it into two sentences at the comma:

> She joined the army. And she traveled overseas. (The split makes sense.)

If you put the comma in the wrong place, after the coordinating conjunction, your split sentences would be

> She joined the army and. She traveled overseas. (The split doesn't make sense.)

This test helps you see whether the comma has been placed correctly—*where the first independent clause ends.* (Notice that you can begin a sentence with *and.* You can also begin a sentence with *but, or, nor, for, yet,* or *so*—as long as you're writing a complete sentence.)

Caution: Do *not* put a comma every time you use the words *and, but, or, nor, for, yet,* or *so;* use a comma only when the coordinating conjunction joins independent clauses. Do not use a comma when the coordinating conjunction joins words:

> blue and gold   tired but happy   hot or cold

Do not put the comma when the coordinating conjunction joins phrases:

> on the chair or under the table
> in the water and by the shore
> with a smile but without an apology

The comma is used when the coordinating conjunction joins two independent clauses. Another way to say the same rule is to say that the comma is used when the coordinating conjunction joins two simple sentences.

Placing the Comma by Using Subject-Verb (*S-V*) Patterns

An independent clause, or simple sentence, follows one of these basic patterns:

> S V
> He ran.

> S   S V
> He and I ran.

> S V   V
> He ran and swam.

> S   S V   V
> He and I ran and swam.

Study all four patterns for the simple sentence, and you will notice you can draw a line separating the subjects on one side and the verbs on the other:

S	V
SS	V
S	VV
SS	VV

Whether the sentence has one or more subjects and one or more verbs, in the simple sentence the pattern is subject(s) followed by verb(s).

When you combine two simple sentences, the pattern changes:

two simple sentences:

S   V   S V
He swam. I ran.

two simple sentences combined:

S   V   S V
He swam, but I ran.

In the new pattern, *SVSV*, you cannot draw a line separating all the subjects on one side, and all the verbs on the other. This new pattern, with two simple sentences, (or independent clauses) joined into one, is called a *compound sentence*.

Recognizing the *SVSV* pattern will help you place the comma for compound sentences. Here is another way to remember this rule. If you have this pattern

SV   SV

use a comma in front of the coordinating conjunction. Do not use a comma in front of the coordinating conjunction with these patterns:

S	V
SS	V
S	VV
SS	VV

For example, use a comma for this pattern:

S   V   , S V
Jane followed directions, but *I rushed* ahead.

Do not use a comma for this pattern:

S   V   V
Carol cleans her kitchen every week but never *wipes* the top of the refrigerator.

You have just studied one way to combine simple sentences. If you are going to take advantage of this method, you have to memorize the coordinating conjunctions—*and, but, or, nor, for, yet,* and *so*—so that your use of them, with the correct punctuation, will become automatic.

Exercise 1

Practice

Recognizing Compound Sentences and Adding Commas

Add commas only where they are needed in the following sentences. Do not add any words.

1. Cody was hungry but he was also broke.

2. The girl with the tray of perfume samples approached the shoppers and offered them a small tube of the new scent.

3. After class I made a peanut butter sandwich and I ate it in front of the television.

4. The kindergartners are dressing up for Halloween and are having a party in their classroom.

5. The snow was heavy so the skiing was great.

6. Anthony was a quiet man at home yet his children treated him with affection and respect.

7. Eva badly needed some quiet time at home but couldn't ask her boss for a day off.

8. Sometimes you can get a good deal on sneakers at Athlete Heaven or you can check the sales racks at Sporty Feet.

9. He was thrilled with his grade in geometry for he had studied hard all term.

10. The heart specialist was not optimistic about the operation nor was she convinced it was necessary.

| Exercise 2 | **More on Recognizing Compound Sentences and Adding Commas** |

Practice

Add commas only where they are needed in the following sentences. Do not add any words.

1. Rudy drove to the airport in twenty minutes but he couldn't find the right terminal for his flight.

2. A few of my friends bought a get-well card and sent it to their speech teacher.

3. The mall was crowded so Anthony decided to come back later.

4. Love stories in movies are unrealistic yet they are a good escape from everyday life.

5. Stella baked a cake and Brian made homemade ice cream.

6. Stella and Brian baked a cake and made homemade ice cream.

7. Tom appears to be outgoing yet is rarely seen at parties or other gatherings.

8. Next week the manager will meet with the safety committee or he will speak to them individually.

9. The apartment has high ceilings and a kitchen with room for a small table.

10. The entrance to our apartment complex is neither lighted nor clearly marked with a large sign.

OPTION 2: USING A SEMICOLON BETWEEN TWO SIMPLE SENTENCES

Sometimes you want to combine two simple sentences (independent clauses) without using a coordinating conjunction. If you want to join two simple sentences that are related in their ideas and you do not use a coordinating conjunction, you can combine them with a semicolon.

two simple sentences:

S   V   S   V

I cooked the turkey. *She made* the stuffing.

two simple sentences combined with a semicolon:

S   V   ; S   V

I cooked the turkey; *she made* the stuffing.

Here's another example of this option in use:

S   V   V   V   ; S   V

Rain can be dangerous; *it makes* the roads slippery.

Notice that when you join two simple sentences with a semicolon, the second sentence begins with a lowercase letter, not a capital letter.

You need to memorize the seven coordinating conjunctions so that you can make a decision about punctuating your combined sentences. Remember these rules:

- If a coordinating conjunction joins the combined sentences, put a comma in front of the coordinating conjunction.

  S   V   ,   S   V

  Tom had a barbecue in his back yard, and the *food was* delicious.

- If there is no coordinating conjunction, put a semicolon in front of the second independent clause.

  S   V   ;   S   V

  Tom had a barbecue in his back yard; the *food was* delicious.

OPTION 3: USING A SEMICOLON AND A CONJUNCTIVE ADVERB

Sometimes you may want to join two simple sentences (independent clauses) with a connecting word called a **conjunctive adverb.** This word points out or clarifies a relationship between sentences. Here is a list of some conjunctive adverbs:

> **Info BOX**
>
> ### Some Common Conjunctive Adverbs
>
> | | | | |
> |---|---|---|---|
> | also | furthermore | likewise | otherwise |
> | anyway | however | meanwhile | similarly |
> | as a result | in addition | moreover | still |
> | besides | in fact | nevertheless | then |
> | certainly | incidentally | next | therefore |
> | consequently | indeed | now | thus |
> | finally | instead | on the other hand | undoubtedly |

You can use a conjunctive adverb (CA) to join simple sentences, but when you do, you still need a semicolon in front of the adverb:

two simple sentences:

S   V   S V

My *parents checked* my homework every night. *I did* well in math.

two simple sentences joined by a conjunctive adverb and a semicolon:

$$\text{S} \qquad \text{V} \qquad\qquad\qquad\qquad \text{; CA S V}$$

My *parents checked* my homework every night; *thus I did* well in math.

$$\text{S} \quad \text{V} \qquad\qquad \text{;} \qquad \text{CA} \quad \text{S} \quad \text{V}$$

She gave me good advice; *moreover, she helped* me follow it.

Punctuating After a Conjunctive Adverb

Notice the comma after the conjunctive adverb in the preceding sentence. Here is the generally accepted rule:

Put a comma after the conjunctive adverb if the conjunctive adverb is more than one syllable long.

For example, if the conjunctive adverb is a word like *consequently, furthermore,* or *moreover,* you use a comma. If the conjunctive adverb is one syllable, you do not have to add a comma after it. One-syllable conjunctive adverbs are words like *then* or *thus.*

I saw her cruelty to her staff; *then* I lost respect for her.

We worked on the project all weekend; *consequently,* we finished a week ahead of the deadline.

Exercise 3

Practice

Combining Simple Sentences Three Ways

Add a comma, a semicolon, or a semicolon and a comma to the following sentences. Do not add, change, or delete any words; just add the correct punctuation.

1. My father is nodding over the newspaper soon he will be fast asleep.

2. Buying toys for children makes them happy but toys cannot replace attention.

3. The driver was arrested for driving under the influence moreover, he was charged with leaving the scene of an accident.

4. Mints have changed they now come in fancy tins at fancy prices.

5. Gardening is a good way to relieve stress furthermore it is good exercise.

6. The coach's face was bright red with anger and the players looked embarrassed.

7. The coach's face was bright red with anger the players looked embarrassed.

8. You can exchange this shirt for another one however you can't get your money back.

9. My sister made a cup of coffee then she watched the morning news.

10. Paul's wife just had a baby consequently he is beaming with pride.

Exercise 4

Practice

More on Combining Simple Sentences Three Ways

Add a comma, a semicolon, or a semicolon and a comma to the following sentences. Do not add, change, or delete any words; just add the correct punctuation.

1. Brian drove to Louisville with a friend for he wanted some company on the long ride.

2. The adults sat around the table and told stories meanwhile the children played with their toys.

3. The coat was extremely simple in design yet it cost a fortune.

4. They didn't want another Toyota instead they bought a Saturn.

5. The speaker started with a child's poem next she told a true story about the impact of violent crime on one family.

6. My boss never gave me a raise nor did he ever give me paid vacation days.

7. Once I was afraid of meeting people now I work with the public every day in my job at a hotel.

8. I like my apartment still I prefer living in a house.

9. My brother woke up late yesterday so he missed the breakfast special at Harbor Grill.

10. A platter of dishes crashed to the floor two waiters scrambled to clean up the mess.

 **Exercise 5**

Collaborate

Combining Simple Sentences

Below are pairs of simple sentences. Working with a partner or partners, combine each pair into one sentence in two different ways. You have three options: (1) use a comma and a coordinating conjunction, (2) use a semicolon or (3) use a semicolon and a conjunctive adverb (with a comma if it is needed). Pick the options that makes the most sense for each sentence. The first one is done for you.

1. Jim missed the beginning of the movie.
   I had to explain the story to him.
   combinations:

   a. Jim missed the beginning of the movie, so I had to explain the

      story to him.

   b. Jim missed the beginning of the movie; therefore, I had to explain

      the story to him.

2. Edna was exhausted at the end of the trip.
   She was glad she had made the journey.
combinations:

a. _____

_____

b. _____

_____

3. Adam pulled down the bed covers.
   He saw a large snake in his bed.
combinations:

a. _____

_____

b. _____

_____

4. Someone left the car windows open.
   A rain storm damaged the interior of the car.
combinations:

a. _____

_____

b. _____

_____

5. You can get a half-price ticket at a special ticket booth.
   You have to stand in line at the booth for hours.
combinations:

a. _____

_____

b. _____

_____

Exercise 6

Editing a Paragraph for Errors in Coordination

Connect

Edit the following paragraph for errors in coordination. Do not add or change words; just add, delete, or change punctuation. There are six errors in the paragraph.

A bad cold is a minor illness but it can be one of the most miserable ailments in the world. Most people soon forget their own colds, and don't sympathize with someone else's bad cold. A cold is supposed to be a silly, sniffling disturbance in the head however, the person with a cold feels very sick. He or she is sneezing, wheezing, and grabbing at tissues. Fever, headache, and stuffiness suddenly attack the sufferer and no remedy seems to work. Cold pills cannot make a person feel less congested nor can chicken soup clear up a headache. The victim of a cold can only wait for the misery to pass then the cold bug brings its nasty symptoms to a new victim.

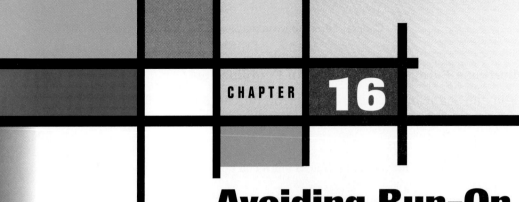

CHAPTER 16

Avoiding Run-On Sentences and Comma Splices

RUN-ON SENTENCES

Run-on sentences are independent clauses that have not been joined correctly. This error is also called a fused sentence.

> **run-on sentence error**
> Carol cleans her kitchen every week she shines every pot and pan.
>
> **run-on sentence error corrected**
> Carol cleans her kitchen every week; she shines every pot and pan.
>
> **run-on sentence error**
> I studied for the test all weekend I am well prepared for it.
>
> **run-on sentence error corrected**
> I studied for the test all weekend, so I am well prepared for it.

STEPS FOR CORRECTING RUN-ON SENTENCES

When you edit your writing, you can correct run-on sentences by following these steps:

> **Step 1:** Check for two independent clauses.
> **Step 2:** Check that the clauses are separated either by a coordinating conjunction and a comma or by a semicolon.

Follow the steps in checking this sentence:

The meeting was a waste of time the club members argued about silly issues.

> **Step 1:** Check for two independent clauses. You can do this by checking for the subject-verb, subject-verb pattern that indicates two independent clauses:

S V   S   V
The *meeting was* a waste of time the club *members argued* about
   silly issues.

The pattern indicates that you have two independent clauses.

Step 2: Check that the clauses are separated either by a coordinating
   conjunction (*and, but, or, nor, for, yet, so*) and a comma or
   by a semicolon.

There is no punctuation between the independent clauses, so you have a
run-on sentence. You can correct the run-on sentence two ways:

**run-on sentence corrected with a coordinating conjunction
and a comma:**

The meeting was a waste of time, *for* the club members argued about
   silly issues.

run-on sentence corrected with a semicolon:

The meeting was a waste of time; the club members argued about
   silly issues.

Follow the steps, once more, as you check this sentence:

I had the flu I missed class last week.

Step 1: Check for two independent clauses. Do this by checking the
   subject-verb, subject-verb pattern:

S V   S   V
I had the flu *I missed* class last week.

Step 2: Check that the clauses are separated either by a coordinating
   conjunction (*and, but, or, nor, for, yet, so*) and a comma or
   by a semicolon.

There is no punctuation between the independent clauses, so you have a
run-on sentence. You can correct the run-on sentence two ways:

**run-on sentence corrected with a coordinating conjunction and
a comma:**

I had the flu, *so* I missed class last week.

run-on sentence corrected with a semicolon:

I had the flu; I missed class last week.

Using the steps to check for run-on sentences can also help you avoid
unnecessary punctuation. Consider this sentence:

The manager gave me my schedule for next week and told me about
   a special sales promotion.

Step 1: Check for two independent clauses. Do this by checking the
   subject-verb, subject-verb pattern:

S   V   V
The *manager gave* me my schedule for next week and *told* me about
   a special sales promotion.

The pattern is *SVV*, not *SV,SV*. The sentence is not a run-on sentence, so it
does not need any additional punctuation.

Following the steps in correcting run-on sentences can help you avoid
a major grammar error.

Exercise 1

Practice

Correcting Run-on (Fused) Sentences

Some of the sentences below are correctly punctuated. Some are run-on (fused) sentences; that is, they are two simple sentences run together without any punctuation. If a sentence is correctly punctuated, write OK in the space provided. If it is a run-on sentence, put an X in the space provided and correct the sentence above the lines.

1. _____ David took me to the dentist's yesterday I had a sharp pain in my lower jaw.

2. _____ I never liked science fiction movies then Marisol dragged me to a great one yesterday.

3. _____ From the top of the mountain came a cry for help rescuers rushed toward the stranded climbers.

4. _____ The most famous stars in action films use a stunt double for their most dangerous scenes or rely on computerized special effects.

5. _____ The refugee's account of her escape was startling it revealed the danger and horror around her.

6. _____ Fat-free cookies are actually full of calories and taste sickly sweet.

7. _____ My brother's car needs a tune-up it hasn't been tuned in a year.

8. _____ I love all kinds of Latin music yet don't know many words of Spanish.

9. _____ Charlotte makes a good salary she never worries about money.

10. _____ Sometimes my day starts off badly but ends with a piece of luck.

Exercise 2

Practice

More on Correcting Run-On (Fused) Sentences

Some of the sentences below are correctly punctuated. Some are run-on (fused) sentences; that is, they are two simple sentences run together without any punctuation. If a sentence is correctly punctuated, write OK in the space provided. If it is a run-on sentence, put an X in the space provided and correct the sentence above the lines.

1. _____ Sam wants some time with his family then he wants some time alone.

2. _____ No one alive today has seen the inside of that house it has been locked and bolted since 1890.

3. _____ Commuters on subways and passengers in airplanes share the stresses of crowded spaces and unhealthy air.

4. _____ A membership in a health club was the perfect gift for my grandmother she loves her aerobics and swimming classes.

5. _____ Mr. and Mrs. Sunderson had no flood insurance thus they were afraid of damage to their house during a hurricane.

6. _____ The doctor checked my throat and gave me a prescription for some cough medicine.

7. _____ First the long distance company called at dinner time next it called in the early morning.

8. _____ The carpenters worked with the finest wood the panels looked rich and elegant.

9. _____ There are too many mosquitoes on the beach I'm going home.

10. _____ I am planning a small wedding at a local park instead of a big celebration with hundreds of people in a big hall.

COMMA SPLICES

A **comma splice** is an error that occurs when you punctuate with a comma but should use a semicolon instead. If you are joining two independent clauses without a coordinating conjunction (*and, but, or, nor, for, yet, so*) you must use a semicolon. A comma is not enough.

comma splice error
The crowd pushed forward, people began to panic.

comma splice error corrected
The crowd pushed forward; people began to panic. (Notice there is no conjunction.)

comma splice error
I forgot my glasses, thus I couldn't read the small print in the contract.

comma splice error corrected
I forgot my glasses; thus I couldn't read the small print in the contract.

CORRECTING COMMA SPLICES

When you edit your writing, you can correct comma splices by following these steps:

Step 1: Check for two independent clauses.

Step 2: Check that the clauses are separated by a coordinating conjunction (*and, but, or, nor, for, yet, so*). If they are, then a comma in front of the coordinating conjunction is sufficient. If they are not separated by a coordinating conjunction, you have a comma splice. Correct the comma splice by changing the comma to a semicolon.

Follow the steps to check for a comma splice in this sentence:

I dropped the glass, it shattered on the tile floor.

Step 1: Check for two independent clauses. You can do this by checking for the subject-verb, subject-verb pattern that indicates two independent clauses.

   S   V   S   V
I dropped the glass, *it shattered* on the tile floor.

The pattern indicates that you have two independent clauses.

Step 2: Check that the clauses are separated by a coordinating conjunction.

There is no coordinating conjunction. To correct the comma splice error, you must use a semicolon instead of a comma.

comma splice error corrected
I dropped the glass; it shattered on the tile floor.

Be careful not to mistake a short word like *then* or *thus* for a coordinating conjunction. Only the seven coordinating conjunctions (*and, but, or, nor, for, yet, so*) with a comma in front of them can join independent clauses.

comma splice error
Susie watched television, then she went to bed.

comma splice error corrected
Susie watched television; then she went to bed.

Then is not a coordinating conjunction; it is a conjunctive adverb. When it joins two independent clauses, it needs a semicolon in front of it.

Also remember that conjunctive adverbs that are two or more syllables long (like *consequently, however,* and *therefore*) need a comma after them as well as a semicolon in front of them when they join independent clauses:

Harry has been researching plane fares to New York; consequently, he knows how to spot a cheap flight.

(For a list of some common conjunctive adverbs, see Chapter 2.)

Sometimes writers see commas before and after a conjunctive adverb and think the commas are sufficient. Check this sentence for a comma splice by following the steps:

Jonathan loves his job, however, it pays very little.

Step 1: Check for two independent clauses by checking for the subject-verb, subject-verb pattern.

   S   V   S   V
Jonathan loves his job, however, *it pays* very little.

The pattern indicates that you have two independent clauses.

Step 2: Check for a coordinating conjunction.

There is no coordinating conjunction. *However* is a conjunctive adverb, not a coordinating conjunction. Because there is no coordinating conjunction, you need a semicolon between the two independent clauses.

comma splice error corrected
Jonathan loves his job; however, it pays very little.

| Exercise 3 | **Correcting Comma Splices** |

Practice

Some of the sentences below are correctly punctuated. Some contain comma splices. If the sentence is correctly punctuated, write OK in the space provided. If it contains a comma splice, put an X in the space provided and correct the sentence above the lines. To correct a sentence, add the necessary punctuation. Do not add any words.

1. _____ The cookies were soft and chewy, some had raisins, nuts, or chocolate chips.

2. _____ Megan lost her cell phone, she is looking for it now.

3. _____ One of the customers at the health food store bought a dozen boxes of herbal tea then he asked for a separate bag for each box.

4. _____ We always start our drive early in the morning, thus we get to the mountains for a full day of fun.

5. _____ Joseph needed a new pair of shoes, but he didn't like any of the styles in the store window.

6. _____ I had to wait four hours for those tickets, nevertheless, the wait was worth it.

7. _____ Sheila had to borrow money from her father, otherwise she would have had to drop out of college.

8. _____ George is not particularly good-looking or smart, yet all the ladies like him.

9. _____ Kendra kicked the back of the driver's seat for an hour, then she began to pull her little sister's hair.

10. _____ Border collies are wonderful dogs, however, they need a great deal of exercise.

| Exercise 4 | **More on Correcting Comma Splices** |

Practice

Some of the sentences below are correctly punctuated. Some contain comma splices. If the sentence is correctly punctuated, write *OK* in the space provided. If it contains a comma splice, put an *X* in the space provided and correct the sentence above the lines. To correct a sentence, do not add any words; just correct the punctuation.

1. _____ Mike forgot to turn off the oven, as a result, the turkey was dry.

2. _____ Our cat loves tuna, so we give her tiny pieces for a treat.

3. _____ Our seats were at the back, I could barely see the stage.

4. _____ Ben loves chocolate, but he will not eat anything with white chocolate in it.

5. _____ One kind of pen has a felt tip, another uses ink from a bottle.

6. _____ One good thing about the class is the time period, and another is the teacher.

7. _____ We can still get to work on time, anyway, we can try.

8. _____ Christine makes all her own clothes, so she always has her own style.

9. _____ Christine makes all her own clothes, therefore she always has her own style.

10. _____ Here comes the bill, I will pay it.

Exercise 5

👥 *Collaborate*

Completing Sentences

With a partner or group, write the first part of each of the following incomplete sentences. Make your addition an independent clause. Be sure to punctuate your completed sentences correctly. The first one is done for you.

1. <u>The driver ignored the railroad warning signals,</u> and his car was hit by the train.

2. _____ then Kayla heard a mysterious noise.

3. _____ furthermore, you are constantly complaining.

4. _____ or the food will get cold.

5. _____ now I need a long vacation.

6. _____ somebody took it.

7. _____ however, it lasted too long.

8. _____ but I learned from the
experience.

9. _____ Carlos refused to
apologize to her.

10. _____ otherwise, we will miss the
movie.

Exercise 6   **Editing a Paragraph for Run-On Sentences and Comma Splices**

Practice   Edit the following paragraph for run-on sentences and comma splices.
There are seven errors.

> Choosing a career is difficult I am torn between two fields. My best
> grades have been in my math classes and my father wants me to be an
> accountant. Accountants make a good salary in addition, they are always in
> demand. My uncle is an accountant and has found good jobs in four exciting
> cities. I would like the security and opportunity of such employment on the
> other hand, I dream of a different career. I have been working at a restau-
> rant for four years as a result, I have learned about the inner workings of
> the restaurant business. The job is tough nevertheless, I would love to have
> my own restaurant. Everyone warns me about the huge financial risks and
> long hours yet these challenges can be exciting. Someday I will have to
> choose between a risky venture in the restaurant business and a safe, well-
> paying career in accounting.

CHAPTER 17

Beyond the Simple Sentence: Subordination

MORE ON COMBINING SIMPLE SENTENCES

Before you go any further, look back. Review the following:

- A clause has a subject and a verb.
- An independent clause is a simple sentence; it is a group of words, with a subject and verb, that makes sense by itself.

There is another kind of clause called a **dependent clause.** It has a subject and a verb, but it does not make sense by itself. It cannot stand alone. It is not complete by itself. That is, it *depends* on the rest of the sentence to give it meaning. You can use a dependent clause in another option for combining simple sentences.

OPTION 4: USING A DEPENDENT CLAUSE TO BEGIN A SENTENCE

Often, you can combine simple sentences by changing an independent clause from one sentence into a dependent clause and placing it at the beginning of the new sentence.

two simple sentences:

S V   S   V
I was late for work. My *car had* a flat tire.

changing one simple sentence into a beginning dependent clause:

S V   S V
Because my *car had* a flat tire, *I was* late for work.

OPTION 5: USING A DEPENDENT CLAUSE TO END A SENTENCE

You can also combine simple sentences by changing an independent clause from one sentence into a dependent clause and placing it at the end of the new sentence:

S V   S   V
I was late for work because my *car had* a flat tire.

Notice how one simple sentence can be changed into a dependent clause in two ways:

two simple sentences:

S   S   V   S V
Mother and *Dad* wrapped my presents. *I slept.*

changing one simple sentence into a dependent clause:

S   S   V   S V
Mother and *Dad* wrapped my presents while *I slept.*

or

S V   S   S   V
While *I slept, Mother* and *Dad wrapped* my presents.

Using Subordinating Conjunctions

Changing an independent clause to a dependent one is called **subordinating.** How do you do it? You add a subordinating word, called a **subordinating conjunction,** to independent clauses, making them dependent—less "important," or subordinate—in the new sentence.

Keep in mind that the subordinate clause is still a clause; it has a subject and a verb, but it does not make sense by itself. For example, let's start with an independent clause:

S   V
Caroline studies.

Somebody (Caroline) does something (studies). The statement makes sense by itself. But if you add a subordinating conjunction to the independent clause, the clause becomes dependent, incomplete, unfinished, like this:

When Caroline studies (When she studies, what happens?)
Unless Caroline studies (Unless she studies, what will happen?)
If Caroline studies (If Caroline studies, what will happen?)

Now, each dependent clause needs an independent clause to finish the idea:

dependent clause   independent clause
When Caroline studies, she gets good grades.

dependent clause   independent clause
Unless Caroline studies, she forgets key ideas.

dependent clause   independent clause
If Caroline studies, she will pass the course.

There are many subordinating conjunctions. When you put any of these words in front of an independent clause, you make that clause dependent. Here is a list of some subordinating conjunctions:

Info BOX			
Subordinating Conjunctions			
after	before	so that	whenever
although	even though	though	where
as	if	unless	whereas
as if	in order that	until	whether
because	since	when	while

If you pick the right subordinating conjunction, you can effectively combine simple sentences (independent clauses) into a more sophisticated sentence pattern. Such combining helps you add sentence variety to your writing and helps to explain relationships between ideas.

simple sentences:

   S   V   V   S   V
Leo could not *read* music. His *performance was* exciting.

new combination:

dependent clause   independent clause
Although Leo could not read music, his performance was exciting.

simple sentences:

 S V   S   V
I caught a bad cold last night. *I forgot* to bring a sweater to the
   baseball game.

new combination:

independent clause   dependent clause
I caught a bad cold last night because I forgot to bring a sweater to
   the baseball game.

Punctuating Complex Sentences

A sentence that has one independent clause and one or more dependent clauses is called a **complex sentence.** Complex sentences are very easy to punctuate. See if you can figure out the rule for punctuating by yourself. Look at the following examples. All are punctuated correctly.

dependent clause   independent clause
Whenever the baby smiles, his mother is delighted.

independent clause   dependent clause
His mother is delighted whenever the baby smiles.

dependent clause   independent clause
While you were away, I saved your mail for you.

independent clause   dependent clause
I saved your mail for you while you were away.

In the examples above, look at the sentences that have a comma. Look at the ones that do not have a comma. Both kinds of sentences are punctuated correctly. Do you see the rule?

If the dependent clause comes at the beginning of the sentence, put a comma after the dependent clause. If the dependent clause comes at the end of the sentence, do not put a comma in front of the dependent clause.

Although we played well, we lost the game.
We lost the game although we played well.

Until he called, I had no date for the dance.
I had no date for the dance until he called.

Exercise 1

Practice

Punctuating Complex Sentences

All the sentences below are complex sentences; that is, they have one independent and one or more dependent clauses. Add a comma to each sentence that needs one.

1. Until you taste the pizza at Spiral Pizza you haven't tasted real pizza.

2. Give me a call when you get home from school.

3. After Maureen and David got married they moved to a small town in Montana.

4. Maureen and David moved to a small town in Montana after they got married.

5. I always watch television while I iron my clothes.

6. Because they never invited me to their house I stopped inviting them to mine.

7. Larry's hair doesn't look good unless he cuts it regularly.

8. Eddie did his studying in the hours before dawn while his children were asleep.

9. If Desmond can get some overtime next week he will buy new tires for his car.

10. Before the neighbors put up a fence their dog was always digging in our back yard.

Exercise 2

Practice

More on Punctuating Complex Sentences

All the sentences below are complex sentences; that is, they have one independent clause and one or more dependent clauses. Add a comma to each sentence that needs one.

1. My parents will have a good time at the reunion even if the weather is too cold for a barbecue.

2. Whether they stay overnight or for the weekend the boys can stay in the guest room.

3. Frank took his collie to the veterinarian since the dog was not eating or playing much.

4. While I read the newspaper article about the rescue at sea my brother called the Coast Guard.

5. Call your mother at her house before you leave for work.

6. Unless I get a big bonus at work I won't be able to pay my credit card bills.

7. When Penelope starts talking about her boyfriend she becomes a different person.

8. My niece wants to come with me on the camping trip even if it will be a rough and rugged vacation.

9. After the mechanic checked the car he gave me a shocking estimate of the cost of repairs.

10. As John waited for the bus the rain began to fall.

Combining Sentences: A Review of Your Options

As you've seen, there are several ways to combine simple sentences. The following chart will help you to see them all, at a glance.

Info BOX

Options for Combining Sentences

Coordination

Option 1
Independent clause { , and / , but / , or / , nor / , for / , yet / , so } independent clause

Option 2
Independent clause   ;   independent clause

Option 3
Independent clause
{ ; also
; anyway,
; as a result,
; besides,
; certainly,
; consequently,
; finally,
; furthermore,
; however,
; incidentally,
; in addition,
; in fact,
; indeed,
; instead,
; likewise,
; meanwhile,
; moreover,
; nevertheless,
; next
; now
; on the other hand,
; otherwise,
; similarly,
; still
; then
; therefore,
; thus
; undoubtedly, } independent clause

Subordination

Option 4		
Independent clause	after although as as if because before even though if in order that since so that though unless until when whenever where whereas whether while	dependent clause
Option 5	After Although As As if Because Before Even though If In order that Since So that Though Unless Until When Whenever Where Whereas Whether While	Dependent clause, independent clause. (Put a comma at the end of the dependent clause.)

Note: In Option 5, words are capitalized because the dependent clause will begin your complete sentence.

Exercise 3

Practice

Using the Five Options for Combining Sentences

Add missing commas and/or semicolons to the following sentences. Some sentences are correct.

1. Terry can get a good deal on the plane fare to Venezuela if he buys his ticket now.

2. My coworker never complains about the customers or the long hours so she is a calm and positive influence on me.

3. I rarely take long trips consequently my five-year-old car has very low mileage.

4. Get something cold for dessert ice cream would be great.

5. Unless I read Kimberly a story she will not go to sleep.

6. When February comes around the stores sell romantic perfumes and offer beautiful boxes of chocolates for Valentine's Day.

7. Derek and Nora got a divorce even though they seemed so happy together.

8. The old building kept deteriorating and was finally torn down.

9. Someone behind the rope barrier started pushing then everyone in the crowd began to push against the rope.

10. After the storm passed the residents inspected the damage to their homes and gardens.

11. Two of my roommates are moving to Arizona they have been offered jobs there.

12. The restaurant around the corner offers great dinner specials however it takes only cash, not credit cards.

13. Melinda tied her son's shoes while he told her all about his day in preschool.

14. Even though Mr. Cohen is a tough instructor he is the best psychology teacher at this college.

15. Larry couldn't believe it when his name was announced.

16. My neighbor works behind the counter at a supermarket all day and he has a second job at night.

17. Nelson never took music lessons instead he taught himself to play the piano.

18. Your hair is beautiful but it needs a good trimming.

19. Since Henry is good with numbers he can figure out the tax on this bill.

20. My dog came home filthy and smelly he had been rolling around in the mud.

Collaborate

Exercise 4   **Combining Sentences**

Do this exercise with a partner or a group. Combine each pair of sentences below into one clear, smooth sentence in two different ways. You can add words as well as punctuation. The first pair of sentences is done for you.

1. I love the music store in the mall.
   The owners let me browse in it for hours.

   combination 1: I love the music store in the mall because the owners

   let me browse in it for hours.

   combination 2: I love the music store in the mall; the owners let me

   browse in it for hours.

2. Camille never went to the beach.
   She was afraid of the ocean.

   combination 1: _____

   _____

   combination 2: _____

   _____

3. Ted broke his wrist.
   He couldn't play on the team for two months.

   combination 1: _____

   _____

   combination 2: _____

   _____

4. Mark wanted a new Lexus.
   He bought a used Camaro.

   combination 1: _____

   _____

   combination 2: _____

   _____

5. The engagement ring was too much money for Mike's budget.
   Mike insisted on getting it for his fiancée.

   combination 1: _____

   _____

combination 2: _____

_____

6. Martha is taking a class in computers.
She wants to find a better job.

combination 1: _____

_____

combination 2: _____

_____

7. Hail as big as baseballs pounded the street.
The truck began to skid.

combination 1: _____

_____

combination 2: _____

_____

8. I loved the movie *Rush Hour.*
Rush Hour 2 was better.

combination 1: _____

_____

combination 2: _____

_____

9. My brother never changes the oil in his car.
He never checks the air in his tires.

combination 1: _____

_____

combination 2: _____

_____

10. George and Lisa hate shopping in crowded malls.
They get bargains at flea markets and garage sales.

combination 1: _____

_____

combination 2: _____

_____

Exercise 5

Collaborate

Create Your Own Text on Combining Sentences

Below is a list of rules for coordinating and subordinating sentences. Working with a group, write two examples for each rule.

Option 1: You can join two simple sentences (two independent clauses) into a compound sentence with a coordinating conjunction and a comma in front of it.
(The coordinating conjunctions are *and, but, or, nor, for, yet, so.*)

example 1: _____

_____

example 2: _____

_____

Option 2: You can combine two simple sentences (two independent clauses) into a compound sentence with a semicolon between independent clauses.

example 1: _____

_____

example 2: _____

_____

Option 3: You can combine two simple sentences (two independent clauses) into a compound sentence with a semicolon and a conjunctive adverb between independent clauses. (Some conjunctive adverbs are *also, anyway, as a result, besides, certainly, consequently, finally, furthermore, however, incidentally, in addition, indeed, in fact, instead, likewise, meanwhile, moreover, nevertheless, next, now, on the other hand, otherwise, similarly, still, then, therefore, thus, and undoubtedly.*)

example 1: _____

_____

example 2: _____

_____

Option 4: You can combine two simple sentences (two independent clauses) into a complex sentence by making one clause dependent. The dependent clause starts with a subordinating conjunction. Then, if the dependent clause begins the sentence, the clause ends with a comma.
(Some common subordinating conjunctions are *after, although, as, as if, because, before, even though, if, in order that, since, so that, though, unless, until, when, whenever, where, whereas, whether, while.*)

example 1: _____

_____

example 2: _____

_____

Option 5: You can combine two simple sentences (two independent clauses) into a complex sentence by making one clause dependent. Then, if the dependent clause comes after the independent clause, no comma is needed.

example 1: _____

_____

example 2: _____

_____

Exercise 6

 Connect

Editing a Paragraph for Errors in Coordination and Subordination

Edit the following paragraph for errors in coordination and subordination. Do not add words to the paragraph; just add, delete, or change punctuation. There are ten errors.

I am beginning to realize the importance of punctuality. This lesson came to me the hard way when I almost lost my job. I am a receptionist at a small, friendly insurance office certainly, I felt at ease with its casual and open atmosphere. I think I confused friendliness with slackness and soon found trouble. Since my boss and the other agents are often busy on the road they rely on me to open up in the morning. I usually arrived on time anyway I tried to get there on time. I figured it didn't matter if I was ten or fifteen minutes late. When I arrived late last Friday it did matter. My boss came in thirty minutes after I did so I figured everything was fine. As soon as she took one call she came up to my desk and started shouting. The call was a customer with an emergency. That customer had called the office six times early in the morning no one had answered. Of course, I had not yet opened the office. My boss explained the seriousness of the problem finally, she gave me one more chance. I'll be on time from now on for I will not risk losing that chance.

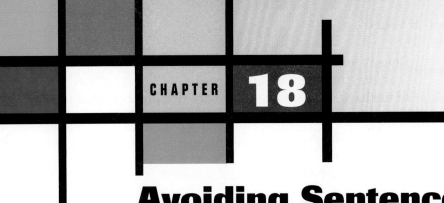

CHAPTER 18

Avoiding Sentence Fragments

A **sentence fragment** is a group of words that looks like a sentence and is punctuated like a sentence but is not a sentence. Writing a sentence fragment is a major error in grammar because it reveals that the writer is not sure what a sentence is.

The following groups of words are all fragments:

Because customers are often in a hurry and have little time to look for bargains.
My job being very stressful and fast-paced.
For example, the introduction of salads into fast-food restaurants.

There are two easy steps to help you check your writing for sentence fragments:

Info BOX

Two Steps in Recognizing Sentence Fragments

Step 1: Check each group of words punctuated like a sentence, looking for a subject and a verb.

Step 2: If you find a subject and a verb, check that the group of words makes a complete statement.

RECOGNIZING FRAGMENTS: STEP 1

Step 1: Check for a subject and a verb. Some groups of words that look like sentences may actually have a subject but no verb, a verb but no subject, or they may have no subject or verb.

The puppy in the pet store window. (*Puppy* could be the subject of a sentence, but there's no verb.)

Doesn't matter to me one way or the other. (There is a verb, *Does matter*, but there is no subject.)

In the back of my mind. (There are two prepositional phrases, *In the back* and *of my mind*, but there is no subject or verb.)

Remember that an *-ing* verb by itself cannot be the main verb in a sentence. Therefore, groups of words like the ones below may look like sentences, but they lack a verb and are really fragments:

Your sister having all the skills required of a good salesperson.

The two top tennis players struggling with exhaustion and the stress of a highly competitive tournament.

Jack being the only one in the room with a piece of paper.

An infinitive (*to* plus a verb) cannot be a main verb in a sentence, either. The following groups of words are also fragments:

The manager of the store to attend the meeting of regional managers next month in Philadelphia.

The purpose to explain the fine points of the game to new players.

Groups of words beginning with words like *also, especially, except, for example, in addition,* and *such as* need subjects and verbs, too. Without subjects and verbs, these groups can be fragments, like the ones below:

Also a good place to grow up.

Especially the youngest member of the family.

For example, a person without a high school diploma.

Exercise 1

Practice

Checking Groups of Words for Subjects and Verbs

Some of the following groups of words have subjects and verbs; these are sentences. Some groups are missing subjects, verbs, or both; these are fragments. Put an *S* by each sentence and an *F* by each fragment.

1. _____ For example, bright colors represent happiness.

2. _____ For instance, a bowl of hot soup on a snowy day.

3. _____ The police officer standing next to my open car window, writing my ticket in his ticket book.

4. _____ Doesn't ever say anything unkind about the people at the office.

5. _____ Especially a house with a basement for storage.

6. _____ Rick has done his income taxes and is looking forward to a small refund.

7. _____ In an argument with no room for compromise on either side.

8. _____ In addition, the job is part-time.

9. _____ Daniel giving me no excuse for his rudeness to my best friend.

10. _____ At the end of the road was an abandoned farm.

Exercise 2

Practice

More on Checking Groups of Words for Subjects and Verbs

Some of the following groups of words have subjects and verbs; these are sentences. Some are missing subjects, verbs, or both; these are fragments. Put an *S* by each sentence; put an *F* by each fragment.

1. _____ Senator Noda to consider running for president.

2. _____ Anyone with an ounce of common sense and some patience.

3. _____ One possible motive being revenge against a rival leader.

4. _____ The cookies from the oven need to cool for ten minutes.

5. _____ Should have been more careful with a valuable antique.

6. _____ Vinnie giving me encouragement from the sidelines and Elena cheering me on.

7. _____ The child pulling back from the little boy with a frog in his pocket.

8. _____ Except the apartments on the third floor of the building.

9. _____ At the door was a smiling salesperson.

10. _____ Will think about the chances of getting a job in engineering.

RECOGNIZING FRAGMENTS: STEP 2

Step 2: If a group of words has both a subject and a verb, check that it makes a complete statement. Many groups of words that have both a subject and a verb do not make sense by themselves. They are **dependent clauses.** How can you tell if a clause is dependent? After you have checked each group of words for a subject and verb, check to see if it begins with one of the subordinating conjunctions that start dependent clauses. (Here are some common subordinating words: *after, although, as, as if, because, before, even though, if, in order that, since, so that, though, unless, until, when, whenever, where, whereas, whether, while.*)

A clause that begins with a subordinating conjunction is a dependent clause. When you punctuate a dependent clause as if it were a sentence, you have a kind of fragment called a **dependent clause fragment:**

After I woke up this morning.
Because he liked football better than soccer.
Unless it stops raining by lunchtime.

It is important to remember both steps in checking for fragments:

Step 1: Check for a subject and a verb.
Step 2: If you find a subject and a verb, check that the group of words makes a complete statement.

Exercise **3**

Practice

Checking for Dependent Clause Fragments

Some of the following groups of words are sentences. Some are dependent clauses punctuated like sentences; these are sentence fragments. Put an *S* by each sentence and an *F* by each fragment.

1. _____ As the teacher passed out the tests and explained the essay questions to the students.

2. _____ Above the desk was a small painting.

3. _____ Because of street flooding in the lower part of town and loss of electricity in many areas.

4. _____ Although we married young and struggled to make a living.

5. _____ Most of the expensive toys in Bobby's room no longer interested him.

6. _____ While Bernadette celebrated the birth of her sister's first child.

7. _____ Yet most people try to save some money for family emergencies.

8. _____ If we could preserve the beauty of our natural environment for future generations.

9. _____ Since I gave Dan the book about skindiving in the Florida Keys.

10. _____ When the team starts spring training near my house.

Exercise **4**

Practice

More on Checking for Dependent Clause Fragments

Some of the following groups of words are sentences. Some are dependent clauses punctuated like sentences; these are sentence fragments. Put an *S* by each sentence and an *F* by each fragment.

1. _____ After a refreshing swim in the new community pool.

2. _____ Down the ladder came a firefighter with a child in his arms.

3. _____ Since we met at the student center for a cup of coffee.

4. _____ Near the hospital is a huge medical building.

5. _____ Suddenly my car alarm sounded.

6. _____ Because anyone could have broken into the gym.

7. _____ While Sergei painted the green trim on the outside of the house.

8. _____ Before I had a chance to put the key in the door.

9. _____ Unless you can give me a better deal on this DVD player.

10. _____ Whenever Tony borrows my clothes.

Exercise 5   **Using Two Steps to Recognize Sentence Fragments**

Practice

Some of the following are complete sentences; some are fragments. To recognize the fragments, check each group of words by using the two-step process:

Step 1: Check for a subject and a verb.
Step 2: If you find a subject and verb, check that the group of words makes a complete statement.

Then put an *S* by each sentence and an *F* by each fragment.

1. _____ The reason being a lack of guidance from his parents.

2. _____ As my sister walked down the aisle in her wedding dress.

3. _____ Ken's neighbors are being very cooperative about the parking problem.

4. _____ Whenever I go into that store and look through the sales rack.

5. _____ Without the right kind of clothes for a cold winter.

6. _____ Around the edge of the mirror was a gold wreath of flowers.

7. _____ Without saying good-bye, Terry left.

8. _____ Because of Marcy's good grades in political science and her volunteer work in voter registration.

9. _____ Fast cars meant freedom to the troubled teenager.

10. _____ It turned out to be the opposite of the truth.

11. _____ Armand painting Haitian scenes in blazing colors.

12. _____ For example, a relationship with no future.

13. _____ Although Luis rarely spent time with his girlfriend's family.

14. _____ A new edition of the game to be available at electronics stores next month.

15. _____ The little league's sponsor supplying all the team members with uniforms.

16. _____ While the puppies tumbled into a drowsy heap around their mother.

17. _____ From the back of the room came the sound of children giggling.

18. _____ When he'd taken a day off to enroll his daughter in school.

19. _____ Then the clock on the mantel began chiming in a loud tone.

20. _____ Out of a sense of duty and concern for his mother.

CORRECTING FRAGMENTS

You can correct fragments easily if you follow the two steps for identifying them.

Step 1: Check for a subject and a verb. If a group of words is a fragment because it lacks a subject, a verb, or both, *add what is missing.*

> **fragment:** My father being a very strong person. (This fragment lacks a main verb.)
> **corrected:** My father is a very strong person. (The verb *is* replaces *being*, which is not a main verb.)

> **fragment:** Doesn't care about the party. (This fragment lacks a subject.)
> **corrected:** Alicia doesn't care about the party. (A subject, *Alicia*, is added.)

> **fragment:** Especially on dark winter days. (This fragment has neither a subject nor a verb.)
> **corrected:** I love a bonfire, especially on dark winter days. (A subject, *I*, and a verb, *love*, are added.)

Step 2: If you find a subject and a verb, check that the group of words makes a complete statement. To correct the fragment, you can turn a dependent clause into an independent one by removing the subordinating conjunction, *or* you can add an independent clause to the dependent one to create a sentence.

> **fragment:** When the rain beat against the windows. (The statement does not make sense by itself. The subordinating conjunction *when* leads the reader to ask, "What happened when the rain beat against the windows?" The subordinating conjunction makes this a dependent clause, not a sentence.)
> **corrected:** The rain beat against the windows. (Removing the subordinating conjunction makes this an independent clause, a sentence.)
> **corrected:** When the rain beat against the windows, I reconsidered my plans for the picnic. (Adding an independent clause turns this into a sentence.)

Note: Sometimes you can correct a fragment by linking it to the sentence before it or after it.

> **fragment (underlined):** I have always enjoyed outdoor concerts. <u>Like the ones at Pioneer Park.</u>

corrected: I have always enjoyed outdoor concerts like the ones at Pioneer Park.

fragment (underlined): <u>Even if she apologizes for that nasty remark.</u> I will never trust her again.

corrected: Even if she apologizes for that nasty remark, I will never trust her again.

You have several choices for correcting fragments: you can add words, phrases, or clauses; you can take words out; or you can combine independent and dependent clauses. You can transform fragments into simple sentences or create compound or complex sentences. To punctuate your new sentences, remember the rules for combining sentences.

Exercise 6

Practice

Correcting Fragments

Correct each sentence fragment below in the most appropriate way.

1. When I want to brighten up my day, I buy a bunch of colorful flowers. Such as carnations or daisies.

corrected: _____

_____

2. If I can finish writing my paper tonight. I can go to the gym with you tomorrow.

corrected: _____

_____

3. Taking a shortcut through the side streets. Nelson avoided the traffic jam at the center of the city.

corrected: _____

_____

4. Eric made a shopping list and bought everything he needed for the barbecue. Except some sturdy paper plates.

corrected: _____

_____

5. The thief's real motive being to get out of the building before the disappearance of the diamond necklace was discovered.

corrected: _____

_____

6. Then sent Ms. Martinez the box of oranges from Florida.

corrected: _____

_____

7. Because the speeches lasted too long. There was no time for a question-and-answer period.

corrected: _____

_____

8. The landlord pounded on the door. As Jill rushed to turn down the music.

corrected: _____

_____

9. He quit his job at the mall. To look for one with better hours and a higher salary.

corrected: _____

_____

10. No one has to do the cleaning all alone. If we can all agree on a plan for dividing the work.

corrected: _____

_____

Exercise 7

👥 *Collaborate*

Correcting Fragments

Working with a partner or group, correct each fragment below in two ways. The first one is done for you.

1. Whenever I am waiting for an important phone call.

corrected: I am waiting for an important phone call.

corrected: Whenever I am waiting for an important phone call, I am

extremely impatient and nervous.

2. Alicia watched cartoons on television. While her mother finished dressing for work.

corrected: _____

_____

corrected: _____

_____

3. Unless I write a note to remind him. My boy friend forgets to take the garbage out on Wednesdays.

corrected: _____

_____

corrected: _____

_____

4. Lamar having a better understanding of organic chemistry than anyone else in the class.

corrected: _____

_____

corrected: _____

_____

5. With a nod of his head to the guest of honor. He began his introduction.

corrected: _____

_____

corrected: _____

_____

6. Although I had never played soccer before.

corrected: _____

_____

corrected: _____

_____

7. At the end of the movie, when the battle began.

corrected: _____

_____

corrected: _____

8. The dinner party will be a disaster. If my cousins are invited.

corrected: _____

_____

corrected: _____

_____

9. Which is the best restaurant in town.

corrected: _____

_____

corrected: _____

_____

10. The audience roared with laughter. As the comedian told joke after joke.

corrected: _____

_____

corrected: _____

_____

Exercise 8

 *Collaborate*

Editing a Paragraph for Sentence Fragments

Correct the sentence fragments in the following paragraph. There are six fragments.

Nick would love to meet a celebrity. Like a famous athlete. He sees these celebrities on television. Where they drive expensive cars and wear wild clothes. They seem to have it all. Talent, looks, money, and fame. They all appear to come easily to celebrities. They can live anywhere they want and buy anything they desire. These famous people filling Nick's dreams. To talk to one basketball or music star and get the man's photograph. Being close to a celebrity would make Nick feel important. Since Nick is only six years old. He has plenty of time to find other dreams..

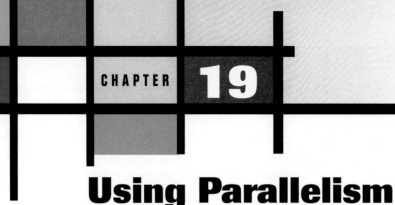

CHAPTER 19

Using Parallelism in Sentences

Parallelism means balance in a sentence. To create sentences with parallelism, remember this rule:

> **Similar points should get a similar structure.**

Often, you will include two or three (or more) related ideas, examples, or details in one sentence. If you express these ideas in a parallel structure, they will be clearer, smoother, and more convincing.

Here are some pairs of sentences with and without parallelism:

not parallel: Of all the sports I've played, I prefer tennis, handball, and playing golf.

parallel: Of all the sports I've played, I prefer *tennis, handball, and golf.* (Three words are parallel.)

not parallel: If you're looking for the car keys, you should look under the table, the kitchen counter, and behind the refrigerator.

parallel: If you're looking for the car keys, you should look *under the table, on the kitchen counter,* and *behind the refrigerator.* (Three prepositional phrases are parallel.)

not parallel: He is a good choice for manager because he works hard, he keeps calm, and well-liked.

parallel: He is a good choice for manager because *he works hard, he keeps calm,* and *he is well-liked.* (Three clauses are parallel.)

From these examples, you can see that parallelism involves matching the structures of parts of your sentence. There are two steps that can help you check your writing for parallelism:

Info BOX

Two Steps in Checking a Sentence for Parallel Structure

Step 1: Look for the list in the sentence.

Step 2: Put the parts of the list into a similar structure. (You may have to change or add something to get a parallel structure.)

ACHIEVING PARALLELISM

Let's correct the parallelism of the following sentence:

> **sample sentence:** The committee for neighborhood safety met to set up a schedule for patrols, coordinating teams of volunteers, and also for the purpose of creating new rules.

To correct this sentence, we'll follow the steps.

> **Step 1:** Look for the list. The committee met to do three things. Here's the list:
> 1. to set up a schedule for patrols
> 2. coordinating teams of volunteers
> 3. for the purpose of creating new rules
>
> **Step 2:** Put the parts of the list into a similar structure:
> 1. *to set up* a schedule for patrols
> 2. *to coordinate* teams of volunteers
> 3. *to create* new rules

Now revise to get a parallel sentence:

> **parallel:** The committee for neighborhood safety met *to set up* a schedule for patrols, *to coordinate* teams of volunteers, and *to create* new rules.

If you follow steps 1 and 2, you can also write the sentence like this:

> **parallel:** The committee for neighborhood safety met to *set up* a schedule for patrols, *coordinate* teams of volunteers, and *create* new rules.

But you cannot write a sentence like this:

> **not parallel:** The committee for neighborhood safety met *to set up* a schedule for patrols, *coordinate* teams, and *to create* new rules.

Think of the list again. You can have

> The committee met
> 1. to set up
> 2. to coordinate   } parallel
> 3. to create

Or you can have

> The committee met to
> 1. set up
> 2. coordinate   } parallel
> 3. create

But your list cannot be

The committee met to
1. set up
2. coordinate   } not parallel
3. to create

In other words, use the *to* once (if it fits every part of the list), or use it with every part of the list.

Caution: Sometimes making ideas parallel means adding something to a sentence because all the parts of the list cannot match exactly.

sample sentence: In his pocket the little boy had a ruler, rubber band, baseball card, and apple.

Step 1: Look for the list. In his pocket the little boy had a
1. ruler
2. rubber band
3. baseball card
4. apple

As the sentence is written, the *a* goes with *a ruler, a rubber band, a baseball card,* and *a apple.* But *a* isn't the right word to put in front of *apple.* Words beginning with vowels (*a, e, i, o, u*) need *an* in front of them: *an apple.* So to make the sentence parallel, you have to change something in the sentence.

Step 2: Put the parts of the list into a parallel structure.

parallel: In his pocket the little boy had *a ruler, a rubber band, a baseball card,* and *an apple.*

Here's another example:

sample sentence: She was amused and interested in the silly plot of the movie.

Step 1: Look for the list. She was
1. amused
2. interested in
the silly plot of the movie.

Check the sense of that sentence by looking at each part of the list and how it works in the sentence: "She was *interested in* the silly plot of the movie." That part of the list seems clear. But "She was *amused* the silly plot of the movie"? Or "She was *amused in* the silly plot of the movie"? Neither sentence is right. People are not *amused in.*

Step 2: The sentence needs a word added to make the structure parallel.

parallel: She was *amused by* and *interested in* the silly plot of the movie.

When you follow the two steps to check for parallelism, you can write clear sentences and improve your style.

Exercise 1

Practice

Revising Sentences for Parallelism

Some of the following sentences need to be revised so that they have parallel structures. Revise the ones that need parallelism.

1. The chapter starts on page 129; page 144 is where it ends.

   revised: _____

   _____

2. Betty is pretty, kind, and has charm.

   revised: _____

   _____

3. Leo's day is so long that he gets up at 5:00 A.M., leaves for work at 5:30 A.M., eating dinner at 10 P.M., and goes to bed at 1:00 A.M.

   revised: _____

   _____

4. You can go to the movies with me or without me.

   revised: _____

   _____

5. If you go to the drug store, please remember to pick up Nick's prescription, buy some toothpaste, and to look for a birthday card.

   revised: _____

   _____

6. I spent an hour with Ms. King, reviewing my job performance, assessing my goals, and my future with the company was discussed also.

   revised: _____

   _____

7. The dog's size, how friendly he was, and temperament made him a good choice for our family.

   revised: _____

   _____

8. To some people, driving an expensive car can be compared to when you become a success.

   revised: _____

   _____

9. Janice was the most admired person in the family, also the most independent person and the most ambitious.

   revised: _____

   _____

10. It is safer to read the label on so-called diet foods than automatically thinking they are low in calories.

    revised: _____

    _____

Exercise **2**

👥 *Collaborate*

Writing Sentences with Parallelism

Complete this exercise with a partner or a group. First, brainstorm a draft list; then, revise the list for parallelism. Finally, complete the sentence in parallel structure. You may want to assign one step (brainstorming a draft list, revising it, etc.) to each group member, then switch steps on the next sentence. The first one is done for you.

1. Three habits I'd like to break are

draft list	revised list
a. worry too much	a. worrying too much
b. talking on the phone for hours	b. talking on the phone for hours
c. lose my temper	c. losing my temper

   sentence: Three habits I'd like to break are worrying too much, talking on the phone for hours, and losing my temper.

2. Three ways to meet new people are

draft list	revised list
a. _____	a. _____
b. _____	b. _____
c. _____	c. _____

   sentence: _____

   _____

3. Two reasons to get regular exercise are

draft list	revised list
a. _____	a. _____
b. _____	b. _____

sentence: _____

_____

4. Three small pleasures in my daily life are

    draft list   revised list

    a. _____   a. _____

    b. _____   b. _____

    c. _____   c. _____

    sentence: Answers will vary. _____

_____

5. Getting enough sleep is important because (add three reasons)

    draft list   revised list

    a. _____   a. _____

    b. _____   b. _____

    c. _____   c. _____

    sentence: _____

_____

6. Ending a relationship can be stressful because (add three reasons)

    draft list   revised list

    a. _____   a. _____

    b. _____   b. _____

    c. _____   c. _____

    sentence: _____

_____

7. Five years from now, I want to (add two goals)

    draft list   revised list

    a. _____   a. _____

    b. _____   b. _____

    sentence: _____

_____

8. I am most carefree when (add two times or occasions)

    draft list   revised list

    a. _____   a. _____

    b. _____   b. _____

    sentence: _____

    _____

9. Three characteristics of a good parent are

    draft list   revised list

    a. _____   a. _____

    b. _____   b. _____

    c. _____   c. _____

    sentence: _____

    _____

10. Two experiences most people dread are

    draft list   revised list

    a. _____   a. _____

    b. _____   b. _____

    sentence: _____

    _____

Exercise 3

Practice

Combining Sentences and Creating a Parallel Structure

Combine each cluster of sentences below into one clear, smooth sentence that includes some parallel structure. The first one is done for you.

1. Before you buy a used car, you should research what similar models are selling for.
It would be a good idea to have a mechanic examine the car.
Also, how much mileage it has racked up is a consideration.

combination: *Before you buy a used car, you should compare prices of*

similar models, get a mechanic to examine the car, and think carefully

about the mileage.

2. Look for the keys in my jacket pocket.
You can also look on the sofa.
Check the area under the kitchen table.

combination: _____

_____

3. When I finish college, I'm going to move to a big city.
Getting a job at a bank or brokerage company is something else I will do.
In addition, I plan to get my own apartment.

combination: _____

_____

4. Whenever I am in trouble, I go to Ernesto, who is understanding.
Ernesto has patience.
Generosity is one of his good qualities.

combination: _____

_____

5. The car was an antique.
It had leather seats.
The chrome was polished.
The dashboard was dark wood.
It was an elegant car.

combination: _____

_____

6. Bookstores sell books and magazines.
CDs are available.
Greeting cards are sold.
You can get coffee and snacks.
They attract a wide variety of customers by selling these things.

combination: _____

_____

7. My father joined a community theater.
He worked on every production.
He eventually became the stage manager.

combination: _____

_____

8. At the concert, hundreds of pre-teenage girls crowded the stage
entrance.

The girls were hoping to see the boy singers arrive.
The girls' other goal was to get the singers' autographs.

combination: _____

_____

_____

9. Noisy was the funniest dog I ever had.
He was more intelligent than any other dog I owned.
His bravery was the greatest, too.

combination: _____

_____

10. Lucy's job includes answering the phone.
She has to take dinner reservations.
When customers arrive, she walks them to their tables.

combination: _____

_____

Exercise 4   **Editing a Paragraph for Errors in Parallelism**

Connect

Correct any errors in parallelism in the following paragraph. There are four errors.

I cannot understand why my brother is a big baseball fan; I think the game is slow, full of boring moments, and outdated. My brother always drags me to baseball games where he pays close attention to every minute of the game. Meanwhile, I am waiting for the action to begin. I can see only men standing around the field, talking to each other, chewing gum, or they spit tobacco juice. I don't see why this behavior is exciting. In addition, there are the boring moments when the game seems to stop completely. Then the coaches or the umpire or the players seem to be having a conference on the field. These little talks seem endless. My last complaint is about the atmosphere of a ball game. Even the big, nationally televised games seem old-fashioned. The games feature the same kinds of uniforms, music playing and fans as a baseball game in a fifty-year old movie. While my brother enjoys this slow, traditional game, I want the action, excitement, and sense of aggression of modern football or basketball.

CHAPTER 20

Using Adjectives and Adverbs

WHAT ARE ADJECTIVES?

Adjectives describe nouns (persons, places, or things) or pronouns (words that substitute for nouns).

> **adjectives:**
> She stood in a *dark* corner. (*Dark* describes the noun *corner.*)
> I need a *little* help. (*Little* describes the noun *help.*)
> She looked *happy*. (*Happy* describes the pronoun *she.*)

An adjective usually comes before the word it describes.

> He gave me a *beautiful* ring. (*Beautiful* describes *ring.*)
> A *small* horse pulled the cart. (*Small* describes *horse.*)

Sometimes it comes after a being verb, a verb that tells what something is. Being verbs are words like *is, are, was, am,* and *has been.* Words like *feels, looks, seems, smells, sounds,* and *tastes* are part of the group called being verbs.

> He seems *unhappy*. (*Unhappy* describes *he* and follows the being verb *seems.*)
> Alan was *confident*. (*Confident* describes *Alan* and follows the being verb *was.*)

 Exercise 1

Practice

Recognizing Adjectives

Circle the adjective in each of the following sentences.

1. Marty painted a beautiful picture.

2. The counselors are wonderful with children.

3. I needed a quiet room.

4. The milk in the refrigerator tastes sour.

5. A sleepy student began to yawn.

6. An enormous rock fell from the cliff.

7. You look handsome in your suit.

8. My mother gave me a small allowance.

9. Turkey and fish are good sources of protein.

10. Ed blinked in the bright sunshine.

ADJECTIVES: COMPARATIVE AND SUPERLATIVE FORMS

The **comparative** form of an adjective compares two persons or things. The **superlative** form compares three or more persons or things.

comparative: Your car is *cleaner* than mine.
superlative: Your car is the *cleanest* one in the parking lot.

comparative: Hamburger is *cheaper* than steak.
superlative: Hamburger is the *cheapest* meat on the menu.

comparative: Lisa is *friendlier* than her sister.
superlative: Lisa is the *friendliest* of the three sisters.

For most adjectives of one syllable, add *-er* to form the comparative, and add *-est* to form the superlative:

The weather is *colder* than it was yesterday, but Friday was the *coldest* day of the year.
Orange juice is *sweeter* than grapefruit juice, but the *sweetest* juice is grape juice.

For longer adjectives, use *more* to form the comparative, and use *most* to form the superlative:

I thought algebra was *more difficult* than composition; however, physics was the *most difficult* course I ever took.
My brother is *more outgoing* than my sister, but my father is the *most outgoing* member of the family.

The three forms of adjectives usually look like this:

Adjective	Comparative	Superlative
	(two)	(three or more)
sweet	sweeter	sweetest
fast	faster	fastest
short	shorter	shortest
quick	quicker	quickest
old	older	oldest

They may look like this instead:

Adjective	Comparative	Superlative
	(two)	(three or more)
confused	more confused	most confused
specific	more specific	most specific

dangerous	more dangerous	most dangerous
confident	more confident	most confident
beautiful	more beautiful	most beautiful

However, there are some irregular forms of adjectives:

Adjective	Comparative (two)	Superlative (three or more)
good	better	best
bad	worse	worst
little	less	least
many, much	more	most

Exercise 2

Practice

Selecting the Correct Adjective Form

Write the correct form of each adjective in parentheses in the following sentences.

1. Marvin was a _____ (good) friend than Harry.

2. I have read books by Stephen King, Clive Barker, and Anne Rice; Stephen King is the _____ (good) of the three writers.

3. My mother says finding the right person to love is _____ (hard) than getting married, but she swears that staying married is the _____ (difficult) part of the whole process.

4. Of the two highways, Federal Highway is _____ (old).

5. We rented three videos this weekend, and *Swordfish* was the _____ (bad) of the three.

6. Working with a tutor can be _____ (good) for you; however, studying and working on your own can be _____ (good) than expecting a tutor to do all your work for you.

7. Which one of these four shirts is the _____ (fashionable)?

8. I looked at two new cars with very little trunk space; however, the Corolla has _____ (little) trunk space than the Taurus.

9. This summer I wrote _____ (many) emails, but my friend Kevin wrote _____ (many) emails than I did.

10. Getting the flu is _____ (bad) than catching a cold.

Exercise 3

 *Collaborate*

Writing Sentences with Adjectives

Working with a partner or group, write a sentence that correctly uses each of the following adjectives. Be prepared to share your answers with another group or with the class.

1. best _____

2. more polite _____

3. coldest   _____

4. thinnest   _____

5. worst   _____

6. most caring _____

7. darker   _____

8. less   _____

9. taller   _____

10. much   _____

WHAT ARE ADVERBS?

Adverbs describe verbs, adjectives, or other adverbs.

adverbs:

As she spoke, Steve listened *thoughtfully*. (*Thoughtfully* describes the verb *listened*.)

I said I was *really* sorry for my error. (*Really* describes the adjective *sorry*.)

The cook worked *very* quickly. (*Very* describes the adverb *quickly*.)

Adverbs answer questions like "How?" "How much?" "How often?" "When?" "Why?" and "Where?"

 Exercise 4

Practice

Recognizing Adverbs

Circle the adverbs in the following sentences.

1. Tim answered foolishly when the police asked him where he had been.

2. Yesterday, Willie was very kind to the homeless man.

3. My parents are really happy with the addition to their home.

4. The manager sent a carefully written letter of apology to the dissatisfied customer.

5. I am getting a completely new bedroom set.

6. Our firm is fully committed to a new marketing plan.

7. The slightly tilted deck of the boat worried me.

8. When my sister and her husband lived in the neighborhood, they visited me frequently.

9. If the traffic is heavy, I sometimes stay at work a little later and wait for rush hour to subside.

10. We were late getting to the airport and nearly missed our plane.

Writing Sentence with Adverbs

Working with a partner or group, write a sentence that correctly uses each of the following adverbs. Be prepared to share your answers with another group or with the class.

1. usually _____

2. never _____

3. often _____

4. strangely _____

5. quickly _____

6. neatly _____

7. eagerly _____

8. always _____

9. cheerfully _____

10. very _____

HINTS ABOUT ADJECTIVES AND ADVERBS

Do not use an adjective when you need an adverb. Some writers make the mistake of using an adjective when they need an adverb.

not this: Talk to me honest.
but this: Talk to me *honestly.*

not this: You can say it simple.
but this: You can say it *simply.*

not this: He was breathing deep.
but this: He was breathing *deeply.*

Exercise 6

Practice

Changing Adjectives to Adverbs

In each pair of sentences, change the underlined adjective in the first sentence to an adverb in the second sentence. The first one is done for you.

1. a. She is a <u>graceful</u> dancer.

   b. She dances ____<u>gracefully</u>____ .

2. a. His speech was <u>soft</u>.

b. He spoke _____

3. a. The supervisor's reply was <u>sarcastic</u>.

b. The supervisor replied _____ .

4. a. Albert took a <u>reckless</u> jump into the river.

b. Albert jumped _____ into the river.

5. a. The store made a <u>cheap</u> version of the antique necklace.

b. The store's version of the antique necklace was _____ made.

6. a. His reaction seemed <u>rude</u>.

b. He reacted _____.

7. a. Gary is <u>patient</u> when he trains his dog.

b. Gary trains his dog _____.

8. a. After his favorite team lost, Brett's complaints about the coach were <u>constant</u>.

b. After his favorite team lost, Brett _____ complained about the coach.

9. a. The attorney was <u>aggressive</u> in questioning the witness.

b. The attorney questioned the witness _____.

10. a. Mr. Woo was a <u>regular</u> visitor to the nursing home.

b. Mr. Woo visited the nursing home _____.

Don't Confuse Good and Well, or Bad and Badly

Remember that *good* is an adjective; it describes nouns. *Well* is an adverb; it describes verbs. The only time *well* can be used as an adjective is when it means "healthy": *I feel well today.*

not this: You ran that race ~~good~~.
but this: You ran that race *well*.

not this: I cook eggs ~~good~~.
but this: I cook eggs well.

not this: How ~~good~~ do you understand grammar?
but this: How *well* do you understand grammar?

Bad is an adjective; it describes nouns. It also follows being verbs like *is, are, was, am,* and *has been.* Words like *feels, looks, seems, smells, sounds,* and *tastes* are part of the group called being verbs. *Badly* is an adverb; it describes action verbs.

not this: He feels ~~badly~~ about his mistake.
but this: He feels bad about his mistake. (*Feels* is a being verb; it is described by the adjective *bad*.)

not this: That soup smells ~~badly~~.
but this: That soup smells *bad*. (*Smells* is a being verb; it is described by the adjective *bad*.)

not this: He dances ~~bad~~.
but this: He dances *badly*.

Exercise 7

Practice

Using *Good* and *Well*, *Bad* and *Badly*

Write the appropriate word in each of the following sentences.

1. Jackie spends every penny she makes, but her sister handles her money _____ (good, well).

2. I'm not sure if I will be feeling _____ (good, well) enough to go to your party tomorrow.

3. Our classroom was small and _____ (bad, badly) designed.

4. After the exam, Rick thought he had done _____ (good, well) on the multiple choice part.

5. She and her new roommate do not get along _____ (good, well) anymore.

6. My brother feels _____ (bad, badly) about the argument since he started it.

7. Mrs. Dominguez hurt her knee _____ (bad, badly).

8. I bought a tape of the concert, but the music sounds _____ (bad, badly).

9. Your beard looks _____ (good, well) on you.

10. The woman without health insurance needed help _____ (bad, badly).

Not More + -er, or Most + -est

Be careful. Never write both an *-er* ending and *more* or an *-est* ending and *most*.

not this: I want to work with someone ~~more smarter~~.
but this: I want to work with someone *smarter*.

not this: Alan is the ~~most richest~~ man in town.
but this: Alan is the *richest* man in town.

Use Than, not Then, in Comparisons

When you compare things, use *than*. *Then* means "at a later time."

not this: You are taller then I am.
but this: You are taller *than* I am.

not this: I'd like a car that is faster then my old one.
but this: I'd like a car that is faster *than* my old one.

When Do I Need a Comma Between Adjectives?

Sometimes you use more than one adjective to describe a noun.

I visited a cold, dark cave.
The cat had pale blue eyes.

If you look at the preceding examples, one has a comma between the adjectives *cold* and *dark*, but the other does not have a comma between the adjectives *pale* and *blue*. Both sentences are correctly punctuated. To decide whether you need a comma, try one of these tests:

Test 1: Try to put *and* between the adjectives. If the sentence still makes sense, put a comma between the adjectives.

> **check for comma:** I visited a cold, dark cave. (Do you need the comma? Add *and* between the adjectives.)
> **add *and*:** I visited a cold *and* dark cave. (Does the sentence still make sense? Yes. You need the comma.)
> **correct sentence:** I visited a cold, dark cave.

> **check for comma:** The cat had pale blue eyes. (Do you need the comma? Add *and* between the adjectives.)
> **add *and*:** The cat had pale *and* blue eyes. (Does the sentence still make sense? No. You do not need the comma.)
> **correct sentence:** The cat had pale blue eyes.

Test 2: Try to reverse the order of the adjectives. If the sentence still makes sense, put a comma between the adjectives.

> **check for comma:** I visited a cold, dark cave. (Do you need the comma? Reverse the order of the adjectives.)
> **reverse order:** I visited a dark, cold cave. (Does the sentence still make sense? Yes. You need the comma.)
> **correct sentence:** I visited a cold, dark cave.

> **check for comma:** The cat had pale blue eyes. (Do you need the comma? Reverse the order of the adjectives.)
> **reverse order:** The cat had blue pale eyes. (Does the sentence still make sense? No. You don't need a comma.)
> **correct sentence:** The cat had pale blue eyes.

You can use test 1 or test 2 to determine whether you need a comma between adjectives.

Exercise 8

Connect

Editing for Errors in Adjectives and Adverbs

Edit the following paragraph, correcting all the errors in the use of adjectives and adverbs. Write your corrections above the errors. There are eight errors.

Last night I became a hero. Well, I wasn't exactly a great hero, but I was

most heroic then most people in similar circumstances would be. It all

began at 1:00 A.M. when I was driving on a narrow stretch of highway. There

weren't many cars on the road. Suddenly, I heard a sound like metal being

torn apart. The noise didn't sound well. While the other cars on the road

sped on, I stopped on the shoulder of the road. It was dark, but I could hear

a faint, whining sound in the distance. I moved toward the sound and saw a

car that had been smashed into flat, jagged pieces of metal and glass. The

sound came from the driver of the car, who had managed to crawl out of the

wreck. He was alone and cut bad; he needed help. I ran the most fastest I've

ever run to get my cell phone out of my car. After I called the emergency

number to get help, I went back to the injured man and prayed the crisis

would end good. It did—the ambulance came quickly. Later, I was real glad

to hear the driver was going to be all right.

CHAPTER 21

Correcting Problems with Modifiers

Modifiers are words, phrases, or clauses that describe (modify) something in a sentence. All the underlined words, phrases, and clauses below are modifiers:

> the *blue* van (word)
> the van *in the garage* (phrase)
> the van *that she bought* (clause)

> *foreign* tourists (word)
> tourists *coming to Florida* (phrase)
> tourists *who visit the state* (clause)

Sometimes modifiers limit another word. They make another word (or words) more specific.

> the girl *in the corner* (tells exactly which girl)
> *fifty* acres (tells exactly how many acres)
> the movie *that I liked best* (tells which movie)
> He *never* calls. (tells how often)

Exercise 1

Practice

Recognizing Modifiers

In each sentence below, underline the modifiers (words, phrases, or clauses) that describe the italicized word or phrase.

1. The *refrigerator* with the ice maker costs too much.

2. The security officer noticed a *man* carrying a bulging suitcase.

3. A lifeguard rescued the *swimmer* trapped in the undercurrent.

4. *The students* studying in the library shared their class notes.

5. Lori and Sonny brought a birthday *cake.*

6. I bought a creaky kitchen room *table* and repaired it.

7. Dancing around the room, *the children* expressed their happiness.

8. The tiny *box* tied with gold ribbon contained a surprise.

9. Swooping down toward my face, *the bat* frightened me.

10. A talented young *singer* with an appealing personality got the part in the movie.

CORRECTING MODIFIER PROBLEMS

Modifiers can make your writing more specific and more concrete. Used effectively and correctly, modifiers give the reader a clear, exact picture of what you want to say, and they help you to say it precisely. But modifiers have to be used correctly. You can check for errors with modifiers as you revise your sentences.

Info BOX

Three Steps in Checking for Sentence Errors with Modifiers

Step 1: Find the modifier.

Step 2: Ask, "Does the modifier have something to modify?"

Step 3: Ask, "Is the modifier in the right place, as close as possible to the word, phrase, or clause it modifies?"

If you answer no in either step 2 or step 3, you need to revise your sentence. Let's use the steps in the following example:

sample sentence: I saw a girl driving a Mazda wearing a bikini.

Step 1: Find the modifier. The modifiers are *driving a Mazda,* and *wearing a bikini.*

Step 2: Ask, "Does the modifier have something to modify?" The answer is yes. The girl is driving a Mazda. The girl is wearing a bikini. Both modifiers go with *a girl.*

Step 3: Ask, "Is the modifier in the right place?" The answer is yes and no. One modifier is in the right place:

I saw *a girl driving a Mazda*

The other modifier is *not* in the right place:

a Mazda wearing a bikini

The Mazda is not wearing a bikini.

revised: I saw a girl *wearing a bikini and driving a Mazda.*

Let's work through the steps once more:

> **sample sentence:** Scampering through the forest, the hunters saw two rabbits.

> **Step 1:** Find the modifier. The modifiers are *Scampering through the forest* and *two*.
> **Step 2:** Ask, "Does the modifier have something to modify?" The answer is yes. There are two rabbits. The rabbits are scampering through the forest. Both modifiers go with *rabbits*.
> **Step 3:** Ask, "Is the modifier in the right place?" The answer is yes and no. The word *two* is in the right place:

> > *two* rabbits

But *scampering through the forest* is in the wrong place:

> > *Scampering through the forest*, the hunters

The hunters are not scampering through the forest. The rabbits are.

> > **revised:** The hunters saw two rabbits *scampering through the forest*.

Caution: Be sure to put words like *almost, even, exactly, hardly, just, merely, nearly, only, scarcely,* and *simply* as close as possible to what they modify. If you put them in the wrong place, you may write a confusing sentence.

> **sample sentence:** Etienne only wants to grow carrots and zucchini. (The modifier that creates confusion here is *only*. Does Etienne have only one goal in life—to grow carrots and zucchini? Or are these the only vegetables he wants to grow? To create a clearer sentence, move the modifier.)
> **revised:** Etienne wants to grow *only* carrots and zucchini.

The examples you have just worked with show one common error in using modifiers. This error involves **misplaced modifiers,** words that describe something but are not where they should be in the sentence. Here is the rule to remember:

> **Put a modifier as close as possible to the word, phrase, or clause it modifies.**

Exercise 2

Practice

Correcting Sentences with Misplaced Modifiers

Some of the following sentences contain misplaced modifiers. Revise any sentence that has a misplaced modifier by putting the modifier as close as possible to whatever it modifies.

> **1.** Wedged between the cushions of the sofa, I saw my lost wallet.
>
> revised: _____
>
> _____
>
> **2.** Cindy nearly jogged for thirty minutes in the afternoon.
>
> revised: _____
>
> _____

3. If I major in accounting, I only need one history course.

revised: _____

_____

4. Fresh from the oven, I tasted the cookies.

revised: _____

_____

5. Struck by lightning, the old tree split in two.

revised: _____

_____

6. On her vacation, she wants to read only entertaining books.

revised: _____

_____

7. Dipped in chocolate, he was sure the strawberries would taste delicious.

revised: _____

_____

8. Andrew and Carl saw a fox and a raccoon on their way to the airport.

revised: _____

_____

9. I donated the gifts to a local charity that I couldn't use.

revised: _____

_____

10. The city has a famous zoo where my father was born.

revised: _____

_____

Correcting Dangling Modifiers

The three steps for correcting modifier problems can help you recognize another kind of error. Let's use the steps to check the following sentence.

sample sentence: Strolling through the tropical paradise, many colorful birds could be seen.

Step 1: Find the modifier. The modifiers are *Strolling through the tropical paradise* and *many colorful*.

Step 2: Ask, "Does the modifier have something to modify?" The answer is yes and no. The words *many* and *colorful* modify birds. But who or what is *strolling through the tropical paradise*? There is no person mentioned in this sentence. The birds are not strolling.

This kind of error is called a **dangling modifier.** It means that the modifier does not have anything to modify; it just dangles in the sentence. To correct this kind of error, you cannot just move the modifier:

still incorrect: Many colorful birds could be seen strolling through the tropical paradise. (There is still no person strolling.)

The way to correct this kind of error is to add something to the sentence. If you gave the modifier something to modify, you might come up with several different revised sentences:

As I strolled through the tropical paradise, I saw many colorful birds.

or

Many colorful birds could be seen *when we were strolling through the tropical paradise.*

or

While the tourists strolled through the tropical paradise, they saw many colorful birds.

Try the process for correcting dangling modifiers once more:

sample sentence: Ascending in the glass elevator, the hotel lobby glittered in the light.

Step 1: Find the modifier. The modifiers are *Ascending in the glass elevator* and *hotel.*

Step 2: Ask, "Does the modifier have anything to modify?" The answer is yes and no. The word *hotel* modifies lobby, but *ascending in the glass elevator* doesn't modify anything. Who is ascending in the elevator? There is nobody mentioned in the sentence.

To revise this sentence, put somebody or something in it for the modifier to describe:

As the guests ascended in the glass elevator, the hotel lobby glittered in the light.

or

Ascending in the glass elevator, she saw the hotel lobby glitter in the light.

Remember that you cannot correct a dangling modifier just by moving the modifier. You have to give the modifier something to modify; you have to add something to the sentence.

Exercise 3

Practice

Correcting Sentences with Dangling Modifiers

Some of the following sentences use modifiers correctly, but some have dangling modifiers. Revise the sentences with dangling modifiers by adding words or changing words.

1. Sitting by the fire and telling ghost stories, a strange feeling seeped into the atmosphere.

   revised: _____

   _____

2. While taking a shower, the doorbell rang.

   revised: _____

   _____

3. At the age of four, my mother had my baby brother.

   revised: _____

   _____

4. Without a good background in mathematics, a college algebra course can be difficult.

   revised: _____

   _____

5. Lying awake in the dark all night, her plan was slowly formed.

   revised: _____

   _____

6. Lost in the blizzard, we could not see our lighted cabin.

   revised: _____

   _____

7. Having run out of time, George's paper was never finished.

   revised: _____

   _____

8. To rent that apartment, a two months' rent deposit is required.

   revised: _____

   _____

9. Feeling confident about the job interview, Beverly made a good impression.

revised: _____

_____

10. When troubled by a difficult decision, the advice of a trusted friend can help.

revised: _____

_____

REVIEWING THE STEPS AND THE SOLUTIONS

It is important to recognize problems with modifiers and to correct these problems. Modifier problems can result in confusing or even silly sentences. And when you confuse or unintentionally amuse your reader, you are not making your point.

Remember to check for modifier problems in three steps, then correct each kind of problem in the appropriate way.

Info BOX

A Summary of Modifier Problems

Checking for Modifier Problems

Step 1: Find the modifier.
Step 2: Ask, "Does the modifier have something to modify?"
Step 3: Ask, "Is the modifier in the right place?"

Correcting Modifier Problems
If the modifier is in the wrong place (a misplaced modifier), put it as close as possible to the word, phrase, or clause it modifies.
If the modifier has nothing to modify (a dangling modifier), add or change words so that it has something to modify.

Exercise 4

Practice

Revising Sentences with Modifier Problems
The following sentences have modifier problems. Write a new, correct sentence for each one. You may move words, add words, change words, or remove words. The first one is done for you.

1. Stopping suddenly, the box with the cake in it fell from the seat of the car.

revised: When I had to stop suddenly, the box with the cake in it fell

from the seat of the car.

2. Having discussed the details all morning, the plan for the new town hall was finally accepted.

revised: _____

_____

3. Caught putting a frog in the bathtub, the mother disciplined the child.

revised: _____

_____

4. The old farm truck bounced down the bumpy roads loaded with fresh vegetables.

revised: _____

_____

5. After digging up gardens all over the block, the neighbors were angry enough to complain to the dog's owner.

revised: _____

_____

6. Slathered in hot butter, Peter offered the popcorn to his friend.

revised: _____

_____

7. Because she was late for class, Sarah almost missed all the notes.

revised: _____

_____

8. Before buying a house, enough money for a down payment has to be saved.

revised: _____

_____

9. I could see the wildfire burning from my bedroom window.

revised: _____

_____

10. When working with small children, imagination and enthusiasm are definite assets.

revised: _____

_____

Exercise 5

◎◎ *Connect*

Editing a Paragraph for Modifier Problems

Correct any errors with modifiers in the following paragraph. There are four errors. Write your corrections above the line.

When entering a new school, it is difficult to make new friends. If the school is a college, the process can be especially hard. Colleges have students of all ages, and new students may think they can only see a few people of their own age. Everyone else may look much younger or older. College also seems to be a more serious place than high school, so students may feel shy about starting a conversation. Standing alone in the hall before class, nervousness paralyzes a newcomer. It may seem as if everyone else has a close friend to talk to. Then, when the newcomer starts to meet one or two people, another problem arises. A new student, may hesitate before giving a phone number or e-mail address to a classmate fearing too much intimacy too soon. Fortunately, time passes, and new students become a part of school and of new friendships.

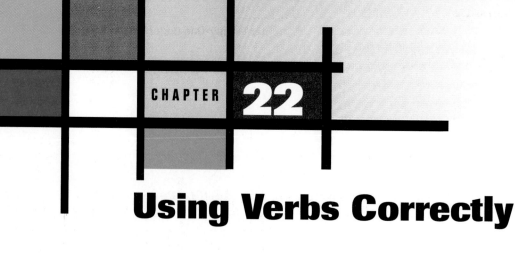

CHAPTER 22

Using Verbs Correctly

Verbs are words that show some kind of action or being. These verbs show action or being:

> verb
> He *runs* to the park.

> verb
> Melanie *is* my best friend.

> verb
> The pizza *tastes* delicious.

Verbs also tell about time.

> He *will run* to the park. (The time is future.)
> Melanie *was* my best friend. (The time is past.)
> The pizza *tastes* delicious. (The time is present.)

The time of a verb is called its *tense*. You can say a verb is in the *present tense*, *future tense*, or many other tenses.

Using verbs correctly involves knowing which form of the verb to use, choosing the right verb tense, and being consistent in verb tense.

USING STANDARD VERB FORMS

Many people use nonstandard verb forms in everyday conversation. But everyone who wants to write and speak effectively should know different levels of language, from the slang and dialect of everyday conversation to the **standard English** of college, business, and professional environments.

In everyday conversation, you may use **nonstandard forms** like these:

I goes	he don't	we was
you was	it don't	she smile
you be	I be	they walks

480   But these are not correct forms in standard English.

THE PRESENT TENSE

Look at the standard verb forms for the present tense of the word *listen:*

verb: listen

I listen	we listen
you listen	you listen
he, she, it listens	they listen

Take a closer look at the standard verb forms. Only one form is different:

he, she, it *listens*

This is the only form that ends in *s* in the present tense.

Info BOX

In the present tense, use an -<u>s</u> or -<u>es</u> ending on the verb only when the subject is <u>he</u>, <u>she</u>, or <u>it</u> or the equivalent.

He calls his mother every day.
She chases the cat away from the birdcage.
It runs like a new car.

Jim calls his mother every day.
Samantha chases the cat away from the birdcage.
The jalopy runs like a new car.

Take another look at the present tense. If the verb is a standard verb, it will follow this form in the present tense:

I attend every lecture.
You care about the truth.
He visits his grandfather regularly.
She drives a new car.
The new album *sounds* great.
We follow that team.
You work well when you both compromise.
They buy the store brand of cereal.

Exercise 1

Practice

Picking the Correct Verb in the Present Tense

Underline the subject and circle the correct form of the verb in parentheses in each sentence below.

1. A ticket in the front row (cost, costs) more than one in the balcony.

2. On rainy days I (sell, sells) many umbrellas.

3. Winning at chess (demand, demands) all your concentration.

4. The garage at the back of my house (need, needs) a coat of paint.

5. He sometimes (sleep, sleeps) through the loudest alarm clock.

6. Leonard (dislike, dislikes) cookies with raisins in them.

7. In the tree by patio (live, lives) a bird with yellow feathers.

8. Without a trace of fear, Sheila and Frank (explore, explores) shark-infested waters.

9. It (taste, tastes) like chicken.

10. Sympathy (motivate, motivates) people to perform acts of kindness.

Exercise 2

Practice

More on Picking the Correct Verb in the Present Tense

Underline the subject and circle the correct form of the verb in parentheses in each sentence below.

1. On warm days, our cat (doze, dozes) on the patio.

2. You (talk, talks) about yourself too much.

3. The chief of detectives (drive, drives) an unmarked car.

4. A clean house (make, makes) a good impression.

5. Behind the skyscrapers (sit, sits) a small stone house.

6. The towels with the green stripes (match, matches) our shower curtain.

7. Every Saturday night, they (rent, rents) an old horror movie.

8. Humor (get, gets) people through tough situations.

9. A representative of the student government (attend, attends) the conference.

10. At that price, it (sound, sounds) like a bargain.

THE PAST TENSE

The past tense of most verbs is formed by adding *-d* or *-ed* to the verb.

verb: listen
I listened	we listened
you listened	you listened
he, she, it listened	they listened

Add *-ed* to *listen* to form the past tense. For some other verbs, you may add *-d*.

The sun *faded* from the sky.
He *quaked* with fear.
She *crumpled* the paper into a ball.

Exercise 3	**Writing the Correct Verb Forms of Past Tense**

Practice

Write the correct past tense form of each verb in parentheses in each sentence below.

1. Last night, Dr. Patel _____ (call) me from the hospital.

2. My favorite Mexican restaurant _____ (close) last week.

3. The tornado _____ (move) dangerously close to my house.

4. In his teen years, Sean _____ (impress) me with his ambition.

5. My mother _____ (volunteer) at a soup kitchen for three years.

6. Yesterday, the actors _____ (rehearse) the first act of the play.

7. The old raincoat _____ (last) through hundreds of storms.

8. Three years ago, the marriage _____ (end) in divorce.

9. In fifth grade, I _____ (annoy) my older sister all the time.

10. You _____ (answer) my question with a nasty remark.

THE FOUR MAIN FORMS OF A VERB: PRESENT, PAST, PRESENT PARTICIPLE, AND PAST PARTICIPLE

When you are deciding what form of a verb to use, you will probably rely on one of four forms: the present tense, the past tense, the present participle, and the past participle. Most of the time, you will use one of these forms or add a helping verb to it. As an example, look at the four main forms of the verb, *listen:*

Present	**Past**	**Present Participle**	**Past Participle**
listen	listened	listening	listened

You use the four verb forms—present, past, present participle, and past participle—alone or with helping verbs to express time (tense). Forms of regular verbs like *listen* are very easy to remember. Use the present form for the present tense:

We *listen* to the news on the radio.

The past form expresses past tense:

I *listened* to language tapes for three hours yesterday.

The present participle, or *-ing* form, is used with helping verbs:

He *was listening* to me.
I *am listening* to you.
You *should have been listening* more carefully.

The past participle is the form used with the helping verbs *have*, *has*, or *had*:

I *have listened* for hours.
She *has listened* to the tape.
We *had listened* to the tape before we bought it.

Of course, you can add many helping verbs to the present tense:

present tense:
We *listen* to the news on the car radio.

add helping verbs:
We *will* listen to the news on the car radio.
We *should* listen to the news on the car radio.
We *can* listen to the news on the car radio.

When a verb is regular, the past form is created by adding *-d* or *-ed* to the present form. The present participle is formed by adding *-ing* to the present form, and the past participle form is the same as the past form.

IRREGULAR VERBS

Irregular verbs do not follow the same rules for creating verb forms that regular verbs do. Three verbs that we use all the time—*be, have, do*—are irregular verbs. You need to study them closely. Look at the present tense forms for all three, and compare the standard present tense forms to the nonstandard ones. *Remember to use the standard forms for college or professional writing.*

verb: be

Nonstandard	Standard
I be or I is	I am
you be	you are
he, she, it be	he, she, it is
we be	we are
you be	you are
they be	they are

verb: have

Nonstandard	Standard
I has	I have
you has	you have
he, she, it have	he, she, it has
we has	we have
you has	you have
they has	they have

verb: do

Nonstandard	Standard
I does	I do
you does	you do
he, she, it do	he, she, it does
we does	we do
you does	you do
they does	they do

Caution: Be careful when you add *not* to *does*. If you are writing a contraction of *does not*, be sure you write *doesn't*, not *don't*.

not this: The light don't work.
but this: The light doesn't work.

Exercise 4

Practice

Choosing the Correct Form of *be, have,* or *do* in the Present Tense

Circle the correct form of the verb in parentheses in each sentence below.

1. Most of the time, I (is, am) a fast runner.

2. On a sunny day, he (has, have) no excuse for staying indoors.

3. That discount store (don't, doesn't) have a children's department.

4. In an emergency, it (be, is) wrong to refuse to help.

5. When she speaks, she (has, have) a slight Jamaican accent.

6. Every weekend, Sammy and Dana (do, does) the yard work.

7. Parents of small children (has, have) many responsibilities.

8. If lightning is nearby, we (be, are) extra careful about staying inside.

9. You (do, does) the best work in the department.

10. The ants (be, are) coming in through an open window.

Exercise 5

Practice

More on Choosing the Correct Form of *be, have,* or *do* in the Present Tense

Circle the correct form of the verb in parentheses in each sentence below.

1. Consequently, her son (do, does) nothing about the arguments.

2. Today I (be, am) the youngest member of the football team.

3. Lamont (has, have) nothing but praise for his boss.

4. Regular exercise is important; it (do, does) affect your health.

5. Even though you pretend to be carefree, you (do, does) too much worrying.

6. Most of the time, a paperback book (doesn't, don't) cost as much as a hardcover book.

7. At New Year's, we (has, have) a traditional meal.

8. My shoelaces (be, are) too long; I keep tripping on them.

9. The new gym (has, have) great air conditioning.

10. If you (has, have) a student ID, you can get a discount.

The Past Tense of *be, have, do*

The past forms of these irregular verbs can be confusing. Again, compare the nonstandard forms to the standard forms. *Remember to use the standard forms for college or professional writing.*

verb: be

Nonstandard	Standard
I were	I was
you was	you were
he, she, it were	he, she, it was
we was	we were
you was	you were
they was	they were

verb: have

Nonstandard	Standard
I has	I had
you has	you had
he, she, it have	he, she, it had
we has	we had
you has	you had
they has	they had

verb: do

Nonstandard	Standard
I done	I did
you done	you did
he, she, it done	he, she, it did
we done	we did
you done	you did
they done	they did

Exercise 6

Practice

Choosing the Correct Form of *be, have,* or *do* in the Past Tense

Circle the correct verb form in parentheses each sentence below.

1. The top of the table (was, were) cracked and dirty.

2. The professor from Washington (done, did) an interesting presentation on the census.

3. Although it lost two key players to injuries, the team (has, had) a good year.

4. Yesterday at noon, we (was, were) at my son's soccer game.

5. Last month, I (has, had) a bad case of the flu.

6. At seven, Courtney (was, were) already acting in television commercials.

7. Without expecting any payment, the strangers (done, did) a favor for the stranded motorists.

8. A week ago, I (was, were) hoping for a good grade in my algebra class.

9. In high school, you (was, were) my partner in biology lab.

10. My training in CPR (done did) a good job of preparing me for work as a lifeguard.

 Exercise 7

Practice

More on Choosing the Correct Form of *be, have,* or *do* in the Past Tense

Circle the correct form of the verb in parentheses in each sentence below.

1. Lorenzo and I (was, were) once in love with the same woman.

2. Last winter, my sister (have, had) an encounter with a baby bear.

3. I learned Portuguese when I (was, were) a student in Brazil.

4. Brendan (done, did) what he could to help his parents find a place to live.

5. We (was, were) minding our own business when the robbery occurred.

6. Last month, my cousin Lewis (have, had) a job interview with the parks department.

7. Yesterday, you and I (was, were) calm and confident.

8. After the car accident, Monique (have, had) to fill out a statement for the police.

9. I have the evening free because I (done, did) the laundry and the ironing yesterday.

10. The student lounge at the college (have, had) comfortable chairs.

More Irregular Verb Forms

Be, have, and *do* are not the only verbs with irregular forms. There are many such verbs, and everybody who writes uses some form of an irregular verb. When you write and you are not certain if you are using the correct form of a verb, check the list of irregular verbs on pages 488 and 489.

For each irregular verb listed, the *present,* the *past,* and the *past participle* forms are given. The present participle isn't included because it is always formed by adding *-ing* to the present form.

Irregular Verb Forms

Present	Past	Past Participle
(Today I *arise*.)	(Yesterday I *arose*.)	(I have/had *arisen*.)
arise	arose	arisen
awake	awoke, awaked	awoken, awaked
bear	bore	born, borne
beat	beat	beaten
become	became	become
begin	began	begun
bend	bent	bent
bite	bit	bitten
bleed	bled	bled
blow	blew	blown
break	broke	broken
bring	brought	brought
build	built	built
burst	burst	burst
buy	bought	bought
catch	caught	caught
choose	chose	chosen
come	came	come
cling	clung	clung
cost	cost	cost
creep	crept	crept
cut	cut	cut
deal	dealt	dealt
draw	drew	drawn
dream	dreamed, dreamt	dreamed, dreamt
drink	drank	drunk
drive	drove	driven
eat	ate	eaten
fall	fell	fallen
feed	fed	fed
feel	felt	felt
fight	fought	fought
find	found	found
fling	flung	flung
fly	flew	flown
freeze	froze	frozen
get	got	got, gotten
give	gave	given
go	went	gone
grow	grew	grown
hear	heard	heard
hide	hid	hidden
hit	hit	hit
hold	held	held
hurt	hurt	hurt
keep	kept	kept
know	knew	known
lay (means to put)	laid	laid

Present	**Past**	**Past Participle**
lead	led	led
leave	left	left
lend	lent	lent
let	let	let
lie (means to recline)	lay	lain
light	lit, lighted	lit, lighted
lose	lost	lost
make	made	made
mean	meant	meant
meet	met	met
pay	paid	paid
prove	proved	proved, proven
ride	rode	ridden
ring	rang	rung
rise	rose	risen
run	ran	run
say	said	said
see	saw	seen
sell	sold	sold
send	sent	sent
sew	sewed	sewn, sewed
shake	shook	shaken
shine	shone, shined	shone, shined
shrink	shrank	shrunk
shut	shut	shut
sing	sang	sung
sit	sat	sat
sleep	slept	slept
slide	slid	slid
sling	slung	slung
speak	spoke	spoken
spend	spent	spent
stand	stood	stood
steal	stole	stolen
stick	stuck	stuck
sting	stung	stung
stink	stank, stunk	stunk
string	strung	strung
swear	swore	sworn
swim	swam	swum
teach	taught	taught
tear	tore	torn
tell	told	told
think	thought	thought
throw	threw	thrown
wake	woke, waked	woken, waked
wear	wore	worn
win	won	won
write	wrote	written

Exercise 8

Practice

Choosing the Correct Form of Irregular Verbs

Write the correct form of the verb in parentheses in each sentences below. Be sure to check the list of irregular verbs.

1. We looked for the stolen necklace, but the thief had _____ (hide) it too well.

2. I should have _____ (know) about the surprise party; my boyfriend gave quite a few hints.

3. Mrs. O'Neill _____ (string) colored lights across the front of the restaurant.

4. I tried to help the toddler open his birthday presents, but he had already _____ (tear) the brightly colored wrapping into shreds.

5. He said he wouldn't accept the job, and he _____ (mean) what he said.

6. Last week, my parents _____ (lend) me the money for my first month's rent.

7. Over the weekend, Andy got a sunburn because he _____ (lie) in the sun too long.

8. The western ranch scared Cody because he had never _____ (ride) a horse before.

9. Sally took the report card and _____ (fling) it into the lake.

10. Luke called me to see the enormous bubble, but before I got there, it had _____ (burst).

11. When my aunt came back from India, she _____ (bring) me some beautiful silk fabric.

12. For years, Mr. Kowolski _____ (teach) tennis at the city tennis center.

13. Yesterday I _____ (lay) out all the items for the garage sale.

14. For years, I have _____ (dream) of a long, dark hall.

15. After the mysterious woman opened the door, she _____ (lead) me to a small room.

16. I could have _____ (swear) the door was locked.

17. Keith was in a great deal of pain, but he _____ (bear) his pain without complaining.

18. Someone had _____(stick) a note in my lunch box.

19. The committee has _____(tell) us its decision and will not change it.

20. Dennis has often _____(think) of going back to school.

Exercise 9   **Writing Sentences with Correct Verb Forms**

👥 *Collaborate*

Working with a partner or a group, write two sentences that correctly use each of the verb forms below. In writing these sentences, you may add helping verbs to the verb forms, but do not change the verb form itself. The first one is done for you.

1. sent

   a. _He sent her a dozen roses on Valentine's Day._

   b. _I have sent him all the information he needs._

2. swum

   a. _____

   b. _____

3. shrunk

   a. _____

   b. _____

4. drawn

   a. _____

   b. _____

5. stunk

   a. _____

   b. _____

6. lain

   a. _____

   b. _____

7. crept

   a. _____

   b. _____

8. proven

a. _____

b. _____

9. became

a. _____

b. _____

10. eaten

a. _____

b. _____

Exercise 10

Connect

Editing a Paragraph for Correct Verb Forms

Correct the errors in verb forms in the following paragraph. There are seven errors.

My responsibilities at home often interferes with my responsibilities at school. I am not a parent, but I live with my parents and my two younger brothers. Because my mother and father work full time, they turn to me when they has a family emergency. Last week, my five-year-old brother was sick and feverish. My mother thought he had catched a cold and wanted to keep him out of school. That meant I had to stay out of school, too. I missed a quiz in my English class because I was stuck in the house with my sick brother. Something similar happened yesterday. My father's car breaked down on the highway, so he called me at school on my cell phone. He needed help, so I leaved my math class and picked him up on the road. Some students skip class because they have sleeped through the alarm or spent all night at a party, but I miss class because I be busy with my family.

CHAPTER 23

More on Verbs: Consistency and Voice

Remember that your choice of verb form indicates the time (tense) of your statements. Be careful not to shift from one tense to another unless you have a reason to change the time.

CONSISTENT VERB TENSES

Staying in one tense (unless you have a reason to change tenses) is called **consistency of verb tense.**

incorrect shifts in tense:

The waitress *ran* to the kitchen with the order in her hand, *raced* back to her customers with glasses of water, and *smiles* calmly.
He *grins* at me from the ticket booth and *closed* the ticket window.

You can correct these errors by putting all the verbs in the same tense.

consistent present tense:

The waitress *runs* to the kitchen with the order in her hand, *races* back to her customers with glasses of water, and *smiles* calmly.
He *grins* at me from the ticket booth and *closes* the ticket window.

consistent past tense:

The waitress *ran* to the kitchen with the order in her hand, *raced* back to her customers with glasses of water, and *smiled* calmly.
He *grinned* at me from the ticket booth and *closed* the ticket window.

Whether you correct by changing all the verbs to the present tense or by changing them to the past tense, you are making the tenses consistent. Consistency of tense is important in the events you are describing because it helps the reader understand what happened and when it happened.

Practice

Correcting Sentences That Are Inconsistent in Tense

In each sentence following, one verb is inconsistent in tense. Cross it out and write the correct tense above it.

1. Every Saturday I change the sheets on my bed and the towels in my bathroom; then I went to the laundromat to wash the dirty items.

2. In an interview, the star of the film talked about the special effects and explained the stunt work, but she never mentions her costars.

3. Whenever Isabel has a chance, she spends some time at the beach or relaxes in the backyard because she loved the outdoors and enjoys nature.

4. Sometimes I get five or six calls a day, but at other times, my phone rang a dozen times an hour, especially when I am too busy to answer it.

5. The football coach pushed the players through a long, sweltering practice yesterday; consequently, one of the players passes out and wound up in the hospital.

6. My husband pulled strange pieces of metal from the box as he tried to assemble the tricycle; meanwhile, I struggle with the complex directions.

7. Whenever the first snow falls, my aunt makes cocoa and cookies and invited all the neighborhood children.

8. Since the movie was a blockbuster, we come an hour early and got the best seats.

9. Dealing with unhappy customers is difficult for me because I am not allowed to refund their money, and they got angry when they learn this policy.

10. Although Vincent says he studies every day, he never had a book when I see him at school or at home.

Editing Paragraphs for Consistency of Tenses

Connect

Read the following paragraphs. Then cross out any verbs that are inconsistent in tense and write the corrections above. There are four errors in the first paragraph and four errors in the second.

1. My first dinner with my girlfriend's parents was a disaster. I arrived in a dress shirt and tie, but everyone else is wearing shorts and tee shirts. When we sit down to eat, I sat in her father's place and had to move. Then I couldn't think of a word to say, and when I finally did speak, I spoke with my mouth full. Worst of all, I was so nervous that I ate everything on my plate very quickly. I finish my dinner thirty minutes before the rest of the group. I felt like a starving animal that had gobbled its food. I want to crawl under the table.

2. The people in line for concert tickets turned the long wait into an event. People began lining up twenty hours before the ticket booth opened. Some brought lawn chairs or sleeping bags. Everyone brought food and bottles of water. At first everyone is quiet, but as the line grew longer, strangers began to open up. Some hold other people's place in line. Some began to play CDs. Then people began talking about music or how much they wanted to see the concert. Soon people were sharing their food, swapping tapes and CDs, telling jokes, and playing cards. There is an atmosphere of cheerful excitement as time passes. No one got much sleep. By the time the ticket window opened, most people seemed like old friends.

Writing a Paragraph with Consistent Verb Tenses

Collaborate

The paragraph following on page 496 shifts between past and present tenses. Working with a group, write two versions of the paragraph, one in the present tense and one in the past tense. Half the group may write the paragraph in one tense while the other half writes it in the other tense. After both rewrites are complete, read the new paragraph aloud to the whole group.

The day starts off well, but it doesn't end that way. At first, I am confident about taking my driving test and getting my driver's license. Then I got into the car with the examiner and wait for him to tell me to start. When he does, I turned the key in the ignition and slowly pull out of the parking lot. For some rerason, I am sweating with fear, but I tried not to show it. I managed to drive without hitting another car. I remember to stop at a stop sign. But when it came to parallel parking, I knocked down all those orange markers! My driving examiner never cracks a smile or even talked to me. He just gives instructions. But I knew what he was thinking, and I know I won't get a license. I feel like the worst driver in the world.

Paragraph Revised for Consistent Tenses:

_____

_____

_____

_____

_____

_____

_____

_____

_____

_____

_____

_____

_____

_____

_____

_____

THE PRESENT PERFECT TENSE

When you are choosing the right verb tense, you should know about two verb tenses, the present perfect and the past perfect, that can make your meaning clear.

The **present perfect tense** is made up of the past participle form of the verb plus *have* or *has* as a helping verb. Use this tense to show an action that started in the past but is still going on in the present.

> **past tense:** My father *drove* a truck for five months. (He doesn't drive a truck any more, but he did drive one in the past.)
> **present perfect tense:** My father *has driven* a truck for five months. (He started driving a truck five months ago; he is still driving a truck.)
>
> **past tense:** For years, I *studied* ballet. (I don't study ballet now; I used to.)
> **present perfect tense:** For years, I *have studied* ballet. (I still study ballet.)

Remember, use the present perfect tense to show that an action started in the past and is still going on.

Practice

Distinguishing Between the Past Tense and the Present Perfect Tense

Circle the correct verb in parentheses in each sentence below. Be sure to look carefully at the meaning of the sentences.

1. Last night Brad (called , has called) me about the rumor.

2. We (volunteered, have volunteered) at the animal shelter for many years now.

3. My arthritis (was, has been) bothering me, but I don't want to go to the doctor.

4. Yesterday I set the table and (cooked, have cooked) the dinner.

5. The two actors (starred, have starred) in the play for a year and are still playing to large audiences every night.

6. Two of the coaches (were, have been) players on professional teams but left as a result of injuries.

7. The restaurant (was, has been) offering the special dinner for months now.

8. While Jeanne was recovering from the accident, she (remembered, has remembered) the events leading to it.

9. Charles (interviewed , has interviewed) ten applicants for the job and hired the one who spoke the most intelligently.

10. Maureen (accepted, has accepted) the position two weeks ago.

THE PAST PERFECT TENSE

The **past perfect tense** is made up of the past participle form of the verb and *had* as a helping verb. You can use the past perfect tense to show more than one event in the past—that is, when two or more things happened in the past but at different times.

> **past tense:** He *washed* the dishes.
> **past perfect tense:** He *had washed* the dishes by the time I came home. (He washed the dishes before I came home. Both actions happened in the past, but one happened earlier than the other.)

> **past tense:** Susan *waited* for an hour.
> **past perfect tense:** Susan *had waited* for an hour when she gave up on him. (Waiting came first; giving up came second. Both actions are in the past.)

The past perfect tense is especially useful because you write most of your essays in the past tense, and you often need to get farther back into the past. Remember, to form the past perfect tense, use *had* with the past participle of the verb.

 Exercise 5

Practice

Distinguishing Between the Past Tense and the Past Perfect Tense

Circle the correct verb in parentheses in each sentence below. Be sure to look carefully at the meaning of the sentences.

1. Yesterday I asked my dentist to look at a tooth I (chipped, had chipped) a week ago.

2. Bernie got soaked last night because he forgot he (gave, had given) his umbrella to his daughter.

3. Everyone (ate, had eaten) all the good desserts by the time I arrived.

4. Don and I visited an old cabin that (sheltered, had sheltered) soldiers in the Civil War.

5. My mother asked whether I (cleaned, had cleaned) my room yet.

6. As the airline passengers (shoved, had shoved) their luggage into the overhead compartments, they dreamed of more spacious airplanes.

7. Late shoppers found that the early birds (took, had taken) all the best bargains.

8. She (wrapped, had wrapped) the gift in silver paper and tied it with a silver bow.

9. My father was not sure whether my brother (borrowed, had borrowed) the truck earlier that morning.

10. Mike (completed, had completed) the project before Diane offered to help with it.

PASSIVE AND ACTIVE VOICE

Verbs not only have tenses, but they also have voices. When the subject in the sentence is doing something, the verb is in the **active voice.** When something is done to the subject, when it receives the action of the verb, the verb is in the **passive voice.**

> **active voice:**
>
> I painted the house. (*I*, the subject, did it.)
> The people on the corner made a donation to the emergency fund. (The *people*, the subject, did it.)

> **passive voice:**
>
> The house was painted by me. (The *house*, the subject, didn't do anything. It received the action—it was painted.)
> A donation to the emergency fund was made by the people on the corner. (The *donation*, the subject, didn't do anything. It received the action—it was given.)

Notice what happens when you use the passive voice instead of the active:

> **active voice:** I painted the house.
> **passive voice:** The house was painted by me.

The sentence in the passive voice is two words longer than the one in the active voice. Yet the sentence that uses the passive voice does not say anything different, and it does not say it more clearly than the one in the active voice.

Using the passive voice can make your sentences wordy, it can slow them down, and it can make them boring. The passive voice can also confuse readers. When the subject of the sentence is not doing anything, readers may have to look carefully to see who or what *is* doing something. Look at this sentence:

> A decision to fire you was reached.

Who decided to fire you? In this sentence, it is hard to find the answer to that question.

Of course, there will be times when you have to use the passive voice. For example, you may have to use it when you do not know who did something:

> Our house was broken into last night.
> A leather jacket was left behind in the classroom.

But in general, you should avoid using the passive voice and rewrite sentences so they are in the active voice.

  Rewriting Sentences, Changing the Passive Voice to the Active Voice

Practice

In the following sentences, change the passive voice to the active voice. If the original sentence does not tell you who or what performed the action, add words that tell who or what did it. An example is done for you.

example: Sandy Adams was appointed chief negotiator last night.

rewritten: The union leaders appointed Sandy Adams chief negotiator

last night.

1. The famous bank robber was caught in Wichita yesterday.

rewritten: _____

_____

2. An agreement has been signed by the high school coaches.

rewritten: _____

_____

3. An attempt to contact the owner was made last night.

rewritten: _____

_____

4. At last, a motel was found by the weary travelers.

rewritten: _____

_____

5. Every effort is being made to locate your missing luggage.

rewritten: _____

_____

6. Finally, the winners of the contest were announced by the judge.

rewritten: _____

_____

7. Once a month, the trees and bushes are trimmed by a landscaping service.

rewritten: _____

_____

8. Those beautiful fabrics are designed by a group of Guatemalan artists.

rewritten: _____

_____

9. The truth about Aaron's accident is not known by his mother.

rewritten: _____

_____

10. The strange disease is being studied by medical authorities.

rewritten: _____

_____

Avoiding Unnecessary Shifts in Voice

Just as you should be consistent in the tense of verbs, you should be consistent in the voice of verbs. Do not shift from active voice to passive voice, or vice versa, without some good reason to do so.

> active   passive
> **shift:** _I designed_ the decorations for the dance; _they were put up_
> by Chuck.

> active   active
> **rewritten:** _I designed_ the decorations for the dance; _Chuck put_
> them _up._

> passive
> **shift:** Many _problems were discussed_ by the council members,
> active
> but _they found_ no easy answers.

> active
> **rewritten:** The council _members discussed_ many problems, but
> active
> _they found_ no easy answers.

Being consistent in voice can help you write clearly and smoothly.

| Exercise 7 | **Rewriting Sentences to Correct Shifts in Voice** |

Practice

Rewrite the sentences below so that all the verbs are in the active voice. You may change the wording to make the sentences clear, smooth, and consistent in voice.

1. One mosquito bit Todd, but I was bitten by a hundred mosquitoes.

rewritten: _____

_____

2. A new set of guidelines for campus campaigning is being prepared by the student election board; the board is also working on a campaign timetable.

rewritten: _____

_____

3. Since you are a trusted friend, Dina can be guided by your advice.

rewritten: _____

_____

4. Textbooks were slammed shut by students as the bell rang.

   rewritten; _____

   _____

5. It was decided by a panel of experts that the pollution poses no threat to human beings.

   rewritten: _____

   _____

6. A heroic police officer has been named Citizen of the Year by the town; Officer Espinoza rescued a man from a burning car.

   rewritten: _____

   _____

7. Some people are pack rats; useless items like old magazines and broken appliances are saved by such people.

   rewritten: _____

   _____

8. Denise expressed her happiness when her father was praised by the mayor.

   rewritten: _____

   _____

9. If a crime was committed by my brothers, they never told me about it.

   rewritten: _____

   _____

10. Most of the tourists didn't think about the danger of sharks until one swimmer was viciously attacked by a shark.

   rewritten: _____

   _____

Small Reminders About Verbs

There are a few errors that people tend to make with verbs. If you are aware of these errors, you'll be on the lookout for them as you edit your writing.

Used to: Be careful when you write that someone *used to* do, say, or feel something. It is incorrect to write *use to.*

not this: Janine ~~use to~~ visit her mother every week.
They ~~use to~~ like Thai food.
but this: Janine *used to* visit her mother every week.
They *used to* like Thai food.

Could Have, Should Have, Would Have: Using *of* instead of *have* is another error with verbs.

not this: I ~~could of~~ done better on the test.
but this: I *could have* done better on the test.

not this: He ~~should of~~ been paying attention.
but this: He *should have* been paying attention.

not this: The girls ~~would of~~ liked to visit Washington.
but this: The girls *would have* liked to visit Washington.

Would Have/Had: If you are writing about something that might have been possible, but that did not happen, use *had* as the helping verb.

not this: If I ~~would have~~ taken a foreign language in high school, I wouldn't have to take one now.
but this: If I *had* taken a foreign language in high school, I wouldn't have to take one now.

not this: I wish they ~~would have~~ won the game.
but this: I wish they *had* won the game.

not this: If she ~~would have~~ been smart, she would have called a plumber.
but this: If she *had* been smart, she would have called a plumber.

Exercise 8

 *Collaborate*

Writing Sentences with the Correct Verb Forms

Complete this exercise with a partner or a group. Follow the directions to write or complete each sentence below.

1. Complete this sentence and add a verb in the correct tense: I had concealed the evidence by the time

_____

_____

2. Write a sentence that is more than eight words long and that uses the words *have been friends* in the middle of the sentence.

_____

_____

3. Write a sentence that uses the past tense form of these words: *mix* and *pour.*

_____

_____

4. Write a sentence in the passive voice.

_____

_____

5. Write a sentence in the active voice.

_____

_____

6. Write a sentence that uses _would have_ and _had_.

_____

_____

7. Write a sentence that is more than six words long and that uses the words _had prepared_ and _before_.

_____

_____

8. Write a sentence of more than six words that uses the words _used to_.

_____

_____

9. Write a sentence that contains two verbs in the same tense.

_____

_____

10. Write a sentence that uses the words _should have_.

_____

_____

 Exercise **9**

⊙⊙⊙ _Connect_

Editing a Paragraph for Errors in Verbs: Consistency, Correct Tense, and Voice

Edit the following paragraph for errors in verb consistency, tense, or voice. There are seven errors.

Last week, a tragedy struck our town, and it was particularly terrible

because it was so senseless. Two cars sped down a dark country road, one driver loses control, and four high school students died. The dangers of that road were known by everyone at the high school; two accidents already occurred there earlier in the year. It was a notoriously unsafe road for years, yet nothing was done by the local police. More and better enforcement could have saved lives. Even speed bumps could have helped. Of course, the two drivers who drove down that stretch of concrete at over 80 m.p.h. do not use their heads. They chose to risk their lives long before they crashed. If they were more rational and less in love with street racing, four people would be alive today.

CHAPTER 24

Making Subjects and Verbs Agree

Subjects and verbs have to agree in number. That means a singular subject must be matched to a singular verb form and a plural subject must be matched to a plural verb form.

> **singular subject, singular verb:**
> My *sister walks* to work every morning.

> **plural subject, plural verb:**
> *Mary, David,* and *Sam believe* in ghosts.

> **singular subject, singular verb:**
> That *movie is* too violent for me.

> **plural subject, plural verb:**
> Bulky *packages are* difficult to carry.

Caution: Remember that a regular verb has an *s* ending in one singular form in the present tense—the form that goes with *he, she, it,* or their equivalents:

> He *makes* me feel confident.
> She *appreciates* intelligent conversation.
> It *seems* like a good buy.
> Bo *runs* every day.
> That girl *swims* well.
> That machine *breaks* down too often.

 Exercise 1

Practice

Subject-Verb Agreement: Selecting the Correct Verb Form

Select the correct form of the verb in parentheses in each sentence following.

1. My sisters (spend, spends) too much time writing and reading email.

2. If the weather is cold, I (like, likes) to drink coffee with cream.

3. Shyness (keep, keeps) many people from making friends.

4. Interesting conversations always (start, starts) at the end of our psychology class.

5. When he (want, wants) something done right, Jimmy can be very demanding.

6. The basement and attic (need, needs) a good cleaning.

7. I see that cat every night; it (belong, belongs) to the people across the street.

8. I have to get away from Sharon because her whining (make, makes) me want to scream.

9. An alarm system (cost, costs) more than I want to pay.

10. You (is, are) my best friend, and I trust you with my secrets.

Exercise 2

Connect

Correcting Errors in Subject-Verb Agreement in a Paragraph

There are errors in subject-verb agreement in the paragraph below. If a verb does not agree with its subject, change the verb form. Cross out the incorrect verb form and write the correct one above it. There are five errors in agreement in the paragraph.

On weekends, my father love to go to flea markets. He says he can find all kinds of interesting merchandise at the markets, but I think what he like best is negotiating the prices. If he sees an item that catch his eye, he first offers a ridiculously low price for it. The seller respond with an insulted look, and then the two are off, each trying to get the best of the deal. I can see the gleam in my father's eye when he argues over a price. He enjoys the give-and-take of the haggling. He is even happier when he walk off with what he thinks is a bargain.

PRONOUNS AS SUBJECTS

Pronouns can be used as subjects. Pronouns are words that take the place of nouns. **When pronouns are used as subjects, they must agree in number with verbs.**

Here is a list of the subject pronouns and the regular verb forms that agree with them, in the present tense:

Info **BOX**

Subjective Pronouns and a Present Tense Verb

pronoun	verb	
I	listen	
you	listen	all singular forms
he, she, it	listens	
we	listen	
you	listen	all plural forms
they	listen	

In all the sentences below, the pronoun used as the subject of the sentence agrees in number with the verb:

singular pronoun, singular verb:
I make the best omelet in town.

singular pronoun, singular verb:
You dance very well.

singular pronoun, singular verb:
She performs like a trained athlete.

plural pronoun, plural verb:
We need a new refrigerator.

plural pronoun, plural verb:
They understand the situation.

SPECIAL PROBLEMS WITH AGREEMENT

Agreement seems fairly simple: If a subject is singular, you use a singular verb form, and if a subject is plural, you use a plural verb form. However, there are special problems with agreement that will come up in your writing. Sometimes, it is hard to find the subject of a sentence; at other times, it is hard to determine if a subject is singular or plural.

Finding the Subject

When you are checking for subject-verb agreement, you can find the real subject of the sentence by first eliminating the prepositional phrases. To find the real subject, put parentheses around the prepositional phrases. Then it is easy to find the subject because nothing in a prepositional phrase is the subject of a sentence.

prepositional phrases in parentheses:

S   V
One (of my oldest friends) *is* a social worker.

S   V
A *student* (from one) (of the nearby school districts) *is* the winner.

The *store* (across the street) (from my house) *is* open all night.

Jim, (with all his silly jokes), *is* a nice person.

Note: Words and phrases such as *along with, as well as, except, in addition to, including, plus,* and *together with* introduce prepositional phrases. The words that follow them are part of the prepositional phrase and cannot be part of the subject.

My *sister,* (along with her husband), *is* planning a trip to Bolivia.

Tom's *house,* (as well as his apartment), *is* part of a family inheritance.

Exercise 3

Practice

Finding the Real Subject by Recognizing Prepositional Phrases

Put parentheses around all the prepositional phrases in the sentences below. Put an *S* above each subject and a *V* above each verb.

1. Three of the baseball cards in his collection are worth a great deal of money.

2. Leticia, along with her cousins, is taking a trip to Los Angeles this summer.

3. One of the four members of the band is a graduate of our college.

4. The last of the new students comes from a small town near Denver.

5. A spokesperson for the electric company, in addition to a city planner, was scheduled to speak about the new power plant.

6. The mansion behind the row of pine trees has a long history of ghostly sightings.

7. At the end of the day, a security guard locks all the rooms on the third floor.

8. With a calm and friendly voice, the veterinarian coaxes frightened dogs onto the examining table.

9. The door with all the nicks and scratches needs a new coat of paint.

10. Colin, as well as his brother, regularly donates blood to the local blood bank.

Practice

Selecting the Correct Verb Form by Identifying Prepositional Phrases

Put parentheses around all the prepositional phrases in the sentences below. Then circle the correct verb in parentheses in each sentence.

1. A volunteer from Citizens for Better Emergency Services (is , are) speaking at the town meeting on Wednesday.

2. Several of the winners of the state semifinals, plus last year's champion, (is, are) at the opening ceremonies.

3. One of the photographs from Mr. Khouri's portfolio (is , are) on exhibit at the Photography Center.

4. The protestors at the international trade conference (come , comes) from all parts of the world.

5. A person without a knowledge of accounting (has , have) little chance of success in business.

6. With his huge dark eyes and easy grin, my dog (rank, ranks) far above the other dogs in the dog show.

7. One of the bushes at the edge of the fields (is , are) a rare type of wildflower from England.

8. Spending beyond your means (lead, leads) to money problems.

9. Her impressive background in medicine, together with her calm and soothing bedside manner, (make, makes) Dr. Iyanla the most respected doctor at the clinic.

10. A college with a diverse student body, good teachers, and small classes (is , are) located within ten miles of your house.

Changed Word Order

You are probably used to looking for the subject of a sentence in front of the verb, but not all sentences follow this pattern. Questions, sentences beginning with words like *here* or *there*, and other sentences change the word order, making subjects harder to find. So you have to look carefully to check for subject-verb agreement.

>   V   S
> Where *are* my *friends*?

>   V S V
> When *is he going* to work?

>   V   S
> Behind the elm trees *stands* a huge *statue*.

>   V   S
> There *are potholes* in the road.

>   V   S
> There *is* a *reason* for his impatience.

Exercise 5

Practice

Making Subjects and Verbs Agree in Sentences with Changed Word Order

In each of the sentences below, underline the subject and circle the correct verb in parentheses.

1. Below the full-page offer for a miracle hair cream (was , were) a list of warnings in very small print.

2. Among the list of things to do (is , are) a scrawled reminder about cleaning the garage.

3. Along the edge of the property (is / are) a barbed-wire fence with glass at the top of the posts.

4. There (is, are) a new Lexus and an old Dodge truck in the parking lot.

5. There (was , were) a choice of vegetables on the menu.

6. Behind the lawsuit (is / are) a complicated tale of family struggle and betrayal.

7. There (was , were) a murmur of discontent during the governor's speech.

8. Under his bed (is , are) a surprise birthday gift for his mother.

9. Where (is, are) the boxes with the toys for the children's shelter?

10. Here (is, are) your bagel and coffee mug.

Exercise 6

Practice

More on Making Subjects and Verbs Agree in Sentences with Changed Word Order

In each sentence on page 512, underline the subject and circle the correct verb in parentheses.

1. Apart from Trina's promotion at work, there (is/ are) her academic and personal successes.

2. Outside the city (is , are) an area of prosperous farms.

3. Suddenly, there (was , were) the clatter of pots and pans.

4. Beneath all his tough talk (is / are) a strong concern for children in trouble and a commitment to helping them.

5. Where on earth (is, are) your father and sister?

6. Sitting on lounge chairs at the beach (was, were) a tall, dark man and two elegant ladies.

7. Inside the birthday card from my grandmother in Chicago (was /were) a check for fifty dollars.

8. Between the pages of the old book (is, are) pressed and faded flowers.

9. Recently there (was, were) two accidents at the intersection.

10. Near the college (is , are) an indoor mall with a food court.

COMPOUND SUBJECTS

A **compound subject** is two or more subjects joined by *and*, *or*, or *nor*. When subjects are joined by *and*, they are usually plural:

S   S   V
Jermaine and *Lisa are* bargain hunters.

S   S   V
The *house* and the *garden need* attention.

S   S   V
A *bakery* and a *pharmacy are* down the street.

Caution: Be careful to check for a compound subject when the word order changes.

V   S   S
There *are* a *bakery* and a *pharmacy* down the street. (Two things, a *bakery* and a *pharmacy*, *are* down the street.)

V   S   S
Here *are* a *picture* of your father and a *copy* of his birth certificate. (A *picture* and a *copy*, two things, *are* here.)

When subjects are joined by *or*, *either . . . or*, *neither . . . nor*, or *not only . . . but also*, the verb form agrees with the subject closer to the verb:

                         singular S   plural S, plural V
Not only the restaurant *manager* but also the *waiters were* pleased with the new policy.

                plural S   singular S, singular V
Not only the *waiters* but also the restaurant *manager was* pleased with the new policy.

plural S   singular S, singular V
Either the *parents* or the *boy walks* the dog every morning.

singular S   plural S, plural V
Either the *boy* or the *parents walk* the dog every morning.

 Exercise 7

Practice

Making Subjects and Verbs Agree: Compound Subjects

Circle the correct form of the verb in parentheses in each sentence below.

1. Neither the apartment nor the house (has , have) enough closet space.

2. When the weather turns cold, Richard and Eileen (make , makes) a fire in the fireplace.

3. Here (is, are) the soap and the towel.

4. Either my brother or my uncles (is, are) supposed to check on my grandmother's empty house.

5. After class, either the students or the teacher (put, puts) the desks back in order.

6. Cookies and a cake (was, were) on the dessert table.

7. In the bottom drawer of the desk there (is, are) a diary and a yearbook.

8. Either Manny or Lisa (is , are) picking me up.

9. Not only the children but also their mother (enjoy, enjoys) swimming in the pool.

10. Talking to strangers and finding the right classrooms (was/ were) my greatest fears on my first day at a new school.

Exercise 8

Practice

More on Making Subjects and Verbs Agree: Compound Subjects

Circle the correct form of the verb in parentheses in each sentence below.

1. Not only the sausages but also the garlic bread (was , were) dripping with olive oil.

2. Neither the tires nor the shock absorbers (is/ are) in good shape.

3. There (is, are) a small boy and his parents waiting at the end of the line.

4. Certainly, either Mr. Lopez or Mr. Woo (qualifies , qualify) for the position.

5. Here (was, were) my parents, tired after the long trip.

6. Kindness and generosity (make , makes) a person welcome in any group.

7. Here (is, are) a video of the crime and eyewitness testimony from a neighbor.

8. Whenever I come home for a visit, either my father or my brothers (say , says) I look tired.

9. Within weeks of Mike's graduation, there (was, were) a family crisis and an accident facing him.

10. On Fridays, neither crazy drivers nor my nasty boss (spoil, spoils) my good mood.

INDEFINITE PRONOUNS

Certain pronouns called **indefinite pronouns** always take a singular verb.

Info BOX			
Indefinite Pronouns			
one	nobody	nothing	each
anyone	anybody	anything	either
someone	somebody	something	neither
everyone	everybody	everything	

If you want to write clearly and correctly, you must memorize these words and remember that they always take a singular verb. Using your common sense is not enough because some of these words seem plural: for example, *everybody* seems to mean more than one person, but in grammatically correct English, it takes a singular verb. Here are some examples of the pronouns used with singular verbs:

singular S   singular V
Everyone in town *is talking* about the scandal.

singular S   singular V
Each of the boys *is* talented.

singular S   singular V
One of their biggest concerns *is* crime in the streets.

singular S   singular V
Neither of the cats *is* mine.

Hint: You can memorize the indefinite pronouns as the *-one*, *-thing*, and *-body* words (*everyone*, *everything*, *everybody*, and so forth) plus *each*, *either*, and *neither*.

Exercise 9

Practice

Making Subjects and Verbs Agree: Using Indefinite Pronouns

Circle the correct verb in parentheses in each sentence following.

1. Anybody with the right maps (is, are) capable of making the trip.

2. Nothing on the library shelves (appeal, appeals) to me.

3. Somebody (want, wants) another vote on the issue of downtown development.

4. Everything from the kitchen cabinets and from the pantry shelves (is , are) sorted and packed.

5. (Is , Are) anyone watching this television program?

6. Everybody in the suburbs (face, faces) a long drive to the city.

7. Nobody from the airlines (was, were) willing to estimate a time of arrival.

8. Anything under the boys' beds (need, needs) to be cleaned out.

9. One of his kindest gestures (was , were) his offer of financial help to the homeless family.

10. Here (is , are) someone with the latest news about the game.

Exercise 10

Practice

**More on Making Subjects and Verbs Agree:
Using Indefinite Pronouns**

Circle the correct verb in parentheses in each sentence below.

1. (Has , Have) anybody tried the math problems yet?

2. Either of the applicants for the job (is , are) a good choice.

3. Someone (deliver, delivers) the paper early in the morning.

4. Each of Michael's business trips (cost, costs) the office thousands of dollars.

5. Neither of Dana's aunts (has , have) seen her in weeks.

6. On the Fourth of July, everyone in the neighborhood (go, goes) to see the fireworks in the park.

7. Something in the stranger's explanation (hint, hints) at a mystery.

8. Beneath the stack of documents, there (was , were) nothing except a rusty key.

9. At the end of the movie, (was , were) anyone crying?

10. Everything about soccer (confuse, confuses) me.

COLLECTIVE NOUNS

Collective nouns refer to more than one person or thing:

team	company	council
class	corporation	government
committee	family	group
audience	jury	crowd

Collective nouns usually take a singular verb:

> singular S, singular V
> The *committee is sponsoring* a fund-raiser.

> singular S, singular V
> The *audience was* impatient.

> singular S, singular V
> The *jury has reached* a verdict.

The singular verb is used because the group is sponsoring, or getting impatient, or reaching a verdict, *as one unit.* Collective nouns take a plural verb only when the members of the group are acting individually, not as a unit.

> The sophomore *class are fighting* among themselves. (The phrase *among themselves* shows that the class is not acting as one unit.)

Making Subjects and Verbs Agree: Using Collective Nouns

Practice

Circle the correct verb in parentheses in each sentence below.

1. The family (is , are) adopting a shelter dog.

2. A company with a reputation for community involvement (is , are) moving into the office park.

3. His class (has , have) fewer rules than my class.

4. The Athletic Council (decide, decides) on a game schedule tomorrow.

5. The group of visitors (was, were) exploring Washington, D.C.

6. A team of experts in contagious diseases (is , are) studying the origins of the West Nile virus.

7. On Sundays, the crowd for brunch (fill/ fills) the restaurant.

8. A bored audience often (start, starts) fidgeting and coughing.

9. The board of education (approve, approves) of the new plan.

10. Every spring, the garden club (sponsor, sponsors) a plant sale.

MAKING SUBJECTS AND VERBS AGREE: THE BOTTOM LINE

As you have probably realized, making subjects and verbs agree is not as simple as it first appears. But if you can remember the basic ideas in this section, you will be able to apply them automatically as you edit your own writing. Below is a quick summary of subject-verb agreement.

Info BOX

Making Subjects and Verbs Agree: A Summary

1. Subjects and verbs should agree in number: singular subjects get singular verb forms, and plural subjects get plural verb forms.

2. When pronouns are used as subjects, they must agree in number with verbs.

3. Nothing in a prepositional phrase can be the subject of the sentence.

4. Questions, sentences beginning with *here* or *there*, and other sentences can change word order, making subjects harder to find.

5. Compound subjects joined by *and* are usually plural.

6. When subjects are joined by *or, either . . . or, neither . . . nor,* or *not only . . . but also*, the verb form agrees with the subject closest to the verb.

7. Indefinite pronouns always take singular verbs.

8. Collective nouns usually take singular verbs.

 Exercise 12

Practice

A Comprehensive Exercise on Subject-Verb Agreement

Circle the correct verb in parentheses in each sentence below.

1. One of the runners at the Olympics (come, comes) from my home town.

2. Anybody with common sense (avoid, avoids) the blazing summer sun.

3. When (was/ were) the suitcases placed on the plane?

4. Each of the witnesses to the accident (was , were) interviewed at the scene.

5. Within the tight-knit group of friends (is , are) a gifted leader.

6. Neither the sheriff nor his deputies (was, were) fooled by the suspect's story.

7. Sometimes, courtesy and respect (go , goes) a long way in creating new friendships.

8. Nothing in the boxes (was , were) broken except a glass dish.

9. Each year, the manager with the best record in sales and service (receive, receives) an award.

10. Not only the kittens but also the mother cat (is , are) living under the porch.

11. Everything in the old photo albums (look, looks) fragile, faded, and strange.

12. Around the corner from the club there (is, are) a coffee shop and a convenience store.

13. The jury (is , are) sent out of the courtroom whenever the lawyers and judge want to argue.

14. The insurance company (like, likes) to hire graduates of this college.

15. A sense of humor and a positive attitude (help , helps) you get through a difficult situation.

16. If that splintered step is not repaired, someone (is , are) going to get hurt.

17. Yesterday there (was, were) a cardinal and two blue jays at my birdfeeder.

18. Neither of your jackets (has , have) a thick lining.

19. Either my cousins or my uncle (stay, stays) with my grandmother when she is ill.

20. Megan, as well as Eric, (take, takes) the bus to work.

Exercise 13

Practice

Collaborate: Writing Sentences with Subject-Verb Agreement

Working with a partner or a group, turn each of the following phrases into a pair of sentences. That is, write two sentences for each phrase. Use a verb that fits, and put the verb in the present tense. Be sure that the verb agrees with the subject.

1. A small packet of diamonds _____

_____

A small packet of diamonds _____

_____

2. Either butter or margarine _____

_____

Either butter or margarine _____

_____

3. The committee _____

   _____

   The committee _____

   _____

4. Ken and Barbie _____

   _____

   Ken and Barbie_____

   _____

5. Everything in the refrigerator _____

   _____

   Everything in the refrigerator _____

   _____

6. Someone from the police department _____

   _____

   Someone from the police department _____

   _____

7. Not only the students but also the instructor _____

   _____

   Not only the students but also the instructor _____

   _____

8. Anybody from our school _____

   _____

   Anybody from our school _____

   _____

9. One of his worst faults _____

   _____

   One of his worst faults _____

   _____

10. Neither Carla nor her parents _____

_____

Neither Carla nor her parents _____

_____

Exercise 14

Collaborate

Create Your Own Text on Subject-Verb Agreement

Working with a partner or a group, create your own grammar handbook. Below is a list of rules on subject-verb agreement. Write one sentence that is an example of each rule. The first one is done for you.

Step 1: Subjects and verbs should agree in number: singular subjects get singular verb forms, and plural subjects get plural verb forms.

example: A battered old car stands in the front yard.

Step 2: When pronouns are used as subjects, they must agree in number with verbs.

example: _____

Step 3: Nothing in a prepositional phrase can be the subject of a sentence.

example: _____

Step 4: Questions, sentences beginning with *here* or *there*, and other sentences can change word order, making subjects harder to find.

example: _____

Step 5: When subjects are joined by "and," they are usually plural.

example: _____

Step 6: When subjects are joined by *or, either . . . or, neither . . . nor,* or *not only . . . but also*, the verb form agrees with the subject closest to the verb.

example: _____

Step 7: Indefinite pronouns always take singular verbs.

example: _____

Step 8: Collective nouns usually take singular verbs.

example: _____

Exercise 15

Connect

Editing a Paragraph for Errors in Subject-Verb Agreement

Edit the following paragraph by correcting any verbs that do not agree with their subjects. Write your corrections above the lines. There are five errors.

There is two simple lessons adults could learn from very young children. First of all, have anybody ever seen a toddler hesitate to have fun?

Small children do not hold back; they run directly toward the joy of a bright flower or a pet or a parent's embrace. Yet everybody over the age of fifteen seem to worry about enjoying a moment of happiness. People debate whether they have time to enjoy the flower or play with the dog. They think hugging a child can be done later, after they have gone to work and made the money to support the child. Toddlers, in contrast, lives fully in the moment, and that is the second lesson we can learn from them. When small children are building a house with their plastic bricks, they are fully focused on that project. Adults may be building a patio out of real bricks, but at the same time they are also talking on their cell phones and obsessing about tomorrow's workload. The adults have lost their ability to enjoy and to focus on a single, present moment. A group of children are often wiser than stressed and anxious grownups.

CHAPTER 25

Using Pronouns Correctly: Agreement and Reference

NOUNS AND PRONOUNS

Nouns are the names of persons, places, or things.

> *Jack* is a good friend. (*Jack* is the name of a person.)
> The band is from *Orlando*. (*Orlando* is the name of a place.)
> I hated the *movie*. (*Movie* is the name of a thing.)

Pronouns are words that substitute for nouns. A pronoun's **antecedent** is the word or words the pronoun replaces.

> antecedent   pronoun
> *Jack* is a good friend; *he* is very loyal.

> antecedent   pronoun
> I hated the *movie* because *it* was too violent.

> antecedent   pronoun
> *Playing tennis* was fun, but *it* started to take up too much of my time.

> antecedent   pronoun
> *Mike and Michelle* are sure *they* are in love.

> antecedent   pronoun
> *Sharon* gave away *her* old clothes.

> antecedent   pronoun
> The *dog* rattled *its* dish, begging for dinner.

Exercise 1

Practice

Identifying the Antecedents of Pronouns

Underline the word or words that are the antecedent of the italicized pronoun in each sentence below.

1. Carter and I are studying Spanish because *we* want to learn a second language.

2. Visiting a sick friend is important; *it* shows you care.

3. My sisters knew *they* had made a big mistake.

4. The zoo opened *its* new reptile house last week.

5. Andrea, will *you* ever tell me the truth?

6. Kayla learned how to skate by watching *her* sister.

7. Arnelle wants to try skydiving, but I am afraid of *it*.

8. We asked the landlord for an extension on the rent, and *he* was very understanding.

9. The students in the health class get *their* final grades today.

10. Regular exercise is important for children because *it* can lessen the risk of certain adult health problems.

AGREEMENT OF A PRONOUN AND ITS ANTECEDENT

A pronoun must agree in number with its antecedent. If the antecedent is singular, the pronoun must be singular. If the antecedent is plural, the pronoun must be plural.

singular antecedent   **singular pronoun**
Susan tried to arrive on time, but *she* got caught in traffic.

plural antecedent   **plural pronoun**
Susan and Ray tried to arrive on time, but *they* got caught in traffic.

plural antecedent   **plural pronoun**
The *visitors* tried to arrive on time, but *they* got caught in traffic.

Agreement of pronoun and antecedent seems fairly simple. If an antecedent is singular, use a singular pronoun. If an antecedent is plural, use a plural pronoun. There are, however, some special problems with agreement of pronouns, and these problems will come up in your writing. If you become familiar with the explanations, examples, and exercises that follow, you will be ready to handle the special problems.

INDEFINITE PRONOUNS

Certain words called **indefinite pronouns** are always singular. Therefore, if one of these indefinite pronouns is the antecedent, the pronoun that replaces it must be singular. Here are the indefinite pronouns:

Info BOX

Indefinite Pronouns

one	nobody	nothing	each
anyone	anybody	anything	either
someone	somebody	something	neither
everyone	everybody	everything	

You may think that *everybody* is plural, but in grammatically correct English, it is a singular word. Therefore, if you want to write clearly and correctly, memorize these words as the *-one*, *-thing*, and *-body* words: every*one*, every*thing*, every*body*, and so on, plus *each*, *either*, and *neither*. If any of these words is an antecedent, the pronoun that refers to it is singular.

singular antecedent   singular pronoun
Each of the Boy Scouts received *his* merit badge.

singular antecedent   singular pronoun
Everyone in the sorority donated *her* time to the project.

Avoiding Sexism

Consider this sentence:

Everybody in the math class brought _____ own calculator.

How do you choose the correct pronoun to fill in the blank? If everybody in the class is male, you can write

Everybody in the math class brought *his* own calculator.

Or if everybody in the class is female, you can write

Everybody in the math class brought *her* own calculator.

Or if the class has students of both sexes, you can write

Everybody in the math class brought *his or her* own calculator.

In the past, most writers used the pronoun *his* to refer to both men and women. Today, many writers try to use *his or her* to avoid sexual bias. If you find using *his or her* is getting awkward or repetitive, you can rewrite the sentence and make the antecedent plural:

correct: *The students* in the math class brought *their* own calculators.

But you cannot shift from singular to plural:

incorrect: ~~Everybody in the math class brought their own calculators.~~

Exercise 2

Practice

Making Pronouns and Antecedents Agree

Write the appropriate pronoun in the blank in each sentence below. Look carefully for the antecedent before you choose the pronoun.

1. The bracelet is stylish and pretty; I really admire _____.

2. A hundred years ago, people in this town left their doors unlocked; _____ were not afraid of crime.

3. I wonder if the man with the messy yard will ever mow _____ lawn.

4. All of my friends buy _____ clothes at Midland Mall.

5. As soon as my brother saw the loft on Mill Street, _____ wanted to convert it into an apartment.

6. A boy growing up without much guidance at home may have to rely on _____ instincts in choosing between right and wrong.

7. Either of the men in the run-offs for student government president will do _____ best for the college.

8. Everyone nominated for Outstanding Female Athlete had proven _____ commitment and ability many times.

9. Each of my sisters received praise for _____ work in the state attorney's office.

10. I love my new computer; _____ is so much faster than my old one.

Exercise 3

Practice

More on Making Pronouns and Antecedents Agree

1. Bring home anything from Perfect Pizzas; _____ will taste good to me.

2. At the women's basketball tournament, one of the players hurt _____ back.

3. Every Saturday, Lennie and Geraldo take _____ cars to the car wash.

4. One of my antique cups is cracked so badly that _____ cannot be repaired.

5. All my aunts gave me _____ version of the family feud that has been going on for years.

6. Everyone in the sorority wore _____ best dress to the homecoming ball.

7. Ray cleaned his house thoroughly because he wanted everything to look _____ best for the visitors.

8. I think somebody from the men's bowling league left _____ shoes behind.

9. Nothing at the movies looked as if _____ would appeal to a teenage audience.

10. Either of the men could have given _____ seat to the elderly lady.

COLLECTIVE NOUNS

Collective nouns refer to more than one person or thing:

team	company	council
class	corporation	government
committee	family	group
audience	jury	crowd

Most of the time, collective nouns take a singular pronoun.

collective noun   **singular pronoun**
The *team* that was ahead in the playoffs lost *its* home game.

collective noun   **singular pronoun**
The *corporation* changed *its* policy on parental leave.

Collective nouns are usually singular because the group is losing a game or changing a policy as one, as a unit. Collective nouns take a plural pronoun only when the members of the group are acting individually, not as a unit.

The *class* picked up *their* class rings this morning. (The members of the class pick up their rings individually.)

Exercise 4

Practice

Making Pronouns and Antecedents Agree: Collective Nouns

Circle the correct pronoun in each sentence below.

1. Even when the economy is in a slump, the electronics company knows how to increase (its, their) profits.

2. I will never fly with that airline again because of the rudeness of (its, their) flight attendants.

3. Although the committee tried to be fair, (its /their) decision was somewhat biased.

4. The audience lost (its, their) patience when the singer was an hour late.

5. Several of the groups have petitioned to get (its, their) money back.

6. A family near the forest fires had to flee from (its, their) home.

7. Steven quit working at the United Furniture Company because (it, they) wouldn't give him vacation time.

8. The committee divided the fund-raising chores among (itself, themselves).

9. The president was concerned that the army keep up (its, their) morale.

10. The vicious gang began to disintegrate when the leaders started fighting among (themselves /itself).

Exercise 5

👥 *Collaborate*

Writing Sentences with Pronoun-Antecedent Agreement

With a partner or group, write a sentence for each pair of words below, using each pair as a pronoun and its antecedent.
    The first pair is done for you.

1. women . . . their

    sentence: <u>Women who work outside the home have to plan their</u>

    <u>time carefully.</u>

2. government . . . its

sentence: _____

_____

3. someone . . . his or her

sentence: _____

_____

4. parents . . . they

sentence: _____

_____

5. driving . . . it

sentence: _____

_____

6. neither . . . his

sentence: _____

_____

7. each . . . his or her

sentence: _____

_____

8. Mexico . . . it

sentence: _____

_____

9. movies and popular music . . . they

sentence: _____

_____

10. credit card debt . . . it

sentence: _____

_____

Exercise 6

Connect

Editing a Paragraph for Errors in Pronoun-Antecedent Agreement

Read the following paragraph carefully, looking for errors in agreement of pronouns and their antecedents. Cross out each pronoun that does not agree with its antecedent and write the correct pronoun above it. There are seven pronouns that need correcting.

My recent discussion with the Institutional Foods Corporation led to some positive changes on our campus. This corporation runs the cafeteria at my college, and I wrote them a letter about improving the food service. A manager from Institutional Foods Corporation responded and invited me to meet with representatives of the corporation to discuss my views. We met a week later, and I began by saying everybody has their own ideas about the cafeteria, but I had talked to many students, and he or she agreed on two points. One is that the company should lower their prices. Each of the students felt that they were paying too much at the cafeteria. Another point was that each section of the cafeteria needs to add healthy foods to their selections. For example, the beverages should include real juices, not sugary substitutes, and the snacks should include fresh fruit. Meals should not be limited to pizza, burgers, and fries, but should include broiled chicken, fish, and vegetarian dishes. The representatives of the corporation listened to me and acted quickly. Within a month, the menu at the cafeteria began to improve, and while prices are still not great, they are slightly lower. The corporation turned out to be willing to change their practices.

PRONOUNS AND THEIR ANTECEDENTS: BEING CLEAR

Remember that pronouns are words that replace or refer to other words, and the words that are replaced or referred to are antecedents.

Make sure that a pronoun has one clear antecedent. Your writing will be vague and confusing if a pronoun appears to refer to more than one antecedent or if it doesn't have any specific antecedent to refer to. In grammar, such confusing language is called a problem with *reference of pronouns*.

When a pronoun refers to more than one thing, the sentence becomes confusing or silly. The following are examples of unclear reference:

Jim told Leonard his bike had been stolen. (Whose bike was stolen? Jim's? Leonard's?)

She put the cake on the table, took off her apron, pulled up a chair, and began to eat it. (What did she eat? The cake? The table? Her apron? The chair?)

If there is no one clear antecedent, you must rewrite the sentence to make the reference clear. Sometimes, the rewritten sentence may seem repetitive, but a little repetition is better than a lot of confusion.

unclear: Jim told Leonard his bike had been stolen.
clear: Jim told Leonard Jim's bike had been stolen.
clear: Jim told Leonard, "My bike has been stolen."
clear: Jim told Leonard Leonard's bike had been stolen.
clear: Jim told Leonard, "Your bike has been stolen."

unclear: She put the cake on the table, took off her apron, pulled up a chair, and began to eat it.
clear: She put the cake on the table, took off her apron, pulled up a chair, and began to eat the cake.

Sometimes the problem is a little more tricky. Can you spot what's wrong with this sentence?

unclear: Bill decided to take a part-time job, which worried his parents. (What worried Bill's parents? His decision to work part time? Or the job itself?)

Be very careful with the pronoun *which*. If there is any chance that using *which* will confuse the reader, rewrite the sentence and get rid of *which*.

clear: Bill's parents were worried about the kind of part-time job he chose.
clear: Bill's decision to work part time worried his parents.

Sometimes, a pronoun has nothing to refer to; it has no antecedent.

no antecedent: When Bill got to the train station, they said the train was going to be late. (Who said the train was going to be late? The ticket agents? Strangers Bill met on the tracks?)
no antecedent: Maria has always loved medicine and has decided that's what she wants to be. (What does that refer to? The only word it could refer to is medicine, but Maria certainly doesn't want to be a medicine. She doesn't want to be an aspirin or a cough drop.)

If a pronoun lacks an antecedent, add an antecedent or get rid of the pronoun.

add an antecedent: When Bill got to the train station and asked the ticket agents about the schedule, they said the train was going to be late. ("They" refers to the ticket agents.)

drop the pronoun: Maria has always loved medicine and has decided she wants to be a physician.

Note: To check for clear reference of pronouns, underline any pronoun that may not be clear. Then try to draw a line from that pronoun to its antecedent. Are there two or more possible antecedents? Is there no antecedent? In either case, you need to rewrite.

Exercise 7

Practice

Rewriting Sentences for Clear Reference of Pronouns

Rewrite the following sentences so that the pronouns have clear references. You may add, take out, or change words.

1. Don told Brian, that he needed a shave and a shower.

2. Whenever I fly on Sun Airlines, they are friendly and helpful.

3. At the electronics store, Jerome was given a discount which surprised him.

4. I don't like Mountain High School; they are all snobs there.

5. Alicia's brother is a mechanical engineer, but she is not interested in it.

6. Husbands may resist their wives' suggestions because they are domineering.

7. Dr. Cohen told Dr. Roselli that her patient needed further tests.

8. The speedboat bumped the edge of the dock, but it didn't need many repairs.

9. When I was a child, they used to give me a lollipop after I had a vaccination.

10. Dana blamed her boyfriend for the accident. which was foolish.

Exercise 8

∞ *Connect*

Editing a Paragraph for Errors in Pronoun Agreement and Reference

Correct any errors in pronoun agreement or reference in the following paragraph. There are six errors. Write your corrections above the line.

The food at Casa Taco is good, but the real attraction is the atmosphere. They are so friendly that a visit to the restaurant can seem like a family reunion. From the cashier to the counter staff, everybody does their best to make the customers feel special. For example, the people behind the counter know my order before I tell them, and they often tease me about being adventurous and trying some new item. In addition, the lady at the cash register always has a smile and a joke for me. The good feeling spreads to all the customers. Nobody loses their temper or raises their voice over an incorrect order or a long wait. Even if the restaurant is crowded, the crowd never loses their patience. Casa Taco treats each customer like a special person and invites them into a special place.

CHAPTER 26

Using Pronouns Correctly: Consistency and Case

When you write, you write from a point of view, and each point of view gets its own form. If you write from the first person point of view, your pronouns are in the *I* (singular) or *we* (plural) forms. If you write from the second person point of view, your pronouns are in the *you* form, whether they are singular or plural. If you write from the third person point of view, your pronouns are in the *he*, *she*, or *it* (singular) or *they* (plural) forms.

Different kinds of writing may require different points of view. When you are writing a set of directions, for example, you may use the second person (*you*) point of view. An essay about your childhood may use the first person (*I*) point of view.

Whatever point of view you use, be consistent in using pronouns. That is, you should not shift the form of your pronouns without some good reason.

> **not consistent:** Every time *I* go to that mall, the parking lot is so crowded *you* have to drive around for hours, looking for a parking space.
>
> **consistent:** Every time *I* go to that mall, the parking lot is so crowded *I* have to drive around for hours, looking for a parking space.

 Exercise 1

Practice

Consistency in Pronouns

Correct any inconsistency in point of view in the sentences below. Cross out each incorrect pronoun and write the correct pronoun above it.

1. I often have times when I want to sit back and let go of all the stresses that you accumulate during the working day.

2. After the hospital patients have breakfast, the nurse comes in and checks your charts.

3. Students starting college must be sure to keep up with assigned reading; once you get behind, they will have a hard time catching up.

4. Yvette likes shopping at Fine Designs because you can always find a bargain or two.

5. The passengers waiting for takeoff were so tired that they were asleep by the time the flight attendant told them to fasten your seatbelts.

6. My brother and I never challenged my father's crazy ideas because you couldn't argue with my father.

7. Even though we always have flashlights in the house, we often forget that you have to have batteries, too.

8. When Laura went to the beach yesterday, the sun was so strong that you needed heavy sunscreen.

9. Whenever I eat at Claudia's restaurant, you know the food is fresh.

10. The first time I visited the amusement park, I had so much fun that I realized it was a place you would return to many times.

Exercise 2

Practice

Correcting Sentences with Consistency Problems

Rewrite the following sentences, correcting any errors with consistency of pronouns. To make the corrections, you may have to change, add, or take out words.

1. You can sense the tension in his voice when we listen to him speak in class.

   rewrite: _____

   _____

2. In elementary school, Mr. Kolsky was my favorite teacher; he always let you express your creativity in drawing and music.

   rewrite: _____

   _____

3. A rude salesperson can lose customers for good if you leave them feeling dissatisfied and insulted.

rewrite: _____

_____

4. People who have recently moved to the area are surprised by all the green space; you are overwhelmed by all the trees and parks.

rewrite: _____

_____

5. Maya loves big cities; she even enjoys the constant noise of drivers caught in traffic, the crowds of people pushing against you, and the towering skyscrapers blocking out the sky.

rewrite: _____

_____

_____

6. I won't lend money to Sammy because he always gives you some excuse for not paying it back.

rewrite: _____

_____

7. I've stopped trying to get a better grade in Health Science; you can't get an A in that class.

rewrite: _____

_____

8. Students who apply for scholarships will be considered only if you have three letters of recommendation from teachers, employers, or community leaders.

rewrite: _____

_____

_____

9. The best part of working at a bakery is that you get to bring home the leftovers.

rewrite: _____

_____

10. If a parent wants to help a child through a divorce, you shouldn't force the child to take sides.

rewrite: _____

_____

CHOOSING THE CASE OF PRONOUNS

Pronouns have forms that show number and person, and they also have forms that show **case.**

Singular Pronouns	Subjective Case	Objective Case	Possessive Case
1st person	I	me	my
2nd person	you	you	your
3rd person	he, she, it	him, her, it	his, her, its

Plural Pronouns			
1st person	we	us	our
2nd person	you	you	your
3rd person	they	them	their

The rules for choosing the case of pronouns are simple:

1. When a pronoun is used as a subject, use the subjective case.
2. When a pronoun is used as the object of a verb or the object of a preposition, use the objective case.
3. When a pronoun is used to show ownership, use the possessive case.

pronouns used as subjects:
He practices his pitching every day.
Bill painted the walls, and *we* polished the floors.

pronouns used as objects:
Ernestine called *him* yesterday.
He gave all his money to *me*.

pronouns used to show possession:
I am worried about *my* grade in Spanish.
The nightclub has lost *its* popularity.

Problems Choosing Pronoun Case

One time when you need to be careful in choosing case is when the pronoun is part of a related group of words. If the pronoun is part of a related group of words, isolate the pronoun. Next, try out the pronoun choices. Then decide which pronoun is correct and write the correct sentence. For example, which of these sentences is correct?

Aunt Sophie planned a big dinner for Tom and *I*.

or

Aunt Sophie planned a big dinner for Tom and *me*.

Step 1: Isolate the pronoun. Eliminate the related words *Tom and.*

Step 2: Try each case:

> Aunt Sophie planned a big dinner for *I.*
>
> or
>
> Aunt Sophie planned a big dinner for *me.*

Step 3: The correct sentence is

> Aunt Sophie planned a big dinner for Tom and me.

The pronoun acts as an object, so it takes the objective case.

Try working through the steps once more to be sure that you understand this principle. Which of the following sentences is correct?

> Last week, *me* and my friend took a ride on the new commuter train.
>
> or
>
> Last week, *I* and my friend took a ride on the new commuter train.

Step 1: Isolate the pronoun. Eliminate the related words *and my friend.*

Step 2: Try each case:

> Last week, *me* took a ride on the new commuter train.
>
> or
>
> Last week, *I* took a ride on the new commuter train.

Step 3: The correct sentence is

> Last week, I and my friend took a ride on the new commuter train.

The pronoun acts as a subject, so it takes the subjective case.

Note: You can also write it this way:

Last week my friend and I took a ride on the new commuter train.

COMMON ERRORS WITH CASE OF PRONOUNS

Be careful to avoid these common errors:

1. *Between* is a preposition, so the pronouns that follow it are objects of the preposition: between *us,* between *them,* between *you and me.* It is never correct to write *between you and I.*

    not this: The plans for the surprise party must be kept a secret between you and I.
    but this: The plans for the surprise party must be kept a secret between you and me.

2. Never use *myself* as a replacement for *I* or *me.*

    not this: My father and myself want to thank you for this honor.
    but this: My father and I want to thank you for this honor.

    not this: She thought the prize should be awarded to Arthur and myself.
    but this: She thought the prize should be awarded to Arthur and me.

3. The possessive pronoun *its* has no apostrophe.

not this: The car held it's value.
but this: The car held its value.

not this: The baby bird had fallen from it's nest.
but this: The baby bird had fallen from its nest.

4. Pronouns that complete comparisons can be in the subjective, objective, or possessive case.

subjective: Christa speaks better than *I.*
objective: The storm hurt Manny more than *her.*
possessive: My car is as fast as *his.*

To decide on the correct pronoun, add the words that complete the comparison and say them aloud:

Christa speaks better than I *speak.*
The storm hurt Manny more than *the storm hurt* her.
My car is as fast as his *car.*

Exercise 3

Practice

Choosing the Right Case of Pronoun

Circle the correct pronoun in parentheses in each sentence below.

1. The car dealership has lost (its, it's) reputation for honest negotiating.

2. The family and (I, myself) are consulting an attorney about filing charges in this case.

3. If my cousins are not home today, I will try calling (they, them) and Pierre tomorrow.

4. I'm a good hockey player, but Richie is a much better player than (I, me).

5. When it started to rain, Casey and (she, her) ran to the bus stop.

6. You should know that whatever is said in this conference is strictly between you and (I, me).

7. The judges deliberated for an hour; then they chose Rigoberto and (me, myself) as the regional winners of the science contest.

8. Now that I am older, staying out all night has lost (its, it's) attraction for me.

9. The new president of the company hinted at a promotion for my supervisor and (me, myself).

10. A highway patrol officer and (we, us) saw the accident at the same time and stopped to help.

More on Choosing the Right Case of Pronoun

Practice

Circle the correct pronoun in parentheses in each sentence below.

1. After I met Frank at my sister's house, life began to change for (me , I) and him.

2. Before breakfast, Sylvia and (she , her) went out for an early-morning run.

3. Dr. Leah Goldstein is a dedicated researcher, but Dr. Andrew McKenna is just as committed as (she , her).

4. Marty is a much better listener than (he , him).

5. My husband planned a big surprise for the children and (I, me).

6. Even though you both speak Spanish, your accent is different than (him, his).

7. James and I visited the old football stadium, but it didn't have any of (its , it's) former magic.

8. I spent the whole afternoon looking for Tim and (she, her), but they must have gone out of town.

9. My grandfather's will left a small sum of money to be divided between my sister and (me, myself).

10. Lieutenant Bakara and (he , him) are looking into suspicious activity at the waterfront.

Write Your Own Text on Pronoun Case

Collaborate

Working with a partner or group, write two sentences that could be used as examples for each of the following rules. The first one is done for you.

Rule 1: When a pronoun is used as a subject, use the subjective case.

examples: He complained about the noise in the street.

Tired and hungry, they stopped for lunch.

Rule 2: When a pronoun is used as the object of a verb or the object of a preposition, use the objective case.

examples: _____

_____

Rule 3: When a pronoun is used to show ownership, use the possessive case.

examples: _____

_____

Rule 4: When a pronoun is part of a related group of words, isolate the pronoun to choose the case. (For examples, write two sentences in which the pronoun is part of a related group of words.)

examples: _____

_____

 Exercise 6

Connect

Editing a Paragraph for Errors in Pronoun Consistency and Case

Correct any errors in pronoun consistency and case in the following paragraph. There are seven errors. Write your corrections above the line.

I love to go to the Downtown Flea Market because there are so many things you can do and buy there. My brother and me often spend a whole Saturday afternoon at the market, snacking on the many varieties of ethnic food, listening to the music, and watching the performers. My favorite place for shopping is the used furniture area; I am always looking for an old lamp or a framed poster for my room. My brother loves the Greek market; he says it's pastry is the best in the city. We both like to sit and listen to the music. Each weekend, a different group plays, and some of the music is excellent. My friend Dave takes his girlfriend to hear the groups every Friday night. Dave and her like to catch all the new talent. Even my best friend Carlos, who plays guitar in a local band, says some of the performers are as good as him. In addition, the market has street entertainers. Little girls can visit a friendly clown and get your faces painted, and street dancers crowd the sidewalks, making dramatic moves to the sounds of a portable CD player. I think anyone can spend a pleasant afternoon at the flea market. It's been the highlight of many days for myself.

CHAPTER 27

Punctuation: The Period and the Question Mark

THE PERIOD

Periods are used two ways:

1. Use a period to mark the end of a sentence that makes a statement:

   We invited him to dinner at our house.
   When Richard spoke, no one paid attention.

2. Use a period after abbreviations:

   Mr. Ryan
   James Wing, Sr.
   10:00 P.M.

Note: If a sentence ends with a period marking an abbreviation, do not add a second period.

Exercise 1 — Using Periods

Practice

Add periods where they are needed in each sentence following.

1. Harry brought soft drinks, popcorn, chips, etc to the picnic

2. I hope Ms Petrosky arrives at the airport before 5:00 so I don't have to drive her home in rush-hour traffic

3. Jonelle got her B A in music from the University of Colorado

4. Ask Mr. Benadir or Mr Samuels about how to apply for financial aid.

5. Lisa doesn't like her new doctor because she wants someone like Dr Ramirez

6. Last night I stayed up until nearly 2:00

7. Salvatore Ruffino, Jr is the president of the company

8. I invited Aunt Jessica and Uncle Aaron to the wedding

9. In elementary school, my favorite teacher was Miss Carlson

10. You must have put about two lbs of chocolate into those brownies

THE QUESTION MARK

Use a question mark after a direct question:

Isn't she adorable?
Do you have car insurance?

If a question is not a direct question, it does not get a question mark:

They asked if I thought their grandchild was adorable.
She questioned whether I had car insurance.

Exercise 2
Practice

Punctuating with Periods and Question Marks

Add any missing periods and question marks to each sentence below.

1. My grandmother offered me some cookies and iced tea, and she tried to get me to eat a sandwich, too

2. Is Nadina still working at the credit card company

3. Felice thinks Mr Johannsen is a great math teacher

4. Manny is not sure whether his father has health insurance

5. Is he bringing his guitar

6. Lorene will try to get there at 3:30 PM, but she may be a little late

7. Carmela wanted to know when the movie started

8. My girlfriend asked me if I was taking a break from studying

Exercise 3
Practice

More on Punctuating with Periods and Question Marks

Add periods and question marks only where they are needed in the following sentences. Do not change or omit any words.

1. I wonder why he is always twenty minutes late for class

2. Did you know Francis Adams, Sr, before he moved to California

3. Haven't you finished changing that tire yet

4. How has Bill been feeling since his knee surgery

5. I'm not sure whether Mr Diaz is still in town

6. Mrs. Shimura has a BA in biology and teaches at my sister's school

7. Is there any more orange juice in the refrigerator

8. Hillary and Keith have been asking about tickets for the game

9. Will we ever find out who committed that murder

10. Are the neighbors planning to sell their house

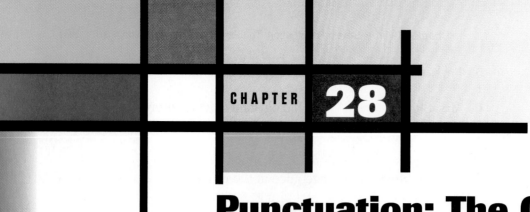

Punctuation: The Comma

There are four main ways to use a comma, as well as other, less important ways. *Memorize the four main ways.* If you can learn and understand these four rules, you will be more confident and correct in your punctuation. That is, you will use a comma only when you have a reason to do so; you will not be scattering commas in your sentences simply because you think a comma might fit, as many writers do.

The four main ways to use a comma are as a lister, a linker, an introducer, or an inserter (use two commas).

USE A COMMA AS A LISTER

Commas support items in a series. These items can be words, phrases, or clauses:

> **comma between words in a list:** Her bedroom was decorated in shades of blue, green, and gold.
> **comma between phrases in a list:** I looked for my ring under the coffee table, between the sofa cushions, and behind the chairs.
> **comma between clauses in a list:** Last week he graduated from college, he found the woman of his dreams, and he won the lottery.

Note: In a list, the comma before *and* is optional, but most writers use it.

 Exercise 1

Practice

Using a Comma as a Lister

Add commas only where they are needed in the following sentences. Do not add any other punctuation or change existing punctuation.

1. Soon I will meet the perfect woman she will fall in love with me and we will get married.

2. The lost suitcase had my best sweaters newest pants nicest shoes and favorite shirts in it.

3. Brownies cake and pies are my son's favorite foods.

4. I particularly like my new car because it has leather seats a sun roof and a CD player.

5. My sister is prepared for a power outage during a snowstorm; she has wood in the fireplace candles in all the rooms and blankets on the beds.

6. My family never had pets until my little brother started bringing home frogs mice gerbils and snakes.

7. Eric will do the dusting vacuuming mopping and washing if you ask him to help.

8. The head of the rescue team looked focused fearless and exhausted.

9. Ben can pick up the plane tickets I can make hotel reservations and Todd can rent a car for the trip.

10. Cough drops hot tea chicken soup and Vitamin C are popular treatments for a cold.

USE A COMMA AS A LINKER

A comma and a coordinating conjunction link two independent clauses. The coordinating conjunctions are *and, but, or, nor, for, yet,* and *so.* The comma goes in front of the coordinating conjunction:

> I have to get to work on time, or I'll get into trouble with my boss.
> My mother gave me a beautiful card, and she wrote a note on it.

Exercise 2

Practice

Using a Comma as a Linker

Add commas only where they are needed in the following sentences. Some sentences do not need commas. Do not change words or add any other punctuation.

1. Mr. Stein knows a great deal about Israel yet he has never been there.

2. No one told me about the college holiday so I arrived at an empty campus.

3. My new boss is calm and never loses her temper with the employees.

4. Pablo doesn't get home from work until midnight yet never seems tired in his early morning class.

5. Chrissy was expecting an argument with Rob but nothing happened.

6. I hope it rains tomorrow for I'm sick of playing softball every weekend.

7. Darryl couldn't borrow the money nor could he earn it.

8. Too much time in front of a computer makes my eyes hurt and my back ache.

9. Alan can drive you home after work or you can catch a ride with me.

10. Dr. Zielinski needed an office assistant and he offered me the job.

USE A COMMA AS AN INTRODUCER

Put a comma after introductory words, phrases, or clauses in a sentence.

comma after an introductory word:
Yes, I agree with you on that issue.
Dad, give me some help with the dishes.

comma after an introductory phrase:
In the long run, you'll be better off without him.
Before the anniversary party, my father bought my mother a
  necklace.

comma after an introductory clause:
If you call home, your parents will be pleased.
When the phone rings, I am always in the shower.

 Exercise 3

Practice

Using a Comma as an Introducer

Add commas only where they are needed in the following sentences. Some sentences do not need commas. Do not change words or add any other punctuation.

1. Honestly you are the biggest whiner in America.

2. If it rains we'll move the party indoors.

3. Under the circumstances Helen should get a refund from the company.

4. Under the bed are enormous balls of dust and piles of dirt.

5. While Jean-Pierre reads his sociology assignment I will start my math homework.

6. On humid summer days I wish for an air-conditioned house.

7. Margie may I use your computer tomorrow?

8. No I do not want to buy more insurance.

9. Until I get my next check I can't afford to repair the car.

10. In my wallet is an old photograph of Debbie.

USE A COMMA AS AN INSERTER

When words or phrases that are *not* necessary are inserted into a sentence, put a comma on *both* sides of the inserted material:

> The game, unfortunately, was rained out.
> My test score, believe it or not, was the highest in the class.
> Potato chips, my favorite snack food, are better tasting when
>   they're fresh.
> James, caught in the middle of the argument, tried to keep the peace.

Using commas as inserters requires that you decide what is essential to the meaning of the sentence and what is nonessential.

Here are the rules:

> **If you do not need material in a sentence, put commas around the material.**
> **If you need material in a sentence, do not put commas around the material.**

For example, consider this sentence:

> The girl who called me was selling magazine subscriptions.

Do you need the words *who called me* to understand the meaning of the sentence? To answer that question, write the sentence without those words:

> The girl was selling magazine subscriptions.

Reading the shorter sentence, you might ask, "Which girl?" The words *who called me* are essential to the sentence. Therefore, you do not put commas around them.

> **correct:** The girl who called me was selling magazine subscriptions.

Remember that the proper name of a person, place, or thing is always sufficient to identify it. Therefore any information that follows a proper name is inserted material; it gets commas on both sides.

> Video Views, which is nearby, has the best prices for video rentals.
> Sam Harris, the man who won the marathon, lives on my block.

Note: Sometimes, the material that is needed in a sentence is called *essential* (or *restrictive*), and the material that is not needed is called *nonessential* (or *nonrestrictive*).

 Using Commas as Inserters

Practice

Add commas only where they are needed in the following sentences. Some sentences do not need commas.

1. The man with the strange golf swing won the charity golf tournament.

2. Philadelphia where I grew up attracts millions of visitors to its historical buildings.

3. The black BMW at the back of the car lot is the best bargain.

4. National Gym which is a mile from the college is popular with students and instructors.

5. *The Matrix* one of my favorite movies contains some groundbreaking special effects.

6. My best friend a dog lover has three mixed-breed dogs.

7. Students who get to school early can get closer parking spaces.

8. You can of course take a bus to work.

9. My sister her hair soaked by the rain ran for shelter.

10. A box of new crayons makes a good gift for a five-year-old girl.

Remember the four main ways to use a comma—as a lister, a linker, an introducer, and an inserter—and you'll solve many of your problems with punctuation.

Punctuating with Commas: The Four Main Ways

Practice

Add commas only where they are needed in the following sentences. Do not add any other punctuation, and do not change any existing punctuation. Some of the sentences do not need commas.

1. If you like hiking you will love this trip to Colorado.

2. Marisela told me to pack sweaters gloves boots and jackets for my visit to Vermont.

3. He was tired of standing around and waiting for the guest of honor to arrive.

4. The book with photographs of Cambodia is the most interesting one in the store.

5. The Owl Café the nearest coffee shop has great cinnamon buns.

6. Sure I'll give you a lift to work when you take your car to the repair shop.

7. Angry and hurt Scott lashed out at the people closest to him but his hurt remained.

8. Andy couldn't spend another day in San Diego for he had run out of money.

9. My apartment is above a restaurant so I hear dishes clattering all the time.

10. Before I get married I want to see some of the world meet some new people and make some money.

More on Punctuating with Commas: The Four Main Ways

Add commas only where they are needed in the following sentences. Do not add any other punctuation, and do not change any existing punctuation. Some sentences do not need commas.

1. Whenever I have a cold my mother gives me orange juice and my girlfriend brings me chicken soup.

2. Arguing with my boss made me anxious and ready to look for a job with better working conditions.

3. Maureen will you lend me your bracelet with the turquoise beads?

4. I spend every weekend it seems cleaning my apartment doing my laundry repairing my car and paying my bills.

5. Well the judge doesn't think you are telling the truth.

6. The cookies from the supermarket are better than the cookies from the expensive bakery.

7. Marva was talking on her cell phone of course and paying no attention to her driving.

8. A house that has a patio always seems as if it has an extra room.

9. The leather boots his favorite footwear were spotted with water stains.

10. As I sorted through the junk mail I found a card in a familiar handwriting.

Other Ways to Use a Comma

There are other places to use a comma. Reviewing these uses will help you feel more confident as a writer.

1. Use commas with quotations. Use a comma to set off a direct quotation from the rest of the sentence:

My father told me, "Money doesn't grow on trees."
"Let's split the bill," Raymond said.

Note that the comma that introduces the quotation goes before the quotation marks. But once the quotation has begun, commas or periods go inside the quotation marks.

2. Use commas with dates and addresses. Use commas between the items in dates and addresses:

August 5, 1980, is Chip's date of birth.
We lived at 133 Emerson Road, Lake Park, Pennsylvania, before we moved to Florida.

Notice the comma after the year in the date and the comma after the state in the address. These commas are needed when you write a date or address within a sentence.

3. Use commas in numbers. Use commas in numbers of one thousand or larger:

The price of equipment was $1,293.

4. Use commas for clarity. Put a comma when you need it to make something clear:

Whoever it is, is about to be punished.
While hunting, the eagle is swift and strong.
I don't like to dress up, but in this job I have to, to get ahead.

Exercise 7

Practice

Punctuation: Other Ways to Use a Comma

Add commas only where they are needed in the following sentences. Do not add any other punctuation, and do not change any existing punctuation.

1. Mrs. Liu said "You are the best student in the class."

2. My aunt and uncle were married on November 1 2000 in Atlanta Georgia.

3. "Don't ever lie to me again " my girlfriend warned.

4. Danny looked at the dent in his car and wailed "This is going to cost me a fortune in repairs."

5. My grandfather came to this country on October 5 1970 and started a small lawn business in Springfield Illinois.

6. My trip to the emergency room cost me $1173.

7. Fire damage to the old theater is estimated at $450000.

8. Jeanette came in in an expensive evening dress.

9. On February 14 1999 my boyfriend murmured "I want to spend the rest of my life with you."

10. "I wish it would stop raining " Alex said.

Exercise 8

Practice

Punctuating with Commas: A Comprehensive Exercise

Add commas only where they are needed in the following sentences. Do not add any other punctuation, and do not change any existing punctuation. Some of the sentences do not need commas.

1. Navy white and yellow were the colors she wanted for her bathroom so I bought her some yellow and white towels.

2. I graduated from Benjamin Franklin High School on June 10 2001.

3. I can only hope Sarah that you have learned your lesson.

4. My mother wanted a house with a laundry room but had to settle for a washer and dryer in the garage.

5. My brother Nelson the smartest member of our family is a heart surgeon.

6. Lisa spent the weekend answering her email doing research on the Internet and working on her resume.

7. The car that caused the accident was speeding.

8. Whether I get the job or not I have learned to practice my interviewing skills.

9. "I'll be with you in a minute " the bank clerk said.

10. Unfortunately the store no longer carries that brand of paint.

11. He whined at me he threatened me he pleaded with me but he couldn't get me to change my mind.

12. Professor Ramsammy the best teacher in the college is retiring next year.

13. Nick can fly to Philadelphia or take an early train.

14. At the top of his lungs the small boy shrieked "I want my Mommy!"

15. Students who come late to class often miss important announcements and explanations.

16. My only niece who has a real talent for dance is appearing on a local television show.

17. Clothes that need ironing just give me extra work.

18. My house was old and decrepit yet it was home to me.

19. When you complain complain politely.

20. The customer couldn't find a shirt that fit him nor could he find slacks that he liked.

CHAPTER 29

Punctuation: The Semicolon and the Colon

THE SEMICOLON

There are two ways to use semicolons:

1. Use a semicolon to join two independent clauses:

Michael loved his old Camaro; he worked on it every weekend.
The situation was hopeless; I couldn't do anything.

Note: If the independent clauses are joined by a conjunctive adverb, you still need a semicolon. You will also need a comma after any conjunctive adverb that is more than one syllable long.

He was fluent in Spanish; *consequently*, he was the perfect companion for our trip to Venezuela.

I called the hotline for twenty minutes; *then* I called another number.

A list of common conjunctive adverbs is on page 419.

Independent clauses joined by coordinating conjunctions (the words *and, but, or, nor, for, yet*, and *so*) do not need semicolons. Use a comma in front of the coordinating conjunction:

Michael loved his old Camaro, *and* he worked on it every weekend.

He was fluent in Spanish, *so* he was the perfect companion for our trip to Venezuela.

2. Use semicolons to separate items on a list that contains commas. Adding semicolons will make the list easier to read:

The contestants came from Rochester, New York; Pittsburgh, Pennsylvania; Trenton, New Jersey; and Boston, Massachusetts. (The semicolons show that Rochester is a city in the state of New York, Pittsburgh is a city in the state of Pennsylvania, and so forth.)

The new officers of the club will be Althea Bethell, president; François Rivière, vice-president; Ricardo Perez, secretary; and Lou Phillips, treasurer. (The semicolons link the person, Althea Bethell, with the office, president, and so forth.)

Exercise 1

Practice

Punctuating with Semicolons

Add any missing semicolons to the following sentences. In some sentences, you may have to change commas to semicolons.

1. Last night, Geraldo apologized to me about the accident finally, he admitted he was wrong about something.

2. You can order tickets on the Internet or go to a ticket outlet in the mall.

3. My plane was late thus I missed my connecting flight to Mexico City.

4. The best players on our team are Ricky Gonzalez, first baseman, Dan Stein, catcher, Mitchell Lindquist, pitcher, and Sean Scott, right fielder.

5. Something is wrong with the radio I can't turn down the volume.

6. We expected a scared little kitten instead, we got an adventurous young cat.

7. Cable television costs money, but network television is free.

8. The day began with my father shouting at me to wake up then my brother pulled the covers off my bed.

9. A month ago, my little sister couldn't ride a two-wheeler bike now she is very confident on one.

10. I was trying to get dressed for work meanwhile, my three-year-old was playing with his cereal and milk.

THE COLON

A colon is used at the end of a complete statement. It introduces a list or an explanation:

colon introduces a list: When I went grocery shopping, I picked up a few things: milk, eggs, and coffee.

colon introduces an explanation: The room was a mess: dirty clothes were piled on the chairs, wet towels were thrown on the floor, and an empty pizza box was tossed in the closet.

Remember that the colon comes after a complete statement. What comes after the colon explains or describes what came before the colon. Look once more at the two examples, and you'll see the point:

> When I went grocery shopping, I picked up a few things: milk, eggs, and coffee. (The words after the colon—*milk, eggs, and coffee*—explain what few things I picked up.)

> The room was a mess: dirty clothes were piled on the chairs, wet towels were thrown on the floor, and an empty pizza box was tossed in the closet. (In this sentence, all the words after the colon describe what the mess was like.)

Some people use a colon every time they put a list in a sentence, but this is not a good rule to follow. Instead, remember that a colon, even one that introduces a list, must come after a complete statement:

> **not this:** When I go to the beach, I always bring: suntan lotion, a big towel, and a cooler with iced tea.
> **but this:** When I go to the beach, I always bring my supplies: suntan lotion, a big towel, and a cooler with iced tea.

A colon may also introduce long quotations:

> On December 8, 1941, the day after the Japanese attacked Pearl Harbor, President Franklin Delano Roosevelt summed up the situation: "Hostilities exist. There is no blinking at the fact that our people, our territory, and our interests are in grave danger." (Note that what comes after the colon explains what came before it.)

Exercise 2

Practice

Punctuating with Colons

Add colons where they are needed in the following sentences. Some sentences do not need a colon.

1. For this trip, Celia is packing three sweaters a lightweight one, a cotton turtleneck, and a heavy pullover.

2. My first attempt at cooking dinner was a disaster the spaghetti was limp, the sauce was greasy, and the garlic bread was burnt.

3. I have two kinds of books books I have to read for college and books I like to read for pleasure.

4. If you want to contribute to the party, you can bring paper plates, paper napkins, plastic forks and spoons, and a large bag of ice.

5. My little brother's birthday is costing me a fortune money for the fancy birthday cake, money for the decorations, and more money for his surprise gifts.

6. Mom always leaves me hints about getting a haircut a coupon for half-price haircuts on my desk, a photo of a stylish cut on my bed.

7. When we left the garage sale, we were carrying two small lawn chairs, an old tea kettle, a green glass candle holder, and a dog leash.

8. After Nick got paid, he bought some treats for Nina fresh-squeezed orange juice, red grapes, and a bunch of flowers.

9. The office looked like a tornado had hit it papers all over the floor, boxes flowing with trash, file cabinets jammed to bursting, and books spilling from every chair.

10. If you send me your old computer, be sure you include the owner's manual, user's guide, and any warranties.

Exercise 3

Practice

Using Semicolons and Colons

Add semicolons and colons where they are needed in the following sentences. You might have to change a comma to a semicolon.

1. Eileen picked me up at the train station then she drove me to my sister's house.

2. Every Thanksgiving, we have the same meal roast turkey, stuffing, cranberry sauce, and pumpkin pie.

3. You should bring a jacket to the game otherwise, you're going to get cold.

4. When I started working at the restaurant, I had to be trained in customer relations, menu selections, and financial procedures.

5. Last night the Athletic League voted Greg Parro, president, Lisa Tobin, vice president, Graham Pritchard, second vice president, and Daisy Fiero, treasurer.

6. You can keep an eye on the baby, meanwhile, I'll call the doctor about the baby's fever.

7. If you're going to the bakery, bring me some bagels, a loaf of whole grain bread, and some cinnamon buns.

8. Frank arrived at nine he's always prompt.

9. You can pick up a bath mat at Wal-Mart, and don't forget your son's goodies a new Barney toy for the tub and a small stuffed animal.

10. I would never eat broccoli the very thought of it makes me sick.

CHAPTER 30

Punctuation: The Apostrophe

Use the apostrophe in the following ways:

1. Use an apostrophe in contractions to show that letters have been omitted.

do not = don't
I will = I'll
is not = isn't
she would = she'd
will not = won't

Also use the apostrophe to show that numbers have been omitted:

the summer of 1998 = the summer of '98

Exercise 1	**Using Apostrophes in Contractions**
Practice	

Add apostrophes where they are needed in each sentence below.

1. Next week, Im taking my sister to the big water slide in Mango Park; youre welcome to come along.

2. If you were driving at night, you couldnt have gotten a good look at the car ahead of you.

3. Hillary hadnt planned on staying so late, but she wasnt at all sorry about leaving after midnight.

4. Whats the matter with the clothes dryer?

5. If youll lend me the money, I think Ill buy a new car.

6. When people refer to the American Revolution, they often refer to the fighting spirit as the Spirit of 76.

7. If theres no violence in the movie, I think shell like it.

8. If youre curious about the ring, you should see a jeweler; hell tell you if it s real gold.

9. Dogs make the best companions; theyll cheer you up whenever youre feeling down.

10. Surprises dont always come when were ready for them; thats why theyre called surprises.

2. **Use an apostrophe to show possession.** If a word does not end in *s*, show ownership by adding an apostrophe and *s*.

the ring belongs to Jill = Jill's ring
the wallet belongs to somebody = somebody's wallet
the books are owned by my father = my father's books

If two people jointly own something, put the 's on the last person's name.

Ann and Mike own a house = Ann and Mike's house

If a word already ends in *s* and you want to show ownership, just add an apostrophe.

the ring belongs to Frances = Frances' ring
two boys own a dog = the boys' dog
the house belongs to Ms. Jones = Ms. Jones' house

Caution: Be careful with apostrophes. These words, the possessive pronouns, do not take apostrophes: *his, hers, theirs, ours, yours, its.*

not this: The pencils were their's.
but this: The pencils were theirs.

not this: The steak lost it's flavor.
but this: The steak lost its flavor.

Exercise 2

Practice

Using Apostrophes to Show Possession

Add apostrophes where they are needed in the following sentences. Some sentences do not need apostrophes.

1. Oscar and Ernesto share an office on Bright Street; the mens office is full of files and legal documents.

2. I am giving the turquoise bracelet to Nina, so the crystal bracelet is yours.

3. Yolanda says she likes Tracy and Matthews budget proposal better than ours.

4. Sometimes, ice cream that has been kept in the freezer too long loses its flavor.

5. Now that Chris has moved to Phoenix, he loves its weather, but he misses New Yorks excitement.

6. Malcolm found someones book bag next to some old boxes in the empty classroom.

7. Even though I am standing on the stage with Leah Albury, this award for service to the community is strictly hers.

8. In a hurry to get to out of a tight parking space, I scratched my cars fender against somebodys bumper.

9. If you give me Michael and Dennis address, I will send them a card.

10. Because she was not paying attention to where she was walking, Mrs. Nair tripped and fell against the tables sharp edge.

3. **Use the apostrophe for special uses of time and to create a plural of numbers mentioned as numbers, letters mentioned as letters, and words that normally do not have plurals.**

   special uses of time: It will take a *week's* work.
   numbers mentioned as numbers: Take out the *5's.*
   letters mentioned as letters: Cross your *t's.*
   words that normally do not have plurals: I want no more *maybe's.*

Caution: Do not add an apostrophe to a simple plural.

   not this: He lost three suitcase's.
   but this: He lost three suitcases.

Exercise 3

Practice

Special Uses of Apostrophes

Add apostrophes where they are needed in the following sentences. Some sentences do not need apostrophes. Do not change or add any words.

1. Kelly has been taking lessons in martial arts for three years.

2. The repairs to my car cost me the equivalent of a whole semesters tuition.

3. When you write, your *7*s look different than mine.

4. You need two *f*s in the word *traffic.*

5. Mary is getting fed up with all of your *somedays*; she would like you to act now.

6. Lance waited for three weeks before he complained about the neighbors.

7. Traci dots her *i*s with a tiny circle.

8. What Professor DeGroot expects us to do for one class is a weeks worth of homework in other classes.

9. Noreen brought eighteen doughnuts to the meeting; Keith brought two gallons of orange juice.

10. Nicki thinks she can get two Bs and a C in her winter term classes.

Exercise 4

Practice

A Comprehensive Exercise in Using Apostrophes

Circle the correct form in parentheses in each sentence below.

1. I began working at my father's office in the summer of (99, '99).

2. Over the years, the old car lost (its, it's) shiny paint job.

3. May I borrow (someone, someone's) pencil?

4. Larry was on the wrestling team for three (years, year's).

5. When you polish the table, it (doesnt, doesn't) look too bad.

6. Melanie met (Kevin's and Mike's, Kevin and Mike's) mother yesterday.

7. The company I work for has (its, it's) own day care center for the children of employees.

8. The repairs to my car cost me a (weeks, week's) salary.

9. A neighbor admired my two (son's, sons') computer skills and offered them a job at his computer store.

10. When you visit Aunt LaShonda, do not forget to say your (thank yous, thank you's).

11. That adorable puppy belongs to (James, James').

12. The teacher collected (everyones, everyone's) assignment.

13. I love to watch (women's, womens') basketball on television.

14. Kevin has too many mood swings; I cannot figure out that (mans, man's) personality.

15. Yesterday, Angela tried to concentrate on her reading, but she faced many (interruptions, interruption's).

16. The schoolchildren were fascinated by the (museums, museum's) dinosaur exhibit.

17. Mrs. (Morris, Morris') house is the oldest on our street.

18. The award-winning photograph was (hers, her's).

19. The restaurant has managed to maintain (its, it's) reputation for fine food.

20. Many (students, student's) go to the library for a quiet place to study.

Using Apostrophes: Another Comprehensive Exercise

Practice

Add apostrophes where they are needed in the following sentences. Some sentences do not need apostrophes. Do not change or add any words.

1. Manny accepted Charles apology and forgot about the argument.

2. My car wouldnt start this morning; its battery was dead.

3. My neighbors are wonderful hosts, but I cant stand watching their home videos.

4. Joel and I love to cook, so almost all the cookbooks on the shelves are ours.

5. Because she has never seen snow, Kelly is looking forward to Massachusetts winter weather and its winter activities.

6. My sisters have always dreamed of writing childrens stories.

7. The captain and one crew member were the only survivors, so the press was eager to hear the mens stories.

8. Hes one of the greatest experts in physics.

9. Theyll never see a smarter dog than James and Lauras border collie.

10. You may not like the boys, but most of the credit for winning the game is theirs.

11. Leon has such bad handwriting that his *7*s look like *9*s.

12. If somethings wrong at home, its hard for me to focus on my responsibilities at work.

13. My little boy is just learning the alphabet; right now we are working on the *d*s and *e*s.

14. The foolish mistakes were ours; the smart moves were theirs.

15. Tyrese wont miss Marcia and Luis wedding; its a family gathering that will create lifelong memories.

16. I wonder whos selecting the speakers for the seminar on mens health.

17. Try not to use so many *whatever*s at the end of your sentences.

18. For a while, fashion returned to the 70s for its ideas.

19. Im going to take a months vacation and then start looking for a job like yours.

20. Some entertainers have private jets with luxurious interiors.

CHAPTER 31

Other Punctuation and Mechanics

THE EXCLAMATION MARK

The exclamation mark is used at the end of sentences that express strong emotion:

> **appropriate:** You've won the lottery!
> **inappropriate:** We had a great time! (*Great* already implies excitement.)

Be careful not to overuse the exclamation mark. If your choice of words is descriptive, you should not have to rely on the exclamation point for emphasis. Use it sparingly, for it is easy to rely on exclamations instead of using better vocabulary.

THE DASH

Use a dash to interrupt a sentence. It usually indicates a dramatic shift in tone or thought:

> I picked up the crystal bowl carefully, cradled it in my arms, walked softy—and tripped, sending the bowl flying.

Two dashes set off dramatic words that interrupt a sentence.

> Ramón took the life preserver—our only one—and tossed it far out to sea.

Since dashes are somewhat dramatic, use them sparingly.

PARENTHESES

Use parentheses to enclose extra material and afterthoughts:

> I was sure that Ridgefield (the town I'd just visited) was not the place for me.
> Her name (which I have just remembered) was Celestine.

Note: Commas in pairs, dashes in pairs, and parentheses are all used as inserters. They set off material that interrupts the flow of the sentence. The least dramatic and smoothest way to insert material is to use commas.

THE HYPHEN

A hyphen joins two or more descriptive words that act as a single word.

> The old car had a souped-up engine.
> Bill was a smooth-talking charmer.

Exercise 1
Practice

Punctuating with Exclamation Marks, Dashes, Parentheses, and Hyphens

Add any exclamation marks, dashes, parentheses, and hyphens that are needed in the sentences below.

1. Mr. DiSouza was a warm hearted and generous friend to the poor.

2. The Carlton Cascade Room where my parents held a party for my fifteenth birthday is a great place for wedding receptions or anniversary parties.

3. Stop, or I'll shoot

4. Carefully, I placed my old textbooks on the ground, neatly stacked my notes and papers on top of them and lit a match to the whole pile.

5. Spring River where I grew up is a country town thirty miles from the nearest city.

6. How dare you talk to me like that

7. Linda ran to the cliff her only way out and jumped.

QUOTATION MARKS

Use quotation marks for direct quotes, for the titles of short works, and for other special uses.

1. Put quotation marks around direct quotes, a speaker or writer's exact words:

   My mother told me, "There are plenty of fish in the sea."
   "I'm never going there again," said Irene.
   "I'd like to buy you dinner," Peter said, "but I'm out of cash."
   My best friend warned me, "Stay away from that guy. He will break your heart."

Look carefully at the preceding examples. Notice that a comma is used to introduce a direct quotation and that at the end of the quotation, the comma or period goes inside the quotation marks:

> My mother told me, "There are plenty of fish in the sea."

Notice how direct quotations of more than one sentence are punctuated. If the quotation is written in one unit, quotation marks go before the first quoted word and after the last quoted word:

> My best friend warned me, "Stay away from that guy. He will break your heart."

But if the quote is not written as one unit, the punctuation changes:

> "Stay away from that guy," my best friend warned me. "He will break your heart."

Caution: Do *not* put quotation marks around indirect quotations:

> **indirect quotation:** He asked if he could come with us.
> **direct quotation:** He asked, "Can I come with you?"
> **indirect quotation:** She said that she wanted more time.
> **direct quotation:** "I want more time," she said.

2. Put quotation marks around the titles of short works. If you are writing the title of a short work like a short story, an essay, a newspaper or magazine article, a poem, or a song, put quotation marks around the title:

> In middle school, we read Robert Frost's poem, "The Road Not Taken."
> My little sister has learned to sing "Itsy Bitsy Spider."

If you are writing the title of a longer work like a book, movie, magazine, play, television show, or CD, underline the title:

> Last night I saw an old movie, <u>Stand By Me</u>.
> I read an article called "Campus Crime" in <u>Newsweek</u>.

In printed publications such as books or magazines, titles of long works are put in italics. But when you are handwriting, typing, or using a word processor, underline the titles of long works.

3. There are other special uses of quotation marks. You use quotation marks around words mentioned as words in a sentence:

> When you said "never," did you mean it?
> People from the Midwest pronounce "water" differently than I do.

If you are using a quotation within a quotation, use single quotation marks:

> My brother complained, "Every time we get in trouble, Mom has to say 'I told you so.'"
> Kyle said, "Linda has a way of saying 'Excuse me' that is really very rude."

CAPITAL LETTERS

There are ten main situations in which you capitalize:

1. Capitalize the first word of every sentence:

> Yesterday we saw our first soccer game.

2. Capitalize the first word in a direct quotation if the word begins a sentence:

> My aunt said, "This is a gift for your birthday."

"Have some birthday cake," my aunt said, "and have some more ice cream." (Notice that the second section of this quotation does not begin with a capital letter because it does not begin a sentence.)

3. Capitalize the names of persons:

Nancy Perez and Frank Murray came to see me at the store.
I asked Mother to feed my cat.

Do not capitalize words like *mother*, *father*, or *aunt* if you put a possessive in front of them.

I asked my mother to feed my cat.

4. Capitalize the titles of persons:

I spoke with Dr. Wilson.
He has to see Dean Johnston.

Do not capitalize when the title is not connected to a name:

I spoke with that doctor.
He has to see the dean.

5. Always capitalize countries, cities, languages, nationalities, religions, races, months, days of the week, documents, organizations, holidays, and historical events or periods:

In high school, we never studied the Vietnam War.
The Polish-American Club will hold a picnic on Labor Day.

Use small letters for the seasons:

I love fall because I love to watch the leaves change color.

6. Capitalize the names of particular places:

We used to hold our annual meetings at Northside Auditorium in Springfield, Iowa, but this year we are meeting at Riverview Theater in Langton, Missouri.

Use small letters if a particular place is not given:

We are looking for an auditorium we can rent for our meeting.

7. Use capital letters for geographic locations:

Jim was determined to find a good job in the West.

But use small letters for geographic directions:

To get to my house, you have to drive west on the turnpike.

8. Capitalize the names of specific products:

I always drink Diet Pepsi for breakfast.

But use small letters for a kind of product:

I always drink a diet cola for breakfast.

9. Capitalize the names of specific school courses.

I have to take Child Psychology next term.

But use small letters for a general academic subject.

My advisor told me to take a psychology course.

10. Capitalize the first and last words in the titles of long or short works, and capitalize all other significant words in the titles:

I've always wanted to read <u>The Old Man and the Sea</u>.

Whenever we go to see the team play, my uncle sings "Take Me Out to the Ballgame."

(Remember that the titles of long works, like books, are underlined; the titles of short ones, like songs, are quoted.)

Practice

Punctuating with Quotation Marks, Underlining, and Capital Letters.

Add any missing quotation marks, underlining, and capital letters to the sentences below.

1. I'll make you a deal, my sister said, if you promise not to tell Mother.

2. All my friends told me to see The fast and the furious, but by the time I got to the Regency mall theaters, the movie was no longer playing.

3. Lonette, don't bother me right now, her mother warned; I'm too busy to listen to your complaining.

4. The word love has different meanings for different people.

5. My boyfriend has a sports scholarship to Michigan state university; his brother attends a university in the south.

6. For a while, I watched television every week just to see the latest episode of Survivor, but now I think that show was silly.

7. My cousin and mother had free tickets to the concert at the Smith center for the Performing Arts; however, they gave them to dr. O'Brien and a doctor friend of his.

8. This time, my girlfriend said, you had better say 'please' when you ask me for a favor.

9. I know my aunt Ella has a good heart, but my aunt is also known for her hot temper.

10. Marcy is nearly finished with college, but she still has to take courses in mathematics, art, and physical education.

NUMBERS

Spell out numbers that take one or two words:

Alice mailed two hundred brochures.
I spent ninety dollars on car repairs.

Use the numbers themselves if it takes more than two words to spell them out:

We looked through 243 old photographs.
The sticker price was $10,397.99.

Also use numbers to write dates, times, and addresses:

We live at 24 Cambridge Street.
They were married on April 3, 1993.

ABBREVIATIONS

Although you should spell out most words rather than abbreviate them, you may abbreviate <u>Mr., Mrs., Ms., Jr., Sr., Dr</u>. when they are used with a proper name. You should abbreviate references to time and to organizations widely known by initials.

The moderator asked Ms. Steinem to comment.
The bus left at 5:00 P.M., and the trip took two hours.
He works for the FBI.

You should spell out the names of places, months, days of the week, courses of study, and words referring to parts of a book:

not this: I missed the last class, so I never got the notes for
Chap. Three.
but this: I missed the last class, so I never got the notes for Chapter
Three.

not this: He lives on Chestnut Street in Boston, Mass.
but this: He lives on Chestnut Street in Boston, Massachusetts.

not this: Pete missed his trig. test.
but this: Pete missed his trigonometry test.

 Using Numbers and Abbreviations

Practice

Correct any errors in the use of numbers or abbreviations in the following sentences. Some sentences may not need corrections.

1. We are looking for Thomas Pittman, Jr., the man who wrote the

editorial in today's paper.

2. My mother was born in Philadelphia, Penn., the youngest of

4 children, all girls.

3. The rent for the one-room apartment on Orchard St. was $1,250 a month.

4. I graduated from high school on June fourth, 2002, and I started my new job the following Mon.

5. The new biology prof. takes 2 weeks to return our test papers.

6. The answer to the psych. question is in Chap. 2 of the child psychology textbook.

7. The alarm went off at 7:00 A.M., so I had plenty of time to get ready for the trip to Orlando, Fla.

8. Dr. Chen found seventeen new specimens of a rare tropical insect; she will study them in her research facility at the Charter Chemical Co.

9. I sorted through three hundred and fifty photographs before I came across the one of our old house on Monroe Ave. in Pasadena, Cal.

10. Mario missed his econ. class last Weds. because he fell and twisted his ankle about fifty ft.from the classroom building.

 Exercise 4

Practice

A Comprehensive Exercise on Punctuation and Mechanics

Add any missing punctuation to the following sentences. Correct any errors in capitalization and in use of numbers or abbreviations.

1. Louisa moved her two cats food dishes, but they refused to eat in the new location.

2. The hike will take me through some rough terrain nevertheless I intend to make it.

3. Cinnamon toast which used to be my favorite breakfast food is the most popular item at the downtown coffee shop.

4. Whenever I ask you a question, she complained you answer it with another question.

5. I will wash the kitchen floor Sal will vacuum the living room and Lisa will clean the bathroom if you will do the laundry.

6. Trevor just spent five hundred and forty-six dollars on car repairs.

7. My little boy recently watched the lion king, and now he keeps singing the circle of life from the movie.

8. Luis can't cook without the proper equipment good knives copper pans deep bowls and a food processor.

9. Somebody left a textbook in the classroom so I took the book to the lost-and-found department.

10. Lenny got his first job in Scottsdale Arizona on March 21 1999 when he was 18.

11. Elaine Kovody who was my lab partner in biology class is now a surgeon at Livingston hill hospital.

12. My sister's smile a defiant sign of victory made me angry.

13. You know mom that you've hurt uncle James feelings.

14. Until you get rid of that broken down car you will always have to worry about lastminute repairs.

15. The tourist asked Is there a restaurant nearby

16. The tourist asked if there was a restaurant nearby.

17. Bill took several english courses in high school, and now he is taking an advanced communications course at Beacon college.

18. The man staring at me from the back of the room began to wave then he started walking toward me and called my name.

19. The pizza shop near the college is known for its low prices and good deals thus its always full of hungry students.

20. For years my mother has been pushing me to read a book called chicken soup for the soul but I hate chicken soup.

Practice

Another Comprehensive Exercise on Punctuation and Mechanics

Add any missing punctuation to the following sentences. Correct any errors in capitalization and in use of numbers or abbreviations.

1. When I was a child my favorite movie was The lion king I still like the movie and its music.

2. Take the leftovers home with you my mother said and share them with your roommates.

3. Mr Duval is a famous mathematician incidentally he is also a great skateboarder.

4. Four yrs. at Eagle High school taught me to respect others viewpoints explore others cultures and examine my own values.

5. If youre going to take Intro to Drawing you must buy everything on this list a large sketch pad three no. 3 pencils a box of charcoal, and a large eraser.

6. Why isnt there any milk in the refrigerator Sam asked.

7. Sam wanted to know why there wasn't any milk in the refrigerator.

8. Its too late mother for you to change Kirk and Lewis bad habits, but you can certainly object to them.

9. A woman pushing a baby stroller stopped in the middle of the sidewalk she then knelt down to check on the baby inside.

10. Smoking was making my clothes smell it was costing me money and it was wrecking my health so I decided to quit.

11. My sister still cries every time she hears the song, My heart will go on from the movie Titanic.

12. The meeting hall was beautifully decorated bright cotton tablecloths fresh flowers on every table and pale ivory candles in clear glass candlesticks among the flowers.

13. The hospital bill was $2,339 consequently I had to dip into my savings.

14. Alex Spiros my best friend is thinking about moving to Chicago Ill. at the end of Sept.

15. A diamond even a small one costs more than a plain gold ring.

16. Theres a small dog digging in Marcia and Kevins garden maybe the dog is theirs.

17. When it comes to talking about our raises, our boss is generous with his *hopefullys* but not with his *definitelys*.

18. After I finish this semester I ll ask my brother in law to help me paint my apartment.

19. At the end of the dinner the club members applauded the newly elected officers Dana Chodhury president Darius Lebow vice president Elaine Cohen secretary and Brett Anderson treasurer.

20. Theres nothing wrong with the car it just needs some oil.

CHAPTER 32

Spelling

No one is a perfect speller, but there are ways to become a better speller. If you can learn a few spelling rules, you can answer many of your spelling questions.

Vowels and Consonants

To understand the spelling rules, you need to know the difference between vowels and consonants. **Vowels** are the letters *a, e, i, o, u* and sometimes *y*. **Consonants** are all the other letters.

> The letter *y* is a vowel when it has a vowel sound.
>> silly (The *y* sounds like *ee*, a vowel sound.)
>> cry (The *y* sounds like *i*, a vowel sound.)
> The letter *y* is a consonant when it has a consonant sound.
>> yellow (The *y* has a consonant sound.)
>> yesterday (The *y* has a consonant sound.)

SPELLING RULE 1: DOUBLING A FINAL CONSONANT

Double the final consonant of a word if all three of the following are true:

1. The word is one syllable, or the accent is on the last syllable,
2. The word ends in a single consonant preceded by a single vowel, and
3. The ending you are adding starts with a vowel.

begin	+	ing	=	beginning
shop	+	er	=	shopper
stir	+	ed	=	stirred
occur	+	ed	=	occurred
fat	+	est	=	fattest
pin	+	ing	=	pinning

Exercise 1

Practice

Doubling a Final Consonant

Add -*ed* to the following words by applying the rules for doubling a final consonant.

1. simmer _____   **6.** expel _____

2. pat _____   **7.** reveal _____

3. kick _____   **8.** mop _____

4. murder _____   **9.** repel _____

5. permit _____   **10.** prefer _____

SPELLING RULE 2: DROPPING THE FINAL *e*

Drop the final *e* before you add an ending that starts with a vowel.

observe	+	ing	=	observing
excite	+	able	=	excitable
fame	+	ous	=	famous
create	+	ive	=	creative

Keep the final *e* before an ending that starts with a consonant:

love	+	ly	=	lovely
hope	+	ful	=	hopeful
excite	+	ment	=	excitement
life	+	less	=	lifeless

Exercise 2

Practice

Dropping the Final *e*

Combine the following words and endings by following the rule for dropping the final *e*.

1. evacuate + tion _____

2. love + less _____

3. engage + ment _____

4. peace + ful _____

5. amaze + ing _____

6. care + less _____

7. defense + ive _____

8. exquisite + ly _____

9. deplore + able _____

10. excuse + ing _____

SPELLING RULE 3: CHANGING THE FINAL *y* TO *i*

When a word ends in a consonant plus *y*, change the *y* to *i* when you add an ending:

try	+	es	=	tries
silly	+	er	=	sillier
rely	+	ance	=	reliance
tardy	+	ness	=	tardiness

Note: When you add *-ing* to words ending in *y*, always keep the *y*.

cry	+	ing	=	crying
rely	+	ing	=	relying

Exercise 3

Practice

Changing the Final *y* to *i*

Combine the following words and endings by applying the rule for changing the final *y* to *i*.

1. friendly + er _____

2. buy + ing _____

3. slay + er _____

4. mercy + less _____

5. carry + ed _____

6. supply + es _____

7. rely + ance _____

8. defy + ant _____

9. steady + ness _____

10. try + ing _____

SPELLING RULE 4: ADDING *-s* OR *-es*

Add *-es* instead of *-s* to a word if the word ends in *ch*, *sh*, *ss*, *x*, or *z*. The *es* adds an extra syllable to the word.

box	+	es	=	boxes
witch	+	es	=	witches
class	+	es	=	classes
clash	+	es	=	clashes

Exercise 4

Practice

Adding *-s* or *-es*

Apply the rule for adding *-s* or *-es* to the following words.

1. vanish _____	6. mix _____
2. repeat _____	7. glass _____
3. church _____	8. crash _____
4. clock _____	9. attack _____
5. impress _____	10. relax _____

SPELLING RULE 5: USING *ie* OR *ei*

Use *i* before *e*, except after *c*, or when the sound is like *a*, as in *neighbor* and *weigh*.

i before e:
relief   convenience   friend   piece

e before i:
conceive   sleigh   weight   receive

Exercise 5

Practice

Using *ie* or *ei*

Add *ie* or *ei* to the following words by applying the rule for using *ie* or *ei*.

1. dec___t	6. th___f
2. ___ghteen	7. n___ce
3. rec___pt	8. p___ce
4. rel___f	9. repr___ve
5. prem___re	10. ach___ve

Exercise 6

Practice

Spelling Rules: A Comprehensive Exercise

Combine the following words and endings by applying the spelling rules.

1. prefer   +   ed   _____
2. bury   +   ed   _____
3. buzz   +   s or es   _____
4. happy   +   er   _____
5. smash   +   s or es   _____
6. mass   +   s or es   _____
7. slip   +   ed   _____
8. steady   +   ness   _____

9. ply   +   able   _____

10. infer   +   ed   _____

11. surrender +   ed   _____

12. promote   +   ion   _____

13. hate   +   ful   _____

14. create   +   ive   _____

15. discourage +   ment   _____

16. defy   +   es   _____

17. convey   +   ance   _____

18. hatch   +   s or es _____

19. offer   +   ed   _____

 Exercise 7

Practice

Editing a Paragraph for Spelling

Correct the spelling errors in the following paragraph. Write your corrections above each error. There are fourteen errors.

Until recently, I did all my writeing assignments at the last minute, but I have finaly learned how much more effecttive it is to do my work in stepps. For example, if I have a paper to write, I start thinking about it right away. I make time to freewrite because freewriteing is a relyable way for me to get started, and it stimulates my createvity. Outlining is the next important step; I start with a list of ideas, and later I develop a more organized plan. I beleive this step is the most valueable one for me; I feel more confident if I work through this planing stage. Once I have my plan, I find drafting and revising less stressful than it used to be when I tryed to do everything at the last minute. Now that I am spliting my work into small tasks, I feel as if a great wieght has fallen off my shoulders, and I am more hopful about my abilities.

DO YOU SPELL IT AS ONE WORD OR TWO?

Sometimes you can be confused about certain words. You are not sure whether to combine them to make one word or to spell them as two words. The lists below show some commonly confused words.

Words That Should Not Be Combined

a lot	each other	high school	every time
even though	good night	all right	no one
living room	dining room	in front	

Words That Should Be Combined

another	newspapers	bathroom
bedroom	playroom	good-bye, goodbye, or good-by
bookkeeper	roommate	cannot
schoolteacher	downstairs	southeast, northwest, etc.
grandmother	throughout	nearby
worthwhile	nevertheless	yourself, himself, myself, etc.

Words Whose Spelling Depends on Their Meaning

one word: *Already* means "before."
  He offered to do the dishes, but I had *already* done them.
two words: *All ready* means "ready."
  My dog was *all ready* to play Frisbee.

one word: *Altogether* means "entirely."
  That movie was *altogether* too confusing.
two words: *All together* means "in a group."
  My sisters were *all together* in the kitchen.

one word: *Always* means "every time."
  My grandfather is *always* right about baseball statistics.
two words: *All ways* means "every path" or "every aspect."
  We tried *all ways* to get to the beach house.
  He is a gentleman in *all ways*.

one word: *Anymore* means "any longer."
  I do not want to exercise *anymore*.
two words: *Any more* means "additional."
  Are there *any more* pickles?

one word: *Anyone* means "any person at all."
  Is *anyone* home?
two words: *Any one* means "one person or thing in a special group."
  I'll take *any one* of the chairs on sale.

one word: *Apart* means "separate."
  Liam stood *apart* from his friends.
two words: *A part* is "a piece or section."
  I read *a part* of the chapter.

one word: *Everyday* means "ordinary."
Tim was wearing his *everyday* clothes.
two words: *Every day* means "each day."
Sam jogs *every day.*

one word: *Everyone* means "all the people."
Everyone has bad days.
two words: *Every one* means "all the people or things in a specific group."
My father asked *every one* of the neighbors for a donation to the Red Cross.

Exercise 8

Practice

Do You Spell It as One Word or Two?

Circle the correct word in parentheses in each sentence below.

1. Sarah said she couldn't promise a fancy dinner, just an (every day, everyday) sort of meal.

2. I was away at college when my sister started (high school, high-school).

3. Norma isn't working at the bank (any more, anymore).

4. It is difficult to say (good bye, goodbye) when you don't know when you will see (each other, eachother) again.

5. Nathan hates to see his little girl ice skate; he is afraid she will fall and hurt (her self, herself).

6. Jimmy and Guido sat and talked about the times they were (room mates, roommates).

7. (Every time, Everytime) Enrique calls, he asks about Gloria.

8. Harry told me the news about his job, but I had (all ready, already) heard it.

9. You can borrow (any one, anyone) of the shirts in my closet.

10. Mack has been in a car accident; I hope he is (all right, allright).

Exercise 9

Practice

Do You Spell It as One Word or Two? Correcting Errors in a Paragraph

The following paragraph contains errors in word combinations. Correct the errors above each line. There are ten errors.

I know that every one has bad days, but lately it seems that every one of my days has been a disaster. On Monday, for instance, I tripped on some sneakers that were right infront of me and fell in my bed room. My room mate thought it was the funniest thing he had ever seen. Then, on Tuesday, I was driving north west on Charles Avenue when I got stuck in a traffic jam at the highschool and bumped into the car in front of me. Any one can have an accident like that, but I cannot stop blaming my self. Since Wednesday, I have been at home with the flu and feeling altogether miserable. I don't want to get out of bed any more because I may discover more bad luck, and I have all ready had enough of it.

COMMONLY MISSPELLED WORDS

Following is a list of words you use often in your writing. Study this list and use it as a reference.

1. absence	29. August	57. buried
2. absent	30. aunt	58. business
3. accept	31. author	59. busy
4. accommodate	32. automobile	60. calendar
5. ache	33. autumn	61. cannot
6. achieve	34. avenue	62. career
7. acquire	35. awful	63. careful
8. across	36. awkward	64. catch
9. actually	37. balance	65. category
10. advertise	38. basically	66. caught
11. again	39. because	67. cemetery
12. a lot	40. becoming	68. cereal
13. all right	41. beginning	69. certain
14. almost	42. behavior	70. chair
15. always	43. belief	71. cheat
16. amateur	44. believe	72. chicken
17. American	45. benefit	73. chief
18. answer	46. bicycle	74. children
19. anxious	47. bought	75. cigarette
20. apparent	48. breakfast	76. citizen
21. appetite	49. breathe	77. city
22. apology	50. brilliant	78. college
23. appreciate	51. brother	79. color
24. argue	52. brought	80. comfortable
25. argument	53. bruise	81. committee
26. asked	54. build	82. competition
27. athlete	55. bulletin	83. conscience
28. attempt	56. bureau	84. convenient

85. conversation
86. copy
87. cough
88. cousin
89. criticism
90. criticize
91. crowded
92. daily
93. daughter
94. deceive
95. decide
96. definite
97. dentist
98. dependent
99. deposit
100. describe
101. desperate
102. development
103. different
104. dilemma
105. dining
106. direction
107. disappearance
108. disappoint
109. discipline
110. disease
111. divide
112. doctor
113. doesn't
114. don't
115. doubt
116. during
117. dying
118. early
119. earth
120. eighth
121. eligible
122. embarrass
123. encouragement
124. enough
125. environment
126. especially
127. etc. (et cetera)
128. every
129. exact
130. exaggeration
131. excellent
132. except
133. excite
134. exercise
135. existence

136. expect
137. experience
138. explanation
139. factory
140. familiar
141. family
142. fascinating
143. February
144. finally
145. forehead
146. foreign
147. forty
148. fourteen
149. friend
150. fundamental
151. general
152. generally
153. goes
154. going
155. government
156. grammar
157. grateful
158. grocery
159. guarantee
160. guard
161. guess
162. guidance
163. guide
164. half
165. handkerchief
166. happiness
167. heavy
168. height
169. heroes
170. holiday
171. hospital
172. humorous
173. identity
174. illegal
175. imaginary
176. immediately
177. important
178. independent
179. integration
180. intelligent
181. interest
182. interfere
183. interpretation
184. interrupt
185. iron
186. irrelevant

187. irritable
188. island
189. January
190. jewelry
191. judgment*
192. kindergarten
193. kitchen
194. knowledge
195. laboratory
196. language
197. laugh
198. leisure
199. length
200. library
201. listen
202. loneliness
203. lying
204. maintain
205. maintenance
206. marriage
207. mathematics
208. meant
209. measure
210. medicine
211. millennium
212. million
213. miniature
214. minute
215. muscle
216. mysterious
217. naturally
218. necessary
219. neighbor
220. nervous
221. nickel
222. niece
223. ninety
224. ninth
225. occasion
226. o'clock
227. often
228. omission
229. once
230. operate
231. opinion
232. optimist
233. original
234. parallel
235. particular
236. peculiar
237. perform

*judgement is also correct; students often omit the "d."

238. perhaps
239. permanent
240. persevere
241. personnel
242. persuade
243. physically
244. pleasant
245. possess
246. possible
247. potato
248. practical
249. prefer
250. prejudice
251. prescription
252. presence
253. president
254. privilege
255. probably
256. professor
257. psychology
258. punctuation
259. pursue
260. quart
261. really
262. receipt
263. receive
264. recognize
265. recommend

266. reference
267. religious
268. reluctantly
269. remember
270. resource
271. restaurant
272. ridiculous
273. right
274. rhythm
275. sandwich
276. Saturday
277. scene
278. schedule
279. scissors
280. secretary
281. seize
282. several
283. severely
284. significant
285. similar
286. since
287. sincerely
288. soldier
289. sophomore
290. strength
291. studying
292. success

293. surely
294. surprise
295. taught
296. temperature
297. theater
298. thorough
299. thousand
300. tied
301. tomorrow
302. tongue
303. tragedy
304. trouble
305. truly
306. twelfth
307. unfortunately
308. unknown
309. until
310. unusual
311. using
312. variety
313. vegetable
314. Wednesday
315. weird
316. which
317. writing
318. written
319. yesterday

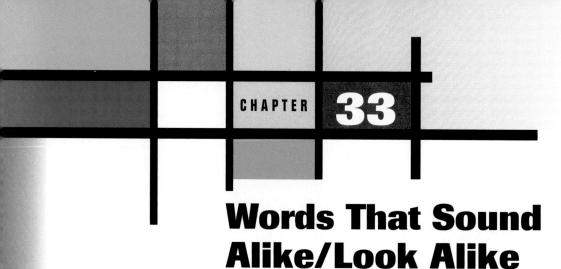

Words That Sound Alike/Look Alike

WORDS THAT SOUND ALIKE/LOOK ALIKE

Words that sound alike or look alike can be confusing. Here is a list of some of the confusing words. Study this list, and make a note of any words that give you trouble.

a/an/and *A* is used before a word beginning with a consonant or consonant sound:

> Jason bought *a* car.

An is used before a word beginning with a vowel or vowel sound:

> Nancy took *an* apple to work.

And joins words or ideas:

> Pudding *and* cake are my favorite desserts.
>
> Fresh vegetables taste delicious, *and* they are nutritious.

accept/except *Accept* means "to receive":

> I *accept* your apology.

Except means "excluding":

> I'll give you all my books *except* my dictionary.

addition/edition An *addition* is something that is added:

> My father built an *addition* to our house in the form of a porch.

An *edition* is an issue of a newspaper or one of a series of printings of a book:

> I checked the latest *edition* of the *Daily News* to see if my advertisement is in it.

advice/advise *Advice* is an opinion offered as a guide; it is what you give someone:

> Betty asked for my *advice* about finding a job.

Advise is what you do when you give an opinion offered as a guide:

> I couldn't *advise* Betty about finding a job.

affect/effect *Affect* means "to influence something":

> Getting a bad grade will *affect* my chances for a scholarship.

Effect means "a result" or "to cause something to happen":
>Your kindness had a great *effect* on me.
>The committee struggled to *effect* a compromise.

allowed/aloud *Allowed* means "permitted":
>I'm not *allowed* to skateboard on those steps.

Aloud means "out loud":
>The teacher read the story *aloud*.

all ready/already *All ready* means "ready":
>The dog was *all ready* to go for a walk.

Already means "before":
>David had *already* made the salad.

altar/alter An *altar* is a table or place in a church:
>They were married in front of the *altar*.

Alter means "to change":
>My plane was delayed, so I had to *alter* my plans for the evening.

angel/angle An *angel* is a heavenly being:
>That night, I felt an *angel* guiding me.

An *angle* is the space within two lines:
>The road turned at a sharp *angle*.

are/our *Are* is a verb, the plural of *is:*
>We *are* friends of the mayor.

Our means "belonging to us":
>We have *our* family quarrels.

beside/besides *Beside* means "next to":
>He sat *beside* me at the concert.

Besides means "in addition":
>I would never lie to you; *besides*, I have no reason to lie.

brake/break *Brake* means "to stop" or "a device for stopping":
>That truck *brakes* at railroad crossings.
>When he saw the animal on the road, he hit the *brakes*.

Break means "to come apart" or "to make something come apart":
>The eggs are likely to *break*.
>I can *break* the seal on that package.

breath/breathe *Breath* is the air you take in, and it rhymes with *death:*
>I was running so fast that I lost my *breath*.

Breathe means "to take in air":
>He found it hard to *breathe* in high altitudes.

buy/by *Buy* means "to purchase something":
>Sylvia wants to *buy* a shovel.

By means "near," "by means of," or "before":
>He sat *by* his sister.
>I learn *by* taking good notes in class.
>*By* ten o'clock, Nick was tired.

capital/capitol *Capital* means "city" or "wealth":
>Albany is the *capital* of New York.
>Jack invested his *capital* in real estate.

A *capitol* is a building:
>The city has a famous *capitol* building.

cereal/serial *Cereal* is a breakfast food or type of grain:
My favorite *cereal* is Cheerios.
Serial means "in a series":
Look for the *serial* number on the appliance.

choose/chose *Choose* means "to select." It rhymes with *snooze:*
Today I am going to *choose* a new sofa.
Chose is the past tense of *choose:*
Yesterday I *chose* a new rug.

close/clothes/cloths *Close* means "near" or "intimate." It can also mean "to end or shut something":
We live *close* to the train station.
James and Margie are *close* friends.
Noreen wants to *close* her eyes for ten minutes.
Clothes are wearing apparel:
Eduardo has new *clothes.*
Cloths are pieces of fabric:
I clean the silver with damp *cloths* and a special polish.

coarse/course *Coarse* means "rough" or "crude":
The top of the table had a *coarse* texture.
His language was *coarse.*
A *course* is a direction or path. It is also a subject in school:
The hurricane took a northern *course.*
In my freshman year, I took a *course* in drama.

complement/compliment *Complement* means "complete" or "make better":
The colors in that room *complement* the style of the furniture.
A *compliment* is praise:
Trevor gave me a *compliment* about my cooking.

conscience/conscious Your *conscience* is your inner, moral guide:
His *conscience* bothered him when he told a lie.
Conscious means "aware" or "awake":
The accident victim was not fully *conscious.*

council/counsel A *council* is a group of people:
The city *council* meets tonight.
Counsel means "advice" or "to give advice":
I need your *counsel* about my investments.
My father always *counsels* me about my career.

decent/descent *Decent* means "suitable or proper":
I hope Mike gets a *decent* job.
Descent means "going down, falling, or sinking":
The plane began its *descent* to the airport.

desert/dessert A *desert* is dry land. To *desert* means "to abandon":
To survive a trip across the *desert*, people need water.
He will never *desert* a friend.
Dessert is the sweet food we eat at the end of a meal:
I want ice cream for *dessert.*

do/due *Do* means "perform":
I have to stop complaining; I *do* it constantly.

Due means "owing" or "because of":
> The rent is *due* tomorrow.
> The game was canceled *due* to rain.

does/dose   *Does* is a form of *do:*
> My father *does* the laundry.

A *dose* is a quantity of medicine:
> Whenever I had a cold, my mother gave me a *dose* of cough syrup.

fair/fare   *Fair* means "unbiased." It can also mean "promising" or "good":
> The judge's decision was *fair.*
> José has a *fair* chance of winning the title.

A *fare* is the amount of money a passenger must pay:
> I couldn't afford the plane *fare* to Miami.

farther/further   *Farther* means "a greater physical distance":
> His house is a few blocks *farther* down the street.

Further means "greater" or "additional." Use it when you are not describing a physical distance:
> My second French class gave me *further* training in French conversation.

flour/flower   *Flour* is ground-up grain, an ingredient used in cooking:
> I use whole-wheat *flour* in my muffins.

A *flower* is a blossom:
> She wore a *flower* in her hair.

forth/fourth   *Forth* means "forward":
> The pendulum on the clock swung back and *forth.*

Fourth means "number four in a sequence":
> I was *fourth* in line for tickets.

hear/here   *Hear* means "to receive sounds in the ear":
> I can *hear* the music.

Here is a place:
> We can have the meeting *here.*

heard/herd   *Heard* is the past tense of *hear:*
> I *heard* you talk in your sleep last night.

A *herd* is a group of animals:
> The farmer has a fine *herd* of cows.

hole/whole   A *hole* is an empty place or opening:
> I see a *hole* in the wall.

Whole means "complete" or "entire":
> Silvio gave me the *whole* steak.

isle/aisle   An *isle* is an island.
We visited the *isle* of Capri.
An *aisle* is a passageway between sections of seats.
The flight attendant came down the *aisle* and offered us coffee.

its/it's   *Its* means "belonging to it":
> The car lost *its* rear bumper.

It's is a shortened form of *it is* or *it has:*
> *It's* a beautiful day.
> *It's* been a pleasure to meet you.

knew/new *Knew* is the past tense of *know:*
I *knew* Teresa in high school.
New means "fresh, recent, not old":
I want some *new* shoes.

know/no *Know* means "to understand":
They *know* how to play soccer.
No is a negative:
Carla has *no* fear of heights.

Exercise **1**

Practice

Words That Sound Alike/Look Alike

Circle the correct words in parentheses in each sentence below.

1. When the bride and groom stood at the (altar, alter), my daughter, the (flour, flower) girl behind them, looked like a little (angel, angle).

2. Everyone (accept, except) Karen is ready to take Victor's (advice, advise) about an appropriate (coarse, course) of action.

3. Too much criticism can have a negative (affect, effect) on a child; it can (brake, break) a child's spirit.

4. Eric never (allowed, aloud) himself to spend any money on the day the rent was (do, due).

5. I ran out of (breath, breathe) trying to make it to work (buy, by) 9:00 A.M.

6. I don't like the (close, clothes) that Ingrid bought, but she can (choose, chose) what she wants.

7. You deserve a complement, compliment) for the way you explained (are, our) store policy and (knew, new) how to handle the angry customer.

8. Tom thinks (its, it's) only (fair, fare) to pay the guest of honor's plane (fair, fare).

9. This discussion has lost (its, it's) point; let's not take it any (farther, further).

10. The (hole, whole) issue is a matter of each individual's (conscience, conscious).

Exercise **2**

👥 *Collaborate*

Words That Sound Alike/Look Alike

Working with a partner or group, write one sentence for each word below.

1. a. hear _____

   b. here _____.

2. a. coarse _____

   b. course _____

3. a. council _____

   b. counsel _____

4. a. forth _____

   b. fourth _____

5. a. capital _____

   b. capitol _____

6. a. desert _____

   b. dessert _____

7. a. cereal _____

   b. serial _____

8. a. does _____

   b. dose _____

9. a. know _____

   b. no _____

10. a. addition _____

   b. edition _____

Exercise 3   **Editing a Paragraph for Words That Sound Alike/Look Alike**

Practice   The following paragraph has errors in words that sound alike/look alike. Correct each error in the space above it. There are eight errors.

I am taking my sister's advise and reading allowed to my daughter

every night. My sister, who teaches elementary school, says that reading to

a child helps the child associate books with pleasure. I no my three-year-old

loves to here the stories and to see the pictures in the books I share with

her. She especially likes to hear the same stories over and over again so that

she is sure of what is coming next. Beside, a bedtime story helps to create a

feeling of closeness between me and my little girl. As I read to her, I am conscience of her snuggling up to me, her soft breathe against my cheek.

Most of all, it's a time when I realize how lucky I am to be the father of such

an angle.

MORE WORDS THAT SOUND ALIKE/LOOK ALIKE

lead/led When *lead* rhymes with *need*, it means "to give directions, to take charge." When *lead* rhymes with *bed*, it is a metal:
> The marching band will *lead* the parade.
> Your bookbag is as heavy as *lead*.

Led is the past form of *lead* when it means "to give direction, to take charge":
> The cheerleaders *led* the parade last year.

loan/lone A *loan* is something you give on the condition that it be returned:
> When I was broke, I got a *loan* of fifty dollars from my aunt.

Lone means "solitary, alone":
> A lone *shopper* stood in the checkout line.

loose/lose *Loose* means "not tight."
> In the summer, *loose* clothing keeps me cool.

To *lose* something means "to be unable to keep it":
> I'm afraid I will *lose* my car keys.

lessen/lesson *Lessen* means make less or reduce.
> I took an aspirin to *lessen* the pain of my headache.
> A *lesson* is something to be learned or studied.
> I had my first guitar *lesson* yesterday.

moral/morale *Moral* means "upright, honorable, connected to ethical standards":
> I have a *moral* obligation to care for my children.

Morale is confidence or spirit:
> After the game, the team's *morale* was low.

pain/pane *Pain* means "suffering":
> I had very little *pain* after the surgery.

A *pane* is a piece of glass:
> The girl's wild throw broke a window *pane*.

pair/pear A *pair* is a set of two:
> Mark has a *pair* of antique swords.

A *pear* is a fruit:
> In the autumn, I like a *pear* for a snack.

passed/past *Passed* means "went by." It can also mean "handed to":
> The happy days *passed* too quickly.
> Janice *passed* me the mustard.

Past means "the time that has gone by":
> Let's leave the *past* behind us.

patience/patients *Patience* is calm endurance:
> When I am caught in a traffic jam, I should have more *patience*.

Patients are people under medical care:
> There are too many *patients* in the doctor's waiting room.

peace/piece   *Peace* is calmness:

> Looking at the ocean brings me a sense of *peace*.

A *piece* is a part of something:

> Norman took a *piece* of coconut cake.

personal/personnel   *Personal* means connected to a person. It can also mean intimate.

> Whether to lease or own a car is a *personal* choice.

> That information is too *personal* to share.

Personnel are the staff in an office.

> The Digby Electronics Company is developing a new health plan for its *personnel*.

plain/plane   *Plain* means "simple, clear, or ordinary." It can also mean "flat land."

> The restaurant serves *plain* but tasty food.

> Her house was in the center of a windy *plain*.

A *plane* is an aircraft:

> We took a small *plane* to the island.

presence/presents   Your *presence* is your attendance, your being somewhere.

> We request your *presence* at our wedding.

Presents are gifts:

> My daughter got too many birthday *presents*.

principal/principle   *Principal* means "most important." It also means "the head of a school":

> My *principal* reason for quitting is the low salary.

> The *principal* of Crestview Elementary School is popular with students.

A *principle* is a guiding rule:

> Betraying a friend is against my *principles*.

quiet/quit/quite   *Quiet* means "without noise":

> The library has many *quiet* corners.

Quit means "stop":

> Will you *quit* complaining?

Quite means "truly" or "exactly":

> Victor's speech was *quite* convincing.

rain/reign/rein   *Rain* is wet weather:

> We have had a week of *rain*.

To *reign* is to rule; *reign* is royal rule:

> King Arthur's *reign* in Camelot is the subject of many poems.

A *rein* is a leather strap in an animal's harness:

> When Charlie got on the horse, he held the *reins* very tight.

right/rite/write   *Right* is a direction (the opposite of left). It can also mean "correct":

> To get to the gas station, turn *right* at the corner.

> On my sociology test, I got nineteen out of twenty questions *right*.

A *rite* is a ceremony:

> I am interested in the funeral *rites* of other cultures.

To *write* is to set down in words:

> Brian has to *write* a book report.

sight/site/cite   A *sight* is something you can see:

> The truck stop was a welcome *sight*.

A *site* is a location:

The city is building a courthouse on the *site* of my old school.

Cite means to "quote an authority." It can also mean "to give an example":

In her term paper, Christina wanted to *cite* several computer experts.

When my father lectured me on speeding, he *cited* the story of my best friend's car accident.

sole/soul A *sole* is the bottom of a foot or shoe:

My left boot needs a new *sole*.

A *soul* is the spiritual part of a person:

Some people say meditation is good for the *soul*.

stair/stare A *stair* is a step:

The toddler carefully climbed each *stair*.

A *stare* is a long, fixed look:

I wish that woman wouldn't *stare* at me.

stake/steak A *stake* is a stick driven into the ground; it also means "in question":

He was nervous because his career was at *stake*.

The gardener put *stakes* around the tomato plants.

A *steak* is a piece of meat or fish:

I like my *steak* cooked medium rare.

stationary/stationery *Stationary* means "standing still":

As the speaker presented his speech, he remained *stationary*.

Stationery is writing paper:

For my birthday, my uncle gave me some *stationery* with my name printed on it.

steal/steel To *steal* means to take someone else's property without permission, especially secretly or by force:

Last night someone tried to *steal* my car.

Steel is a form of iron:

The door is made of *steel*.

than/then *Than* is used to compare things:

My dog is more intelligent *than* many people.

Then means at that time.

I lived in Buffalo for two years; *then* I moved to Albany.

their/there/they're *Their* means "belonging to them":

My grandparents donated *their* old television to a women's shelter.

There means "at that place." It can also be used as an introductory word:

Sit *there*, next to Simone.

There is a reason for his happiness.

They're is a contraction of *they are:*

Jaime and Sandra are visiting; *they're* my cousins.

thorough/through/threw *Thorough* means complete:

I did a *thorough* cleaning of my closet.

Through means "from one side to the other." It can also mean "finished":

We drove *through* Greenview on our way to Lake Western.

I'm *through* with my studies.

Threw is the past tense of throw:

I threw the ball to him

to/too/two *To* means "in a direction toward." It is also a word that can go in front of a verb:

I am driving *to* Miami.

Selena loves *to* write poems.

Too means "also." It also means "very":

Anita played great golf; Adam did well, *too*.

It is *too* kind of you to visit.

Two is the number:

Mr. Almeida owns *two* clothing stores.

vain/vane/vein *Vain* means "conceited." It also means "unsuccessful":

Victor is *vain* about his dark, curly hair.

The doctor made a *vain* attempt to revive the patient.

A *vane* is a device that moves to indicate the direction of the wind:

There was an old weather *vane* on the barn roof.

A *vein* is a blood vessel:

I could see the *veins* in his hands.

waist/waste The *waist* is the middle part of the body:

He had a leather belt around his *waist*.

Waste means "to use carelessly." It also means "thrown away because it is useless":

I can't *waste* my time watching trashy television shows.

That manufacturing plant has many *waste* products.

wait/weight *Wait* means "to hold yourself ready for something":

I can't *wait* until my check arrives.

Weight means "heaviness":

He tested the *weight* of the bat.

weather/whether *Weather* refers to conditions outside:

If the *weather* is warm, I'll go swimming.

Whether means "if":

Whether you help me or not, I'll paint the hallway.

were/we're/where *Were* is the past form of *are*:

Only last year, we *were* scared freshmen.

We're is the contraction of *we are*:

Today *we're* confident sophomores.

Where refers to a place:

Show me *where* you used to play basketball.

whined/wind/wined *Whined* means "complained":

Polly *whined* about the weather because the rain kept her indoors.

Wind (when it rhymes with *find*) means to "coil or wrap something" or "to turn a key":

Wind that extension cord, or you'll trip on it.

Wind (when it rhymes with *sinned*) is air in motion:

The *wind* blew my cap off.

If someone *wined* you, he or she treated you to some wine:

My brother *wined* and dined his boss.

who's/whose *Who's* is a contraction of *who is* or *who has*:

Who's driving?

Whose means "belonging to whom":

I wonder *whose* dog this is.

woman/women *Woman* means "one adult female person":

A *woman* in the supermarket gave me her extra coupons.

Women means "more than one woman":
Three *women* from Missouri joined the management team.

wander/wonder *Wander* means to move about without a definite purpose. It may also mean to become lost:
I love to *wander* around antique stores and flea markets.
The child *wandered* the streets, looking for his parents.
Wonder means to think or be curious about something:
Jill *wonders* if she will ever see Thomas again.

wood/would *Wood* is a hard substance made from trees:
I have a table made of a polished *wood.*
Would is the past form of *will:*
Albert said he *would* think about the offer.

your/you're *Your* means "belonging to you":
I think you dropped *your* wallet.
You're is the contraction of *you are:*
You're not telling the truth.

Exercise 4

Practice

More Words That Sound Alike/Look Alike

Circle the correct words in each sentence below.

1. Queen Victoria of England is known for her long (rain, reign, rein) and for the (moral, morale) standards that came to be named after her.

2. (Their, There, They're) is a (woman, women) in my anthropology class who is writing her research paper on the initiation (rights, rites, writes) of an African tribe.

3. Since the (principal, principle) investor at the company complained about money (waisted, wasted) on unnecessary staff, most of the (personal, personnel) have been worried about job security.

4. If you (wood, would) like to see which way the (whined, wind, wined) is blowing, check the (weather, whether) (vain, vane, vein) on the top of the barn.

5. (Were, We're, Where) taking the (lead, led) pipe out of the old house.

6. Once we do a (thorough, through, threw) inventory of the stockroom, we will be (thorough, through, threw) with today's work.

7. Even though that movie star is extremely (vain, vane, vein) and difficult to deal with, his (presence, presents) at our charity concert will bring in more money (than, then) we could ever make without him.

8. (Your, You're) having trouble writing (your, you're) paper because (your, you're) not sure how to (sight, site, cite) the sources you used.

9. Elsa was (to, too, two) angry (to , too, two) respond when a (woman , women) at work called her a fool.

10. Jennifer (thorough, through, threw) a baseball (thorough, through, threw) her neighbor's window and had to pay $100 to replace a (pain, pane) of glass.

Exercise 5

👥 *Collaborate*

More Words That Sound Alike/Look Alike

Working with a partner or group, write one sentence for each of the words below. When you have completed this exercise, exchange work with another for evaluation.

1. a. loose _____

   b. lose _____

2. a. stationary _____

   b. stationery _____

3. a. loan _____

   b. lone _____

4. a. passed _____

   b. past _____

5. a. plain _____

   b. plane _____

6. a. who's _____

   b. whose _____

7. a. sole _____

   b. soul _____

8. a. stake _____

   b. steak _____

9. a. wait _____

   b. weight _____

10. a. stair _____

   b. stare _____

Exercise 6

Practice

Editing a Paragraph for Errors in More Words That Sound Alike/Look Alike

The following paragraph has errors in words that sound alike or look alike. Correct each error in the space above it. There are thirteen errors.

When and where to attend college is a personnel decision; everyone

must decide what is rite for him or her. Some people are quiet happy to start

college as soon as they finish high school. They don't want to waist time.

Others choose to take some time off between high school and college.

Maybe there financial or family situation requires them too earn some

money before they continue they're education, or maybe they just want to

weight and explore their options before they start more schooling. Where to

go to college is also a major decision. Many choose a college close to home

so they don't have to give up friends, family, or jobs. Others want to explore

a new environment; their principle reason for leaving home is to put their

teen years in the passed. Whatever the choices are, they should be the soul

choice of the person who's future is at steak.

Exercise 7

Practice

Words That Sound Alike/Look Alike: A Comprehensive Exercise

Circle the correct words in parentheses in each sentence below.

1. Michael got some interesting (stairs, stares) from his supervisors when he said he (wood, would) rather (quiet, quit, quite) his job (than, then) be (quiet, quit, quite) on a matter of ethics and (moral, morale) values.

2. In (addition, edition) to having monogrammed (stationary, stationery), Gus has monogrammed luggage.

3. Keith was (all ready, already) to offer us some ice cream when he realized we had (all ready, already) had (desert, dessert) at home.

4. The old house is full of narrow corridors and sharp (angels, angles), so (its, it's) easy to (loose, lose) (your, you're) way.

5. The accident victim was barely (conscience, conscious) and moaning in (pain, pane) while the other (patience, patients) slept.

6. I (knew, new) Martha would (loose, lose) her temper; I told her to take a deep (breath, breathe) and count to ten.

7. Learning to (accept, except) what you cannot change can bring you a feeling of (peace, piece).

8. My advisor told me that the (close, clothes, cloths) I wear to an interview can (affect, effect) my chances of getting a (decent, descent) job.

9. Keshia needs bus (fair, fare) in case the (weather, whether) is (to, too, two) wet for her to walk.

10. My car payment is (do, due) on the (forth, fourth) of the month, but I don't have the money to pay the (hole, whole) amount.

11. The (coarse, course) wool (close, clothes, cloths) that the campers used as blankets made my skin itch.

12. Phillip tightened the (rains, reigns, reins) as the horse galloped (thorough, through, threw) the meadow.

13. Take my (advice, advise): serve your family (plain, plane) food like (stake, steak) or chicken.

14. (Their, There, They're) traveling (farther, further) (than, then) I am to get to the governor's economic (council, counsel) meeting.

15. I won't apply for a job at the new health food market because I (heard, herd) a rumor about poor working conditions at that store; (beside, besides), it offers no health benefits.

16. My grandmother is (vain, vein) about her (flour, flower) garden.

17. Mrs. Portrusky is a (woman, women) who (choose, chose) to study law at a time when few (woman, women) had entered the profession.

18. Of (coarse, course), you can have (cereal, serial) for breakfast, but I've (all ready, already) made bacon and eggs.

19. (Buy, by) the time we were (allowed, aloud) to board the (plain, plane), we had lost all (are, our) (patience, patients).

20. Whenever Alan comes over, he brings (presence, presents) for my children and he (complements, compliments) my cooking.

 Exercise 8

Practice

Editing a Paragraph for Errors in Words That Sound Alike/Look Alike: A Comprehensive Exercise

The following paragraph has errors in words that sound alike or look alike. Correct each error in the space above it. There are twelve errors.

I new I had found the right apartment the first time I saw it. I had

spent all day looking at places to rent, going threw dirty apartments, ugly apartments, and depressing apartments without finding a single descent one out of the hole bunch. Just when I thought I wood never find a place to live, I discovered a perfect home. It has to large rooms, big windows with solid pains of glass, and a small but clean bathroom. I particularly like the high ceilings, which are higher then the ceilings in any of the other apartments I saw. There are many other attractive features. The apartment is on the second floor, so I won't have to climb too many stares. The previous tenant left blinds on the windows, so I won't have to spend money on window coverings. In edition, my new home is within walking distance of the college, and its only a few blocks from my job. I can't weight to move in.

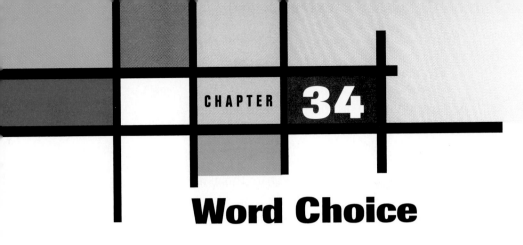

CHAPTER 34

Word Choice

One way to improve your writing is to pay attention to your choice of words. As you revise and edit, be careful to use precise language and to avoid wordiness and clichés.

PRECISE LANGUAGE

Try to be as specific as you can in explaining or describing. Replace vague, general words or phrases with more precise language.

not this: Last night, I made a lot of money in tips.
but this: Last night, I made *$50* in tips.

not this: He gave me a nice smile.
but this: He gave me a *friendly* smile.
or this: He gave me a *reassuring* smile.
or this: He gave me a *welcoming* smile.

not this: Maggie is a good friend.
but this: Maggie is a *loyal* friend.
or this: Maggie is a *devoted* friend.

Exercise 1 **Using Precise Language**

Practice

Replace the italicized word or phrase in each sentence following with a more precise word or phrase. Write your revisions above the lines.

1. Derek has a *nice* car.

2. Over the weekend, my girlfriend and I rented *a lot* of movies.

3. When I was younger, I used to play games at the video arcade *often*.

4. My math teacher is *nice*.

5. Last night, my brother got some *bad* news.

6. I want to read a story that is *interesting*.

7. It took me *a lot* of time to write this paper.

8. Adnan had a *bad* day.

9. That shirt looks *funny* on you.

10. The basketball game was *great*.

WORDINESS

As you revise and edit your work, check for *wordiness*, the use of extra words. If you can say the same thing in fewer words, do so. You can be precise *and* direct.

not this: After the accident, I thought in my mind that I was to blame.
but this: After the accident, *I thought* I was to blame.

not this: In my opinion, I think children should exercise daily.
but this: *I think* children should exercise daily.

not this: Jorge bought a CD for the price of $10.95.
but this: Jorge bought a CD *for* $10.95.

Here is a list of some wordy expressions and possible substitutes:

Wordy Expressions	Possible Substitutes
attach together	attach
at that time	then
at the present time	now
basic essentials	essentials
blend together	blend
by means of	by
by the fact that	because
day in and day out	daily
deep down inside he believed	he believed
due to the fact that	because
each and every one	each one
for the reason that	because
have a need for	need
have a realization of	realize
I felt inside	I felt
I personally feel	I feel
I thought in my head	I thought
I thought to myself	I thought
in the field of art (music, etc.)	in art (music, etc.)
in the near future	soon
in this day and age	today
in this modern world	today
in my mind, I think	I think

in my opinion, I think	I think
in order to	to
in today's society	today
maximum amount	maximum
of a remarkable kind	remarkable
on a daily basis	daily
on a regular basis	regularly
past experience	experience
point in time	time
really and truly	really
refer back	refer
repeat again	repeat
short in stature	short
small in size	small
the reason being	because
top priority	priority
two different kinds	two kinds
very unique	unique

Exercise 2

Practice

Revising for Wordiness

Revise the following sentences, eliminating the wordiness. Write your revisions in the space above the lines.

1. I try to work out on a daily basis due to the fact that my health is my top priority.

2. In today's society, many people have to work hard in order to provide the basic essentials for their families.

3. For the reason that my past experience was not in the field of business, I was not eligible for the job.

4. The only way I can refer back to that point in time is by means of checking my records.

5. I personally feel that the product is very unique.

6. I quit my receptionist job for the reason that I was sick of repeating "How can I help you?" again and again.

7. In the near future, we can expect to receive email on a regular basis.

8. At the present time, we are studying the two different kinds of programs to see if they would blend together efficiently.

9. Even though he was short in stature, deep down in his mind he believed he could make the team.

10. The salesman promised that the car would provide a maximum amount of satisfaction at a reasonable price.

CLICHÉS

Clichés are worn-out expressions. Once they were a new way of making a point, but now they are old and tired. You should avoid them in your writing.

not this: I know that Monica will always be there for me.
but this: I know that Monica will always support me.

not this: Alan experienced the trials and tribulations of late registration.
but this: Alan experienced the difficulties of late registration.

Following are some common clichés. If you spot clichés in your writing, replace them with more direct or thoughtful statements of your own.

Some Common Clichés

all in all	in the final analysis
beat around the bush	I wouldn't be where I am today
between a rock and a hard place	information superhighway
break the ice	last but not least
break new ground	let bygones be bygones
climb the ladder of success	light as a feather
cry my eyes out	live life to the fullest
cutting edge	make ends meet
dead as a doornail	one day at a time
down in the dumps	on top of the world
down on his luck	quick as a wink
a drop in the bucket	shoulder to cry on
few and far between	sick as a dog
free as a bird	state of the art
first and foremost	through thick and thin
give it your best shot	tried and true
go the distance	up at the crack of dawn
grass is always greener	when all is said and done
hard as a rock	without a shadow of a doubt
hit the nail on the head	worked and slaved
hustle and bustle	work like a dog

Exercise 3 *Collaborate*

Revising Clichés

The following sentences contain clichés (italicized). Working with a partner or group, rewrite the sentences, replacing the cliches with more direct or thoughtful words or phrases. Write your revisions above the lines.

1. I lent my brother $100 because he was *down on his luck*.

2. I can sell you a *state-of-the-art* home entertainment system.

3. Tonight, you are going to enjoy the comedy of Steve Ross and the singing of Talia Brooks; *last but not least*, you will thrill to the dancing of The Planets.

4. When Gordon called you stubborn, he really *hit the nail on the head.*

5. I *worked and slaved* to make that dinner, and now you tell me you don't like Chinese food.

6. Jorge and Greta are so much in debt that their salaries are just *a drop in the bucket* compared to what they owe on their credit cards.

7. I tried to heat the rolls in the microwave, but they turned out *hard as a rock.*

8. Dr. Lin's studies on the virus are *on the cutting edge.*

9. If you want to go fishing with me, you have to get *up at the crack of dawn.*

10. Once the semester was over, I felt *as free as a bird.*

 Identifying Clichés

Practice

Underline all the clichés in the following paragraph. There are nine clichés.

I am sure I wouldn't be where I am today if I hadn't had Bill as my older brother. People like Bill are few and far between; he has a kind, generous, and compassionate spirit. Whenever I need good advice about my job or education, I turn to Bill because he is wise and practical. He doesn't scold me when I make the wrong choices, nor does he criticize. With his tried and true suggestions, he simply helps me find the best way to solve my problems. Bill is also the first to work like a dog when I need help finishing a project like painting my room or typing a report. He is always there for me, even when I have cried my eyes out over a fight with my boyfriend. Quick as a wink, he appears, offering me a shoulder to cry on. Bill is the ideal big brother, for his big heart has helped me through thick and thin.

 Editing for Precise Language, Wordiness, and Clichés

Practice

Edit the following paragraph for precise language, wordiness, and clichés. Write your revisions above the lines. There are nine places that need editing.

When I started my new job, my supervisor advised me about the qualities I need to succeed. First, she said I had to be willing to work hard and put in a lot of overtime each week. She explained that I must expect to stay late on a regular basis if I want to start climbing the ladder of success. In addition, my knowledge of computers should be on the cutting edge since all the company's equipment is state of the art. In this modern world, she warned, hard work and technical skills are the basic essentials for a nice career. I personally feel that her advice hit the nail on the head.

CHAPTER **35**

Sentence Variety

One way to polish your writing is to work on *sentence variety*, the use of different lengths and kinds of sentences. You can become skilled in sentence variety by (1) revising your writing for a balance of short and long sentences and for a mix of sentence types and (2) being aware of the kinds of sentences you can use.

BALANCING LONG AND SHORT SENTENCES

There are no grammar errors in the following paragraph, but it needs revision for sentence variety.

> I have a routine for waking up. First, I grab a can of Diet Pepsi. I gulp it down. I turn on the TV at the same time. I watch cartoons. I sit for about half an hour. Then the caffeine in the Pepsi starts working. I move to the shower. I make the water temperature very hot. Steam fills the bathroom. My muscles come alive. I begin to feel fully awake.

The paragraph is filled with short sentences. Read it aloud, and you will notice the choppy, boring style of the writing. Compare it to the following revised paragraph, which contains a variety of short and long sentences:

> I have a routine for waking up. First, I grab a can of Diet Pepsi and gulp it down while I turn on the TV. Then I watch cartoons for about half an hour. When the caffeine in the Pepsi starts working, I move to the shower. I make the water temperature so hot that steam fills the bathroom. My muscles come alive as I begin to feel fully awake.

The revised paragraph balances short and long sentences. Read it aloud, and you will notice the way the varied lengths create a more flowing, interesting style.

Some writers rely too heavily on short sentences; others use too many long sentences. The following paragraph contains too many long sentences:

Randall wanted to make new friends because his old friends had become a bad influence. Randall loved his old friends, especially Michael, but they had begun to be involved in some dangerous activities, and Randall didn't want to be part of these crimes because Randall wanted to apply to the police academy, and he knew that having a record would destroy his chances of admission. Consequently, Randall was honest with Michael, and Randall told him that Randall couldn't risk his future by mixing with people who liked to joyride in stolen cars or steal from neighborhood stores. Soon Randall's friends stopped asking him out, and for a while Randall felt lonely and isolated, but eventually, Randall formed some new friendships, and he was happy to be part of a new group and happy it was one that didn't break the law.

Read the previous paragraph aloud, and you will notice that the sentences are so long and complicated that part of their meaning is lost. Piling on one long sentence after another can make a paragraph boring and difficult to follow. Compare the previous paragraph to the following revised version:

Randall wanted to make new friends because his old friends had become a bad influence. Randall loved his old friends, especially Michael. However, they had begun to be involved in some dangerous activities, and Randall didn't want to be a part of these crimes. He wanted to apply to the police academy and knew that having a record would destroy his chances of admission. Consequently, Randall spoke honestly to Michael. Randall explained that he couldn't risk his future by mixing with people who liked to joyride in stolen cars or steal from neighborhood stores. Soon Randall's friends stopped asking him out, and for a while, Randall felt lonely and isolated. Eventually, Randall formed some new friendships and was happy to be part of a new, law-abiding group.

Read the revised paragraph aloud, and you will notice the combination of long and short sentences makes the paragraph clearer and smoother. Careful revision helps you achieve such a mix.

Exercise 1

Practice

Revising Short Sentences

The following paragraph is composed entirely of short sentences. Rewrite it so that it contains a mix of short and long sentences. Write your revisions above the lines.

My grandmother is committed to staying healthy. She has an exercise routine every week. She walks to the store instead of driving. She takes a class in aerobics. She takes it at the adult education center. The center is near her house. She also tries to eat right. She checks the labels on food. She looks for the fat and cholesterol content. She tries to eat at least four servings of fruit and vegetables every day. She tries to limit the amount of beef she eats. She also tries to cut back on pork in her diet. All her efforts have paid off. My grandmother is healthy. She also looks healthy. She looks at least ten years younger than her age.

Exercise 2

Practice

Revising Long Sentences

The following paragraph is composed entirely of long sentences. Rewrite it so that it contains a mix of short and long sentences. Write in the space above the lines.

Yesterday was one of those rare days when I had spare time to myself and the opportunity to enjoy it. I had the day off at work, and my five-year-old was at kindergarten while my twelve-year-old was in middle school, and my husband was at work. So I realized I had about five hours to myself, and at first I thought about all the chores I had to do, but I remembered the house was clean since I had cleaned it over the weekend, and I had done the laundry the night before, so all I had to do was enjoy myself. I began by making myself another cup of coffee and sipping it while I watched one of the morning news shows I never get to see when I am rushing my children out the door every morning and racing to get ready for my job. Then I took a long, leisurely walk, enjoying the neighborhood and looking in the store windows, imagining all the items I would buy if I had the money, and ending with a stop at my favorite bakery, where I bought some peanut butter cookies for my family. When I got home, I fell asleep on the couch until my five-year-old arrived and asked me what I had been doing all day. I said, "Playing and taking a nap," and he said, "Mommy! That's what we do in kindergarten!"

USING DIFFERENT WAYS TO BEGIN SENTENCES

Most of the time, writers begin sentences with the subject. However, if you change the word order, you can break the monotony of using the same pattern over and over.

Begin with an Adverb

One way to change the word order is to begin with an **adverb,** a word that describes verbs, adjectives, or other adverbs. (For more on adverbs, see

Chapter 20.) You can move adverbs from the middle to the beginning of the sentence as long as the meaning is clear.

> **adverb in middle:** Ricky opened the package *carefully* and checked the contents.
> **adverb at beginning:** *Carefully*, Ricky opened the package and checked the contents.
>
> **adverb in middle:** The police officer *calmly* issued a ticket to the aggressive driver.
> **adverb at beginning:** *Calmly*, the police officer issued a ticket to the aggressive driver.

 Exercise 3

Practice

Writing Sentences That Begin with an Adverb

Rewrite each sentence below so that it begins with an adverb. Write your revisions above the lines.

1. The poodle and the fox terrier quickly ran to the front door.

2. The petals of the rose drifted gently through the air.

3. One gang leader hissed hatefully at his rivals.

4. He opened the door quietly and looked inside.

5. Our landlord waited patiently for the rent check.

6. My father usually watches television on Monday nights.

7. The police officer watched suspiciously as the driver reached for her license.

8. The little boy impulsively reached for a peanut butter cookie.

9. My brother reluctantly gave me his credit card.

10. One driver wove recklessly in and out of the traffic lanes.

Begin with a Prepositional Phrase

A **prepositional phrase** contains a preposition and its object. (For more on prepositions, see Chapter 14.) You can change the usual word order of a sentence by moving a prepositional phrase from the end of a sentence to the beginning. You can do this as long as the meaning of the sentence remains clear.

prepositional phrase at the end: A gleaming silver convertible suddenly passed me *in the left lane.*

prepositional phrase at the beginning: *In the left lane,* a gleaming silver convertible suddenly passed me.

prepositional phrase at the end: The bulldog growled and snarled *with fierce intensity.*

prepositional phrase at the beginning: *With fierce intensity,* the bulldog growled and snarled.

Note: Most of the time, you put a comma after a prepositional phrase that begins a sentence. However, you do not need a comma if the prepositional phrase is short.

Practice

Writing Sentences That Begin with a Prepositional Phrase

Rewrite the following sentences, moving a prepositional phrase to the beginning of the sentence. Write your revisions above the lines.

1. Nelson is writing a research paper for extra credit.

2. A small child stood crying outside the apartment door.

3. Tiffany did her homework in the early morning hours.

4. You can see some beautiful quilts at the Museum of Folklore.

5. A gray cat dozed blissfully on a satin pillow.

6. I'll give you a ride home after my last class.

7. James fought his disease with hope and determination.

8. Two rain-drenched people took shelter beneath the big trees.

9. Harry will approach this new challenge in his usual way.

10. The hitchhikers made it home before dark.

Collaborate

Creating Sentences That Begin with Prepositional Phrases

Working with a partner or group, write sentences that begin with the following prepositional phrases.

1. At our house _____

2. With a tear-stained face _____

3. Near the two boys _____

4. Between classes _____

5. Before dinner _____

6. Under stress _____

7. For five dollars _____

8. After the party _____

9. On the kitchen table _____

10. In a loud voice _____

USING DIFFERENT WAYS TO JOIN IDEAS

Another way to create sentence variety is to try different methods of combining ideas. Among these methods are (1) using an *-ing* modifier, (2) using an *-ed* modifier, (3) using an appositive, and (4) using a *who*, *which*, or *that* clause.

Use an *-ing* Modifier

You can avoid short, choppy sentences by using an *-ing* modifier. This way, one of the short sentences becomes a phrase. (For more on modifiers, see Chapter 21.)

> **two short sentences:** Sarah was talking on her cell phone. She drove into a tree.
> **combined with an *-ing* modifier:** *Talking on her cell phone,* Sarah drove into a tree.

Note: If the modifier begins the sentence, be sure that the next word is the one the modifier describes.

> **two short sentences:** Mr. Martinez loves to read travel books. He plans his next vacation.
> **combined with an *-ing* modifier:** Mr. Martinez loves to read travel books, *planning his next vacation.*

 Exercise 6

Practice

Using *-ing* Modifiers

Following are pairs of sentences. Combine each pair by using an *-ing* modifier.

1. Mr. Johannsen lit a big cigar. He filled the room with smoke.

combined: _____

_____

2. My mother saw someone at the window. She screamed at the top of her lungs.

combined: _____

_____

3. Ernesto sent Marcy roses. He was trying to win her love.

combined: _____

_____

4. The rain pounded the roof. It kept me awake all night.

combined: _____

_____

5. A few people talk on their cell phones at the movie theater. They do not pay attention to other people's rights.

combined: _____

_____

6. Two scientists worked through the night. They struggled to identify the strange virus.

combined: _____

_____

7. Mrs. Delgado wrote a letter to the housing commission. She is complaining about her landlord.

combined: _____

_____

8. George slapped me on the back. He congratulated me on my job promotion.

combined: _____

_____

9. The roller coaster loomed in front of me. It offered me terror and thrills.

combined: _____

_____

10. A red convertible waited in front of the house. Its horn was beeping.

combined: _____

_____

Use an *-ed* Modifier

You can also avoid short, choppy sentences by using an *-ed* modifier. This way, one of the short sentences becomes a phrase. (For more on modifiers, see Chapter 21.)

> **two short sentences:** The fish was broiled with lemon and butter. The fish was delicious.
>
> **combined with an *-ed* modifier:** *Broiled with lemon and butter,* the fish was delicious.

Note: If the modifier begins the sentence, be sure that the next word is the one the modifier describes.

> **two short sentences:** Sam gave me a jewelry box. It was painted with silver and blue flowers.
>
> **combined with an *-ed* modifier:** Sam gave me a jewelry box *painted with silver and blue flowers.*

 Exercise 7

Practice

Using *-ed* Modifiers

Following are pairs of sentences. Combine each pair by using an *-ed* modifier.

1. The golden bowl was cracked in two places. It could not be mended.

combined: _____

_____

2. The filling of the cake is made of chocolate. The chocolate is mixed with heavy cream.

combined: _____

_____

3. Victor was called in to work. Victor missed the farewell party.

combined: _____

_____

4. I found my grandfather's medal. The medal was awarded during the Vietnam War.

combined: _____

_____

5. The old kettle was coated with grease. The kettle was difficult to clean.

combined: _____

_____

6. Lieutenant Andrea Meyer was interviewed on television. She rescued two victims of a train wreck.

   combined: _____

   _____

7. My cat was tangled in yarn. He looked like an unraveling sweater.

   combined: _____

   _____

8. I bought a new toothbrush. It is designed to reach every tooth.

   combined: _____

   _____

9. Caroline was offered a job in Trinidad. She asked her father for advice.

   combined: _____

   _____

10. Henry and Kalida love their new computer. It is filled with the latest features.

    combined: _____

    _____

Exercise 8

👥 *Collaborate*

Completing Sentences with *-ing* or *-ed* Modifiers

Working with a partner or group, complete each sentence below.
Answers will vary.

1. Stuck in the elevator _____

2. Trying to apologize _____

3. Rushing out the door _____

4. Convinced of her honesty _____

5. Encouraged by my coach's advice _____

6. Struggling with two heavy suitcases _____

7. Heated in the microwave _____

8. Clapping his hands _____

9. Enraged by my comment _____

10. Carefully inspecting the car _____

Use an Appositive

Another way to combine short, choppy sentences is to use an appositive. An **appositive** is a phrase that renames or describes a noun. Appositives can go in the beginning, middle, or end of a sentence. Use commas to set off the appositive.

> **two short sentences:** Chocolate milk contains calcium and vitamins. It is a favorite of children.
> **combined with an appositive:** Chocolate milk, *a favorite of children*, contains calcium and vitamins.

> **two short sentences:** Richard is my best friend. He has been a wrestler for several years.
> **combined with an appositive:** Richard, *my best friend*, has been a wrestler for several years.

> **two short sentences:** I am looking forward to Thanksgiving. It is my favorite holiday.
> **combined with an appositive:** I am looking forward to Thanksgiving, *my favorite holiday*.

Exercise 9

Practice

Using Appositives

Following are pairs of sentences. Combine each pair by using an appositive.

1. Anna is a brilliant skater. She is trying out for the Olympics.

combined: _____

_____

2. Carter Elementary is my old school. It is being turned into a state museum.

combined: _____

_____

3. You must taste Anthony's barbecued ribs. They are the best ribs in town.

combined: _____

_____

4. My sister is driving to Disney World. It is my favorite place in the world.

combined: _____

_____

5. Lorraine is a trusted employee. She was promoted to head of security.

combined: _____

_____

6. Jeans and tee shirts are my favorite clothes. They are all I wear on the weekends.

combined: _____

_____

7. My father is very careful of his health. He is a cancer survivor.

combined: _____

_____

8. Everyone likes a single rose. It is a perfect gift.

combined: _____

_____

9. Mario is the smallest in his gym class. He is the best runner.

combined: _____

_____

10. Cynthia Nguyen is a well-known lawyer. She is a graduate of our high school.

combined: _____

_____

Use a *Who, Which,* or *That* Clause

Clauses beginning with *who, which,* or *that* can combine short sentences.

two short sentences: Jacob is my favorite cousin. He won the golf tournament.

combined with a *who* clause: Jacob, *who is my favorite cousin,* won the golf tournament.

two short sentences: Good running shoes can be expensive. They make running easier.

combined with a *which* clause: Good running shoes, *which can be expensive,* make running easier.

two short sentences: The cinnamon buns were delicious. I tasted them.

combined with a *that* clause: The cinnamon buns *that I tasted* were delicious.

Punctuating *who*, *which*, or *that* clauses requires some thought. Decide whether the information in the clause is *essential* or *nonessential*. If the information is essential, do not put commas around it:

> **essential clause:** Students *who like history* will love the movie.

(Without the clause *who like history*, the sentence would not have the same meaning. Therefore, the clause is essential and is not set off by commas.)

> **nonessential clause:** Mel, *who has been singing for years*, deserves to win. (The clause *who has been singing for years* is not essential to the meaning of the sentence. Therefore, it is set off by commas.)

If you have to choose between *which* and *that*, *which* usually begins a nonessential clause, and *that* usually begins an essential clause.

> **essential clause:** The car *that he was driving* is expensive.
> **nonessential clause:** The car, *which I've had for years*, needs a new muffler.

Note: Essential and nonessential clauses are also referred to as "restrictive" and "nonrestrictive" clauses.

 **Exercise 10**

Practice

Using *Who, Which,* or *That* Clauses

Following are pairs of sentences. Combine each pair by using a *who*, *which*, or *that* clause.

1. Nelson wrote me a letter. The letter changed my life.

combined: _____

_____

2. Caviar is an expensive delicacy. Caviar is fish eggs.

combined: _____

_____

3. Angela met a handsome man. He plays the drums in a Latin band.

combined: _____

_____

4. Tony Lopata loves to write poetry. He has had a poem published in the college magazine.

combined: _____

_____

5. People dream of winning the lottery. They will stand in line for hours to purchase lottery tickets.

combined: _____

_____

6. Barbie dolls have been little girls' favorite toys for years. The dolls are now collector's items.

combined: _____

_____

7. Shawna needs a new bike. The bike must be suitable for country roads.

combined: _____

_____

8. I have always loved the movie *Rush Hour*. It is now available on DVD.

combined: _____

_____

9. Santiago is giving a party for his wife. She graduated from college yesterday.

combined: _____

_____

10. Sushi used to make me sick. It is now my favorite food.

combined: _____

_____

Exercise 11

 Connect

Revising for Sentence Variety: A Comprehensive Exercise

Rewrite the following paragraph, combining each pair of underlined sentences using one of the following: an *-ing* modifier, an *-ed* modifier, an appositive, or a *who, which,* or *that* clause. Write your revisions above the lines.

<u>My first love was a little girl. She sat next to me in first grade.</u> She never seemed to notice me. <u>I was determined to get her attention. I used to act up in class.</u> I fidgeted, made smart remarks, and threw little balls of paper across the room. <u>My teacher was Miss Lavona. She was very strict.</u> She often made me take a time-out in the corner. <u>I would be sulking and pouting about my punishment. I wondered if the little girl had ever even glanced my way.</u> Maybe she saw me as a fool, I thought. Then one day, I was hit by a small ball of paper. <u>I turned and saw my beloved little girl. She was throwing balls of paper at me!</u> My first romance began.

Grammar for ESL Students

NOUNS AND ARTICLES

A **noun** names a person, place, or thing. There are count nouns and noncount nouns.

> **Count nouns** refer to persons, places, or things that can be counted: three *doughnuts*, two *kittens*, five *pencils*
>
> **Noncount nouns** refer to things that can't be counted: *medicine, housework, mail*

Here are some more examples of count and noncount nouns.

count	noncount
rumor	gossip
violin	music
school	intelligence
suitcase	luggage

One way to remember the difference between count and noncount nouns is to put the word *much* in front of the noun. For example, if you can say *much luggage*, then *luggage* is a noncount noun.

Exercise 1

Practice

Identifying Count and Noncount Nouns

Write count or noncount next to each word below.

1. _____ sailboat

2. _____ button

3. _____ time

4. _____ sympathy

5. _____ clock

6. _____ health

7. _____ food

8. _____ milk

9. _____ banana

10. _____ tree

Using Articles with Nouns

Articles point out nouns. Articles are either **indefinite** (*a, an*) or **definite** (*the*). There are several rules for using these articles:

- Use *a* in front of consonant sounds and use *an* before vowel sounds:

a card	an orange
a radio	an answer
a button	an entrance
a thread	an invitation
a nightmare	an uncle

- Use *a* or *an* in front of singular count nouns (*a* or *an* mean "*any one.*")

  I ate *an* egg.
  James planted *a* tree.

- Do not use *a* or *an* with noncount nouns:

  not this: Selena filled the tank with ~~a~~ gasoline.
  but this: Selena filled the tank with gasoline.

  not this: I am studying ~~an~~ algebra.
  but this: I am studying algebra.

- Use *the* before both singular and plural count nouns whose specific identify is known to the reader:

  The dress with the sequins on it is my party dress.
  Most of *the* movies I rent are science fiction films.

- Use *the* before noncount nouns only when they are specifically identified:

  not this: I need ~~the~~ help. (Whose help? What help? The noncount noun *help* is not specifically identified.)
  but this: I need *the help* of a good plumber. (Now *help* is specifically identified.)

  not this: ~~Kindness~~ of the people who took me in was remarkable. (The noncount noun *kindness* is specifically identifed, so you need *the.*)
  but this: *The kindness* of the people who took me in was remarkable.

Exercise 2

Practice

Using *a* or *an*

Put *a* or *an* in the spaces where it is needed. Some sentences are correct as they are.

1. Mrs. Verinsky took us to _____ movie.

2. I need to buy _____ furniture for my new house.

3. My cat was playing with _____ insect.

4. My brother is studying _____ medicine and taking _____ course in _____ chemistry.

5. Keith had _____ accident on Wednesday.

6. I can bring _____ coffee and _____ ice cream to Joe's birthday party.

7. Jimmy took me to _____ concert and _____ exhibition of famous racing cars.

8. All she wants is _____ respect.

9. Mark was carrying _____ umbrella with _____ hole in it.

10. Joanna has _____ confidence and _____ sense of humor.

<table>
<tr><td>Exercise 3
Practice</td><td>

Using *the*

Write *the* in the spaces where it is needed. Some sentences are correct as they are.
</td></tr>
</table>

1. Larry missed _____ dinners his mother used to make.

2. Eventually, you will develop _____ patience to succeed in _____ child psychology.

3. I have always wanted to swim in _____ ocean.

4. With _____ support of my family, I managed to graduate from _____ high school.

5. Stephanie goes to _____ supermarket near her house because that store has _____ best selection of _____ vegetables.

6. _____ newspapers in _____ garage need to be thrown out.

7. Because of _____ hard work of _____ volunteers at our community garage sale, we made $500 for _____ community garden.

8. Getting a good job takes _____ determination to keep looking and _____ hard work.

9. Every Sunday, Leon watches _____ television.

10. Tom cleaned out _____ trash in _____ back yard but left _____ dead leaves under _____ porch for another day.

<table>
<tr><td>Exercise 4
Practice</td><td>

Correcting a Paragraph with Errors in Articles

Correct the errors with *a*, *an*, or *the* in the following paragraph. You may need to add, change, or eliminate articles. Write the corrections in the space above the errors. There are eleven errors.
</td></tr>
</table>

When I was twelve years old, I had a dog like no other dog in a world.

This dog had the intelligence and the courage, and he also had a crazy

streak in his personality. His name was Buzzy, and he was the border collie.
On farms of England and Scotland, border collies are used to herd sheep,
and these dogs love to chase anything that moves. They are full of the energy and have stamina of much larger dogs. Buzzy loved to run, and he could
chase and herd almost any animals. I remember him herding five ducks into
a quacking group and pushing them into a pond. He was always looking for
a opportunity to run and play. If he couldn't find anything to herd, he loved
to play fetch. He would retrieve a old tennis ball for a hour. He ran as fast
as the bullet.

NOUNS OR PRONOUNS USED AS SUBJECTS

A noun or a pronoun (a word that takes the place of a noun) is the subject
of each sentence or dependent clause. Be sure that all sentences or dependent clauses have a subject:

> **not this:** Drives to work every day.
> **but this:** *He* drives to work every day.

> **not this:** My sister is pleased when gets a compliment.
> **but this:** My sister is pleased when *she* gets a compliment.

Be careful not to *repeat* the subject:

> **not this:** The police officer ~~she~~ said I was speeding.
> **but this:** The police officer said I was speeding.

> **not this:** The car that I needed ~~it~~ was a sportscar.
> **but this:** The car that I needed was a sportscar.

Exercise 5

Practice

Correcting Errors with Subjects

Correct any errors with subjects in the sentences below. Write your corrections above the errors.

1. Anthony he never gets up when hears the alarm clock.

2. In the summer, my car it often gets overheated.

3. Action movies with a good sound track they are the best.

4. After a long day, is difficult to concentrate on homework.

5. Sweatshirts are warm in winter; are also very comfortable.

6. My friend Inez she likes to walk in all kinds of weather.

7. Yesterday, the right rear tire on my truck it was flat.

8. Always comes to visit on New Year's Day and brings a special gift.

9. Whenever sees a coupon in the newspaper, he cuts it out.

10. The scariest part of the amusement park it was a haunted house.

VERBS

Necessary Verbs

Be sure that a main verb isn't missing from your sentences or dependent clauses.

not this: My boyfriend very ambitious.
but this: My boyfriend *is* very ambitious.

not this: Sylvia cried when the hero in the movie.
but this: Sylvia cried when the hero in the movie *died.*

-s Endings

Be sure to put the *-s* on present tense verbs in the third person singular:

not this: He ~~run~~ in the park every morning.
but this: He *runs* in the park every morning.

not this: The concert ~~start~~ at 9:00 P.M.
but this: The concert *starts* at 9:00 P.M.

-ed Endings

Be sure to put an *-ed* ending on the past participle form of a verb when necessary. There are three main forms of a verb:

present: Today I walk.
past: Yesterday I walked.
past participle: I *have* walked. He *has* walked.

The past participle form is also used after *were, was, had,* and *has*:

not this: He has ~~call~~ me every day this week.
but this: He has *called* me every day this week.

not this: My neighbor was ~~surprise~~ by the sudden storm.
but this: My neighbor was *surprised* by the sudden storm.

Do not add *-ed* endings to infinitives. An infinitive is the verb form that uses *to* plus the present form of the verb:

infinitives: to consider to obey

not this: Dean wanted me to ~~considered~~ the proposal.
but this: Dean wanted me to *consider* the proposal.

not this: I taught my dog to ~~obeyed~~ commands.
but this: I taught my dog to *obey* commands.

Exercise 6

Practice

Correcting Errors in Verbs: Necessary Verbs, Third Person Present Tense, Past Participles, and Infinitives

Correct any errors in verbs in the sentences below. Write your corrections above the lines. Some sentences do not need any corrections.

1. The letter was mail at the post office where my uncle work.

2. After I got divorced, I wanted to examined the good and bad points of moving to Texas.

3. As a child, I was fascinated by dinosaurs and other prehistoric creatures.

4. Once a week, Lucy calls her family in Manila and tells them all her news.

5. Your new haircut look good on you; it make you look very handsome.

6. Laura had wrap all the gifts before the children arrived.

7. Two of the most generous neighbors in my building Mike and Alice Hennessy, from the third floor.

8. Do not come to the dinner table unless you have wash your hands.

9. Good communication skills essential in any close relationship.

10. When Mrs. Simone need to relaxed, she lie on the couch and read a mystery novel.

Practice

Correcting a Paragraph with Errors in Necessary Verbs, Third Person Present Tense, Past Participles, and Infinitives

Correct the verb errors in the following paragraph. Write your corrections above the lines. There are seven errors.

Whenever we have a sale at the store where I work, we have to prepared for it for days. If the sale start on a Wednesday, for example, we work for hours on Monday and Thursday, sorting the sale items and marking the merchandise with special sales tags. All this sorting and marking must be done after the store close, so the work continue late into the night. Then, at about 5:00 A.M. on Wednesday morning, the really hard work begins. We rush to put up the "Sale" signs, to displayed the marked-down items, and to be ready when the customers come in at 9:00. Before a sale begins, I have often earn as much as fifteen hours of overtime. A sale is fun for customers, but for salespeople it a hard way to make extra money.

Two-Word Verbs

Two-word verbs contain a verb plus another word, either a preposition or an adverb. The meaning of each word by itself is different from the meaning the two words have when they are together. Look at this example:

Sometimes Consuelo *runs across* her sister at the park.

You might check *run* in the dictionary and find that it means "to move quickly." *Across* means "from one side to the other." But *run across* means something different:

> **not this:** Sometimes Consuelo ~~moves quickly from one side to the other of~~ her sister at the park.
> **but this:** Sometimes Consuela *encounters* her sister at the park.

Sometimes, a word or words come between the words of a two-word verb:

> On Friday night, I *put* the garbage *out*; the sanitation department collects it early Saturday morning.

Here are some common two-word verbs:

ask out	Jamal wants to *ask* Teresa *out* for dinner.
break down	I hope my car doesn't *break down*.
call off	You can *call* the party *off*.
call on	I need to *call on* you for help.
call up	Jim will *call* Ken *up* tomorrow.
come across	I often *come across* bargains at thrift shops.
drop in	Let's *drop in* on Claude.
drop off	My father will *drop* the package *off*.
fill in	You can *fill in* your name.
fill out	Danny has to *fill out* a complaint form.
hand in	We have to *hand in* our assignments.
hand out	I hope the theater *hands out* free passes.
keep on	You must *keep on* practicing your speech.
look into	Jonelle will *look into* the situation.
look over	Jake needs to *look* the plans *over*.
look up	I had to *look* the word *up* in the dictionary.
pick up	Tomorrow I *pick up* my first paycheck.
quiet down	The teacher told the class to *quiet down*.

run into	Nancy will *run into* Alan at the gym.
run out	The family has *run out* of money.
think over	I like your idea; let me *think* it *over.*
try on	Before you buy the shirt, *try* it *on.*
try out	She wants to *try* the lawnmower *out.*
turn on	*Turn* the television *on.*
turn down	Sal thinks Wayne should *turn* the job *down.*
turn up	Nick is sure to *turn up* at the party.

Exercise 8

Practice

Writing Sentences with Two-Word Verbs

Write a sentence for each of the following two-word verbs. Use the examples above as a guide, but consult a dictionary if you are not sure what the verbs mean.

1. call off _____

2. look up _____

3. keep on _____

4. fill out _____

5. run across _____

6. turn up _____

7. drop off _____

8. pick up _____

9. try out _____

10. ask out _____

Contractions and Verbs

Contractions often contain verbs you may not recognize in their shortened forms.

contraction: *I'm* losing weight.
long form: *I am* losing weight.

contraction: *She's* been my best friend for years.
long form: *She has* been my best friend for years.

contraction: *He's* leaving tomorrow.
long form: *He is* leaving tomorrow.

contraction: *They'll* never know.
long form: *They will* never know.

contraction: The *truck's* in the garage.
long form: The *truck is* in the garage.

9

Practice

Contractions and Verbs

In the space above each italicized contraction, write its long form. The first one is done for you.

       She would
1. *She'd* let me know if she needed help.

2. *Alberto's* building a new house.

3. *Alberto's* built a new house.

4. *You'll* be sorry you missed the game.

5. The *car's* in the body shop for repairs.

6. On a rainy day, *I'm* likely to stay home and sleep.

7. *They'll* never sell their boat.

8. Do you think *you'd* like to visit Hong Kong?

9. *You've* given me a good idea.

10. The neighbors *won't* turn down their television.

PREPOSITIONS

Prepositions are little words such as *with, for, of, around,* or *near.* Some prepositions can be confusing; these are the ones that show time and place.

Prepositions That Show Time

Use *at* to show a specific or precise time:

> I will call you *at* 7:30 P.M.
> The movie starts *at* midnight.

Use *on* with a specific day or date:

> The meeting is *on* Friday.
> Frances begins basic training *on* June 23.

Use *by* when you mean "no later than that time":

> Jean has to be at work *by* 8:00 A.M.
> We should be finished with the cleaning *by* 5:00 P.M.

Use *until* when you mean "continuing up to a time":

> Yesterday I slept *until* 10:00 A.M.
> The dentist cannot see me *until* tomorrow.

Use *in* when you refer to a specific time period (minutes, hours, days, months, years):

> I'll be with you *in* a minute.
> Nikela works *in* the morning. (You can also say *in* the afternoon, or *in* the evening, but *at* night.)

Use *during* when you refer to a continuing time period or within the time period:

> I fell asleep *during* his speech.
> My sister will study management *during* the summer.

Use *for* to tell the length of a period of time:

> We have been married *for* two years.
> Wanda and Max cleaned the attic *for* three hours.

Use *since* to tell the starting time of an action:

> He has been calling *since* 9:00 A.M.
> We have been best friends *since* third grade.

Prepositions That Show Place

Use *in* to refer to a country, area, state, city, or neighborhood:

> He studied *in* Ecuador.
> Mr. Etienne lives *in* Houston.

Use *in* to refer to an enclosed space:

> He put the money *in* his wallet.
> Delia waited for me *in* the dining room.

Use *at* to refer to a specific address:

> The repair shop is *at* 7330 Glades Road.
> I live *at* 7520 Maple Lane.

Use *at* to refer to the corner or intersection:

> We went to a garage sale *at* the corner of Spring Street and Lincoln Avenue.
> The accident occurred *at* the intersection of Madison Boulevard and Temple Road.

Use *on* to refer to a street or a block:

> Dr. Lopez lives *on* Hawthorne Street.
> Malcolm bought the biggest house *on* the block.

Use *on* to refer to a surface:

> Put the sandwiches *on* the table.
> There was a bright rug *on* the floor.

Use *off* to refer to a surface:

> Take the sandwiches *off* the table.
> She wiped the mud *off* the floor.

Use *into* and *out of* for small vehicles such as cars:

> Our dog leaped *into* the convertible.
> The children climbed *out of* the car.

Use *on* and *off* for large vehicles like planes, trains, buses, and boats:

> I was so seasick, I couldn't wait to get *off* the ship.
> I like to ride *on* the bus.

Practice

Correcting Errors in Prepositions

Correct any errors in prepositions in the following sentences. Write your corrections above the lines.

1. The dinner begins on 7:30 P.M. and will be over by 9:30 P.M.

2. I studied biology during two years until I changed my major to botany.

3. Come and see me on an hour, and we can talk about old times at Mexico City.

4. We got into the plane two hours before it left the runway.

5. The stack of mail in the table has been sitting there since a week.

6. The restaurant is at the corner of Second Street and Washington Avenue, but my house is farther down at Third Street.

7. I've been studying at my room since 4:00 P.M.

8. We walked to a sunny patio with bright wicker furniture in the tile floor.

9. Take my keys off the counter and put them on your backpack.

10. How long have you lived on 5545 Hammond Lane?

TEXT CREDITS

Page 39: "Sticky Stuff" by Kendall Hamilton & Tessa Namuth. From Newsweek Extra, winter 97–98, p. 27. Copyright © 1998 Newsweek. All rights reserved. Reprinted by permission.

Page 62: From "Spanglish Spoken Here" by Janice Castro, with Dan Cook & Christina Garcia. Time, July 11th, 1988. Copyright © 1988 Time, Inc. Reprinted by permission.

Page 87: "A Present for Popo" by Elizabeth Wong. From The Los Angeles Times, December 30, 1992. Copyright © 1992 Elizabeth Wong. Reprinted by permission of the author.

Page 113: "Rocky Rowf" from "The Corpse Had A Familiar Face" by Edna Buchanan, pp. 242–246. Copyright © 1987 by Edna Buchanan. Reprinted by permission of Random House, Inc.

Page 138: From "We Are Still Married," by Garrison Keillor. Published by Viking Penguin, Inc. Reprinted by permission of International Paper Company Copyright © 1987 by International Paper Company. (Originally titled "How to Write a Personal Letter.")

Page 170: "Against All Odds, I'm Just Fine" by Brad Wackerlin. Originally appeared in Newsweek Special Edition, June 1990, vol. CXV, no. 27, p. 22. Reprinted by permission of the author.

Page 190: "Three Disciplines for Children" is reprinted by permission from "Freedom and Beyond" by John Holt. Copyright © 1995, 1972 by Holt Associates. Published by Heinemann, a division of Reed Elsevier, Inc. Portsmouth, NH.

Page 213: "Breaking the Bonds of Hate" from My Turn Essays by Virak Khiev. Originally appeared in Newsweek, April 27, 1992, p. 8. Reprinted by permission of the author.

Page 240: "Students in Shock" by John Kellmayer from "A Basic Reader for College Writers" by David I.

Daniels, Janet M. Goldstein & Christopher Hayes. Reprinted by permission of Townsend Press.

Page 266: "Athletics Heroes" by James Beekman. Newsweek My Turn Essays: More Student Opinion. Originally appeared in Newsweek Education Programs, 1996. Reprinted by permission of the author.

Page 269: "Too Tired to Appreciate the Revolution?" by Jeremy Rifkin, author of "The Age of Access." (Tarcher/Putnam 2000). Originally published in the Los Angeles Times. Reprinted by permission of the author.

Page 310: "Eleven" from "Woman Hollering Creek" by Sandra Cisneros. Copyright © 1991 by Sandra Cisneros. Published by Vintage Books, a division of Random House, Inc. and originally printed in hardcover by Random House, Inc. Reprinted by permission of Susan Berghol.

Page 313: "Althea Gibson: Never Give Up" by Varla Ventura, excerpted from "Sheroes" by Varla Ventura. Copyright © 1998 by Varla Ventura. Reprinted by permission of Conari Press.

Page 315: "Send Your Children to the Library" by Arthur Ashe. New York Times, February 6, 1977. Copyright © 1977 The New York Times. Reprinted by permission.

Page 369: "A Ridiculous Addiction" by Gwinn Owens. Originally appeared in Newsweek, December 4th, 1989, My Turn, p.17. Reprinted by permission of the author.

Page 389: "My Daugther Smokes" from "Living by the Word" by Alice Walker. Copyright © 1987 by Alice Walker. Reprinted by permission of Harcourt, Inc.

Page 393: "Parental Discretion" by Dennis Hevesi. New York Times Educational Supplement, 1990. Copyright © 1990 by The New York Times. Reprinted by permission.

PHOTOGRAPH CREDITS

Page 36: Tony Stone Images; **Page 36:** Myrleen Ferguson/PhotoEdit; **Page 36:** PhotoDisc, Inc.; **Page 59:** Jim Muth/Western Development Corporation; **Page 60:** Richmond Smith/Omni-Photo Communications, Inc.; **Page 85:** PhotoDisc, Inc.; **Page 85:** Tony Stone Images; **Page 111:** Tony Stone Images; **Page 111:** Pearson Education/PH College; **Page 135:** Getty Images Inc./Stone; **Page 136:** Tony Stone Images; **Page 168:** Will & Deni McIntyre/Photo Researchers, Inc.; **Page 168:** Omni-Photo Communications, Inc.; **Page 188:** Robert Harbison; **Page 211:** Tony Stone Images; **Page 237:** Tony Stone Images; **Page 238:** Felicia Martinez/PhotoEdit; **Page 264:** Bill Bachmann/Photo Researchers, Inc.; **Page 264:** PhotoDisc, Inc.; **Page 308:** Michael Newman/PhotoEdit; **Page 308:** PhotoDisc, Inc.

INDEX

Note: Itemized listings for **Florida Exit Test** competencies and **Texas Academic Skills Program** test objectives are on pages 629 and 634, respectively.

A

a/an/and, 580
a/an (indefinite articles), 615
abbreviations, 539, 565
accept/except, 580
acronyms, 565
action verbs, 399–400
   with adverbs, 467–68
active voice, 499, 501
addition/edition, 580
adjectives, 462–66
   comparative forms, 463–64, 468–69
   good/bad, 467–68
   superlative forms, 463–64
   + *than*, 469
   using commas with, 469
adverbs, 407–8, 465–66
   beginning sentences, 603–4
   conjunctive, 419–20, 428, 550
   sequencing, 473
   well/badly, 467–68
advice/advise, 580
affect/effect, 580–81
agreement
   of pronouns, 522–30
   between subject and verb, 506–21
agreement/disagreement writing, 381–84
   brainstorming, 382
   drafting, 383
   final lines, 383–84
   freewriting, 381–82
   outlines, 383
   proofreading, 383–84
   revising, 383
   rough lines, 383
allowed/aloud, 581
all right, 575
a lot, 575
already/all ready, 575, 581
altar/alter, 581
altogether/all together, 575
always/all ways, 575
angel/angle, 581
antecedents, 522–30
anymore/any more, 575
anyone/any one, 575
apart/a part, 575
apostrophes, 554–59

   in contractions, 554
   indicating possession, 555
   its/it's, 536
   with letters, 556
   with numbers, 554, 556
   with plural forms, 556
   in time expressions, 556
appositives, 610–11
are/our, 581
argument essays, 360–66
   drafting, 363–64
   final lines, 364–65
   outlines, 362–63
   proofreading, 364–65
   revising, 363–64
   rough lines, 363–64
   the thesis, 360
   thought lines, 361–62
argument paragraphs, 244–71
   audience, 245
   drafting, 256–57
   final lines, 260
   grouping ideas, 249
   outlines, 251–53
   peer review forms, 265
   proofreading, 260
   revising, 252, 256
   rough lines, 256–57
   sequencing, 252–53
   thought lines, 248–49
   topic sentences, 244–45
   transitions, 257
articles, 615–17
ask out, 620
at, 622–23
attitude, 367–68
audience, 4
   argument essays, 360–61
   argument paragraphs, 245
a while, 575

B

bad/badly, 467–68
being verbs, 399–400
   with adjectives, 462, 467
beside/besides, 581
between, 535
brainstorming, 4–5
   adding details, 9–11
   classification paragraphs, 176–77
   reaction writing, 382

brake/break, 581
break down, 620
breath/breathe, 581
but also, 512
buy/by, 581
by, 622

C

call off/on/up, 620
capital/capitol, 581
capitalization, 562–64
   of course names, 563
   of names of persons, 563
   of place names, 563
   of product names, 563
   in quotations, 562–63
   of titles of persons, 563
   of titles of works, 564
   when using a semicolon, 419
cause and effect essays, 355–60
   drafting, 358
   final lines, 358–59
   outlines, 357
   proofreading, 358–59
   rough lines, 358
   the thesis, 356–57
   thought lines, 355–57
cause and effect paragraphs, 217–43
   drafting, 229–30
   final lines, 234
   freewriting, 220–22
   linking, 229–30
   outlines, 225–26
   peer review forms, 239
   proofreading, 234
   revising, 225, 229–30
   rough lines, 229–30
   sequencing, 225–26
   thought lines, 220–22
   topic sentences, 218, 222
cereal/serial, 582
checklists
   argument paragraphs, 252, 256
   basic paragraphs, 22
   cause and effect, 225, 229
   classification paragraphs, 180, 182
   comparison and contrast paragraphs, 160
   definition paragraphs, 201, 204

descriptive paragraphs, 78
essays, 284, 289–90, 294
illustration paragraphs, 53
irregular verbs, 488–89
narrative paragraphs, 103
prereading, 368
process paragraphs, 124, 129
topic sentences, 289
choose/chose, 582
classification essays, 344–49
drafting, 346–47
final lines, 347–48
outlines, 345–46
proofreading, 347–48
revising, 346–47
rough lines, 346–47
sequencing, 344
the thesis, 345
thought lines, 344–45
classification paragraphs, 172–92
brainstorming, 176–77
drafting, 182
explanation, 172–73
final lines, 184–85
outlines, 179–80
peer review forms, 189
proofreading, 184–85
revising, 182
sequencing, 179–80
thought lines, 176–77
topic sentences, 177
transitions, 182–83
clauses
See also sentences
definition, 399
dependent, 432–42, 445–48,
617–18
punctuation, 612–13
that modify, 471
using *who/which/that*, 611–13
clichés, 598–99
close/clothes/cloths, 582
coarse/course, 582
coherence, 22–23
collective nouns, 516, 525–26
colons, 551–53
introductions, 551
combining sentences, 436–37
See also complex sentences;
compound sentences;
run-on sentences
come across, 620
commas
in addresses, 548
between adjectives, 469
with coordinating conjunctions,
415–18, 543

in dates, 548
insertions, 561
with insertions, 545
with introductions, 544
as links, 543
lists, 550–51
in lists, 542
in numbers, 548
in proper names, 545
in quotations, 547, 561–62
splices, 427–29
commonly misspelled words,
577–79
comparative forms, 463–64,
468–69
pronouns, 536
+ *than*, 469
comparison and contrast essays,
337–44
drafting, 341–42
final lines, 342–43
outlines, 340–41
point-by-point organization,
338–39
proofreading, 342–43
revising, 341–42
rough lines, 341–42
sequencing, 337–38
the thesis, 337
thought lines, 338–39
comparison and contrast paragraphs, 142–71
adding details, 153–54
choosing a topic, 142–43
drafting, 159–62
final lines, 162–66
outlines, 155–59
peer review form, 169
point-by-point organization,
146–47, 162–63
proofreading, 162–66
revising, 159–62
rough lines, 159–62
subject-by-subject organization,
144–46, 163–64
thought lines, 150–55
topic sentences, 142–43
transitions, 148
complement/compliment, 582
complex sentences, 432–42
punctuation of, 434
using dependent clauses, 432–33
using subordinating conjunctions, 433–34, 436, 445–46
compound sentences, 414–23
using conjunctive adverbs,
419–20, 550

using coordinating conjunction,
415–18
using semicolons, 418–19,
550–51
compound subjects, 512–13
conclusions
in essays, 291–92
in illustration paragraphs, 56–57
conjunctions
adverbial, 419–20, 428
coordinating, 415–18, 425, 428,
436
in run-on sentences, 425
subordinating, 433–34, 436,
445–46
conscience/conscious, 582
consonants, 570
contractions, 407–8, 485, 554,
621–22
contrast. *See* comparison and
contrast
coordinating conjunctions,
415–18, 425, 428, 436
could have, 503
council/counsel, 582
count nouns, 614

D

dashes, 560–61
decent/descent, 582
definite articles, 615
definition essays, 349–55
drafting, 352–53
final lines, 353–54
outlines, 351–52
proofreading, 353–54
revising, 352–53
rough lines, 352–53
the thesis, 349–50
thought lines, 350–51
definition paragraphs, 193–216
drafting, 203–4
final lines, 208–9
outlines, 201–2
peer review forms, 212
proofreading, 208–9
revising, 201–2, 204
rough lines, 203–4
thought lines, 198–99
topic sentences, 194, 199
transitions, 203
using examples, 194–95
dependent clauses, 432–42,
445–48, 617–18
description essays, 323–28
drafting, 325–26

final lines, 326–27
outlines, 324–25
proofreading, 326–27
revising, 325–26
rough lines, 325–26
sequencing, 323
thought lines, 324
using details, 323
description paragraphs, 65–89
choosing a dominant impression, 72
choosing specific words, 65–66, 69
colons, 551–52
drafting, 78
final lines, 82
outlines, 74–75
peer review form, 86
proofreading, 82
revising, 78
rough lines, 78
sequencing your information, 74–75
thought lines, 71–72
topic sentences, 72, 74
transitions, 80–81
writing from reading, 87–89
descriptive words, 65–66, 69, 462–70
desert/dessert, 582
details, 9–12, 19–21
in comparison and contrast paragraphs, 153–54
in definition paragraphs, 198–99
in description essays, 323
in essays, 282–83
in illustration paragraphs, 45–46
in narrative paragraphs, 100–101, 103–4
using questions, 198
differences. *See* comparison and contrast
dining room, 575
directional writing, 118, 127, 332
See also process paragraphs
do/due, 582–83
does/dose, 583
drafting, 1, 27, 286–97
argument essays, 363–64
argument paragraphs, 256–57
cause and effect essays, 358
cause and effect paragraphs, 229–30
classification essays, 346–47
classification paragraphs, 182
comparison and contrast essays, 341–42

comparison and contrast paragraphs, 159–62
definition essays, 352–53
definition paragraphs, 203–4
description essays, 325–26
descriptive paragraphs, 78
illustration essays, 321
illustration paragraphs, 53–54
narrative essays, 330
narrative paragraphs, 103
process essays, 334–35
process paragraphs, 127–29, 131
reaction writing, 383
summaries, 379–80
drop in/off, 620
during, 623

E

each other, 575
editing, 27
either, 512, 514
emphatic order, 225–26, 252–53
English as a second language, 614–24
essays, 3, 272–317
argument, 360–66
body, 282, 289–90
body of, 274
cause and effect, 355–60
classification, 344–49
clustering ideas in, 278–79
comparison and contrast, 337–44
conclusions, 274, 291–92
definition of, 349–55
description, 323–28
details in, 282–83
drafting of, 286–97
final lines, 301–2
illustration, 318–23
introductions, 273, 286–88
lists, 278
narrative, 328–32
outlines, 281–85
peer review form, 309
process, 332–37
proofreading, 301–2
reading steps, 384
revising, 283–85, 293–94
rough lines, 286–97
subpoints of, 272, 274–75
the thesis, 273–75, 286–87, 292
thought lines, 277–79, 283–84
titles of, 301
topic sentences, 272–73, 282–83, 289

transitions, 294–96
using repetition, 295–96
vs. single paragraphs, 272–73
essay tests, 384–87
essential clauses, 612
essential phrases, 545
even though, 575
every day/every day, 576
everyone/every one, 576
every time, 575
examples
in definition paragraphs, 194–95
in illustration essays, 318–19
exclamation marks, 560–61

F

fair/fare, 583
farther/further, 583
fill in/out, 620
final lines, 1, 30–37, 301–2
argument essays, 364–65
argument paragraphs, 260
cause and effect essays, 358–59
cause and effect paragraphs, 234
classification essays, 347–48
classification paragraphs, 184–85
comparison and contrast essays, 342–43
comparison and contrast paragraphs, 162–66
definition essays, 353–54
definition paragraphs, 208–9
description essays, 326–27
descriptive paragraphs, 82
essay tests, 385
illustration essays, 322
illustration paragraphs, 56–57
narrative essays, 330–31
narrative paragraphs, 108
process essays, 335–36
process paragraphs, 131–32
reaction writing, 383–84
summaries, 380–81
Florida Exit Test competencies
effectively using transitions, 27, 53, 80–81, 106–7, 128–29, 148, 182–83, 203, 257, 294–96
understanding topic sentences, 13–21, 23, 46–47, 72, 74, 90–92, 98–99, 104, 122, 142–43, 177, 194, 199, 218, 222, 244–45, 272–73, 282–83, 289
understanding word choice/vocabulary, 595–600

understanding homonyms, 580–94

recognizing misplaced modifiers, 473–75

effectively using subordination, 432–42, 445–46

parallelism, 453–61

recognizing sentence fragments, 443–52

recognizing comma splices, 427–29

effectively using coordination, 415–18, 425, 428, 436

recognizing fused sentences, 424–31

effectively using verb tense/consistency, 493, 501

effectively using irregular verbs, 484–89

effectively using verb tense, 480–84, 493, 497–98

subject-verb agreement, 506–21

pronoun reference, 522–30

pronoun consistency, 531–34

recognizing unclear pronoun reference, 522–30

pronoun case, 534–38

understanding adjectives/adverbs, 407–8, 419–20, 428, 462–79, 550, 603–4

understanding comparatives/superlatives, 463–64, 469, 536

spelling, 570–79

effectively using semicolons, 418–20, 427–29, 550–51

understanding apostrophes/possessives, 554–59

capitalization, 419, 562–64

flour/flower, 583

focusing ideas, 12–19

descriptive paragraphs, 72

lists, 12, 15

maps, 13

topic sentences, 13–19

for, 623

formal outlines, 281

forth/fourth, 583

fragments, 443–52

freewriting, 4

cause and effect writing, 220–22

narrative writing, 97

reaction writing, 381–82

selecting a topic, 9

fused sentences, 424–31

G

general statements, 318

good night, 575

good/well, 467

grammar for ESL students

articles, 614–17

contractions, 621–22

idiomatic expressions, 620–21

necessary verbs, 618

nouns, 614, 617

prepositions, 622–24

pronouns, 617–18

subjects of sentences, 617–18

two-word verbs, 620–21

grammatical person, 127–28

grouping ideas, 249

H

hand in/out, 620

heard/herd, 583

hear/here, 583

helping verbs, 400, 483–84

have and *had*, 503

with past participles, 618–19

past perfect tense, 498

present perfect tense, 497

using *of*, 503

Here is/are/was/were, 406

here/there

compound subjects, 512

subject-verb agreement, 511

high school, 575

himself/herself, 575

hole/whole, 583

homonyms, 580–94

See also sound alike/look alike words, e.g., *altar/alter*

hyphens, 561

I

idiomatic expressions, 620–21

illustration essays, 318–23

drafting, 321

final lines, 322

outlines, 320–21

proofreading, 322

revising, 321

rough lines, 321

the thesis, 320

thought lines, 319–20

illustration paragraphs, 42–64

adding details, 45–46

concluding sentences, 56–57

drafting, 53–54

final lines, 56–57

gathering ideas, 45

general statements, 42–43

outlines, 50–51

peer review form, 61

proofreading, 56–57

revising, 53–54

rough lines, 53–54

specific statements, 42–43

topic sentences, 46–47

transitions, 53

writing from reading, 61–63

in, 623

indefinite articles, 615

indefinite pronouns, 514, 523–24

independent clauses. *See* sentences

infinitives, 408–9, 618–19

informational writing, 118, 127, 332

See also process paragraphs

in front, 575

into/out of, 624

introductions

in essays, 273, 286–88

punctuation of, 544, 551

irregular verbs, 484–89

checklist, 487–89

isle/aisle, 583

italic print, 562

its/it's, 536, 583

J

journal writing, 5

K

keep on, 620

knew/new, 584

know/no, 584

L

lead/led, 586

lessen/lesson, 586

letters. *See* spelling

linking cause and effect, 229–30

lists, 10–12, 15

with essays, 278

using colons, 551–52

using semicolons, 550–51

living room, 575

loan/lone, 586

look into/over/up, 620

loose/lose, 586

M

main ideas, 377–78

maps, 13
modifiers, 471–79
   See also adjectives; adverbs
   dangling, 474–75
   -ed modifiers, 608–10
   -ing modifiers, 606–7
   misplaced, 473
   phrases, 471
moral/morale, 586
more/most, 468–69

N

narrative essays, 328–32
   drafting, 330
   final lines, 330–31
   outlines, 329–30
   proofreading, 330–31
   revising, 330
   rough lines, 330
   sequencing, 328
   thought lines, 328–29
narrative paragraphs, 90–117
   choosing a topic, 98–99
   clarity and interest, 94
   drafting, 103
   final lines, 108
   freewriting, 97
   having a point, 90, 95, 98–99
   outlines, 100–101
   peer review form, 112
   proofreading, 108
   quotations, 95
   relevance, 100
   rough lines, 103–4
   selecting details, 100–101, 103–4
   sequencing events, 94–95,
      100–101, 106–7
   thought lines, 96–100
   topic sentences, 90–92, 98–99,
      104
   transitions, 106–7
   writing from reading, 113–17
neither, 512, 514
noncount nouns, 614
nonessential clauses, 612
nonessential phrases, 545
nonrestrictive clauses, 612
nonrestrictive phrases, 545
nonstandard English, 480–81
no one, 575
not, 407–8
note taking, 372–75
not only, 512
nouns, 522
   appositives, 610–11
   articles with, 614–17

collective, 516, 525–26
contractions, 621–22
proper names, 545
numbers, 554, 556, 565

O

off, 624
on, 622–24
one, 508, 514, 524
or, 512
order. *See* sequencing
organization abbreviations, 565
outlines, 1, 19–27, 281–85
   argument essays, 362–63
   argument paragraphs, 251–53
   cause and effect essays, 357
   cause and effect paragraphs,
      225–26
   classification essays, 345–46
   classification paragraphs,
      179–80
   comparison and contrast
      essays, 340–41
   comparison and contrast
      paragraphs, 155–59
   definition essays, 351–52
   definition paragraphs, 201–2
   description essays, 324–25
   descriptive paragraphs, 74–75
   essay tests, 385
   illustration essays, 320–21
   illustration paragraphs, 50–51
   narrative essays, 329–30
   narrative paragraphs, 100–101
   process essays, 333–34
   process paragraphs, 122–23
   reaction writing, 383
   summaries, 379

P

pain/pane, 586
pair/pear, 586
paragraphs, basic, 3–41
   See also specific types of
      paragraphs, e.g., descriptive
      paragraphs
   choosing a topic, 6–7
   coherence, 22–23
   details, 9–12, 19–21
   drafting, 27
   focusing ideas, 12–19
   generating ideas, 4–6
   length, 3
   outlining, 19–27
   peer review form, 38
   revising, 27–30

sequencing ideas, 22–23
   titles, 30–31
   topic sentences, 13–19
   transitions, 27
   unity, 3
   vs. essays, 272–73
   writing from reading, 40–41
parallelism in sentences, 453–61
parentheses, 560–61
passed/past, 586
passive voice, 499, 501
past participles, 483–84, 497–98,
      618–19
past perfect tense, 498
past tense, 482–83, 497–98
patience/patients, 586
peace/piece, 587
peer review forms
   argument paragraphs, 265
   basic paragraphs, 38
   cause and effect, 239
   classification paragraphs, 189
   comparison and contrast, 169
   definition paragraphs, 212
   descriptive paragraphs, 86
   essays, 309
   illustration paragraphs, 61
   narrative paragraphs, 112
   process paragraphs, 137
   writing from reading, 388
periods, 561–62
person, shifts in, 127–28
personal/personnel, 587
pick up, 620
plain/plane, 587
planning. *See* thought lines
plural verbs. *See* subject-verb
      agreement
point-by-point organization,
      146–47, 162–63, 338–39
possessive forms
   of pronouns, 534–36, 555
   using apostrophes, 555
precise language, 595–96
prepositional phrases, 402–3
   between, 535
   beginning sentences with,
      604–6
   not the subject of a sentence,
      508–9
   pronoun case in, 535
   showing place, 623–24
   showing time, 622–23
prereading, 368–71
presence/presents, 587
present participles, 408, 444, 483
present perfect tense, 497

present tense, 481, 483–84
  -s endings, 618
principal/principle, 587
process essays, 332–37
  drafting, 334–35
  final lines, 335–36
  outlines, 333–34
  proofreading, 335–36
  revising, 334–35
  rough lines, 334–35
  sequencing, 332
  the thesis, 332
  thought lines, 333
process paragraphs, 118–41
  choosing a topic, 119, 121
  drafting, 127–29, 131
  final lines, 131–32
  grammatical person, 127–28
  outlines, 122–23
  peer review form, 137
  proofreading, 131–32
  rough lines, 127–29, 131
  sequencing, 118–22, 128–29
  thought lines, 121–22
  topic sentences, 122
  transitions, 128–29
pronouns
  agreement with nouns, 522–30
  antecedents of, 522–30
  apostrophes with, 555
  avoiding sexism, 524
  case, 534–38
  for collective nouns, 525–26
  comparative forms, 536
  consistency of, 531–34
  contractions, 621–22
  indefinite, 514, 523–24
  myself, 535
  spelled as one word, 575
  objective case, 534–36
  points of view, 531
  possessive case, 534–36, 555
  in prepositional phrases, 535
  punctuation of, 536
  subjective case, 534–36
  subject-verb agreement,
    507–8
  they/their, 524, 529
proofreading, 1, 30, 301–2
  argument essays, 364–65
  argument paragraphs, 260
  cause and effect essays, 358–59
  cause and effect paragraphs,
    234
  classification essays, 347–48
  classification paragraphs,
    184–85

comparison and contrast
    essays, 342–43
comparison and contrast para-
    graphs, 162–66
definition essays, 353–54
definition paragraphs, 208–9
description essays, 326–27
descriptive paragraphs, 82
illustration essays, 322
illustration paragraphs, 56–57
narrative essays, 330–31
narrative paragraphs, 108
process essays, 335–36
process paragraphs, 131–32
reaction writing, 383–84
summaries, 380–81
proper names, 545
punctuation
  of addresses, 548
  after conjunctive adverbs, 420
  apostrophes, 554–59
  capitalization, 562–64
  colons, 551–53
  commas, 427–29, 469, 542–49,
    561
  in complex sentences, 434
  in compound sentences, 415–20
  dashes, 560–61
  of dates, 548
  exclamation marks, 560–61
  hyphens, 561
  inserters, 560–61
  of numbers, 548
  parentheses, 560–61
  periods, 539–40, 561
  of possessive pronouns, 536
  question marks, 540
  quotation marks, 561–62
  of quotations, 547, 552, 561–62
  in run-on sentences, 425
  semicolons, 418–20, 427–29,
    550–51
  in titles of works, 562
  underlining, 562
  in *who/which/that* clauses,
    612–13
purpose of writing, 4

Q

questions
  for identifying details, 198
  punctuation of, 540
  for reading, 369, 372
  subject-verb agreement in, 511
  word order of, 406–7
quiet down, 620

quiet/quit/quite, 587
quotation marks, 561–62
quotations
  capitalization in, 562–63
  indirect, 562
  in narrative writing, 95
  within other quotations, 562
  punctuation of, 547, 552, 561–62

R

rain/reign/rein, 587
reaction writing, 381–84
  brainstorming, 382
  drafting, 383
  final lines, 383–84
  freewriting, 381–82
  outlines, 383
  points of agreement/disagree-
    ment, 382–83
  proofreading, 383–84
  revising, 383
  rough lines, 383
reading selections
  "Against All Odds, I'm Just
      Fine" (Wackerlin), 170–71
  "Althea Gibson: Never Give Up"
      (Ventura), 313–14
  "A Present for Popo" (Wong),
      87–89
  "A Ridiculous Addiction"
      (Owens), 369–71, 373–75
  "Athletic Heroes" (Beekman),
      266–68
  "Breaking the Bonds of Hate"
      (Khiev), 213–16
  "Eleven" (Cisneros), 310–12
  "How to Write a Personal
      Letter" (Keillor), 138–41
  "My Daughter Smokes"
      (Walker), 389–92
  "Parental Discretion" (Hevesi),
      393–96
  "Rocky Rowf" (Buchanan),
      113–17
  "Send Your Children to
      Libraries" (Ashe), 315–17
  "Spanglish" (Castro, Cook and
      Garcia), 61–63
  "Sticky Stuff" (Hamilton and
      Namuth), 39–40
  "Students in Shock"
      (Kellmayer), 240–43
  "Three Disciplines for Children"
      (Holt), 190–92
  "Too Tired to Appreciate the
      Revolution" (Rifkin),
      269–71

reading steps, 368–75, 384
reasons. *See* cause and effect
    paragraphs
relevance, 100
repetition, 295–96
rereading, 372–75
restating an idea, 295
restrictive clauses, 612
restrictive phrases, 545
results. *See* cause and effect
    paragraphs
reviewing. *See* final lines
revising, 1, 27–30, 283–85, 293–94
    See also checklists
    argument essays, 363–64
    argument paragraphs, 252, 256
    cause and effect essays, 358
    cause and effect paragraphs,
        225, 229–30
    classification essays, 346–47
    classification paragraphs, 180,
        182
    comparison and contrast
        essays, 341–42
    comparison and contrast
        paragraphs, 159–62
    definition essays, 352–53
    definition paragraphs, 201–2,
        204
    description essays, 325–26
    descriptive paragraphs, 78
    illustration essays, 321
    illustration paragraphs, 53–54
    narrative essays, 330
    narrative paragraphs, 103–4
    process essays, 334–35
    process paragraphs, 128–29
    reaction writing, 383
    summaries, 379–80
right/rite/write, 587
rough lines, 1, 27–30, 286–97
    argument essays, 363–64
    argument paragraphs, 256–57
    cause and effect essays, 358
    cause and effect paragraphs,
        229–30
    classification essays, 346–47
    classification paragraphs,
        182–83
    comparison and contrast
        essays, 341–42
    comparison and contrast para-
        graphs, 159–62
    definition essays, 352–53
    definition paragraphs, 203–4
    description essays, 325–26
    descriptive paragraphs, 78

essay tests, 385
illustration essays, 321
illustration paragraphs, 53–54
narrative essays, 330
narrative paragraphs, 103–4
process essays, 334–35
process paragraphs, 127–29,
    131
reaction writing, 383
summaries, 379–80
transitions, 53
run into/out, 621
run-on sentences, 424–31

S

semicolons, 418–20, 427–29,
    550–51
sense words, 69
sentences
    See also punctuation
    balancing length, 601–3
    beginning with an adverb,
        603–4
    beginning with a prepositional
        phrase, 604–6
    combining, 29, 414–23, 550–51
    complex, 432–42
    compound, 415–20, 550
    with compound subjects,
        512–13
    definition of, 399
    fragments, 443–52
    joining ideas, 608–13
    parallelism, 453–61
    prepositional phrases in, 402–3
    recognizing subjects of, 401–2
    recognizing verbs in, 399–400,
        402
    run-on, 424–31
    simple, 399–413, 416–17
    subject-verb patterns of, 416–17
    subordination, 432–42
    using adverbs, 407–8
    using appositives, 610–11
    using -ed modifiers, 608–10
    using *here is/are/was/were*, 406
    using -ing modifiers, 606–7
    using semicolons, 550–51
    using *there is/are/was/were*,
        406
    using *who/which/that* clauses,
        611–13
    variety, 601–13
    word order, 405–7, 511, 603–6
sequencing, 22–23
    See also word order

argument paragraphs, 252–53
cause and effect paragraphs,
    225–26
classification essays, 344
classification paragraphs,
    179–80
comparison and contrast
    essays, 337–38
description essays, 323
description paragraphs, 74–75
emphatic order, 225–26, 252–53
logical order, 22–23, 225–26,
    245–46
modifiers, 472–73
narrative essays, 328
narrative paragraphs, 94–95,
    100–101, 106–7
point-by-point organization,
    146–47, 162–63, 338–39
process essays, 332
process paragraphs, 118–22,
    128–29
subject-by-subject organization,
    144–46, 163–64
time order, 225–26
sexism in writing, 524
shifts in person, 127–28
should have, 503
sight/site/cite, 587–88
similarities. *See* comparison and
    contrast paragraphs
simple sentences, 399–413,
    416–17
since, 623
singular verbs. *See* subject-verb
    agreement
sole/soul, 588
sound alike/look alike words,
    580–94
    See also specific words, eg.
        altar/alter
specific words and phrases,
    42–43, 65–66, 69, 318
spelling, 570–79
    adding -s or -es, 572–73
    changing final *y* to *i*, 572
    combining words, 575
    commonly misspelled words,
        577–79
    doubling final consonants,
        570–71
    dropping final *e*, 571
    sound alike/look alike words,
        580–94
    using *ie* or *ei*, 573
stair/stare, 588
stake/steak, 588

standard English forms, 480–81, 484, 486
stationary/stationery, 588
steal/steel, 588
story telling. *See* narrative paragraphs
subject-by-subject organization, 144–46, 163–64
subject of a sentence, 401–3, 406, 617–18
  collective nouns, 516
  compound, 512–13
  hard-to-find, 508–9
  reversed word order, 511
  in sentence fragments, 448
subject pronouns, 507–8, 617–18
subject-verb agreement, 506–21
  collective nouns, 516
  compound subjects, 512–13
  hard-to-find subjects, 508–9
  indefinite pronouns, 514
  number, 506–8
  one, 508
  reversed word order, 511
subordinating conjunctions, 433–34, 436, 445–46
subpoints of essays, 272, 274–75
summaries, 376–81
  drafting, 379–80
  final lines, 380–81
  outlines, 379
  proofreading, 380–81
  revising, 379–80
  rough lines, 379–80
  thought lines, 376–78
superlative adjectives, 463–64, 468–69
synonyms
  in comparison and contrast paragraphs, 162
  for essay transitions, 295–96

T

tense, 480, 493
  See also verbs
  past, 482–83, 497–98
  past perfect, 498
  present, 481, 483–84, 618
  present perfect, 497
Texas Academic Skills Program
  test objectives
  appropriateness, 4, 245, 360–61
  unity and focus, 12–19
  prewriting skills, 1, 4–19 (*See also* thought lines)

thesis statements, 272–75, 286–87, 292, 320, 332, 337, 345, 349–50, 356–57, 360
  development, 1, 4–19 (*See also* thought lines)
  introductions and conclusions, 56–57, 273, 286–88, 291–92, 544, 551
  concrete examples, 194–95, 318–19
  organization, 1, 27–30 (*See also* rough lines)
  rough outline of essay, 19–27, 281–85 (*See also* outlines)
  timing, 384–87
  recognizing purpose and audience, 4, 245, 360–61
  recognizing unity, focus and development, 4–19, 30–37 (*See also* final lines)
  recognizing effective organization, 27–37 (*See also* final lines)
  recognizing effective sentences, 399–423
  subject-verb agreement, 506–21
  recognizing run-on sentences, 424–31
  recognizing fragments, 443–52
  recognizing dangling modifiers, 474–75
  recognizing ineffective word choice, 595–600
  recognizing standard American English, 480–81, 484, 486
  comparatives/superlatives, 463–64, 469, 536
  adjectives and adverbs, 407–8, 419–20, 428, 462–79, 550, 603–4
  verb forms, 480–89, 493, 497–98, 501
than, 469
than/then, 588
that clauses, 611–13
the (definite articles), 615
their/there/they're, 588
then, 428, 469
There is/are/was/were, 406
thesis of an essay, 272–75, 286–87, 292
  argument essays, 360
  cause and effect essays, 356–57
  classification essays, 345
  comparison and contrast, 337
  definition essays, 349–50
  illustration essays, 320

  process essays, 332
they/their, 524, 529
think over, 621
thorough/through/threw, 588
thought lines, 1, 4–19, 277–79, 283–84
  argument essays, 361–62
  argument paragraphs, 248–49
  cause and effect essays, 355–57
  cause and effect paragraphs, 220–22
  classification essays, 344–45
  classification paragraphs, 176–77
  comparison and contrast essays, 338–39
  comparison and contrast paragraphs, 150–55
  definition essays, 350–51
  definition paragraphs, 198–99
  description essays, 324
  descriptive paragraphs, 71–72
  essay tests, 385
  focusing ideas, 12–19
  illustration essays, 319–20
  illustration paragraphs, 45–50
  narrative essays, 328–29
  narrative paragraphs, 96–100
  process essays, 333
  process paragraphs, 121–22
  summaries, 376–78
time abbreviations, 565
time order, 225–26
titles, 30
  abbreviations of, 565
  capitalization of, 563–64
  of essays, 301
  of persons, 563, 565
  punctuation of, 561–62
  using italic print, 562
to be, 484, 486
to do, 484–86
to have, 484, 486
topic sentences, 13–19
  argument paragraphs, 244–45
  cause and effect, 222
  cause and effect paragraphs, 218
  classification paragraphs, 177
  comparison and contrast paragraphs, 142–43
  definition paragraphs, 194, 199
  descriptive paragraphs, 72, 74
  essays, 272–73, 282–83, 289
  illustration paragraphs, 46–47
  location of, 23, 91–92

narrative paragraphs, 90–92,
98–99, 104
process paragraphs, 122
staying on one point, 283
supporting details, 19–21
to/too/two, 588–89
to + verb, 408–9, 444
transitions, 27, 294–96
argument paragraphs, 257
classification paragraphs,
182–83
comparison and contrast
paragraphs, 148
definition paragraphs, 203
descriptive paragraphs, 80–81
illustration paragraphs, 53
narrative paragraphs, 106–7
between paragraphs, 295–96
within paragraphs, 294–95
process paragraphs, 128–29
restating an idea, 295
using synonyms, 295–96
try on/out, 621
turn on/down/up, 621
two-word verbs, 620–21

U

underlining, 562
until, 623
used to, 502–3

V

vain/vane/vein, 589
verbs, 480–92
See also subject-verb agreement
active voice, 499, 501
with adverbs, 620–21
consistency, 493, 501
contractions, 407–8, 621–22
-*d* or -*ed* endings, 482–83
-*ed* endings, 618–19
for ESL students, 618–22

helping, 400, 483–84, 497–98,
503, 618
infinitives, 408–9, 444, 618–19
-*ing* verbs, 408, 444, 483
irregular, 484–89
irregular verb checklist, 487–89
passive voice, 499, 501
past participles, 483–84, 497–98,
618–19
past perfect tense, 498
past tense, 482–83, 497–98
with prepositions, 620–21
present participles, 408, 444,
483
present perfect tense, 497
present tense, 481, 483–84, 618
the pronoun test, 408
-*s* endings, 618
sentence fragments, 448
in simple sentences, 399–400,
402
-*s* or -*es* endings, 481, 483
standard English forms,
480–81, 484
tense, 480, 493
used to, 502–3
using *have* and *had*, 503
using *of*, 503
voice, 499, 501
voice, 499, 501
vowels, 570

W

waist/waste, 589
wait/weight, 589
wander/wonder, 590
weather/whether, 589
were/we're/where, 589
which clauses, 611–13
whined/wind/wined, 589
who clauses, 611–13
who's/whose, 589

woman/women, 589
wood/would, 590
word choice, 595–600
clichés, 598–99
precision, 595–96
wordiness, 596–97
word order
in questions, 406–7
in sentences, 405–7, 603–6
would have, 503
writing from reading, 367–96
argument paragraphs, 266–71
asking questions, 369, 372
attitude, 367–68
basic paragraphs, 40–41
cause and effect paragraphs,
240–43
classification paragraphs,
190–92
comparison and contrast
paragraphs, 170–71
definition paragraphs, 213–16
descriptive paragraphs, 87–89
essays, 310–17
essay tests, 384–87
illustration paragraphs, 61–63
main ideas, 377–78
narrative paragraphs, 113–17
note taking, 372–75
peer review form, 388
prereading, 368–71
process paragraphs, 138–41
reaction writing, 381–84
reading steps, 368–75
rereading, 372–75
summaries, 376–81

Y

y (letter), 570
your/you're, 590
yourself, 575